Videos on Art

a resource guide to films and videos available worldwide
from the Roland Collection

Contents

This resource guide introduces a comprehensive international collection of films and videos on art, architecture and modern literature available for sale worldwide.

Introduction

Over some thirty-three years the Roland Collection has selected from thousands of titles worldwide those that will be of lasting importance rather than of transient interest. It is continually developing and being updated and outstrips in breadth and depth anything comparable in the commercial or educational sphere. Bringing together films with an original production value of $50 million, it not only represents a learning resource that is flexible to the varied needs of users and audiences, it also embodies a philosophy and a vision.

The Roland Collection has rediscovered and preserved many rare films dating from the mid-twentieth century to the present which would otherwise have been lost. It is inspired by the conviction that the arts are of the highest imaginable importance – not as a desirable luxury in times of prosperity, but as a life-force indispensable to all our futures.

The films chosen by the collection reflect the notion of art as life-integral and life-giving; they also interconnect and cross-fertilize in unexpected ways, making the collection a significant whole. Every film sets up creative dialogs that cut across boundaries of epoch, culture, nationality and medium.

The Roland Collection offers inexhaustible worlds of history, culture, philosophy, emotion, human document, celebration, protest, moral challenge and imaginative liberation – all embodied in the forms of art. *Videos on Art* is designed to give free access to those worlds.

Film on art: film as art

Anthony Roland, the curator and owner of the collection, is himself a film-maker who has directed sixteen of the key films in this resource guide. His central, holistic concept, that a film on art must convey the life of the works shown and be a work of art with a parallel life of its own, sets the agenda for the whole collection. A rich interplay is established between artist, art work, film-director-as-artist, and viewer; and the collection itself, it can be said, has in some senses become for its creator an extended work of art.

Directors, composers, scriptwriters

In keeping with the concept of the art film as a 'holistic' medium, Anthony Roland pays great attention to the merit of a film's music and narration as well as to the force and vision of the director. Several films are made by directors who have gone on to make feature films, many of the filmscripts are by the most authoritative art historians, and many of the original scores are by top-ranking contemporary composers.

Directors who are especially in accord with Anthony Roland's ethos are often represented by several films. They include Carlo Ragghianti, a major figure in the Italian art world, who edited influential journals and pioneered the making and publicizing of art films. He developed his 'crito-film' genre, in which camera movements convey, almost subliminally, the structure of works to the viewer. There are also the powerful films of the French art critic Max-Pol Fouchet, which achieve a haunting quality through poetic and perceptive voice-overs set against slow, atmospheric camera movements and dramatic lighting. Harold Van de Perre, another director selected by the collection, draws challenging parallels between the imagery of his artists and other sources in both art and life. He also constructs remarkable linear or coloristic 'overlays' upon the paintings to analyze with graphic clarity the formal qualities which make them so expressive.

The contributions of directors, composers and scriptwriters are scrupulously credited in the resource guide and are separately indexed to allow users who have appreciated a particular film to find others similarly directed, scored or narrated.

Using 'Videos on Art'

Videos on Art is far more than just a list of international films and videos available from a single source; it is designed and structured to reflect the richness of the whole collection and of individual programs.

The main resource guide is divided into thirty-seven sections on art and architecture, with titles that relate to several sections appearing more than once. Sections 1–23 introduce films chronologically, from the art of the earliest times to the present day, with some subdivisions by country or school. Sections 24–37 group films by subject, to help readers appreciate and assimilate the breadth of the collection. This presentation should make it easy for readers to find the right films for their needs and also prompt them to sample related titles and put together their own combinations from the range of the collection.

The rest of the resource guide, from page 329, is divided into five parts that provide supplementary information about the collection: an overview of film and video series; comprehensive indexes to the programs on art and architecture; details of videos on modern literature; background information about the making of the collection; and everything you need to know when placing an order. The Key to the Collection on pages 412–33 gives prices and technical details for the entire collection; use it both as a checklist before ordering and as a starting point if you want to choose titles on the basis of period, art discipline or age-range.

To show how the different sections of the guide interrelate and how easy it is to find your way around, we have included some examples of how the resource guide can be used on pages 10–12, If You're Interested In… We hope these pages will act as a springboard that will allow you to make the most of this unique resource.

During his early career as a highly successful dealer in
Old Master and modern paintings, Anthony Roland realized
the importance of communicating the art experience.
He felt that through film he could capture the cinematographic
qualities in art. Art film was to become his vocation.

Anthony Roland

His first film was an immediate success, and subsequent titles won
wide acclaim and numerous awards. He developed a technique of filming
without narration, creating an aesthetic continuity that emotionally
envelops the audience, allowing them to sense the 'soul' of the artist.

The founder of the collection

Anthony Roland has devoted himself to the
medium of film on art and its promotion,
unearthing the best examples of the genre –
those which combine filmic excellence
with real empathy for the art they deal
with – steadily developing his collection and
establishing efficient worldwide distribution
for its titles.

He has lectured, conducted workshops and
acted as consultant to museums and public
bodies internationally. During the late 1960s
he founded the two-cinema Art Film Centre
in central London. Then in the 1980s in
Edinburgh, Washington DC and New York
he presented the revolutionary 'Artscope',
a traveling art museum in motion-picture
form, consisting of sixteen open-air
cinemas, which took his collection literally
'to the people.'

The passion and integrity with which
Anthony Roland crusades for the cause of
the art film is evident in the quality
of his collection. Many of the titles have
been secured only through enormous
determination and against the odds –
saving unique material, pursuing film rights,
tracking down negatives, transferring
footage laboriously on to new formats
compatible with developing technology. At
the same time he is committed to keeping
original, superior-quality formats available.
Where possible, he offers programs in one
or more languages in addition to English.

If you're interested in...

... an artist

- look in the **General Index**, pages 338–58, under the artist's name. For instance, if you are interested in Picasso, you'll find seven programs about Picasso's work and nine others in which it is featured. Because of the diversity of his art, you will find films about him in the sections Modern and Contemporary Sculptors, Drawing and the Graphic Arts, and The Photographic Image as well as in Modern Masters.

... an architect

- look in the **General Index** under the architect's name. For instance, if you are interested in Le Corbusier, you'll find six programs about Le Corbusier's work and six others in which it is featured. Section 23, Modern Architecture and Design, includes a vast panorama of the architect's work as well as programs about specific buildings.

... a writer

- look in the section **Videos on Modern Literature**, which begins on page 375. The series *Writers Talk: Ideas of Our Time* lists writers in alphabetical order, with the topics they speak about. For example, in the case of Maya Angelou, topics include writing through the black experience and the human spirit in adversity.

... an art discipline

- look in the **General Index**, where all the programs on that discipline are listed together by period and by country.

- look at the **Key to the Collection**, which begins on page 412. Each discipline – painting, drawing and graphics, sculpture, architecture and design, photography and video art – has its own color code to show instantly every program that features it.

  If you are interested in sculpture, section 20 is dedicated to Modern and Contemporary Sculptors. Stonecarving is covered in Techniques of the Artist.

... a style

- look in the **General Index**. For instance, under Gothic you'll find four programs on Gothic painting, sculpture, stained glass and architecture and three on the Gothic revival.

- look at the **Contents** pages. The first part of the catalog introduces films chronologically; section 5 covers programs on the Gothic and Romanesque styles.

... the art and architecture of **a period**,

- turn to the **Key to the Collection**, which begins on page 412. The column 'period covered' will show you at a glance all the programs that cover your period. For instance, there are thirty-six programs on the eighteenth century.

- turn to the **Contents** pages. Section 9, Baroque and Rococo, has twenty-three illustrations and details of the series The Age of Baroque and The Enlightenment.

... a theme

- look in the **General Index**. For instance, under 'women as artists' you'll find eighteen programs, ranging from Angelica Kauffman of the Royal Academy and the Impressionist Berthe Morisot, to the emotionally powerful German pacifist Kathe Kollwitz and the dazzling pure color of the British artist Bridget Riley.

... a cultural group

- look in the **General Index**. For example, the Aztecs are covered in section 4, Pre-Columbian America.

... the art and architecture of **a country**

- look under that country's name in the **General Index**. All the ninety-five programs featuring the art and architecture of, say, Britain, are listed by century. You'll find countries as diverse as Denmark, Iraq, Mexico, Russia...

... the art and architecture of **a city**

- look up the city in the **General Index**. For instance, you'll find nineteen different programs listed under 'Paris', covering art movements, buildings, gardens and museums of the city as well as its art.

... a building, or a type of building

- look in the **General Index**. For instance, you'll find twenty-four programs listed under 'churches and cathedrals.'

... a series of programs

- look at the section **Film and Video Series**, pages 330–3, for summary information about the whole series.

- look up the title of the series in the **Index of Film and Video Titles**, which begins on page 359, to find the full catalog entries.

... the work of **a director** or **a scriptwriter**

- look in the **Index of Directors** on pages 364–5, or the **Index of Scriptwriters** on pages 366–7.

... a narrator

- see the **Index of Narrators and Presenters**, page 368. It includes artists – Alexander Calder, Marcel Duchamp, Max Ernst, Andy Goldsworthy, Eugène Ionesco; actors – Glenda Jackson, Peter Ustinov; feature-film-makers – Agnes Varda.

... **awards** won by the films and videos

- look at the **Index of Awards**, pages 370–1. Awards are listed by country and by festival.

… programs suitable for **younger audiences**

- look at the **Key to the Collection**, pages 412–29. The color-coded columns on the left show at a glance which programs are suitable for different age ranges. The fourth column after the title indicates the precise recommended age. You will find thirty-two titles suitable for six-year-olds, forty titles for eight-year-olds and seventy titles for ten-year-olds.

- turn to **Section 31**, which is dedicated to Films for Younger Audiences

… programs suitable for **deaf, hearing-impaired** or **multi-lingual audiences**

- look in the **General Index**, pages 338–58, under 'Narration, films with little or no.' This entry lists thirty films or videos, among the best in the collection, where the visual continuity and musical scores preclude the need for spoken narration.

… programs available in **other languages** as well as English

- look up the language in the **General Index**. You'll find complete lists of all the programs available in Arabic, Chinese, Danish, Dutch, Estonian, Finnish, French, German, Greek, Hebrew, Italian, Japanese, Norwegian, Portuguese, Russian, Spanish and Latin American Spanish.

… videos that cost less than $100 each

- you will find them all straight away in the **Key to the Collection** price list, starting page 412. There are 470 videos costing between $69 and $99.

… especially **short** or **long** programs

- see the column of running times in the **Key to the Collection**, pages 412–33. There are fifty-three programs of twelve minutes or under, and eighty-eight programs of fifty-three minutes and up.

… the techniques of an art form

- see **section 36**, Techniques of the Artist. Thirty programs range from enameling and lithography to photomontage and stonecarving, and allow you to see artists at work.

- the **Draw with Don** series for five- to twelve-year-olds, in Films for Younger Audiences, teaches drawing and painting, balancing instruction with fun.

- to teach yourself (or your class) creative writing, discover the only course of its kind, **Writers on Writing**, page 386.

… how the Roland Collection programs can **help your pupils**

- see pages 408–11 to understand the **United States National Visual Arts Standards** and their student achievement standard definitions; these are color-coded Grades K–4, 5–8, 9–12 for each title on art and architecture pages 412–29.

- turn to page 435, which outlines the **educational services** offered by the Roland Collection. These include sale of stock footage, transcripts of narrations and program notes.

… **video rental**

- see the **Price and Availability Details** on page 434, which lists rental prices for the USA and Canada.

… videos for **individual home use**

- bear in mind that the prices throughout the catalog are for institutional use. Enquiries from individuals and private collectors are welcome.

Acknowledgments

Without my late father introducing me to the inner sensitivities of art and their influence on the outer world, the Roland Collection would not have been possible.

Many individuals have been generous in offering advice, assistance and support. I am honored by their valuable contribution, in particular:

Mildred Gordon, United States office manager for seventeen years

Anne Short, my invaluable personal assistant for thirteen years

Tom Buckley, USA

Daniel Cohen, France

Renate Fortescue, Britain

Marie Gordon, USA

Diane Hills, Britain

Anna Kelby, Britain

Jim Knox, USA

Anne Livingstone, Britain

Glenys Melgaard, Australia

Howard C Miskin, USA

Henk Newenhouse, USA

Gail Nicoll, Britain

Ida Roland, Denmark

Marc Roland, Britain

Saskia Roland, Britain

John Walker Jnr, USA

The Roland Collection is indebted to the expertise and long-term commitment of Humphries Video Services, London:

David Brown, Executive Co-ordinator

Censi Cabrera, Supervising Videotape Editor

Demetrakis Michael, Videotape Master Librarian and Resources Executive

Mark Summers, Head of Technical Services

Research has been facilitated by the endeavors of numerous organizations, including:

Biennale International du Film sur l'Art, Musée Nationale d'Art Moderne, Centre Georges Pompidou, Paris

Centre du Films sur l'Art, Brussels

Euro Aim-Mediabase, Brussels

Festival International du Film sur l'Art, Montréal

Program for Art on Film, Columbia University, New York (founded as a joint venture of the J Paul Getty Trust and the Metropolitan Museum of Art)

UNESCO (United Nations Educational Scientific and Cultural Organization), Paris

European home video publication has been aided by Espace Vidéo Européen, an initiative of the Irish Film Institute and the Médiathèque de la Communauté française de Belgique within the framework of the MEDIA program of the Commission of the European Union.

English language versions of some titles have been made with the assistance of:

BABEL (Broadcasting Across the Barriers of European Language)

EBU (European Broadcasting Union)

MEDIA (Commission of the European Communities)

EATC (European Alliance for Television and Culture)

And finally I should like to thank my diverse clients worldwide – from the Central Library in Berlin that acquired the entire collection to a small international school in Papua New Guinea. In recognition of the breadth of support given to the collection in the United States, a detailed list of American clients is given on pages 396-406.

Anthony Roland

1 Early Cultures

Film – history's newest art form – reaches back to some of the earliest images ever created by human beings. The two films which frame this first section of the Roland Collection's history of art set the keynote of the collection: art on film, and film as art.

This section of 5 programs can be purchased on VHS for $435

Television rights and prices on request

For the particular effects achieved in *Tassili N'Ajjer*, the director, JD Lajoux, booked what was then the only camera of its kind in Europe (being used at the time in the filming of the feature *The Longest Day*), and traveled on camel-back to the Sahara, with all equipment, including that necessary for 'bouncing' natural daylight in the absence of power supply.

The Origins of Art in France presents near-hallucinatory sequences of artefacts and figures, alternated with images of the landscape, flora and fauna and rough-hewn architecture that were the backdrop to Gallic agrarian society, and to Druidic religion.

While the direction of these and other films in the Roland Collection is arresting and dramatic, it illuminates, rather than competes with, the art shown – neolithic rock paintings of animals, carved stone effigies, decorative artefacts, coins, cromlechs. These images are the antecedents of all the art of succeeding centuries. Bound up with lost social beliefs and customs, they yet retain in themselves aesthetic force and eloquence.

10 Tassili N'Ajjer
Prehistoric Rock Paintings of the Sahara

Four thousand years ago the people who inhabited the Tassili N'Ajjer, a group of mountains in the eastern Sahara, painted the rocks with scenes of their daily life. Why? Probably they were making magic; we can only guess. But from the hundreds of thousands of pictures they left (nowhere else is prehistoric art to be found in such abundance) we learn that the desert then was no desert at all: it was a place of flourishing community life, of flowers and waterholes and herds of antelope. To our eyes these vivid and colorful humans and animals in motion, farming and hunting and making war, look astonishingly 'modern,' preserved as they have been by the dry climate. Today, however, they are in danger, since many have been defaced by tourists and some have already entirely disappeared. To film this invaluable record of the paintings, some of the most recent technical developments in the art of film have been used to capture some of the most ancient images we still have. At the very dawning of artistic activity, the images human beings create are bound up with the politics and economics of their existence – the animals they hunt, the forces, natural and supernatural, that sustain their lives, the battles they fight. And their pictures are inscribed on the very fabric of the environment they inhabit – the rocks and cave walls – prefiguring the graffiti or public murals of today, giving expression to social concerns and passions.

'Very beautiful, with a very fine subject'
UNESCO

Director	**16 minutes**
Jean-Dominique Lajoux	**Color**
Narration	**Age range 6–adult**
Max-Pol Fouchet	**Film $553** Rental $169
Original music	**VHS $79**
Maurice Le Roux	

Awards
Gold Medal, Venice
Bronze Medal, Bilbao
Quality Award and Prize,
French National Film Center

◀◀ 10
Five-thousand-year-old
rock painting

▼ 13
Stonehenge

13 Prehistoric Sites
From Stonehenge to the Moorlands of Western Britain

Prehistoric sites are often difficult to understand; this video looks at a wide variety – from Stonehenge, in Wiltshire, England, to less well-known monuments high on the moorlands of western Britain – and helps to explain them. It also sets out to tell part of the story of the ancient peoples who built them. We can see the evidence – tools, stone buildings, earthworks, burial chambers, stone circles and long lines of upright stones – but how are we to interpret it? Many clues are pointed out to help work out what the monuments might have been used for. Reconstruction paintings of prehistoric times bring to life the remains of ancient communities: the makers of these structures were farmers, and we assume that the henges had ritual and religious significance in their lives. The construction of the later hillforts of the Iron Age, including Maiden Castle, is also looked at. An excavation of a long barrow is used to show how much of the evidence that we do have has been recovered by archaeological investigation. We also see a school party using a detailed map as they set out to explore a monument. The video ends by making clear just how many such ancient remains there are. It is a useful general guide to any study of prehistory.

Part of the series *Looking at...*

English Heritage	**20 minutes**
	Color
	Age range 11–14
	VHS $89

14 Grimes Graves
Neolithic Flint Mines and the Techniques of Flint Knapping

The strange landscape of pits and mounds known as Grimes Graves near Thetford in Norfolk, England, is the site of one of Britain's earliest industries, flint mining, and its associated craft of flint knapping. This industry was carried on in the area within living memory – the craft survived long enough to be filmed in the 1940s and historic footage of this is included. Next, the mines are investigated and examined for evidence of how neolithic miners extracted the flint – the pits are the filled-in entrances to mine shafts. A school party is shown beginning their investigation of the mines. A professional flint knapper, John Lord, takes the viewer on a tour of the mines, including one of the deepest that is not open to the public. The flint is found underground embedded in the chalk, and the best is at the bottom of the pit, 60 feet down. Here tunnels lead off the central chamber into a maze of galleries beyond. John Lord demonstrates how the neolithic miners must have worked, using antler picks, by scraping away the chalk to loosen the large flint boulders. In the last part of the video he demonstrates the skills needed to make an axe head by using a pebble to split the flintstone and shape it. Finally the cutting edge of the axe head is put on, using an antler to flake off smaller pieces.

Part of the series *Evidence on Site*

Director/Writer	**12 minutes**
Philip Sugg	**Color**
English Heritage	**Age range 6–14**
Also available in French	**VHS $79**

The Origins of Art in France
Celtic Art Treasures

Bringing together an unprecedented range of artefacts – jewels, animals in stone, carved figures and heads, abstract decorations on standing stones and primitive architecture – this film presents Celtic art in the context of Gallic civilization as a whole. The poetic and penetrating narrative by Max-Pol Fouchet stresses the art's supernatural roots in Druidic cults of gods, goddesses and heroes. For the Celts, we are told, 'the spirit and the head are inseparable', and 'eternity is in the gaze.' Theirs is 'a religion of spiritual intensity', of 'transcendence', concerned with forces beyond human control. Fouchet hints at how the reduction of artistic forms to their expressive essentials relates to Scandinavian art of the period, to the distant oriental connections of the Celtic peoples, and indeed to modern Cubism and Abstraction. In Gallic art, we learn, abstraction and representation co-exist and merge. Fouchet's narration accompanies mesmeric sequences of intricate metalwork, ornaments, charms, 'souvenirs', helmets (symbols of the French 'Gauloise' cigarette), and shots of desolate fortresses, tombs, and above all gazing, timeless heads. We learn how Gallic culture developed against the backdrop of a yet more ancient prehistory, recorded in cromlechs and stone circles that the sculptor Rodin came to consider 'the predecessors to the great Gothic cathedrals.' We learn too how, with the coming of the Romans, Romano-Gallic art extended to the building of bridges, aqueducts and ornamented, columned façades. It is thus out of an extremely rich brew of cultures that French art evolves.

'A masterly production. An enormous amount of documentary evidence shown very successfully.'
UNESCO

Directors	**38 minutes**
Max-Pol Fouchet	**Black and white**
Jean L'Hote	**Age range 12–adult**
Narration	**Film $693** Rental $199
Max-Pol Fouchet	**VHS $99**

Also available in French

◀◀ 13, page 15
Castleriggg Stone Circle

▶ 16
Reconstruction drawing

◀ 20
Celtic dancer

17

Working on the Evidence: Maiden Castle
Modern Archaeology at the Iron Age Hillfort

A group of young people visit the hillfort of Maiden Castle in Dorset, England, and think themselves back in time. They realize that archaeology is all about building up a picture of what life was like in the past. The archaeologist at work explains the techniques of modern archaeology and what his team is actually doing at Maiden Castle. Reconstruction paintings based on real evidence help to show life in the Iron Age, as does a visit to an experimental farm which uses the farming 'technology' employed by people over two thousand years ago. The children work on the evidence on site and in the local museum in Dorchester. Through a series of 'dissolves' they are transformed into the Iron Age people who defended the fort and the Roman soldiers who stormed it, while archive film shows Sir Mortimer Wheeler giving a vivid analysis of the battle of AD 43, based on what he learned from his excavations.

Part of the series *Evidence on Site*

Director/Writer	**20 minutes**
David Collison	**Color**
	Age range 9–14
Narrator	
Magnus Magnusson	**VHS $89**

English Heritage

Also available in French

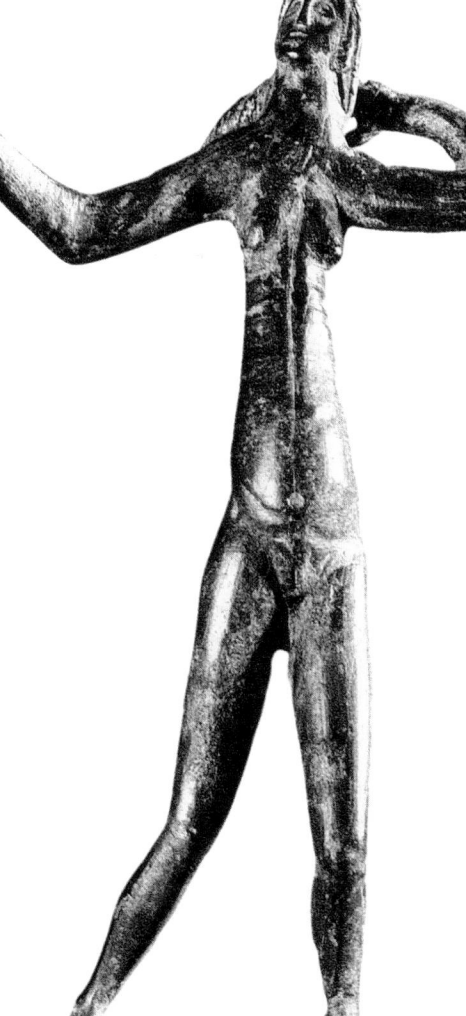

2

3500 BC–AD 1000

The films in this section deal with the world's first developed cultures, those that provide the classical precedents and standards for many of our aesthetic judgments.

First Civilizations

This section of 13 programs can be purchased on VHS for $1257

Television rights and prices on request

'Classicism' and 'the classics' are terms used extremely broadly in art. At times 'classical' means simply 'traditional' (as opposed to avant-garde or innovatory), or of a high standard as judged against some accepted canon of earlier masterpieces. At other times it refers strictly to works from, or in the style of, the ancient Greek and Roman civilizations. Notions of order and harmony derived from those civilizations have had an incalculable influence upon subsequent western culture – its taste, its ideas, its sense of proportion, its definitions of beauty. They inform Romanesque or 'Roman-like' architecture in the Middle Ages. Similarly the Renaissance was seen as a 'rebirth' of classical humanist arts, sciences and learning. In the later eighteenth century Neo-classicism again consciously sought to revive the forms of the ancient world in all the arts. In the modern period Classicism informed work as different as Maillol's serene statuary, de Chirico's haunted piazza scenes, Picasso's heavy, robed figures of the 1920s, Nazism's sinister 'body beautiful' monuments, and even the uncluttered functionalism of the Bauhaus.

The Graeco-Roman culture, however, was not the only one to reach supreme heights of political power, social organization and cultural sophistication in Europe and the Middle East in the millennia leading up to the advent of Christianity. The films in this section also cover the Egyptian, Babylonian and Hittite kingdoms, which have all left their own 'classical' legacies.

To all these civilizations modern and future culture owes its identity. In the words of the great British archaeologist Sir Leonard Woolley, quoted in the first film in this section, 'we cannot detach ourselves from our past. We are always conscious of precedents, not least when we flout them. So we let experience shape our views and actions. This is so much the case that when tradition is absent, progress stops.'

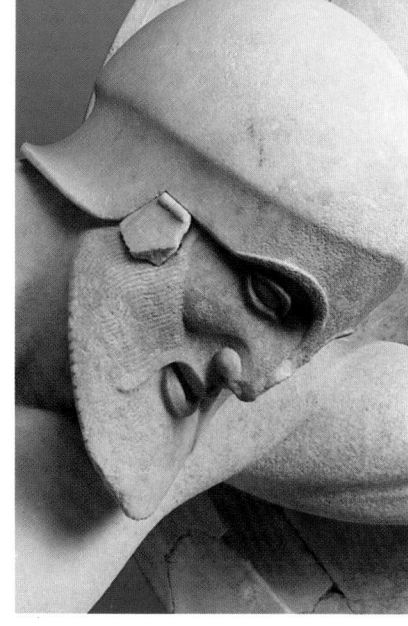

30
Abu Simbel, detail

40A/B
Royal Trojan head

30
Precise contour drawing
generated by stereoscopic
photography

30 Nubia '64

Saving the Temples of Ancient Egypt

The ancient Egyptians built colossal temples and shrines along the banks of the River Nile, because they knew that from its yearly flooding came the whole prosperity of their land. But when the modern rulers of Egypt decided to dam the Nile in Nubia, to ensure regular irrigation along 600 miles of its course, they knew that the river's level was bound to rise and rise until some of the monuments on the former banks were completely submerged. Only a huge exercise in conservation, in which the experts of many nations had to co-operate, could save these priceless treasures from death by water. What had taken hundreds of years and thousands of slaves to build had to be moved and reassembled in months on the new banks of the Nile. Presented as a human document rather than as art history, dramatically and powerfully directed, this film will fascinate old and young viewers alike. Locations featured include the Aswan Dam, the Tomb of Pennenout, the Temple of Deer, the Shrine of Gaarf Hussein, the Temple of Dakka, the Temple of Ramses, the Temple of Philae, the Temple of Abu Simbel, the Temple of Amada and the Temple of Kalaboha.

Director	**42 minutes**
Robert Genot	**Color**
Narration	**Age range 12–adult**
Desroches-Noblecourt	**Film $833** Rental $249
Award	**VHS $119**
Grand Prix, Cannes	

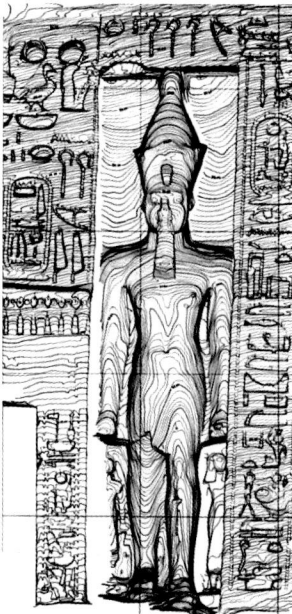

40A Digging for the History of Man
40B

Art and Architecture of the Babylonians, Sumerians, Hittites, Greeks, Romans and Sassanians
40A Part One, 40B Part Two

A voyage of discovery into man's earliest civilizations, those which developed in the countries we know today as Turkey, Iran and Iraq. The special merit of this film is that works of art scattered throughout the great collections and museums of the world have been brought back to be shown as if at their original sites, helping us to recreate in our imagination the cultures that produced them. As the film explores the findings of many different archaeologists over the years, it points out the refinements in techniques of exploration and improvements in methods of research that have taken place. One of the first highly developed civilizations which has been discovered is the state of Sumer. It is possible to reconstruct vast cathedral-like buildings and the first Mesopotamian 'pyramid temples.' Relief carvings, vases and statues speak to us of the spiritual and material preoccupations of this ancient society. Excavations in Turkey have revealed the vast empire of the Hittites which dated from the seventeenth to the thirteenth century BC. A rich and great civilization emerges from the relief carvings and many thousands of clay tablets worked on and interpreted by different scholars. Many ancient cities have been discovered in Asia Minor, meeting-ground of East and West. The most remarkable examples of Hellenistic art and architecture were found in Pergamum and Troy. Alexander the Great set out to destroy the Persian empire and died in Babylon, having built a new empire which he believed incorporated the best of Greece and the best of the Orient. Under the Sassanian kings, the greatest civilization in Persian history arose. Royal palaces of the ancient kings and sanctuaries of mysterious elemental powers rise from the volcanic desert. Persepolis still stands as a symbol of the empire of Darius and Xerxes which stretched from the Indus to the Nile and west to the Bosporus. Locations featured include the Tower of Babel, Uruk, Warka, Hattusas, Yazili-Kaya, Ephesus, Myus, Magnesia, Priene, Miletus, Herakleia, Euromus, Didyma, Pergamum, Troy, Takhht-i-Sulaiman, Zendan-i-Sulaiman, Ctesiphon, and Persepolis.

'Outstandingly successful, in supreme command of its material. Reliable and precise, it is, at the same time, light and elegant, particularly penetrating in the shots of early portrayals of mankind. It transmits a wealth of knowledge. The greatest moments are the interpretations of the history of civilization in conjunction with individual sculptural, architectural and scenic objects.'
German Center for Film Classification

Director/Narration	**40A 30 minutes**
H J Hossfeld	**40B 25 minutes**
Original music	**Color**
Enno Dugend	**Age range 12–adult**
Awards	
Gold Ribbon, Berlin	**Each part**
International Status,	**Film $693** Rental $199
German Government	**VHS $99**
Highly Commended,	
German Center for	
Film Classification	

Ancient Cultures of Mesopotamia

Five documentaries filmed in Iraq about the old Mesopotamian cultures. A Finnish team travel the length and breadth of Iraq, giving the viewer the chance to see, in addition to the ruins themselves, a magnificent collection of exhibits including those in the Iraq Museum. This series is also a tribute to the tenacious archaeologists who, in exhausting heat and harsh sandstorms, in peril of their lives, revealed the glorious history of Mesopotamia for generations to come.

This series of
5 programs
can be purchased
on film for $3465 or
on VHS for $495
Reference S1

21 The Sumerian Kingdom of Ur

A culture considered to be the beginning and root of western civilization flourished more than five thousand years ago in the area of ancient Mesopotamia. Ur was one of the great Sumerian urban states; it has traditionally been identified with the Garden of Eden, or Paradise. The ruins of Ur, the most impressive of which is the temple tower, or ziggurat, are seen in the film in their present-day condition, and collections from the National Museum of Iraq present the variety and high level of the Sumerian culture. Ancient 'reed culture' can still be found in modern Iraq, at the point where the Euphrates and Tigris turn into one river; the Marsh Arabs consider themselves to be descendants of the ancient Chaldeans. The film covers also the history of archaeology and excavators at Ur.

Part of the series
Ancient Cultures of Mesopotamia

Director
Antti Kaskia
Also available in Finnish

25 minutes
Color
Age range 14–adult
Film $693 Rental $199
VHS $99

◀ 23
Brick with pattern, detail

◀ 25
Royal Mosque, Isfahan, detail

▶▶ 23
Assyrian wall relief

22 Babylon – The Gate of the Gods

The legendary, holy Babylon, a city which flourished for thousands of years, an ancient metropolis also called the Gate of the Gods, is still a mysterious place, stimulating the curiosity of scientists even though they have already worked on its mystery for more than one hundred years. This film explores the immense ruined city of Babylon and, at the same time, the whole Babylonian empire. Two of the eight Wonders of the World, the Tower of Babel (the temple tower of Babylon) and the Hanging Gardens, have been located here. Even the present ruins impress the visitor, who can follow in the footsteps of the ancient kings through the Ishtar Gate and along the Procession Street past the vast ruin-field of the Southern Palace. The Babylonians occupied themselves with almost all the fields of science known in our times. For example, they were masters in trigonometry two thousand years before the Greeks. And they were great legislators, basing their laws on the Code of King Hammurabi. Babylon, a huge city in its time, was a peaceful meeting place of all the nations, races and religions of those days.

Part of the series
Ancient Cultures of Mesopotamia

Director
Antti Kaskia
Also available in Finnish

25 minutes
Color
Age range 14–adult
Film $693 Rental $199
VHS $99

Assurnasirpal is not considered to be one of the great Assyrian kings, like Assurbanipal, but he had all the characteristics of a typical ruler of that time. The film focuses on the Assyrian era mostly through the medium of his life. We start from Nineveh – present-day Mosul, a town in northern Iraq – with its magnificent walls and gates. The town plan gives a good impression of the vivid life of Nineveh and its great importance as the center of a superpower. With the help of enormous reliefs of carved stone at the museum, we familiarize ourselves with the king's favorite hobby – lion hunting, a typical leisure activity for the well-off at that time. Warfare was almost a science and war strategy, as well as the highly advanced technology, with its equipment for wall-breaking purposes, and tanks, was surprisingly modern. The victorious king organized parades and feasts which were then memorialized in carved stone. The Assyrians admired and honored power; the well-shaped muscles of human figures were emphasized in their art and the king was portrayed as a mighty bull with a pair of wings – an early form of propaganda. The Assyrians were also skilled constructors, especially expert in town and city culture. Their buildings were decorated with glass bricks and there were parks, squares and fountains between the blocks. Both the public buildings and the private houses were decorated with many reliefs and wall paintings, and the furniture, beds and so on were decorated with splendid ivory carvings. King Assurnasirpal founded his villa at Nimrud some 60 miles south of Nineveh along the course of the River Tigris. It was actually a town with its palace, temple, fortress and harbor. Several texts with relatively detailed descriptions of the events of the king's life and life at Nimrud in general have been preserved for posterity there. Material for this film was shot at Nineveh, Nimrud and the museums of Iraq.

Part of the series
Ancient Cultures of Mesopotamia

Director	**25 minutes**
Antti Kaskia	**Color**
Also available in Finnish	**Age range 14–adult**
	Film $693 Rental $199
	VHS $99

Hatra is a fortress-like town in the barren desert area in north-west Iraq, between Mosul and Samarra. The Hatra era lasted from about 400 BC to AD 300, and was at its height during the first century AD. Although the earliest phases of its history remain unknown, it can perhaps be considered the most important monument of the ancient Mesopotamian cultures. It was a major staging-post on the famous oriental silk road and its prosperity was based on the international caravan traffic. The center of Hatra consists of a group of temples. The most important is the temple dedicated to the Shamash or sun god; other heavenly bodies had temples of their own. The group of temples has been partly restored and exemplifies the unique Hatran architecture: an elegant combination of eastern and western influences. Excavations of Hatra have only just started. The town itself has not been uncovered yet but we are able to see the temples, the tombs, the wall and the remains of towers. Impressive examples of Greek-influenced Hatran art, with its statues of kings and all kinds of smaller items, can be admired at the National Museum of Iraq.

Part of the series
Ancient Cultures of Mesopotamia

Director	**25 minutes**
Antti Kaskia	**Color**
Also available in Finnish	**Age range 14–adult**
	Film $693 Rental $199
	VHS $99

This film follows a path from the five-thousand-year-old Sumerian architecture, the temple tower of Ur and its construction, the tower of Aqaquf, the Marsh Arabs and their reed culture, the ruin-field and culture of Babylon, to the Assyrian Nineveh and the architecture of Nimrud. We seek for common features and lines of development to give us some idea of the tradition and influence of those times on Islamic architecture, which has itself had a substantial influence on western architecture, either directly or through Spain, Italy and the Crusades. We visit the cinema city of Habaniya – the 'Hollywood' of Iraq – where colorful scenes of an Assyrian town have been reconstructed. We call at Hatra to see the architectural integration of two cultures and admire the work of the constructors of the huge arch and temple of Ctesiphon near Baghdad, clearly influenced by Greek culture. The age of the arch is not known. Among numerous other monuments, we visit the Wasit Gate in the middle of the desert in the southern part of Iraq, a relic of a large mosque surrounded by a so far uncovered town. It may originate from the eleventh century – its ornaments are of the same style as those at the Mustansiriya School in the center of Baghdad. Mustansiriya School has been called the oldest university in the world. The building is under restoration and it will be converted into a cultural center. Its ornaments are unique in their splendor. The mosques of Karbala and Najaf with the graves of Caliphs Ali and Hussein are the most impressive in the world, and there are several different types of mosques, originating from different eras and used by different sects, at Mosul in northern Iraq. Tradition is still alive in the mosque architecture of our times, and modern Islamic architecture flourishes and gains inspiration from these traditions.

Part of the series
Ancient Cultures of Mesopotamia

Director	**29 minutes**
Antti Kaskia	**Color**
Also available in Finnish	**Age range 14–adult**
	Film $693 Rental $199
	VHS $99

2 First Civilizations

27   **Borobudur: Beyond the Reach of Time**
Restoring Indonesia's Great Shrine

Dating from a thousand years ago – four centuries before the great Gothic cathedrals of Europe – the Buddhist temple of Borobudur stands in Java, a 400 feet square terraced pyramid festooned with stone carvings and reliefs and featuring five hundred figures of Buddha. The carvings tell stories of the life of Buddha, and the film retells (with the aid of traditional Indonesian dancers) the myths of the great world religion called after him. It also charts in some depth the enormous reconstruction and restoration project to which Borobudur has been subjected in recent years, for the monument has suffered erosion by the elements and subsidence, and the greatest efforts have been needed to counteract these.

Director
Francine Vande Wiele

Narration
Brian Featherstone

Principal adviser
Professor
Dr Haryati Soebadio

UNESCO

Also available in
French, Portuguese,
Russian and Spanish

32 minutes
Color
Age range 14–adult
Film $763 Rental $199
VHS $109

50   **Greek Pottery**

These superb examples from the Louvre in Paris show the development of Greek vases, their variations of shape and size and the techniques used in their decoration. Oddly enough, of all classical Greek art the frail pots, urns and vases have endured the best, and they are of the greatest use to us as illustrations of Greek life and culture. Practically every activity of the ancient Greeks – their work and their play, their pets, their games, their amusements, their history and their religion – were portrayed on the pottery they used every day.

Director/Narration
Pierre Alibert

Original music
Francis Seyrig

Award
Quality Award, French
National Film Center

19 minutes
Color
Age range 12–adult
Film $623 Rental $189
VHS $89

◀◀ 50
Athens vase c 680 BC

◀ 27
Restored Buddha

70   **Etruscan Tombs of Volterra**

Sculpted during the twilight of Etruscan independence, the great beauty of the sarcophagi of Volterra stems from a nostalgia for the past. Believing the dead to be more important and more powerful than the living – the burial grounds were spread over a much greater area than the living were allowed to inhabit – the anonymous artists fashioned memorials, not only to the individual Etruscan dead, but also to a culture and an age that they knew was lost to them for ever. Their refined and gentle figures, so graphic, vibrant and full of life, owe little to the Greek style that prevailed elsewhere, but later were to inspire great Italian masters like Leonardo and Michelangelo.

'Accentuates the vitality and force of the art presented. The analysis of the bas-reliefs enhances the value…of these works from the Hellenic-Roman Period of the Etruscans.'
UNESCO

Director/Narration Carlo L Ragghianti	**11 minutes** **Color**
Original music Giorgio Fabor	**Age range 14–adult** **Film $483** Rental $149
Award Exceptional Quality, Italian Government	**VHS $69**

80   **Pompeii, City of Painting**

Virtually destroyed on one terrible day in AD 79 by the eruption of Mount Vesuvius, Pompeii has been almost completely excavated to reveal a treasure-house of paintings preserved under the cinders and ashes which buried the city – the only paintings of all classical antiquity to have survived. Hellenistic and Roman, the variety of the artists is great: the pictorial panorama presents styles derived from the theater, fabulous depictions of Trojan legends, serenely contemplative views, and vibrantly impressionistic representations of myth and reality. Regal portraits alternate with epic characters and men and women of Pompeii. In the silent houses, in slow progression along the walls of precious, glowing color, the eternal vitality of art brings to life for us the serene spirit, the harmony and humanity of classical times.

'Points out what one does not normally see and captures the exuberant nature of this rich art.'
UNESCO

Director/Narration Carlo L Ragghianti	**12 minutes** **Color**
Original music Franco Potenza	**Age range 12–adult** **Film $553** Rental $169
Award Exceptional Quality, Italian Government	**VHS $79**

327   **Classical Sculpture and the Enlightenment**

The Grand Tour took many people of taste and wealth to Italy in the eighteenth century and encouraged the collecting of antique works of art. This program concentrates on one important British collector, Charles Townley, whose collection of marbles is in the British Museum. Gerard Vaughan of Oxford University talks to Colin Cunningham of the Open University about a number of Townley's most important marbles. They discuss the problems of interpreting the subject of sculptures, including the work of the eighteenth-century scholar Winckelmann, the question of restoration and the difficulties of exporting major works from Italy. Publications illustrating Greek and Roman works of art influenced British taste, as did the displays of the works themselves by Townley and other collectors. Among the volumes shown in the programs are the works from Pompeii and Herculaneum published by the King of Naples, and Townley's own catalog of the collection displayed in his private house.

Part of the series *The Enlightenment*

Director Robert Philip	**25 minutes** **Color**
Presenters Colin Cunningham Gerard Vaughan	**Age range 18–adult** **VHS $99**
Open University/BBC	

2 First Civilizations

23

3

Africa

For a long time a common error among western commentators was to classify the peoples and traditional arts of Africa, along with those of prehistory, as 'primitive.' In fact, of course, the native cultures of Africa are sophisticated and subtle.

**This section of
5 programs can be
purchased on
VHS for $475**

**Television rights and
prices on request**

In Africa for longer than in Europe arts continued to exist in a social and religious context, as a function of a rich spiritual life and in reverent, mythopaeic relation to their environment. Such attitudes are lost to a post-Industrial Revolution world, which views artists, artworks, and indeed the spiritual, with scepticism, or at least sets them apart from functional life in the 'real world.' The parallels often drawn between tribal art (and indeed prehistoric art) and the modern art of the West, while not invalid, at times disregard the former's true function in its original context. The films in this section variously show art within its social framework or directly presented to the viewer, without narrated explanation, thus respecting the ability of the work of art to operate both as a social tool and as an independent, self-sufficient object of beauty and significance.

10 **Tassili N'Ajjer**
Prehistoric Rock Paintings of the Sahara

Four thousand years ago the people who
inhabited the Tassili N'Ajjer, a group of
mountains in the eastern Sahara, painted
the rocks with scenes of their daily life.
Why? Probably they were making magic;
we can only guess. But from the hundreds
of thousands of pictures they left (nowhere
else is prehistoric art to be found in such
abundance) we learn that the desert then
was no desert at all: it was a place of
flourishing community life, of flowers and
waterholes and herds of antelope. To our
eyes these vivid and colorful humans and
animals in motion, farming and hunting and
making war, look astonishingly 'modern',
preserved as they have been by the dry
climate. Today, however, they are in danger,
since many have been defaced by tourists
and some have already entirely disappeared.
To film this invaluable record of the
paintings, some of the most recent
technical developments in the art of film
have been used to capture some of the
most ancient images we still have. At the
very dawning of artistic activity, the images
human beings create are bound up with the
politics and economics of their existence –
the animals they hunt, the forces, natural
and supernatural, that sustain their lives,
the battles they fight. And their pictures are
inscribed on the very fabric of the
environment they inhabit – the rocks and
cave walls – prefiguring the graffiti or
public murals of today, giving expression to
social concerns and passions.

'Very beautiful, with a very fine subject'
UNESCO

Director	**16 minutes**
Jean-Dominique Lajoux	**Color**
Narration	**Age range 6–adult**
Max-Pol Fouchet	**Film $553** Rental $169
Original music	**VHS $79**
Maurice Le Roux	
Awards	
Gold Medal, Venice	
Bronze Medal, Bilbao	
Quality Award and Prize,	
French National Film	
Center	

◀◀ 85A/B
Ceremonial spoon with
female ancestor figure

85A **The Shape of Darkness**
85B An Exploration of African Art
85A Part One, 85B Part Two

A haunting, poetic quality pervades this
vast panorama of African art, which took
two years of preparation and then nine
months of filming by two camera teams
to draw together. Region by region, the
development of civilization and art is
explored through art objects used in the
daily life of the people. Masks and
ceremonial objects were filmed in remote
parts of Africa where the authentic dances
still take place. African dance under
European influence is rapidly losing its true
form and meaning, so this film is a rare
and notable record. Sections concentrate
on the Nok culture of Northern Nigeria,
the Sao people of the Chad, Ife and Benin,
the Island of Goree, the Bawongo tribe,
the Ivory Coast, the Abomey in Dahomey,
the Senufo tribe, the Bamileke tribe (with
dancers belonging to the Kanze Secret
Society), the Dogon of Sudan, Batouffan
Camaroons and Senegal.

Director/Narration	**85A 26 minutes**
Max-Pol Fouchet	**85B 26 minutes**
	Black and white
	Age range 12–adult

Each part
Film $623 Rental $189
VHS $89

---

88 **Of Leaves and of Earth**
Traditional Tribal Architecture
of the Cameroon

Cameroon is a country where men and
women continue to construct their own
habitats according to ancestral methods
and in perfect harmony with the
environment. From the shores of Lake Chad
to the great equatorial forest, our guides
are the writer André Gide, a pygmy school-
teacher, the chief of a mountain tribe,
and the sultan of the Kotokos. Architecture,
social customs and dance are examined as
we retrace a route followed by Gide in
1926, with excerpts from a journal and
clips of film made on the trip, which gives
us a unique insight.

Director	**45 minutes**
Dominique Theron	**Color**
Awards	**Age range 6–adult**
Canton Prize, Lausanne	**Film $833** Rental $249
City of Bordeaux Prize,	**VHS $119**
FIFARC and FIDEM Awards	

Also available in French

---

87 **The Colonial Encounter**
Past and Present Ways of Representing and
Categorizing the Culture of Ex-French
Colonies in Africa

In the first part of the program Annie
Coombes looks at the ways in which the
culture and history of the French colonies
have been represented to a western
European audience since the turn of the
nineteenth century. These issues are
introduced through an interview with
Joseph Adando, conducted at the Musée de
l'Homme, Paris. Annie Coombes considers
the organization and content of exhibitions,
and the images of colonial culture
disseminated by the popular press and a
growing tourist industry. The program
focuses on the representations of two
African colonies, Dahomey (now the state
of Benin) and Algeria. Dahomey was made
a French colony in 1893, while Algeria was
occupied in 1830. The representation of
these two cultures is considered in the
context of the colonial displays in the
Trocadero Museum, Paris, and the displays
and exhibits in the Paris World Fair of 1900.
Annie Coombes goes on to consider how
forms of ethnographical display and
categorization have been developed in the
organization of two modern collections: the
Rockefeller Collection in the Metropolitan
Museum in New York, and the Museum of
Mankind in London. She argues that the
former tends to emphasize the formal
qualities of these colonial objects,
encouraging us to evaluate them in terms
of western artistic criteria, whereas some
of the displays in the Museum of Mankind
may encourage us to engage with the
contradiction inherent in western
consumption of the artefacts and history
of non-western colonial cultures.

Part of the series
Modern Art, Practices and Displays

Director	**25 minutes**
Nick Levinson	**Color**
Presenter	**Age range 18–adult**
Annie Coombes	**VHS $99**
Open University/BBC	

Part of the fascination of studying early cultures lies in the similarities and contrasts between the major civilizations of the different continents, developing independently of each other.

4

Pre-Columbian America

This section of
5 programs can be
purchased on
VHS for $575

Television rights and
prices on request

Central and South America prior to the Spanish conquest harbored some of the great traditions of the ancient world, traditions which have at times been underplayed by Eurocentric histories: those of the Incas, the Aztecs, and the Mayas. Although they never developed the technology of metalworking, or the use of the wheel, these peoples created an advanced written language, a system of mathematics and a 'proto-Pythagorean' geometry, a sophisticated astronomy and an accurate calendar system. In this respect they were startlingly close to ancient Mesopotamian peoples (see section 2). North America, meanwhile, was the territory of diverse native American tribes whose more organic, less empirical culture again was rich and subtle, but infinitely fragile. As so often, Christian settlers and colonists burst in where angels might fear to tread, both in North and South America. Today the European West increasingly looks to such ancient cultures, in need of their wisdom and their harmony with nature.

90 A Thousand and One Years Ago
Inca Art of Peru

Journeying into the civilization of the Incas, the film uses their pottery, jewels and woven materials to suggest the characters and life of the people. There is very little narration.

'A brilliant presentation of magnificent objects'
UNESCO

Director	13 minutes
Herbert Seggelke	Color
	Age range 12–adult
Original music	
Karl von Feilitzsch	Film $553 Rental $169
	VHS $79

91 Pre-Columbian Art in Mexico

In this film Octavio Paz speaks of his childhood in Mixoac, once an independent town, now a suburb of Mexico City, from whence he made visits to an Aztec shrine nearby. For him the site was 'a kind of doorway that led to another part of Mexican tradition that I didn't know and could only guess at…mine, yet also distant from me.' We are taken to Aztec locations such as that of the Coatlicue colossal figure found in Mexico City. Paz introduces us to the complex cosmology of the Aztecs, their notions of time and space, and their symbols, such as the zigzag serpent motif, representing the duality of the life force – rise and fall, growth and death. Also featuring prominently in this film are the great pyramids of Tenayuca, Chichén-Itzá, Teotihuacán and Tajín. We learn that the Mesoamerican religions all share the notion that the gods have sacrificed themselves to create the world, and that human beings must worship so as to keep the gods alive. For these peoples there was no merely aesthetic pleasure, no pure abstraction, no art for art's sake. All the forms in their art and architecture have symbolic meaning.

Part of the series
Mexico through the Eyes of Octavio Paz

Director	56 minutes
Hector Tajonar	Color
Presenter/Writer	Age range 14–adult
Octavio Paz	VHS $139
Special collaboration	
Marie José Paz	
Original music	
Mario Lavista	

Also available in Spanish

92 In Search of the Mayas

An introduction to the geographical area of Mesoamerican culture which gave birth to the pre-Hispanic civilizations of Mexico. Origins and characteristics are discussed: the idea of nature, communication with the gods, the complex theocratic organization and the symbolic nature of their artistic expressions. The cultures of the Olmecs, Mayas, Mixtecs and Zapotecs are examined through a reconstruction of their architecture, sculpture, painting, ceramics and craftsmanship in precious metals.

Part of the series *The Art of Mexico*

Director	56 minutes
Hector Tajonar	Color
Narrator	Age range 14–adult
Ricardo Montalban	VHS $139
Original music	
Mario Lavista	

Also available in Spanish

93 The Aztec Sun

Deals with the pre-Columbian art of the groups of people from Mexico's high central plateau and the Gulf of Mexico. The plastic arts of the Totonac, Toltec and Mexican cultures reveal the continuity of a deeply religious and warlike view of the universe. The violence and beauty of these creations express a dramatic encounter with a mythical reality. The identity of Mesoamerica was preserved for centuries through this extraordinary view of the cosmos.

Part of the series *The Art of Mexico*

Director	56 minutes
Hector Tajonar	Color
Narrator	Age range 14–adult
Ricardo Montalban	VHS $139
Original music	
Mario Lavista	

Also available in Spanish

◀◀ 92, 93
Pyramid of Uxmal,
Yucatan

▼ 92
Mayan figure

95 Maya Terracotta Figurines

The Mayas were founders of the most brilliant of the pre-Columbian civilizations. When their tombs on Jaina Island, off the north-west coast of Yucatán, were opened, they yielded many very fine, lively terracotta figurines, most of them in the forms of whistles and bells, representing nearly every strand of Mayan society – priests, chiefs on their thrones, warriors, ball-players, dancers, musicians, and craftsmen. Mostly produced in what is now Honduras, these figurines, with their dress, attitudes and expressions so carefully observed, are not only a record of Mayan society, but are invaluable for their artistic qualities too. This is a film without narration.

Directors	12 minutes
Carlos Saenz	Color
Slivia Garduno	Age range 14–adult
Original music	Film $553 Rental $169
Rocio Sanz	VHS $79

5

AD 700–1500

Romanesque and Gothic

With the decline of the great classical civilizations, the first coherent artistic style to emerge was the Romanesque, which was established by the mid-eleventh century. Formed of an eclectic combination of Roman, Moorish, Byzantine and Carolingian traits, the style manifests itself primarily in the architecture of Christian churches that were then proliferating, and in the sculptures and wall paintings adorning them, and the illuminated books housed in them.

This section of
33 programs can be
purchased on
VHS for $3117

Television rights and
prices on request

Typical of Romanesque architecture is the rounded arch supported on plain pillars, while carvings are robust, sometimes humorous, sometimes grotesque. By the middle of the twelfth century, increasingly elongated, slender forms and intricate, refined structures were developing in both architecture and in depictions of the figure. The term Gothic, to describe these tendencies, was introduced during the Renaissance, and denoted disapproval of a style supposedly resulting from the destruction of classical art by the Goths' defeat of the Romans. However the Gothic period was itself an artistic golden age, producing, among much else, cathedrals of newly spectacular height and beauty through the deployment of the pointed Gothic arch and the flying buttress. Such developments in turn stimulated the refinement of stained glass. The Romantic movement and artists and architects of the Victorian period harked back to the time, creating a Gothic revival that aspired to spiritual mystery and intensity.

98   Carved in Ivory

Between the seventh and twelfth centuries
a highly sophisticated tradition of carving
in ivory developed in Britain, beginning in
the monasteries before their devastation by
the Vikings and continuing until it was
superseded by the French style in the
twelfth century. In this film Lord Clark
argues that, at its height, the English
tradition was characterized by a sense of
humanity lacking in its European
counterparts. The earliest pieces shown,
including the 'non-style' of the Frank's
Casket and other examples in the Celtic or
'folk-wandering' cursive style, pre-date the
classic period. Lord Clark illustrates this
classic era, the hundred years around the
Norman Conquest, with ivories from
Winchester, a Giottesque nativity scene,
small figures which show a 'complete
disregard for conventional grace' and a
small box which attains a 'classic grandeur
worthy of a great Renaissance fresco.' The
eleventh century saw the gradual revival of
the cursive style, but while some pieces
reveal a cold ornamental 'un-British' style,
others continue the classic tradition,
including in particular a 'Tau' cross from
Winchester and a crozier made in
Canterbury. Lord Clark sees the ensuing
dominance of the French style as an end to
a period in which the anonymous English
sculptures were the best in the world.
Carved in Ivory was filmed at the exhibition
'Ivory Carvings in Early Medieval England
700–1200,' staged at the Victoria and Albert
Museum, and Kilpeck Church, Herefordshire.

Director	**30 minutes**
Michael Gill	**Color**
Writer/Narrator	**Age range 14–adult**
Lord Clark	**Film $693** Rental $199
Arts Council of	**VHS $99**
Great Britain	

99A   Looking at a Castle
The Complex Arrangements of Medieval Life

The remains of the fortifications and
domestic quarters of Goodrich Castle, near
Ross-on-Wye, Hereford and Worcester,
England, show the complex arrangements
of life in a medieval castle. The presenter
acts as a detective, identifying and reading
the clues which the building contains. For
example, how was the castle defended
against attack? There is a pit for a
drawbridge; sockets and grooves in the
gatehouse point to doors and a portcullis;
and there are 'murder holes' and arrow slits.
A castle is essentially a collection of houses
with a strong outer wall. But where are the
houses? Looking carefully, it is possible to
see angles where roofs, long since gone,
were once sealed and joined to the main
structure. Fireplaces and the remains of the
ovens reveal where the kitchen was, and
there is evidence for a covered way that
provided a service passage between houses
and kitchen. Looking up at the different
floor levels in the towers and large buildings
enables the presenter to show that there
was space here for five separate households.
A useful introduction to castles in general,
since most medieval castles have layouts
similar to Goodrich's.

Part of the series *Looking at…*

Writer/Narrator	**14 minutes**
Howard Williams	**Color**
English Heritage	**Age range 9–13**
	VHS $79

99B Castles of Northumberland

This video has been designed for use in five sections, each leading into a study of a particular aspect of castles – any castles of a similar type, not just the many in Northumberland. The first part, *Siting a Castle,* opens by setting the context for castle building. Children are shown how to relate the building to the landscape and to understand that castles were built both to control the land and to give security. Siting was crucial, especially if the castle's rôle was largely defensive. In the second section, *Elements of a Castle,* we are introduced to the two basic earthworks common to most castles of the period, the motte and bailey. To these are added buildings such as the keep, curtain wall, towers, stables and outhouses. *Defending a Castle* forms the third section, looking at the purely defensive features of a castle. All castles had various lines of defence: defended entrances such as barbicans and gateways with drawbridge and portcullis were combined with strong walls and towers. We also learn the best way of attacking castles. The fourth section introduces the skills of observation and deduction involved in *Looking at a Wall.* We are shown how to look for clues to alterations and how stone was used. Lines of old roofs, doorways, fireplaces, slots for timber floor supports and other construction clues can be seen. The final section, *A Place to Live In,* looks at a fortified manor house before moving on to larger castles. We see where families lived in a castle and how it could be both a home and a refuge in times of attack.

Part of the series *Evidence on Site*

Director	**24 minutes**
Frank Harris	**Color**
Writer	**Age range 9–15**
Michael Scarborough	**VHS $99**
Narrator	
Judi Dench	
English Heritage	

100 French Romanesque Art

Emerging from the long dark age of savagery which followed the collapse of the Roman empire, the Christian Church began once more to assert herself. Craftsmen of the eleventh and twelfth centuries covered France with what one of them called 'the white ornament of churches.' Since the most impressive buildings still standing were Roman, it was natural that they should follow the Roman pattern, at least in their earlier works – hence the name, Romanesque. The people who turned to the Church for a message of hope had no access to books; they learned the great stories of sacred history from the stone statuary and symbolic carvings that adorned the churches – here, Jonah stepping from the whale's jaws, there, an angel dragging Adam out of Eden by his beard. A superbly filmed account of some of the finest Romanesque sculpture and architecture in France.

Director	**21 minutes**
Edouard Logereau	**Black and white**
Original music	**Age range 12–adult**
Andre Jolivet	**Film $623** Rental $189
Award	**VHS $89**
Quality Prize, French National Film Center	

110 Romanesque Painters

Using vast unbroken wall spaces in comparatively windowless buildings, Romanesque fresco painters created scenes of heroic proportions. Brilliant in color, these served as illustrated Bible history lessons for the people of the late Middle Ages in France.

'A very beautiful film, all the more important as all the paintings were filmed on site'
UNESCO

Director	**12 minutes**
Edouard Logereau	**Color**
Original music	**Age range 12–adult**
Yves Baudrier	**Film $483** Rental $149
Awards	**VHS $69**
Mention d'Excellence, Cannes	
Outstanding Merit, Bergamo	
Merit of Honor, Venice	
Quality Prize, French National Film Center	

◀◀ 99B
Warkworth Castle

▲ 119
Virgin and child

117 Pierres d'Etoiles (Gems of Stone)
Romanesque Art in Medieval France
and Spain

The *pierres d'étoiles* or 'gems of stone'
were the stages of the pilgrim route from
Aubrac to Santiago de Compostela. This
film about sacred sites of Romanesque art
in France and Spain is divided into four
parts: *The Resurrection, The Paths of
Eternity, The Sphere of the Stars,* and
The Courses of the Sea. It analyzes the
Visigothic, Carolingian and Mozarabic
influences on Romanesque style in the
context of this sacred network of sites –
Sainte-Foy de Conques, Perse, Bessuéjouls,
Sainte-Marie de Souillac, Saint-Pierre de
Moissac, Eunate, San Millan de la Cogolla,
San Miguel de la Escalada, Foncebadon,
Leboreiro, Santiago de Compostela, and
Castro de Barona. And finally, it examines
the spiritual and material considerations
that influenced the fertile imagination of
Romanesque sculptors and architects.

Director/Scenario	**54 minutes**
Gerard Raynal	**Color**
Original music	**Age range 14–adult**
David Hykes	**Film $1043** Rental $299
Also available in French	**VHS $149**

118 The Norman Conquest of England

The Norman Conquest was not just a
political or military achievement: it altered
the language, the landscape and the
building styles of England. Who were the
Normans? They were really French-speaking
Vikings, who controlled large parts of Italy,
Sicily and Antioch in Syria as well as
conquering England and parts of Scotland
and Ireland. To protect and control their
conquest they built a vast number of motte
and bailey castles. At first these were
wooden structures, but many were later
developed further in stone. The most
impressive of all is the Tower of London,
begun in 1068 as a simple earth fort and
developed to display the importance of the
king. The Normans also erected a great
many ecclesiastical buildings, such as
Rochester Cathedral. Norman features are
pointed out – many churches were later
altered, so their Norman features are no
longer obvious. Examples shown include
Durham Cathedral, the tiny church of
Kilpeck in Hereford and Worcester, and a
Norman house in Lincoln that has the same
shaped windows and doors as the churches.
The landscape also holds many clues to the
Norman Conquest. Besides the ditches,
mottes and earth banks of the early castles,
there are the remains of the great open
fields preserved as ridge and furrow strips.
Then there are the royal forests the
Normans created, such as the New Forest.
The *Domesday Book* is a great property
survey of the kingdom; and a glance at the
dictionary shows many words still in
everyday use that were originally Norman
French. The clues to the conquest are still all
around us.

English Heritage	**15 minutes**
	Color
	Age range 8–15
	VHS $79

119 English Romanesque Art

This video was inspired by the 'English
Romanesque Art' exhibition held at the
Hayward Gallery in London, and features
the art and architecture of the period
1066–1200 – a time of intense creative
activity which gave rise to some of
England's greatest buildings and works of
art. It includes an examination of the
Bayeux Tapestry, plus sections on
architecture, sculpture, manuscripts,
stained glass, metal, wood and ivory.

'…the production is clear, comprehensive,
and professional. Music and sound
effects enhance the quality visuals, which
include many close-ups of intricate carvings
…succeeds in capturing the importance
of building such massive edifices with
relatively simple tools and so much
humble manpower. This is a fine choice
for art teachers.'
Video Rating Guide for Libraries, USA

Director	**56 minutes**
Brian Taylor	**Color**
	Age range 12–18
	VHS $129

French Romanesque

A tour of some of the most celebrated and some of the lesser-known Romanesque sites in France. Our guides are historians, priests and artisans, who initiate us into the philosophy behind the sculptural and architectural splendors of the medieval churches, abbeys and cathedrals. Each of the films in this series is distinctively and imaginatively made by a different feature-film director.

This series of 6 programs can be purchased on film for $4158 or on VHS for $594
Reference S4

'A rich introduction to a cultural and architectural revolution that set fire to Europe…The script explains what lay behind Romanesque art, when man achieved a perfect communion between art and the holy…Marvellous.'
La France Catholique, Paris

'This series…restores to imaginations numbed by innumerable guided tours… a deep sense of a movement that for two whole centuries – and for the first time in history – gave the West a common language…'
L'Humanité, Paris

'This approach to Romanesque France province by province aims to appeal to the emotional and spiritual dimensions and to combat the ugliness and stupidity of today's world…Each film brings together three characters: a historian, a craftsman or artist, and a director who, eschewing the usual documentary style, applies his own personal stamp. The threefold object being to show Romanesque man and the world around him as they really were, together with his dreams of heaven and earth and his masks with their symbols and ciphers.'
L'Eveil, Caen

111 Romanesque Architecture of Alsace
Men of Stone, Men of Faith

'Architecture is the only art where I can enter into the interior…A master builder, whether he be a monk or a layman…when he builds a temple, he knows that a kind of hymn will emanate from the internal spaces. I can pray in any temple as long as the architects and builders gave it that rhythm which brings me silence, meditation and peace…I believe that Romanesque architecture is the most authentic manifestation of the mentality and soul of the people who lived in the eleventh and twelfth centuries. Life wasn't funny; when a little bit of happiness was found somewhere it was taken advantage of to the detriment of civil and religious laws. The important thing was not to get caught…but that was a period when people were straightforward, they sinned heavily, and they repented a great deal!' In such terms the monk Brother Pascal takes us engagingly into the world of Romanesque Alsace, and provides the philosophical and social background for a discussion of the conservation of medieval buildings. Churches looked at include those of Ottmarsheim, Murbach, Epfig, Rosheim, and Neuwiller-les-Saverne.

Part of the series *French Romanesque*

Director
Alain Schwarzstein

Historian
Roland Oberle

Participant
Brother Pascal

Series concept/Producer
Clara Ford

Also available in French

26 minutes
Color
Age range 14–adult
Film $693 Rental $199
VHS $99

112 Romanesque Architecture of Burgundy
Eve, Stone and the Serpent

Approaching the year 2000, this film looks back to the year 1000 for a view of the human condition. Burgundy – destination of pilgrims and cradle of the crusades; a land scattered with churches and shrines, and saturated with vital, often crude faith. In this film we are initiated into the beliefs and ways of the medieval masons who created the Romanesque churches. The central examples of their work here are at Vézelay and Autun, pilgrims' stopping places decorated with fabulous carvings, including those by Gislebertus, one of the few sculptors whose name has come down to us.

Part of the series *French Romanesque*

Director
Jean-François Comte

Historian
Raymond Oursel

Participants
Pierre Grior (sculptor)
Brother Pascal

Series concept/Producer
Clara Ford

Original music
F Verken

Also available in French

26 minutes
Color
Age range 14–adult
Film $693 Rental $199
VHS $99

▲ 112
Gislebertus
Eve

▶ 113
Head of the prophet Jeremiah

113 Romanesque Architecture of Languedoc
Aude: Crossroads of the Romanesque

Languedoc: land of passage, land of refuge, where the mountains still reverberate to the murmur of prayer and the clash of combat. The Spaniards were here, and the Moors have left their imprint, as in the church of Rieux on the road to Compostela; the memory of the Lombards also endures. Here, legends and tales are greatly appreciated. With a historian and artisans as our very informative guides, we rediscover that universal desire to be in osmosis with heaven and earth, which is the prime ambition of the Romanesque. In this way we journey around Caunes-Minervois, Rieux, Montbun, Escales, St Hilaire, St Gilles du Gard and Fontfroide. Many of the sites are ruined, and this film proposes a surprising alternative to the familiar desire to see Romanesque churches rebuilt and their original purpose restored – there is a verity and an authenticity in their ruined condition, testifying to time, and change, yet enduring in fragmented form.

Part of the series *French Romanesque*

Director	**26 minutes**
Bernard Monsigny	**Color**
Historian	**Age range 14–adult**
André Bonnery	**Film $693** Rental $199
Series concept/Producer	**VHS $99**
Clara Ford	

Also available in French

114 Romanesque Architecture of Normandy
Narrow Naves, Mighty Vessels

Abbot Le Gard, ecclesiastic and builder at the Abbey of La Lucerne, brings back to life the great figures of Romanesque creation in Normandy. The legend and reality in the story of William the Conqueror are blended in the course of this evocation of the period. Cerisy, Jumièges, St Etienne and the Trinité of Caen, Essay, St Martin de Boscherville – these are the great medieval buildings the film examines. Abbot Le Gard deals with the technical issues of restoration and reconstruction, as well as those of aesthetic appreciation, and above all conveys his respect for and responsiveness to all that the Romanesque has left us.

Part of the series *French Romanesque*

Director	**26 minutes**
Bernaud Saint-Pierre	**Color**
Historian	**Age range 14–adult**
Maylise Bayle	**Film $693** Rental $199
Participant	**VHS $99**
Abbot Le Gard	
Series concept/Producer	
Clara Ford	

Also available in French

115 Romanesque Architecture of Poitou-Charente
Stone, Mystery and Light

Several sensational Romanesque churches are explored in this film. Villesalem in Poitiers is seen under restoration, with its outstanding carvings of animals and figures, often depicting virtues and vices. The 100-foot-long Charroux is presented as one of the finest creations of the whole Romanesque period. The narrator, Raymond Ourset, talks inspiringly of his love of the period, and he makes connections with our own day (he cites the architecture of Le Corbusier). Other churches in and around Poitiers which are looked at include St Hilaire, St Radigund, Juan-de-Marnes, Melle, Talmont and Lichères.

Part of the series *French Romanesque*

Director	**26 minutes**
Bernard Monsigny	**Color**
Narration	**Age range 14–adult**
Raymond Ourset	**Film $693** Rental $199
Historian	**VHS $99**
Marie-Thérèse Camus	
Series concept/Producer	
Clara Ford	

Also available in French

116 Romanesque Architecture of Provence
The 'Three Sisters'

The 'Three Sisters' are the churches of Thoronet, Senanque and Silvacane. The narration of this film is not an analytical discourse on Romanesque architecture or history but an intuitive exploration of its principles – faith in God and in nature as his creation. Light, proportion, harmony, geometry – with these elements the medieval builder played out his life between heaven above and earth beneath, and created his buildings to the glory of God. Like others in this series, this film emphasizes that Romanesque style is not just one of surface decoration but of structure and proportion.

Part of the series *French Romanesque*

Director	**26 minutes**
Dominique Delouche	**Color**
Historians	**Age range 14–adult**
Maurice Rouquette	**Film $693** Rental $199
Yves Esquieú	**VHS $99**
Series concept/Producer	
Clara Ford	

Also available in French

120 **Pisa, Story of a Cathedral Square**

One of the most famous squares in the
world, the Piazza del Duomo in Pisa, Italy,
was built over a period of several centuries.
But since styles of architecture changed
very slowly at the time, and hundreds
of years of the elements have since washed
over the piazza, the many buildings look
to us like the result of a single act of
creation. These magnificent monuments,
best known of which is the campanile,
or Leaning Tower, bear witness to a time
when Pisa was a powerful seaport.

'Varied and brilliant shots cause an interplay
of the close and distant shapes...or stress
the contrast between the architectural
masses and the horizontal nature of the
countryside. It is obvious that if the
important monuments of various countries
were studied in this way, a tremendously
useful pictorial history of architecture
could be established, of considerable
didactic interest.'
UNESCO

Director/Narration	**11 minutes**
Carlo L Ragghianti	**Color**
Original music	**Age range 14–adult**
Giorgio Fabor	**Film $483** Rental $149
Award	**VHS $69**
Exceptional Quality,	
Italian Government	

123 **The Romanesque in Austria**

This video takes us on a journey back to the
time of the Babenbergs, who, as rulers of
what was then Ostmark, were the real
founders of Austria. The Romanesque covers
the period 1000 to 1250. This program
not only shows world-famous Romanesque
buildings in Austria such as the mighty
churches of Gurk and Seckau, the renowned
cloister of Millstatt, or the Romanesque
chapter house and dormitory at Zwettl
Monastery, it also takes us to less well-
known places, like St John's Church
in Pürgg in the province of Styria, and
the tiny church of St Nikolaus near
Matrei in East Tyrol.

Director	**44 minutes**
Kuri Junek	**Color**
Also available in German	**Age range 15–adult**
	VHS $119

125 **And They Sang a New Song**
Twenty-four Musical Elders at
Santiago de Compostela

The cathedral shrine of Santiago or St
James of Compostela was the destination of
thousands of pilgrims from all over the
Christian world, since St James was the only
one of Christ's apostles supposedly buried
in western Europe. Above the Portico de la
Gloria are sculpted the twenty-four elders
of the Apocalypse, musicians surrounding
the figure of Christ, all holding musical
instruments remarkable both for their
variety and the accuracy of their detail.
Why did the twelfth-century artist place
the elders there? Was he depicting real
instruments? And were they actually played
in the cathedral at the time, despite the
opinion of scholars that instruments were
not used in most liturgical ceremonies?
Our examination of the sculptures is
accompanied by music of the period,
including pilgrim songs taken from the
Codex Calixtinus, a twelfth-century
guidebook for pilgrims to Santiago.

'...accurate and interesting examination of
musical iconography and medieval artistic
license. It also provides a glimpse at the life
of a twelfth-century pilgrim...highly
recommended for music, art, and history
classes. Public libraries would also find it
a valuable addition.'
Video Rating Guide for Libraries, USA

Directors/Narration	**28 minutes**
Susan Havens Caldwell	**Color**
Eugene Enrico	**Age range 14–adult**
	VHS $99

130 **Popular Art in Brittany**

Few parts of the world during the Middle
Ages had a popular art form so fully
developed and of such exceptional quality
as Brittany, home of a multitude of saints.
Architecture, sculpture, and paintings are
shown here in their original settings, in the
fields and on the seashore. Most of these
works of art can be found only in out-of-
the-way places and are rarely, if ever, seen.

Director/Narration	**19 minutes**
Max-Pol Fouchet	**Black and white**
Also available in French	**Age range 14–adult**
	Film $553 Rental $169
	VHS $79

136 The Master Builders: The Construction of a Great Church

Medieval builders produced some of the finest structures that the world has seen in terms of technical sophistication, engineering skill, grace in design, and sheer size. This video follows the building of a cathedral from the earliest stages of fundraising and planning to its construction from the foundations to the roof. By looking at the existing fabric of Beverley Minster, England, in an archaeological light, the video reconstructs some of the methods used to design and build it. Firstly a present-day architect shows how the master builders used the principle of proportional geometry to develop the complicated design with a minimum of equipment. Excavations show evidence of how the foundations support the colossal weight of the building and overcome the problems of the ground beneath.
A draftsman uses modern techniques to create a template for cutting the stone based on surviving working drawings. Construction methods are shown, including the use of scaffolding and cranes, and the building of curved arches to form an interior framework, and flying buttresses to stop the walls from bulging. Many of the individual tool marks left by the masons, plumbers and joiners survive today and help to date the various stages in the building project. Finally, the cracks in the central tower serve as a reminder that not even the master builders were infallible.

Part of the series *Frameworks of Worship*

Director	21 minutes
John Murray	Color
Writer	Age range 8–15
Richard Morris	VHS $89
Presenter/Narrator	
Roberta Gilchrist	
English Heritage	

137 Looking at an Abbey
How Cistercian Monks Organized their Lives

The *Looking at…* series uses real sites to investigate the clues left behind in the buildings and monuments of the past. The partly ruined Rievaulx Abbey in North Yorkshire, England, has a lot to tell the visitor about monastic life. There were many different orders of Cistercian monks, but they all followed the same rule laid down by St Benedict. Moreover, the layout of monasteries followed a common plan. The communities lived round a central cloister, a kind of village green, with a covered way all round. The spiritual center of their lives was worship, and so the most important building was the cross-shaped church to the north of the cloister. The Cistercians were a self-sufficient order: at Rievaulx they had up to five hundred lay brethren, who farmed the lands but were not permitted to worship with the monks – they had to stay behind a screen which divided the church in two. It is possible to see where the dormitories, kitchens, refectory and infirmary were, and also how the Chapter House was reduced in size and rebuilt as the numbers of monks at Rievaulx dwindled over the centuries. The community was advanced for its time: in particular, it made provision for an unusually effective sewerage system.

Part of the series *Looking at…*

Narration	17 minutes
Howard Williams	Color
English Heritage	Age range 8–15
	VHS $89

138 Building an Abbey: Rievaulx
Approaching Technology through an Historic Building

Rievaulx is a twelfth-century Cistercian abbey set in a beautiful and secluded valley in North Yorkshire, England. Children from a local primary school are shown looking for clues to the design and engineering problems faced by the monks who built this large group of buildings. A great deal can be learned from looking carefully at both the buildings and the remains of fallen masonry. For example, it is possible to work out how the monks built such tall columns and high walls. We see how the buttresses and pinnacles, beautiful as they are, have more than a mere decorative function, being an integral part of the engineering. Weight, stresses and load-bearing in a vaulted stone roof are introduced through the medium of an instructive children's game. While the magnificent nave and choir are the central core of Rievaulx, the remains of the extensive monastic buildings are also examined for clues to the way of life of the monks who lived, worked and worshiped here. Evidence of the hearths, the kitchens and refectory all add to our understanding of how they lived. The film is a stepping-off point for a multi-disciplinary study of the history of any abbey or cathedral.

Part of the series *Evidence on Site*

Director	14 minutes
Frank Harris	Color
Writer	Age range 8–15
Michael Scarborough	VHS $79
English Heritage	

140 Villard de Honnecourt, Builder of Cathedrals

The thirty-three pages of this parchment 'album', covered with notes and drawings, speak directly to us of a world about which we know very little. Villard de Honnecourt, thirteenth-century architect, engineer and journalist, 'greets you and bids all of those laboring at the tasks described in this book to pray for his soul and remember him kindly, for herein-contained is information of great value' – not only about the practical problems of stone and timberwork, but also about what he saw on his travels around France and to Hungary, his working sketches for the cathedrals he built or planned along the way, and the principles of the Gothic architecture which expressed so magnificently the spirit of his times.

Directors/Narration	**15 minutes**
Georges Rebillard	**Black and white**
Yves Thaler	**Age range 14–adult**
Award	**Film $553** Rental $169
Quality Prize, French	**VHS $79**
National Film Center	

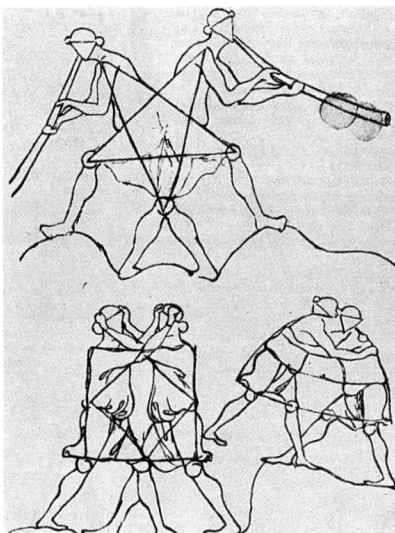

150 Visions of Light
Gothic Stained Glass

For medieval western society, Christianity was the overriding structural force. No area of life was untouched by it, and artists did not seek to be individual, original or subversive, or to give expression to private vision; they were the servants of religious authority, employed to convey the Christian message and thus reinforce society's coherence and stability. The stained-glass windows in the cathedral at Bourges in France are superb examples of how this art form was used to illustrate the Bible for people who could not read, as well as to light up formerly dim interiors: a stained-glass cinema of the Middle Ages. They tell, in the simplest of human terms, the Gospel stories, beginning with the birth of the world, when God ordered the sun to warm the earth, and brilliantly colored birds and strange animals burst out upon scenes of fantastic vegetation. They also show the works of man – cities and buildings, and houses, and tables and chairs and cups – everyday things, all recreated by the unknown window painters, so that what they intended for the instruction of the people of their own time serves to tell us, now, how they lived.

Directors/Narration	**15 minutes**
Louis Cuny	**Color**
M Malvaux	**Age range 9–adult**
Original music	**Film $553** Rental $169
Marcel Dellanoy	**VHS $79**

160 Antelami: The Baptistery of Parma

In 1196 the City Council of Parma commissioned a whole building to be erected to the glory of God – the baptistery, which stands close by the cathedral. At that time Christian baptism was a ceremony which happened only three times a year, so that a large building had to be set aside for it. Everything about this great marble baptistery – the design, the walls, the sculpture with which it was adorned, even the choice of materials – was the work of one man, Benedetto Antelami. Given such an opportunity, many architects would have spoiled their design with too much decoration. Antelami, however, restrained by his feeling for classical simplicity, composed the baptistery as one might compose a classical symphony, from a few very simple elements. Distinguished by the unusual quality of the camera work, this film reveals the whole building as if it were in the film studio, enabling the viewer to see every part from different angles.

'A film of tremendous richness and with remarkable virtuosity in the rotating movements of the camera'
UNESCO

Director/Narration	**16 minutes**
Carlo L Ragghianti	**Color**
Original music	**Age range 14–adult**
Daniele Paris	**Film $553** Rental $169
Award	**VHS $79**
Exceptional Quality,	
Italian Government	

163 **Art in the Making:**
Italian Painting before 1400

Filmed in Siena and at The National Gallery,
London, this video examines the
methods and techniques of Tuscan panel
paintings of the fourteenth century. Using
the detailed instruction in Cennino Cennini's
Libro dell'Arte (c1397), experts from
The National Gallery conservation and
framing departments demonstrate
the many stages of creating an altarpiece,
including making gesso, water gilding,
burnishing, pigment grinding, and painting
with egg tempera. The demonstrations
are linked with paintings by Duccio, Nardo
and Jacopo di Cione.

'An interesting combination of history
and technique…Direction and technical
qualities are excellent. Of particular
importance is the lighting, which shows
off the vivid colors and exquisite gold leaf.
The script is concise and clear…The topic
is fascinating.'
Video Rating Guide for Libraries, USA

Part of the series *Art in the Making*

Presenter	**20 minutes**
James Heard	**Color**
Audio Visual Unit	**Age range 14–adult**
The National Gallery	**VHS $89**

The following book of the same title gives
an extensive overview of the subject –
an ideal companion to the video.

164 **Art in the Making:**
Book **Italian Painting before 1400**

In Italy between 1270 and 1370 the whole
tradition of European painting underwent a
radical and enduring change of direction.
Through their study of The National
Gallery's rich holdings of works from the
early Renaissance, the authors examine
the materials and techniques of painting
which effected this transformation. They
survey the primarily religious function of
the works commissioned, the system of
patronage, the operation of painters' guilds
and contracts of employment and the
organization of workshops. This is followed
by a comprehensive and very readable
account of panel-painting techniques.
The substantial sections on pigments and
color represent original research done
at the gallery. The book discusses great
masterpieces of this period, with full-page
color reproductions, cross-sections
showing layers of paint and gilding and
their composition, X-rays, infra-red
photographs and reflectograms.

Authors from	**10.75 x 8.75 inches**
The National Gallery	**273 x 224 mm**
	236 pages
	303 illustrations
	174 in color
	Book $33

165 **The Birth of European Painting**

The roots of European painting lie in an
awakening experience of Christianity which
spread through the whole of Europe during
the later Middle Ages. Painting offered a
golden image of heaven. The very earliest
paintings were accessories of the Christian
faith, but gradually, especially in Italy, there
developed the concept of a 'picture.' Works
of art began to relate the Christian
experience to life in this world. This new
approach is most powerfully seen in the
works of Giotto, who introduced the
element of narrative. Giotto cared less
about being realistic than expressing
human feeling. While introducing many
realistic elements, Duccio kept well within
the Sienese tradition, painting in warm rich
colors, lavishly applying texture and gold
leaf. The Black Death halted the course of
realism for a while and artists reverted to a
more ritualistic style of devotional painting.
This intense religious mood gave way to an
increasingly elaborate style, elegant and
decorative, known as International Gothic.

Part of the series
The National Gallery – A Private View

Director	**28 minutes**
Henry Lewes	**Color**
Writer/Narrator	**Age range 12–adult**
Edwin Mullins	**Film $693** Rental $199
	VHS $99

37

170 Dijon: The Four Grand Dukes of Burgundy

For nearly one hundred years the house of Burgundy was one of the most powerful in all western Europe. Its dominion stretched from the North Sea to the Loire and from the Loire to the Rhine, while Dijon, the duchy's capital, became an important center of both the religious and secular arts, and the scene of glittering festivities. Four dukes ruled at the height of the family's prosperity: Philip the Rash, who founded its fortunes; John the Fearless, who engaged in feuds that almost destroyed it; Philip the Good, who sold Joan of Arc to the English; and Charles the Bold, perhaps the richest of them all. The film is an historic journey: it shows many of the fine paintings, sculptures, and other *objets d'art* in the Musée des Beaux Arts at Dijon and the Carthusian monastery at Champmol.

Director/Narration Jacques Berthier	**14 minutes**
	Color
Original music	**Age range 14–adult**
Pierre Spiers	**Film $553** Rental $169
	VHS $79

171 An Eye for Detail
Early Netherlandish Paintings

The fine detail of early Netherlandish paintings has continued for over five centuries to delight all who see them. Lifelike illusionism based on the imitation of light effects and surface textures characterizes both portraits and devotional pictures. This video explores some outstanding examples of early Netherlandish paintings from The National Gallery's collection, including works by Jan Van Eyck, Robert Campin and Rogier van der Weyden.

Audio Visual Unit The National Gallery	**21 minutes**
	Color
	Age range 14–adult
	VHS $89

◄ 174
Jan Van Eyck
The Marriage of Arnolfini, detail
and
► enlarged detail

173 Van Eyck, Part One
Beauty in All Its Mystery

Part One deals exclusively with *The Adoration of the Lamb* polyptych (a picture or relief made up of two or more panels) in St Baaf's Cathedral, Ghent, believed to be the work of both Van Eyck brothers. This masterpiece is often described as an all-encompassing painted inventory of man and his world-view. But the film-makers go beyond iconography: entranced by the glowing vitality of the work, they try to explore the mystery of beauty itself. At the International Monte Carlo Television Festival in February 1990, Part One was honored with the URTI prize. URTI (International Radio and Television University) groups together around fifty official radio and television broadcasters whose objective is to promote the increase of cultural programing on the small screen. The jury praised the quality of direction, the rhythm and the contemplative approach to the work, referring to it as a breakthrough in television viewing.

'...very satisfying...would interest the serious art student or collector...'
Video Rating Guide for Libraries, USA

Part of the series
The Genius of Flemish Painting

Screenplay Harold Van de Perre	**55 minutes**
	Color
Director	**Age range 14–adult**
Anton Stevens	**VHS $139**
Award URTI Prize, Monte Carlo	
Also available in Dutch, French and German	

174 Van Eyck, Part Two
The Mystery of Painting

Three masterpieces by Jan Van Eyck, are studied: *The Madonna with Chancellor Rolin, The Madonna with Canon Van der Paele* and *The Marriage of Arnolfini*. By comparing these paintings with the Italian School, contemporary Flemish and ancient Egyptian works, the film-makers try to clarify the abstract idea of 'style.'

'Of especial interest is Van Eyck's use of dots (called vibration), lines (engraving) and patches (modeling) to suggest depth. Narration is excellent...Highly recommended for its novel approach to the subject. Universities and libraries... should certainly consider purchase.'
Video Rating Guide for Libraries, USA

Part of the series
The Genius of Flemish Painting

Screenplay Harold Van de Perre	**55 minutes**
	Color
Director	**Age range 14–adult**
Anton Stevens	**VHS $139**
Award Best Educational Documentary, International Festival of Art Films UNESCO, Paris	
Also available in Dutch, French and German	

175 Beaune: Rogier van der Weyden

Considering its size, nowhere in the whole of western Europe was richer in the later Middle Ages than Burgundy; but the ostentation and extravagance of the wealthy only served to highlight the misery of the poor, who were dependent on their charity. Nicholas Rolin, Chancellor to Philip the Good, built the Hôtel de Dieu at Beaune in the fifteenth century as a combined hospital and chapel for the sick, the aged, and the poor. For the chapel, Rolin commissioned Rogier van der Weyden to create a many-paneled painting of the Last Judgment, which was unshuttered only on holy days. This powerful work of art – the good flying heavenwards to eternal bliss, the wicked pulled down to the fiery depths of hell – was a stark reminder to the invalids that they must always be prepared to meet their God...

Director/Narration	**15 minutes**
Jacques Berthier	**Color**
Original music	**Age range 14–adult**
Pierre Spiers	**Film $553** Rental $169
Also available in French	**VHS $79**

176 Buildings and Beliefs
Medieval Social Structure and Spirituality

This exploration of a typical parish church – All Saints, York, England – shows how much can be learned about the social and religious beliefs of those who built it and extended it over the centuries. The starting point is the structure itself. The surviving fabric can tell us a great deal about the sequence of construction; a model is used to show the development and enlargement of the building and its division into different parts. All Saints was situated in the industrial part of the city – evidence of various trades and industries can be seen in the symbols on coffin lids. Further evidence comes from written records such as fourteenth-century wills, which contain a wealth of information about funeral arrangements and bequests for improvements to the church – these indicate the increasing prosperity of the local merchants and tradesmen. New glass windows were inserted, and the aisles were divided and widened to put in more side chapels so that masses could be said for the departed who had left money for the purpose. At one time there were five separate altars. Merchants also gave money for the establishment of a hospice for the poor and sick. Altogether the fabric of the building, together with its records, is a rich source of historical information.

This program is particularly suitable for teacher training.

Part of the series *Frameworks of Worship*

Director	**20 minutes**
John Murray	**Color**
Writer	**Age range 16–adult**
Richard Morris	**VHS $89**
Narrator	
Roberta Gilchrist	
English Heritage	

178 Ecce Homo
Richly Painted and Gilded Wood Sculptures

Already two centuries old in France and Italy, Gothic art reached eastern Europe much later. The most beautiful examples are to be found in Czechoslovakia; the richly painted and gilded wood sculptures of the birth, life, death and resurrection of Christ were made (as the Romanesque sculptures had been several hundred years before) by anonymous craftsmen, telling the simple people who could neither read nor write the basic stories of the New Testament. The most humble peasants could relate what they saw – birth, suffering, death – to their own life in their village, while the color and richness of the robes and diadems, more splendid than anything they were used to, served to impress the Gospel story on their mind. Too often today our notion of Gothic art and architecture is one of static forms and pale, neutral colors. Such restrained qualities, however, are due to the bleaching of age and the deliberate Puritan 'toning down' of original colors to suit post-Reformation tastes. In their day Romanesque and Gothic churches and cathedrals were ablaze with color, closer to the scintillation of Byzantine churches and Moslem temples than to the piously whitewashed northern church interiors we know today. The statuary was painted in gaudy and lifelike color, and was carried in processions down aisles and out into the streets, draped in finery and flickering in the light of candles. Church ritual and pageantry had the immediacy and drama then that movies have for modern audiences. This film shows rare statues which have retained their original colors, and restores to them something of their processional drama and mystery through the control of camera-angle and cinematic technique. Anthony Roland considers it to be one of the jewels of his collection. There is no narration.

Director	**9 minutes**
Bruno Sefranka	**Color**
Award	**Age range 12–adult**
Merit of Honor,	**Film $483** Rental $149
Bergamo	**VHS $69**

The history of western art is one of movements and counter-movements, actions and reactions. In particular there is the alternation between the tendency towards balance and rationality and the urge towards emotive elaboration or distortion. A typical example is the contrast between the Renaissance art of the fourteenth to fifteenth centuries, which sought to re-establish the rules of grand design and proportion of classical art after the overarching strains of the Gothic, and the Mannerist art which followed in the sixteenth century, which elaborates upon, and even perversely bends and breaks, the classical rules.

1400–1600

6 Renaissance and Mannerism

With early Renaissance painters such as Giotto, Masaccio and Piero, and with High Renaissance masters like Leonardo, Raphael and Michelangelo, come poised, architectonic arrangements of the human form. The development of their art coincided with a flowering of the natural sciences and of Christian humanist philosophy which, while deeply religious, marked a demystification and a new urbanity in human thought.

By the end of Michelangelo's career, however, we can perceive a distortion of figures and an exaggeration of musculature characteristic of Mannerism. The term 'mannerist' is one of the most problematic in art history, frequently used disparagingly to suggest affectation, often from an opposing 'classical' point of view. The original Mannerism of the sixteenth century certainly tended to heighten color and employ exaggerated, articulated pose or contrapposto to achieve emotional and spiritual charge. In architecture, at the same time, the elegance of Palladian proportion began to be subject to inventive, if not willful, variation, inversion, and parody. Thus the way opened up for the even greater and more florid artifices of the Baroque and Rococo.

◀◀ 223, page 42
Giovanni Bellini
The Madonna of the Meadow

▶ 179
Andrea Mantegna
The Agony in the Garden

◢ 200
Piero della Francesca
The Baptism of Christ

179　Early Renaissance in Italy

The word 'renaissance' means 'rebirth'; what was reborn in Italy during the fifteenth century was an interest in the classical art and ideas of Ancient Greece and Rome. Scholars, writers and painters found in these civilizations before Christ a golden age of wisdom and art, and sought to bring it alive once more. The rediscovery of this classical world radically altered their vision of their own, and gave to the art of painting a new variety of style and of purpose. By the year 1500, the Renaissance had immensely broadened the scope of art – both in its range of subject and in its range of human experience. Technically the artist could now do almost anything. The spiritual content of painting changed too, as devotional art became humanized; artists no longer revered dead heroes and formalized saviors. The work of the following is featured: Uccello, Masaccio, Masolino, Fra Angelico, Piero della Francesca, Filippo Lippi, Verrochio, Baldovinetti, Botticelli, Piero di Cosimo, Luca Signorelli, Andrea Mantegna, Antonello da Messina and Crivelli.

Part of the series
The National Gallery – A Private View

Director Henry Lewes	**28 minutes** **Color**
Writer/Narrator Edwin Mullins	**Age range 12–adult** **Film $693**　Rental $199 **VHS $99**

180　Fra Angelico

This film is preserved in the Roland Collection primarily as an example of early experiments in art-critical film by Carlo Ragghianti, who was to become one of Italy's most influential art critics and educators. The film presents a critical analysis of Fra Angelico's style, which blended traditional Gothic forms with the revolutionary ideas of his contemporaries, Masaccio and Brunelleschi.

Director/Narration Carlo L Ragghianti	**10 minutes** **Color**
Original music Giorgio Fabor	**Age range 14–adult** **Film $483**　Rental $149 **VHS $69**
Award Exceptional Quality, Italian Government	

200　Piero della Francesca

A fine example of early experiments in art-critical film by Carlo Ragghianti. It examines the work of this very individual master who was perhaps the first to exploit the subduing and soothing qualities of light. His ability to endow the world with majesty and calm has never been surpassed.

Director/Narration Carlo L Ragghianti	**10 minutes** **Color**
Original music Giorgio Fabor	**Age range 14–adult** **Film $483**　Rental $149 **VHS $69**
Award Exceptional Quality, Italian Government	

210　Jean Fouquet

Jean Fouquet was one of the greatest artists of the fifteenth century. Among his patrons was Etienne de Chevalier, Grand Treasurer of France, who commissioned from him a *Book of Hours*: a strange mixture of amusing picturebook and devotional manual, linking the chronicles of Christianity to the hours of the day. Fouquet conceived this *Book of Hours* long before he began to work at it. Round each central picture, illustrating some incident from the life of Christ or the Virgin or some other important story from the Bible, he painted scenes of the places he and his patron had known in the king's service – Touraine and Italy, the castle of Vincennes, the streets of Paris. And, where it was appropriate, he portrayed people of his time – among the suppliants at the feet of the Virgin is Etienne de Chevalier himself, and the Three Kings coming to Bethlehem are King Charles VII and his two sons. In introducing these likenesses Fouquet anticipated the liberties later Renaissance painters were to take with religious subject matter.

For more information see page 230

Director/Narration Jacques Berthier	**15 minutes** **Color**
Original music Pierre Spiers	**Age range 14–adult** **Film $553**　Rental $169 **VHS $79**
Also available in French	

215 Guido Mazzoni

The Master of Ecclesiastical Lifesize Statuary Groups

While following the restoration of the monumental *Porrini* group by Guido Mazzoni, this documentary also presents an overview of the sculptures of this marvellous but little-known Renaissance artist.

Director	**30 minutes**
Marco Speroni	**Color**
Original music	**Age range 14–adult**
Angelo Bergamini	**VHS $99**
Also available in Italian	

220 Botticelli's Calumny of Apelles

Italy was indisputably the cradle of Renaissance civilization, and Sandro Botticelli was one of her greatest artists. During the early part of his long career he was a painter of religious frescoes; in the mid-1480s he attempted a new concept in the painting of women, personifying the Goddess of Love and the Seasons, and it is for this that he is most famous; but at the end of his life he was influenced by the teachings of the reforming friar Savonarola, who denounced the corruption of society. Henceforward Botticelli abandoned the feminine beauties of his earlier work; his imagination became darker and more anguished, as we can see from his allegory of the *Calumny of Apelles,* one of his masterpieces. Calumny, preceded by Jealousy, drags an innocent man to the judgment throne of Midas; Suspicion and Deceit whisper in Midas's ear, while Remorse gazes downcast at naked Truth. How distant these impassioned mortals are from Botticelli's legendary gods basking in the sun. This is the best short example of director Ragghianti's pioneering 'crito-film.' All aspects of the film work like an in-depth criticism of Botticelli's painting.

Director/Narration	**12 minutes**
Carlo L Ragghianti	**Color**
Original music	**Age range 14–adult**
Daniele Paris	**Film $483** Rental $149
Award	**VHS $69**
Exceptional Quality,	
Italian Government	

223 The Age of Titian

In the sixteenth century the republic of Venice was the wealthiest trading power in the Mediterranean. Merchants brought precious goods from the East; she adorned herself with riches and offered lavish patronage to architects and artists. Perhaps the greatest of these was Titian. During the next century, Titian and his fellow artists in Venice became the idols of artistic Europe, and right up to our own time painters continue to turn for inspiration to the art of the golden age of Venice. Besides Titian's work, the film features that of Bellini, Giorgione, Tintoretto, Veronese, Antonello da Messina, Palma Vecchio, Lorenzo Lotto, and Jacopo Bassano.

Part of the series
The National Gallery – A Private View

Director	**28 minutes**
Henry Lewes	**Color**
Writer/Narrator	**Age range 12–adult**
Edwin Mullins	**Film $693** Rental $199
	VHS $99

The Age of Leonardo and Raphael

If European art ever reached its zenith, it was surely in Italy in the period after 1500 known as the High Renaissance. Painters were no longer simply traditional craftsmen; they were men of intellect and vision, and their art expressed the supreme value placed in Renaissance Italy on knowledge – the knowledge of humanity. And yet, though the High Renaissance may have been the finest flower of art to date, a citizen of Florence could have watched it bud and wither in his own lifetime. The following artists are featured: Leonardo, Filippino Lippi, Michelangelo, Botticelli, Andrea del Sarto, Perugino, Raphael, Sebastiano del Piombo, Garofalo, Lorenzo Costa, Correggio, Parmigianino, Pontormo and Bronzino.

Part of the series
The National Gallery – A Private View

Director
Henry Lewes

Writer/Narrator
Edwin Mullins

29 minutes
Color
Age range 12–adult
Film $693 Rental $199
VHS $99

226 **The Restoration of a Leonardo da Vinci**

The *Virgin and Child with St Anne and the Infant St John*, Leonardo da Vinci's famous cartoon of 1506/8 which had been at The National Gallery since 1962, was attacked with a shotgun on July 17, 1987. This video, compiled from footage exclusive to The National Gallery, records all the stages of the two-year restoration. It offers a unique and fascinating insight into the methods of a modern conservator and those of past centuries, and into the working practices of Leonardo himself.

Audio Visual Unit
The National Gallery

20 minutes
Color
Age range 12–adult
VHS $89

223
Titian
Bacchus and Ariadne

215
Guido Mazzoni
Deposition

225
Leonardo da Vinci
The Virgin of the Rocks

225
Raphael
An Allegory 'Vision of a Knight'

230A Michelangelo
230B 230A Part One, 230B Part Two

Accorded divine status in the world of art, Michelangelo Buonarroti was a beginning and an end unto himself. Regardless of the media in which he worked – painting, sculpture or architecture – there is a breathtaking perfection to the finished product. This film marks the high point of the art film-making of Carlo Ragghianti. The most technically ambitious and innovative film on art in its period, *Michelangelo* is still unsurpassed as an exposition of an artist's vision in painting, architecture, drawing and sculpture. A camera was designed and built specifically for this film to achieve the sense of a completely free, fluid, infinitely varied viewpoint, weaving at will around the artist's forms. Our conception of the genius of Michelangelo is one of a master able to move between and within his various media, bending and twisting his forms freely into the dramatic contrapposto which marks the transition from late Renaissance to Mannerism. It is this soaring, spiralling fluency that Ragghianti's unique camera work supported by music by Johann Sebastian Bach conveys.

'…absolutely new and hitherto unexplored possibilities of the film camera in the analysis of artistic forms'
La Nazione, Florence

'Leaves an impression of weightlessness, even brevity, as well as force'
Corriere della Sera, Milan

'We can feel the thematic and stylistic unity in the art of Michelangelo'
La Stampa, Turin

Director/Narration
Carlo L Ragghianti

Awards
Exceptional Quality,
Quality Prize,
Outstanding Merit,
Italian Government

35 minutes each part
Age range 14–adult
Color

Each part

Film $763 Rental $199
VHS $109

232 The Miracle of Palladio

In northern Italy in the sixteenth century it was Andrea di Pietro, called Palladio, who renewed the art of architecture in the spirit of classical antiquity. The starting point for this journey is the Church of San Giorgio Maggiore in Venice, which the master planned in 1565. By way of Padua, where Palladio was born on November 30, 1508, the trip continues to Vicenza, which was Palladio's artistic home. Here twelve of his buildings can still be admired, first and foremost the famous basilica, the city hall, whose Gothic structure the master dressed in a splendid coat of two-storey Renaissance loggias. Palladio also built magnificent country villas in a wide area surrounding the city. There is, for instance, the Villa Barbaro in Maser, which Paolo Veronese painted so marvellously that it vies with Palladio's architecture, or the Villa Cornaro in Piombina Dese, a perfect example of the classical temple front which was to influence later architecture as far away as America.

Director	43 minutes
Georg Madeja	Color
Also available in German	Age range 15–adult
	VHS $119

233 Rome under the Popes: Church and Empire

It was only in the sixteenth century that successive popes began to develop the medieval walled area of Rome into a papal city. Until then the Vatican and the Castel Sant' Angelo had been little more than a church and a fortress. Great urban schemes were carried out to assist pilgrims (today we might call them tourists) to visit the new St Peter's and other churches. 'Jubilee' years also swelled the number of visitors, who found that new obelisks and fountains had been built, the water supply renewed, and that antique remains had been 'christianized', providing added attractions for the sightseer.

Part of the series
Culture and Belief in Europe 1450–1600

Director	25 minutes
Charles Cooper	Color
Presenter	Age range 18–adult
Tim Benton	VHS $99
Open University/BBC	

◀◀ 230B
Biblioteca Laurenziana,
anteroom, detail

▲ 233
Sala Paolina, in
Castel Sant' Angelo

◀ 230B
Michelangelo Buonarroti
Sistine Chapel
The Last Judgment,
detail

252 Seville: The Edge of Empire

Once the opulent capital of the Moorish kingdom of Al Andalus, Seville was reconquered and 'christianized' in 1248, its mosques were transformed into churches, but the new cathedral, the largest in Spain, kept the former minaret as a bell tower, and the royal palace, the Alcazar, retained its Moorish character. Successive Christian kings were eager to exploit Moorish craftsmanship and design. In the sixteenth century Seville reached a new zenith. Trade with the New World brought fabulous wealth to the city, and she began to see herself as the new Rome, needing new civic buildings to match her stature. In a private palace, the Casa Pilatos, we trace the evolution on a smaller scale of traditional christianized Moorish design into the humanism and classicism of the Italian Renaissance.

Part of the series
Culture and Belief in Europe 1450–1600

Director	**24 minutes**
Charles Cooper	**Color**
Presenters	**Age range 18–adult**
Tim Benton,	**VHS $99**
Stephen Earle	

Open University/BBC

Also available in Spanish

254 El Escorial: Palace, Monastery and Mausoleum

The Palace of El Escorial in Spain, built by Philip II in the second half of the sixteenth century, was intended to combine all the functions of Church and state. It also contains the bodies of all but two of the kings of Spain from Charles V to Alfonso XIII. From the outside it appears drab and austere, but from within it gives us an intriguing insight into the mind of Philip II, who erected it in a barren and severe setting as a memorial to his father, 'to offer respect and honor to death', and to commemorate Spain's victory at San Quentin in 1557. At close range the beauty of the palace's ornamentation and of its pools and gardens can be seen; but one can also view the small, bare and poorly furnished cell in which Philip chose to die. It is this mixture of royal grandeur and monastic austerity that makes El Escorial unique.

Part of the series
Culture and Belief in Europe 1450–1600

Director	**24 minutes**
Amanda Willett	**Color**
Presenter	**Age range 18–adult**
Tim Benton	**VHS $99**

Open University/BBC

Also available in Spanish

256 Ottoman Supremacy: The Suleimaniye, Istanbul

By the reign of Suleiman I (1520–66), known to the West as the Magnificent, the Ottoman empire had come to dominate the whole of the eastern Mediterranean and North Africa. In many ways conditions paralleled those of the Italian Renaissance, enormous wealth and long history giving rise to a taste for antique classical architecture. In 1550 Suleiman commissioned his architect Sinan to build a mosque complex, the Suleimaniye, which also included a university, a hospital, a public kitchen and a religious hostel. We examine the symbolism of the design and decoration and the varied functions of this, the greatest building completed since Roman times.

Part of the series
Culture and Belief in Europe 1450–1600

Director	**24 minutes**
Charles Cooper	**Color**
Presenter	**Age range 18–adult**
Godfrey Goodwin	**VHS $99**

Open University/BBC

259 Germain Pilon
Sculptor of Royal Tombs

The universe of sculptor Germain Pilon, the creator of tomb effigies to the French kings, was controlled by the power-politics of the sixteenth century. This film was made for the four-hundredth anniversary of Pilon's death, an occasion for which no conventional exhibition could be mounted, as the majority of his works cannot be moved. They are, however, absolutely representative of his period, when the Renaissance was already in decline and humanism was showing a superficially cultured front, beneath which lay violence, perversion, superstition, and anguish.

Directors	15 minutes
Bertrand Dessolier	**Black and white**
Paule Muxel	**Age range 15–adult**
Also available in French	**Film $623** Rental $189
	VHS $89

261 Discovering Sixteenth-century Strasbourg

To walk through the old quarters of Strasbourg in France today is to be faced on all sides by ancient buildings; but how much can we learn from them about the city as it was in the sixteenth century? Using contemporary sources such as maps, engravings and other documents, we investigate what remains and what has changed.

Part of the series
Culture and Belief in Europe 1450–1600

Director	**24 minutes**
Nick Levinson	**Color**
Presenters	**Age range 18–adult**
Rosemary O'Day	**VHS $99**
Tim Benton	

Open University/BBC

260 Fontainebleau: The Changing Image of Kingship

When Francis I decided to convert the royal hunting lodge at Fontainebleau into a sumptuous palace, he invited artists such as Rosso Fiorentino and Francesco Primaticcio to France to decorate it. These two were among the greatest Italian Mannerists of the time. Mannerism was a self-consciously artificial, 'mannered' style that placed the importance of subjective inner vision above the authority of classicism or naturalism. The influence of the Mannerist style – particularly on the stucco reliefs and mural paintings in the Galerie François II, the rooms of Madame d'Etampes, and the ballroom built later by Henry II – spread throughout northern Europe. And as court life changed under Francis I and his successors, the palace's architecture evolved with it.

Part of the series
Culture and Belief in Europe 1450–1600

Director	**24 minutes**
Charles Cooper	**Color**
Presenter	**Age range 18–adult**
Tim Benton	**VHS $99**

Open University/BBC

This section of
15 programs can be
purchased on
VHS for $1535

Television rights and
prices on request

7

1400–1600

Northern Renaissance

'Two groups of mankind have been, and still are, the principal factors of modern civilization; on the one hand, the Latin or Latinized people – the Italians, French, Spanish and Portuguese – and on the other, the Germanic people – the Belgians, Dutch, Germans, Danes, Swedes, Norwegians, English, Scots and Americans. In the Latin group the Italians are undeniably the best artists; in the Germanic group they are indisputably the Flemings and the Dutch.'
Hippolyte Taine

There has been a long-accepted division in art history between northern and southern culture. In his study of Netherlandish art, the nineteenth-century French writer and critic Hippolyte Taine elaborately characterizes northern temperament, physique and custom and their reflection in northern art. He notes in particular northern realism, and the tendency to proliferate detail, the freedom from any desire to over-refine or idealize nature or the human form, and the preference for landscape subjects.

It is of course important not to over-emphasize national or racial characteristics. The Renaissance after all was a period of great metropolitanism, and the beginning of cultural 'tourism' for both collectors and artists, who would often cross Europe, live abroad for long periods, absorb styles and exchange ideas. Nevertheless the Germanic/ Latin divide cannot be entirely denied, as Michelangelo recognized: 'In Flanders they prefer to paint what are called landscapes and many figures scattered here and there … There is neither art nor reason in this, no proportion, no symmetry, no careful selection, no grandeur … If I speak so ill of Flemish painting it is not because it is wholly bad, but because it seeks to render in perfection so many objects of which one alone, through its importance, would suffice…'

205 The Northern Renaissance

Five and a half centuries ago in the Netherlands, artists were learning for the first time that a painted image on a flat surface could actually be made a mirror of reality; and in part this achievement was made possible through an exciting discovery – oil painting. The Northern Renaissance painter minutely examined every aspect of his expanding world. He scrutinized its surface; he also peered beneath, searching for a significance deeper than what is visible. It was a search for the truth, and the Northern Renaissance rooms in The National Gallery, London, document the many stages of that search. The work of the following is featured: Jan Van Eyck, Robert Campin, Dirk Bouts, Gerard David, Jan Provoost, Geertgen, Hans Memlinc, Rogier van der Weyden, Hieronymus Bosch, Pieter Bruegel, Marinus, Lucas Cranach, Jan Gossaert, Albrecht Dürer, Hans Holbein.

Part of the series
The National Gallery – A Private View

Director	**28 minutes**
Henry Lewes	**Color**
Writer/Narrator	**Age range 12–adult**
Edwin Mullins	**Film $693** Rental $199
	VHS $99

236 Venice and Antwerp, Part One: The Cities Compared

Two great sixteenth-century cities contrasted: one a booming commercial center, the other an ancient European power. Between 1496 and 1538, a major change of attitude towards public building and public spaces took place in Venice, and this led to the development of the area around the Piazza San Marco and the Rialto. Antwerp, on the other hand, simply exploded outwards from its medieval core, the Grote Markt and the cathedral. Both cities were extremely rich; both reached a peak of prosperity and then declined – one through Spanish conquest, the other through exhausting wars and the new trade with the Americas.

Part of the series
Culture and Belief in Europe 1450–1600

Director	**25 minutes**
Nick Levinson	**Color**
Presenter	**Age range 18–adult**
Tim Benton	**VHS $99**
Open University/BBC	
Also available in Spanish	

237 Venice and Antwerp, Part Two: Forms of Religion

In the sixteenth century religion had a far greater impact on society in general; it dominated many aspects of life now presided over by government and social services. On location in Venice and Antwerp, we see that the two great cities were no exception to this rule; and yet, despite the supremacy of the Catholic Church, vital minorities such as Jews, Greeks and Germans were also allowed relative freedom to practice their own religions.

Part of the series
Culture and Belief in Europe 1450–1600

Director	**25 minutes**
Nick Levinson	**Color**
Presenter	**Age range 18–adult**
David Englander	**VHS $99**
Open University/BBC	
Also available in Spanish	

▼ 205
Hieronymus Bosch
Christ Mocked

▲ 205
Gerard David
Christ Nailed to the Cross

238 Christopher Plantin, Polyglot Printer of Antwerp

Christopher Plantin's successful printing and publishing business, founded in Antwerp in the 1560s, brought together many scholars, linguists and theologians and produced a wide range of scholarly books including the highly complex Polyglot (or 'many language version') Bible. We tour the Plantin Moretus Museum and find that, in the sensitive political and religious climate of Antwerp at the time, printing was not only lucrative and full of exciting technical innovations, but sometimes dangerous as well.

Part of the series
Culture and Belief in Europe 1450–1600

Director	25 minutes
Nick Levinson	Color
Presenters	Age range 18–adult
Rosemary O'Day	VHS $99
Noel Coley	
Open University/BBC	

240 At the Turn of the Age: Hans Holbein

As the new age of the Renaissance began to flower, Hans Holbein the Younger, born in 1497 and at first apprenticed to his father, discovered his vocation – portrait painting. His picture of the most famous scholar of his age, Erasmus of Rotterdam, reveals the complexity of his subject's character. Erasmus introduced him to Sir Thomas More, through whom Holbein came to know, and paint, other members of Henry VIII's court. The new patrons of the time, merchants and bankers and rulers who ran their kingdoms like business empires, required a new kind of painter who would depict them surrounded by all the trappings of their wealth and power, and by objects symbolizing their cultural interests. In 1532 Holbein went to England for the second time and remained there, becoming court painter to Henry and portraying many of the courtiers – and queens – who came within the king's orbit. In 1543 the plague ravaged London once more; it was a 'Dance of Death' such as Holbein had illustrated earlier in his career, and this time the painter himself fell victim to it.

Director/Narration	13 minutes
Herbert E Meyer	Color
Original music	Age range 12–adult
Jakob Trommer	Film $553 Rental $169
	VHS $79

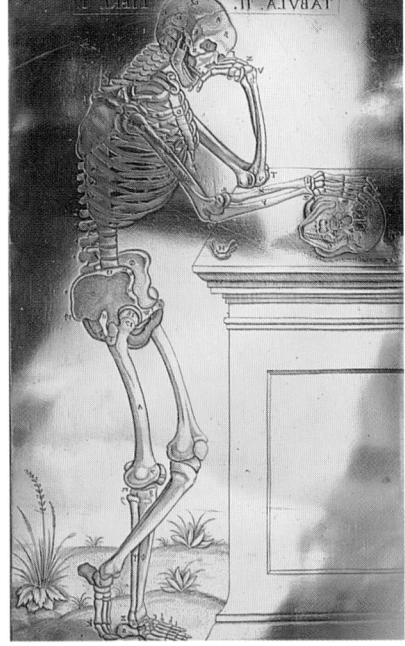

242 Maarten van Heemskerck: Humanism and Painting in Northern Europe

The brilliant young artist Maarten van Heemskerck, born in Holland in 1498, learned to imitate the Italianate manner while still at home – his early *St Luke Painting the Virgin* is almost a parody of the Italian style. But in 1532 he became one of the first artists to travel to Rome and immerse himself in the humanist art made famous by Michelangelo and his contemporaries. Here we trace the development of Heemskerck's work, and also study some of the drawings he made in Rome. From his sketchbooks we have valuable evidence of the monuments of antiquity as they existed in the sixteenth century, and of the building of the new St Peter's.

Part of the series
Culture and Belief in Europe 1450–1600

Director	24 minutes
Charles Cooper	Color
Presenter	Age range 18–adult
Catherine King	VHS $99
Open University/BBC	

Bruegel, Part One
True to Life: Prophet for All Seasons

Pieter Bruegel stands out as the greatest novelist–painter in history. He closely observes the rich pattern of life unfolding around him and in true-to-life style ruthlessly paints his vision of man and the world, stories of village life (*The Battle between Carnival and Lent*), peasant life (*The Wedding Dance, The Harvest*), the city (*The Tower of Babel*), war (*Mad Margot*) and the Gospel (*The Procession to Calvary*). The film-makers investigate Bruegel's paintings together with our time, by using contemporary photographs. In this way they demonstrate how Bruegel's time differed little from our own – a mirror image which can leave no viewer unmoved.

'…most enlightening in the way the viewer is taken step-by-step to the nucleus of these vast panoramas, a process that provides a means of critically studying any work of art. The graphics are top rate, especially when used in the analyses. For example, parts of a painting are faded out to focus in on what is being emphasized, or paintings are divided by graphics to illustrate composition. Bruegel's *Tower of Babel* is given a side-by-side comparison with photos of the Colosseum of Rome (where Bruegel travelled) in order to depict their similarities and resemblance… accessible to both those without an art education background and those with previous experience…a wonderful acquisition for both school and public libraries alike.'
Video Rating Guide for Libraries, USA

Part of the series
The Genius of Flemish Painting

Screenplay	**50 minutes**
Harold Van de Perre	**Color**
Director	**Age range 14–adult**
Anton Stevens	**VHS $139**

Also available in Dutch, French and German

▼▼ 240
Hans Holbein the Younger
The Ambassadors

◀◀ 238
Original copper plate for anatomical illustration

▶ 244
Pieter Bruegel the Elder
The Adoration of the Kings

Bruegel, Part Two
True to Life: Painter for All Seasons

As well as showing sharp insight into the good and evil of his times, Bruegel was a genius as a painter. This second part of the Bruegel story investigates his highly original way of painting, his feeling for composition, his brushwork, and his use of color. His style is as complex as life itself, making his work a documentary of the village and at the same time universal. Particular attention is paid to the landscapes which fill Bruegel's paintings. The second part concentrates on *The Parable of the Blind, The Return of the Herd, The Conversion of Paul, The Magpie on the Gallows* and *The Gloomy Day*.

'The color rendition is very good…very interesting and beautiful to watch'
Video Rating Guide for Libraries, USA

Part of the series
The Genius of Flemish Painting

Screenplay	**50 minutes**
Harold Van de Perre	**Color**
Director	**Age range 14–adult**
Anton Stevens	**VHS $139**

Also available in Dutch, French and German

Pieter Bruegel and Popular Culture

The old nickname of 'Peasant Bruegel' is misleading; although he painted peasant life, Pieter Bruegel was a highly educated townsman. He had also traveled to France and Italy, although the art of Italy seems to have left little impression on him. His scenes of village life in sixteenth-century Flanders, pictures like *The Return of the Herd, The Hunters in the Snow*, and *The Battle between Carnival and Lent*, are not merely realistic, but show the influence of humanist ideas about rural life, which were themselves derived from classical writers. These works also form part of the tradition of rural paintings derived from medieval books of hours – and they express a satirical approach to drunkeness, gluttony and other sins.

Part of the series
Culture and Belief in Europe 1450–1600

Director	**24 minutes**
Robert Philip	**Color**
Presenter	**Age range 18–adult**
Ivan Gaskell	**VHS $99**
Open University/BBC	

Also available in Spanish

The Past Replayed: Kirby Hall

A Living History Project for Special-needs Schoolchildren

Special-needs schoolchildren experience a day out in the sixteenth century at Kirby Hall, Northamptonshire, England. The first part of this video is an account of the planning and organization that preceded the event: the teachers attended courses to study music, dancing, costume-making, cooking and the history of Kirby Hall. Next, the children were given careful preparation for the day in the classroom. This part of the video also includes a brief resumé of the day's events and a look at the follow-up work carried out by the schools. The second part of the video is intended for classroom use; it is a detailed record of the day itself. Each child was dressed in authentic costume, and took part in two work groups in order to experience different aspects of life in a grand country house in 1590. Lunch was authentic too – the pea soup was not popular! In the afternoon each school presented some aspect of their work as the last event of the day.

This program is particularly suitable for teacher training.

Director	38 minutes
Alan McPherson	**Color**
English Heritage	**Age range 9–13**
	VHS $99

265   **Shropshire in the Sixteenth Century**

Surviving buildings in Shrewsbury, England, and the surrounding Shropshire countryside tell us much about the area in the sixteenth century. The most important cash commodity of the time was wool. Wool production had hitherto been concentrated on the great monastic estates, but when these were divided up and sold during the Reformation, it was lawyers and merchants who had the ready money to buy them. Local merchants with London and Welsh links took over the marketing of wool and cloth after the break with Rome and the departure of the Italian bankers. The ownership, the materials, the function and the style of the buildings they put up or adapted were all influenced by the social, political and economic changes of the time.

Part of the series
Culture and Belief in Europe 1450–1600

Director	24 minutes
Nick Levinson	**Color**
Presenter	**Age range 18–adult**
Nick Rowling	**VHS $99**
Open University/BBC	

266   **Hardwick Hall: Power and Architecture**

'Hardwick Hall, more glass than wall,' as astonished contemporaries described it, was one of the most innovative houses of its period in Europe. At the same time, it is a typical, though exceptionally well-preserved, English house of the Elizabethan period. The video looks at the factors which influenced its design, the powerful personality of its owner-builder, Elizabeth, Countess of Shrewsbury, or 'Bess of Hardwick', and the brilliance of her architect, Robert Smythson.

Part of the series
Culture and Belief in Europe 1450–1600

Director	24 minutes
Nick Levinson	**Color**
Presenter	**Age range 18–adult**
Nick Rowling	**VHS $99**
Open University/BBC	

271 **Jan Bruegel the Elder**

Jan Bruegel the Elder
A Painter between Two Periods

Jan Bruegel the Elder is one of the most interesting artists working at the turn of the sixteenth and seventeenth centuries. The second son of Pieter Bruegel the Elder, he was known as 'Flower Bruegel' and 'Velvet Bruegel.' The incredibly detailed accuracy of his works, which were painted in jewel-like colors, made him one of the most respected and financially successful painters of his time. The film is based on the results of more than ten years' research by Dr Klaus Ertz, author of a critical catalog of Bruegel's works. The life and work of this Flemish artist is described mainly through his paintings. His fruitful cooperation with other artists such as Rubens, Joos de Momper the Younger, Hendrik van Balen, Hans Rottenhammer and others is examined in depth, while shots of the town and countryside of modern Flanders enable us to make both artistic and biographical comparisons. The wealth of material in the commentary is structured by headings which emphasize the concepts central to his work, such as scenes of the world, images of village life, new landscape compositions, flowers, scenes set in paradise, mythology and allegories. Contemporary music, anecdotes and quotations contribute entertainingly to our understanding of Jan Bruegel's importance. The film touches on the controversial theme of the attribution and authenticity of many works, including the distinctions between a copy, an artistic interpretation and a forgery.

Director	45 minutes
Dr Klaus Ertz	Color
Also available in German	Age range 14–adult
	VHS $119

269 **Moscow: The Gold-domed Capital**

Moscow: The Gold-domed Capital

The Gold-domed Capital tells the story of Moscow, of how it has grown and changed since the time of Dmitry Donskoy, Tsar Ivan the Terrible, in the sixteenth century. The luxurious palaces of the Russian Tsars, the world-famous St Basil's Cathedral on Red Square, the Ascension Cathedral – 'the Russian Parthenon' – in Kolomenskoye, the ancestral estate of the Tsars at Izmailovo, the splendors of the numerous ancient Orthodox churches – all these and others make up the character of Moscow today.

Part of the series
The Beautiful City of Moscow

Director/Script	30 minutes
Vladimir Benidiktov	Color
Art Video International	Age range 14–adult
Also available in Russian	VHS $99

270 **Renaissance Architecture in Slovakia**

Renaissance Architecture in Slovakia

From Italy the styles of the Renaissance began to travel northwards into what is now East Slovakia. Because the Slavs were not familiar with the new principles of design and architecture, they invited foreigners to supervise their new buildings. But Italy was not the only source of influence; from the west – from Silesia and Saxony, where Gothic was changing to a more intimate and human style – came builders, architects and sculptors. Indeed, for students of the Renaissance to see only the well-known High Renaissance buildings gives a false view of what most towns were like. The merchants and princes of this area were rich enough to build great houses, but far away enough from the center of the new movement to have minds and wills of their own; a new type of architecture came into being, uniting the best of sunny south and solemn west.

Director/Narration	12 minutes
Pavel Miskuv	Color
	Age range 14–adult
	Film $483 Rental $149
	VHS $69

7 Northern Renaissance

53

'I have concentrated on expressing the greatest inward emotion and feeling'
Rembrandt

1600–1700

8 Rembrandt

This section of
9 programs can be
purchased for $3861:
5 titles on film,
4 titles on VHS

Television rights and
prices on request

Rembrandt is one of the handful of artists from the past whose names are familiar even to those who know little of art. Frequently he is referred to as the greatest artist who ever lived. Yet, while his name is synonymous with unquestioned genius, we may fail to see beyond the aura or to penetrate the particularity of his art, which anticipates so much of Romanticism, Expressionism, the deep humanism of Van Gogh and the tremulous scrutiny of Cézanne, but which remains unique. The films in this section take us beyond the myth to the man, his materials and his methods. They explore the background of his age (see also section 7 for the broader backdrop of *The Northern Renaissance*) and investigate his techniques, chronicle his life story, fathom his personality and follow the spiritual pilgrimage of his art.

295   The Age of Rembrandt

In the seventeenth century a small Spanish colony on the North Sea won its independence. The northern Spanish Netherlands became Holland; and in a remarkably short time this energetic new nation rose to pre-eminence in science, trade, learning and art. It was the golden age of Holland. Suddenly there was a popular demand for painting, and Dutch artists in general concentrated on popular subjects: in this young nation, the largest market for painting was the private home. With thoroughness and objectivity the Dutch artists recorded every aspect of their world. At no time in history has the art of painting occupied so natural a rôle in the daily life of man. Although focusing on Rembrandt, the outstanding artist of his age in northern Europe, the work of the following is also shown: Jan Steen, Aelbert Cuyp, Berckheyde, Metsu, Koninck, Avercamp, Jan van der Cappelle, Gerrit Dou, Fabritius, Vermeer, Wouvermans, Gérard ter Borch, Van Hoogstraten, and Ferdinand Bol.

Part of the series
The National Gallery – A Private View

Director	**28 minutes**
Henry Lewes	**Color**
Writer/Narrator	**Age range 12–adult**
Edwin Mullins	**Film $693** Rental $199
	VHS $99

296   Art in the Making: Rembrandt

Rembrandt is universally recognized as an artist of intense feeling, but here less well-known aspects of the seventeenth-century Dutch master are revealed. He was a brilliant craftsman and his calculated painting methods, studio organization and ingenious use of certain pigments, as well as his dramatic use of thick, impasted color, are all explored through The National Gallery's own unrivalled collection.

'…successfully combines scenic outside footage with more technical interior shots and museum stills. Heard is articulate and scholarly; he has a keen sense of timing. He knows how to present technical information in a pleasingly beneficial format. The program informs the artist and art historian, teaches the student, and entertains the layperson.'
Video Rating Guide for Libraries, USA

Part of the series *Art in the Making*

Presenter	**20 minutes**
James Heard	**Color**
	Age range 12–adult
Audio Visual Unit	**VHS $89**
The National Gallery	

The following book of the same title gives an extensive overview of the subject – an ideal companion to the video.

297   Art in the Making: Rembrandt
Book

A revealing and pioneering study of Rembrandt's style and technique. The National Gallery's Rembrandts have a remarkable chronological spread, representing most of his major preoccupations as a mature painter. This book describes Rembrandt's technical procedures – how he prepared his canvases and panels, first laid in the composition, made alterations on the canvas, and so on. This technical examination of The National Gallery Rembrandts enables the authors to make a major contribution to the controversial issue of establishing an authentic Rembrandt *œuvre*. The book presents an account of the subject matter of each painting and fully illustrated technical analyses. There is also a chronology of Rembrandt's life and important works; essays on training and studio practice in the Netherlands, and on Rembrandt's painting materials and techniques; a survey of his paint medium; a glossary of technical terms; and an extensive, annotated bibliography.

Authors from	**10.75 x 8.75 inches**
The National Gallery	**273 x 224mm**
	160 pages
	189 illustrations
	88 in color
	Book $33

298 **Rembrandt: Painter of Stories**

Painter of Stories focuses on Rembrandt's foremost artistic ambition – history painting. He made certain developments in his technique in order to achieve this aim, and numerous pupils and followers were attracted to this aspect of his art. Fifty of Rembrandt's masterpieces were chosen in a survey of his artistic development as well as twenty paintings formerly attributed to him that are in fact the work of identified pupils – a juxtaposition that will introduce a large public to the continual debate on authenticity among Rembrandt experts. This video complements *Art in the Making* (296) and is itself both purposeful and enlightening.

Audio Visual Unit	**24 minutes**
The National Gallery	**Color**
Also available in Dutch	**Age range 14–adult**
	VHS $99

300 **Rembrandt's Christ**
Drawings of the Life of Christ

Anthony Roland's *Rembrandt's Christ* is a difficult film to define. More penetrating and demanding than a simple celebration of Rembrandt's drawings (though it is certainly that too), yet more imaginative and poetic than any formal study of the artist's graphic work, the film takes the form of a seamless sequence of images choreographed to the specially composed music of Henry Barraud. The central theme is provided by Rembrandt's depictions of Christ which have never before been gathered together in this way; 160 drawings from sixty-two collections in twelve countries were drawn upon for the film. Rembrandt is shown to be one of the great geniuses of graphic art, and at a time when the authenticity of many of his canvases is being questioned, it is perhaps appropriate to look again to the more intimate medium of his drawings for an insight into the artist's real character. The film reveals the huge breadth of his techniques, from subtly modeled tone to almost violent pen strokes, sensitive fine line, or the almost oriental virtuosity of brush and ink (picked up in Barraud's occasionally somewhat oriental, staccato score). The film intersperses the images of Christ with other biblical motifs, and, significantly, with scenes of landscape and street life of Rembrandt's Holland: children at play, crowds gathering, men and women going about their business. The artist's models are his friends, neighbors and family. The multi-layered nature of the film reflects the interconnections between Old and New Testaments, between past and present, and above all between sacred and secular life, which were universally felt in Rembrandt's day, particularly in Protestant Holland, where religion was being brought from the confines of church ceremony into the wider world of daily life. Thus in the film we see, for example, a parent and child such as those observed countless times by the artist in a domestic setting. Yet Rembrandt's addition of an angel to the scene immediately gives a biblical dimension, and in the same spirit the film director juxtaposes images from other drawings with it – images of violence that might anticipate the Massacre of the Innocents or Abraham's sacrifice of Isaac. Henry Barraud's score, meanwhile, gives musical expression to the concept of Christ as at once human and divine. There is no narration.

'Of universal interest…penetrates very deeply…the mystery of creative activity in an artist of genius. And the result is a masterly film, which can, like a poem by Andrew Marvell or a sonata by Scarlatti, bear endless repetition, each time yielding something fresh and valuable to the spirit.'
Arts Review, London

'An extremely important work in the History of Film…an aesthetic work as an end in itself…the spectator will feel extraordinarily enriched by deep thought and new ideas'
From the book *Christo nel Mondo,* Assisi

Director	**40 minutes**
Anthony Roland	**Black and white**
Original music	**Age range 14–adult**
Henry Barraud	**Film $763** Rental $199
Awards	**VHS $109**
Art Documentary of	
the Year, Assisi	
Chriss Award, Columbus	

56

The Kenneth Clark Rembrandt series

'In these five films I have tried first to convey the character of Rembrandt, then to follow the course of his art, and finally to look more closely at the subject which meant most to him, the illustration of the Bible. Rembrandt was not only one of the greatest artists that ever lived, but one who touches us almost personally in a way that no other great artist does.'

This series of
5 programs
can be purchased
on film for $3465
Reference S9

301   Rembrandt – The Self-Portraits

We know a lot about Rembrandt from his self-portraits; he was the first artist to make the self-portrait a major means of artistic expression. The series begins with the image of a vigorous roughneck, passes through confident celebrity, and ends with the penetrating visions of a solitary old man.

'A blend of interpretation and scholarship, will delight those for whom Rembrandt is the most majestic and human of all artists'
Financial Times, London

Part of the *Kenneth Clark Rembrandt* series

Writer/Narrator	30 minutes
Kenneth Clark	Color
Director	Age range 14–adult
Colin Clark	Film $693 Rental $199

302   Rembrandt – The Rebel

The second film considers Rembrandt as a rebel. This aspect of his character is clear enough in his early work, both in his sympathetic etchings of tramps and beggars and in some major paintings such as *The Blinding of Samson;* it is repressed in his period of prosperity, but it never disappears entirely.

'A homage to the whole man; essential viewing'
Observer, London

Part of the *Kenneth Clark Rembrandt* series

Writer/Narrator	30 minutes
Kenneth Clark	Color
Director	Age range 14–adult
Colin Clark	Film $693 Rental $199

303   Rembrandt – The Success

The third film is concerned with Rembrandt's worldly success as a portrait painter in Amsterdam, which culminated in his enormous portrait group known as *The Night Watch.*

'Lord Clark's ability to direct the eye to greatness, and to identify the intellectual ingredients which indicate genius in art, remains unrivalled'
Daily Telegraph, London

Part of the *Kenneth Clark Rembrandt* series

Writer/Narrator	30 minutes
Kenneth Clark	Color
Director	Age range 14–adult
Colin Clark	Film $693 Rental $199

304   Rembrandt – The Withdrawal

Rembrandt was a careless and prodigal spender, and by the age of fifty he was threatened with bankruptcy. He 'escaped' from the prosperous life of his middle age, but this was a spiritual rather than a material withdrawal, and was also the period of his greatest work, in which his painting achieved a richer color and a new spirituality.

'A display of how a worthwhile subject and an illuminating mind can turn the most simple of formulas into riveting viewing'
Sunday Times, London

Part of the *Kenneth Clark Rembrandt* series

Writer/Narrator	30 minutes
Kenneth Clark	Color
Director	Age range 14–adult
Colin Clark	Film $693 Rental $199

305   Rembrandt – The Bible

Rembrandt's last years were spent entirely alone, but his love of art and of his fellow man made him unconquerable. As an illustrator of the Bible he is unsurpassed; he brooded over every episode of it in the light of his own experience, and gave to it a vivid and dramatic form. In consequence he is really the only great Protestant artist.

'Lord Clark achieves the impossible. He cuts away the cant from culture and makes it understandable to millions'
Daily Express, London

Part of the *Kenneth Clark Rembrandt* series

Writer/Narrator	30 minutes
Kenneth Clark	Color
Director	Age range 14–adult
Colin Clark	Film $693 Rental $199

301
Rembrandt Harmensz van Rijn
Self Portrait Aged Thirty-four

298
Rembrandt Harmensz van Rijn
Belshazzar's Feast

300
Rembrandt Harmensz van Rijn
Christ visiting Mary and
Martha, detail

305
Rembrandt Harmensz van Rijn
Isaac's Sacrifice

Baroque and Rococo art may be seen as the extension of Mannerist artifice, carried to extremes into the seventeenth and even eighteenth centuries. One driving force behind this energizing of artistic form was the Catholic Counter-Reformation, a resurgence of religious fervor during which artists were urged to inspire and carry their audiences away into delirious rapture. Yet inventiveness for its own sake became the heart of the Rococo. The characteristics of the style are serpentine curves, convoluted compositions, weightlessness and a preponderance of organic rather than geometric form.

1600–1800

9 Baroque and Rococo

This section of 41 programs can be purchased on VHS for $4379

Television rights and prices on request

The term 'rococo' comes from the French word *rocaille*, referring to the fantastical, coral-like forms which in much Rococo ornament surround figures and flora as sheer visual improvisation. Such frivolity was inevitably to provoke a return to stern Neo-classical forms.

Yet it is over-simplistic, of course, to view the progress of art as a schematic pattern of swing and counter-swing from classical to Gothic, Renaissance to Baroque, Neo-classicism to Romanticism, Impressionism to Expressionism and so forth. Nowhere more clearly than in the Baroque and Rococo do we see how within any period various and contrasting elements coexist and merge in unpredictable ways. Thus Watteau mixes classical with romantic traits, Chardin celebrates the homely and unrhetorical in the midst of eighteenth-century grandiosity, Bellotto and Canaletto depict townscapes with a near-Impressionist lucidity, while Wright of Derby concentrates attention on scientific subjects that herald a new age of progress and industry.

273 Rubens, Part One
Classical Synthesis: Prophet of Modern Art

Starting from the wide-ranging and varied works of Peter Paul Rubens, this first part gives an overview of some of the most important periods and influences in the history of western painting. In Italy, where he stayed for eight years as a student, Rubens made antique and Renaissance culture his own. He was also aroused by the new Baroque style, which he brought back to Flanders and gave a typical Flemish character. Rubens is famous for his exuberant nudes. No one has rendered different types of nude better than he did: they are ecstatic, aesthetic and even ethereal. We see each type later in the work of other painters such as Watteau, Fragonard and Delacroix. We also see Rubens at work as a landscape painter, at which point it is easy to step from his work into the pre-Impressionist landscapes of Constable. At the end of the story, which also introduces us to Cubism, Futurism and even the beginnings of film, we recognize in Rubens a painter who brings life in all its variety to the canvas.

Part of the series
The Genius of Flemish Painting

Screenplay	**55 minutes**
Harold Van de Perre	**Color**
Director	**Age range 14–adult**
Anton Stevens	**VHS $139**

Also available in Dutch,
French and German

◀◀ 307, page 60
Studio of El Greco
*The Agony in the
Garden of Gethsemane*

▼ 273
Peter Paul Rubens
*An Autumn Landscape
with a View of Het Steen*

274 Rubens, Part Two
Celebrating the Art of Painting

The second part of this documentary deals mainly with Rubens's own *œuvre* and the evolution of his style. It is divided into three periods. The first concerns his early work: though still classical, it shows the influence of the Baroque. The paintings are clearly and easily interpreted and make full use of diagonal axes (*The Elevation of the Cross, The Descent from the Cross*). Later he begins to give his own interpretation to the subjects he portrays. His composition becomes more complex, disturbing, and dynamic (*The Mystic Wedding of Saint Catharina, The Virgin Venerated by the Saints*). In his third period Rubens breaks all bounds and dispenses with the rules. We see an explosion of style in which composition becomes a whirlpool, the brush strokes swirl and dive, color vibrates in the light (*The Ascension of Mary*). We also see Rubens at work in the studio among his pupils. How do we recognize the hand of the master? What techniques does he employ? How does he arrive at his lyrical style? Finally, Rubens's *Allegory of War* is compared with Picasso's *Guernica*.

Part of the series
The Genius of Flemish Painting

Screenplay	**55 minutes**
Harold Van de Perre	**Color**
Director	**Age range 14–adult**
Anton Stevens	**VHS $139**

Also available in Dutch,
French and German

275 The Age of Rubens

This film particularly honors two of the greatest Flemish painters of the seventeenth century, Rubens and Van Dyck. Rubens had the brilliant gift of taking themes from classical mythology and making them live for his own time. He would tackle with dramatic verve large-scale complex work for altarpieces and ceilings, many showing evidence of his early study of Italian art; and all his pictures reveal the pleasure he took in painting them. His tremendous output of works of every kind included highly skilled portraits and landscapes expressing his delight in observing nature and people. Van Dyck, the most gifted of Rubens's assistants, was an outstanding painter of portraits. As court painter to Charles I of England, he created a majestic image of kingship. Other artists featured are Jan Bruegel the Elder, Frans Snijders, Jacob Jordaens and Teniers the Younger.

Part of the series
The National Gallery – A Private View

Director	**28 minutes**
Henry Lewes	**Color**
Writer/Narrator	**Age range 12–adult**
Edwin Mullins	**Film $693** Rental $199
	VHS $99

289 Portrait of Frans Hals

Few facts are known about the Dutch
painter Frans Hals as a person, but
one can learn a lot about him as an
artist by observing his paintings closely.
In this film many of Hals's paintings –
all portraits, for no other work is
known – are shown chronologically.
From time to time, however, earlier and
later portraits are compared, thus
showing his progress in mastering his
material and his unique brushwork.

Director	17 minutes
Frans Dupont	Color
Awards	Age range 14–adult
Award of Merit, Edinburgh	Film $623 Rental $189
Golden Gate Award,	VHS $89
San Francisco	
British Academy Award,	
London	
Best Art Film, San Francisco	
First Prize, La Felguera	
Gran Premio, Bergamo	
Grand Prix, Montevideo	
Best Art Film, Guadalajara	

Also available in French,
German and Spanish

290 Matthew Merian
European Engraver and Historian

Copperplate engraving is an art that has
almost been forgotten; Matthew Merian
was its master. During a working life that
almost exactly spanned the Thirty Years
War, he produced thousands of engravings,
filling thick portfolios with scenes of
Europe and its towns, its people and its
history – a record of a world on the brink
of its own destruction.

For more information see page 235

Director	15 minutes
Th N Blomberg	Black and white
Original music	Age range 12–adult
Horst Dempwolff	Film $553 Rental $163
Award	VHS $79
International Status,	
German Government	

306 Mexico: The Grandeur of New Spain

This historical account of events in
Mesoamerica after the arrival of the
Spaniards describes the complex nature of
the conquest and the evangelization. The
religious and civil art of the viceregal period
expresses the new dawn of Mexican culture
as a product of the fusion of indigenous
and Spanish traditions. A sample is offered
of the applied arts of the sixteenth,
seventeenth and eighteenth centuries, as
well as the architectural, sculptural and
pictorial styles known as tequitqui,
Plateresque, Baroque, Churrigueresque and
Neo-classical.

Part of the series *The Art of Mexico*

Director	56 minutes
Hector Tajonar	Color
Narrator	Age range 14–adult
Ricardo Montalban	VHS $139

Also available in Spanish

307 Spanish Art: El Greco to Goya

Spanish art flourished in its prime under
two patrons, the Church and the royal
court. In El Greco's day Spain was a country
inflamed by the Counter-Reformation and
the teachings of the Jesuits. El Greco
presented religious subjects as visions,
conveying a spirit of passionate nervous
energy. Velázquez sought inspiration in the
world of common everyday experience.
A brilliant portrait painter, his interest was
in people and human incident. He
celebrated man's physical reality. Goya is
the natural heir to Velázquez in his power
to observe and record people as they really
are, but he also brings to his observation a
new brand of awareness, revealing the inner
psychology of the people he painted.
Two threads seem to run through more
than 250 years of Spanish painting: a sense
of drama, and a trust in realism. In the
context of European painting as a whole,
Spanish art is unswervingly candid.
Paintings by Zurbarán, Giordano and Murillo
are also featured.

Part of the series
The National Gallery – A Private View

Director	28 minutes
Henry Lewes	Color
Writer/Narrator	Age range 12–adult
Edwin Mullins	Film $693 Rental $199
	VHS $99

◀◀ 289
Frans Hals
The Laughing Cavalier

◥ 307
Diego Velázquez
The Toilet of Venus

◀ 309, 309A
Claude Lorraine
*Seaport: The Embarkation
of St Ursula*

309   Baroque Painting in France and Italy

The immense variety of style and purpose
in French and Italian painting of the
seventeenth and eighteenth centuries is
vividly demonstrated by this survey of the
period. Beginning with the dramatic realism
of Caravaggio, the period ends with
Guardi's atmospheric landscapes. Inspired
by classical antiquity, Poussin created idyllic
landscapes and harmonious arrangements
of human figures. With Claude, nature
becomes the central theme in landscapes
reaching to infinity. Watteau turned to
human nature and the expression of love.
Boucher set out to please, while Chardin
painted domestic scenes of moving
simplicity. Tiepolo was a master of
decorative painting, and Canaletto the
chronicler of Venice in pageant. Other
artists featured are Carracci, Domenichino,
Philippe de Champaigne, Vernet, Lancret,
and Perroneau.

Part of the series
The National Gallery – A Private View

Director	**28 minutes**
Henry Lewes	**Color**
Writer/Narrator	**Age range 12–adult**
Edwin Mullins	**Film $693** Rental $199
	VHS $99

309A   Claude

The Roman Landscape

'Calm beautiful and serene…' is how Turner,
the great nineteenth-century landscape
painter, described the landscapes of the
seventeenth-century master, Claude
Lorraine. This video examines the ways in
which Claude drew his inspiration from
classical and contemporary poetry,
the remains of ancient, medieval and
Renaissance Rome and the countryside
around the city. Shot on location in Italy
and from original paintings and drawings,
it demonstrates not only the artist's powers
of evocation but also the naturalism
which dazzled his contemporaries, and
caused Turner's rival Constable to claim
that it was Claude who first taught him
'how to look at nature.'

Audio Visual Unit	**25 minutes**
The National Gallery	**Color**
	Age range 14–adult
	VHS $99

310   Via Dolorosa (Stations of the Cross)

Early Baroque Lifesize Sculpture in Slovakia

We normally associate the Baroque style
with high art by sophisticated sculptors and
painters, although it was often intended to
impress a religious message on the common
people as well as the intelligentsia. This film,
however, focuses on what could be called
'folk baroque,' created by artisans – lifelike
carvings making up an extraordinary
Stations of the Cross series at Rimov, a
remote mid-seventeenth-century shrine in
southern Bohemia. Here, a series of twenty-
five white chapels, ranged over a five-mile
route, contain lifesized figures enacting the
fourteen traditional scenes from the last
hours along the 'way of sorrows' leading up
to Christ's crucifixion. The creation of the
series was conceived and organized by a
Jesuit, Jan Gurre, and throughout the
Baroque period the Jesuit influence almost
succeeded in turning art into a propaganda
tool for the Counter-Reformation.
Overwhelming church environments were
created with all-encircling images and
staggeringly illusionistic painted ceilings,
which, combined with impassioned pulpit
performances, were designed to sweep the
congregation into unquestioning religious
fervor. There was a general urge towards a
'total art' that involved the audience
completely (opera was developing at the
same time). This is powerfully demonstrated
by the work shown in this film, which is a
kind of forerunner of modern 'environment'
and 'installation' art. Tellingly, as we pass
the figures in the film, experiencing them
as did the pilgrims to the shrine, the total
work is described in terms of its 'actors,'
its 'sets' and its 'director,' emphasizing its
dramatic, even cinematic force.

Director	**11 minutes**
Hugo Huska	**Black and white**
Original music	**Age range 14–adult**
Vladimir Brabec	**Film $483** Rental $149
	VHS $69

The Age of Baroque

Baroque, an epoch which emerged from the agony of Europe after decades of warfare, is not only the expression of an art form but also an awareness of life, an ideology. It was an age which produced great talents: architects, painters, musicians, poets and philosophers of a quality unknown in previous centuries. Frontiers were crossed; man was eager for everything new. He wanted to know more, feel more, experience more. It was an age of excesses, discoveries and renovations. The series tries to bring those turbulent times to life again – not as a lesson in art history but as a feast for both eyes and ears.

This series of 6 programs can be purchased on VHS for $954 Reference S10

▲ 314
Canaletto
The Customs Point, detail

◤ 315
Michelangelo Merisi da Caravaggio
The Supper at Emmaus

▶ 314
Canaletto
Venice: The Doge's Palace

314 **All the World on Stage**

This program gives a stimulating introduction to the Baroque age, opening with an evocation of Louis XIV, the Sun King, ostentatiously dressed for a ballet at the palace of Versailles. We learn of the period's preoccupation with dance, opera, drama and all forms of pageantry. We see the florid sculpture of Bernini (including a bust of Louis XIV), the inventive buildings of Guarini at Turin, the detailed views painted by Bellotto and Canaletto. We chart the spread of the Baroque craze for artifice, fantasy and energy in England, Belgium, Spain and eastern Europe; and we learn about the music, philosophy, science and economics of this paradoxical phase of European history.

Part of the series *The Age of Baroque*

Directors	**60 minutes**
Folco Quilici	**Color**
Jean Antoine	**Age range 15–adult**
	Film $1113 Rental $299
	VHS $159

315 **The Wizards of the Marvellous**

Underlying this period was a fascination with the grotesque, the outlandish and the ghoulish. Focusing on Rome, in many ways the center of the Baroque style, this film looks at some of the forerunners of the movement. In painting these are Caravaggio, with his dramatic, strained realism, Pietro da Cortona and the Carraccis, with their softer, sometimes more informal atmosphere, and Guercino, whose sweetness has often been considered cloying, but whose importance is increasingly recognized. Rubens personifies the transition between Renaissance and Baroque, with his sinuous lines and diaphanous vitality. These characteristics are also exemplified in the Baroque fountains of Rome, the inventive buildings of Borromini, and in the virtuosity of Bernini's swirling sculptures, such as his Daphnis and Chloe.

Part of the series *The Age of Baroque*

Directors	**60 minutes**
Folco Quilici	**Color**
Jean Antoine	**Age range 15–adult**
	Film $1113 Rental $299
	VHS $159

9 Baroque and Rococo

Steadily through the seventeenth century
the ethos of the Baroque spread from
its birthplace in Rome northwards to
central and eastern Europe, flourishing
in centers such as Venice, Vienna, Prague,
Württemberg and Salem. The paintings
of Tiepolo and Morazzone testify to
the fervor of Counter-Reformation ideology,
or propaganda (a word of Baroque origin),
in the face of the severe Protestant
movement in northern Europe. In addition
to painters, the film discusses the work of
composers such as Mozart and Beethoven,
and architecture by masters like Hildebrandt
and von Erlach. The new concept of town
planning is touched upon in connection
with Karlsruhe in southern Germany,
built as a Utopian 'new city' in 1715 and
anticipating the nineteenth-century
planning schemes of Haussmann and others,
not least in its expression of prestige power
politics. Exploring the Baroque fascination
with theater, and showmanship of all kinds,
the film discusses on the one hand the
phenomenon of carnival in Venice, and
on the other the pious, lifelike sculptures
by Ignaz Günther at the isolated Bavarian
church of Rott-am-Inn.

Part of the series *The Age of Baroque*

Directors	60 minutes
Folco Quilici	Color
Jean Antoine	Age range 15–adult
	Film $1113 Rental $299
	VHS $159

316
Giovanni Battista Tiepolo
Carnival Scene

▶ 318
Thomas Gainsborough
Mr and Mrs Andrews

▶▶ 316
Giovanni Battista Tiepolo
*An Allegory with Venus
and Time*

One aspect of the Baroque too rarely recognized is the colonial dissemination of the style from central and southern Europe, southward to Sicily, South America and even South Africa and India. It was the Dutch who created the Cape Colony in South Africa, building Baroque-style homes in their new territory of Stellenbosch. However, the film depicts Spain as the cradle of the most characteristically florid styles, both in architecture and painting, which are then shown to have been transferred to Sicily, virtually a province of Spain in the period, and of course to Latin America, the 'New Spain', where an architect such as Alehjadino could continue to practice in such modes into the nineteenth century. Even more surprising, perhaps, we learn of a Baroque colony at Goa in India, created by the Portuguese.

Part of the series *The Age of Baroque*

Directors	60 minutes
Folco Quilici	Color
Jean Antoine	Age range 15–adult
	Film $1113 Rental $299
	VHS $159

From Rubens to Gainsborough analyzes the development of the Baroque in Flanders, northern Europe, and especially France. We look at the Jesuit church in Antwerp, decorated by Rubens, Jordaens and Van Dyck. We visit the palace of Vaux-le-Vicomte built by Louis Le Vau, with gardens by André Le Nôtre. We see Le Nôtre's work again in the Tuileries Gardens stretching before Bernini's façades of the Palais du Louvre in Paris, and, across the Seine, the Hôtel des Invalides with its dome by Jules Hardouin; and in England we visit Wren's Greenwich Hospital and Vanburgh's Castle Howard.

Part of the series *The Age of Baroque*

Directors	60 minutes
Folco Quilici	Color
Jean Antoine	Age range 15–adult
	Film $1113 Rental $299
	VHS $159

The last in this series deals with the manifestations of the Baroque style in Russia and Poland. It begins at the court of Frederick the Great in Potsdam, where Frederick entertained both Voltaire and Johann Sebastian Bach; it moves on to Poland, and then to Russia – both St Petersburg and Moscow are essentially Baroque cities, the former being modeled on Peter the Great's memories of Amsterdam and Versailles. We visit Krakow, with its Wawel Cathedral and mausoleum of Stanislaw, and the monastery of Kalwaria, surrounded by lifesize tableaux of the Stations of the Cross (which can be compared with the Stations at Rimov in southern Bohemia in film 310, *Via Dolorosa*). *The Baroque of Extremes* also discusses the largely unknown influence, or perhaps parallel appearance, of the Baroque in Japan.

Part of the series *The Age of Baroque*

Directors	60 minutes
Folco Quilici	Color
Jean Antoine	Age range 15–adult
	Film $1113 Rental $299
	VHS $159

9 Baroque and Rococo

65

Teaching on Site
Seventeenth-century Merchants' Houses

The visit of a group of six-year-old children to two seventeenth-century merchants' houses in Great Yarmouth, Norfolk, England. Their teacher had already visited the site and planned how the children should prepare in school for their outing, what they should do during the visit, and the follow-up work they could do afterwards. Beforehand, they were encouraged to compare houses from past centuries with those they were used to themselves, and to develop skills of observation which would be useful on the day. A local museum education service provided relevant objects which they could handle and familiarize themselves with in the classroom. Their work in the medieval houses built on the comparisons the children had been making between old and new, but the historic buildings and the variety of objects displayed in them also helped them to imagine what life might have been like in the past. The class worked in three small groups on observation, artwork and creating stories – work which was shared in the whole class back at school, in discussion, writing, art and technology lessons, the class teacher showing how this was a useful progression from the visit itself. This video will be useful for teachers wishing to investigate the possibility of using the historic environment for their teaching.

This program is particularly suitable for teacher training.

Director/Writer
Patrick Redsell

English Heritage

19 minutes
Color
Age range 6–9
VHS $89

Evidence on Site: Boscobel House
Where Charles II Hid from Parliament

An introduction to a house where Charles II hid from the Roundheads. Boscobel, near Wolverhampton, England, was an isolated hunting lodge in a forest when the future king fled there after his defeat at Worcester in 1651. While Parliament's forces searched the area, Charles, dressed in servant's clothes, hid in an oak tree and later in a priest's hole within the house. This single dramatic event acted like a time-bomb on Boscobel. When the story became public after Charles's coronation, seventeenth-century tourists flocked to see the oak tree, tearing off branches as souvenirs and eventually killing it – but the house was unaffected. Not until it was sold in the early nineteenth century did the time-bomb explode. The new owners celebrated Boscobel's past by remodeling the house as they thought it might have been in Charles's time. Their view of history was an entertaining mixture of fact and fiction, so many features of the house are not what they seem to be, and need close inspection before one can assess their origins. This documentary explains the complicated history of the house, and the effects of an historic event on a quiet country dwelling. It also raises questions about how we look at the past which are applicable to any site.

Part of the series *Evidence on Site*

Director/Writer
Philip Sugg

English Heritage

10 minutes
Color
Age range 9–14
VHS $69

Chapels: The Buildings of Nonconformity
Baptist, Unitarian, Quaker, Methodist and Others

Chapels commemorates the three-hundredth anniversary of the passing of the Act of (religious) Toleration in England in 1689 by celebrating varied local buildings which often receive little attention. The Act stimulated the building of chapels for all types of Nonconformist worship; the video compares the archaeology of remaining buildings of different denominations and asks what these reveal about the kinds of religious practices they sheltered and about how the chapels are related to the human and industrial landscape of villages and towns. Baptist and Unitarian chapels, for example, are compared with contemporary Church of England chapels of ease (built for the convenience of remote parishioners) and Quaker meeting houses. Early primitive Methodist houses in which the 'Ranters' preached are contrasted with the cavernous grandeur of Victorian Methodist churches built in major industrial towns like York. *Chapels* relates to a wide range of studies: history, geography, religion, conservation and social development. It is also of importance to planners and architects, and to chapel-goers in an age when many Nonconformist buildings face redundancy, and thousands have already disappeared.

This program is particularly suitable for teacher training.

Part of the series *Frameworks of Worship*

Director/Writer
John Murray

Narrator
Roberta Gilchrist

English Heritage

18 minutes
Color
Age range 16–adult
VHS $89

The beginning of the eighteenth century was a time of curious indecision. Men were losing faith in the old beliefs, yet were wary of placing themselves in the hands of politics and science. Most artists reflect in their work the insecurity of these times, but a few painters deliberately ignored it and invented pleasing fantasies which bore little relation to the world outside the studio. The French painter Antoine Watteau was fascinated by the world of the sophisticated Italian theater, the *commedia dell'arte*, and portrayed its characters in some of his major paintings. Harlequin and Columbine, the Doctor and Mezzetino, and all the other figures of the wistful theater of unrequited love, were good symbols for a time in which no men, and few women, seemed to be faithful. Watteau, in many canvases now scattered throughout the world, pinpointed the glitter and heartlessness of his times – one reaction to an age of uncertainty. Ironically, in view of the artist's own poverty, he unwittingly created a fashion in high society for dressing 'à la Watteau' – after the style of characters in his paintings.

Director	**18 minutes**
Yvan Jouannet	**Color**
	Age range 14–adult
Original music	
Oliver Bernard	**Film $623** Rental $189
	VHS $89

Although the Church in the eighteenth century was losing its hold over the minds of scientists and philosophers, it was able to keep a grip on the imaginations of simpler people by telling them the stories of their faith in a way which was easy for them to understand. The most important story, of course, was that of the birth of Christ; but to the peasants of southern Italy who knew nowhere but their own villages, it was useless to talk of inns in Bethlehem or the Roman governor of Judea. The Church therefore had local woodcarvers make figures, none more than a handspan high, of the Holy Family, dressed in the familiar clothes of the peasants' own time and place. The three shepherds who come to worship the newborn baby are obviously based on three local shepherds; the innkeeper who has no room is a grasping Neapolitan; and Herod and his soldiers massacring the innocents are dressed as Turks, the cruellest enemy of whom the peasants would have heard, or as Moslems, the arch-enemies of Christianity. There is no narration.

Director	**12 minutes**
Dr Doederlein	**Color**
	Age range 6–adult
Original music	
Mark Lothan	**Film $483** Rental $149
	VHS $69

◀◀ 312
Boscobel: house and
farmyard

▲ 330
Neapolitan crib scene,
detail

▶ 320
Jean-Antoine Watteau
La Gamme d'Amour,
detail

9 Baroque and Rococo

67

The Enlightenment

This Open University/BBC series explores the culture of the age of reason at its height, through some of its great works of art and through the achievements of leading figures of the time.

This series of 16 programs can be purchased on VHS for $1584 Reference S11

323 Chardin and the Female Image

In the eighteenth century there was a great demand for images of women, and depictions of aristocratic intrigues and love affairs were also popular. Here we compare Chardin's pictures, particularly of women, with those of his contemporaries such as Fragonard, Watteau, Boucher and Greuze, and see where they stand in the European tradition of painting the female image. We also investigate beliefs at the time about the rôle and behavior of women, and the position of the male spectator of the female nude. The moral message of a picture such as Chardin's *The Diligent Mother* is explained; we also see how he painted children, and the different ways in which he portrayed girls and boys. Finally we explore the question of why Chardin's paintings are still popular today.

Part of the series *The Enlightenment*

Director
Paul Kafno
Presenter
Francis Frascina
Open University/BBC

24 minutes
Color
Age range 18–adult
VHS $99

325 Montgeoffroy: Life in a Château

A tour of the country house of Montgeoffroy in Anjou brings to life the French aristocracy on the eve of the Revolution. As we see the arrangement of the rooms and gardens, the furniture and the decoration, the mirrors and the gaming tables, we gain a vivid impression of the daily pastimes and the nightly amusements of a society which regarded marriage as a practical necessity, and expected romance to come later. The owner of the château, the Marquis de Contades, had several mistresses; the apartments of his companion in later life, Madame Hérault, are examined in some detail, as is the tiny, concealed room at the top of a spiral staircase which housed Madame's maid – in an eighteenth-century château the servants, although their lives were so different from those of their masters, were never far away.

Part of the series *The Enlightenment*

Director
Paul Kafno
Presenter
Belinda Thomson
Open University/BBC

23 minutes
Color
Age range 18–adult
VHS $99

333 Freedom and Plenty: England through Foreign Eyes

To visiting Europeans during the second quarter of the eighteenth century, England appeared a haven of intellectual freedom and material prosperity. Beginning with Voltaire's description of his arrival at Greenwich in 1726, we hear how continental thinkers reacted to English developments in commerce, agriculture, philosophy, science, literature, painting and music. The patriotic symbolism of the Royal Naval Hospital's Painted Hall, the aristocracy's interest in trade as typified by *Mr and Mrs Andrews* in Gainsborough's portrait, political corruption and satire as shown in Hogarth's engravings and in *The Beggar's Opera*, sculptures of Handel and Pope – these and many other examples demonstrate the ascent of both realism and classicism in the arts. And they also express the happiness of the Englishman who was free – or so it seemed to envious foreigners – to speak his mind, rise through the class system, and gorge himself on the roast beef of Old England.

Part of the series *The Enlightenment*

Director
Paul Kafno
Presenter
Angus Calder
Open University/BBC

25 minutes
Color
Age range 18–adult
VHS $99

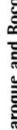

Opening shots of a Palladian or classical house leave us in no doubt about Horace Walpole's tastes: this is the very style of domestic architecture which he disliked so much. In 1747 his move to Strawberry Hill, Twickenham, near London, gave him the chance to express his aversion by redesigning the original house there and to realize, aided by his 'Committee on Taste,' his dream of a 'Little Gothick Castle.' After views of Strawberry Hill at night, the 'gothic' atmosphere enhanced by organ music, thunderclaps and readings from Walpole's sensational novel *The Castle of Otranto,* we are taken on a tour of Strawberry Hill, showing how Walpole drew inspiration from Westminster Abbey and old St Paul's, how he chose the design and the decorative details, and what Victorian alterations were made later. Walpole's enthusiasm for painted glass and for gardening is also described, and his reaction to the crowds of visitors who descended upon his 'castle.' And then comes the final question – what was the real importance of Strawberry Hill?

Part of the series *The Enlightenment*

Director	**22 minutes**
Paul Kafno	**Color**
	Age range 18–adult
Presenter	
Gill Perry	**VHS $99**
Open University/BBC	

335
William Hogarth
Scene from
Marriage à la Mode

337
Joseph Wright of Derby
*The Experiment with
the Air Pump*

336
William Kent
Temple of Echo
Rousham Park

English Landscape Gardens

English gardens in the late seventeenth century had been formal in design, imitating the French example, supremely that of Versailles; but in the early eighteenth century attempts were made to bring the surrounding countryside into garden design, a development that still seems more in keeping with the English gardener's temperament today. Exploring Rousham House garden in Oxfordshire, planned by William Kent in about 1735 and the best surviving example of early English landscape gardening, we see how serpentine paths and informal clumps of trees break up the rigidity of the design and create unexpected vistas. Kent also introduced classical motifs into the garden, including buildings of classical design and statues based on Roman and Greek originals. His style influenced Capability Brown and was itself imitated in France and Germany.

Part of the series *The Enlightenment*

Director	24 minutes
Robert Philip	Color
Presenter	Age range 18–adult
Colin Cunningham	VHS $99
Open University/BBC	

335   **Innocents: Images in Hogarth's Painting**

Why are children so often shown imprisoned in Hogarth's pictures? And why do his dogs appear to parody the behavior of humans? From this investigation we learn how Hogarth's own childhood fueled his obsession with the corruption of society and its treatment of innocence. We see how animals and children in his early work represent small, socially acceptable disruptions of an otherwise strict social order, a muted comment on the behavior or character of the adults who are the main subjects of paintings like *The Wollaston Family* and *A Modern Midnight Conversation*. In his later work his social criticism becomes harsher as the innocents are themselves corrupted and, as in *Marriage à la Mode*, destroyed. Finally *The Shrimp Girl* is identified as Hogarth's quintessential portrait of uncorrupted purity, although the painting's style reveals his bitter view that such purity is always ephemeral.

Part of the series *The Enlightenment*

Director	23 minutes
Tony Coe	Color
Presenter	Age range 18–adult
Ronald Paulson	VHS $99
Open University/BBC	

337   **Joseph Wright of Derby: Images of Science**

A painter who interested himself in the scientific, technological and philosophical issues of his day, Joseph Wright still needed to sell his paintings in the market-place. Here we examine two of his works in detail: *A Lecture on the Orrery* (an orrery was a clockwork model of the solar system) and *The Alchemist*. We also see a demonstration of an orrery and a short sequence of other pictures by Wright in the Derby Art Gallery, plus a discussion of three more of his paintings, *The Experiment with the Air Pump*, *The Blacksmith's Shop*, and *Hermit Studying Anatomy*.

Part of the series *The Enlightenment*

Director	25 minutes
Peter Walton	Color
Presenter	Age range 18–adult
Gerard Benson	VHS $99
Open University/BBC	

9 Baroque and Rococo

71

322 The Encyclopédie

The *Encyclopédie*, probably the greatest single enterprise of the Enlightenment, was published in France between 1751 and 1772 and edited by Diderot and d'Alembert. Giles Barber, Curator of the Taylorian Institution, Oxford, looks at the intentions of its editors, the problems associated with its publication and the importance of its illustrative plates. Robert Fox, Professor of the History of Science, University of Oxford, discusses the emphasis in the *Encyclopédie* on science and technology, and Christopher Lawrence of the Wellcome Institute talks about the attitudes to medicine and surgery shown by the writers of the *Encyclopédie*.

Part of the series *The Enlightenment*

Director	**25 minutes**
Robert Philip	**Color**
Presenters	**Age range 18–adult**
Giles Barber	**VHS $99**
Robert Fox	
Christopher Lawrence	
Open University/BBC	

324 Chardin and the Still Life

Chardin became known as the supreme master of the still life in eighteenth-century France. The program begins by discussing the hierarchy of genres in the eighteenth century, among which the still life was the lowest category. Examples are shown of paintings by earlier French and Dutch still-life painters, by whom Chardin was influenced. Then Chardin's own methods are discussed, his subtle use of light, shade and color, and his loose application of paint to create vivid textures. The quiet sentiments of Chardin's paintings are contrasted with the highly emotional style coming into fashion in the late eighteenth century. The program is punctuated throughout by quotations from the *Salons* of Diderot, who was one of the first critics to admire Chardin.

Part of the series *The Enlightenment*

Director	**25 minutes**
Robert Philip	**Color**
Open University/BBC	**Age range 18–adult**
	VHS $99

326 Frederick the Great and Sans Souci

Frederick the Great ruled Prussia from his new palace at Potsdam, Sans Souci. It was built to his own design and reveals much about his character as a ruler who wanted to be seen as an 'enlightened' philosopher. The palace is small, lavishly decorated and includes a library, a music room and a guest wing. The significance of each of these is discussed in turn. It does not include a chapel, which reflects Frederick's views on religious freedom. The grounds contain busts of Roman emperors, decorative statues and a Chinese teahouse. After the Seven Years War he built a much larger new palace but rarely used it. Throughout the program, the contrast is drawn between the man of letters, philosopher, musician and friend of the Enlightenment and the aristocratic ruler whose foreign policy included the eighteenth-century equivalent of a world war.

Part of the series *The Enlightenment*

Director	**25 minutes**
Robert Philip	**Color**
Presenters	**Age range 18–adult**
Tony Lentin	**VHS $99**
Colin Cunningham	
Open University/BBC	

327 Classical Sculpture and the Enlightenment

The Grand Tour took many people of taste and wealth to Italy in the eighteenth-century and encouraged the collecting of antique works of art. This program concentrates on one important British collector, Charles Townley, whose collection of marbles is in the British Museum. Gerard Vaughan of Oxford University talks to Colin Cunningham of the Open University about a number of Townley's most important marbles. They discuss the problems of interpreting the subject of sculptures. Publications illustrating Greek and Roman works of art influenced British taste, as did the displays of the works themselves by Townley and other collectors. Among the volumes shown in the programs are the works from Pompeii and Herculaneum published by the King of Naples, and Townley's own catalog of the collection displayed in his private house.

Part of the series *The Enlightenment*

Director	**25 minutes**
Robert Philip	**Color**
Presenters	**Age range 18–adult**
Colin Cunningham	**VHS $99**
Gerard Vaughan	
Open University/BBC	

328 Kedleston Hall (Robert Adam)

This program examines one of Robert Adam's architectural masterpieces – Kedleston Hall. It attempts to explain Adam's neo-classical designs, to look at the changes between design and construction and to consider the purpose for which the hall was built.

Part of the series *The Enlightenment*

Director	25 minutes
Amanda Willett	Color
Presenter	Age range 18–adult
Colin Cunningham	VHS $99

Open University/BBC

329 Scotland in the Enlightenment

The program looks at some of the buildings and paintings of eighteenth-century Scotland and discusses them in the context of society, politics and intellectual currents of the time, particularly in relation to the Enlightenment. It begins at Fort George, near Inverness, a barracks built as a defence against the Highlands, and then moves to Edinburgh and considers the building of the New Town in the late eighteenth century. This is seen in the context of Scottish aspirations to equality with the English following the parliamentary union of the two countries. The model village of Gifford is included as an example of rational town-planning by the Scottish aristocracy.

Part of the series *The Enlightenment*

Director	25 minutes
Robert Philip	Color
Presenter	Age range 18–adult
Colin Cunningham	VHS $99

Open University/BBC

333A Angelica Kauffman, RA, and the Choice of Painting

A founder member of the Royal Academy of Art in London and one of the first women to achieve an international reputation as a painter, today Kauffman is much less well known than her male contemporaries such as Reynolds or Gainsborough. The program traces her early life in Switzerland, her artistic training in Italy and the patronage that brought her to London. It examines her contribution as a history painter to the Neo-classical style of her day.

Part of the series *The Enlightenment*

Director	25 minutes
Charles Cooper	Color
Presenters	Age range 18–adult
Gill Perry	VHS $99
Professor Wendy Wassyng Rosworth	

Open University/BBC

336A Poetry and Landscape

Professor John Barrell of Sussex University looks at eighteenth-century landscape paintings and poetry which describes landscapes, in the context of their social and political background. He argues that landscape was seen as a metaphor for society, providing either a justification for, or a critique of, the established order. The program falls into four parts:

1 The organization of eighteenth-century landscape painting to look like theatre sets and a comparison with equivalent techniques in poetry

2 The political significance of such a procedure, related to the different layers of society

3 The contrast in paintings between formalized landscape gardens and 'natural' landscape and its significance as a metaphor for degrees of freedom

4 The layering of society represented in rural poetry and in visual representations of rural life

Part of the series *The Enlightenment*

Director	25 minutes
Robert Philip	Color
Presenter	Age range 18–adult
Professor John Barrell	VHS $99

Open University/BBC

337A Nature Displayed

Eighteenth-century Concepts of Women and Nature depicted in Art and Science

Professor Ludmilla Jordanova explains the connections between the concept of woman and botany (flowers, gardens, nurturing), health, charity (breastfeeding) and truth (as unveiled by science). She shows how the obstetric atlases of the day (Hunter and Jenty) depicted the dissected pregnant female torso in relation to classical art forms; and how even anatomical models were sexualized (wax model from the Science Museum, London). She discusses how the debates about midwifery, particularly the appearance of male midwives and the use of obstetric instruments such as forceps, polarized views in society about what was natural and what constituted 'meddling with nature.' Finally she makes reference to Mary Shelley's *Frankenstein* as encapsulating fears that the Enlightenment obsession with science had gone too far. Quotations from George Crabbe's *The Parish Register*, telling the story of Leah Cousins, the village midwife, and Doctor Glibb, illustrate the midwifery debate, with contemporary caricatures by Thomas Rowlandson and pamphlets.

Part of the series *The Enlightenment*

Director	25 minutes
Alison Tucker	Color
Presenter/Consultant	Age range 18–adult
Professor Ludmilla Jordanova	VHS $99

Open University/BBC

◀◀ 326
Frederick the Great reviewing his troops

340 Royal Rococo

A study of the Rococo style, characterized by small curves, counter-curves, prettiness and gaiety, as exemplified in Schloss Brühl, an old water castle remodeled in 1725 by the prince-archbishop of Cologne, Germany. Taste at this time was dominated by the French, so an architect and a landscape gardener from France were brought in to 'Frenchify' the Schloss; the interior was adorned with shell-work and scroll-work, the walls and ceilings covered with paintings. Every detail inside and out was brought into exquisite harmony. The film is accompanied by the music of Handel and others. There is no narration.

Director	13 minutes
Dr Carl Lamb	Color
Award	Age range 12–adult
Highly Commended,	Film $553 Rental $169
German Center for	VHS $79
Film Classification	

341 Moscow: Showing a Youthful Look to the World

Fluent, lyrical camera work carries us through the stunning buildings and monuments of Baroque nineteenth-century Moscow: Peter the Great's eighteenth-century Arsenal; sculptor Ivan Martos's monuments; Matvei Kazakov's Senate building; the beautiful façades and Triumphal Arch of architect Osip Bove; the breathtaking Bolshoi Theatre, and many more. The program's voice-over informs us of the historic and cultural events to which the ornate forms and pastel colors of Moscow's buildings were the backdrop: wars with Sweden; resistance to Napoleon; the Great Fire of 1737; the lives of writers Pushkin and Gogol…

Part of the series
The Beautiful City of Moscow

Director/Script	30 minutes
Vladimir Benidiktov	Color
Art Video International	Age range 14–adult
Also available in Russian	VHS $99

338 George Stubbs
The Most Original and Searching of All Animal Painters

Stubbs, labeled 'Mr Stubbs the Horse Painter,' was undervalued for far too long. Now he is recognized as the equal of his contemporaries, Gainsborough and Reynolds. He is the most original and searching of all animal painters, whether his subject is a brood-mare and foal, a monkey or a poodle in a punt; he is also a realistic and perceptive portraitist of human beings, as much a master of the art of class-distinction in eighteenth-century England as he is of the anatomy of the horse. Above all, he is a master of design, able to translate faithful observations from nature into unforgettable images. This is a unique record of the most important exhibition of Stubbs ever held, described by the *Times Educational Supplement* as 'wild, exotic and modern.'

'…succeeds in presenting many of his paintings and etchings in a comprehensive and interesting fashion. Recommended for art classes, especially those that emphasize the painting of animals.'
Video Rating Guide for Libraries, USA

Script	26 minutes
Simon Wilson	Color
Tate Gallery	Age range 12–adult
	VHS $99

339 The Hand of Adam
Robert Adam: Architect and Designer

The life and achievements of this outstanding Scottish architect and designer set against an exploration of his most outstanding work. The film ranges from the ruins of the Emperor Diocletian's palace at Split, Yugoslavia, which Adam visited in 1757, to his reinterpretation of a Roman palace at Kedleston Hall in Derbyshire, England, and across the Irish Sea to Headfort House to show a selection of Adam interiors. In order to relate Adam's decorative detail to his feeling for interior space, the film-maker devised complex camera movements involving large lighting plans in preference to a series of fragmented shots. The resulting sequences, at Syon House and Osterley Park, are beautifully counterpointed by an inventive musical score. Robert Adam never lost sight of Scotland, and one side of his genius derived inspiration from her great medieval castles or ruins like the peel tower on his family estate in Fife. Throughout his life he designed schemes in the Gothic as well as the classical style – and sometimes a fusion of both.

Director	33 minutes
Murray Grigor	Color
Awards	Age range 14–adult
Silver Plaque,	Film $763 Rental $199
Chicago	VHS $109
Gold Medal, Madrid	
Golden Palm, Seaborne	

 338
George Stubbs
Horse Attacked by a Lion

▶▶ 339
Audley End House,
ceiling detail

10 Neo-classicists and Romantics

Partly as a reaction to the capricious artificiality of the Rococo, there emerged in the arts from the mid-eighteenth century a growing trend for imitating the austere forms of the classical world. The vogue for Greek pottery grew steadily, and from 1748 there began to be startling archaeological discoveries in Herculaneum and Pompeii which revealed the true forms of classical painting and sculpture.

This section of
24 programs can be
purchased on
VHS for $2496

Television rights and
prices on request

Under the influence of the esthetic theories of Winkelmann and others, grandeur, balance and sobriety came to be considered the essential artistic virtues. Perhaps the supreme Neo-classical painters were David, Gros and Ingres in France, alternating mythological subjects with classicized contemporary ones, and capable of depicting the political figures of their day – Robespierre, Bonaparte – as Roman emperors.

As is evident from certain films in the last section (eg *The Hand of Adam*, page 73) Neo-classicism also manifested itself in architecture, frequently mingled with Baroque and Rococco traits. In particular there were Palladian country houses and their landscape gardens, in which nature was subtly 'improved' and harmonized into Italianate order, often featuring classical style temples, grottos, and antique or pseudo-antique statuary.

Though developing almost simultaneously with Neo-classicism, and at times shading imperceptibly into it (as in the work of Géricault), the Romantic movement contrasts with it in seeking to liberate the inner passions of the individual, rather than to impose order and rationality. The dawn of the nineteenth century, with its political revolts and the social disorientations of the Industrial Revolution, provides the tumultuous backdrop for the energetic and sometimes propagandist art of Delacroix and Géricault in France, for Blake's forceful mysticism in England, and for Friedrich's desolate spirituality in Germany. Where Neo-classicists celebrated social order, the Romantics sang the supremacy of the individual struggling to be liberated from, rather than lost without, ordered beliefs and customs. Thus they anticipate many of the concerns of Modernist and Expressionist artists.

◀◀ 342
Jean-Auguste-Dominique Ingres
Madame Moitessier Seated

▲ 342
William Blake
*Satan Smiting Job with
Sore Boils*

▲ 345
Sir Joshua Reynolds
General Sir Banastre Tarleton

342 The Multiplication of Styles 1700–1900

This film gives a rudimentary 'exposure' to a broad range of art for young audiences. Until the eighteenth century western art tended to have one dominant style at a time, but from 1700 onwards a multitude of innovations and revivals expressed the confusion and curiosity of the new scientific humanism. This film offers a survey of the painting, sculpture and architecture of the period. A filming technique was evolved whereby brief instalments of information are followed by long sections without narration, designed to capture the spirit of each style that has been discussed. Film sequences include: Baroque in Europe, Watteau, Chardin, Palladianism, Neo-classicism in European and American art, Romantic Classicism, Romantic Naturalism, Constable, Turner, Goya, Blake, French Romanticism, English Gothic Revival, the Pre-Raphaelites, Social Realists, Daumier, Rodin, suspension bridges, prefabrication, Eiffel Tower, Missouri skyscraper, Impressionism, Cézanne, Monet, Renoir, Pissarro, Whistler, Sickert and Toulouse-Lautrec.

Part of the series *Western Art 1700–1970*

Director	26 minutes
Anthony Roland	Color
Narration	Age range 12–adult
Anthony Bertram	Film $693 Rental $199
Original music	VHS $99
Adrian Wagner	

343 Moscow: In the Quiet of Its Country Estates

An opportunity to stroll around famous country estates of the eighteenth and nineteenth centuries, now mere islands surrounded by the spreading tide of Moscow. Kouskov, Ostankino…glorious palaces and landscapes created by the labor and talent of the serfs, who, like their creations, were owned by the foremost patrons of art in Russia.

Part of the series
The Beautiful City of Moscow

Director/Script	30 minutes
Vladimir Benidiktov	Color
Art Video International	Age range 14–adult
Also available in Russian	VHS $99

345 The British Achievement

The theme of this film is the contribution made by British painters towards revitalizing the art of Europe. For this one long period, from 1720 to 1850, British art seems to be anchored to Europe instead of floating somewhere offshore. But even so there is something very British about it: there are no gods or saints; it is essentially factual, recording the daily life of England right across the social spectrum. Hogarth painted the London poor and the greed and ruthlessness of the rich. Gainsborough flattered high society, portraying its fashionable elegance; he was a master at combining portraiture with landscape. Reynolds emphasized the grand presence of his sitters. Stubbs excelled in animal portraiture. Nature began to take over from society as the main theme: Constable painted the English countryside with a freshness and spontaneity not seen before. Turner responded to the elemental powers of nature – wind, water and heat – as being greater than the powers of humankind.

Part of the series
The National Gallery - A Private View

Director	28 minutes
Henry Lewes	Color
Writer/Narrator	Age range 12–adult
Edwin Mullins	Film $693 Rental $199
	VHS $99

Credited with liberating color from its rôle of merely describing the subject of a painting, Turner evoked an intensity of feeling in his landscapes that future Impressionists and abstract artists were to try to capture years later. This internationally acclaimed film, which shows why Turner is regarded as the father of modern art, is a cinematographic essay on the most important period of Turner's work, the last twenty-five years. A selection made from ten thousand paintings illustrates Turner at the height of his creative powers. Most of the works filmed have never been photographed or exhibited before. The original music captures the ethereal quality of Turner's work. There is no narration.

'A first rate film. A very successful choice of the late Turner period at the time when, having become a master of color, his extraordinary qualities as a colorist are at their peak. Turner is depicted as a phenomenon. The faithful color reproduction, the richness of the music, and the care and elegance of presentation.'
UNESCO

'Here is Turner exposed to public view in a way no exhibition, however ambitious, could match'
Art and Antiques Weekly, London

Director Anthony Roland	**12 minutes**
	Color
Original music Marius Constant	**Age range 12–adult**
	Film $623 Rental $189
Awards Silver Cup, Salerno	**VHS $89**
Certificate of Merit, Vancouver	
Highly Commended, German Center for Film Classification	
Quality Award and Prize French National Film Center	
Chriss Award, Columbus	
Koussivitzky Award, USA prize for the year's best piece of European contemporary music	

355   Constable: The Changing Face of Nature

Leslie Parris, co-selector of the 1991 Tate Gallery Constable exhibition, introduces his hero with great knowledge lightly worn. 'We all know Constable,' he says. 'It is difficult to escape *The Haywain* as it trundles from one biscuit tin to another. But if we look instead at the real thing, we may find an artist more varied and more exciting than we imagined.' Largely filmed direct from the paintings themselves, this is a valuable introduction to Constable's art.

'Teachers, programmers, and independent students of art…will find this video useful.'
Video Rating Guide for Libraries, USA

Writer/Presenter Leslie Parris	**25 minutes**
	Color
Audio Visual Unit The National Gallery	**Age range 14–adult**
	VHS $99

▲ 360
Joseph Mallord William Turner
Rain, Steam and Speed

◥ 360
Joseph Mallord William Turner
Rainclouds at sea

◥ 365
Théodore Géricault
The Raft of the 'Medusa'

▶▶ 370
Eugène Delacroix
Artist's model

356   Constable: The Leaping Horse

The Leaping Horse is one of John Constable's most celebrated pictures – celebrated at the time of its creation as well as subsequently. The artist exhibited it at the Royal Academy in 1825, having made many studies for the work (one full size, now in the Victoria and Albert Museum), and he was to make a second finished version of the composition, in which he omits the detail of the horse itself. The painting was done at a time when Constable's fame was at last growing, especially in France. The king of France had presented him with a gold medal for paintings exhibited at the Louvre, including *The Haywain*, and he was to come to be seen in that country as a precursor of Impressionism. The video takes *The Leaping Horse* as a starting point for a broad discussion of the conventions of landscape depiction of the period.

Part of the series
Culture and Society in Britain 1850–90

Director Charles Cooper	**25 minutes**
	Color
Presenter Briony Fer	**Age range 18–adult**
	VHS $99
Open University/BBC	

365 Géricault: The Raft of the 'Medusa'

Painter and lithographer Théodore Géricault was the leader of the French Romantic movement; *The Raft of the 'Medusa'* was his most ambitious work. In this film we see how he consciously sought for 'headline' public events to provide a subject for a major work that would launch his career. The *Medusa*, a government vessel, had foundered off the West African coast, and 150 people tried to escape on a raft. After thirteen days, only fifteen were rescued alive. They had had nothing but a few drops of wine – and human meat – to sustain them. The tragedy was blamed on official negligence and created a political scandal. Géricault depicted the instant when the survivors first saw the rescue ship, and he went to extraordinary lengths to achieve authenticity: he interviewed survivors and drew their portraits, he had a model of the raft built, he even studied corpses in the morgue. Such a choice of subject matter, and the presentation of a dramatic moment, is typical of Romantic painting, and forcefully illustrates the extent of Géricault's break from the balance and chill calm of the prevailing Neo-classical school.

Director Adrien Touboul	**21 minutes** **Color**
Script Georges-Antoine Borias	**Age range 12–adult**
	Film $623 Rental $189
Original music Jacques Lasru	**VHS $89**

370 Delacroix

Human and Animal Movement Expressed in Drawings

Born into an age marked by revolution and extremes, Eugène Delacroix was an arch-romanticist; he was also one of the finest French draftsmen, influencing not only many of his contemporaries but also modern masters such as Van Gogh, Gauguin, Cézanne, Rodin and Matisse. In this film, the theme of movement in the human and animal form builds up through tightly woven sequences to a climax. Delacroix's drawings make us understand the basic value of his art, his intimate thoughts and his daring invention. This is the only film of its kind made in the famous Louvre Drawing Collection. There is no narration.

'Delacroix is magic. We seem to be sharing the artist's most intimate thoughts in a strange land where the creativity of Delacroix is perfectly matched with the equally creative powers of the film-maker… a very strong feeling for the artist's style, ideas, and moods… notable for unity of purpose and coherence, for synchronization of visuals and music… shows real feeling for the artist.'
Vancouver International Film Festival

'Startling musical score; excellent photography; unusual treatment of subject; artistically authentic… turned stills into a moving scene showing the art and genius of the artist… exciting… intimate; unity like a poem.'
Canada's Documentary Film Festival

For more information see pages 225 and 237

Director Anthony Roland	**13 minutes** **Black and white**
Original music Marius Constant	**Age range 6–adult**
	Film $623 Rental $189
Awards Silver Cup, Salerno Diplôme d'Honneur, Cannes First Prize, Canada's International Film Festival, Yorkton Certificate of Merit, Vancouver Commended, German Center for Film Classification Quality Award, French National Film Center Chriss Award, Columbus	**VHS $89**

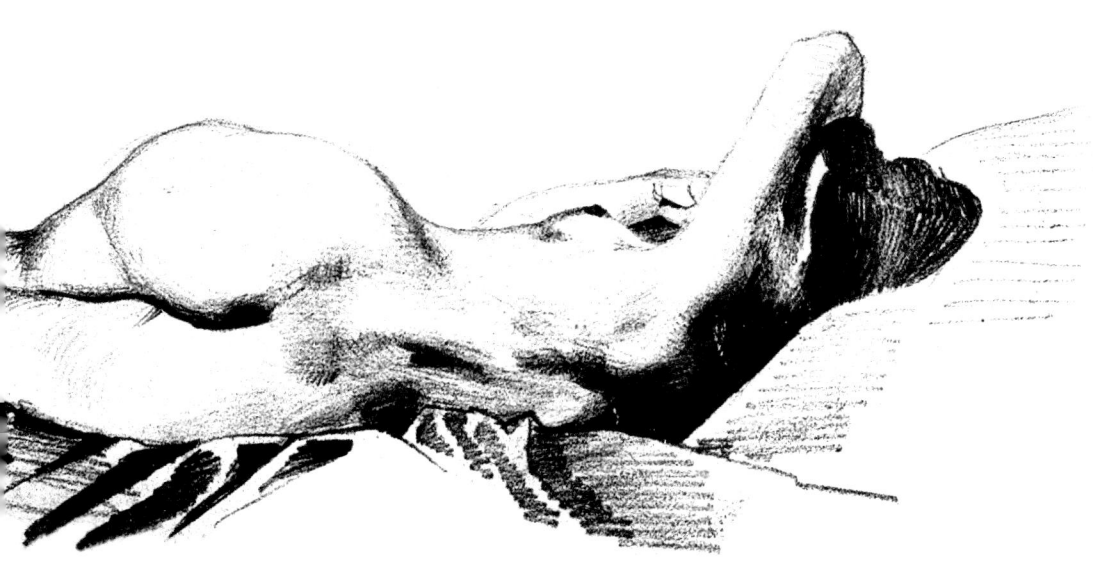

▲ 380
Jean-Baptiste-Camille Corot
Tivoli, The Villa d'Este Gardens

◥ 390
Honoré-Victorin Daumier
Don Quixote and Sancho Panza

◥ 400
Victor Hugo
Imaginary landscape

◢◣ 389
Honoré-Victorin Daumier
Jean-Claude Persil
Politician, French peer and
magistrate under Louis-Philippe

346 The Road to Modern Art

Between 1800 and 1900 so much happened
in French painting that the period seems
like several centuries compressed into one.
Delacroix expressed energy in a free
handling of brilliant color, as opposed to
the classically smooth and perfect finish of
Ingres. Courbet painted with a hard, bright
realism, and Corot with fresh spontaneity.
Impressionism was not only a bold new
style; it also represented a new range of
subject matter, a new way of looking at the
world. It was a re-evaluation of what art
should be about. One of its chief concerns
was with light and its ability to dissolve
forms and modify colors. Detail was
sacrificed to the overall momentary
impression. While using the bright palette
of Impressionism, some artists could not
entirely abandon line and structure.
Cézanne in particular had different
objectives, seeking to express the
geometrical basis of all forms, thereby
pointing the way to Cubism and ultimately
to abstract painting. Other painters
featured are Pissarro, Monet, Manet, Renoir,
Degas, Seurat, Van Gogh and Rousseau.

Part of the series
The National Gallery – A Private View

Director Henry Lewes	**28 minutes** **Color**
Writer/Narrator Edwin Mullins	**Age range 12–adult**
	Film $693 Rental $199 **VHS $99**

380 Corot

Like Constable, Corot was one of the first
artists to take his easel out of doors.
Like Constable again, he developed a
new approach to landscape painting
through his sensitive treatment of light,
form and distance. This film is concerned
with his visit to Rome in 1825 and his
interest in Poussin. It shows his early
historical compositions and his later
landscapes; it also attempts to assess his
place among other great landscape painters
of the English, Dutch and Barbizon schools,
such as Constable, Hobbema, Millet, and
the Impressionist Sisley.

Director/Writer Roger Leenhardt	**18 minutes** **Color**
Original music Guy Bernard	**Age range 12–adult**
Awards Quality Prize and Quality Award, French National Film Center	**Film $623** Rental $189 **VHS $89**
Also available in French	

389 Parliamentarians: Daumier Sculpture

Honoré Daumier is better known to most people as a graphic artist, and perhaps as a painter, than as a sculptor, yet he created many sculptures, which often preceded the lithographs and drawings that relate to them. His modeled heads of politicians, originally painted in polychrome (though also cast in bronze) are part caricatures of notables of the time and part physiological human 'types.' Using creative lighting, sound and camera work, the film brings alive the *Parliamentarians* and other works by Daumier, setting them in dramatic context and deploying the figures almost as if they are in a puppet theater. This is one of the many rare film discoveries which the Roland Collection has brought out of undeserved obscurity.

Director
Jiri Jahn

Scenario
Eric Legler

Original music
Rolf Kuhl

Also available in German

18 minutes
Black and white
Age range 9–adult

Film $623 Rental $189
VHS $89

390 Daumier

Of all the visual wits of the nineteenth century, none was more sharp or observant than the painter, sculptor and engraver Honoré Daumier. He was jailed early in his career for caricaturing King Louis-Philippe as Gargantua, wolfing the taxes paid by the little people, but his time in the dank cells of St Pélagie prison seems only to have fueled his left-wing beliefs. He took the part of the common man against kings and princes, of the poor against the rich, of social justice against inequality. He mocked those whom he considered to be on the wrong side, and in doing so he gave enormous pleasure to their opponents. But his canvases, which today are worth millions, were ignored by the art-lovers of his time, and he was often faced with the direst poverty himself.

Directors/Writers
Roger Leenhardt
Henry Sarrade

Original music
Guy Bernard

Award
Special Mention, Locarno

Also available in French

15 minutes
Black and white
Age range 12–adult

Film $553 Rental $169
VHS $79

400 Victor Hugo Drawings

Moody scenes of old castles in the mist, the moon on dark waters… Known as a great French writer, playwright and poet, Victor Hugo was also a remarkable draftsman. Unknown drawings, filmed from the only important collection of Hugo's work, reveal a world of mystery, poetry and dramatic power that is exceptionally cinematographic. More intimate and direct than Hugo's writings, these drawings have the power to take us into the Gothic world of his imagination. There is no narration.

Director
Anthony Roland

Original music
Michel Phillipot

14 minutes
Black and white
Age range 12–adult

Film $553 Rental $169
VHS $79

Arnold Böcklin

The fantastical work of the Swiss painter Arnold Böcklin forms a keystone in the bridge from nineteenth-century Romantic and Neo-classical trends to the Modernism of the twentieth century. In particular his work was important for Surrealists such as Dali or de Chirico. And yet, like many other influential artists of his era – such as the Italian Segantini or the Frenchmen Moreau and Carrière – Böcklin's reputation has been neglected, his preoccupation with subject and symbol being incompatible with the prevailing view of modern art as a progression away from 'content' toward the pure 'form' of abstraction. Böcklin's style, by contrast, was close to that of many Victorian artists in Britain, artists who were also derided for being narrative, fanciful, meticulous. Today, however, with the breakdown of such doctrinaire definitions of Modernism, the importance of Böcklin and his contemporaries is recognized anew, and he has become a touchstone for contemporary artists.

401 Rodin

At his death, Rodin was the most famous artist in the western world but the critical reception of his works was far from positive. As a sculptor making public works, Rodin was exposed to public criticism. The modernity of his works was ridiculed by critics. Even his famous *Thinker* and his *Balzac* attracted scorn and, in the case of the *Thinker*, physical violence. The explicit sexuality of Rodin's sculpture was often seen as scandalous but contemporary taste was tolerant of the erotic as long as it represented the female form. Nude women were ubiquitous in nineteenth-century art. Rodin's *Balzac* sexualized the male form; critical anger did not focus directly on its phallic nature, but saw the sculpture as incomprehensible. Rodin's career marks the transition from the public role of the nineteenth-century sculptor to the more private consumption of modern art.

Part of the series
Modern Art, Practices and Displays

Director	25 minutes
Nick Levinson	Color
Presenter	Age range 18–adult
Annie Wagner	VHS $99
Open University/BBC	

349 Arnold Böcklin
A Biography – His Vision of Nature

This film provides an overview of Böcklin's career, of the *œuvre* he created during his extensive travels, and of the personal hardships and complications of his life.

For more information see page 208

Director/Writer	96 minutes
Bernhard Raith	Color
Narrator	Age range 14–adult
Peter Ustinov	Film $1533 Rental $449
Award	VHS $219
Special Jury Prize, Montreal	
Also available in German	

 349
Arnold Böcklin
Playing in the Waves

 401
Auguste Rodin
Nijinsky

351
Biedermeier furniture

Biedermeier Style

'Biedermeier' is a term used to describe a style of furniture and painting, and the bourgeois lifestyle in general that flourished in Austria, Germany and Scandinavia in the first half of the nineteenth century. Many artistic movements (for example, Impressionism and Fauvism) have acquired their names from satirical or pejorative epithets given by hostile critics. Biedermeier was named after a fictional character called Gottfried Biedermeier, created by the poet Ludwig Eichrodt, who typified middle-class bad taste and vulgarity. The Biedermeier sensibility was parallel to that of Victorian England. Its décors had a heavy, ornate respectability, and its painting tended toward a highly detailed, anecdotal illusionism close to that of the Pre-Raphaelites and their contemporaries. As with Victorian art and design, the Biedermeier style is no longer dismissed as simply vulgar and oppressive. Today it is recognized as the crystallization of a unique historical moment in manners and mores in Europe, deploying a wide design vocabulary that relates backwards to the French Empire style and forward to Art Nouveau, and even to the functionalism of modern mass-production.

350 **The Happiness of Still Life**
Scenes from the Austrian Biedermeier

A poetic depiction of the cultural life of Vienna from 1815 to 1848, which focuses on the Biedermeier lifestyle, a middle-class way of life in a society which was still aristocratic. The film combines pictures of period paintings and furniture, music from Schubert, and extracts from private letters and diaries of contemporaries. This period of calm came between the Napoleonic Wars and the initial upheavals of the Industrial Revolution, when Austria was the dominant power of Europe.

Director/Scenario Andrea Simon	**27 minutes**
	Color
Also available in German	**Age range 15–adult**
	Film $693 Rental $199
	VHS $99

At the beginning of the nineteenth century, Napoleon brought fear and terror to Europe. After his defeat at Waterloo, his victorious opponents set about rebuilding Europe at the Congress of Vienna; and in Austria, pre-revolutionary conditions were re-established under the iron heel of Prince Metternich. During this period, known as Vormärz, the masses lived in poverty, and even middle-class citizens enjoyed very few freedoms. Dancing became an 'opiate of the people;' Strauss and other composers of the waltz competed for fame, and ballet and theater – albeit a theater much subject to censorship – were typical Viennese entertainments. It was also a period of technical innovation, with the introduction of the steamship and steam railway, sewing machines, gas lighting, and mass-production of various kinds. But the 'Biedermeier person' prided himself on his artistic taste, and preferred craftsmen's work to machine-made items. Furniture was simple and functional. Tableware and glassware, adorned with transparent miniature paintings of landscape motifs, portraits, flowers and animals, became a Viennese speciality; porcelain flourished, as did fashion, which became simpler and free of earlier pretentiousness. In architecture, the influence of Neo-classicism was still in evidence, but domestic architecture for the middle classes became simple and modest. In painting it became the custom to copy nature. Biedermeier landscape painting, though not without atmosphere or feeling, is laboriously detailed and precise. In portraiture, bourgeois realism prevailed, enhanced by subtly observed psychological detail. Cosy idylls of family life were popular, for the bourgeois parlour, seen as a place of refuge from rough reality, was at the very heart of the Biedermeier ethos. But the most typical Biedermeier painting was the genre picture. In 1848 another revolution took place in Paris, and on March 13, the people of Vienna also rose. They were promised a constitution, and the lifting of censorship. Metternich, after more than thirty years in power, resigned and fled. The Biedermeier age was gone for ever.

Austria Wochenshau	**25 minutes**
	Color
Also available in German	**Age range 15–adult**
	VHS $99

10 Neo-classicists and Romantics

347 Caspar David Friedrich

In 1987 The National Gallery in London bought *Winter Landscape* by Caspar David Friedrich, a German landscape painter. Like so many of his paintings, it is full of a sense of mystery. Friedrich's paintings are not well known in Britain, and this was the first oil painting by him to enter a public collection in England. His life and the development of his extraordinary landscape imagery are the subjects of this production.

'…intelligent, informative, and tightly written…solid piece of artistic analysis… most useful to students of art'
Video Rating Guide for Libraries, USA

Writer/Presenter William Vaughan	**25 minutes**
	Color
Audio Visual Unit The National Gallery	**Age range 14–adult**
	VHS $99

348 Caspar David Friedrich: Landscape as Language

In Germany, as in England, landscape was the finest achievement of Romantic painting, and Friedrich is the outstanding German painter in this field. His landscapes symbolize and express subjective human experience; his approach to nature is naïve and his religious thought has a melancholy aspect. The pantheistic interpretation of landscape in Friedrich's art – that is to say, the sense of God informing the universe – made an important break with tradition.

For more information see page 232

Director Dr Walter Koch	**18 minutes**
	Color
Original music Pavel Blatny Johannes G Fritsch	**Age range 14–adult**
	Film $623 Rental $149
	VHS $89

353 A View from the Mountains: The Oscar Reinhart Foundation

Set in the heart of Europe, Switzerland shares much of the culture of its neighbours, yet retains its distinct individuality, shaped by the mountains to which it owes its existence. The Oscar Reinhart Foundation in Winterhur, while containing magnificent paintings from other countries, also houses a 'local' collection celebrating that special 'view from the Alps.' This video, filmed on location in Switzerland and from original paintings, illustrates work by many of the major and unfamiliar artists exhibited there – Swiss painters such as Wolf, Böcklin and Hodler, the great Romantic artists Runge and Friedrich, the Austrian Waldmüller and others – and records the landscape which inspired some of their greatest works.

Audio Visual Unit The National Gallery	**20 minutes**
	Color
	Age range 14–adult
	VHS $89

◀◀ 405
José Maria Velasco
Volcano

◤ 348
Caspar David Friedrich
Chalk Cliffs on Rügen

405   Modern Mexican Art

Words and painting meet on the television screen to deliver an enriching vision of José Maria Velasco, the painter, and José Guadalupe Posada, the engraver. We also discover a great but little known portraitist, Hermenegildo Bustos, as Octavio Paz illuminates the creations of these masters of the nineteenth century. Velasco painted breathtaking scenes of South American landscape in a precise yet fresh style unique to himself. He captured the strong, expansive light of the continent, picking out trembling water, glittering grasses, radiant cloud. In contrast, Posada's engravings, executed for the press, captured and caricatured the personalities and political and social events of his day in a style somewhere between eighteenth-century political cartoons and Germanic Expressionism of the twentieth century. Bustos provides an equally fascinating chapter in the history of South American art. He was self-taught, close in some ways to the naïve painters of religious images in his culture, yet endowed with a gift that makes his portraits arresting and authentic.

Part of the series
Mexico through the Eyes of Octavio Paz

Director	**56 minutes**
Hector Tajonar	**Color**
Presenter/Writer	**Age range 14–adult**
Octavio Paz	**VHS $139**
Special collaboration	
Marie José Paz	
Original music	
Mario Lavista	
Also available in Spanish	

406   Modern Mexico: The Artistic Identity

This view of the development of the art of painting in Mexico in the nineteenth and twentieth centuries shows how the country responded to artistic movements of the time. The works shown enable us to recreate the cultural history of a country that experienced two decisive conflicts, the War of Independence and the revolution. These events gave birth to an overwhelming spirit of nationalism which was powerfully expressed in the provinces and which culminated in the Muralist movement of the twenties and in contemporary Mexican sculpture.

Part of the series *The Art of Mexico*

Director	**56 minutes**
Hector Tajonar	**Color**
Narrator	**Age range 14–adult**
Ricardo Montalban	**VHS $139**
Original music	
Mario Lavista	
Also available in Spanish	

▶ 402
Opera House and
surrounding area of
Haussmann's Paris

402 Paris: Story of a City
Medieval to Modern within a Century

In 1853 Napoleon III appointed
Baron Georges-Eugène Haussmann, a
lawyer and civil servant, to the post of
prefect of the Seine *département* of France.
His brief was to improve Paris's planning,
and for the following two decades he swept
away acres of rambling medieval streets
and substituted his own concept of a
modern city – wide, straight boulevards
with imposing façades, converging at major
junctions marked by monuments, public
buildings and points of importance such as
city gates or railway stations. Paris became
the yardstick by which all European cities
were judged. This film was made to mark
the centenary of the death of Baron
Haussmann in 1891. Historian Francis Loyer
combs the city, scrutinizing objects that are
so familiar we no longer see them: a
wooden shutter, the angle of a street, a
carving on a façade. 'Haussmannism' is
often seen as a kind of urban vandalism
presaging the great modern devastations in
the name of progress; it can also look like
totalitarian imposition by an authority
eager to control and police its populace and
to suppress revolution. In this film, however,
Haussmann's scheme is considered as a
rigorous and coherent means of controlling
the growth of a city.

Director
Stan Neumann

Scenario
Stan Neumann
Francis Loyer

Art historian
Francis Loyer

Awards
Grand Prix, Bordeaux
Environmental Film
of the Year,
National Geographic,
Washington DC

Also available in French

52 minutes
Black and white
Age range 14–adult

Film $903 Rental $299
VHS $129

403 Paris, Spectacle of Modernity

The program is presented by three art
historians, all experts on different aspects
of nineteenth-century French art and
urbanism, who display their own particular
methodology. Francis Frascina's approach
is informed by a Marxist view of history
in which the reconstruction of Paris under
its prefect Baron Haussmann is seen as
determined by the political and economic
forces of capitalism. Tim Benton explores
the history of urban development and
outlines the positive improvements against
the social cost of such rapid change.
Hollis Clayson's argument centers on the
huge public concern over the growth of
prostitution in the city. The program
suggests ways in which these historical
interpretations can inform our reading of
Impressionist art in the 1870s.

Part of the series
Modern Art, Practices and Debates

Director
Nick Levinson

Presenters
Francis Frascina
Tim Benton
Hollis Clayson

Open University/BBC

25 minutes
Color
Age range 18–adult

VHS $99

Between the Romantic rebellion, marked by revolution in France and America, and the kindred traumas of the Modernism ushered in by the First World War, comes the long and fascinating interlude of the Victorian period.

1850 – 1900

11
The Victorians

This section of 16 programs can be purchased on VHS for $1584

Television rights and prices on request

As with certain aspects of the Baroque and Rococo, twentieth-century popular and scholarly taste has often disparaged Victoriana for its ornate heaviness and supposed decadence. However, Victorian art and culture have been rediscovered in recent years as rich and compelling, rather than simply reflecting stuffy respectability overlaid with complacency, moral corruption, class injustice and exploitation – realities though these were. The films in this section illustrate the complexity of English culture between 1850 and 1900.

◀◀ 373, page 87
St Barnabas, London

▼ 356
John Constable
The Haywain

356   **Constable: The Leaping Horse**

John Constable was, with Turner, the foremost English landscape painter of the nineteenth century; *The Haywain* is his most famous picture. Of the green watermeadows and windswept skies of Suffolk he remarked, 'These scenes made me a painter.' Here we analyze his *Leaping Horse* in terms of landscape genre painting as a whole, and look at the skills and techniques available to the artist. We also consider the constraints and possibilities with which the landscape painter worked, including the current market in art and the ideas of Constable's contemporaries about how the countryside could be represented.

Part of the series
Culture and Society in Britain 1850–90

Director	**25 minutes**
Charles Cooper	**Color**
Presenter	**Age range 18–adult**
Briony Fer	**VHS $99**
Open University/BBC	

Culture and Society in Britain 1850–90

This series, made up of videos produced by the Open University/BBC and concentrating chiefly on Victorian buildings, is not really art-historical in intention; rather it shows how various types of architecture – chapels, grand houses, town halls – came into being and were used by the different members of society.

This series of 10 programs can be purchased on VHS for $990 Reference S12

371   **Cragside**

When the Victorian architect Norman Shaw began building Cragside in Northumberland in 1863, it was intended to be a relatively modest country retreat for the great armaments manufacturer Lord Armstrong. But as Armstrong's business expanded, a mere lodge was not enough for him, and the house developed into something almost palatial – the Prince and Princess of Wales were among the first visitors after its completion. Its size, its grandeur and its references to the past gave Cragside, and its owner, an appearance of pedigree: the house is made to look as if it had grown over centuries as the ancestral home of a noble family. Examining the different architectural styles that Shaw employed, we can see how each one is related to the ways in which Armstrong, his guests and his servants used the house.

Part of the series
Culture and Society in Britain 1850–90

Director	**25 minutes**
Tony Coe	**Color**
Presenter/Writer	**Age range 17–adult**
Colin Cunningham	**VHS $99**
Open University/BBC	

372 The Albert Memorial

The popularity that the German Prince
Consort had never really enjoyed in his
lifetime seemed to be lavished on him
once he was dead, and the Albert Memorial
was Britain's greatest expression of its
loss – or was it? Were the details of its
decoration and style, and the identities of
the 169 lifesized figures from the history of
art that are sculpted round its base, over
which the seated figure of the Prince
presides, really a monument to Albert and
his achievements? Or do they tell us more
about the society that planned and built
the memorial, and its desire to reinforce the
image of British supremacy in the eyes of
the rest of the world?

Part of the series
Culture and Society in Britain 1850–90

Director
Nick Levinson

Presenter/Writer
Colin Cunningham

Open University/BBC

25 minutes
Color
Age range 17–adult

VHS $99

The Roland Collection

373 The Victorian High Church

The Anglo-Catholic or 'high-church' movement, which was seen by its opponents as a dangerous and unforgivable effort to move the Church of England nearer to Rome, and by its adherents as an attempt to restore a spiritual dimension which the conventional, worldly Church of England had lost, gave rise to enormous upheaval and conflict during the Victorian era. All Saints Church, Margaret Street, was built in 1849 to serve Anglo-Catholics in what was then a poor part of London. Here its architecture and design, and its rich decoration, are examined in the light of what we know about its 'ritualistic' purpose. All Saints is also compared with its near contemporary, St Marks in Dalston, London, which was designed for more orthodox Anglican worship.

Part of the series
Culture and Society in Britain 1850–90

Director	25 minutes
Nick Levinson	Color
Presenter/Writer	Age range 17–adult
Colin Cunningham	VHS $99
Open University/BBC	

374 Victorian Dissenting Chapels

This film features four chapels designed for Dissenters or Nonconformists: Dukinfield Unitarian in Manchester, which was built to assert the new respectability that Nonconformists had attained in the eyes of the law; King Street Congregational in Newcastle-under-Lyme, which with its range of weektime activities became the center of its congregation's life; Bethesda Methodist Chapel in Hanley, a 'Nonconformist cathedral'; and Saltaire Congregational near Bradford, a model church designed for a model town. In each case their architecture can be seen as expressive of the kind of worship which they were intended to shelter.

Part of the series
Culture and Society in Britain 1850–90

Director	25 minutes
Nick Levinson	Color
Presenter/Writer	Age range 17–adult
Colin Cunningham	VHS $99
Open University/BBC	

375 Religion and Society in Victorian Bristol

The Victorian religious buildings of Bristol are explored for what they reveal about the spiritual activities of their congregations and about the worshipers' daily lives. Around the streets in which the poorer classes eked out a living several religious alternatives were on offer, many of them housed in buildings which have now been adapted to modern secular uses. Among those visited here are the widely differing St Agnes' Church, the Salvation Army Citadel in the St Paul's district, Clifton College Chapel and Mount Zion Chapel, Bedminster.

Part of the series
Culture and Society in Britain 1850–90

Director	25 minutes
Nick Levinson	Color
Presenter/Writer	Age range 17–adult
John Kent	VHS $99
Open University/BBC	

374
Saltaire, England

372
The Albert Memorial, London

375
St Paul's, Bristol, England

A New Museum in South Kensington

The story of the development of the new museum buildings which eventually, in the early years of the twentieth century, became the Victoria and Albert Museum. The idea for the museum grew out of Prince Albert's Great Exhibition of 1851, which had attracted over six million visitors, and also out of the government's wish to improve the education of British designers. The fascinating if fractured growth of the buildings reflects the parallel growth of the museum's status from its beginnings as a rather suspect pioneering venture, and also the development of taste between 1850 and 1890. It also illustrates conflicting contemporary attitudes toward the economics of education and manufacture, craftsmanship and collecting, and bringing art to the people – or at least to those who had the leisure to visit museums.

Part of the series
Culture and Society in Britain 1850–90

Director	**25 minutes**
Tony Coe	**Color**
Presenter/Writer	**Age range 17–adult**
Colin Cunningham	**VHS $99**
Open University/BBC	

377 **King Cotton's Palace: Manchester Town Hall**

The huge growth of trade and manufacturing business in Manchester in the nineteenth century – when 'cotton was king' – meant that the city needed a new town hall for practical reasons alone. But the new building was also intended to impress the rest of the world: nobody who saw it was to be left in any doubt about Manchester's economic status. Detailed investigation of the town hall's planning and design show how deliberately its builders set out to create a visible symbol of the city's mushrooming wealth and power.

Part of the series
Culture and Society in Britain 1850–90

Director	**25 minutes**
Tony Coe	**Color**
Presenter/Writer	**Age range 17–adult**
Colin Cunningham	**VHS $99**
Open University/BBC	

378 **Rural Life: Image and Reality**

Many Victorian landowners took a passionate interest in the creation of ideal villages for their workers and workers' families. Usually, of course, the cottages they built were a great deal better than what their inhabitants had been used to; but it also meant that the landlords could gain far greater control over every aspect of their tenants' lives. Here three Victorian villages are explored: Old Warden and Steppingley in Bedfordshire, which were each improved by a single landowner, and Wortham in Suffolk, which was not. Drawings by Richard Cobbold, the rector, of the people and scenes of Wortham are used to reconstruct the greater diversity of life to be found in an 'unmodel' village.

Part of the series
Culture and Society in Britain 1850–90

Director	**25 minutes**
Nick Levinson	**Color**
Presenters/Writers	**Age range 17–adult**
Gerry Roberts	**VHS S99**
Colin Cunningham	
Open University/BBC	

◀◀ 379
385, page 91
Arab Hall,
Leighton House, London

▲ 376
Victoria and Albert Museum,
London

379 **The Melbury Road Set**
Important Aesthetic and Architectural Monuments

Most of the building plots in Melbury Road, built in the second half of the nineteenth century in Holland Park in west London, were bought by a group of artists who made this area the center of a new aesthetic élite. They moved in fashionable society, and in keeping with their social and financial position – artists were never held in higher esteem than in the closing decades of the nineteenth century – they built themselves expensive and modish studio houses which stood out from the common run of suburban architecture around them. The fantastic interior of Leighton House, built by Lord Leighton, with its Arab Hall decorated with tiles he had brought back from his travels and cooled by an indoor pool, and Tower House, designed as a Gothic castle by the architect William Burges for himself, stand out as important aesthetic and architectural monuments of the period.

Part of the series
Culture and Society in Britain 1850–90

Director	**25 minutes**
Charles Cooper	**Color**
Presenter/Writer	**Age range 17–adult**
Colin Cunningham	**VHS $99**
Open University/BBC	

11 The Victorians

The Roland Collection

Painters to the People
The Golden Age of Victorian Painting

The critic and art historian Christopher Wood writes: 'English art, according to my studies at Cambridge, somehow stopped dead with Constable and Turner. After that loomed a great dark void, the Victorian period, an epoch so unmentionable that only the brave dared to confess an interest in it. The very word Victorian was likely to arouse mirth and derision, and its art, along with everything else, was instantly consigned to oblivion. In spite of this, Victorian art beckoned me, perhaps with the irresistible attraction of the forbidden. In the mid-1960s, I would creep guiltily into the Tate Gallery at weekends and gaze at the Pre-Raphaelites, then all in the basement, along with the lavatories.

'Two artists, above all, fascinated me – Dante Gabriel Rossetti and Edward Burne-Jones. Even their names seemed mysteriously romantic. Some of Burne-Jones's bigger pictures, such as *Love and the Pilgrim* and *King Cophetua and the Beggar Maid,* still hung upstairs at the Tate, so big that perhaps no one could be bothered to take them down.

'At that time, there were very few books on Victorian painting, but I read them avidly. I visited provincial art galleries, especially Birmingham and Manchester, where the great collections of Victorian art were to be found. Gradually, it began to dawn on me that here was an entire continent of English art, submerged, waiting to be rediscovered and explored.'

This series of
6 programs
can be purchased on
VHS for $594
Reference S13

381   **The Pre-Raphaelites**

Christopher Wood presents a very personal view of paintings from the reign of Queen Victoria. In this first program of the series, he tells how he discovered Pre-Raphaelite paintings for himself. At the time they were unfashionable and hidden away in the basements of galleries. The magic names of Rossetti, Millais and Holman Hunt revealed their secrets, and he learned of the tragedy behind one particular painting.

Part of the series *Painters to the People*

Director of photography Edwin Mickleburgh	**26 minutes**
	Color
Presenter/Writer Christopher Wood	**Age range 15–adult**
	VHS $99
Original music Ed Shearmur	

382   **The Followers of the Pre-Raphaelites**

This program explores how the Pre-Raphaelite Brotherhood turned English painting upside down, but only lasted four short years. Its influence was immediately felt in the work of its two best-known followers, William Morris and Edward Burne-Jones. Art moved into design, and Rossetti responded by producing some of his finest work, in voluptuous portraits of beautiful women.

Part of the series *Painters to the People*

Director of photography Edwin Mickleburgh	**26 minutes**
	Color
Presenter/Writer Christopher Wood	**Age range 15–adult**
	VHS $99
Original music Ed Shearmur	

◄◄ 382
Sir Edward Coley Burne-Jones
The Wheel of Fortune,
detail

▼ 381
John Everett Millais
Ophelia

383 Victorian Painting – Modern Life

Christopher Wood demonstrates how
Victorian painting consisted of much more
than wistful maidens and knights in armor.
Painters turned for inspiration to what they
saw around them. They incorporated visual
clues in their pictures for the public to seek
out and interpret, and they illustrated the
social issues of the day. The public's
enthusiastic reception of each new canvas
confirmed their close relationship with this
new school of painters.

Part of the series *Painters to the People*

Director of photography Edwin Mickleburgh	**26 minutes** **Color**
Presenter/Writer Christopher Wood	**Age range 15–adult** **VHS $99**
Original music Ed Shearmur	

384 Victorian Painting – High Life and Low Life

The new patrons of Victorian painting were
often men of industry. They encouraged a
new-look realistic approach to subjects
which reflected the nature of Victorian
society at all levels. Fildes, Holl and
Herkomer contrast with Tissot in the kind
of society they portrayed, and they created
uniquely strong images of their times.

Part of the series *Painters to the People*

Director of photography Edwin Mickleburgh	**26 minutes** **Color**
Presenter/Writer Christopher Wood	**Age range 15–adult** **VHS $99**
Original music Ed Shearmur	

385 Victorian Painting – Aesthetes and Dreamers

There was a group of painters in Victorian
times fascinated by classical themes.
Alma-Tadema portrayed day-to-day life in
ancient Greece and Rome, whereas Moore
saw his paintings as color compositions for
which a title would be inappropriate.
G F Watts painted superb portraits of great
figures of the day – and murky abstractions
of his own favorite themes. All won great
honors, but Lord Leighton was the first
painter to become a peer. Christopher
Wood guides the viewer through this
school of Victorian painters.

Part of the series *Painters to the People*

Director of photography Edwin Mickleburgh	**26 minutes** **Color**
Presenter/Writer Christopher Wood	**Age range 15–adult** **VHS $99**
Original music Ed Shearmur	

386 Victorian Painting – Country Life and Landscapes

The most popular Victorian paintings were
of the countryside – picturesque cottages,
pretty milkmaids, perfect cattle. This
unrealistic image of the English landscape
is still with us, but as painters moved away
from the towns which had been ravaged
by the Industrial Revolution, they escaped
as far as the Great Western Railway
would take them, and found themselves
in Cornwall. Here they contemplated
the lessons learned from the French
Impressionists, and Stanhope Forbes
founded the Newlyn School. Christopher
Wood brings the series to a close in the
place where Victorian painting moved into
the twentieth century.

Part of the series *Painters to the People*

Director of photography Edwin Mickleburgh	**26 minutes** **Color**
Presenter/Writer Christopher Wood	**Age range 15–adult** **VHS $99**
Original music Ed Shearmur	

12 Impressionists and Post-Impressionists

The familiarity of Impressionist and Post-Impressionist paintings today (reproduced on greetings cards, calendars and note pads) makes it hard for us to appreciate how radical the work of Manet, Pissarro, Degas, Monet, Renoir, Lautrec and their colleagues first appeared.

This section of 22 programs can be purchased on VHS for $2188

Television rights and prices on request

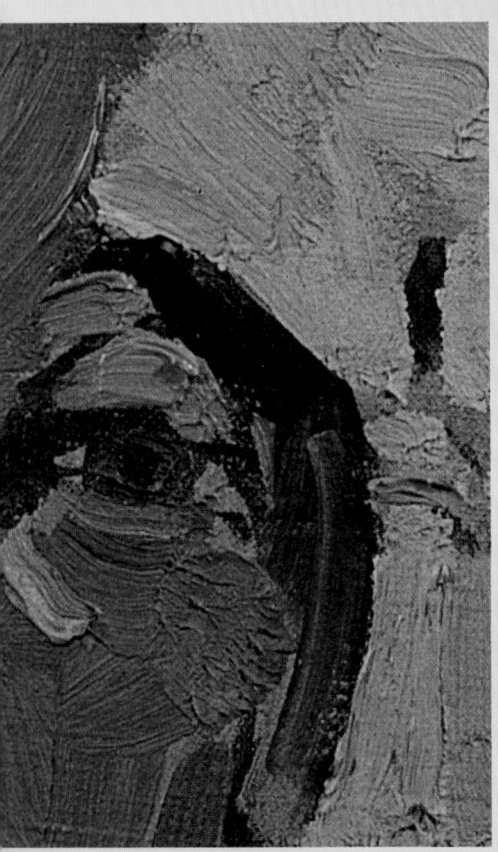

In the course of the nineteenth century the painting of grand historical and mythological subjects favored in the Paris Salon exhibitions had grown academic and formulaic. A challenge had already come in the realism of Courbet, Millet, Manet and others, and in the 'alternative' graphic work of artists such as Daumier and Steinlen. Apart from a newly robust technique, realism's opposition to history painting lay primarily in depicting scenes of rural or urban labor, everyday life or even low-life.

In a way, Impressionism was to go one step further, adopting not provocatively debased subjects, but provocatively *neutral* images. Landscape, traditionally considered a minor genre, was promoted to a major position, taking its cues from Corot and the Barbizon painters in France, and from English Romantic painting, especially Constable.

The Impressionists' major preoccupations were with the perception and recording of light and color. Composition became daringly cropped and seemingly arbitrary, related in a way to the developing medium of photography. Other factors affecting the Impressionists' work included scientific research into color theory (encouraging their use of pure hue, rather than tonal gradation in creating illusion), and the new vogue for eighteenth-century Japanese prints (confirming them in their radical compositional tendencies). The development of tube paints facilitated the artists' outdoor (*plein-air*) approach to painting the subject directly before them (*sur le motif*) as opposed to 'reconstructing' it in the studio.

Inevitably there were reactions to, and developments from, Impressionism. Experiments with color became schematized in the neo-Impressionism (or Pointillism or divisionism) of Seurat and his followers, who painted with myriad dots of pure color. Cézanne, dissatisfied with the lack of structure and solidity in the Impressionist surface, moved to more constructed and schematic composition. The term Post-Impressionism, however, is an extremely loose label applied primarily to Cézanne, Van Gogh, Gauguin, Lautrec and Seurat, but often used to describe other progressive artists after the great decade of Impressionism (1870–80), such as Matisse or Bonnard.

346 The Road to Modern Art

Between 1800 and 1900 so much happened
in French painting that the period seems
like several centuries compressed into one.
Delacroix expressed energy in a free
handling of brilliant color, as opposed to the
classically smooth and perfect finish of
Ingres. Courbet painted with a hard, bright
realism, and Corot with fresh spontaneity.
Impressionism was not only a bold new
style, it represented a new range of subject
matter, a new way of looking at the world.
It was a re-evaluation of what art should be
about. One of its chief concerns was with
light and its ability to dissolve forms and
modify colors. Detail was sacrificed to the
overall momentary impression. While using
the bright palette of Impressionism, some
artists could not entirely abandon line and
structure. Cézanne in particular had
different objectives, seeking to express the
geometrical basis of all forms, thereby
pointing the way to Cubism and ultimately
to abstract painting. Other painters
featured are Pissarro, Monet, Manet, Renoir,
Degas, Seurat, Van Gogh and Rousseau.

Part of the series
The National Gallery – A Private View

Director	28 minutes
Henry Lewes	Color
Writer/Narrator	Age range 12–adult
Edwin Mullins	Film $693 Rental $199
	VHS $99

391 Art in the Making: Impressionism

A group of pictures in The National Gallery,
London, cleaned to restore the original
brilliant colors and textures, exemplifies
the aims and methods of the Impressionist
painters. This video, filmed on location
in France and England, looks at the
Impressionists' color theories and their
use of newly available pigments, and
demonstrates the ways in which modern
technology made possible the development
of Impressionism.

'This high-quality program provides a focused
overview of a significant period in painting
history…well scripted with high-quality
photography of the paintings…lighting that
shows the texture of the paint on the surface,
both important characteristics of this style…
recommended for audiences who are
interested in learning more about how the
impact of new materials and knowledge
affect the way artists paint.'
Video Rating Guide for Libraries, USA

Part of the series *Art in the Making*

Presenter	22 minutes
James Heard	Color
Audio Visual Unit	Age range 14–adult
The National Gallery	VHS $89

The following book of the same title gives an
extensive overview of the subject – an ideal
companion to the video.

392 Art in the Making: Impressionism
Book

While Impressionist art appears to be
effortless and spontaneous, it actually
involves an intricate and varied approach
to painting. This book investigates how
Impressionist paintings were made and
what materials were used. Impressionist
artists came to the fore during a period
of dramatic change in patterns of artistic
training and patronage. The book begins
with an essay that sets their techniques
within the wider context of French
nineteenth-century painting. The authors
discuss such subjects as open-air painting,
the Impressionist use of color, and the
paint layers and surfaces of Impressionist
paintings. Focusing in particular on the
new synthetic pigments that became
available in tubes, the authors show how
this development allowed artists to free
themselves from traditional studio
practice and to render their subject
matter more vividly. Fifteen paintings
from The National Gallery are examined,
using X-rays, infra-red photography and
the analysis of pigments and paint media.
An analysis of the artists' palette, a
chronology, biographies of the artists
discussed, a glossary and an extensive
bibliography complete this interesting
and valuable work.

Authors from	10.75 x 8.75 inches
The National Gallery	273 x 224 mm
	316 illustrations
	218 in color
	Book $33

◀◀ 426, page 98
André Derain
Henri Matisse, detail

▼ 346
Pierre-Auguste Renoir
The Cabaret

This video celebrates the complexity and richness of Manet's painting and its intriguing blend of tradition and modernity. News of the execution of the Emperor Maximilian in Mexico in the summer of 1867 provided Manet with the chance to depict a current event which could match the epic dramas of past history. The video examines Manet's commitment to painting the history of his own era, which his friend Baudelaire characterized as the 'heroism of modern life.' It traces the development of Manet's art during the 1860s and explores the ways in which he used painting to comment on his own time. Many of Manet's most celebrated works are examined, and their debt to Spanish art, especially the paintings of Velazquez and Goya, is assessed. Manet's visit to Spain in 1865 is documented with footage shot on location.

Audio Visual Unit	**25 minutes**
The National Gallery	**Color**
	Age range 14–adult
	VHS $89

Why was Edouard Manet's painting *Olympia* received with such hostility at the Salon of 1865? And were criticisms of the 'incoherence' of his *Bar at the Folies Bergère*, painted sixteen years later, really justified? Both of these notorious pictures appear to represent aspects of prostitution in nineteeth-century Paris; but do we react to them in the same way as Manet's contemporaries?

Part of the series *Modern Art and Modernism: Manet to Pollock*

Director	**25 minutes**
Nick Levinson	**Color**
Presenter/Writer	**Age range 17–adult**
TJ Clark	**VHS $99**
Open University/BBC	

During the 1880s, when he was already more than fifty years old, Camille Pissarro was forced to reassess and then change the subject of his work. As this appraisal shows, although he did not, or could not, break away from the principles of Impressionism to which he had hitherto given his allegiance – he was the only artist to exhibit in all eight of the Impressionist exhibitions – his increasing commitment to left-wing political ideas altered more than his outlook on life. Now, as a painter of peasants and peasant life, he faced new problems that were both technical and ideological.

Part of the series *Modern Art and Modernism: Manet to Pollock*

Director	**25 minutes**
Nick Levinson	**Color**
Presenter/Writer	**Age range 17–adult**
TJ Clark	**VHS $99**
Open University/BBC	

410 Degas' Dancers

In this film, as in other key titles in the Roland Collection, a meeting takes place between several media: the dance of Degas' subject matter, the dynamism of his draftsmanship, the drama of the score by Marius Constant, and the exploratory and expressive direction of the film-maker's camera work. The elements are mutually illuminating. Degas anticipates photographic and filmic qualities in his use of light and the 'verism' of his cropping and composition. The dancers 'draw' and compose in space, transposing music into visual form, which is in turn reinterpreted in the score, synchronized with Anthony Roland's moving, extemporizing camera work. This film, like others in the collection, collaborates with its subject in a way that complements and perhaps challenges more cerebral, analytical films in this and other sections. Where a more conventional narrator might hasten to make a didactic point about Degas – for example, about the frequent misery of girls forced into the 'marriage market' of ballet training – this film, with no narration, respects the silence and inscrutability of the artist's images. It permits us a slower, more meditative entry into the pictures, during which we may indeed come to sense tensions, ambivalences, even pain, existing side by side with delicacy and beauty.

Director	13 minutes
Anthony Roland	**Black and white**
Documentation	**Age range 10–adult**
Lilian Browse	**Film $623** Rental $189
Original music	**VHS $89**
Marius Constant	

Awards
Silver Cup, Salerno
Chriss Award, Columbus

◀◀ 394
Edouard Manet
*Fragments of the
Execution of Maximilian*

◀ 410
Edgar Degas
Two dancers, detail

411 Renoir

Renoir's greatest fame came from his association with the French Impressionist painters of the later nineteenth century. The Impressionists captured their immediate surroundings in richly colored, fluently sketched canvases often executed out of doors rather than in the studio. But Renoir's long career encompassed a wide range of styles and there is a world of difference between the ambitious subject pictures he painted in the 1860s and the glowing nudes that he produced in the final years before his death in 1919. This video explores the full range of Renoir's extraordinary talent through detailed photography and an illuminating script by John House, one of the selectors of the Renoir exhibition seen in London, Paris and Boston.

Script	**28 minutes**
John House	**Color**
Narrator	**Age range 14–adult**
Sir Anthony Quayle	**VHS $99**

412 The Bathers by Cézanne and Renoir: Modernism and the Nude

The program is shot in the Philadelphia Museum of Art and deals with the nude bathers that Renoir and Cézanne painted in the 1870s. It adopts a feminist angle in trying to understand why the nude remains an important subject in the modern period. Cézanne and Renoir approach the nude very differently. While Renoir's nudes conform to stereotypical images of woman as fertile, fecund and consumable, Cézanne seems to offer a more complex reading. His nudes are not conventionally feminine; they resist the predominantly male gaze. Despite this, Tamar Garb argues that Cézanne is locked into the same pictorial tradition that produced Renoir's nudes.

Part of the series
Modern Art, Practices and Debates

Director	**25 minutes**
GD Jayalakshmi	**Color**
Presenter	**Age range 18–adult**
Tamar Garb	**VHS $99**
Open University/BBC	

413 Monet

Monet is often seen as the archetypal Impressionist painter, conveying unstructured, sensual 'impressions' of 'real' scenes, but this view may be misleading. Paintings like *Bathers at La Grenouillère* and *Gare St Lazare* are not, perhaps, 'sliced from life', but are highly worked and tightly structured to produce an almost flat, decorative effect. In later years Monet worked more and more from inspiration provided by the famous water-garden he had made at Giverny, culminating in the great series of waterlily paintings; but even in these, it is possible to demonstrate that clear artistic principles of organization are at work. It seems that whatever his subject, Monet was well aware of the part that illusion and artifice must play in any work of art.

Part of the series *Modern Art and Modernism: Manet to Pollock*

Director	**25 minutes**
Tony Coe	**Color**
Presenter/Writer	**Age range 17–adult**
Dr Anthea Callen	**VHS $99**
Open University/BBC	

12 Impressionists and Post-Impressionists

95

The Roland Collection

Seurat Drawings

Seurat's drawings, like those of other great artists – Rembrandt and Daumier, for example – contain his talent in its entirety. This film brings together nearly all of Seurat's drawings and demonstrates how pointillism can work in monochrome; looking at them, the pleasures of color seem to lose their importance. Nothing is more interesting than to see great artists reveal themselves in their drawings. Something seems to be created out of nothing in this naked confrontation between the artist and his medium. Seurat advances with infinite caution; yet however methodical his approach, the passion and the vigor are never lost, the reserve and the ardor reinforce one another. This deliberate, sophisticated, almost monumental art is frequently inspired by the most ephemeral, banal reality – by figures of anonymous passers-by in the street. These drawings have surprising dramatic force: the strange, precise silhouettes, moving in a kind of tragic silence, make one think of ghosts, soon to melt back into the darkness from which they have briefly emerged. There is very little narration.

Director
Anthony Roland
Music
Claude Debussy

17 minutes
Black and white
Age range 12–adult
Film $623 Rental $189
VHS $89

Seurat

Georges Seurat had a brief working life during which he produced six major compositions on the theme of modern urban life. The first two, *Bathers at Asnières* and *Sunday Afternoon on the Island of La Grande Jatte*, established him as a leading figure in the avant-garde of the 1880s. The combination of innovatory and classical qualities in his work in terms of formal design make him a forerunner of the geometric and abstract artists of the twentieth century. However Seurat's style of composition and his 'Pointillist', or 'divisionist', technique are not merely ends in themselves, but a means to an end – that of critically describing the modern world.

Part of the series *Modern Art and Modernism: Manet to Pollock*

Director
Tony Coe
Presenter/Writer
Tom Crow
Open University/BBC

24 minutes
Color
Age range 17–adult
VHS $99

Giovanni Segantini

Giovanni Segantini (1858–99) was an Italian painter with a distinctive style ranging from illusionistic Impressionism to a divisionist or pointillist accumulation of paint touches, creating highly atmospheric effects. In his own time his international reputation was such that he had to retreat ever higher into the desolate Alps to escape the adoring fans who hounded him, and to find the spiritual isolation he sought in nature. Today he is often forgotten, though his work was an important transitional influence on later modern artists such as the American painter Marsden Hartley. With the growing recognition of the diversity of trends and influences within Modernism, Segantini, like other artists of his generation, is gaining new respect among viewers.

Giovanni Segantini: Life and Work

This film stresses the mystical content that lies behind the Impressionist technique. It displays neither an art-historical nor a documentary approach, but is centered around the artist's paintings, which are of vital interest for our own times, when humankind's relationship with nature is under threat.

For more information see pages 209 and 260

Director
Gaudenz Meili
Writer
Guido Magnaguagno
Also available in French, Italian and Spanish

45 minutes
Color
Age range 14–adult
Film $833 Rental $249
VHS $119

Japonism, Part One

Japanese Influences on Western Art:
Ukiyo-e/Japonitis/Mood of Light/
Return to the Linear

The western world's fascination with Japan
since 1854 (when her ports were forcibly
opened to the rest of the world by the US
Navy) has caused almost every major artist
up to the end of the last century to adopt
the styles, techniques and ideas of the
Japanese model. This film examines
Japanese influences in the works of the first
and second generations of Impressionists,
including Van Gogh, Gauguin, the Nabis and
Toulouse-Lautrec, and provides a starting-
point for analyzing the influence of
Japanese art on Art Nouveau.

Director	**30 minutes**
Guido De Bruyn	**Color**
Also available in Dutch	**Age range 15–adult**
and French	**VHS $99**

424   **Dreams of Beautiful Japan –**
Van Gogh and Ukiyo-e

Le Père Tanguy, one of Vincent Van Gogh's
best-known works, is a portrait of the
proprietor of an art supply shop in France.
In the background of this nineteenth-
century portrait we are surprised to see
six different Japanese prints, or ukiyo-e,
unmistakably featuring Japanese scenes
and objects, including cherry blossom,
a Japanese courtesan, Mount Fuji, and a
cluster of morning-glory. What inspired
Van Gogh to include these ukiyo-e in the
background of the portrait? This program
explores the fascinating relationship
between Vincent Van Gogh and the Japan
of his dreams, as each of the six ukiyo-e in
the background of *Le Père Tanguy* is traced
back through the 'Japonism' movement of
Van Gogh's Paris to its Japanese origin.

NHK Broadcasting Center	**45 minutes**
Also available	**Color**
in Japanese	**Age range 14–adult**
	VHS $129

393   **The Impressionist Surface**

Dr Paul Smith reviews influential theories
of Impressionism. Clement Greenberg's
Modernist criticism argued that
Impressionism was a critical stage in the
movement toward flatness and abstraction.
In contrast TJ Clark saw flatness in
Impressionism as carrying meaning about
the nature of modern life and as signifying
modernity itself. Paul Smith rejects both
explanations as over-simplified. Flatness,
the use of individual brush strokes, was a
way of rendering 'sensations'. Pissarro and
Monet used scientific color theories to
achieve greater impact and immediacy in
their work. Cézanne's work also showed
that the world depicted depended on the
surface depicting it. His work testifies to
a struggle to hold colors and surface in
balance. Degas' depiction of realistic social
and sexual life depends on the artifical or
factitious technique of representing it.
These artists wanted to convey the
sensations provoked by nature, not just
a notion of 'flatness'.

Part of the series
Modern Art, Practices and Debates

Director	**25 minutes**
Nick Levinson	**Color**
Presenter	**Age range 18–adult**
Dr Paul Smith	**VHS $99**
Open University/BBC	

420   **Toulouse-Lautrec**

Born the heir to a rich and aristocratic
family, Henri de Toulouse-Lautrec seemed
to have everything a young man could
want – until an accident and bone disease
left him with the head and torso of an old
man and the legs of a dwarf. With true
heroism he turned to drawing and painting
the glittering life he could no longer share.
He had been forced on to the sidelines,
made to understand how society treats its
outcasts; and this understanding can be
seen in his portraits of the prostitutes he
visited, the only women who were available
to him. His life was a drama which he
consciously lived to the full, dying at the
age of thirty-seven from alcohol and
venereal disease; but he rejected pity so
rigorously that not even those who knew
him best realized the weight of suffering he
bore. This deeply moving film shows the
artist as a man as well as a creative genius.

Director	**14 minutes**
Jacques Berthier	**Color**
Narration	**Age range 14–adult**
Henri Perruchot	**Film $553** Rental $169
Jacques Berthier	**VHS $79**
Original music	
Pierre Spiers	
Also available in French	

◀◀ 416
Georges-Pierre Seurat
Bathers, Asnières

▶ 418
Giovanni Segantini
The Bad Mother, detail

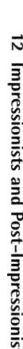

417 **Berthe Morisot**
An Interview with Kathleen Adler

Kathleen Adler, author of a book on Morisot, is interviewed by Bryony Fer. Ms Adler describes the restrictions suffered by a woman artist in Paris in the 1860s and 1870s – Morisot was restricted as to the places she could go and therefore what she might paint. Her subject matter was life in the middle-class suburb of Passy in which she lived. Her special interest in the suburban world informs her painting *View of Paris from the Trocadero,* which can be seen as representing the relationship between suburb and center. Morisot's technique was close to that of the other Impressionists, but her subject matter is of special interest to us now.

Director Nick Levinson	**25 minutes**
	Color
Presenter Bryony Fer	**Age range 18–adult**
Open University/BBC	**VHS $99**

425 **Impressionism and Post-Impressionism**

What is an Impressionist? And how much does one Impressionist have in common with another? This is an attempt to explain how categories like Impressionism and Post-Impressionism come into being in the minds of art historians, and to discover whether the reputation of the artists to whom they give these labels is distorted when we assume that they share more than a certain kind of technique.

Part of the series *Modern Art and Modernism: Manet to Pollock*

Director Charles Cooper	**25 minutes**
	Color
Presenter/Writer Belinda Thomson	**Age range 17–adult**
Open University/BBC	**VHS $99**

426 **Fauvism**

By 1890 Matisse, who was to be the *chef d'école* of the Fauvist movement, had moved to Paris, where he shared a studio with Marquet (another of the future Fauves) right next to the River Seine. After a conventional beginning at the Ecole des Beaux Arts, Matisse studied at the studio of the painter Gustave Moreau, who preferred to develop imagination in his students rather than academic imitation. As early as 1896 Matisse was preoccupied with color, and trips to the Mediterranean, the 'land of light,' encouraged him to persevere in this direction. Cézanne was another important influence, but other painters including Derain and Vlaminck were coming to share Matisse's attraction to light and color. In 1904, Matisse encountered Pointillist painters, including Paul Signac, at St Tropez, and he employed the technique for a few months. In 1905 he discovered the work of Gauguin; and Fauvism was born during the Salon d'Automne exhibition where the works of Matisse, Marquet, Derain and Vlaminck were shown, and a wry critic named them *fauves,* or 'wild beasts.' The Fauvist artists did not form a homogeneous school, but they all tended to use the energetic power of light and color. If power and energy are indeed at the center of their works, then in some sense the Italian Futurists may be said to have taken over from them in expressing movement, power and exhilaration, as can be seen from the paintings of Carrà, Balla, Boccioni, Severini and Russolo, which are introduced toward the end of this film. It also features works by Moreau, Maillol, Dufy and others.

Part of the series
The Adventure of Modern Art

Director Carlos Vilardebo	**53 minutes** **Color**
Writers/Narration André Parinaud Carlos Vilardebo	**Age range 15–adult** **Film $1043** Rental $299 **VHS $149**
Also available in French	

426
André Derain
Henri Matisse

445
Vincent Van Gogh
The Sower

430
Alexander Steinlen
Clown dressing

445 **One Hundred Years of Modern Art, Part One**

This film gives a rudimentary 'exposure' to a broad range of art for young audiences. It offers a survey of the painting and sculpture of the period 1870 to 1907. A filming technique has been evolved, particularly suitable for showing in schools, whereby short instalments of information are followed by long sections without narration, designed to capture the spirit of each style that has been discussed. This conveys dramatically the visual qualities of the major artists involved. The specially composed music draws viewers into even deeper involvement with what they see. Film sequences include: Degas, Cézanne, Monet, Neo-Impressionists, Pointillism, Seurat, Gauguin, Van Gogh, the Nabis, Picasso, Matisse, Rousseau, the Fauves.

Part of the series *Western Art 1700–1970*

Director	**19 minutes**
Anthony Roland	**Color**
Narration	**Age range 12–adult**
Anthony Bertram	**Film $623** Rental $189
Original music	**VHS $89**
Adrian Wagner	

815 **Artists' Techniques**

Any work of art is determined first and foremost by the materials available to the artist and his ability to manipulate them. Here we examine five paintings, Gleyre's *Lost Illusions*, Renoir's *La Parisienne*, Manet's *Déjeuner sur l'Herbe*, Monet's *Autumn at Argenteuil*, and Cézanne's *Mountains Seen from L'Estaque*, for the techniques which each artist employed: the application of paint, the use of color, the brushwork and the type of lighting. Only when these technical limitations are taken into account can one begin to understand what the artist's vision really was.

Part of the series *Modern Art and Modernism: Manet to Pollock*

Director	**23 minutes**
Tony Coe	**Color**
Presenter/Writer	**Age range 17–adult**
Dr Anthea Callen	**VHS $89**
Open University/BBC	

430 **At the Foot of the Tree**
A Homage to Steinlen

The Swiss-born painter, lithographer and draftsman Alexander Steinlen devoted his life to furthering the cause of justice and liberty. He saw himself as a working man whose mission was to express the opinions and reveal the suffering of those who could not speak for themselves, the inarticulate people and the cabhorses and carthorses of Paris. His work comments on the evils of his time – the imprisonment of children, the poverty of the workers, the horrors of war. He drew for magazines such as the anarchist *La Feuille*, considered dangerously revolutionary, and in consequence he often had to escape incognito from the authorities in Paris. The more lyrical and pleasing aspects of the simple working life, in the countryside where he hid himself and also in the city, are also celebrated in his work. But the main aim of his life was the fight to redress wrong. The bold historical and political approach of this film to its subject ensures the viewer's complete involvement.

Director/Narration	**24 minutes**
Alain Saury	**Black and white**
Poem	**Age range 14–adult**
Jean Rictus	**Film $623** Rental $189
Original music	**VHS $89**
Henri Sauget	

Awards
Special Diploma, Bergamo
Quality Award, French
National Film Center

Also available in French

13

Art Nouveau

Primarily a movement of the applied arts – interior and furniture design, architecture, book production and illustration – Art Nouveau, with its sinuous, serpentine lines and exotic, sensuous imagery, is among the most immediately recognizable and widely appreciated of artistic styles. It has important roots in English Romanticism, with the elongated forms and emphatic design of Blake and Fuseli, and later in the floral designs of William Morris and the Arts and Crafts movement. On the Continent influential late Romantic painters like Moreau and Puvis de Chavannes were similarly important. By the turn of the twentieth century, the style had stretched its tentacles across Europe and America. Echoing the almost morbid opulence of the French Symbolist writers, or of Poe in America, the decadent illustrations of Beardsley in England, the rippling architecture of Gaudí in Spain, Horta in Belgium, Endell in Germany, and the extravagant furnishings of Tiffany in the USA all exemplify the 'high' Art Nouveau manner.

This section of 16 programs can be purchased on VHS for $1804

Television rights and prices on request

An important center of Art Nouveau was Belgium, and one sees affinities with the style in the submarine imagery, coral-like color and languorous atmosphere of James Ensor, who was associated with the Belgian Art Nouveau creators. Similarly, in Paris, Lautrec's cabaret posters contributed strongly to the style, as did the work of the Austrian painter Klimt. Affinities also exist between northern European Expressionism and Art Nouveau (or *Jugendstil* as it was called in Germany). Aspects of the work of the Norwegian Munch, for example, can be seen as consonant with Art Nouveau.

The Art Nouveau influence on design has been a lasting one, often reaching into unexpected areas, such as the animated films of the Disney studios, for which the Art Nouveau illustrator Kay Nielsen worked late in his career.

Modernism in Barcelona

Modernismo was the term which in Spain described the *fin-de-siècle* style which in Germany and Austria was called *Jugendstil*, and in France *Art Nouveau*. Rather than focusing on individual artists, this film presents a wealth of stunning visual material from the period – painting, furniture, sculpture, interior design, stained glass and costume. It also describes the social background of growing industrialism, class unrest, civic rationalization and town planning. Especially notable are sequences on graphic design, posters, magazine covers and illustrations, including the journal *L'Avenç*, in which the term 'Modernism' was first used in 1881.

Director	25 minutes
Joan Mallarach	Color
Narration	Age range 14–adult
Teresa Guasch	VHS $99
Ramon Rull	

464 **Modernist Architecture in Barcelona**

Modernism is defined in this program as the revival, beginning toward the end of the nineteenth century, of an inventiveness and exuberance in building and craftsmanship that Spain had not seen since the Middle Ages. The works of three major architects are highlighted: Domenic y Montinair, Pug y Carafalc, and the most famous, Antonio Gaudí. The first wrote an important text in 1870, *In Search of a National Architecture*, and we see spectacular buildings of his, such as the Montinair-Simon Publishing building and the Hospital de la Santa Creu in St Pau. Gaudí's great, organically structured and mosaic-encrusted buildings are also featured, including the celebrated Barcelona cathedral. Pug y Carafalc, meanwhile, a believer like Montinair in Catalan independence, created equally powerful structures, with similar vernacular decoration and archaic, neo-medievalist details.

A sequel to 463 (see above).

Director	25 minutes
Joan Mallarach	Color
Narration	Age range 14–adult
Teresa Guasch	VHS $99
Ramon Rull	

---

701 **The Universal International Exhibition, Paris 1900**

A mammoth, chaotic event, the Universal International Exhibition held in Paris in 1900 can be seen as a late celebration of nineteenth-century values, imperialism and eclecticism. It included displays of real live 'natives' from the colonies and real camels, a complete medieval French village and its inhabitants reconstructed on the Right Bank, and buildings ranging from Serbian Byzantine and English Jacobean to Austrian Gothic. But the exhibition was also intended to look forward to the new century: an elevated electric railway surrounded the site, and it held examples of what the general public considered to be the last word in modern architecture and design, epitomized by the Art Nouveau. Contemporary Pathe News film, still photographs and writings show us the tangle of artistic ideas from which the modern movements of the twentieth century were to emerge.

Part of the series *History of Architecture and Design 1890-1939*

Director	25 minutes
Nick Levinson	Black and white
Presenter/Writer	Age range 18–adult
Tim Benton	VHS $99
Open University/BBC	

460
Hector Guimard
Paris Métro station roof support incorporating drainage system

463
Antonio Gaudí
Ceramic mosaic sculpture
Park Güell, Barcelona

---

460 **Art Nouveau: Equivoque 1900**

The influence of the Art Nouveau, or New Style, was profoundly felt throughout the art, architecture and design of its day. It contradicted everything that had gone before: during the second half of the nineteenth-century, the gap between artist and manufacturer, between custom designer and mass-producer, had grown ever wider. The moving spirits of Art Nouveau attempted to reverse this trend, and soon scarcely a single household object remained untouched by the New Style, while ideas of typography, illustration and graphic design underwent a revolution. The impact on painting and sculpture was less immediate, but it did provide architecture with a new way forward. The film indicates the widespread expression of Art Nouveau ideas, showing among many examples the furniture of Van de Velde, the ironwork of Guimard's famous Paris Métro stations, the houses of Auguste Perret, the posters of Mucha and the painting of the Symbolists.

Directors	14 minutes
Maurice Rheims	Color
Monique Lepeuve	Age range 14–adult
Narration	Film $623 Rental $189
Maurice Rheims	VHS $89
Original music	
Diego Masson	
Awards	
Quality Prize and	
Quality Award, French	
National Film Center	
Also available in French	

La Grande Epoque

This series traces the fascinating remnants of the short-lived but influential epoch, ending in 1914, during which Art Nouveau spread across Europe and beyond, from fine arts to crafts, from architecture to the most mundane objects of everyday life. Vienna, Brussels, Paris, Glasgow, Cape Town, Chicago and Mexico City are all stations on this journey, in which artistic expression is assumed to be inseparable from the spirit of its times.

This series of 4 programs can be purchased on VHS for $636 Reference S14

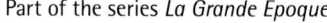

456   **Burning with Life**

This spectacular collage of music and images charts one period of great and momentous change at the end of the nineteenth century and the beginning of the twentieth – the time of the coming of electricity, the development of telecommunications, the invasion of advertising, the birth of film and aviation, and the spread of consumerism and the automobile. The camera discovers and explores the new style in fine and applied art that influenced all these innovations and is mirrored in them. In Italy this new style is called 'Liberty', in France *Art Nouveau*, in England 'New Style', in Germany *Jugendstil*, in Austria *Secession*, in Spain *Modernismo*. Many names for one and the same upheaval, for a major impetus by two extreme creative opposites. In order to give an idea of these opposites, the film observes two strongly contrasted manifestations within the same movement: the Glasgow School, with the moving story of Mackintosh, and the *Modernismo* of the Barcelona School. It is the confrontation of two personalities, two tendencies in architecture and works of art – both in the musical and in the visual sphere.

Part of the series *La Grande Epoque*

Director/Writer Folco Quilici	**60 minutes** **Color**
Also available in Italian	**Age range 15–adult**
	Film $1113 Rental $299
	VHS $159

The film describes the development of the Art Nouveau movement in Brussels, Vienna and Germany and introduces the viewer to fascinating personalities – Horta, Hoffmann, Van de Velde, Ohlbrich, Mahler, Klimt and Schiele. We learn about their artistic and social ideals against the background of a society which is dominated by a bourgeoisie sometimes surprisingly enlightened, sometimes apathetic and hopelessly inured to its own prejudices. In some central European regions, the bourgeoisie mustered the courage to provide financial support for even the most outrageous avant-garde art. In other regions it tended to be conservative and conformist, although an active minority professed its adherence to an innovative socialism. Within this society, unrest of all types, social and individual, was seething – and aggravating this unrest came the psychoanalytical theories of Sigmund Freud.

Part of the series *La Grande Epoque*

Director/Writer	**60 minutes**
Folco Quilici	**Color**
Also available in Italian	**Age range 15–adult**
	Film $1113 Rental $299
	VHS $159

Fin-de-siècle Paris: the Mecca of Art Nouveau. The great 'world exhibitions' of the last decades of the nineteenth century had popularized a series of exceptional new scientific achievements which, via Paris, had spread their fame all over the world. A thousand novelties put an end for ever to the old traditional way of life, replacing it with a totally new technological reality and a new attitude to life, unmistakable in its style. Art Nouveau is not a uniform, codified phenomenon but a rich and varied brew, exemplified by a whole list of different personalities from Eiffel to Debussy, from Toulouse-Lautrec, Gauguin, Gallé and Guimard right up to Lalique – to say nothing of the 'newcomers' like Mucha, from Prague, Bakst, with his Russian ballets or Boldini, with his portraits. It was certainly a great age, a great 'epoch'; but it faded quickly.

Part of the series *La Grande Epoque*

Director/Writer	**60 minutes**
Folco Quilici	**Color**
Also available in Italian	**Age range 15–adult**
	Film $1113 Rental $299
	VHS $159

◀◀ 457
Victor Horta
Tassel House, Brussels

▲ 457
Gustav Klimt
The Music

▼◤ 458
Restaurant scene

◥ 458
Toulouse-Lautrec
The Englishman at the Moulin-Rouge

In *Final Vortex* we find ourselves on the fringe of the creative, innovative movement which characterized the turn of the century. Italy and Spain, Russia, the East, and both North and Latin America are on this fringe, but only in the geographical, not the creative, sense. In these regions there emerge centers which, like Vienna, Paris or Brussels, can boast artistic giants – one need only point to Gaudí in Spain or Tiffany in the United States. The surprising photographs shown in this film (mostly unpublished until now) testify in a spectacular manner to the fantastically rapid spread of this movement all over the world, a phenomenon manifested on this scale and with this directness for the first time in the history of art and customs. This development continued, only to be destroyed in the immense drama of the First World War, which generated a malaise, bitter and destructive, in which the purpose of innovation was reversed. Progress suddenly became an instrument of death: a violent and bitter shattering of mankind's illusions.

Part of the series *La Grande Epoque*

Director/Writer	**60 minutes**
Folco Quilici	**Color**
Also available in Italian	**Age range 15–adult**
	Film $1113 Rental $299
	VHS $159

13 Art Nouveau

480 Hectorologie
Hector Guimard

The leading French Art Nouveau architect and designer Hector Guimard stood aloof from the chaos into which the New Style too often collapsed; he created a style of his own, unique, beautiful and inimitable. His best-known work is the entrances to the original Paris subway stations. He was nicknamed Handsome Hector – his two passions in life were design and pretty women – and it seems that the voluptuous curves of his balconies and balustrades, his lampstands and tablelegs, his bedheads and drinking glasses, drew their inspiration from the opulent curves of his female friends. For Guimard furnished the houses that he built himself, creating a whole world of his own design, and while some of his contemporaries sneered that he was improperly trained, or that he 'scorned history', he became rich and famous. He designed apartment blocks, a girls' school, a concert hall, mansions and villas in the best part of Paris, all in a manner so complex and individual that it was impossible to imitate – in fact, he was the first of the great individualists of twentieth-century design. This stylish film draws the viewer irresistibly into Guimard's world.

Directors/Narration	12 minutes
Yves Plantin	Color
Alain Blondel	Age range 13–adult
Original music	Film $553 Rental $169
Jeff Gilson	VHS $79

Awards
Gold Lion, Venice
Prix Max Ophuls, Paris
Quality Prize and
Quality Award, French
National Film Center

Also available in French

971 Japonism, Part One
Japanese Influences on Western Art: Ukiyo-e/Japonitis/Mood of Light/ Return to the Linear

The western world's fascination with Japan since 1854 (when her ports were forcibly opened to the rest of the world by the US Navy) has caused almost every major artist up to the end of the last century to adopt the styles, techniques and ideas of the Japanese model. This film examines Japanese influences in the works of the first and second generations of Impressionists, including Van Gogh, Gauguin, the Nabis and Toulouse-Lautrec, and provides a starting-point for analyzing the influence of Japanese art on Art Nouveau.

Director	30 minutes
Guido De Bruyn	Color
Also available in Dutch	Age range 15–adult
and French	VHS $99

468 Moscow 1910: Search for Truth

Search for Truth introduces one of the most exciting and complex chapters in the architectural history of Moscow, the transition from the nineteenth to the twentieth century. Buildings such as the Kremlin Palace and the spectacular Yaroslavski railway station are shown and compared with the intricate 'fairy house' of the artist Vasnetsov and later, more humble domestic residences in the modern style. In the period covered, Russia experienced its own version of the Art Nouveau style spreading across Europe and America. It was a period of eclecticism, a curious mixture of nostalgic romanticism, adventurous modernism and decadence. Here we see for the first time the interiors of many of Moscow's finest buildings, long closed to the public, in addition to stained-glass windows, paintings and sculptures by artists such as Vroubel, Serov and Antakolsky.

Part of the series
The Beautiful City of Moscow

Director/Script	30 minutes
Vladimir Benidiktov	Color
Art Video International	Age range 14–adult
Also available in Russian	VHS $99

465 Vienna 1900
The Kiss to the Whole World

Opening with shots of the fabulous (and newly restored) Vienna Secession building, with its painted friezes by Gustav Klimt, *Vienna 1900* investigates the *Jugendstil,* or 'young style', which revived art and craft in the middle of Europe from the late nineteenth century. We see Klimt's development from a style imitative of Michelangelo's Sistine Chapel ceiling to the sinuous, sensuous, dazzling style which made him famous. Architects mentioned in this film include Otto Wagner, Josef Hoffmann and Adolf Loos. Vienna emerges as a city of cultural ferment, a melting-pot of history where Hitler, Lenin, Trotsky and numerous other world-shapers lived, including Sigmund Freud, who developed his revolutionary theories of the unconscious here.

Austrian Wochenschau	18 minutes
Also available in German	Color
	Age range 14–adult
	VHS $89

782 1900
1900–1920

The year 1900 marks the meridian between the Victorian era and our own, modern world. In the two decades that followed – which included both the Great War and the October Revolution – the old ways were lost for ever. A new, Modernist style furnished concrete evidence that the twentieth century was to be a new, forward-looking era. The apotheosis of the popular press as a mass-medium provided a secure framework within which the graphic artist, the cartoonist, the caricaturist and the illustrator joined together to develop comics – the ninth art form. Maurice Horn is interviewed in the film, which features Yellow Kid, Little Nemo, Krazy Kat and the Katzenjammer Kids.

Part of the series *Comics, the Ninth Art*

Director	28 minutes
Alejandro Vallejo	Color
Script	Age range 9–adult
Carmen Dominguez	VHS $99
Alejandro Vallejo	
Maite Ruiz de Austri	

Award
Finalist Award,
New York Film Festival

Also available in French
and Spanish

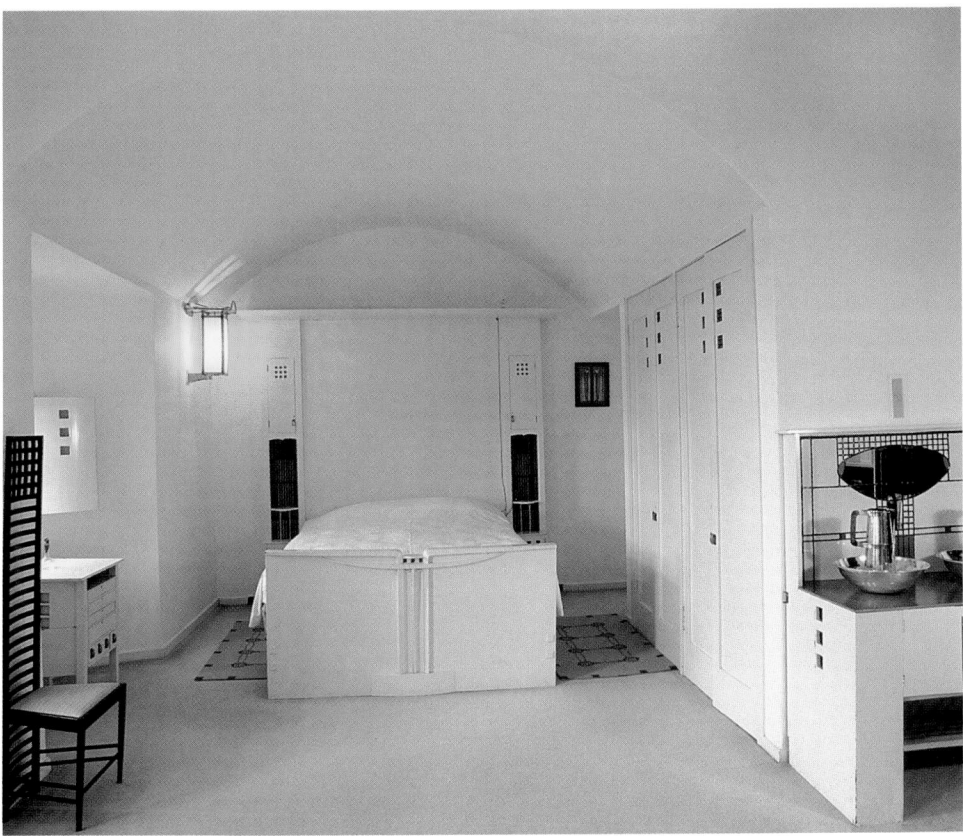

702   Charles Rennie Mackintosh: Hill House

A detailed look at the inside and outside of Hill House, Helensburgh, near Glasgow, with its panoramic view of the Clyde, built by Mackintosh for the publisher Walter Blackie in 1903. In *Memories of Charles Rennie Mackintosh,* Blackie described how he came to commission the house after seeing Mackintosh's Glasgow School of Art. How did the relationship between client and architect and the client's individual needs affect the style of the house, and how are its interior and exterior design related to each other? And how much, or how little, did traditional Scottish forms of architecture influence Mackintosh's work?

Part of the series *History of Architecture and Design 1890–1939*

Director	**25 minutes**
Nick Levinson	**Color**
Presenter/Writer	**Age range 18–adult**
Sandra Millikin	**VHS $99**
Open University/BBC	

470   Charles Rennie Mackintosh

The first British architect to acquire an international reputation since the eighteenth century, Charles Rennie Mackintosh was the leading exponent of the distinctive style known as 'Glasgow Art Nouveau.' He is probably best known for his Glasgow School of Art – it was remarkable that in 1896, when Art Nouveau still made hackles rise, his design should have been accepted – but he was also responsible for several other buildings including private houses and a school. The film examines these projects in detail, and also others that were never realized, such as his proposals for Liverpool Cathedral. Also shown are his posters, furniture, interiors and, notably, Miss Cranston's famous Tea Rooms. Later in his life, when commissions had dried up, Mackintosh turned to painting, and the film concludes with a look at his watercolors.

Director	**22 minutes**
W Thomson	**Color**
Narration	**Age range 14–adult**
R Horn	**Film $623** Rental $189
Original music	**VHS $89**
T Wilson	

471   The Fall and Rise of Mackintosh

When Murray Grigor made his first film on Glasgow's great architect in 1968, practically no one in Glasgow had heard of Mackintosh. And those who knew him were hostile or at best indifferent. The revelation of *The Fall and Rise of Mackintosh* is the process that put Mackintosh on the international map as a great force in contemporary architecture and design. The initiatives came from some quite surprising sources: it was the Italian Connection, through the firm of Cassina, that really launched Mackintosh as a contemporary designer of the 1970s, by appropriating and reproducing his designs. For 1990, Murray Grigor devised an exhibition at the Glasgow School of Art and a seminar as part of the Mackintosh Society's conference. This brought together world-renowned architects who had discovered Mackintosh for themselves back when Mackintosh's reputation was at its lowest. They, along with other long-standing supporters, analyze Mackintosh's architectural legacy as 'an architect's architect.'

For more information see page 312

Director/Writer	**52 minutes**
Murray Grigor	**Color**
Original music	**Age range 14–adult**
David McNiven	**VHS $129**

Interviews/Discussions
Filippo Alison, Italy
Edward Cullinan, UK
Hans Hollein, Austria
Stanley Tigerman, USA
Aldo Van Eyck, Netherlands
Professor Andrew Macmillan, UK
Professor Isi Metzstein, UK
Bruno del Priori, Italy

Special work
Arata Isosaki, Japan

▼ 465
Gustav Klimt
Beethoven Frieze, detail,
The Hostile Forces

▼ 702
Charles Rennie Mackintosh
The white bedroom, Hill House

If one characteristic of twentieth-century art, particularly in its development toward Abstraction, has been the urge toward order, geometrical simplification and objectivity, there have been equally strong counter-currents. Subjective passion, fervor, energy and anguish have been conveyed through various forms of Expressionism. To some extent the two impulses – toward controlled order and toward free energy – correspond with the earlier movements of Neo-classicism and Romanticism and, beyond them, with the traditional division between the southern European Renaissance, seeking balanced harmony, and the Northern Renaissance, emphasizing emotional drama.

c1890 to the present

14

Expressionism

This section of 21 programs can be purchased on VHS for $2289

Television rights and prices on request

The northern tradition of artists, from Bosch and Bruegel to Rembrandt and Rubens, has been felt to anticipate modern Expressionism. (Compare the way an Italian film-maker like Carlo Ragghianti conveys the serene, architectonic structures of Piero della Francesca, Fra Angelico or Michelangelo with the way a Flemish director, Harold Van de Perre, demonstrates the dynamic rhythm and drama of Bruegel, Van Eyck or Rubens and draws specific parallels with modern Expressionists like Ensor.)

Though modern Expressionist trends can be detected right across European and American art, in French artists like Vlaminck and Derain early in the century, then in Soutine, and later in 'Gestural Abstraction' in Europe and the United States, it is in Nordic countries, and especially Germany, that it is strongest.

The term 'expressionist' itself appears to have been coined in the German journal *Sturm* ('Storm') in 1911. The *Blaue Reiter* ('Blue Rider') and *Die Brücke* ('The Bridge') movements were typical manifestations, rejecting the objective, external reality of Impressionism, and picking up on more emotive aspects of Post-Impressionists like Van Gogh, Gauguin and Lautrec. Affected by the anxieties of accelerated social change, and by the anguish of world wars and political upheaval, Expressionist artists employed violent exaggerations and distortions of form and color, and near-brutal handling of materials.

During the Nazi period, the authorities attempted to suppress all progressive forms of art, especially Expressionism, which they termed savage, insane and infantile. Expressionist artists were indeed drawing on the tribal arts of Africa and elsewhere, on the 'outsider' art of psychotics and naïfs, and on the drawings of children, seeing in them a liberation from convention and the truth of inner reality.

Expressionism is the art of the emotive, the art of tension provoked by consciousness of the forces which surround modern humankind. The inevitability of world war, the rise of industrialization, the new power of capitalism – all these things weighed on men's minds at the beginning of the century, especially in Germany. Around 1906, in Dresden, a group of artists, known as *Die Brücke,* developed Expressionism. Its founders had their ancestors: Van Gogh who, according to the view expressed here, fought with his landscapes and his various pictorial subjects to get them to 'express' his feelings; James Ensor, who mocked those things which would stop him from living – society and his own death; Edvard Munch, who tried to cope with the difficulties and torments that faced his existence. Expressionism was therefore to be a way of painting through suffering to cope better with the unhappiness which surrounds everyone. In Vienna, Kokoschka wanted his pictures to make the viewer empathize with the spirit of the subject; the purpose of a painting was not the object painted but the feeling and the impression it made on the person looking at it.

The painters of *Die Brücke* – Kirchner, Schmidt-Rottluff, Heckel – tried to find the primitive nature of man by living in a community and using the expressiveness of color. What counts is not so much their actual paintings and how they painted, but that which is perceived even though it is not formulated. War and all its horrors was to constrain these painters; they could not look away from it. Otto Dix and Georg Grosz forced themselves to depict Germany after the war: the invalids, the misery and the bourgeoisie they blamed for it all. They believed theirs was the 'new objectivity.' After them, Max Beckmann managed to transcend this reality – but what he painted in his allegorical works was the great fear which had taken over the world. The film also features the work of Klimt, Nolde, Meidner, the *Blaue Reiter* group and others.

Part of the series
The Adventure of Modern Art

Director	**53 minutes**
Carlos Vilardebo	**Color**
Writers/Narration	**Age range 15–adult**
André Parinaud	**Film $1043** Rental $299
Carlos Vilardebo	**VHS $149**

Also available in French

The Mexican Muralist movement is the artistic child of post-revolutionary Mexico. Octavio Paz clearly distinguishes the political and ideological elements of the paintings of Diego Rivera, David Alfaro Siqueiros and José Clemente Orozco from their strictly pictorial content. The poet also places the works of these Mexican artists in the wider context of modern world painting. The dynamism of their figures, the distortions and emphatic compositions and the explicit social content of the Muralists' work put them firmly in the Expressionist camp. Some of their works bear comparison with European artists such as Beckmann or Edvard Munch, and perhaps also influenced later artists such as Jackson Pollock. Paz explains how Mexican Muralism was closely linked with the Mexican revolution, which gave the nation a new sense of identity and an impulse to return to its origins; and we learn how José Vasconcelos, Minister for Education, involved creative artists from all the media in the reconstruction of Mexico's identity.

Part of the series
Mexico through the Eyes of Octavio Paz

Director	**56 minutes**
Hector Tajonar	**Color**
Presenter/Writer	**Age range 14–adult**
Octavio Paz	**VHS $139**
Special collaboration	
Marie José Paz	
Original music	
Mario Lavista	

Also available in Spanish

505, page 109
Ernst Ludwig Kirchner
Street Scene

504
Karl Schmidt-Rottluff
Lofthus Landscape

505 Die Brücke (The Bridge)
The Birth of Modern Art in Germany

This movement marks the beginning of modern art in Germany. It is the German equivalent of French Fauvism, from which it draws its main inspiration, but it carries an Expressionist and social emphasis that is characteristic of Nordic 'angst.' The artists of *Die Brücke* were restless creatures, over-sensitive, haunted by religious, sexual, political or moral obsessions. Dramatic landscapes and nudes, mystical and visionary compositions, scenes of the countryside, the streets, the circus, the *café-dansants* and the *demi-monde* were their principal subjects. Their pure colors blaze in acid stridency, encompassed by rough, dry contours which show the influence of African art and primitive woodcuts. The work of the following is shown: Kirchner, Fritz Bleyl, Erich Heckel, Schmidt-Rottluff, Otto Muller, Emil Nolde and Max Pechstein.

Director	**24 minutes**
Dr Walter Koch	**Color**
Also available in German	**Age range 14–adult**
	Film $693 Rental $199
	VHS $99

507 Edvard Munch: The Frieze of Life

'We should no longer paint interiors with men reading and women knitting. We should paint living people who breathe, feel, suffer and love.' This manifesto, written in 1889 by the twenty-six-year-old Norwegian artist Edvard Munch, was implemented by him throughout the 1890s in major works on the universal themes of love, anxiety and death, linked in a 'symphonic arrangement' he titled *The Frieze of Life*. Shot on location in Norway and from original paintings and graphic works, with commentary mainly drawn from Munch's own writings, this video explores the psychological and artistic origins and significance of some of the most arresting images in European art.

Director	**24 minutes**
Jonathan Wright Miller	**Color**
Original music	**Age range 14–adult**
Peter Kiely	**VHS $99**
Audio Visual Unit	
The National Gallery	

506 Edvard Munch: The Restless Years

The Restless Years deals with the life and work of Edvard Munch from his birth in 1863 to the mental and physical breakdown he suffered in 1908. It covers the years when Munch was an eager student of art, a frequenter of intellectual circles, a visitor to the artistic capitals of Europe and, above all, a prolific painter. The narrative sets Munch's development as a painter in the context, first of his early life and dramatic emotional experience, and later against the background of changes in the artistic and intellectual life of Europe. Many of Munch's paintings are examined in detail, and the commentary is interspersed with readings from Munch's own writing about his work. Particular attention is paid to the works that make up *The Frieze of Life,* Munch's most important project, on which he worked for almost thirty years.

'Both the artistic and technical quality of the video are high. The colors are subtle and the close-ups emphasize both the bold and the intentionally blurry features. Edvard Munch's words contrast clearly with the well modulated voice of the narrator.'
Video Rating Guide for Libraries, USA

Director	**21 minutes**
Brian Taylor	**Color**
Narration	**Age range 14–adult**
Christine Newton	**VHS $89**

508 Käthe Kollwitz

Käthe Kollwitz was the most powerfully emotional German artist of this century; this film describes her life and work, and stresses the timelessness and humanity of her art. Its very personal narration is taken wholly from the artist's own diaries. The suffering of Berliners in the 1890s, the cruelty and senselessness of the First World War, in which Kollwitz lost a son, and the anguish of the Second World War are vividly portrayed. Most of her best works are tragic and many of them specifically pacifist. This was a pioneering art film, and the honesty of its approach is unsurpassable.

Director	**16 minutes**
Herbert Apelt	**Black and white**
Original music	**Film $693** Rental $199
Oskar Sala	**VHS $99**
Also available in German	

◀◀ 506
Edvard Munch
Study for *The Scream*

▲ 505
Ernst Ludwig Kirchner
Ballroom

509 **'I'm Mad, I'm Foolish, I'm Nasty'**
A Self-portrait of James Ensor

In this film we see how James Ensor, an
acknowledged initiator of Expressionism,
begins with an essentially Impressionist
style, but gradually introduces more
fantastical, scatological subject matter,
a 'caricature' style of drawing and physical
paint-handling and more artificial color.
The influence on his imagery and color of
the spectacular shells and the exotic masks
and grotesques sold in his parents' and
uncle's souvenir shops in his native Ostend
is suggested in the film, as is the
atmospheric protean presence of the sea.
Subtly it hints at the anxieties and
melancholia at work under the surface of
Ensor's life. We are left to speculate on
the rôle of his dominating mother, and of
his dissolute father who died when the
artist was a young man. Death, and a
strangely whimsical eroticism, were Ensor's
recurrent preoccupations.

'...impressive video...approaches Ensor's
work as he might have approached the
subject himself...leads us directly into the
personality of the artist, discovering the
imagery...intercutting a feast of rich
details from paintings and sketches with
photos of the artist at the same locations
occupied by his subjects...a remarkable and
poetic portrait of the artist who prefigured
Expressionism. The producer's vision and
Ensor's vision blend into one unified whole.
Its lean, economical editing lets every shot
add meaning to the next. This is one of the
finest videos on an artist you're likely to
see. It is highly recommended.'
Video Rating Guide for Libraries, USA

For more information see pages 148
and 286

Director/Script	Awards
Luc de Heush	Best Documentary, Belgium
Texts	Selected European
James Ensor,	Cinema, Berlin
extracts from letters, speeches and orations	Directors' Grand Prix, UNESCO Paris
Ensor's voice	Also available in Dutch
John Boyle	and French
Narrator	**55 minutes**
Richard Wells	**Color**
Original music	**Age range 14—adult**
Denis Pousseur	**Film $1043** Rental $299
	VHS $149

◀◀ 509
James Ensor
Intrigue

▶ 510
Emil Nolde
Breaker

510 **Emil Nolde**

For the whole of his long life Emil Nolde, the leading German Expressionist, luxuriated in color. Before the First World War in Berlin he made many paintings of the theater, music-hall and opera; he loved flowers and even coaxed a garden out of the salty soil of the Baltic coast, where he had built himself an isolated house. His parents were Frisian peasants and he loved the landscape of North Friesland: it was the theme of many of his pictures. But the Nazis disapproved of his work and finally forbade him to paint at all. Although Nolde was already in his seventies when this happened, no political regime could stifle his vision. At great danger to himself he continued to work, making watercolor sketches the size of postcards, which he called 'unpainted pictures,' meaning them to serve as sketches for the large oils he would paint when he was free. And he did outlive the Nazi regime, marrying a twenty-eight-year-old woman in 1948 and painting up until the year before he died.

'…enables the eye to recognize the mystic glow and the structure of painting and form through very careful camera work'
German Center for Film Classification

Director
Friedhelm Heyde

Narration
Dr Martin Urban

Original music
Joachim Ludwig

Awards
Highly Commended,
German Center for
Film Classification
Quality Award,
German Government

12 minutes
Color
Age range 14–adult
Film $553 Rental $169
VHS $79

14 Expressionism

111

511 Part of the Struggle
Art and Politics in the Weimar Republic

Rarely in modern times has art been more intimately involved with the social and political world than during the years of the Weimar Republic in Germany. Expressionism, the vanguard movement before the First World War, created works of spiritual vitality with a strong emotional content. The Expressionists believed that an artistic revolution could help bring about social and political change by transforming the individual. Realism was rejected in favor of a subjective search for an inner reality. But the horror of the First World War and the subsequent political turmoil in Germany thrust many artists into a new relationship with society. The Weimar Republic was formed in 1919 and collapsed in 1933 with Hitler's accession to power. *Part of the Struggle* focuses on the relationship between avant-garde art and left-wing politics during a period of unprecedented social and economic upheaval. It looks in detail at artists based in Dresden and the formation of such political art movements as the Red Group in 1923 and the Association of Revolutionary Artists in 1928. The film uses a minimum of commentary and the artists' own words are heard in dramatized 'interviews' in which actors portray Georg Grosz, Otto Dix, Hans and Lea Grundig and Otto Nagel. It covers the Dada explosion, the abortive German revolution, when Dix, Grosz and Heartfield joined the Spartacists, the move away from Dada towards Verism and the *Neue Sachlichkeit* (the 'New Objectivity'), and finally the Nazis' infamous exhibition of these artists' work as 'degenerate art.'

'For one seeking information about the Weimar era in art and politics, this is one of those titles that belongs in both public and educational libraries. *Part of the Struggle* will probably find a grateful audience in high school students through adults seeking to understand conditions following the First World War. Recommended.'
Video Rating Guide for Libraries, USA

Directors	36 minutes
Norbert Bunge	Color
Ron Orders	Age range 14–adult
Arts Council of	Film $763 Rental $199
Great Britain	VHS $109

512 Beckmann

How far should we trust an artist's own statements about his work? Max Beckmann, a leading Expressionist painter who had been dismissed as 'decadent' in Germany during the 1930s, emigrated to Holland in 1937 and died in America in 1950. When he wrote about his work, particularly after 1937, he stressed the spiritual rôle of the artist and his position as solitary genius, unconcerned with public events; and the triptych *Temptation*, finished in 1937, can be seen as consistent with this view. But an examination of his earlier work, *Departure*, finished in 1933, certainly seems to show that it was intended as a comment on the political and cultural situation in Germany at the time, however hard Beckmann tried to reinterpret it later.

Part of the series *Modern Art and Modernism: Manet to Pollock*

Director	25 minutes
Tony Coe	Color
Presenter/Writer	Age range 18–adult
Gill Perry	VHS $99
Open University/BBC	

706 **Erich Mendelsohn: The Einstein Tower**

The Einstein Tower in Potsdam near Berlin is considered a key Expressionist building – its curved, organic forms depart from all traditional expectations of what a tower should look like. We trace the genesis of its design back to Erich Mendelsohn's letters and sketches sent from the front during the First World War. The rounded, irregular forms of the tower were inspired by his passion for music and his interest in Einstein's revolutionary ideas; but the technical problems were daunting in the extreme. It is a tribute to the brilliance of Mendelsohn and the enthusiasm of his client, Dr Freundlich, that such a complex and beautiful concept ever actually materialized.

Part of the series *History of Architecture and Design 1890–1939*

Director   25 minutes
Nick Levinson   Black and white
Presenter/Writer   Age range 16–adult
Dennis Sharp   VHS $99
Open University/BBC

512B **Contemporary Expression**

On April 26, 1937, the Nazi Condor Legion destroyed the little city of Guernica in Spain; learning of this, Picasso immediately started work on a very large painting which he finished on June 3. *Guernica* can probably be considered the greatest work of our century – and 'contemporary expression', can be defined as the link which every work of art has with a precise time in history. Different artists react differently to the events of their time, and their reactions might be categorized as negative or positive. For example, Vlaminck, whose paintings were full of color during the period of Fauvism, covered his post-war skies with grey clouds. After the First World War, German painters carried an oppressive social weight on their shoulders: Otto Dix portrayed the misery of the soldier in the trenches and the pain of a mutilated person with open wounds, Georg Grosz the loss of hope, inflation, famine. This and other revelations of the guilt of German society in 1933 resulted in painting being censored by the dictatorship. Sometimes, as in the case of Max Beckmann, the painter sought exile. On the other hand, the Muralist Mexican painters Orozco, Rivera and Siqueiros participated positively in the revolution, helping Mexico to discover herself. Their paintings became banners for the peasants who were fighting, messages painted on the walls of public buildings.

After the Second World War, the weight of the world lay even more heavily upon artists. The CoBrA group tried desperately to renew the celebration of life, through humor, by looking into the truth of children, and by the use of brilliant color. The most important painter of this group is the Dane, Asger Jorn; others are Dotremont, Appel, Corneille, Constant and Alechinsky. But form in contemporary expression as we know it today presents two aspects. One is demonstrated in the work of Edward Kienholz, who wanted to recreate the life of society and make us aware of an everyday reality which we have forgotten about or taken for granted; the other is revealed in the work of Francis Bacon, who also wished to be a witness of his times, but only through the dimension of himself. There are no messages in his paintings; Bacon is simply trying to communicate with the people who wish to communicate with him. This art, which might seem to be pessimistic, is merely a way of asserting that life is the first priority – which is why mouths painted by Bacon look as if they are about to bite rather than to scream. Also features the work of Permeke, De Smet, Soutine, Chagall, Dubuffet and others.

Part of the series
The Adventure of Modern Art

Director   53 minutes
Carlos Vilardebo   Color
Writers/Narration   Age range 15–adult
André Parinaud   Film $1043 Rental $299
Carlos Vilardebo   VHS $149

Also available in French

512
Max Beckmann
Odysseus and Kalypso

706
Erich Mendelsohn
Sketch for the
Einstein Tower

113

503E Jackson Pollock: Tim Clark and Michael Fried in Conversation

Art historian TJ Clark and art critic Michael Fried in the past occupied opposing positions. Clark was the eminent advocate of the social history of art, based on a Marxist approach which saw art as produced in a socio-economic context. Fried, on the other hand, was an arch-Modernist, believing art to be about itself alone, separate from social meaning. Now, however, the two have moved closer. Clark accepts the canonical greatness of Pollock's work and Fried no longer claims that art functions only in an 'optical' way. This video is hard work if one has not read the works of Clark and Fried.

Part of the series
Modern Art, Practices and Debates

Directors	**25 minutes**
GD Jayalakshmi	**Color**
Nick Levinson	**Age range 18–adult**
Presenter	**VHS $99**
Paul Wood	
Contributors	
TJ Clark	
Professor M Fried	
Open University/BBC	

513 Kokoschka

The early paintings of Oskar Kokoschka, from 1910 to 1940, show him to be one of the most gifted portrait and townscape painters of our time. His portraits are psychological documents of haunting accuracy and his cities appear to be living beings with legends, stories and secrets of their own. Kokoschka's conception is dramatic, and his work carries an echo of the tradition of dynamic and visionary Baroque painting still strong in Austria before 1914.

Director	**10 minutes**
Giorgio Patara	**Color**
	Age range 14–adult
	Film $483 Rental $149
	VHS $69

554 Abstract Expressionism

In *Abstract Expressionism* the artist Donald Judd, himself very un-Expressionist in style, examines the works of Mondrian, De Kooning, Rothko, Still, Pollock and Newman. He believes that to call the artists of the New York School 'Expressionist' does not give an adequate account of their work, even though an important part of what typifies Expressionism is its use of marks and paint strokes that are dynamic, spontaneous, even violent, making material expressive in itself. The viewer sympathizes with the gesture of the artist. In *Abstract Expressionism* this power of the material itself to 'express' is brought home to us, since often there is no trace of representational imagery to which a painting's force can be attributed.

Part of the series *Modern Art and Modernism: Manet to Pollock*

For more information see page 131

Director	**24 minutes**
Charles Cooper	**Color**
Presenter/Writer	**Age range 18–adult**
Donald Judd	**VHS $99**
Open University/BBC	

503C American Abstraction

The narrator of *American Abstraction* claims that art in the United States always considered itself dependent on European art, particularly when it sustained the shock of modern art arriving from Europe in 1913 to be presented at the Armory Show. American painters tried to adapt these new forms to their own outlook on life, but their art was no more than adaptation. Certain painters looked elsewhere: for example, Arshile Gorky found inspiration in the mythology of his homeland, Armenia, and Mark Tobey painted works of meditation influenced by oriental thought. Little by little the physical element, the 'action', in abstract American painting gave way to the 'sign', in painters such as Gottlieb and Newman. This evolution transformed the spontaneous gesture we find in Pollock into a cultural gesture, a vocabulary. One painter who stands out from these trends is Mark Rothko. In his paintings there is no culture, no sign, no gesture, just color and light. The film also features the work of Rivera, Thomas Hart Benton, Orozco, Stuart Davis, Motherwell, De Kooning, Franz Kline and others.

Part of the series
The Adventure of Modern Art

Director	**53 minutes**
Carlos Vilardebo	**Color**
Writers/Narration	**Age range 15–adult**
André Parinaud	**Film $1043** Rental $299
Carlos Vilardebo	**VHS $149**
Also available in French	

503D Abstraction: The Experience

Artists, like everyone else in Europe, had lived through traumatic experiences by the time the Germans surrendered in 1945. In France, artists such as Wols and Jean Fautrier were trying to hold on to the pre-war Abstraction movement. Wols showed his life of misery in troubled but spontaneous works: his first oil paintings were once described as 'forty moments in the crucifixion of man.' Jean Fautrier revealed a similar experience in his paintings of hostages. Then came the Lyric Abstraction painters, Georges Mathieu, Pierre Soulages, Serge Poliakoff, Hans Hartung. The abstract expression of this period conveys an effort to escape from a world confronted with the problem of having to rebuild itself. This attempt to escape very often resulted in dilemma: for example, Nicholas de Staël committed suicide in 1951. Each artist struggled to find his own way: Lucio Fontana in Italy, Antoni Tàpies in Spain, Jean Dubuffet in France. In the United States, the revolution caused by the paintings of Pollock and De Kooning led to a new humanism, as expressed in the paintings of Mark Rothko and Barnett Newman. From this point onward, American Abstraction evolved progressively toward its downfall, because of a shortage of ideas and new techniques. After Clyfford Still, Sam Francis and Morris Louis, forms and shapes were simplified, colors purified; trying to achieve detachment led to a lack of sensitivity. From Kenneth Noland to Frank Stella, painting turned to parallel lines following the edges of the canvas. It was during this period that Joseph Albers, who had previously been a professor at the Bauhaus, devoted the rest of his life to homage to the square. This asceticism reached its culmination with works such as those of Ad Reinhardt, who said, 'Art is Art. Everything else is everything else.' He painted wholly black canvases, declaring these 'the last painting anyone can hope or wish to paint.' In the meantime, Europeans were attracted to technology. Painting was becoming an attempt to recreate movement; kinetic art – *kinetic* from the Greek verb 'to move' – was a school led by Victor Vasarely. Forms of energy were also being used: magnetic force by Vassilakis Takis and Pol Bury, air in the case of Alexander Calder, and light in the case of

Julio Le Parc. Today the desire to incorporate kinetic works into everyday life still represents the ultimate aim of the abstractional experience. The film also features the work of Bacon, Esteve, Riopelle, Piaubert, Lilyan Lijn, the GRAV group and many others.

Part of the series
The Adventure of Modern Art

Director	**53 minutes**
Carlos Vilardebo	**Color**
Writers/Narration	**Age range 15–adult**
André Parinaud	**Film $1043** Rental $299
Carlos Vilardebo	**VHS $149**
Also available in French	

14 Expressionism

115

Karel Appel

The Dutch painter and sculptor Karel Appel
first came to prominence in the 1940s when
associated with the CoBrA group of artists,
whose name derived from the cities in
which they were most active: Copenhagen,
Brussels and Amsterdam. Like the work of
several CoBrA artists, Appel's paintings are
redolent of the world of trolls, Norse signs
and Nordic myth. Appel settled in Paris,
where other artists such as Dubuffet shared
his interest in the creations of children, the
insane and the socially marginalized, and his
preoccupation with raw matter in painting.
He quickly became aware, too, of affinities
between his own activities and those of
American Abstract Expressionists like
Pollock and De Kooning.

---

596   **The Reality of Karel Appel**

The reality of the painter Karel Appel is an
overcrowded, possessed and frantic world,
a barbaric age in which he can only paint
as a barbarian – as he says in this film.
His paintings are gaudy, his colors vivid, and
he slaps them on the canvas as if in a duel,
using his brushes, paints, putty-knife and
his hands as weapons.

For more information see page 290

Director	**15 minutes**
Jan Vrijman	**Color**
Awards	**Age range 13–adult**
Golden Bear, Berlin	**Film $623** Rental $189
Gran Premio, Bergamo	**VHS $89**
Silver Medal, Barcelona	
Silver Medal, La Felguera	

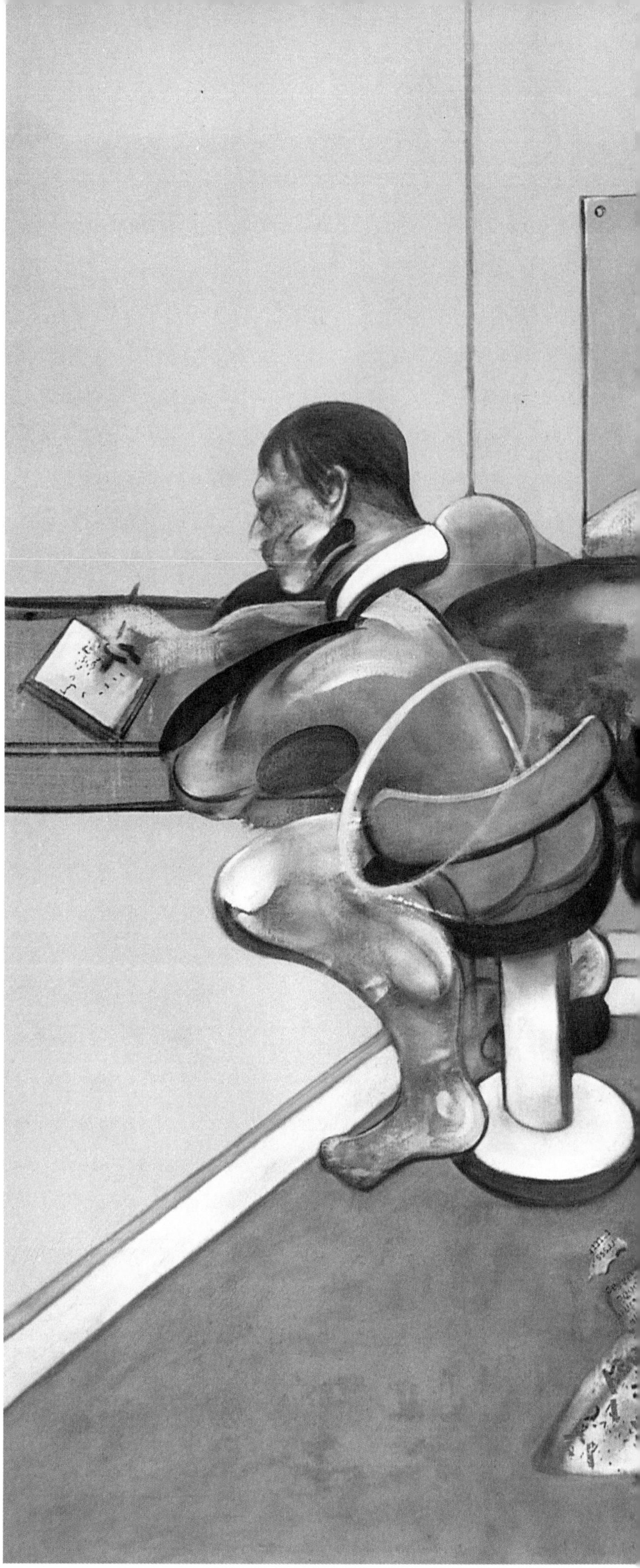

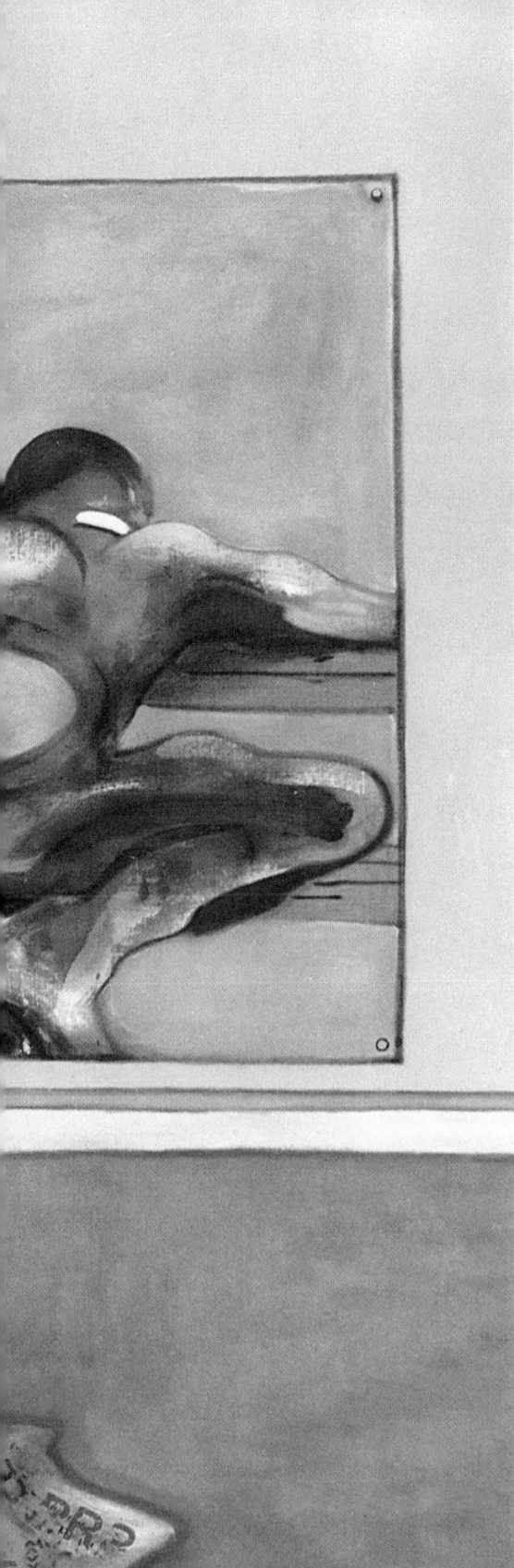

599 Francis Bacon

Francis Bacon's work is not easy to categorize. If he cannot quite be called an Expressionist proper, it is because even when he allows his paint to appear loose and spontaneous, there remains a sense of strict control, even precision. His intense background colors also seem to have been applied with pristine detachment, and his writhing figures seem frozen in time. His use of photographs and medical illustrations give a further quasi-documentary atmosphere that is not typically Expressionist. Nevertheless, Bacon is in accord with Expressionism in his painful abrasions and distortions of faces and flesh, evoking an agonized picture of the world in which individuals are isolated and vulnerable.

'Invaluable... the expertly detailed visual analysis of the imagery leaves the viewer with the uncomfortable but exhilarating sense that Bacon's macabre *œuvre* has been left to percolate under one's own skin. The feeling is transcending... a must-see for serious art students and a compelling experience for the neophyte.'
Video Rating Guide for Libraries, USA

For more information see page 172

Director/Script	**28 minutes**
Richard Francis	**Color**
	Age range 17–adult
	VHS $99

599A Francis Bacon: Paintings 1944–62

The film opens with images that recur in Francis Bacon's paintings – Muybridge photographs of animals in motion, stills from Eisenstein's *The Battleship Potemkin*, a Rembrandt self-portrait, and *Pope Innocent X* by Velázquez. The remainder of the film presents Bacon's interpretation of such images during the period 1944–62. There is no commentary, but through a combination of music, camera movement and editing, the film accentuates the violence and menace of the paintings, and gives an impression of their emotional power.

Director/Writer	**11 minutes**
David Thompson	**Color**
Music	**Age range 17–adult**
Elizabeth Lutyens	**Film $553** Rental $169
Arts Council of	**VHS $79**
Great Britain	

597 Antonio Saura: Confessions

Antonio Saura is considered one of the most important Spanish painters of the post-Picasso generation. From his studio in Paris's thirteenth *arrondissement*, Saura explains how he came to be a painter. We also see him at work: the camera appears to spy on the artist caught up in the act of painting and drawing. Other sequences take us to Saura's native village of Huesca, where he recently finished painting a monumental ceiling for the town hall.

For more information see page 171

Director	**26 minutes**
Jean-Claude Rousseau	**Color**
Original music	**Age range 14–adult**
Jean-Marc Padovani	**VHS $99**
Also available in French	

◄◄ 596
Karel Appel
Figurative Calligraphy

◄◄ 599A
Francis Bacon
Person Writing Reflected in the Mirror

15 Cubism and Futurism

1907–1944

Pioneered in the years before the First World War by the painters Picasso, Braque and Gris, Cubism became a dominant school in European art between the wars and after, to which other movements – Geometric or Painterly Abstraction, Dada and Surrealism, and new forms of Neo-classicism, such as that of Maillol – were partly related and partly opposed.

This section of 5 programs can be purchased on VHS for $585

Television rights and prices on request

A host of other artists adopted the Cubist mode, often on their way to more personal styles: Mondrian developed toward total Abstraction, Derain moved from Fauvism toward classic traditionalism, Franz Marc searched for spirituality animated by modernity.

The style developed through a mixture of influences, particularly the faceted brushwork of Cézanne and the angular distortions of African art, and sought to escape what seemed to be the merely visual concerns of Impressionism's optical recordings and Post-Impressionism's surface patterning. It sought to reintroduce a conceptual content into painting, not via the grand subjects of academic 'history painting', but through developing a kind of intellectual realism, reflecting what the mind knows of the structure of objects, rather than what the eye alone perceives. Such was one rationale, anyway, for simultaneous presentation of different viewpoints, or the 'tipping up' of, for example, the elliptical rim of a jug, to present a plan of its circular structure.

Cubism developed in several directions. On one hand its analytical breaking down of form could become, with Gleizes, Metzinger, Lhote and other theorizers and educators, a respected 'manner' in which to produce modern, angular pictures. At the same time it was developed into the sparser, more design-oriented Purism of Léger and others. Yet again, in the more collage-based 'synthetic' modes toward which the first generation Cubists moved, it could point to a radical Constructivist aesthetic which would eventually produce artists such as Anthony Caro.

Futurist artists like Boccioni, Balla, Carrà in Italy, and Goncharova and Larionov in Russia, fragmented and splintered their forms in a way similar to the Cubists. Their aims were to express movement and particularly the accelerated locomotion of modern technological life. They were politically as well as pictorially revolutionary, and often closer in spirit to Dada than to Cubism, which, while artistically avant-garde, could also be perceived as rational, detached, and platonic. It was a Neo-Futurist work, *Nude Descending a Staircase,* which launched the career of Marcel Duchamp, a name synonymous with Dada and conceptualist subversion.

The opening of the twentieth century marked a period of economic, social and scientific transformation, which was reflected in Cubism as an artistic movement. The Cubists, with Picasso as their foremost member, expressed a new perception of the world. In more traditional painting, the artist is static before the object or scene depicted; but in Cubist art the painter seems to see and render the subject from all sides at once. Cubism constituted an explosion of perception. In 1901 Picasso's first exhibition in Paris showed the influence of Pointillist painters such as Seurat, and throughout his 'Blue Period' and 'Pink Period' his work was powerful yet still fairly conventional in style. But in 1907 came the painting *Les Demoiselles d'Avignon,* showing the influence of Negro sculpture and a distinctly Cubist attempt to give a multiple viewpoint rather than create a realistic imitation of appearances. A critic coined the epithet 'cubist' in 1908. At the same time, Juan Gris associated himself with the movement, establishing himself, with Georges Braque, as its other great practitioner. From around 1910 Picasso and Braque began to apply unusual elements to their canvases – cut-up newspapers, sand, corrugated cardboard. Robert Delaunay painted bright discs of warm color; Fernand Léger developed his passion for the industrial landscape. The movement marked a uniquely inventive and energetic moment of creativity in painting, promising endless areas of investigation for ever more artists. Yet, though many artists did follow the style well into the twentieth century, the First World War marked the end of its most vital period. The film also features the work of Villon, Metzinger, Gleizes, Kupka, de la Fresnaye and others.

Part of the series
The Adventure of Modern Art

Director	53 minutes
Carlos Vilardebo	Color
Writers/Narration	Age range 15–adult
André Parinaud	Film $1043 Rental $299
Carlos Vilardebo	VHS $149

---

534 **Picasso's Collages 1912–13: The Problem of Interpretation**

This program is structured around two interviews with art historians who offer radically different interpretations of Picasso's collages – Patricia Leighten and Rosalind Krauss – and examines what we learn from comparing two contrasting systems of historical and critical explanation.

Part of the series
Modern Art, Practices and Debates

Director	25 minutes
Nick Levinson	Color
Presenter	Age range 18–adult
Francis Frascina	VHS $99

Open University/BBC

529 **Cubism and Modernism**

Cubism grew out of the efforts of Picasso, Braque and others, whose work is explored here, to replace the Impressionist concentration on the surface of objects with a more intellectual concept of color and form, an attempt to express the idea of an object rather than to give any one view of it. Of course the name Cubism was disparaging, for the movement gave rise to just as much opposition as Impressionism had encountered earlier. Cubism has generally been seen as the most important influence in twentieth-century art, solely because of its technical and formal aspects; but perhaps this view ignores some of its other features, particularly its realism. Were these just as influential as its form and technique?

Part of the series *Modern Art and Modernism: Manet to Pollock*

Director	25 minutes
Robert Philip	Color
Presenter/Writer	Age range 18–adult
Francis Frascina	VHS $99

Open University/BBC

◀◀ 521
Robert Delaunay
Disk

▲ 529
Pablo Picasso
Playing Card, Glass and a Bottle on a Guéridon

Vita Futurista

Futurism was the art of the avant-garde in Italy from 1909 to 1944. Its development, its artistic stimuli, its creative influences on art and society and its political implications are all closely linked with the personality of Filippo Marinetti. Futurist theory preceded practice – Futurism itself had no precedent. The Futurists' target was an Italian culture rooted in nineteenth-century values – an immobile society devoted to classicism and operatic melodrama. Against this background Marinetti mobilized young writers, painters, sculptors, inventors and, later, politicians into the Futurist revolution of society by means of creative activism. Art and life fused in a magnificent rhetorical gesture; movement became the supreme quality; irrationalism, adventure and war were glorified. Having given Futurism its prestigious launch in Paris, Marinetti returned to Milan and formed the first group of Futurist artists with the poets Luciani, Palazzeschi, Buzzi and Govani, and the painters Balla, Boccioni, Carrà and Severini; and Russolo joined soon after. Memorably this film includes contemporary versions of performances and 'art of noise' pieces that show Futurism to be the precursor of modern performance art and avant-garde music. Marinetti welcomed the First World War as a cleansing expression of pure energy that would sweep away the old world and replace it with a new Futurist society. He allied himself, and Futurism, to Italian Fascism, which gradually usurped and neutralized the movement. The film, therefore, documents the impact of Futurism on art and society, while charting the social development that led to the establishment of Fascism in Italy and to war. *Vita Futurista* was mainly shot at the huge exhibition of Futurist art at the Palazzo Grassi in Venice. It includes dramatic recreations, rare archive film of the principal characters and a host of artworks. The film is constructed, like Futurism itself, from a montage of ideas and concepts. This is not period imitation but a witty response to Futurist structures and techniques characteristic of the Futurists themselves.

'…well documented, well produced, a production that honors speed and machines. The producers contend that Futurism was the precursor of modern performance art and avant-garde music. They present a montage of ideas with well-edited old footage of museum sculptures and industrial sites. The *Art of Noise* is an ensemble of vocalists and musicians who generate sounds ranging from strange, seemingly prehistoric noises to scraping industrial materials. All this is held together with interviews (for which translators are provided)…the production and editing are done by highly skilled professionals.'
Video Rating Guide for Libraries, USA

Director
Lutz Becker

Arts Council of
Great Britain

52 minutes
Color and
black and white
Age range 16–adult

Film $973 Rental $289
VHS $139

557   Futurism, Modernity and Style

The only modern movement to be largely
independent of Paris, Futurism was
nevertheless born there when an article
was published in *Le Figaro* announcing
'a new beauty … a roaring motor car, which
runs like a machine-gun, is more beautiful
than the *Winged Victory of Samothrace*.
We wish to glorify war.' In 1912 the Futurist
Exhibition was also held in Paris, and then
moved on all over Europe, causing riots
and general uproar. Here we examine
the work of Italian and Russian Futurists
such as Russolo, Boccioni, Larionov and
Goncharova, and their relationship with
the French Cubists. What they all had in
common was an approach to avant-garde
art which can broadly be termed
'dynamism', the attempt to present
movement. As a Futurist manifesto put it:
'universal dynamism must be rendered
as dynamic sensation … motion and light
destroy the substance of objects.'

Part of the series *Modern Art and
Modernism: Manet to Pollock*

Director	**24 minutes**
Robert Philip	**Color**
Presenter/Writer	**Age range 18–adult**
Briony Fer	**VHS $99**
Open University/BBC	

◀◀ 557
Umberto Boccioni
*Unique Forms in the
Continuity of Space*

◥◢ 555
Giacomo Balla
*Mercury Passing
in front of the Sun,
Seen by Telescope*

▲ 555
Gino Severini
Blue Dancers

16

c 1908 to the present

Into Abstraction

For many people the stimulation and challenges and the provocation and perplexities of twentieth-century art lie in its progression away from depicting the world around us toward the creation of abstract works, in which color and form take on a life of their own.

This section of
18 programs can be
purchased on
VHS for $1972

Television rights and
prices on request

Toward the end of the nineteenth century, Post-Impressionist artists had asserted that a picture, whatever it depicted, was just as importantly (if not *more* importantly) an object with its own qualities – an assembly of colors, tones and textures.

In the twentieth century, in Paris, Cubist artists like Picasso, Braque and Gris, apparently taking their starting-point from Cézanne, developed their flattened, faceted forms, fragmenting and refracting the objects they depicted, and constructing a contradictory space that could no longer be seen as a clear window on to an illusionistic world. Painters in other countries, sometimes with very different concerns – Franz Marc in Germany, with his Arcadian visions of animals, Futurists like Boccioni in Italy or Larionov in Russia, seeking to reflect the acceleration and instability of modern life – frequently employed forms similar to those of Cubism.

Other currents, too, can be seen as contributing to the drift away from representation. In Germany Wassily Kandinsky was developing his richly patterned fairytale scenes into dramatic orchestrations of forms, aspiring to manifest directly spiritual forces at work. His swooping lines and amorphous 'thought forms' gradually gave way to clusters and scatterings of more geometric flat shapes. Meanwhile the idiosyncratic, pictographic work of Paul Klee mixed emotive, psychological and mystical concerns with analytical interest in the workings of line, color and visual sign-making.

It is easy to see all these trends as leading directly to the most uncompromising abstraction: the grids and flat colors of Mondrian and van Doesburg or Max Bill; the optical vibrations of Victor Vasarely or Bridget Riley; the notorious monochrome square of Malevich's and El Lissitzky's Russian Suprematism; the more gestural, expansive surfaces of American Abstract Expressionism.

It is interesting, too, to note in certain films preserved in the Roland Collection from the Abstraction-dominated 1960s (for example films 20, 40, 50 on pages 17, 19, 22) the emphasis on distortion, simplification and formal qualities in the art of the past, which is interpreted as anticipating and contributing to the 'discovery' of modern abstract art. Compare also the Op Artist Bridget Riley's concentration on color and form in Old Master paintings (film 487, page 293).

Yet it is important not to see the development of Abstraction as a simple and inevitable drive away from representation and from the kinds of meaning more traditionally associated with painting and sculpture. Two films in section 15, 529 and 557, explicitly urge against this reductive view of Modernism. While emphasizing the formal and concrete identity of their works, modern artists arguably still send out a rich range of personal, political and philosophical messages, although they are compelled to 'scramble' those messages in new ways.

Abstraction: the creation of a mental universe where the idea has as much reality as the material object; where painting addresses itself to the spirit. From 1910 onward Wassily Kandinsky studied the dynamics of colors and the concrete, geometrical elements of painting. At the same time the Dutch painter Piet Mondrian researched the orthogonal simplification of the form of an object such as a tree, while the Russian Malevich expressed in his paintings fascination with the void, ending up with the ultimate Suprematist composition, a white square on a white background (1918). For these artists art is before all else spiritual, yet paradoxically they also influenced the Russian Constructivism of Tatlin and Rodchenko, a movement proclaiming the utilitarian nature of art in the revolutionary period around 1920. Another important element in the development of Abstraction was the foundation of the Bauhaus. Set up by the architect Gropius in 1919 in Weimar, it was a school where artists and designers taught together, influenced each other, and shaped the future of European art and architecture for generations to come. By the Second World War the work of Paul Klee, a major Bauhaus personality, represented the confluence of the creative heritage of artists like Malevich, Kandinsky and Mondrian, but in terms unique to Klee himself. After the war, in the USA artists were developing toward a lyrical, gestural Abstraction that dominated world art for some time. The film also features the work of Moholy-Nagy, El Lissitzky, Naum Gabo, van Doesburg and many others.

Part of the series
The Adventure of Modern Art

Director	**53 minutes**
Carlos Vilardebo	**Color**
Writers/Narration	**Age range 15–adult**
André Parinaud	**Film $1043** Rental $299
Carlos Vilardebo	**VHS $149**
Also available in French	

◀◀ 497
Alexander Rodchenko
Study of head

▲ 497
Kasimir Malevich
Portrait of a Peasant Girl

◢ 497
Piet Mondrian
*Composition with Red,
Yellow and Blue*

123

498 Franz Marc

The great German painter Franz Marc may be regarded as one of the originators of modern art. With his friend Kandinsky he founded the 'Blue Rider' group, and together they propounded new ideas subscribed to by the avant-garde of European painters, including Picasso, Braque and Delaunay. Man plays only a small part in Marc's work; he wrote that 'the irreligious humanity which lived all around me did not excite my true feelings, whereas the virgin feeling for life of the animal world set alight everything good in me.' Animals, particularly horses, are central in his work; at first they are symbols of nature, but later they become the messengers of a higher spiritual world. As time passed, Marc turned increasingly to abstract art. He was killed in action at Verdun in 1916.

Director
Goltz van Helmholt

Narration
Dr K H Rothe

Original music
Karl von Feilitzsch

Award
Highly Commended,
German Center for
Film Classification

Also available in German

21 minutes
Color
Age range 14–adult

Film $623 Rental $189
VHS $89

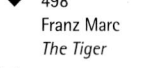

▼ 498
Franz Marc
The Tiger

▶▶ 500
Wassily Kandinsky
St Vladimir

502 Theo van Doesburg
New Aesthetics for a New World

Theo van Doesburg is best known as a painter and as the founder and editor of the avant-garde magazine *De Stijl* (*The Style*, 1917–28). But van Doesburg was also active in other fields: literature, philosophy, architecture, typography. This film explores his life and work, with the emphasis on his architecture, through posthumous works and documentary evidence about the artist and his wife recently given to the Netherlands.

Director
Frank den Oudsten

30 minutes
Color
Age range 14–adult

Film $693 Rental $199
VHS $99

501 Piet Mondrian

The film traces Mondrian's development by comparing some thirty of his paintings and drawings. His career opens with rural landscapes of his native Holland, executed in the atmospheric style of the late nineteenth-century Hague School. The already rather 'schematic' Dutch landscape (flat horizons, vertical towers, the natural geometry of tree and plant structures) is gradually simplified by the artist into abstract elements. Eventually he restricts himself to the black verticals and horizontals and the primary-colored rectangles that came to represent the ultimate modern painting. His writings on art are quoted in the commentary of the film. A portrait of the painter emerges through the use of photographs and other documents evoking his surroundings and activities.

'…clear, lucid narration free from jargon… it elucidates the basic tenets that shaped the Modernist vision…This visually beautiful short production will enhance library and school collections…could be used effectively by students of language as well as by anyone interested in the art and culture of the twentieth century.'
Video Rating Guide for Libraries, USA

Director
Nico Crama

Also available in
Dutch, French, German
and Spanish

18 minutes
Color
Age range 14–adult

Film $623 Rental $189
VHS $89

501A Mondrian

The work of the Dutch painter Piet Mondrian (1872–1944) is conventionally understood as clinical, calculated art from which all traces of life have been expunged. With its bright colors and large, simple shapes it is frequently 'quoted' in interior and product design. Mondrian's own writings lend weight to this image of his art as rational and almost mechanically pure, yet in this program David Batchelor argues that this perspective does scant justice to Mondrian's actual paintings.

Part of the series
Modern Art, Practices and Debates

Director
Tony Coe

Presenter
David Batchelor

Open University/BBC

25 minutes
Color
Age range 18–adult

VHS $99

Abstract art was not 'discovered' by any single artist. Several painters can be seen as working towards total non-representation in the early years of the century, and examples can be cited of 'abstract' works from even earlier (for example, drawings by Victor Hugo or Alexander Cozens), when their full implications could not be recognized. Nevertheless, once the abstract initiative was launched, the idea that momentous breakthroughs had been made quickly took hold, and was seen as akin to an objective scientific discovery. Claims and counter-claims were made as to who was the true 'inventor', to the extent that works were even falsely back-dated! The Russian painter Wassily Kandinsky claimed, or has been credited with, the 'creation' of abstract art. At the core of this film is a dramatic recreation of Kandinsky's account of returning to his studio one dark evening, and being astonished by an unknown masterpiece of abstract art leaning against the easel – a picture which turned out to be one of his own landscapes fallen on its side. 'Now I knew for certain that the object spoiled my pictures.' While this film's narration does indeed emphasize the notion of an inspired breakthrough to Abstraction, the picture it conveys in more purely filmic ways is a rich and complex one. Cuts and fades from Russian folk art, fairytale illustration and icons to Kandinsky's work suggest the intense spiritual content that he hoped not to lose but to intensify as he became more abstract. The dramatic torch-beam lighting, which in the scene of the fallen painting creates a sense of Kandinsky's search and discovery, is also evocative of the supernatural mystery he felt in art. His paintings, propped on the somewhat cruciform easel, echo the devotional images and altars in peasant homes. The film gives a strong feeling of art in the context of everyday life rather than the impersonal museum, and we note how Kandinsky extended his paintings over on to their frames, as if to break the delimiting boundaries of art. (Several Modernist painters, such as Seurat, have felt the same impulse, and for similar reasons, as has a contemporary artist like Howard Hodgkin, who is one of many artists still powerfully influenced by Kandinsky.) At another level, the intimate relation between art and life is underlined in the film where shots of the

Bavarian countryside and domestic architecture strikingly match Kandinsky's seemingly unreal colors and images in his earlier fairytale pictures. The film shows him loath to abandon those images and their associations. The camera tracks move in to reveal two peasant figures in the midst of a seemingly abstract composition, or pan a second time over a passage of free brush-marks that opened the film, and in which we now clearly discern three horsemen. One of the factors that enabled Kandinsky finally to shed figurative imagery was the example of music, which could, while inherently abstract, carry strong spiritual content. The music running through this film serves, subliminally, to make the point that the artist's orchestration of visual shapes is like the composer's manipulation of sounds.

'…has the rare quality of knowing how to present the pictures within their own context.'
UNESCO

For more information see page 147

Director	**15 minutes**
HG Zeiss	**Color**
Narration	**Age range 12–adult**
Susanne Carwin	**Film $553** Rental $169
Original music	**VHS $79**
Winfried Zillig	

Awards
Silver Lion, Venice
Bronze Medal, Brussels
Outstanding Merit, Berlin
First Prize, Cultural Film,
Mannheim International
Recognition, Mannheim
Diplôme d'Honneur, Cannes
Highly Commended,
German Center for
Film Classification

Also available in German

Paul Klee

'Art does not reproduce the visible,
but makes visible.'
Paul Klee

Central for Klee, as for Kandinsky, was the
parallel between visual art and the abstract
medium of music. He was himself a gifted
musician, and though not a composer he
developed motifs, themes, counterpoints
and harmonies in his visual work like a
musical composer.

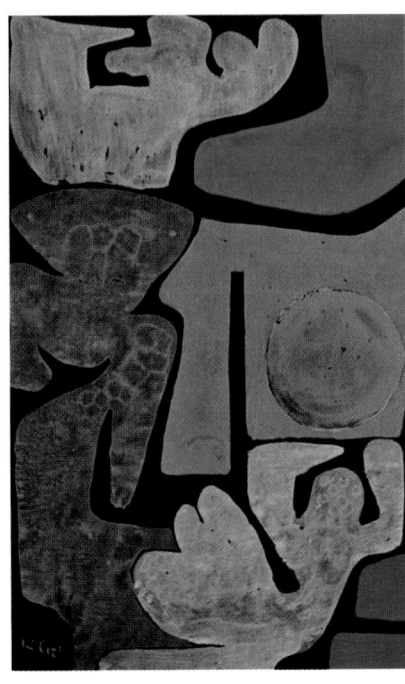

518   Paul Klee

Klee's position among the great painters of
this century is unique. He neither founded
a new style nor belonged to a modern
movement. His achievement was not so
much concerned with the manner of
painting, but with its content. His influence,
though not immediately evident, has been
perhaps the most widely felt of his time.
The script of this film was written by
Professor Will Grohmann, a personal friend
of Paul Klee and the leading authority on
his work. It shows selected examples
taken from nine thousand works created
by Klee, and groups them together not
chronologically but by subject matter.
The commentary describes Klee's life, his
relationships and the different stages in his
artistic career – *Blaue Reiter,* the Bauhaus,
the art academy in Düsseldorf, the end of
his life in Berne. Interpretation is kept as
concise as possible, giving the viewer
time to compare the different pictures with
the suggested interpretations and so gain
personal and direct access to Klee's work.

For more information see page 135

Director	**30 minutes**
Georgia van der Rohe	**Color**
Writer/Narration	**Age range 14–adult**
Will Grohmann	**Film $693** Rental $199
Also available in German	**VHS $99**

528   Klee and the Munich Revolution

Paul Klee was a Swiss painter and etcher
who described his art of free fantasy as
'taking a line for a walk.' He was also an
impassioned teacher and published a great
deal on the theory of art. Here we
concentrate on Klee's work, his writings
and the historical events taking place
during his involvement, and subsequent
withdrawal from, the political ideas and
events of the Munich revolution of
1918-19. In particular we examine the
contrast between his illustrations for
the revolutionary *Potsdamer Platz* and
his painting *Young Proletarian,* all done in
1919, and his fairytale paintings and work
for *Munich Leaves,* which bear witness to
his withdrawal from politics.

Part of the series *Modern Art and
Modernism: Manet to Pollock*

Director	**25 minutes**
Nick Levinson	**Color**
Presenter/Writer	**Age range 18–adult**
Karl Werckmeister,	**VHS $99**
University of California	
Open University/BBC	

502D Art in Revolution

The years between the 1917 revolution and
Lenin's death in 1925 were a period of
experimentation and innovation in Russian
art. Artists of the left – painters, sculptors,
architects, musicians, dramatists, poets, and
designers in all the industrial arts – became
actively involved in the transformation of
society and the creation of a new social
order. This film examines how the close
integration of art and politics produced
revolutionary forms and principles in the
whole range of artistic activities. Using
contemporary film and photographs,
the film gives a detailed account of the
developments after the revolution and
before the inauguration of Stalin's Five
Year Plan. It tells of artists' involvement
with propaganda exercises during the
civil war, winning the peasants over to the
revolution. It shows how street decorations,
pageants and theatrical performances
pointed the way ahead to the use of
Constructivist principles in the theater,
where designers produced machine-like
sets stripped bare of the conventions of
bourgeois illusion. Architects, along with
designers of clothing, furniture and
household goods, introduced an elegant
functionalism into their work, a tradition
continued later by the German Bauhaus.
Some of the greatest innovations were
made in the cinema in typographical
design, where the principles of montage
adopted by artists like Dziga Vertoz and
Rodchenko produced works of tremendous
impact. The film surveys a wide range of
experimental work produced by artists
and designers during this period, and
indicates the extent to which their
innovations have influenced the course
of twentieth-century art.

Director
Lutz Becker

Narration
Edward Braun

Narrator
Chris Stanley

Research
Camilla Gray-Prokovieva

Arts Council of
Great Britain

**50 minutes
Color and
black and white
Age range 14–adult**

Film $973 Rental $289
VHS $139

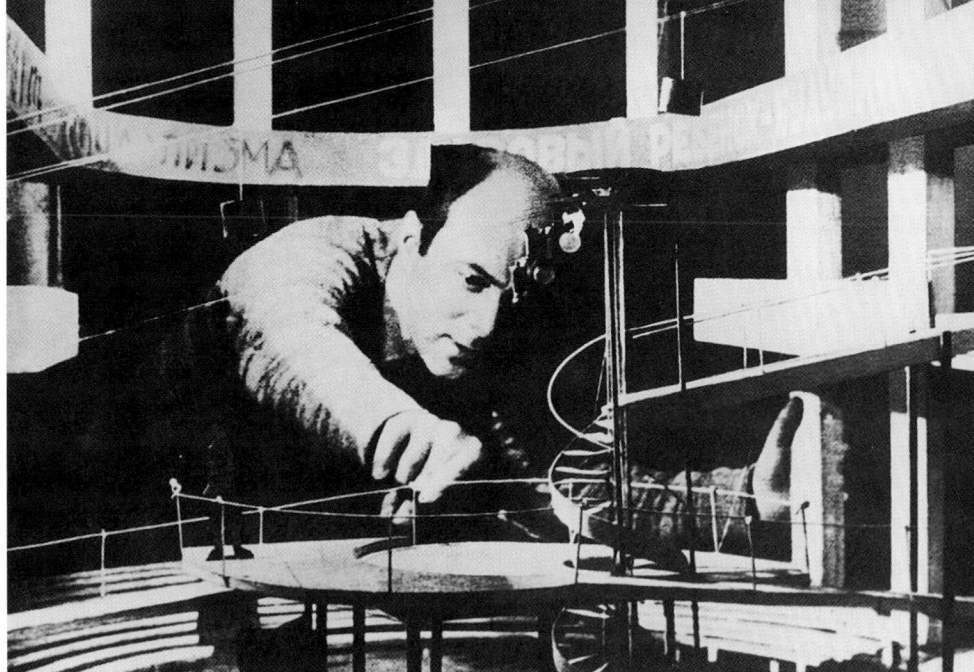

503 El Lissitzky
Constructivist of the Russian Avant-Garde

Leo Lorez portrays the work of the Soviet Constructivist El Lissitzky as an architect, photographer, painter, typographer and designer of exhibitions. Lissitzky's life was that of a pre-war cosmopolitan. Born in 1890 in Smolensk, he went to Germany to study architecture in Darmstadt. He returned to Russia when Marc Chagall invited him to teach at the Vibetsk Art School. Under the influence of the Russian revolution and its fantastic vision of a future to be designed afresh, he became one of the most important artists of the avant-garde led by Malevich. In the 1920s he came in contact with the German Dadaist circle around Kurt Schwitters and Hans Arp. He created his 'Prouns,' a new kind of visual grammar or unit of visual phenomena, which he declared to be 'changing stations' from the two-dimensionality of the canvas to the three-dimensionality of architecture. His architectural projects which were never executed – the Lenin Tribune, a podium from which Lenin could address the masses, and the Wolkenbügel, a skyscraper in Moscow – are realized here by computer animation and shown as if at the sites they were originally planned for. The video draws on authentic picture and sound material, including sequences from Vertov's famous films and original quotes from Lissitzky himself, to portray him as a central figure in classical modern art.

'The cinematography is sharp, distinct, and well lit. Narration is kept to a minimum… Lissitzky's legacy has such a contemporary but classic feel and appearance. Adults, students, and the general public will enjoy this portrait of the artist. For many, Lissitzky will be a serendipitous discovery. Recommended for both public library and college collections.'
Video Rating Guide for Libraries, USA

Director/Scenario	**88 minutes**
Leo Lorez	**Color and**
	black and white
Also available in German	**Age range 14–adult**
	VHS $189

516 A Memory of Moholy-Nagy

The Hungarian artist László Moholy-Nagy was a major propagandist for Abstraction and constructive functionalism in art and design. His exploration of light, space and dynamism, while it employed modern technology and materials, was nevertheless informed by a sense of intuition and even spiritual aspiration. In addition to making avant-garde films and documentaries between 1926 and 1935, he experimented in a wide variety of artistic disciplines: architecture, painting, graphic arts, photography, theater and fashion. Using archive footage, photographs, computer and hand-drawn animation sequences, this film surveys his prolific career.

'…fast paced and information packed, never losing the viewer…crisp with accompanying high-quality narration. The graphics are clever and well done. This video would be a nice addition to collections with a large demand for art titles.'
Video Rating Guide for Libraries, USA

Director	**Not for sale in the USA**
John Halas	**15 minutes**
Animation and artwork	**Color**
Andy Wyatt	**Age range 14–adult**
Models	**VHS $89**
Brian Borthwick	
Phil Gell	
Narration	
Robin Ellis	
Original music	
Boris Karadimchev	
Computer animation	
Tamas Waliczky	
Advice	
Hattula Moholy-Nagy	

This film is a rare document from the period when, in both Europe and America, Abstraction in various forms was becoming dominant, and Victor Vasarely was pioneering 'Op Art.' The film was made at the time of one of the artist's early exhibitions at the progressive Denise René Gallery in Paris – René herself makes a fleeting appearance in Op Art couture. With a soundtrack of contemporary music, and without narration, the film-maker has sought to create a vibrant composition of rhythms and contrasts in the spirit of Vasarely.

Director
Peter Kassovitz

Original music
Ianis Xenakis

9 minutes
Black and white
Age range 12–adult
Film $483 Rental $149
VHS $69

Perceptual art is concerned with the effects and processes of what, in this film, Bridget Riley calls 'the great privilege of sight.' 'Looking,' as she puts it, 'is a pleasure – a continual pleasure.' From the black and white paintings of the early 1960s which first established her international reputation, to her increasing concern with the self-generating luminosity of pure color, the film traces her 'exploration of the truth of what one can see.' In the studio, we see her working on a painting – finding that visual structure which from basic and simple elements will release complex effects of energy, movement, space, light and 'induced' color through the physical act of looking. Certain artists – Van Gogh, Seurat, Monet and the Futurists – are particularly important to her. But the film also shows the inspiration she has always drawn from certain types of visual experiences in nature. 'Painting,' as Bridget Riley says, 'has to obey the laws of painting.' But for her that is a process parallel to nature, dependent on our day-to-day experience of the joy of using our eyes.

Director/Writer
David Thompson

Arts Council of
Great Britain

28 minutes
Color
Age range 12–adult
Film $693 Rental $199
VHS $99

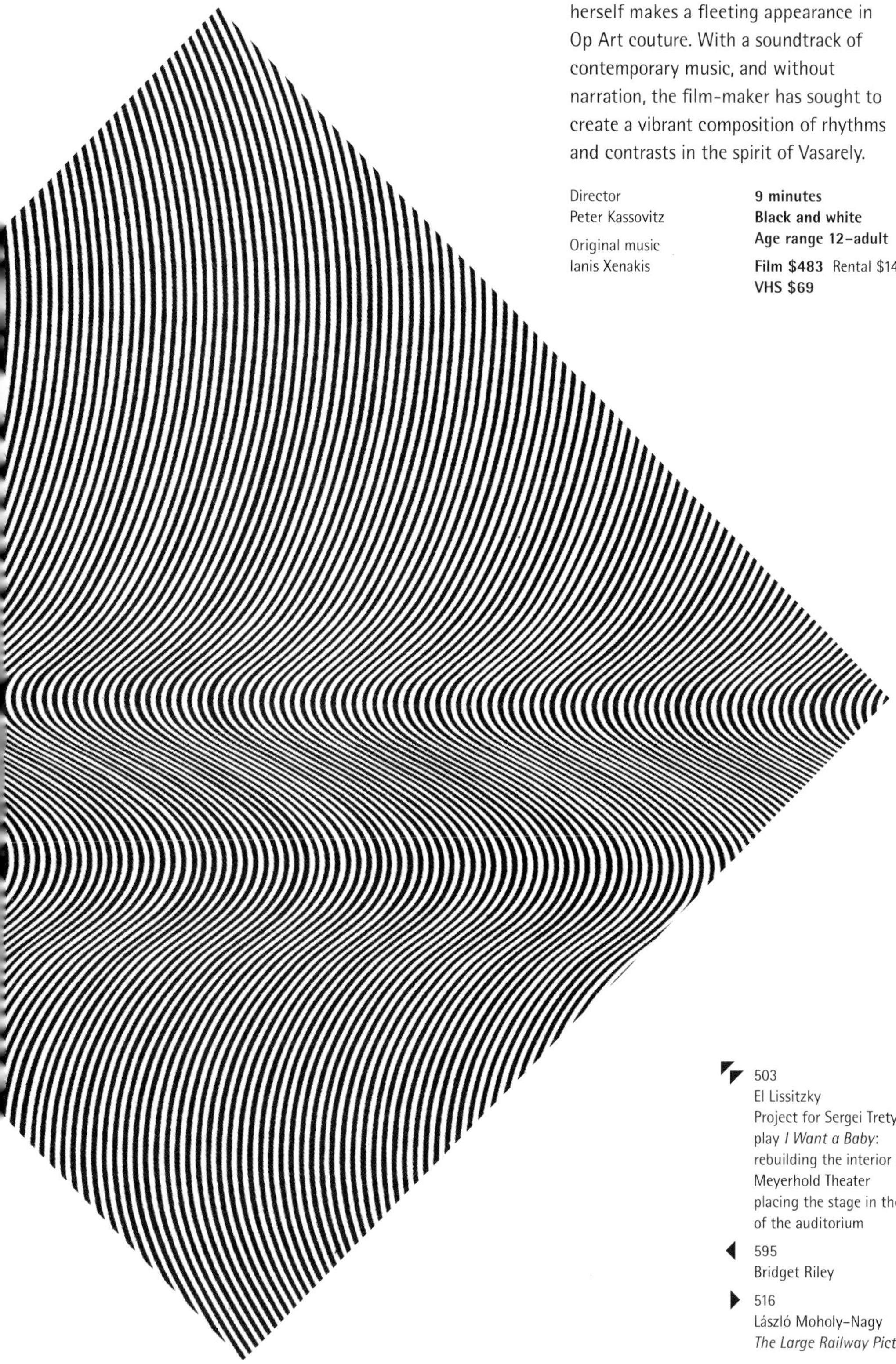

503
El Lissitzky
Project for Sergei Tretyakov's
play *I Want a Baby*:
rebuilding the interior of the
Meyerhold Theater
placing the stage in the center
of the auditorium

◀ 595
Bridget Riley

▶ 516
László Moholy-Nagy
The Large Railway Picture

503E Jackson Pollock: Tim Clark and Michael Fried in Conversation

Art historian TJ Clark and art critic Michael Fried in the past occupied opposing positions. Clark was the eminent advocate of the social history of art, based on a Marxist approach which saw art as produced in a socio-economic context. Fried, on the other hand, was an arch-Modernist, believing art to be about itself alone, separate from social meaning. Now, however, the two have moved closer. Clark accepts the canonical greatness of Pollock's work and Fried no longer claims that art functions only in an 'optical' way. This video is hard work if one has not read the works of Clark and Fried.

Part of the series
Modern Art, Practices and Debates

Directors	**25 minutes**
GD Jayalakshmi	**Color**
Nick Levinson	**Age range 18–adult**
Presenter	**VHS $99**
Paul Wood	
Contributors	
TJ Clark	
Professor M Fried	
Open University/BBC	

503C American Abstraction

The narrator of *American Abstraction* claims that art in the United States always considered itself dependent on European art, particularly when it sustained the shock of modern art arriving from Europe in 1913 to be presented at the Armory Show. American painters tried to adapt these new forms to their own outlook on life, but their art was no more than adaptation. Certain painters looked elsewhere: for example, Arshile Gorky found inspiration in the mythology of his homeland, Armenia, and Mark Tobey painted works of meditation influenced by oriental thought. Little by little the physical element, the 'action,' in abstract American painting gave way to the 'sign,' in painters such as Gottlieb and Newman. This evolution transformed the spontaneous gesture we find in Pollock into a cultural gesture, a vocabulary. One painter who stands out from these trends is Mark Rothko. In his paintings there is no culture, no sign, no gesture, just color and light. The film also features the work of Rivera, Thomas Hart Benton, Orozco, Stuart Davis, Motherwell, De Kooning, Franz Kline and others.

Part of the series
The Adventure of Modern Art

Director	**53 minutes**
Carlos Vilardebo	**Color**
Writers/Narration	**Age range 15–adult**
André Parinaud	**Film $1043** Rental $299
Carlos Vilardebo	**VHS $149**

Also available in French

▲ 503E
Jackson Pollock
Autumn Rhythm

▶▶ 598
Howard Hodgkin
Lunch

598 Howard Hodgkin: A Study

Howard Hodgkin has for some years been one of Britain's leading artists, but the recognition enjoyed by painters such as Peter Blake and David Hockney has come to him only recently. This video sets out to consider the preoccupations and techniques of the artist and his work and to relate these to the wider context of painting, past and present. Recurring themes, such as the intimacy of a moment with friends, are identified and considered alongside the technical devices of Hodgkin's work. This video is a good introduction to abstract painting, since it offers a clear and accessible argument for this kind of work.

'...a sense of Hodgkin's finely tuned use of color, recurring themes, and unique visual language'
Video Rating Guide for Libraries, USA

Director	**16 minutes**
Brian Taylor	**Color**
Script	**Age range 12–adult**
Joe Connolly	**VHS $89**

503D Abstraction: The Experience

Artists, like everyone else in Europe, had lived through traumatic experiences by the time the Germans surrendered in 1945. In France, artists such as Wols and Jean Fautrier depicted lives of misery in troubled but spontaneous works. Wol's first oil paintings were once described as 'forty moments in the crucifixion of man.' Jean Fautrier revealed a similar experience in his paintings of wartime hostages. Then came the Lyric Abstraction painters, Georges Mathieu, Pierre Soulages, Serge Poliakoff, Hans Hartung. The abstract expression of this period conveys an effort to escape from a world confronted with the problem of having to rebuild itself. This attempt to escape very often resulted in dilemma: for example, Nicholas de Staël committed suicide in 1951. Each artist struggled to find his own way: Lucio Fontana in Italy, Antoni Tàpies in Spain, Jean Dubuffet in France. In the United States, the revolution caused by the paintings of Pollock and De Kooning led to a new humanism, as expressed in the paintings of Mark Rothko and Barnett Newman. From this point onward, American Abstraction evolved perhaps reductively, through the works of Clyfford Still, Sam Francis and Morris Louis. Forms and shapes were simplified, colors purified, trying to achieve detachment leading arguably to a lack of sensitivity. From Kenneth Noland to Frank Stella, painting turned to parallel lines following the edges of the canvas. It was during this period that Joseph Albers, who had previously been a professor at the Bauhaus, devoted the rest of his life to homage to the square. This asceticism reached its culmination with works such as those of Ad Reinhardt, who said, 'Art is Art. Everything else is everything else.' He painted wholly black canvases, declaring these 'the last painting anyone can hope or wish to paint.' In the meantime, Europeans were attracted to technology. Painting was becoming an attempt to recreate movement; kinetic art – *kinetic* from the Greek verb 'to move' – was a school led by Victor Vasarely. Forms of energy were also being used: magnetic force by Vassilakis Takis and Pol Bury, air in the case of Alexander Calder, and light in the case of Julio Le Parc.

Today the desire to incorporate kinetic works into everyday life still represents the ultimate aim of the abstractional experience. The film also features the work of Bacon, Esteve, Riopelle, Piaubert, Lilyan Lijn, the GRAV group and many others.

Part of the series
The Adventure of Modern Art

Director	**53 minutes**
Carlos Vilardebo	**Color**
Writers/Narration	**Age range 15–adult**
André Parinaud	**Film $1043** Rental $299
Carlos Vilardebo	**VHS $149**
Also available in French	

554 Abstract Expressionism

A personal account of the artists working in America during the 1940s and 1950s who are connected with so-called Abstract Expressionism. Expressionism itself is the deliberate desertion of naturalism in favor of a simplified style, involving exaggeration and distortion of line and color in order to produce a much greater emotional impact. Piet Mondrian was a Dutch painter who went to America in 1940; much earlier, he had changed his realist landscapes for Cubist ones, and he now became extremely influential with his 'plastic art,' which restricted forms to purely geometrical shapes colored only in the three primary colors and white, black or gray. His work is examined along with that of his fellow abstract artists De Kooning, Rothko, Still, Pollock and Newman.

Part of the series *Modern Art and Modernism: Manet to Pollock*

For more information see page 114

Director	**24 minutes**
Charles Cooper	**Color**
Presenter/Writer	**Age range 18–adult**
Donald Judd	**VHS $99**
Open University/BBC	

16 Into Abstraction

131

17 The Bauhaus and *De Stijl*

Founded by Walter Gropius in 1919, the Bauhaus ('building house') school of design, craft and architecture gathered together the most progressive artists in Germany and eastern Europe, and exerted a dominating influence on art and design throughout the world that is still felt today.

This section of 11 programs can be purchased on VHS for $1109

Television rights and prices on request

The Bauhaus was a self-contained center of artistic instruction and culture with tremendous breadth of scope. The leading teachers, together with Gropius, were Feininger, Klee, Kandinsky, Schlemmer and Moholy-Nagy. Klee taught theory, then painting on glass and tapestry; Kandinsky gave lessons in general theory, but concentrated more on abstract composition and monumental painting. Schlemmer and Moholy-Nagy rejuvenated the techniques of working in metal and plastic, the arts of theater and ballet, photography, typography, publicity and so on. Initially very Expressionist in spirit, the Bauhaus aesthetic became increasingly Constructivist and geometric.

First opening its doors in Weimar in 1919, the school moved to Dessau in 1925, and was housed in a new building designed by Gropius himself. In 1932 it moved again, to Berlin, but in the following year pressure from increasingly right-wing German authorities forced its closure. After the Second World War, however, Bauhaus traditions were continued with the founding under Max Bill of the *Hochschule für Gestaltung und Kunst* (College of Design and Art) in Ulm. The spirit of the Bauhaus also flourished in the United States, where many of its leading lights took refuge during the Nazi period. Moholy-Nagy established the New Bauhaus (later the Institute of Design) in Chicago; Mies van der Rohe became a towering influence in American architecture; Joseph Albers gave seminal tuition at Black Mountain College in North Carolina, and later at Yale, encouraging a generation of younger American artists and anticipating in his own paintings the development of optical and hard-edged Abstraction.

Paralleling the spread of the Bauhaus ethos from Germany, there emerged in Holland *De Stijl*, a movement originating in the work of painters like Mondrian and artist-designers like van Doesburg, van der Leck, Reitverl and Vantongerloo. As with the Bauhaus, *De Stijl* developed an aesthetic of purified geometry, and aimed to unify fine and applied arts. To a great extent the two movements have merged in their huge influence on subsequent art and design developments.

515
The Bauhaus

The Bauhaus

Its Impact on the World of Design

This film draws attention to the great social responsibility of town planners, architects and mass-production designers, whose job it is to design the cities, houses and goods that form our everyday surroundings. It sets out to show that of all art institutions in the 1920s, the Bauhaus was the most intensive in its approach to the task of aestheticizing the modern technical world. At the same time it indicates the importance of design in general, for without it the human need for beauty would remain at least partly unsatisfied.

Director	**19 minutes**
Detten Schliermacher	**Color**
Original music	**Age range 14–adult**
Hans Posegga	**Film $623** Rental $189
Also available in German	**VHS $89**

◀◀ 502B, page 136
Gerrit Rietveld
Rietveld chair

▲ 515
Oskar Schlemmer
Title page drawing for
*Utopia: Document
of Reality*

▲ 515
Walter Gropius
The Bauhaus, Dessau

▶ 515
Peter Keler
Lacquered cradle

A Memory of Moholy-Nagy

The Hungarian artist László Moholy-Nagy played an important rôle in the development of modern art in the first half of the twentieth century. In addition to making avant-garde films and documentaries between 1926 and 1935, he experimented in a wide variety of artistic disciplines – architecture, painting, graphic arts, photography, theater and fashion. Russian Constructivism was a major influence, convincing him of the artist's crucial rôle in the development of western society. Using archive footage, photographs, computer and hand-drawn animation sequences, the film surveys his prolific career: his beginnings in Vienna and Berlin; his teaching at the Bauhaus, where he and colleagues Marcel Breuer, Paul Klee and Herbert Bayer laid the foundations of Functionalism; his English period; and finally in his work in Chicago, where he founded a school in the Bauhaus tradition.

'…fast paced and information packed, never losing the viewer…crisp with accompanying high-quality narration. The graphics are clever and well done. This video would be a nice addition to collections with a large demand for art titles.'
Video Rating Guide for Libraries, USA

Director	**Not for sale in the USA**
John Halas	**15 minutes**
Animation and artwork	**Color**
Andy Wyatt	**Age range 14–adult**
Models	**VHS $89**
Brian Borthwick	
Phil Gell	
Narration	
Robin Ellis	
Original music	
Boris Karadimchev	
Computer animation	
Tamas Waliczky	
Advice	
Hattula Moholy-Nagy	

707 **The Bauhaus at Weimar**

This was the most famous school of architecture, craftsmanship and design in modern times, and has had a huge influence on art-school education all over the world. In its early days it was in Weimar, Germany (it later moved twice and was closed down by the Nazis in 1933). George Adams was a student during the Weimar period. He discusses the attitude of the students toward their work, prevailing trends in art, and their famous tutors, who included Itten and van Doesburg. Some rare artefacts made at the Bauhaus during the early 1920s are also displayed and studied, including tea sets, textiles, silverware and furniture; part of the Bauhaus's importance was that it did not draw back from tackling the problems of mass-production.

Part of the series *History of Architecture and Design 1890–1939*

Director	**25 minutes**
Edward Hayward	**Black and white**
Presenter/Writer	**Age range 18–adult**
Tim Benton	**VHS $99**
Open University/BBC	

▼ 516
László Moholy-Nagy

◄ 707
Henry van der Velde
The Bauhaus, Weimar,
stair detail

◥ 517
Oskar Schlemmer
Scene from a performance
of Form Dance

▶▶ 518
Paul Klee
Turmoil

Paul Klee

The Swiss painter Paul Klee taught at the Bauhaus from 1920 to 1930. He made a central contribution to the life and ethos of the institution, teaching a broad range of practical and theoretical subjects, and publishing, under the Bauhaus imprint, his *Pedagogical Sketchbook*, a textbook which has been continually reprinted worldwide ever since, and is a staple of art education. Film 518 is a retrospective survey of Klee's whole career, including his time at the Bauhaus.

---

518   **Paul Klee**

The script of this film was written by Professor Will Grohmann, a personal friend of Paul Klee and the leading authority on his work. It shows selected examples taken from nine thousand works created by Klee, and groups them together not chronologically but by subject matter. The commentary describes Klee's life, his relationships and the different stages in his artistic career – *Blaue Reiter,* the Bauhaus, the art academy in Düsseldorf, the end of his life in Berne. Interpretation is kept as concise as possible, giving the viewer time to compare the different pictures with the suggested interpretations and so gain personal and direct access to Klee's work.

For more information see page 126

Director	**30 minutes**
Georgia van der Rohe	**Color**
Writer/Narration	**Age range 14–adult**
Will Grohmann	**Film $693** Rental $199
Also available in German	**VHS $99**

Oskar Schlemmer

Oskar Schlemmer (1888–1943) is one of the central personalities of the Bauhaus, and a unique contributor to modern German art, yet his work is not as well known as it deserves to be. Initially Impressionist in style, then passing through a Cubist phase, Schlemmer's mature pictorial work uses human figures, silhouetted in front, back or side view, displaced across the surface in static states or suspended movement. The articulation of limbs is angular, and all lines of direction and composition seem subject to quasi-mechanical regularity. In some paintings the figures are built up into a curious shallow relief. Perhaps his most famous picture depicts wooden-seeming figures ascending an angular modern staircase – the atmosphere is one of Arcadian science fiction. In exploring human figures in spatial relation to each other and to the environment, Schlemmer's concern in his paintings clearly relates to architecture, dance, theater direction and stage design, all of which he was involved with. He was the author of a book, *The Theater of the Bauhaus.*

517   **Man and Mask**
Oskar Schlemmer and the Bauhaus Stage

Oskar Schlemmer did not confine his activities at the Bauhaus to painting and teaching sculpture. He also wanted to put his ideas about ballet into practice, and in 1922 he did so in public for the first time. He planned to free the stage from the trappings of tradition in order to give expression to the 'pure idea.' The central theme of his work was the relation between humankind and space, and the mediator between these two was to be the dancer, stripped of his individual identity by the use of costumes and masks. This documentary film, made with the artistic advice of Oskar Schlemmer's widow, presents an historically faithful, precise reconstruction of some of his dances. More than any other film, it gives a sense of what Bauhaus teaching was really like, and is truly important to an understanding of the origins of contemporary dance.

Director	**27 minutes**
Margarete Hasting	**Color**
Original music	**Age range 10–adult**
Eric Fersti	**Film $693** Rental $199
	VHS $99

▶▶ 502B
Gerrit Rietveld
House for the interior designer
Truus Schröder-Schräder

◢ 497
Kasimir Malevich
Suprematist Painting

501 Piet Mondrian

The film traces Mondrian's development by relating and comparing some thirty of his paintings and drawings. His career opens with rural landscapes of his native Holland, executed in the atmospheric style of the late nineteenth-century Hague School. The already rather 'schematic' Dutch landscape (flat horizons, vertical towers, the natural geometry of tree and plant structures) is gradually simplified by the artist into abstract elements. Eventually he restricts himself to the black verticals and horizontals and the primary-colored rectangles that were to represent for many the ultimate modern painting. His writings on art are quoted in the commentary of the film. A portrait of the painter emerges through the use of photographs and other documents evoking his surroundings and activities.

'…clear, lucid narration free from jargon… it elucidates the basic tenets that shaped the modernist vision…This visually beautiful short production will enhance library and school collections…could be used effectively by students of language as well as by anyone interested in the art and culture of the twentieth century.'
Video Rating Guide for Libraries, USA

Director	**18 minutes**
Nico Crama	**Color**
Also available in	**Age range 14–adult**
Dutch, French, German	**Film $623** Rental $189
and Spanish	**VHS $89**

501A Mondrian

The work of the Dutch painter Piet Mondrian (1872–1944) is conventionally understood as clinical, calculated art from which all traces of life have been expunged. With its bright colors and large, simple shapes it is frequently 'quoted' in interior and product design. Mondrian's own writings lend weight to this image of his art as rational and almost mechanically pure, yet in this program David Batchelor argues that this perspective does scant justice to Mondrian's actual paintings.

Part of the series
Modern Art, Practices and Debates

Director	**25 minutes**
Tony Coe	**Color**
Presenter	**Age range 18–adult**
David Batchelor	**VHS $99**
Open University/BBC	

502 Theo van Doesburg
New Aesthetics for a New World

Theo van Doesburg is best known as a painter and as the founder and editor of the avant-garde magazine *De Stijl* (*The Style,* 1917–28). But van Doesburg was also active in other fields: literature, philosophy, architecture, typography. This film explores his life and work, with the emphasis on his architecture, through posthumous works and documentary evidence about the artist and his wife recently given to the Netherlands.

Director	**30 minutes**
Frank den Oudsten	**Color**
	Age range 14–adult
	Film $693 Rental $199
	VHS $99

502B The Rietveld Schröder House
Restoration of a *De Stijl* Interior and Exterior

In 1924 Mrs Schröder-Schräder of Utrecht commissioned the architect Gerrit Rietveld to build a house for her. Today the result of their co-operation – for the design was truly a combined effort – is considered a monument to Modernism and the purest expression of the principles of *De Stijl.* Mrs Schröder lived in the house until her death in 1985; she was ninety-five years old. Toward the end of her life she decided that she wanted the house to be restored as far as possible to its original condition, and she asked Bertus Mulder, an architect who had worked for Rietveld in the past, to undertake this reconstruction process. The crucial elements of the 'new way of living' for which this house was a manifesto in 1925 – for example, the use of space and the system of sliding panels or walls especially created for Mrs Schröder – had disappeared during sixty years of use, repainting and redecoration; but twenty-four black and white photographs of the house taken shortly after it was built, together with the memories of Mrs Schröder and her three children, became Mulder's primary sources. There were others – for example, he found slivers of paint which revealed the original colors used. All the phases of his effort to reconstruct the house were filmed, and in the film he dwells particularly on the noteworthy aspects of Rietveld's architecture. In 1987 the house was opened to the public, and it is now a museum.

Director	**30 minutes**
Ike Bertels	**Color**
	Age range 16–adult
Restoration-architect	**VHS $99**
Bertus Mulder	
Also available in Dutch	

Abstraction: the creation of a mental universe where the idea has as much reality as the material object; where painting addresses itself to the spirit. From 1910 onward Wassily Kandinsky studied the dynamics of colors and the concrete, geometrical elements of painting.

At the same time the Dutch painter Piet Mondrian researched the orthogonal simplification of the form of an object such as a tree, while the Russian Malevich expressed in his paintings fascination with the void, ending up with the ultimate Suprematist composition, a white square on a white background (1918). For these artists art is before all else spiritual, yet paradoxically they also influenced the Russian Constructivism of Tatlin and Rodchenko, a movement proclaiming the utilitarian nature of art in the revolutionary period around 1920. Another important element in the development of Abstraction was the foundation of the Bauhaus.

Set up by the architect Gropius in 1919 in Weimar, it was a school where artists and designers taught together, influenced each other, and shaped the future of European art and architecture for generations to come. By the Second World War the work of Paul Klee, a major Bauhaus personality, represented the confluence of the creative heritage of artists like Malevich, Kandinsky and Mondrian, but in terms unique to Klee himself. After the war, in the USA artists were developing toward a lyrical, gestural Abstraction that would come to dominate world art for some time. The film also features the work of Moholy-Nagy, El Lissitzky, Nahum Gabo, van Doesburg and many others.

Part of the series
The Adventure of Modern Art

Director	53 minutes
Carlos Vilardebo	Color
Writers/Narration	Age range 15–adult
André Parinaud	Film $1043 Rental $299
Carlos Vilardebo	VHS $149
Also available in French	

741   **The Flame of Functionalism**
The Roots of Modern Design in Finland

The Bauhaus is central in this general survey of modern functional design. Celebrating the spirit of the 1930s, when Scandinavian design first gained wide acclaim, this film juxtaposes period movie clips and documentary footage with images of a wide range of Finnish architecture, interior design and furnishings by Rivel and many others. It explores the idealistic, even naïve, ideology of the day, with its faith in the 'light, health and efficiency' of Functionalism (or *funkkis*, as the Finns call it), and in 'optimism with pragmatism.' The film also charts the continued influence of the epoch in the 'new functionalism' of design today.

Director	40 minutes
Kaisa Blomstedt	Color
Writers	Age range 16–adult
Kaisa Blomstedt	Film $693 Rental $199
Mikael Merenmies	VHS $99
Also available in Finnish	

The spontaneous, the unexpected, the subconscious, the outrageous, the irrational. These were the central concerns of Dada and Surrealism, two closely associated revolutionary artistic movements which flourished between the wars in this century, and continued to have a lasting influence thereafter.

18

Dada and Surrealism

This section of 18 programs can be purchased on VHS for $2002

Television rights and prices on request

Dada originated in Zürich with the activities of Arp, Tzara and others, and quickly spread to Cologne, Berlin, Hanover, New York, Paris, London and Barcelona. Surrealism, which grew alongside and partly out of Dada, was equally cosmopolitan. Among the first leading lights were Picabia, Man Ray, Duchamp, Schwitters, and the writers Breton, Aragon and Soupault. (Man Ray's photographs of many of the confrères feature in a mesmeric sequence in 568, filmed in his studio).

Seeking to overthrow all traditional constraints, Dada tended to break away from the usual media of painting and sculpture. Man Ray and Duchamp, for example, created curious constructions from found objects (*objets trouvés*) which they provocatively exhibited as artworks. Much use was also made of ephemeral forms of publicity – magazines, tracts, bizarrely staged 'events' and addresses. Through artists like Cocteau and Picabia there were strong links with theater and performing arts. Strong Dada influence can be seen in subsequent artistic trends toward events, happenings and body art. (See for instance the crazy machines of Tinguely or the deliberately shocking mutilations of Mark Prent.)

Less wholly anarchic and 'anti-art' than the Dadaists, the Surrealists were not so sweeping in their rejection of the traditional forms of painting. Painters such as Dali and Magritte, de Chirico, Tanguy and often Ernst employed deliberately conservative techniques such as a pseudo-Renaissance chiaroscuro with which they depicted strange, dreamlike, exotic, impossible juxtapositions of objects and symbols. Forerunners of Surrealist painting are the fantastical images of Bosch and Bruegel and later Ensor.

The name Dada was chosen from a dictionary and adopted for its absurdity and arbitrariness; Surrealism, established by Breton, who rejected Dada's extreme nihilism, denoted a less anti-intellectual movement. Yet Surrealism was still very much preoccupied with irrationalism, with Freud's researches into dreams and the unconscious, and with release from conformity and convention. It was opposed to what it saw as the dominant rationalism of Cubism, and many of the major artists of Modernism who strove to establish new forms of expression have some affinity or association with Surrealism: Picasso in his post-Cubist distortions of the body, Miró in his eccentric and mysterious organic forms, Klee in his nervous imagery, Henry Moore in his dreamy, recumbent figures.

561
Joan Miró
*Woman and Bird in the
Moonlight*

558
Salvador Dali
Metamorphosis of Narcissus

558 Europe after the Rain, Part One

Surrealism and Dada from their Beginnings

This feature-length film examines the
movements of Dada and Surrealism, and
follows the development of their main
exponents, Duchamp, Tzara, Arp, Ernst,
Schwitters, Breton and Dali, concentrating
on the contradictions and ambivalences
between their innovatory techniques and
philosophies and their desire to transform
the world. The film uses contemporary
newsreels, some dramatization and
detailed accounts of the artists' work to
show how, building on the nihilism and
anti-aestheticism of Dada and the collage
and Constructivist aspects of Cubism,
the Surrealists attempted to express the
tradition of thought freed from moral
preoccupation. Beginning with the birth of
Dada in Zürich, against the background of
the First World War, the film examines the
different forms the movement assumed in
Berlin, New York and Paris. Following the
collapse of Dada, André Breton more or less
invented Surrealism, which developed in
two phases: the exploration of pure fantasy
via found objects and frottages, and the
depiction of irrationality – the imaginary
landscapes of Yves Tanguy or Salvador Dali,
or Max Ernst's collages from nineteenth-
century illustrations.

Director/Writer	**47 minutes**
Mick Gold	**Color and**
Script consultants	**black and white**
Dawn Ades	**Age range 17–adult**
Robert Short	**Film $833** Rental $249
Arts Council of	**VHS $119**
Great Britain	

559 Europe after the Rain, Part Two

Surrealism and Dada to the 1960s

This film questions the complex relationship
between the Surrealist enterprise, in its
many forms, and politics, particularly in the
light of the rise of Fascism. It charts the rift
between those members who joined the
Resistance and those who went to America,
and considers Breton's unsuccessful attempt
to join the Communist Party, the anti-Nazi
photomontages of John Heartfield, and
Dali's obsession with the image of Hitler as
'the object of my delirium.' The film also
explores the influences of Surrealism on the
art world and on the mass media. It ends
with an interview with Duchamp in the
1960s, discussing the impact of the
movement, its failures and successes.

Director/Writer	**42 minutes**
Mick Gold	**Color and**
Script consultants	**black and white**
Dawn Ades	**Age range 17–adult**
Robert Short	**Film $833** Rental $249
Arts Council of	**VHS $119**
Great Britain	

561 Surrealism

Dada, the nihilistic precursor of Surrealism,
was deliberately anti-art and anti-sense,
intended to outrage and scandalize.
Characteristic of it were Marcel Duchamp's
'readymades' – everyday objects elevated
to the status of art by the mere decision
of the artist to call them such – or his
reproduction of the *Mona Lisa* decorated
with a moustache and an obscene caption.
As Dada burnt itself out, Surrealism was
born, chiefly through the efforts of the
writer André Breton. In both literature and
painting Surrealism explores the same
themes: the exaltation of dreams, the love
of madness and revolt. De Chirico painted
landscapes which provoke disorientation in
the viewer. New materials were called into
service to aid the discovery of the unusual:
collages of photos and illustrations,
or the rubbing of textures, by Max Ernst;
splashes of ink and automatic drawing by
André Masson. Miró revealed the mysteries
and qualities of the void by placing just a
few traces or ideograms on a canvas.
Meanwhile Magritte and Tanguy painted in
a much more traditional, meticulously
illusionistic manner, but created images that
are fantastical, alogical. Dali's techniques
were similar, yet his intentions were more
extreme and outrageous; and following the
Surrealist dictum, 'art is an attitude of
mind,' he was as provocative in his lifestyle
as in his paintings. As the Second World
War approached, many of the movement's
artists fled to America. The Surrealist spirit
was never so intense again. Also features
the work of Balla, Arp, Schwitters, Picabia
and many others.

Part of the series
The Adventure of Modern Art

Director	**53 minutes**
Carlos Vilardebo	**Color**
Writers/Narration	**Age range 15–adult**
André Parinaud	**Film $1043** Rental $299
Carlos Vilardebo	**VHS $149**
Also available in French	

Max Ernst

Surrealism's disturbing send-up of convention has become part of our cultural baggage, and influenced generations not only of artists but also of designers, advertisers, humorists and film-makers. In Max Ernst's animation we see the precedent for the more recent cartoons of Terry Gilliam, made famous in the television comedy *Monty Python's Flying Circus,* itself strongly Surrealist in ethos. Ernst's dislocation of Victorian engraved images is humorous, yet also curiously atmospheric, almost melancholic.

560 Max Ernst: Journey into the Subconscious

The inner world of the great painter Max Ernst is the subject of this film. One of the principal founders of Surrealism, Max Ernst explores the nature of materials and the emotional significance of shapes to combine with his collages and netherworld canvases. The director and Ernst together use the film creatively as a medium to explain the artist's own development.

'A very beautiful film, Max Ernst, the great enchanter, elegant and sensitive, casts a spell over his public. Without priggishness, a poetry of high quality, fairy-like without being imprecise, leads one ultimately into surrealism.'
UNESCO

Directors
Peter Schamoni
Dr C Lamb

Narration/Voice
Max Ernst

Original music
Hans Posegga

Awards
Grand Prix, Oberhausen
Highly Commended,
German Center for
Film Classification

12 minutes
Color
Age range 12–adult

Film $553 Rental $169
VHS $79

570 Kindness Week (Max Ernst)

Max Ernst was one of the young men who returned from the 1914-18 war ready to reject all the standards and customs which society had hitherto taken for granted. If culture and religion had led to nothing better than the past four years of misery and horror, they argued, then it was time to give anarchy and unreason a chance. This film is about the series of 182 collage engravings which illustrate Ernst's irrational novel *Kindness Week,* divided into seven sequences which each represent a day of the week. By animating these fantasy engravings on film, the artist was able to bring yet another absurd element to his protest against reason. The quality of the animation is superb, and the entire film was personally approved by Max Ernst.

'Here the surrealist climate is recreated. High spirits and non-conformism are taken to the limits of the fantastic and of plastic inventiveness.'
UNESCO

Director
Jean Desvilles

Narration/Voice
Max Ernst

Original music
Georges Delerue

Award
Quality Award, French
National Film Center

Also available in French

19 minutes
Black and white
Age range 12–adult

Film $623 Rental $189
VHS $89

▲ 560
Max Ernst
The Bride of the Wind

▲ 560
Max Ernst sculpting
in France

◣ 563
Kurt Schwitters
Relief in the Blue Square

562 Max Ernst and the Surrealist Revolution

The program examines the relationship between the revolutionary rhetoric of Surrealist literature and the works of Max Ernst, which are not obviously about revolutionary subjects. The link is the process whereby Ernst and other Surrealists arrived at their imagery, using methods designed to enable the subconscious mind to express itself. Ernst developed the techniques of collage, grattage and frottage, which relied on 'random' events suggesting or establishing images. The Surrealist revolution lies in this organized artistic expression of the subconscious – to use Ernst's own words, in 'the synthesis of objective and subjective life'.

Part of the series
Modern Art, Practices and Debates

Director	**25 minutes**
Jeremy Cooper	**Color**
Presenter	**Age range 18–adult**
David Batchelor	**VHS $99**
Contributors	
Professor Dawn Ades	
Dr Sarah Wilson	
Open University/BBC	

563 Merz: Kurt Schwitters

Born in Hanover in 1887, Kurt Schwitters is one of the major and most individual figures in modern art. In this film we are guided through his career by his son Ernst Schwitters. Thought of from the first as an eccentric celebrity in his home town, he was naturally drawn to the Dada movement through his anarchic attitudes and creations. 'I am Kurt Schwitters and I nail my paintings together!' he exclaimed of his collages and constructions of everyday detritus. His poems were similarly disjointed, often full of furious, meaningless sounds. Being too much of an individualist to be contained within Dada, Schwitters went on to offer his own 'movement', which he called *Merz*, to the world. It was intended to embrace dance, theater, visual art, poetry and performance. Escaping from the Nazis in Germany, Schwitters traveled to Norway, and to Holland, where he collaborated with Theo van Doesburg to promote the notions of modern art. All the while Schwitters was 'recharging the batteries' of his creativity by painting more conventional portraits and landscapes, but like the architect van Doesburg and other artists such as Mondrian, he aspired to create art that would be an all-encompassing, total environment. To this end he constructed a *Merz-bau*, a modern art house, in which the occupant might 'inhabit' an interior entirely constructed of dynamic shapes created by the artist. The film ends with the tragic destruction by bombing of the Hanover *Merz-bau* and later, by fire, of a second one Schwitters created in Norway. The artist, we are told, went into wartime exile in England, where he died. But as we see in 563A, Schwitters continued to work in England on *Merz* works and on his more traditional paintings, and before his death he began a third *Merz-bau* at Ambleside near his Lake District lodgings.

In Norwegian with English subtitles

Director	**28 minutes**
Päl Sletaline	**Color**
Narration	**Subtitled**
Päl Sletaline	**Age range 14–adult**
Arild Fetveit	
Ole Anders Tandberg	**VHS $99**
Wenche Volle	

563A I Build My Time
Kurt Schwitters in England 1940-48

Kurt Schwitters, born in 1887, was one of the most original and poetic of the German Dada artists. He met Hans Arp and Raoul Hausmann in Zurich in 1918 and in the following year founded a Dada group in Hanover. In the same year he invented *Merz* and worked on his first *Merz-bau* (entitled *The Cathedral of Erotic Misery*) in Hanover between 1923–37, which was bombed in 1943. The second, begun in Norway (1937–40), was destroyed by fire in 1951; only the third, on which he was still working at the time of his death, survives in its incomplete form. The film covers the period spent by Kurt Schwitters in England from his arrival as a refugee in 1940 to his death in 1948. Most of this time was spent in Ambleside in the Lake District with Edith Thomas, whom he met in London in 1941. She recalls her meeting with Schwitters, her introduction to his form of Dada and their life together, talking about the way he would find and keep collections of objects to be used in his assemblages, his work as a conventional landscape and portrait artist from which he made a living, and his responses to the people and scenery of the Lakes. The film tells of Schwitters's growing infirmity and his friends' anxiety for his health. Despite this Schwitters began work on his third *Merz-bau*, the transformation of the interior of a building into an integrated work of art, this time in an old barn. Unlike the first and second attempts, this *Merz-bau* used a natural organic style in keeping with its surroundings. The film shows the single completed wall, which was moved to Newcastle University in 1965. Taking up Schwitters's career at the point where *Merz* (563) leaves off, the film gives a sympathetic account of his last years, showing a range of his work from his conventional pictures and poems to his continuing *Merz* collages.

Director	**30 minutes**
Tristram Powell	**Color**
Writer/Narration	**Age range 14–adult**
William Feaver	**Film $763** Rental $199
Original music	**VHS $109**
John Dalbey	
Arts Council of	
Great Britain	

Marcel Duchamp in His Own Words

This documentary on one of the most important artists of the twentieth century opens with the familiar image of Duchamp studying a chess board – he had a lifelong passion for chess. In recordings made in 1968 in Cadaques, Spain, shortly before his death, Duchamp discusses his work, jokes and reminisces, saying, 'I discarded brushes and explored the mind more than the hands.' This informative and charming film is divided into sections: 'The Art' explores Duchamp's early drawing, painting, and Cubist period, including *Nude Descending a Staircase* and *The Bride Stripped Bare by Her Bachelors, Even (Large Glass)*; 'The Object and the Gesture' is concerned with his 'readymade' objects, 'readymade reciprocals,' and Dada period, including humorous puns such as Mona Lisa's 'L H O O Q'; and the final section chronicles the last major work of his life, *Given: 1 The Waterfall, 2 Illuminating Gas.* This mixed-media assemblage of different materials, techniques and forms was erected at the Philadelphia Museum of Art in 1969. Built to be viewed by only one person at a time, it was produced in secret in the last years of Duchamp's life. Lewis Jacobs approaches the artist through a visual style that reflects Duchamp's energy and humor. Using extensive collage, documentation of his work, photographs, and film footage of the artist, he creates a visual complement to Duchamp's fascinating dialog.

'…Duchamp's narration provides a feeling of intimacy; the viewer is treated to his views on various periods in early twentieth-century art…commands the viewer to pay attention and watch carefully so as not to miss anything…an excellent and very important addition for any art library. Just to hear Duchamp's comments alone is worth its purchase. Highly recommended'. *Video Rating Guide for Libraries,* USA

Director	**34 minutes**
Lewis Jacobs	**Color**
Narration/Voice	**Age range 14–adult**
principally by	**Film $763** Rental $199
Marcel Duchamp	**VHS $109**

BROYEUSE DE CHOCOLAT · 1914

Duchamp

One of Marcel Duchamp's most famous works is *The Bride Stripped Bare by Her Bachelors, Even,* not a painting but a transparent construction of wire and painted foil sandwiched between meticulously dirtied plate glass. Duchamp was born in 1887; by the time of his death in the late 1960s he enjoyed a pre-eminent place in the avant-garde art world. The practicing artist Terry Atkinson was only one of those who saw him then as the ultimate revolutionary, anti-establishment artist; but now Atkinson questions that judgment. He uses interviews from the early 1960s featuring Duchamp himself and a review of his whole artistic output to argue that Duchamp did not, in fact, succeed in establishing a viable counter-tradition to Modernism in art – and that Duchamp himself was well aware of the fact.

Part of the series *Modern Art and Modernism: Manet to Pollock*

Director	**21 minutes**
Tony Coe	**Color**
Presenter/Writer	**Age range 18–adult**
Terry Atkinson	**VHS $99**
Open University/BBC	

567 Theater of Memory: The Dali Museum

Theater of Memory shows the unique theater museum in Catalonia that brings together the works of the self-styled Surrealist genius Salvador Dali. It does not present a conventional survey of the artist's career, but aims to show the museum itself as a work of art. Everything in it is important and significant; nothing is incidental. The voice-over is by Dali himself. He speaks of his pride at being Catalan, of his love for his 'muse' Gala, and of his collaborations with the artist Antoni Pitxot, for whom rock and granite are an obsession. Dali guides us (and a mysterious little girl in a sailor-suit who 'shadows' us throughout) past gilded statues and manikins, past curious columns of tyres, and up and down staircases guarded by bizarre automatons. We see a room in which the furnishings create the illusion of a haunting face, and we see Dali's Cadillac, which, he boasts, is one of only six of its kind, others being owned by Roosevelt, Clark Gable and Al Capone. Dali tells us of the alchemist's fascination with creating gold, and of his own parallel obsession with creating the perfect illusion through his immaculate painting technique, by which he claims (presumably in opposition to Expressionism) to have 'saved modern painting from slackness and chaos.'

Director	**32 minutes**
Joan Mallarach	**Color**
Script	**English narration**
Jesus Garay	**Some subtitles**
Joan Mallarach	**Age range 10–adult**
Original music	**VHS $109**
Javier Navarrete	

Also available in Spanish

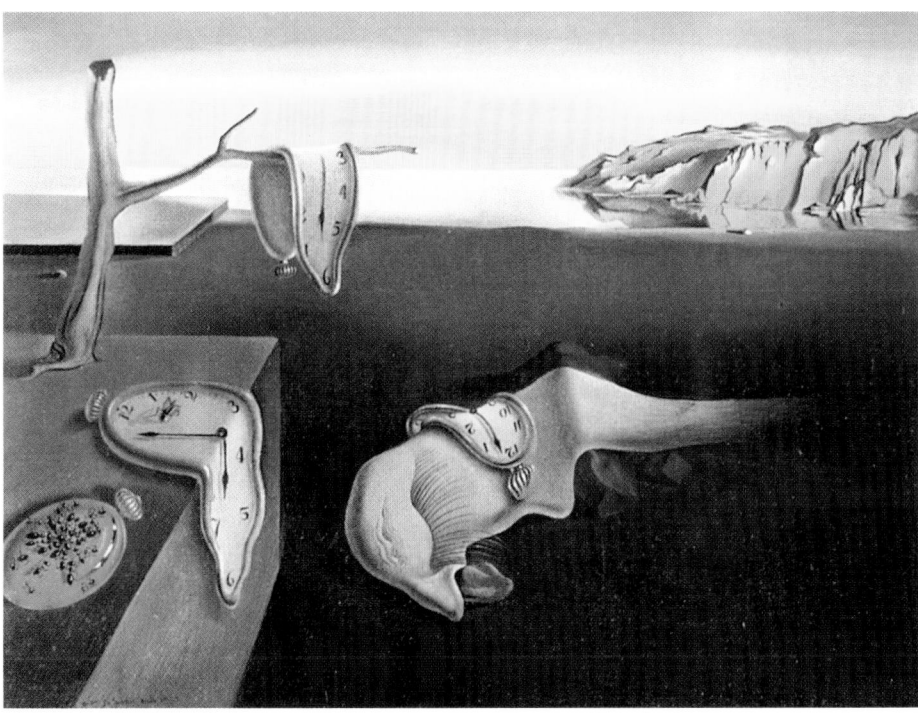

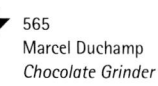
565
Marcel Duchamp
Chocolate Grinder

564
Marcel Duchamp
Nude Descending a Staircase

567C
Salvador Dali
The Persistence of Memory

567B Dali and Surrealism

'As beautiful as the chance encounter of a sewing machine and an umbrella on an operating table,' Surrealism aimed to free the artist from the dictates of moral, aesthetic or intellectual concerns, to create from the unhampered subconscious. During the late 1920s and early 1930s, Salvador Dali became one of the leading Surrealists. But although Dali and the Surrealists shared an interest in the functioning of the subconscious, and in subverting traditional realism, in other ways they diverged widely: some were aiming at an art which could be practiced by anyone, without training, and this was part of their attempt to link the movement with Marxism, whereas Dali continued to base his work on fine technique – and eventually returned to the Catholic Church.

Part of the series *Modern Art and Modernism: Manet to Pollock*

Director	**24 minutes**
Robert Philip	**Color**
Presenter/Writer	**Age range 18–adult**
David Batchelor	**VHS $99**
Open University/BBC	

567C Salvador Dali: His Life through His Paintings

The bizarre and powerful images in the work of Salvador Dali have often been used as the definition of Surrealism, the artistic movement that was born in France in the late 1920s. Such paintings as *The Persistence of Memory* with its soft watches and *The Sacrament of the Last Supper* became widely known as part of the definitive record of twentieth-century art. Salvador Dali introduces us to the magical world of Surrealism, exploring his paintings and explaining the thoughts and experiences that inspired them.

Co-ordination/Script	**45 minutes**
Judith Alanis	**Color**
Research	**Age range 16–adult**
Elisa Y Nava	**VHS $129**
Georgina Hernandez	
Technical directors	
Manuel Garcini	
Pablos Velez	

Also available in Spanish

568 Man Ray
2b Rue Ferou, Paris

This film was made in order to preserve an important aspect of contemporary art – the Parisian studio of the Surrealist artist Man Ray. For twenty-six minutes we are invited to discover what lives on in the silence, under the dust of a place out of time. Since the death of the artist in 1976, everything has remained in place: paintbrushes, canvases, cameras, the darkroom, sculptures, mail, an array of unusual objects, the bedroom. Juliet, Man Ray's muse and companion for over twenty years, remembers. She alone is able to talk about what lives on in the studio. She takes us back to share in his ideas and his friendships – with Duchamp, Giacometti, Breton, Eluard, Paulhan, Dali, and Buñuel. The film is a testimony to a life lived and an art very much alive. It visits, post-mortem, an extraordinary world. The studio was destroyed in December 1989.

Director	26 minutes
François Levy-Kuentz	**Color**
Scenario	**Age range 14–adult**
Stephan Levy-Kuentz	**VHS $99**
François Levy-Kuentz	
Participant	
Juliet Man Ray	

▲ 569
Meret Oppenheim
The Fur-lined Teacup
Photograph Man Ray

▶▶ 568
Man Ray
Ingres' Violin

569 IMAGO Meret Oppenheim

The fame of the Swiss artist Meret Oppenheim rests on one piece, *The Fur-lined Teacup,* which is considered one of the archetypal Surrealist works. By creating it in 1936 at the age of twenty-three, she leapt into the art-history books – but a year later she had retreated from Paris to Basle to study art in order to live up to her worldwide reputation, and plunged into a depression that lasted seventeen years. 'Nobody gives you freedom, you have to take it,' she remarked, and eventually she was able to emerge from the shadow of that teacup and become a mature artist, her links with Dada and Surrealism still alive. Based on Meret Oppenheim's own words and beautifully narrated by Glenda Jackson, this film is an inspiring tribute to a woman who transformed herself after a long crisis.

For more information see page 289

Directors/Writers	**90 minutes**
Pamela Robertson-Pearce	**Color and**
Anselm Spoerri	**black and white**
Narration based on texts,	**Age range 16–adult**
letters, dreams and poems	**Film $1393** Rental $399
by Meret Oppenheim	**VHS $199**
Narrator	
Glenda Jackson	
Awards	
Outstanding Quality Prize,	
The Swiss Film Board	
Gold Apple Award,	
Oakland	
Grand Prix, Mulhouse	
Honorary Mention, Paris	
Also available in French,	
German and Spanish	

570A IMAGO Meret Oppenheim
Part One: 1932–54
Paris of the Surrealists, Creating Crisis and Transformation, Jungian Psychology

An excerpt from 569 (see left), this film begins with Meret Oppenheim leaving home for art school in Paris, seeking 'freedom and independence.' She immediately got to know the Surrealist circle, including Giacometti, Hans Arp and Duchamp, and also a number of other women artists whom she admired very much. For her, Surrealism, although dominated by men, was simply the key to a more liberated life, since the Surrealists accepted women as artists without question. For most of her life the question of self-confidence as an artist (particularly difficult for a woman, she always thought) would be a stumbling-block. Man Ray photographed her, and she fell in love with Max Ernst. Her love was returned, but she felt she had to reject intimacy with Ernst, understanding only later that his maturity as an artist would have stifled her fledgling creativity. In 1936, forced for the first time to try to support herself, she began to design jewelry for the *haute couture.* When she showed Picasso her bracelet of copper lined with sealskin, he remarked that 'many things could be covered in fur,' and this was the inspiration for her fur-lined teacup, which made her famous and was bought by the Museum of Modern Art in New York. But fame was difficult to handle, and from 1937 onward her frequent depressions intensified into a permanent state. For long years she was gripped by a creative crisis. 'I read psychology, primarily Jung,' she said (Jung was a family friend). 'I was looking after my little soul ... During my long crisis, my genius, the animus, the male part of the female soul, that assists the female artist, had abandoned me ... But at the beginning of the fifties, I sensed that things were getting better ...'

Slightly shortened version of the first half of 569

Directors/Writers	**35 minutes**
Pamela Robertson-Pearce	**Color and**
Anselm Spoerri	**black and white**
Narration based on texts,	**Age range 16–adult**
letters, dreams and poems	**VHS $109**
by Meret Oppenheim	
Narrator	
Glenda Jackson	

One Hundred Years of Modern Art, Part Two

This film gives a rudimentary 'exposure' to a broad range art for young audiences; it offers a survey of the painting and sculpture of the period 1907–30. A filming technique was evolved whereby brief instalments of information are followed by long sections without narration, designed to capture the spirit of each style that has been discussed. Within the spectrum of Modernism examined here, Surrealism and Dada are represented by the work of Dali, Ernst and others. Many artists who were not formally members of the Surrealist group are also explored. Film sequences include: Cubism, Picasso, Braque, Independents, Mondrian, Matisse, Expressionism, Rouault, Munch, Abstract, Klee, Chagall, Paul Nash, Picasso's *Guernica.*

Part of the series *Western Art 1700–1970*

Director	**23 minutes**
Anthony Roland	**Color**
Narration	**Age range 12–adult**
Anthony Bertram	**Film $693** Rental $199
Original music	**VHS $99**
Adrian Wagner	

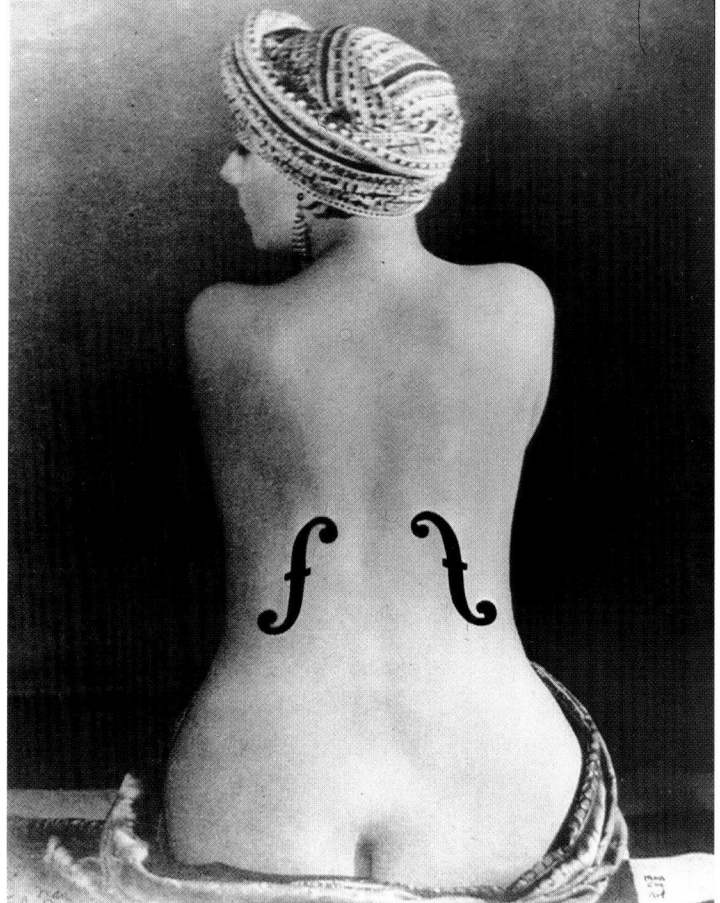

Realms of the Fantastic

This short film about modern fantastic art is not meant to be a didactic or a comprehensive survey. It shows pictures by Arnold Böcklin, Max Klinger, James Ensor, Max Beckmann, Paul Klee, Salvador Dali, Francis Bacon, Paul Delvaux, Yves Tanguy, René Magritte, Konrad Klapheck, and others, and these are set against very personal revelations or fantastic lyrics by the artists themselves. This text collage is preceded by provocative statements about the relationship between art and reality ('Art is what lies beyond reality. But what is reality?') and these are accompanied by unrealistic shots of ordinary, everyday things.

Director	**11 minutes**
Wilhelm Gareis	**Color**
Original music	**Age range 14–adult**
H Heindel	**Film $483** Rental $149
Award	**VHS $69**
Highly Commended,	
German Center for	
Film Classification	

Also available in German

Wilhelm Freddie

Born in Copenhagen, the Danish Surrealist Wilhelm Freddie turned his back on a conventional training at the art academy of his home town, and was largely self-taught as a painter. Ironically he was to return to the college as a master later in life. In the meantime, however, he had become one of the most controversial artists of his generation, and the principal exponent of Surrealism in Scandinavia.

Freddie suffered greatly under the natural conservatism of his country, and especially under the Nazi occupation of Europe. He was vilified for the supposed obscenity of his 'Sex-Surreal' style, and three of his paintings were famously confiscated by Danish authorities and exhibited at the Crime Museum in Copenhagen, where they remained until 1963! Ever a fighter against social and sexual taboos, in the early 1960s Freddie provocatively exhibited identical replica paintings of those that had been confiscated, and this time, when the works were again seized, the public and press outcry was in his favor. Today Freddie is one of the respected 'Old Masters' of European Surrealism.

A Mental State
The Works of Wilhelm Freddie

The quality of the work of Danish artist Wilhelm Freddie was quickly recognized by André Breton and his circle of Paris Surrealists. For years his work was considered scandalous. At the age of eighty-two, however, he looks back at his past without bitterness and recounts his long battle for acceptance by the art world. His works are now exhibited in the most prestigious European and American galleries.

'College art history classes would greatly benefit from this video. It might also be used in general history courses'.
Video Rating Guide for Libraries, USA

In Danish with English subtitles.

Director	**49 minutes**
Per Mossin	**Color**
Narration	**Subtitled**
Per Mossin	**Age range 18–adult**
Wilhelm Freddie	**VHS $129**
Also available in Danish	

The artists in this section come under the category of those whose contributions cannot adequately be understood in terms of style or school. More than any other period in art history, the modern age has been the age of individualism, prizing artists for the novelty or originality of their talents.

1880 – 1970

19
Modern Masters

This section of 23 programs can be purchased on VHS for $2327

Television rights and prices on request

Considerations of individual talent would have been inconceivable among the cathedral masons, manuscript illuminators and painters of church interiors of the Gothic or Romanesque periods, as they would also among the traditional artists of Africa and the Americas. In such traditions, imagery and style are dictated by convention, the artist's job being simply to achieve vitality within the style, and, perhaps, gradually and unconsciously to advance its development.

The notion of unique individuality and of artistic 'masters' of supreme, usually male, creative genius, originates with the Romantic movement, and has informed the standard 'hall of fame' history of modern art. Such ideas have occasionally been challenged, consciously or unconsciously, by movements such as Cubism or Constructivism in which two artists' work may be indistinguishable, or by artists who aspired, whether sincerely, like Mondrian, or somewhat disingenuously, like Duchamp, to anonymous, impersonal statements. Yet even such manifestations as these are still usually discussed in terms of brilliant creative personalities, and much is made of who originated a style, and who merely imitated it. Such deep-rooted ideas are neither to be unquestioningly accepted nor too hastily debunked.

411 Renoir

Renoir's greatest fame came from his association with the French Impressionist painters of the later nineteenth century. The Impressionists captured their immediate surroundings in richly colored, fluently sketched canvases often executed out of doors rather than in the studio. But Renoir's long career encompassed a wide range of styles and there is a world of difference between the ambitious subject pictures he painted in the 1860s and the glowing nudes that he produced in the final years before his death in 1919. This video explores the full range of Renoir's extraordinary talent through detailed photography and an illuminating script by John House, one of the selectors of the Renoir exhibition seen in London, Paris and Boston.

Script	**28 minutes**
John House	**Color**
Narrator	**Age range 14–adult**
Sir Anthony Quayle	**VHS $99**

▮ 535, page 151B
Pablo Picasso
Guernica, detail

▼ 500
Wassily Kandinsky
Cossacks

440 Paula Modersohn-Becker

Paula Modersohn-Becker was the most important woman artist of her day and one of the main forerunners of Expressionism. She lived in Worpswede, in the fens north-east of Bremen in Germany. Little water-courses often dividing, a sand-dune set on the flat marsh, brown moorland, black canals – the power of the landscape is central to her work; it roused in her the faculty to see things as simple, big and monumental. 'If one only could, one should write down the people and the landscape in a sign-language … the great simplicity of form, that is the wonder.' Her diary, which became famous for the way it documented her development, is used for this film's narration. 'I feel how my work startles people. Still … it is the vividness with which one grasps the object which makes beauty in art.'

Director	**12 minutes**
Friedhelm Heyde	**Color**
Awards	**Age range 14–adult**
International Status,	**Film $553** Rental $169
German Government	**VHS $79**
Highly Commended,	
German Center for	
Film Classification	

Also available in German

500 Kandinsky

One of the great innovators of modern art, the Russian Wassily Kandinsky opened the way to non-figurative painting; even now his work continues to influence young painters. At home in Russia his main visual influences had been icons and the naïve paintings and decorations on furniture of local craftsmen. At first, studying in Munich, he painted rather academic pictures, but as he progressed his colors became more violent – no longer the colors of nature, but the colors that seemed to grow out of the feelings aroused by the subject he was seeking to paint. One evening Kandinsky returned to his studio in twilight. Against his easel stood a marvelous painting, full of brilliant forms and enchanting colors. Who could have made it? Looking closely, he realized it was one of his own landscapes, which had fallen on its side. 'Now I know for certain,' he wrote in great excitement, 'that the object spoiled my pictures.' Then began the search for symbols – for example, three parallel lines bent near the top represent three horses pulling a Russian sledge. The symbolic line takes the place of the object. Colors and lines alone remain. Only a genius could have been so inspired by a simple accident, thereby revolutionizing art and giving birth to abstract painting.

'…has the rare quality of knowing how to present the pictures within their own context'
UNESCO

For more information see page 125

Director	**15 minutes**
HG Zeiss	**Color**
Narration	**Age range 12–adult**
Susanne Carwin	**Film $553** Rental $169
Original music	**VHS $79**
Winfried Zillig	

Awards
Silver Lion, Venice
Bronze Medal, Brussels
Outstanding Merit, Berlin
First Prize, Cultural Film,
Mannheim International
Recognition, Mannheim
Diplôme d'Honneur,
Cannes
Highly Commended,
German Center for
Film Classification

Also available in German

509 **'I'm Mad, I'm Foolish, I'm Nasty'**
A Self-portrait of James Ensor

There are two fascinating things about James Ensor: that he was a great painter, perhaps a genius, with a singular way of looking at his fellow human beings, and that his enormous talent apparently burnt itself out without trace before he was forty, although he lived to be eighty-nine. He was born in 1860 in Ostend, of an English father and a Flemish mother, and he lived in Ostend all his life, apart from three years training at the Brussels Academy, 'that blinkered establishment.' He never married, and he stayed with his mother until the age of fifty-five: she gave him money for paint, but she never appreciated what he did with it. The demon-ridden, grotesque world of his paintings is peopled with carnival figures, skeletons and masked men – but the masks are true faces, showing the depravity which is normally hidden in everyday life. Critics labeled him 'mad, foolish and nasty.' When his first major exhibition, in Paris in 1898, was a failure, it seemed to break something in him. He went on painting and drawing all his life, but produced nothing to equal what had gone before. In his old age, years after his creative powers were at their peak, Ensor achieved great acclaim, and he is seen as an initiator of Expressionism. The commentary of this film is largely taken from his own writings, and the music is based on his 'pantomime-ballet,' *The Gamut of Love,* for he was also an amateur musician.

'…impressive video…approaches Ensor's work as he might have approached the subject himself…leads us directly into the personality of the artist, discovering the imagery…intercutting a feast of rich details from paintings and sketches with photos of the artist at the same locations occupied by his subjects…a remarkable and poetic portrait of the artist who prefigured Expressionism. The producer's vision and Ensor's vision blend into one unified whole. Its lean, economical editing lets every shot add meaning to the next. This is one of the finest videos on an artist you're likely to see. It is highly recommended.'
Video Rating Guide for Libraries, USA

For more information see page 110

Director/Script Luc de Heush	**55 minutes** **Color**
Texts James Ensor extracts from letters speeches and orations	**Age range 14–adult** **Film $1043** Rental $299 **VHS $149**
Ensor's voice John Boyle	
Narrator Richard Wells	
Original music Denis Pousseur	
Awards Best Documentary, Belgium Selected European Cinema, Berlin Directors' Grand Prix, UNESCO Paris	
Also available in Dutch and French	

▼ 509
James Ensor in his studio, 1946

▲ 520
Fernand Léger
The Discs in the City

Fernand Léger

In the world of Fernand Léger, machines
are the essential subject matter. After his
country childhood he found the noise and
grinding struggle of city life exciting but
oppressive, so much so that at times the
machine age seems to become an obsession
in his work. In the 1914–18 war he fought
at the front – until he was gassed – and
was overwhelmed by another kind of
mechanical oppression, the tank and the
howitzer, the cannon and the airplane,
all of which appear fragmented in his work.
He painted objects in space without
perspective or support: 'the real subject is
the object.' Later in life he began to free
himself from his fear of the machine,
and he painted, in brilliant colors, humans
and animals attempting to struggle clear
of the geometry of the mechanized world.
At first machinists and mechanics, angular
and cubic figures people his paintings,
but later came his great series of works
on the circus, with all its pageantry and
humanity. Art had conquered the machine.
As a personal declaration combining the
writings as well as the visual work of the
painter, this film is a work of art in itself,
leading the viewer to understand Léger's
search for artistic liberation.

Director	**14 minutes**
Jacques Berthier	**Color**
Narration	**Age range 12–adult**
Fernand Léger	**Film $553** Rental $169
Jacques Berthier	**VHS $79**
Original music	
Marian Kouzay	
Also available in French	

524 Matisse

Henri Matisse's brilliantly colored works are to be found in nearly every museum of modern art throughout the world, and his reputation in Modernist art history is second to none. We examine three paintings in particular – *Bathers by a River, Le Luxe 1* and *Decorative Figure on an Ornamental Background* – to see how he rose to this pre-eminence. We also hear how Modernist art historians categorize his work – and ask whether we should always agree with them.

Part of the series *Modern Art and Modernism: Manet to Pollock*

Director	24 minutes
Charles Cooper	Color
Presenter/Writer	Age range 18–adult
TJ Clarke	VHS $99
Open University/BBC	

527 Nicholson, Wallis and St Ives

The small and charming town of St Ives in Cornwall, England, is still a gathering place for artists today. It played an important part in the life of the English abstract painter Ben Nicholson, who was particularly influenced by his discovery of the local 'primitive' painter Alfred Wallis. Nicholson's own work was geometrically inspired and owed a lot to Cubism; Wallis's was naïvely figurative and descriptive. And yet, paradoxically, his contact with Wallis helped Nicholson to move toward increasingly abstract and formal art.

Part of the series *Modern Art and Modernism: Manet to Pollock*

Director	24 minutes
Nick Levinson	Color
Presenter/Writer	Age range 18–adult
Charles Harrison	VHS $99
Open University/BBC	

 524
Henri Matisse
Luxe, Calme et Volupté

541
Hans Arp
Colored Wooden Forms

541
Auguste Herbin
*Continuous Movement,
Inverted, Internal*

518 Paul Klee

Klee's influential position among the great painters of this century is unique. He neither founded a new style nor belonged to a modern movement; his achievement was not so much concerned with the manner of painting, but with its content. The script of this film was written by Professor Will Grohmann, a personal friend of Paul Klee and the leading authority on his work. It shows selected examples taken from nine thousand works created by Klee, and groups them together not chronologically but by subject matter. The commentary describes Klee's life, his relationships and the different stages in his artistic career – *Blaue Reiter*, the Bauhaus, the art academy in Düsseldorf, the end of his life in Berne. Interpretation is kept as concise as possible, giving the viewer time to compare the different pictures with the suggested interpretations and so gain personal and direct access to Klee's work.

For more information see pages 126 and 135

Director	30 minutes
Georgia van der Rohe	Color
Writer/Narration	Age range 14–adult
Will Grohmann	Film $693 Rental $199
Also available in German	VHS $99

528 Klee and the Munich Revolution

Paul Klee was a Swiss painter and etcher who described his art of free fantasy as 'taking a line for a walk.' He was also an impassioned teacher and published a great deal on the theory of art. Here we concentrate on Klee's work, his writings and the historical background to his involvement with, and subsequent withdrawal from, the Munich revolution of 1918-19. In particular we examine the contrast between his illustrations for the revolutionary *Potsdamer Platz* and his painting *Young Proletarian*, all done in 1919, and his fairytale paintings and work for *Munich Leaves*, which witness his withdrawal from politics.

Part of the series *Modern Art and Modernism: Manet to Pollock*

Director	25 minutes
Nick Levinson	Color
Presenter/Writer	Age range 18–adult
Karl Werckmeister	VHS $99
University of California	
Open University/BBC	

The period between the wars seems, at
first sight, to be a meager period for art.
The First World War had left Europe
virtually bloodless – how many future
geniuses disappeared in the trenches?
On the other hand there were new realities
in a changed world that artists were going
to have to face – the euphoria of victory,
and the boom in technical progress. Many
of the great artists were already on the
scene: Pablo Picasso, for example, and
Henri Matisse, who was well advanced in
his pursuit of line and form when the war
broke out; he was painting *Piano Lesson*
in 1916, the year of Verdun. Forced to turn
his attention to the realities threatened by
humankind, his vision became less severe.
But Matisse is not typical: the life of the
Montparnasse-centered Paris School of the
1920s and 1930s – almost all of whom were
foreigners – was spare and stricken by a
kind of joyful poverty. Montparnasse had
cheap hotels, studios for rent – and other
painters, already there. In many ways it
was a golden age: the same café table
might hold Kisling, or Picasso, together
with other personalities such as the
famous fawn-eyed model Kiki or Amadeo
Modigliani. Then there was Soutine, the
painter of fermentation and love, and the
Russian Jew Marc Chagall, who conceived
his subjects on several levels at once.
Above all there was diversity – perhaps
impelled by the Depression and the inner
knowledge that institutions weren't
working. Le Corbusier and Ozenfant
tried to combine geometry and figures.
A new movement, Purism, attempted to
go beyond the Cubists. Another minor
school centered on the mystical association
of the circle and the square, an ancient
Chinese idea. Then Hitler marched into the
Sudetenland and the new reality was with
them all. The film also features the work of
Pascin, Foujita, Léger, Gorin, Herbin, Helion,
Arp, Dali and others.

Part of the series
The Adventure of Modern Art

Director	**53 minutes**
Carlos Vilardebo	**Color**
Writers/Narration	**Age range 15–adult**
André Parinaud	**Film $1043** Rental $299
Carlos Vilardebo	**VHS $149**

Also available in French

19 Modern Masters

151

525 Matisse and the Problem of Expression

This program focuses on a number of works by Henri Matisse, for whom expressive feeling was the central function of art. Charles Harrison asks how the potential for expression is instilled into painting – how the response of the spectator is conditioned so that certain emotional states rather than others are evoked.

Part of the series
Modern Art, Practices and Debates

Director	25 minutes
Nick Levinson	Color
Presenter	Age range 18–adult
Charles Harrison	VHS $99
Open University/BBC	

547 Public Murals in New York

At the height of the Depression in the USA, Franklin D Roosevelt was elected president. As part of the New Deal program, the Federal Art Project employed artists to paint public murals. There were over 200 in New York alone. The program visits the sites of some of the murals: *The Pursuit of Happiness* by Vertis Hayes in Harlem Hospital, showing phases of life among Negro people in Africa and America; *The Development of Medicine* by William Palmer (two parts remain) in Queens General Hospital, New York; the only abstract work, done for the Williamsburgh Housing Project but now removed to the Brooklyn Museum; James Brooks' *Flight* at La Guardia Airport; and James Michael Newell's *The History of Western Civilization* at Evander Childs High School.

Part of the series
Modern Art, Practices and Debates

Director	25 minutes
GD Jayalakshmi	Color
Presenter	Age range 18–adult
Dr Jonathan Harris	VHS $99
Open University/BBC	

551 On Pictures and Paintings

Charles Harrison conducts us on a tour of selected works in the Tate Gallery, London, exploring different ways of thinking about how works of art represent and, in that sense, have meaning. We tend to expect paintings to be pictures, even though this expectation is not always justified (Kandinsky). Some works represent without being pictures at all (abstracts – Poliakoff). Harrison considers what makes a painting 'modern', starting with Cézanne and moving through Braque, Grosz, Dali, Miró, Jack Smith and Léger, to show how the illusionistic devices of painting become decoupled from the rational compositional themes within which they had previously been controlled.

Part of the series
Modern Art, Practices and Debates

Director	25 minutes
Jeremy Cooper	Color
Presenter	Age range 18–adult
Charles Harrison	VHS $99
Open University/BBC	

▲ 525
Henri Matisse
The Snail

534 **Picasso's Collages 1912–13:**
The Problem of Interpretation

This program is structured around two
interviews with art historians who offer
radically different interpretations of
Picasso's collages – Patricia Leighten
and Rosalind Krauss – and examines
what we learn from comparing two
contrasting systems of historical and
critcial explanation.

Part of the series
Modern Art, Practices and Debates

Director	**25 minutes**
Nick Levinson	**Color**
Presenter	**Age range 18–adult**
Francis Frascina	**VHS $99**
Open University/BBC	

535 **Picasso's Guernica**

Francis Frascina, lecturer in art history at
the Open University, discusses one of
Picasso's best-known works, *Guernica*
(1936). Why did Picasso paint this vast work
representing the destruction of the town of
Guernica during the Spanish Civil War?
How did Picasso tackle a major political,
propagandist work for international
exhibition? What means were at his disposal
and how did he use them? As a work of art
and a political statement, was *Guernica*
successful and what does it signify today?

Part of the series
Modern Art, Practices and Debates

Director	**25 minutes**
Nick Levinson	**Color**
Presenter	**Age range 18–adult**
Francis Frascina	**VHS $99**
Open University/BBC	

531 Picasso: The Forceful Gaze
The Power of his Last Paintings

Pablo Picasso's most famous legacy, *La Mira Fuerte* (*The Forceful Gaze*), was made at the end of his career. The painter and his model in the seclusion of his studio, a symbol of sexuality and creativity, is the tragic story of his last wife, Jacqueline, who was expected to be model, muse and wife, and who was subjected to all the mental and physical metamorphoses of his paintings. *La Mira Fuerte* shows the view that Picasso eventually took of himself, in the figure of the old bearded artist who appeared, like a leitmotif, in numerous paintings. His friends, the writer Pierre Daix and the photographer David Douglas Duncan, speak about Picasso's untiring urge to explore new paths. Viewers are taken to Mougins and Vallauris in the south of France, where Picasso rediscovered his native Spanish culture, and, of course, to Barcelona to see paintings, engravings and sculptures from this brilliant artist's final, and little known, creative period.

Director	26 minutes
Michel Le Bayon	**Color**
Also available in French	**Age range 14–adult**
	VHS $99

530 Picasso: Romancero du Picador
Pen and Wash Drawings of the Bullfight

Based on Picasso's most Spanish series of drawings, this short film is a fusion of art and music. The drawings depict the bullfight, that confrontation between life and death, between man and beast. They show the mounted picador whose *picas* test the bull's bravery, the graceful and heroic matador, the public hooting and applauding in turn. Picasso, Spanish-born, depicts his types with the sardonic eye of a Goya. Dissolves and camera movement trace the vigorous drawings, blending with the clamor of the arena, piercing flamenco coplas and dances accompanied by guitar and castanets. This creates a sense of action in a film which requires minimal narrative. The brilliance of Picasso, the Spanish spirit and the drama of the bullfight merge.

For more information see pages 225 and 241

Director	13 minutes
Jean Desvilles	**Black and white**
Narration	**Age range 12–adult**
Michel Leiris	**Film $553** Rental $169
Original music	**VHS $79**
Georges Delerue	
Awards	
Grand Prix, Vancouver	
Quality Award, French	
National Film Center	
Also available in French	

532 Picasso: A Portrait
The Man behind the Legend

The whole world knows Picasso the genius, but has never been able to agree about Picasso the man. Was he monster or oracle, malevolent or full of wisdom? In 1951 the director Edward Quinn, working as a photographer in the south of France, met Picasso and was allowed to take his picture. Picasso liked the results and gave Quinn permission to visit and photograph him regularly at home and at work, while he continued painting, drawing, sculpting or relaxing with his family and friends. None of the numerous sessions was set up – Picasso simply carried on with his own life and Quinn observed without interfering. The result is this diary of images, revealing as nothing else could Picasso's fascinatingly vital personality and the way he drew on his everyday experience for artistic inspiration.

Director/Writer	60 minutes
Edward Quinn	**Black and white**
Narrator	**Age range 14–adult**
Roland Penrose	**Film $903** Rental $269
Also available in French	**VHS $129**

533 Picasso the Sculptor

Pablo Picasso was born in Malaga, Spain, in 1881, and studied art in Barcelona and Madrid. He moved to Paris in 1904 and rapidly became known as an artist with outstanding innovative powers. Between 1908 and 1914 he developed Cubism in close collaboration with Georges Braque. The value of this film is that it records the comprehensive exhibition of Picasso's sculptures at the Tate Gallery, London, works rarely seen together. It includes works from all periods and in a variety of materials and styles: figurative heads and figures in bronze; sheet metal, wire and tube constructions made with the Spanish sculptor Julio González; a series of massive modelled heads with exaggerated features, dating from the 1930s; the witty assemblages of found materials (the *Bull's Head*, the *Baboon*); ceramic sculptures of the late 1940s and 1950s; and the 'folded' works of the 1960s, in which sheet metal is used as paper. The commentary, written by Sir Roland Penrose, and accompanied by photographs of Picasso at work, describes the various influences – African art, Cubism, Mediterranean fables – on the sculptor and offers some personal interpretations. The film, above all, is a celebration of Picasso's unique ability to transform ordinary materials, even household objects, into poetic statements.

Director/Writer
Roland Penrose

Narrator
Jill Balcon

Arts Council of
Great Britain

27 minutes
Color
Age range 14–adult
Film $693 Rental $199
VHS $99

540 Picasso: Joie de Vivre

Picasso's joy in living is revealed in the Picasso Museum at Antibes. In the summer of 1946, the whole of Europe was recovering from the strain of the war years. Picasso was staying in the south of France where the medieval and long-empty castle at Antibes was offered to him with the idea of making it a permanent Picasso museum. For four months the master worked at sculpture, painting, pottery and covering the walls of the castle with vast murals, each a paean of praise to the new life coming to fruition about him.

Director
Jacques Berthier

Narration
Henri Perruchot
Jacques Berthier

Original music
Pierre Spiers

Also available in French

12 minutes
Color
Age range 12–adult
Film $483 Rental $149
VHS $69

◀◀ 530
Pablo Picasso
Picador looking at
a woman

◤◣ 533
Pablo Picasso
Guitar

▼ 540
Pablo Picasso
The Faun

543 Chagall

The work of Marc Chagall is justly popular for his images of lovers, flowers, musicians and clowns. It also has another side: his response to the world outside the studio, to suffering, to war and a wide cultural heritage. This video-recording of a major retrospective exhibition provides an opportunity to experience the full range of Chagall's art. It includes his mysterious student pictures from St Petersburg, poetic images from pre-war Paris and domestic scenes from further years in Russia. Whereas the early life and work is seen in chronological sequence, the later work is explored by theme and encompasses stained glass and etchings as well as oil paintings. The video not only records an important exhibition, but evokes the special poetic quality of the artist and his work.

Director	28 minutes
Ian Morrison	Color
Script	Age range 14–adult
Susan Compton	VHS $99

546 Edward Hopper

This film is based on a 'search' undertaken by the film-maker into the life and work of the painter Edward Hopper. It uses conversations with Gail Levin, Curator of the Hopper Collection at the Whitney Museum, New York, and author of an exhaustive biography of Hopper, an archive recording of an interview with Hopper and his wife Jo, and a close examination of Hopper's paintings. It visits the places of significance to him – his birthplace in Nyack, his studios at Cape Cod and in Washington Square. It constructs a biography of an artist whose career was, in many ways, an exemplary American success story, both the man and his art sustaining America's image of itself. The film tells of Hopper's visits to Paris, his first studio in New York, his work as a commercial illustrator and his growing concern with the representation of light, but concludes that the biographical approach is limited – the paintings are not direct images of places he knew, they are events in their own right. Looking closely at the paintings and the sketches that Hopper made for them, the film demonstrates that they are constructed landscapes, conveying the idea, not the actuality, of a place – a cinema, a gas station, a hotel room. Similarly the figures are not individuals but types, caught in poses of inaction. Compared with the work of other American artists, like Norman Rockwell and Walker Evans, these scenes are full of contradictions, commenting on, not participating in, the dynamism of city life. The film-maker suggests that these paintings invoke a sense of narrative, like a movie still. The figures seem to be in a relationship to each other, but their story remains hidden and enigmatic, for there is no 'action' to supply this.

Director/Writer	47 minutes
Ron Peck	Color
Narration	Age range 15–adult
Ron Peck	Film $903 Rental $269
Gail Levin	VHS $129
Original music	
David Graham Ellis	
Arts Council of	
Great Britain	

553 One Hundred Years of Modern Art, Part Three

This film gives a rudimentary 'exposure' to a broad range of art for young audiences; it offers a survey of the painting, sculpture and architecture of the period 1930–70. A filming technique was evolved whereby brief instalments of information are followed by long sections without narration, designed to capture the spirit of each style that has been discussed. Film sequences include: Picasso, Sutherland, Bacon, Matisse, Abstract Expressionism, Action Painting, Pollock, Rothko, Figurative Painting, Pop Art, Mixed Media, Kinetic Art, Mobiles, Calder, Illusion, Maillol, Brancusi, Giacometti, González, Moore, Hepworth, Futurism, Dada, Constructivism, Gabo, Frank Lloyd Wright, Le Corbusier, Mies van der Rohe, Alvar Aalto.

Part of the series *Western Art 1700–1970*

Director	26 minutes
Anthony Roland	Color
Narration	Age range 12–adult
Anthony Bertram	Film $693 Rental $199
Original music	VHS $99
Adrian Wagner	

▲ 546
Edward Hopper
Hotel Room

▶ 553
Naum Gabo
Head Number 2

▶▶ 543
Marc Chagall
The Fiddler

20 Modern and Contemporary Sculptors

Increasingly, since the Renaissance, oil paintings on canvas have come to be thought of as the typical artwork – the most important medium, next to which sculpture (along with other important media – see section 22) has been seen as a secondary activity. Sculpture is even at times considered to be, in the words of one modern painter, 'something you bump into when stepping back for a better view of a painting.' Clearly this view is unfair.

This section of
15 programs can be
purchased as
14 titles on
VHS for $1286 plus
1 title on film for $623

Television rights and
prices on request

Sculpture – the making of three-dimensional objects – appears to be an activity as old as, if not older than, flat image-making among human beings, and one which, having produced examples that survive better from antiquity than paintings, exercised the greatest influence on artists from the Renaissance and after – painters included.

In the eighteenth and nineteenth centuries sculpture was admittedly more subject than painting to academicism, providing as it could grand monuments and statuary. Yet in the modern period artists returned to sculpture both as a route to authentic traditionalism (note Henry Moore's or Adam-Tessier's relationship to Egyptian, classical and other ancient sculpture) and conversely as a route forward from familiar artistic modes into the bizarre or challenging (see Tinguely's machines or Mark Prent's shocking 'environments').

519 Dina in the King's Garden
Maillol Sculpture

The sculptor Aristide Maillol was born in the South of France, a man of the Mediterranean, which is itself associated with classical and ancient civilization. He studiously turned his back on the turmoil of our age, reasoning that an attempt to reinterpret the old myths in a twentieth-century manner was perhaps the best way of coming to terms with his own times. As his theme he chose opulent earth goddesses, rich luxuriant mother figures, nubile country girls. He modeled these women in lifelong variations on the theme of natural bounty. One of his most famous models was Dina, and now a great number of bronze statues of Dina are to be seen in the Tuileries gardens of the Louvre, the former royal palace in Paris. Nothing more romantic and poetic can be imagined than these great bronze women of the South, redolent with heat and lazy passion, in the snow-chilled gardens of the North. There is no narration.

Director	**10 minutes**
Dominique Delouche	**Color**
Music	**Age range 12–adult**
Richard Strauss	**Film $483** Rental $149
Award	**VHS $69**
Quality Award, French	
National Film Center	

533 Picasso the Sculptor

It has often been claimed that the most important modern sculpture has been created by artists who were also, or even primarily, painters – Degas, Matisse, Derain and others. This impression has been strengthened by the ever-dominant figure of Picasso, who punctuated his long career with bouts of energetic sculpture-making, almost as time off from painting. Certainly his three-dimensional work, though it relates sometimes to the collage concerns of his pictures, can be deliberately lightweight as well as heavyweight. His pieces range from spindley frameworks of welded rods to huge, bulbous faces built up in plaster and cast in bronze, and humorous farm animals which have all the vitality of folk art. The sculptures sometimes have an almost throw-away charm, as in the famous *Bull's Head* evoked by a bicycle saddle and handlebars. The artist liked to think of the piece being thrown on to a scrap heap where someone might salvage it for bicycle parts – and then the creative cycle would be complete.

Director/Writer	**27 minutes**
Roland Penrose	**Color**
Narrator	**Age range 14–adult**
Jill Balcon	**Film $693** Rental $199
Arts Council of	**VHS $99**
Great Britain	

605, page 164
Andy Goldsworthy
Hazel leaves
Each stitched to next with grass stalks
Gently pulled by the river
Out of a rock pool
Floating downstream
Low water

533
Pablo Picasso
Woman with Pram

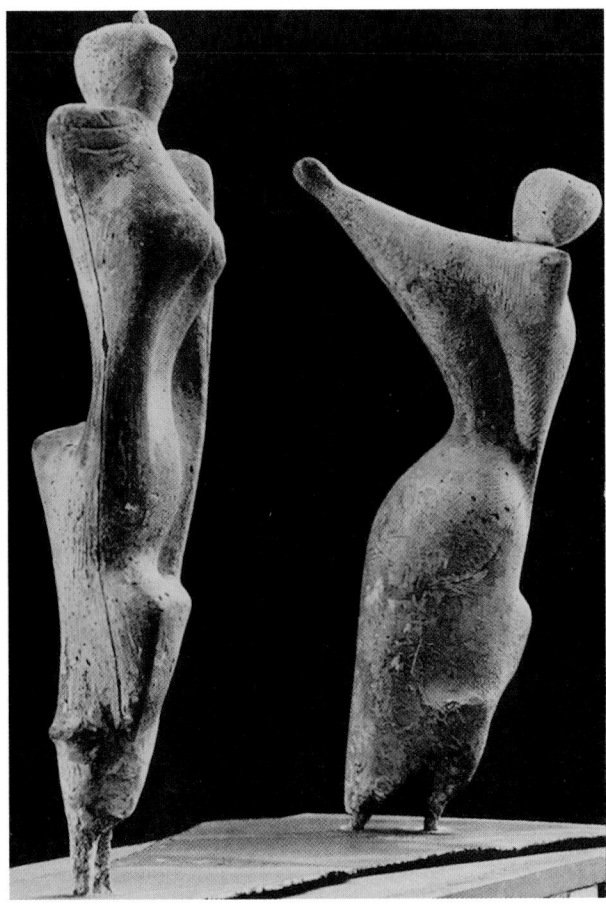

Alexander Calder

Alexander Calder (1898–1976) was, before the American Abstract Expressionists achieved fame, America's best-known modern artist. His constructed sculptures, whether fixed 'stabiles' or moving 'mobiles', were colorful, witty, inventive and celebratory. Visiting Paris between the wars, Calder became associated with Dada and Surrealist artists such as Duchamp, Tanguy and Arp, and with strong abstract or near-abstract artists like Miró, Léger and Mondrian. He also remained very American, however, and in contact with American artists such as Steinberg.

623   Smithson and Serra: Beyond Modernism?

Robert Smithson and Richard Serra both believed that sculpture should have a dialog with its environment. Two sculptures of Richard Serra are shown in an urban environment – *Fulcrum* in the Broadgate development at Liverpool Street in London and *Tilted Arc* in New York – the latter has since been destroyed. *Spin Out*, a tribute to Robert Smithson, is in a rural site at the Kroller-Muller Museum in Holland. Robert Smithson's work is represented by *Broken Circle, Spiral Hill*, which is in a disused quarry in north Holland. Smithson, who died in 1973, greatly influenced Serra's work.

Part of the series
Modern Art, Practices and Debates

Director	**25 minutes**
GD Jayalakshmi	**Color**
Presenter	**Age range 18–adult**
Paul Wood	**VHS $99**
Participant	
Richard Serra	

Open University/BBC

620   Sculpture 58, the Story of a Creation
Bernhard Heiliger

In his Berlin studio, Bernhard Heiliger traces the designs for the large sculpture group to be positioned outside the German Pavilion at the Brussels World Fair. We follow the development from the clay maquette (small model) to the original plaster model. Apart from the physical handicraft involved, we also become aware of the artist's struggle for expression. This is a film without narration, an unsurpassable example of the type of film which shows the artist in the process of creation, ideal for helping the viewer to understand the structure of a sculpture.

Director	**12 minutes**
Herbert Seggelke	**Color**
Original music	**Age range 12–adult**
Boris Blacher	**Film $553** Rental $169
Awards	**VHS $79**
Honor Award, Bergamo	
Honor Award, Cork	
Culture Award,	
German Government	
Highly Commended,	
German Center for	
Film Classification	

621   Calder's Circus

Alexander Calder's fascination with the circus began in his mid-twenties, when he published illustrations in a New York journal of Barnum and Bailey's Circus, for which he held a year's pass. It was in Paris in 1927 that he created the miniature circus celebrated in this film – tiny wire performers, ingeniously articulated to walk tightropes, dance, lift weights and engage in acrobatics in the ring. The Parisian avant-garde would gather in Calder's studio to see the circus in operation. It was, as critic James Johnson Sweeney noted, 'a laboratory in which some of the most original features of his later work were to be developed.' This film exudes the great personal charm of Calder himself, moving and working the tiny players like a ringmaster, while his wife winds up the gramophone in the background. *The Circus* is now housed at the Whitney Museum in New York.

Director	**19 minutes**
Carlos Vilardebo	**Color**
Presenter	**Age range 5–adult**
Alexander Calder	**Film $693** Rental $199
	VHS $99

620
Bernhard Heiliger
Two figures

621
Alexander Calder
Calder's Circus, 1926–31
detail of installation

580 **Henry Moore: London 1940–42**
The Series of Shelter Drawings

A montage, using documentary material filmed during the war, shows the beginnings of an air attack and Londoners entering shelters. From the silent deserted streets, the film moves underground into the world of Henry Moore's shelter drawings. People sit along subway platforms, looking after their children, settling down for the night, sleeping in bunks and on the floor. Above ground London burns. Henry Moore used the eye of a sculptor in portraying the stolidity and enduring patience of a besieged people. This film brings together a unique series of drawings which are some of the most remarkable achievements of an artist during wartime. Eliminating all narration, it explores, on several metaphoric levels, the very nature of human consciousness and creativity. With the image of people descending, before a blitz, to spend a night in the subterranean, artery-like tubes of the subway system, the film draws us into the artist's inner mind, where the creative process occurs, and also into subconscious levels of experience – a dream world where fears and anxieties coexist with a curious stillness. We gain an insight here into how Moore's interests related for a while to those of the Surrealists. The film is calm, yet charged, an atmosphere complemented by the delicate yet tense music of Marius Constant.

Remarkable in the film is the extent to which the illusionism of the drawing technique is sustained even under the camera's close-up scrutiny, so that we appear to be *entering* the tunnels. The organic forms of these caverns echo, but in hollow 'negative' as it were, the forms of the artist's figures: it is as if we were *inside* a Moore sculpture. We think of catacombs in which the faithful of previous eras took shelter. And the tangled lines of Moore's drawings resemble the barbed-wire of the battlefield.

'…pictures of exceptional quality. Silently the film demonstrates that great art can easily dispense with commentary, and the value of the drawings is thus enhanced. The newsreel sequences at the beginning and the end contribute in producing an impressive atmosphere.'
UNESCO

'…captures these drawings and their detail with great mastery…the editing is outstanding. With the aid of music which is very impressive and, at the same time, discreet, the film has succeeded in reproducing the essential feature of these drawings, which is not dependent on the representation of terror itself, nor on any particular milieu or the like, but solely on the greatness and dignity of man, as preserved in these catacombs of terror.'
German Center for Film Classification

'A revelation: a strength and force disclosed, a mastery made clear'
Sunday Times, London

'It's uncanny, Anthony Roland, the master of the montage and dissolve…The film melts moment by moment into a living and breathing homage to the people of London.'
Michigan Education Journal

For more information see pages 221 and 290

Director
Anthony Roland

Original music
Marius Constant

Awards
Silver Cup, Salerno
Honor Award, Vancouver
Certificate of Honor,
Leipzig
Special Excellence,
Mannheim
Exceptional Merit,
Yorkton
Quality Award and
Quality Prize, French
National Film Center
Highly Commended,
German Center for
Film Classification
Chriss Award, Columbus

12 minutes
Black and white
Age range 14–adult

Film $553 Rental $169
VHS $79

Anthony Caro

Anthony Caro is considered by many to be the most significant sculptor of his generation. Born in 1924 near London, Caro worked as an assistant in the early 1950s to Henry Moore. Increasingly Caro became interested in constructing abstract sculptures from scrap metal, in the tradition of Julio González, Picasso and the American David Smith, rather than in carving or clay modeling. He formed important contacts with the American Abstract artists of his day (see section 16), and with formalist critics, such as Clement Greenberg, who were their champions. Not unlike Henry Moore, Anthony Caro has come to be thought of as an official public sculptor in Britain, producing ever-larger works for prestige sites worldwide. He has continued undaunted by the loss of confidence, in some quarters, in purely formalist Abstraction, and his status as an 'institution' in contemporary art has continued to be confirmed by major monographs and museum retrospectives.

625 Anthony Caro

A combination of interviews with the internationally famous sculptor Anthony Caro and material shot at an Arts Council exhibition at the Serpentine Gallery, London. This was the first European retrospective covering Caro's mature work, from 1969 to 1984, and the first time any of the thirty-one important sculptures had been seen in Britain. Included are examples of the brightly painted steel sculptures, several monumental sculptures from welded units of cast and plate steel, and a representative group of smaller table and floor pieces in various media. The exhibition and the video demonstrate the range and beauty of Caro's work, which has been acclaimed as the most significant achievement in sculpture since the days of Abstract Expressionism.

'This should have much appeal to the general audience as well as the true art lover. Because Anthony Caro is not very well known to American viewers, this might be a means of expanding the number of people who appreciate his work. Recommended.'
Video Rating Guide for Libraries, USA

Director	26 minutes
Brian Taylor	Color
	Age range 12–adult
	VHS $99

626 Chadwick

Lynn Chadwick achieved international recognition in 1956 when he won the First Prize for Sculpture at the Venice Biennale. At that time, Chadwick was simply one of the new generation of talented English sculptors; now he is widely acknowledged as the successor to Henry Moore. Chadwick was born in 1914 and began his working life as an architectural draftsman. His later work as a furniture and textile designer led him to sculpture, and he developed an original sculptural technique and a personal vocabulary of fabulous beasts, totemic forms and majestic double figures. For the last thirty years, Chadwick has lived at Lypiatt Manor, deep in the heart of Gloucestershire, keeping his distance from the art world. Despite his use of the human figure, he describes his work as abstract; beyond this he is reluctant to analyze its deeper meaning. Director Barrie Gavin spent some days watching Chadwick at work on a new project, two figures ascending and descending a staircase. By following the process of drawing, the construction of the armature (the metal skeleton used to support the clay or wax during the making of a sculpture), to the foundry and finished piece, this film gives an insight into the artist's physical and mental approach to his work.

For more information see page 223

Director/Writer	51 minutes
Barrie Gavin	Color
Original music	Age range 14–adult
Toru Takemitsu	Film $903 Rental $269
	VHS $129

Jean Dubuffet

Up to the First World War, it is possible, and traditional, to view the progress of modern European art as a series of more or less distinct 'movements' – Neo-classicism, Romanticism, Realism, Impressionism, Post-Impressionism, Cubism and so forth. Between the wars, however, and after the Second World War, as Cubism and Surrealism waned, the absence began to be felt of a dominant 'ism' in Europe. To some extent American art continued the 'relay-race' principle, in which Abstract Expressionism, then Minimalism, were offered as current mainstreams. In Europe individual personalities tended to plow their own separate creative furrow, and chief among these, for many, was Jean Dubuffet, an artist with the breadth and energy to rival Picasso's dominance.

Born in 1901, Dubuffet was close in his youth to many artists and writers such as Léger, Dufy and Ionesco, and by 1918 was a student at the Académie Julien, Paris, where so many major modern artists studied, yet he did not devote himself fully to painting and sculpture until around 1942. Before then he experimented with interior design, philosophy, music and literature, and followed the Dada movement with interest. Once launched, however, his career was meteoric. His preoccupations were with children's art and the art of psychotics – anti-fine-art manifestations which he called *art brut*. His own work depicted cartoonish, seemingly primitive figures, faces and animals. Visits to the Sahara Desert in 1947 and 1948 were critical for him, his own paintings sometimes resembling rock and cave paintings, or referring to the geological and soil structures of the terrain. His pictures consisted, at various times, of abstract surfaces made up of tiny, teeming incidents, of groups of childish figures going about rural or urban business, or of palimpsests of words and objects, both depicted and real, collaged into the surface. He frequently built up surfaces of debris and raw matter, to make volcanic-seeming landscapes relating closely to the *Natural History* series of Max Ernst. Many of his works aspire to the condition of graffiti. In his later painting and sculpture he moves toward a bolder manner, employing only white, black, red and blue, and structuring interlocking, jigsaw shapes that build up into an endless, active jumble.

627 **The Spinney by Jean Dubuffet**

Without narration, we follow all the different stages leading up to the unveiling of *The Spinney*, a monumental sculptural work by Jean Dubuffet, on June 18, 1988 in Flaine, Haute Savoie, France – the location chosen by Dubuffet himself.

'…an inspiration for artists…can at times be mesmerizing…highly artistic…fits together in unexpected ways. This is a video that art discussion groups or those into surrealism may enjoy.'
Video Rating Guide for Libraries, USA

Director
Nedjima Scialom

16 minutes
Color
Age range 12–adult
VHS $79

625
Anthony Caro
Early One Morning

627
Jean Dubuffet
The Spinney
Flaine, France

163

630   **The Genesis of a Sculpture**
Adam-Tessier

This film employs a fascinating technique
to show the various stages of a sculpture
produced by Maxim Adam-Tessier. There
is no narration, but the viewer is able to see
the sculptor's hesitations, his choices –
and his regrets.

'The technique of this research film of
great integrity is remarkable. The care taken
to be truthful extends almost to complete
frankness. This is a courageous film.'
UNESCO

For more information see page 271

Directors	13 minutes
Olivier Clouzot	**Black and white**
Julien Pappe	**Age range 10–adult**
Music	**Film $483** Rental $149
Anton Webern	**VHS $69**
Awards	
Mention d'Excellence,	
Cannes	
Biennale Prize, Paris	

---

605   **Nature and Nature: Andy Goldsworthy**

Andy Goldsworthy, a contemporary sculptor
now living in Scotland, has for years
been exploring various sites of the world,
leaving behind sculptures that are in
harmony with the environment. His
materials are drawn from nature itself and
his works, like many natural things, are
essentially ephemeral. For Goldsworthy,
seeing and understanding nature is a way
of renewing our links with the earth. Here
we meet him in the Scottish countryside
with Colin Renfrew, head of Cambridge
University's Department of Archaeology.
The two men discover surprising similarities
between their interest in and approach to
nature.

Director/Scenario	17 minutes
Camille Guichard	**Color**
Narrators/Participants	**Age range 7–adult**
Andy Goldsworthy	**Film $623** Rental $189
Colin Renfrew	**VHS $89**

---

635   **Sculpture Australia**

In sculpture, as in the other arts, Australia
has achieved a world reputation in recent
years, though often at the cost of
losing some of its most gifted artists to
other countries. In this film Tim Burstall
examines the Australian sculptors working
in Australia and overseas, analyzes their
attitudes and asks them to sum up their
views about modern sculpture. Among
the artists who appear are Norma Redpath,
photographed in her Milan studio at work
on a huge fountain for the National Library,
Canberra, Steven Walker relaxing among
the unusual forms and textures of the
Australian bush from which much of his
inspiration comes, and Ken Reinhart
juxtaposing plastic, sheet-metal and
electric-light globes to create strange
tributes to the technological world.
Robert Klippel, Clement Meadmore,
Vincent Jomantis and many other
sculptors also talk and show their work,
providing a unique insight into this often
misunderstood art.

Director	30 minutes
Tim Burstall	**Color**
Original music	**Age range 12–adult**
Don Burrows	**Film $623**

---

640   **Sculpture in the City – Spoleto**

Spoleto is a medieval Italian city, the
ancient capital of Lombardy. Each year it
has a festival of the arts, and its streets,
squares, steps and old buildings are filled
with new sculpture; on entering the city the
visitor passes under a giant triumphal arch
by the American Alexander Calder.
This unusual film shows how the modern
sculpture achieves new meaning and
proportion when placed in outdoor settings
within a city which already contains every
style of architecture and design from
Roman relic to Baroque. Included in the
film are sculptures by Marino Marini,
Laurens, Perez, Germaine Richier, Giacomo
Manzu, Lynn Chadwick, Alexander Calder,
Pietro Consagra, Ettore Colla, Nino
Franchina, Alberto Viani, Leonardo Leoncillo,
Hans Arp and Henry Moore.

Director	11 minutes
P Schivazap	**Color**
Award	**Age range 12–adult**
Exceptional Quality,	**Film $483** Rental $149
Italian Government	**VHS $69**

---

637   **If Brains Were Dynamite**
The Sculpture of Mark Prent

Hanging like hindquarters in a meat
freezer, bloody butchered human torsos
and limbs simultaneously rivet and repel
viewers of this film's opening footage.
Mark Prent is a Canadian artist whose
exhibitions always provoke outrage and
have resulted in violent reactions and trials
for obscenity. They also reveal the latent
sadism of a certain section of the public –
his *Man Strapped in an Electric Chair*
could be 'executed' by pulling a handle to
activate the chair, and Canadians were
ready to queue for two hours to take a turn.
The film illustrates this, but it allows us to
enter into the artist's work and understand
its personal implications: all these bodies
are his own and have been cast in resin
during a molding session which comes close
to torture. They are then brought to life
with frightening, painstaking care and
accuracy, painted, given hair or a glass eye.
Mark Prent has the support of his father
and his wife, but in the absence of buyers
he has gone into exile in Berlin. The film
examines the relationship between
aesthetic and ethical qualities, the Jewish
memory, and individual complicity in power
and in sadism.

'…provides an interesting look at the
creative process, and it is also timely in its
presentation of the question of government
support for controversial, other-than-
mainstream art. The technical quality is very
good. Recommended for art library
collections and for library media collections
dealing with social issues.'
Video Rating Guide for Libraries, USA

For more information see page 297

Directors	28 minutes
Peter Bors	**Color**
Thom Burstyn	**Age range 18–adult**
	Film $693 Rental $199
	VHS $99

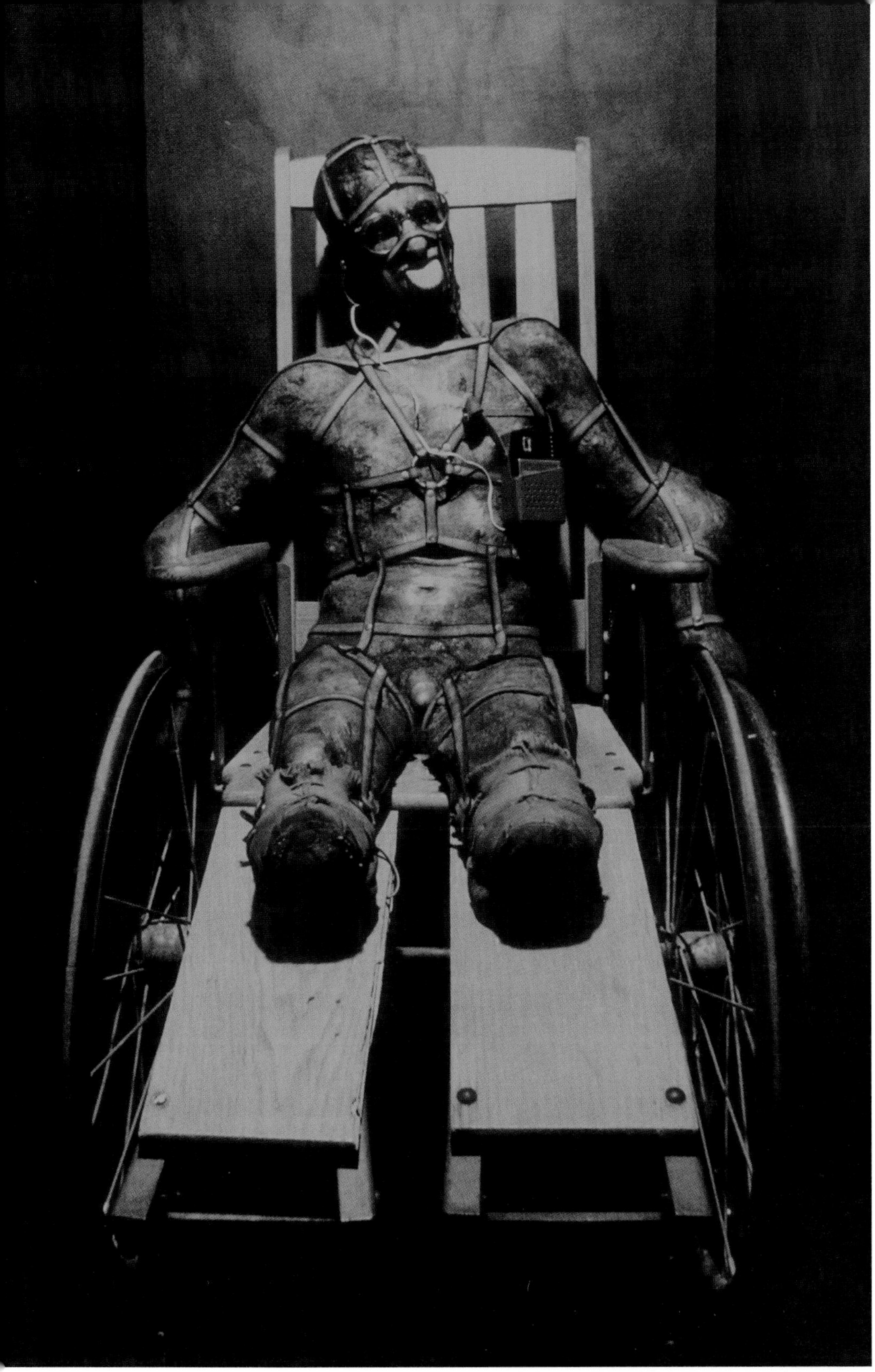

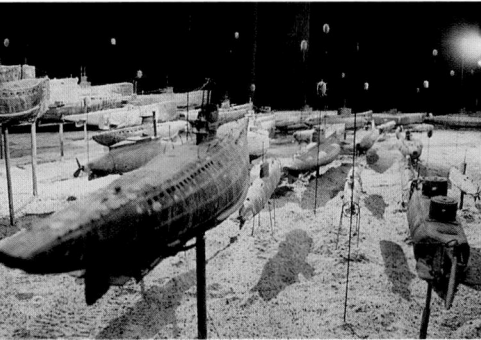

639 Submarine
Dreams and Passions of Tom McKendrick

Artist and sculptor Tom McKendrick grew
up in the shipbuilding town of Clydebank
near Glasgow, Scotland. *Submarine* was the
name of his multi-media exhibition in
Glasgow in 1990, and in this documentary
he explains his childhood obsession with
a device that could 'goe under water unto
the bottome and come up again at your
plaisure' (as it was described in 1578) and
with its development into the deadly
weapon of today. The submarine relies on
invisibility; it operates by stealth. 'These
things are really ugly but that's part of their
attraction for me. They're powerful and
they're brutal and they're vulnerable at
the same time.' Clydebank was almost
completely destroyed by bombing in 1941,
and McKendrick's artistic vision was shaped
by a community scarred physically and
emotionally. He left school at fifteen to
start work in the world-famous John
Brown's shipyard, becoming a 'loftsman,'
a trade now obsolete, but as the yard
experienced its final death-throes, in
common with Clydebank shipbuilding as
a whole, McKendrick moved on to the
Glasgow School of Art. He is now an artist
of international importance, with paintings
on display all over the world.

'…exceptional quality'
Scotsman, Edinburgh

'An artistic triumph…gives the fleeting
impression of other people's lives passing
before your eyes'
Glasgow Herald

For more information see page 300

Director	**52 minutes**
Mark Littlewood	**Color**
Narrator/Participant	**Age range 12–adult**
Tom McKendrick	**Film $903** Rental $269
Original music	**VHS $129**
John Russell	
Tom McKendrick	
Awards	
Best Film, Nova Scotia	
Best Portrait, Montreal	

▲ 637
Mark Prent
Amputation

▶ 639
Tom McKendrick
Part of *Submarine*
multi-media exhibition

165

21 Contemporary Painters

1930 to the present

Although the later twentieth century has been a period of accelerated innovation in the materials of art-making (and it has become almost conventional to be unconventional), nevertheless many artists have kept faith with paint and canvas, demonstrating that the potential and challenges of the conventional media will never be exhausted.

This section of 20 programs can be purchased on VHS for $2200

Television rights and prices on request

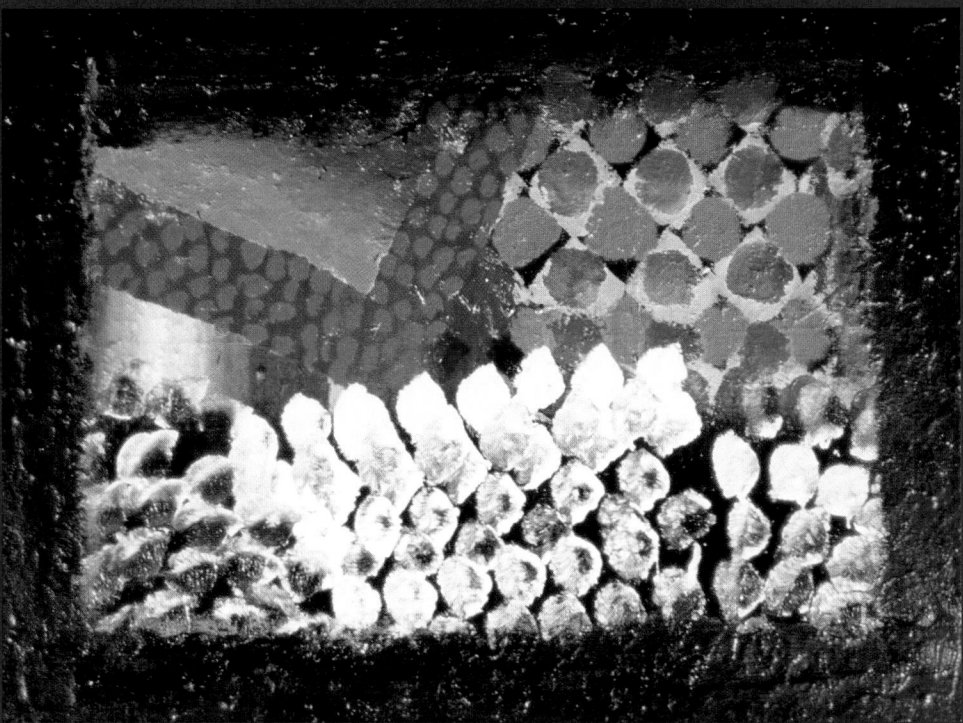

601 Contemporaries – The Quest for Reality

Reality is what every artist searches for, but each artist has a different idea of what reality is. A Renaissance artist did not seek to capture the same reality as an Expressionist; and contemporary creators are just as divided in their quest. This film examines the work of widely differing artists today: men like George Segal, who makes highly detailed plaster casts of the bodies of his own friends, and Antonio Recalcati, who 'prints' real people directly on to canvas. There is Michelangelo Pistoletto, who captures the spectators of his work through mirrors so that they become part of the work of art themselves; Jean-Pierre Reynaud, with his linking of two 'psycho-objects' otherwise quite unrelated; and Gérard Titus-Carmel, who tells an interviewer that the reality of his work is the drawing on the paper – 'right, there is an image somewhere. But … it's not the image I'm interested in. It's the sort of movement … the way things get drawn.' Wolf Vostell, who immortalizes a car or a woman in cement, says that he is seeking to understand the current meaning of life for modern humankind. These, of course, are all Europeans; American 'hyper-realists' like Chuck Close, John de Andrea, Richard MacLean, Don Eddy, Malcolm Morley, Ralph Goings, Richard Estes and Robert Cottingham use photography in their work to juxtapose one reality against another in a 'showdown of visions.' In Spain, by contrast, Antonio Lopez Garcia has been setting up his easel every morning for years in Madrid's Gran Vía, believing he must work from life for the sake of 'naturalness.' Hugo Pratt, comics artist and creator of *Corto Maltese*, tells an interviewer that comics, despised by academia, are a 'modern business' and 'dynamite' for formulating critical and political observation of current events. Jacques Monory works with photography, film and painting 'because if others don't look at me, I'm dead'; while Italian militant artist of the sixties Gianni Spadari has now given up his political struggles because 'in that voluntary commitment, I sacrificed a part of myself.'

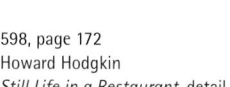

◀◀ 598, page 172
Howard Hodgkin
Still Life in a Restaurant, detail

◥ 601
Yves Klein
Ant 7

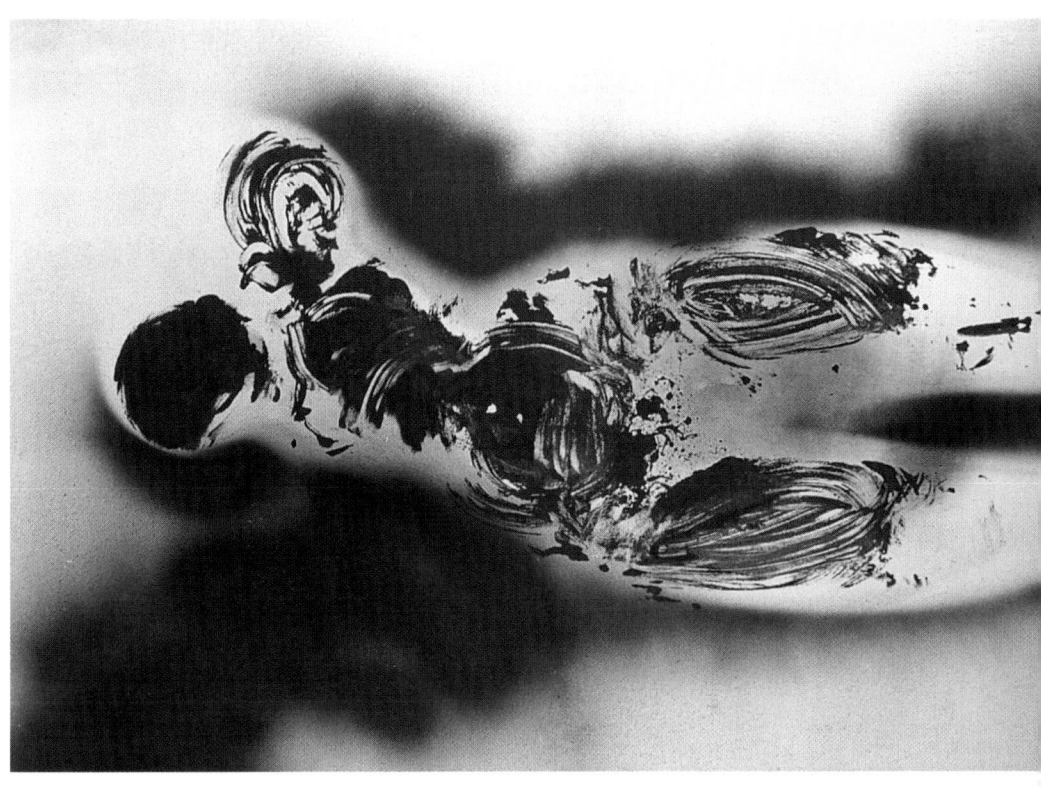

The film also features the work of Camille Bombois, Yves Klein, Jean-Olivier Hucleux, Peter Klasen, Vladimir Velickovic, Gérard Schlosser, Domenico Gnoli, Isabel Quintanilla, Claudio Bravo, Gilles Aillaud, Valerio Adami and others.

Part of the series
The Adventure of Modern Art

Director	**53 minutes**
Carlos Vilardebo	**Color**
Writers/Narration	**Age range 15–adult**
André Parinaud	**Film $1043** Rental $299
Carlos Vilardebo	**VHS $149**
Also available in French	

611 Contemporary Mexican Art

This documentary anthology draws on Octavio Paz's extensive knowledge of contemporary Mexican painters. Although Mexican Modernism was inaugurated by the great Muralists Siqueiros, Orozco and their colleagues, it is important to remember that these men were also studio painters, creating in oils, watercolor, sculpture, engraving and other media. And around 1930 another generation of easel painters appeared on the scene, Tamayo and Castellanos being the best known among them. Paz introduces a range of these artists, many of whom are still living, and some newer talents. We see them at work in their studios, and we learn of their affinities and contrasts with both current European art and their own traditional South American heritage.

Part of the series
Mexico through the Eyes of Octavio Paz

Director	**56 minutes**
Hector Tajonar	**Color**
Presenter/Narration	**Age range 14–adult**
Octavio Paz	**VHS $139**
Also available in Spanish	

167

Vasarely

This film is a rare document from the period when, in both Europe and America, Abstraction in various forms was becoming dominant, and Victor Vasarely was pioneering 'Op Art.' The film was made at the time of one of the artist's early exhibitions at the progressive Denise René Gallery in Paris – René herself makes a fleeting appearance in Op Art couture. With a soundtrack of contemporary music, and without narration, the film-maker has sought to create a vibrant composition of rhythms and contrasts in the spirit of Vasarely.

Director	**9 minutes**
Peter Kassovitz	**Black and white**
Original music	**Age range 12–adult**
Ianis Xenakis	**Film $483** Rental $149
	VHS $69

592 **Lichtenstein in London**

This film is a record of Roy Lichtenstein's retrospective show 'The American Dream' at the Tate Gallery, London, and includes a wide range of his comic-strip paintings, some of his caricatures of modern styles, notably those of Picasso and Mondrian, and a few sculptures. The diverse opinions of members of the public interviewed at the exhibition reveal the controversy surrounding Lichtenstein's work at that time. Lichtenstein talks about the rôle of the cliché in his art, and his attempt to counteract the lack of sensitivity in commercial art while deliberately using the same restricted imagery, materials and conventions. He describes his wish to develop a similar clichéd style for his 'copies' of other artists' work, creating something which is both a caricature and also a genuine statement in its own right.

Director	**20 minutes**
Bruce Beresford	**Color**
Scenario	**Age range 12–adult**
David Sylvester	**Film $623** Rental $189
Narration	**VHS $89**
Roy Lichtenstein	
Arts Council of	
Great Britain	

Tom Phillips works as a painter and graphic artist, and musical composer. He was born in London in 1937 and studied at St Catherine's College, Oxford (1957–66), and at Camberwell School of Art (1961–63). He taught at Wolverhampton College of Art and at Bath Academy of Art, Corsham (1962–70). Since 1965 he has held numerous one-man exhibitions in Britain and abroad, including a retrospective show at the Vaduz Kunsthalle, Basle (1975). A central aspect of Tom Phillips's approach to painting is a concern with process, reflected not only in the structure of individual paintings but in his meticulous documentation of the development of each work. The film is true to the spirit of this concern in its overall shape and the way paintings are shown. A few works – *A Humument* (1971–76), *Benches* (1970–71), *Mappin Wall* (1970–74) – are explored in detail and, by using the artist's own documentation, their development is traced from initial chance encounters (a postcard on Euston Station, for example) to completion. *A Humument*, an on-going element in Phillips's work derived from the Victorian novel *A Human Document*, opens the film and provides linking text and images for the sequences that follow. The artist provides his own particularly clear commentary.

Director
David Rowan

Script Consultant
Eric Rowan

Title music
Michael Nyman

Original music
Gavin Bryars

Arts Council of
Great Britain

50 minutes
Color
Age range 14–adult

Film $973 Rental $289
VHS $139

592
Roy Lichtenstein
Whaam!

592
Roy Lichtenstein at his exhibition

593
Tom Phillips
Camberwell and Peckham Versions

594 **Adventures in Perception**
The Work of the Graphic Artist
Maurits Escher

The work of the graphic artist Maurits Escher is a play on perspectives: it creates an illusion of the impossible. Boundaries expand to infinity and floors become ceilings and vice versa. He repeats forms in an ever-changing perspective, and creates a circle of metamorphosis. Escher's world derives its structure from a lucid intelligence, from a tremendous imagination and from prodigious craftsmanship. It is a revelation, of vital importance to the study of graphic design.

Director
Han van Gelder

Award
First Prize, Cork

Also available in
Dutch, French, German
and Spanish

21 minutes
Color
Age range 14–adult

Film $693 Rental $199
VHS $99

595 **Bridget Riley**

Perceptual art is concerned with the effects and processes of what, in this film, Bridget Riley calls 'the great privilege of sight.' 'Looking,' as she puts it, 'is a pleasure – a continual pleasure.' From the black and white paintings of the early 1960s which first established her international reputation, to her increasing concern with the self-generating luminosity of pure color, the film traces her 'exploration of the truth of what one can see.' In the studio, we see her working on a painting – finding that visual structure which from basic and simple elements will release complex effects of energy, movement, space, light and 'induced' color through the physical act of looking. Certain artists – Van Gogh, Seurat, Monet and the Futurists – are particularly important to her. But the film also shows the inspiration she has always drawn from certain types of visual experiences in nature. 'Painting,' as Bridget Riley says, 'has to obey the laws of painting.' But for her that is a process parallel to nature, dependent on our day-to-day experience of the joy of using our eyes.

Director/Writer
David Thompson

Arts Council of
Great Britain

28 minutes
Color
Age range 12–adult

Film $693 Rental $199
VHS $99

596 **The Reality of Karel Appel**

The reality of the painter Karel Appel is an overcrowded, possessed and frantic world, a barbaric age in which he can only paint as a barbarian – as he says in this film. His paintings are gaudy, his colors vivid, and he slaps them on the canvas as if in a duel, using his brushes, paints, putty-knife and his hands as weapons.

For more information see page 116

Director
Jan Vrijman

Awards
Golden Bear, Berlin
Gran Premio, Bergamo
Silver Medal, Barcelona
Silver Medal, La Felguera

15 minutes
Color
Age range 13–adult

Film $623 Rental $189
VHS $89

973 **Japonism, Part Three**
Japanese Influences on Western Art:
Gesture of the Brush

In recent years, the exchanges between Japanese and western art have been bi-directional. Pierre Alechinsky explains, for example, how the post-war art of the West has been influenced by Japanese calligraphy, and Japanese artist Chinjo Saito reveals his debt to Europe's CoBrA group.

Director
Guido De Bruyn

Also available in Dutch
and French

15 minutes
Color
Age range 15–adult

VHS $79

Antonio Saura

Antonio Saura was born in Madrid in 1930, and began to paint after a long illness in 1947. Initially he was influenced by the Chilean Surrealist Roberto Matta, and from the early 1950s Paris became his base, with his work relating closely to the gestural 'informal' Abstraction of the Ecole de Paris, and of the CoBrA movement of Appel and others. Since the mid-1950s he has been essentially an Abstract Expressionist, reducing color to predominant blacks and whites like those of Still and Motherwell in America. At times, however, discernible imagery has emerged from his violent brushwork – a *Crucifixion* harking back to the traditional iconography of religious art, or a figure which he might entitle *Brigitte Bardot*, reminding us of the fashion-doll *Women* series of Willem De Kooning, or the *Corps de Femmes* of Dubuffet.

597　Antonio Saura: Confessions

Antonio Saura is considered one of the most important Spanish painters of the post-Picasso generation. From his studio in Paris's thirteenth *arrondissement,* Saura explains how he came to be a painter. And we see him at work: the camera appears to spy on the artist caught up in the act of painting and drawing. Other sequences take us to Saura's native village of Huesca, where he recently finished painting a monumental ceiling for the town hall.

Director	**26 minutes**
Jean-Claude Rousseau	**Color**
Original music	**Age range 14–adult**
Jean-Marc Padovani	**VHS $99**
Also available in French	

◀◀ 595
Bridget Riley

◀ 575
Saul Steinberg
Army truck

574　A Mental State
The Works of Wilhelm Freddie

The quality of the work of Danish artist Wilhelm Freddie was quickly recognized by André Breton and his circle of Paris Surrealists. For years his work was considered scandalous and caused Freddie many difficulties, particularly during the war when he had to endure the intolerance of the Nazis. He even spent ten days in prison because of the 'indecency' of his works. For twenty-five years three of his works were exhibited at the Danish Crime Museum, alongside burglar's tools and underworld weaponry. At the age of eighty-two, however, he looks back at his past without bitterness and recounts his long battle for acceptance by the art world. His works are now exhibited in the most prestigious European and American galleries.

'College art history classes would greatly benefit from this video. It might also be used in general history courses'
Video Rating Guide for Libraries, USA

In Danish with English subtitles

For more information see page 145

Director	**49 minutes**
Per Mossin	**Color**
Narration	**Subtitles**
Per Mossin	**Age range 18–adult**
Wilhelm Freddie	**VHS $129**

575　Steinberg

Without narrative, this film takes us on an enchanting path through the American artist Saul Steinberg's witty world of characters, animals and everyday objects, teaching us along the way the delights of drawing with line. Quite close to the doodling most of us indulge in, Steinberg's technique is friendly and unforbidding, yet the artist is clever, thought-provoking and disciplined. In placing himself at the service of the graphic work, the film-maker has created a system of analogies in which lines become movement on the screen. The composer, for his part, has adapted to a similar discipline which is just as strict. From the point of view of production, the film has been conceived as a long journey through the drawings, which are juxtaposed as if in an immense fresco.

'The director has made use of all the resources at the disposal of the cinema to communicate a form of dynamic humor'
UNESCO

Director	**14 minutes**
Peter Kassowitz	**Black and white**
Original music	**Age range 9–adult**
Bernard Parmegiani	**Film $553** Rental $169
	VHS $79

171

Eugène Ionesco: Voices, Silences

As a man of letters, Ionesco is best known for his contributions to the theater, notably *La Cantatrice Chauve (The Bald Prima Donna)*, *Les Chaises (The Chairs)* and *Le Roi Se Meurt (Exit the King)*. When he tires of the clamor of words, Eugène Ionesco starts painting. In a studio in St Gall, Switzerland, he exudes colors and forms as he would words, and he never stops talking, confronting us, laughing at us or himself, expressing the same anxieties and dreams, and interpreting excerpts from his plays. Tragicomic beings appear on the paper: there are false masks and real faces, knights clad in black or sheathed in a multicolored armor; there are the branches of unknown trees, and bursts of grim laughter, and hieroglyphics. Sometimes he accepts a question, shares a confidence, a wink, a smile, then he takes up his brush, leaves time in suspension and traces a line.

'A film of rare quality…The director succeeds in playing down his own rôle, the better to bring out the connections between painting and speech, the image and the voice, abstract thought and the irrepressible burgeoning forth of forms.'
La Libre Belgique, Brussels

'An extraordinary vivid portrait…'
Le Soir, Brussels

'A very fine film…'
Pourquoi pas?, Brussels

'…creativity and old age…a new creative language aptly documented in this video… the artist's own statements and his reading from plays, essays, and fiction on the nature of art, creativity, and aging are worth listening to. Skillful camera weaving of paintings, the artist at work, and the artist musing on creativity in dramatic settings… imbued with intelligence, wit, and wisdom.'
Video Rating Guide for Libraries, USA

Director	**61 minutes**
Thierry Zeno	**Color**
Scenario	**Age range 18–adult**
Thierry Zeno with	**Film $1043** Rental $339
the collaboration	**VHS $149**
of Eugène Ionesco	
Narrator/Participant	
Eugène Ionesco	
Also available in French	

Howard Hodgkin: A Study

Howard Hodgkin has for some years been one of Britain's leading artists, but the recognition enjoyed by painters such as Peter Blake and David Hockney has come to him only recently. This program sets out to consider the preoccupations and techniques of the artist and his work and to relate these to the wider context of painting, past and present. Recurring themes, such as the intimacy of a moment with friends, are identified and considered alongside the technical devices of Hodgkin's work. This video is a good introduction to abstract painting, since it offers a clear and accessible argument for this kind of work.

'…a sense of Hodgkin's finely tuned use of color, recurring themes, and unique visual language'
Video Rating Guide for Libraries, USA

Director	**16 minutes**
Brian Taylor	**Color**
Script	**Age range 12–adult**
Joe Connolly	**VHS $89**

Francis Bacon

Francis Bacon was one of the world's greatest post-war artists. From 1944, when he made his first triptych *Studies for Three Figures at the Base of a Crucifixion*, Bacon painted more than twenty major triptychs which form the core of his work. This video was shot at the Tate Gallery's major exhibition of Bacon's work and focuses on the thirty-six panels that make up twelve of the major works. The images are illuminated by a sound track which is based on an interview given by Bacon himself. Artists often find it difficult to discuss their work, but here Bacon talks about his paintings with great clarity. He explores the themes of morality, realism and sexuality that have always preoccupied him. The result gives an insight into the pictures, the way they are made and the way Bacon saw them.

'Invaluable…the expertly detailed visual analysis of the imagery leaves the viewer with the uncomfortable but exhilarating sense that Bacon's macabre œuvre has been left to percolate under one's own skin. The feeling is transcending…a must-see for serious art students and a compelling experience for the neophyte.'
Video Rating Guide for Libraries USA

For more information see page 117

Director/Script	**28 minutes**
Richard Francis	**Color**
	Age range 17–adult
	VHS $99

Francis Bacon: Paintings 1944–62

The film opens with images that recur in Francis Bacon's paintings – Muybridge photographs of animals in motion, stills from Eisenstein's *The Battleship Potemkin*, a Rembrandt self-portrait, and *Pope Innocent X* by Velázquez. The remainder of the film presents Bacon's interpretation of such images during the period 1944–62. There is no commentary, but through a combination of music, camera movement and editing, the film accentuates the violence and menace of the paintings, and gives an impression of their emotional power.

Director/Writer	**11 minutes**
David Thompson	**Color**
Music	**Age range 17–adult**
Elizabeth Lutyens	**Film $553** Rental $169
Arts Council of	**VHS $79**
Great Britain	

600 Josef Herman Drawings

The great British realist painter
Josef Herman portrays working men –
coal-miners in Wales, grape-harvesters in
Burgundy, Portuguese fishermen and farm
laborers. He gives man's immemorial
struggle for existence the quality of an
epic. His form is simple and monumental,
his drawing, as he says himself, 'true to
experience rather than observation.'
His subject, the immense dignity of the
manual laborer in contact with the realities
of nature, is a dying one in an age of
automation; and the film mirrors the epic
quality of his work. There is no narration.
This is a film which proves that it is up
to individuals to feel what is great in art
rather than simply to accept the opinions
of others.

'With his violent pen and brush it is a
visual triumph of labor. The director has
deliberately chosen the rhythm of the
laborer and the effect is monumental'
UNESCO

For more information see page 244

Director	**15 minutes**
Anthony Roland	**Black and white**
Original music	**Age range 12–adult**
Louis Saguer	**Film $553** Rental $169
Awards	**VHS $79**
Quality Award, French	
National Film Center	
Chriss Award, Columbus	

◀◀ 615
Eugène Ionesco
painting at the lithographer's

▼ 599A
Francis Bacon
Study for a Bullfight

◀ 600
Josef Herman
Man and Ox Ploughing

◀ 603
Colin McCahon
Victory over Death, detail

◢ 569, 570A
Man Ray
Portrait of Meret Oppenheim

602 **Brendan Neiland:**
Evolution of a Commission

This program explores two important aspects of the life of an artist, the commissioning of a work of art by a major institution and the artist's professional practice. It features Brendan Neiland, a well-established British artist whose work is in collections throughout the world. We follow the progress of one of Neiland's paintings commissioned by British Rail, seeing its creation from the start of the commissioning process through the many processes of creation to the reproduction and display of the work as a poster on Kings Cross Station, London. We also see how Neiland practices as a professional artist and we investigate his relations with his gallery and private clients. Featured in the video are art critics from the *Sunday Times* and the *Financial Times* who talk about Neiland's work, the commercial aspects of art and how much compromise the artist has to make in fulfilling the needs of a commission, and Neiland's family, who talk about his success and how it has impinged on their lives.

Director
Gavin Nettleton

37 minutes
Color
Age range 12–adult
VHS $119

603 **Victory over Death:**
The Paintings of Colin McCahon
The Essence of a Young Culture

From the 1930s onward, a kind of cultural nationalism grew up and strengthened in New Zealand: a desire to cut the umbilical cord that joined her to Mother England and to establish an independent identity and culture of her own. The visionary painter Colin McCahon was a major representative of this movement. When he began painting in the 1930s, he sought to express in his work the essence of a young culture. New Zealand, he said, was 'a landscape with too few lovers', and he wanted its people to lay hold of it imaginatively as well as physically. But he was a cultural pioneer in other ways as well: one of the generation of painters who first made it possible to pursue a professional career in his own country, and New Zealand's first and greatest Modernist. Today he has the beginnings of an international reputation – he has been called 'the greatest Australasian artist of all time' (as well as 'a brave man in a provincial culture') – but for most of his career his works (*Victory over Death* is the title of one of the most famous) were often derided and misunderstood: 'They might pass as graffiti on the walls of some celestial lavatory'; 'a bucket of whitewash and a tin of tar.' The director of this documentary, Judy Rymer, has enormous admiration for

McCahon which grew during the months of filming. 'When you look at the years and years and years he kept painting when his work was rejected, the personal certainty he had about his work is fantastic. It became a fascination of mine to examine McCahon's work in relation to international painting and to the environment it came from. It is also a way of looking at the young and still developing cultural nexus of New Zealand.' Filming took place in eight public galleries in New Zealand, numerous private collections and in the landscapes McCahon loved, from Cape Reinga to the Otago Peninsula.

'It deals with an unfamiliar subject carefully and exhaustively, fostering in the viewer a good appreciation of McCahon's contributions and a good understanding of his aims and influences. Recommended.'
Video Rating Guide for Libraries, USA

Director	**52 minutes**
Judy Rymer	**Color**
Scenario	**Age range 14–adult**
Francis Pound	**Film $903** Rental $268
Judy Rymer	**VHS $129**
Original music	
Jan Preston	
Awards	
Gold Plaque, Chicago	
Finalist Award, New York	
Best Film Contemporary	
Art, Montreal	

IMAGO Meret Oppenheim

The fame of the Swiss artist Meret Oppenheim rests on one piece, *The Fur-lined Teacup,* which is considered one of the archetypal Surrealist works. By creating it in 1936 at the age of twenty-three, she leapt into the art-history books – but a year later she had retreated from Paris to Basle to study art in order to live up to her worldwide reputation, and plunged into a depression that lasted seventeen years. 'Nobody gives you freedom, you have to take it,' she remarked, and eventually she was able to emerge from the shadow of that teacup and become a mature artist, her links with Dada and Surrealism still alive. Based on Meret Oppenheim's own words and beautifully narrated by Glenda Jackson, this film is an inspiring tribute to a woman who transformed herself after a long crisis.

Directors/Writers
Pamela Robertson-Pearce
Anselm Spoerri

Narration based on texts, letters, dreams and poems by Meret Oppenheim

Narrator
Glenda Jackson

Awards
Outstanding Quality Prize, The Swiss Film Board
Gold Apple Award, Oakland
Grand Prix, Mulhouse
Honorary Mention, Paris

Also available in French, German and Spanish

90 minutes
Color and
black and white
Age range 16–adult
Film $1393 Rental $399
VHS $199

IMAGO Meret Oppenheim
Part One: 1932–54

Paris of the Surrealists, Creating Crisis and Transformation, Jungian Psychology

An excerpt from 569 (see left), this film begins with Meret Oppenheim leaving home for art-school in Paris, seeking 'freedom and independence.' She immediately got to know the Surrealist circle, including Giacometti, Hans Arp and Duchamp, and also a number of other women artists whom she admired very much. For her, Surrealism, although dominated by men, was simply the key to a more liberated life, since the Surrealists accepted women as artists without question. For most of her life the question of self-confidence as an artist (particularly difficult for a woman, she always thought) would be a stumbling-block. Man Ray photographed her, and she fell in love with Max Ernst. Her love was returned, but she felt she had to reject intimacy with Ernst, only understanding later that his maturity as an artist would have stifled her own fledgling creativity. In 1936, forced for the first time to try to support herself, she began to design jewelry for the *haute couture.* When she showed Picasso her bracelet of copper lined with sealskin, he remarked that 'many things could be covered in fur,' and this was the inspiration for her fur-lined teacup, which was bought by the Museum of Modern Art in New York. But fame was difficult to handle, and from 1937 onward her frequent depressions intensified into a permanent state. Retreating to Basle, she was gripped by a creative crisis. 'I read psychology, primarily Jung,' she said (Jung was a family friend). 'I was looking after my little soul…During my long crisis, my genius, the animus, the male part of the female soul, that assists the female artist, had abandoned me…But at the beginning of the fifties, I sensed that things were getting better…'

Slightly shortened version of the first half of 569.

Directors/Writers
Pamela Robertson-Pearce
Anselm Spoerri

Narration based on texts, letters, dreams and poems by Meret Oppenheim

Narrator
Glenda Jackson

35 minutes
Color and
black and white
Age range 16–adult
VHS $109

IMAGO Meret Oppenheim
Part Two: 1959–85

Rediscovery, Becoming a Contemporary Rôle-model, Feminism, the Playful and the Androgyne

A second excerpt from 569, this film covers the emergence of Meret Oppenheim from her long years of depression and creative block – the transformation of the caterpillar into the imago, the butterfly. Suddenly freed from self-doubt, full of hope, she began working again. Her marriage to a supportive businessman who understood her need for the freedom to lead an independent life made it possible for her to spend her weekends at her studio in Berne; in 1967 her first 'retrospective' took place in Stockholm, and she was rediscovered by the art world. At the end of 1967 her husband died, and her art 'became everything' to her. Meret Oppenheim had a deep trust in the unconscious, and throughout her life she recorded her dreams, which she used as a source of guidance and self-knowledge. She also strongly believed that art had no gender, and strove to balance and unite the opposite sides of her psyche, the spiritual-female and spiritual-male, an effort that was reflected in her appearance and in the dreams of her last years. She felt that, ever since the establishment of patriarchy, the female principle had been devalued and projected on to women. Because of this disturbed balance, she felt that a new direction in the evolution of mankind is needed, where the female principle is not devalued and humanity arrives at wholeness. Younger artists were impressed by her work, and yet, she said, 'I have always been making the same thing.'

Slightly shortened version of the second half of 569.

Directors/Writers
Pamela Robertson-Pearce
Anselm Spoerri

Narration based on texts, letters, dreams and poems by Meret Oppenheim

Narrator
Glenda Jackson

35 minutes
Color and
black and white
Age range 16–adult
VHS $109

Art has perhaps never been so diverse, even fragmented, as it is today. The developments of Modernism, with Abstraction, collage, Constructivism, photographic techniques, and Dadaist and anti-art 'events,' have opened up a bewildering host of avant-garde options for the artist. Many employ photography, film or computer-generated imagery. Others create 'environments' and 'installations.' Some choose to make a social art that tackles issues in the 'real world,' others a private art confronting inward emotions and ideas. This section represents a few of the most diverse creative trends of our day.

1945 to the present

22
New Directions
New Dimensions

This section of 23 programs can be purchased as 22 titles on VHS for $2488 plus 1 title on film for $623

Television rights and prices on request

581 Pop Art: The Test of the Object

After the Second World War came the birth of the consumer society. The American way of life, with its emphasis on growth, quantity, consumption and fun, dominated western values. But underneath, many of the same old dark forces raged on: war – Berlin, Korea, Vietnam; racial unrest; the political intolerance of the early 1950s. Among the young, new values awoke, and protest movements sprang up. While existing abstract painting in America – notably Jackson Pollock's – found itself floundering for ideas, Jasper Johns took notice of the object itself, setting his scenes with icons of the familiar and the everyday. The other great founder of Pop Art, Robert Rauschenberg, considered art as something closer to life – the world as one great painting. Meanwhile in California, another parallel track was emerging, based on the deconstruction of technology (Jim Dine), the nature of silence (John Cage), and Roy Lichtenstein's realization that the medium of the printed plate itself generated fertile subject matter – an art seated on the streetcorner, taking the fullest part in life. Suddenly sociological raw material had become art – Pop Art. There was Tom Wesselmann's American Humdrum, Claes Oldenberg's soda-pop themes – and, inevitably, Andy Warhol, who stuffed the banal images of America back down its throat and then took what was for many the ultimate step and made himself into a living, talking pop object. Yet Pop Art had a third track – for many, its real birthplace was England, where, even more than in California, the most prominent art form was always music. Richard Hamilton also took images from the everyday world, but never abandoned his sensitivity as a painter; nor, in a later period, does David Hockney. In England, Pop Art was never without its personal touch. The film also features the work of Klein, Tinguely, Cesar, Christo, Spoeri, Arman, Raysse and many others.

Part of the series
The Adventure of Modern Art

Director	53 minutes
Carlos Vilardebo	**Color**
Writers/Narration	**Age range 15–adult**
André Parinaud	**Film $1043** Rental $299
Carlos Vilardebo	**VHS $149**
Also available in French	

582 The Sixties: The Art in Question

When, in 1968, the youth of Europe – especially French youth – took to the barricades, they were protesting against… what? Slogans were conveniently vague and motives were mixed and obscure. A quarter of a century later, little has changed politically (if change was the object); however, the art that emerged at the same time – in many ways a natural development of the Pop Art of the earlier sixties – has survived, though it has never ceased to be controversial. The major question that has always hung over the art of the happening, of the performance, of the assemblage, has been: is it art at all? Pre-dating the mass student violence of the late sixties, the first recorded happening was staged by American Alan Kaprow in 1959 in New York. It took many forms thereafter. Chris Burden remained in a room for twenty-two days without eating, hidden away; Gina Pane made gory self-mutilations – a sanguinary direction also pursued with considerably greater elaboration by Michel Journiac and Hermann Nitsch. Minimal art pays close attention to landscape and cityscape; Sol Lewitt programs computer graphics by artificial intelligence algorithms; then there are sculptors as diverse as Naum Gabo, Henry Moore, Jean Dubuffet, Isamu Noguchi, Eduardo Chillida, François Morellet, Alexander Calder and Mark di Suvero. Land artists work outside, like Robert Smithson with his Great Salt Lake Spiral, but Richard Long reverses the same idea, erecting natural-material constructions inside four walls. Finally comes Conceptual Art: the artist makes of himself the work. The film also features the work of Robert Rauschenberg, Jim Dine, Wolf Vostell, Tanaka Min, Arnulf Rainer, Bruce Naman, Larry Bell, Walter de Maria and many others.

Part of the series
The Adventure of Modern Art

Director	53 minutes
Carlos Vilardebo	**Color**
Writers/Narration	**Age range 15–adult**
André Parinaud	**Film $1043** Rental $299
Carlos Vilardebo	**VHS $149**
Also available in French	

◀◀ 618, page 184
Video portrait

▲ 581
Tom Wesselmann
Great American Nude

▲ 581
Andy Warhol
Marilyn

584   The Adventure: Artists on Art

Since Marcel Duchamp, as early as 1914, began exhibiting selected everyday objects – a urinal, a bottle-rack – as 'readymade' works of art, questions about how we define art and what its social function is have been central to all serious artists' concerns. Hosts of Conceptual artists have followed the lead of Duchamp, no longer painting or sculpting in traditional ways, but creating provocative 'gestures' and adopting 'strategies' for making their viewers think about the nature and rôle of art itself, and how it relates to the major concerns of our lives. In this film, Jorn Merckert of the Berlin Academie der Kunst, says: 'Because the human condition today has changed so much, and because there is no longer a system, one single system existing for everybody, giving each person his place, people have lost their identity, they've lost all definition of what they want to do in life and of what they can do in life. And it is there, in that context, that art first of all reflects that identity crisis. Subsequently, art makes us aware of that identity crisis. And finally, every now and then, art provides an answer as to how one might combat that identity crisis.' Artists whose work is looked at include Dutchman Anton Heyboer, who offers as an artistic statement his own taking of multiple 'wives'; Wolf Vostell, who strews a floor with knives, forks and barbed wire, in a reference to the Nazi concentration camps; Christo, whose seventy-five-mile *Running Fence* was erected across California; and Joseph Beuys, who notoriously gave a performance in which he tried to explain art to a dead rabbit. As bizarre as such works will seem to some, this film attempts a thought-provoking exploration of their implications.

Part of the series
The Adventure of Modern Art

Director	**53 minutes**
Carlos Vilardebo	**Color**
Writers/Narration	**Age range 15–adult**
André Parinaud	**Film $1043** Rental $299
Carlos Vilardebo	**VHS $149**

Also available in French

587   Kinetics
The Record of an Exhibition

The film is based on an exhibition of kinetic artists of many nationalities – Takis, Jesús Raphael Soto, Jean Tinguely, Kenneth Martin, Philip Vaughan *et al* – at the Hayward Gallery, London. Kinetic art takes many forms and can be traced to an age-old interest in automata, epitomized by the search for perpetual motion. The film sees this art as a celebration of man-made and natural dynamics, questioning our modes of perception and rejecting the distinction between illusion and reality. Much of the film is given to an exploration of dazzling play of light and movement in the exhibition: pieces that move automatically, some of which require spectator participation, structures of metal and plastic, electronic equipment using neon, ultra-violet and stroboscopic lights.

Director	**14 minutes**
Lutz Becker	**Black and white**
Narration	**Age range 12–adult**
John Adar	**Film $553** Rental $169
Arts Council of	**VHS $79**
Great Britain	

605   Nature and Nature: Andy Goldsworthy

Andy Goldsworthy, a contemporary sculptor now living in Scotland, has for years been exploring various sites of the world, leaving behind sculptures that are in harmony with the environment. His materials are drawn from nature itself and his works, like many natural things, are essentially ephemeral. For Goldsworthy, seeing and understanding nature is a way of renewing our links with the earth. Here we meet him in the Scottish countryside with Colin Renfrew, head of Cambridge University's Department of Archaeology. The two men discover surprising similarities between their interests in and approaches to nature.

Director/Scenario	**17 minutes**
Camille Guichard	**Color**
Narrators/Participants	**Age range 7–adult**
Andy Goldsworthy	**Film $623** Rental $189
Colin Renfrew	**VHS $89**

◀◀ 584
Christo
Valley Curtain

▼ 587
Bryan Wynter
Mobile
Imoos VII

606 **Jean Verame:**
The New Adventurers

The film is about the unique adventure of a
man creating a work of art in the Moroccan
desert near Tafraout. During a period of
three months, Jean Verame utilized
eighteen tons of blue, violet, red and white
paint to cover part of the Anti-Atlas
mountains. His project, fully supported by
King Hassan II, is a striking piece of art.
His work and his presence are not without
effects on the local ethnic group, the
Berbers, whose women still go veiled
in front of every man, though they are
the working force of the region. Often
compared to Christo, Jean Verame offers
a different approach to contemporary
painting: his mountains will last for at
least 100 years.

Director	**52 minutes**
Andrzej Kostenko	**Color**
	Age range 12–adult
Participants	
Jean Verame	**Film $1043** Rental $299
The population of	**VHS $149**
Tafraout (Morocco)	

Also available in French

607 Snow Dream
Gigantic Snow Sculpture

Silence, darkness, cold. Three men working wordlessly in the isolation of a snow-covered, mountainous landscape, sawing, cutting and shaping a huge cube of frozen snow. One of the men is French-Canadian sculptor Réal Bérard, the others his assistants. This film allows us to be spectators at the creation of a work of art far from any art gallery or civic square, a work seemingly made for the satisfaction of its creators alone. Extremes of heat and cold, fire and ice, are contrasted in this film: the men warm themselves all through the night at the campfire, even with the cigarettes they light. The monument they sculpt seems to be a synthesis of Eskimo and Aztec styles and imagery – broad faces, schematic birds, zigzag patterns, blocky forms. The film gives us a brief sequence of the finished work existing mysteriously in the world as the musical score picks up the plaintive theme one of the trio has been playing on a mouth organ by the fire. We see the sculpture survive a dramatic electric storm and torrential rain. Then its makers, still wordless, engulf it in a blazing conflagration. Impermanence would seem to be a major theme of this film, impermanence and the elemental forces at work in life and art.

Director/Writer	**22 minutes**
Claude Grenier	**Color**
Sculptor	**Age range 8–adult**
Réal Bérard	**Film $623** Rental $189
assisted by	**VHS $89**
Nick Burns	
Jim Tallosi	
Original music	
Normand Roger	
National Film Board	
of Canada	

608 Paya et Talla
The Moroccan Painter Farid Belkahia

Farid Belkahia, who was born in Marrakesh, is one of the leading contemporary artists in Morocco. It is his recent works, in leather, that have done most to establish his reputation. On stretched sheepskin, Belkahia draws various clay-inscribed signs and symbols – a secret, arcane language of initiation. What attracted director Raoul Ruiz to this unique work, apart from the subject matter, was the theme of the sign. Like all directors, he is also concerned with the question of 'framing', and is drawn here to the teeming, overflowing, unframeable aspect of Belkahia's works. Lastly, Ruiz profiles the artist himself, a man deeply rooted in the Maghrebin land and culture. The subjects, language and forms of Belkahia inspire and transform the director's way of seeing.

Director/Scenario	**30 minutes**
Raoul Ruiz	**Color**
Also available in French	**Age range 14–adult**
	Film $763 Rental $199
	VHS $109

609 A Day So Red
Homage to the American Indians

All the artists portayed in this video work in different media. Richard Ray Whitman, a photographer, comes from the Yuchi tribe; painter Dan Daminga belongs to the Hopi people; Emmi Whitehorse is a Navajo painter; the Apache Bob Haozous makes constructed, sometimes fetish-like sculptures, while Edgar Heap of Birds, of the Ponca tribe, is a mixed-media artist. As will be evident, these artists are not practicing the traditional arts of their peoples, but using the language of contemporary art to articulate the relationship between their cultural past and present, to testify to their identity, and perhaps to heal the wounds of cultural displacement and discontinuity. Each short video segment takes a raw, matter-of-fact look at an artist against the traditional music of his or her tribe, giving glimpses of personalities 'living' their art.

Director	**42 minutes**
Pierre Lobstein	**Color**
Award	**Age range 13–adult**
Leonardo da Vinci Prize,	**VHS $99**
French Ministry of	
Foreign Affairs	

610A Walls, Walls
The Murals of Los Angeles

A documentary about the murals of Los Angeles: who paints them, who looks at them, who pays for them? The capital of talking pictures has talking walls, through which the people of Los Angeles speak. Naïve, violent, poetic frescos, full of color and humor, reveal the adventure of the city and its inhabitants – black, Mexican, Puerto Rican – images of America caught in the melting-pot at one specific moment in history. Most of these murals will already have been destroyed; only in this film do they still live on.

Director/Writer/Narrator	**81 minutes**
AGNES VARDA	**Color**
Awards	**Age range 12–adult**
Grand Prix, Florence	**Film $1323** Rental $399
Prix Joseph von Sternberg,	**VHS $189**
Mannheim	
Also available with	
French subtitles	

◀◀ 612
Tami Fujie
Art kite

▶ 610B
Berlin Wall, detail

▼ 610A
Painting a mural
on a sausage factory
in Los Angeles

610B The Paintings Came Tumbling Down
Art on the Berlin Wall

Titled in German *The Rapid Disappearance of the Heaviest Paintings in the World,* this color documentary without narration opens by surveying the paintings and graffiti that used to cover the grey concrete of the Berlin Wall on its west side – paintings that were a record of the people's relationship with a totalitarian structure which no longer exists. Faces predominated – all kinds of faces; particularly striking were those of Communist leaders against a red background. Then we see hands raising hammers and chisels, beginning to chip away at the wall. One picture, captioned *Smash All Walls,* seems to encourage its own destruction, and these ordinary Berliners don't want to leave the work to the authorities. Gradually night falls, crowds gather to cheer, the drilling equipment is set in motion, and huge sections of the wall begin to go down. Hundreds of thousands all over the world watched these scenes on television – but only this film is now left to show what was destroyed along with the wall.

Directors of photography	**15 minutes**
Andrzej Kondratiuk	**Color**
Janusz Kondratiuk	**Age range 12–adult**
	VHS $79

612 Pictures for the Sky
Famous Artists Design Kites

Working in conjunction with Japanese master kite-makers, a hundred famous artists from twenty countries all over the world created 'art kites' to turn the sky above Himeji, Japan, into a playground for their world of paintings. *Pictures for the Sky* documents one of the most fascinating international art spectacles of recent years, and is unique in its attractive presentation of a wide range of new works by important representatives of contemporary art. Artists featured include Robert Rauschenberg, Emilio Vedova, Niki de Saint Phalle, Panamarenko, Horst Antes, Frank Stella, Daniel Buren, Kumi Sugai, José de Guimarães, Otto Herbert Hajek, Salome, Tom Wesselmann, Antoni Tàpies, Per Kirkeby, Bukichi Inoue, Chema Cobo, Graham Dean, Griska Bruskin, Rupprecht Geiger, Paul Wunderlich, Mimmo Paladino, Karel Appel, General Idea, Olle Kaks, Zvi Goldberg, Imre Bak, Karl Otto Götz, Ulrike Rosenbach, Kenny Scharf, Gregorij Litischevskij, Sadamasa Motonaga, Tadanori Yokoo, Klaus Staeck, Franz Erhard Walther, and Ivan Rabuzin.

Director/Script	**30 minutes**
Markus Zollner	**Color**
Original sound	**Age range 8–adult**
Jan Kollwitz	**Film $693** Rental $199
Also available in	**VHS $99**
Dutch, French, German,	
Italian, Japanese,	
Portuguese and Russian	

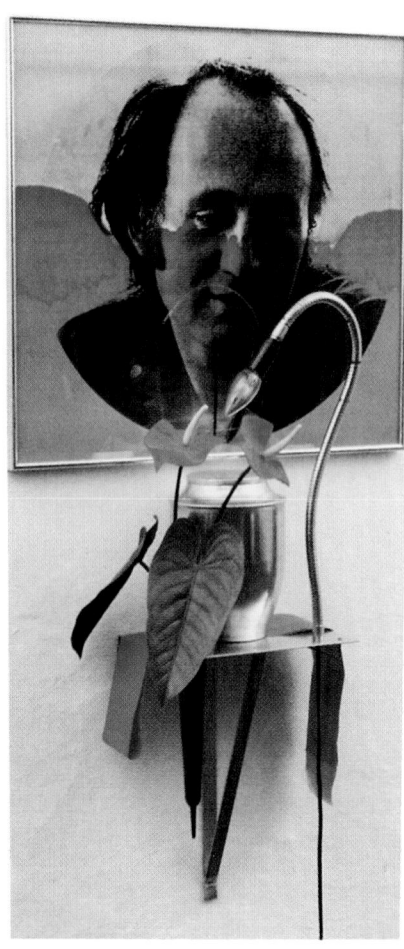

613 Un Mariage d'Amour

Spanish artist Antoni Miralda (born in 1942) has divided his career between New York and Barcelona, exploring the connections between art and culture. He creates artistic events based on everyday rituals. In 1967, he produced his first landscapes in meringue as well as his first colored banquets: examples of edible art. This documentary fable focuses on the monumental project *Honeymoon*, constructed from 1986 to 1992 in celebration of the marriage between the Statue of Liberty in New York and the statue of Christopher Columbus in Barcelona. The film recounts the preparation of the bride's trousseau (on a scale with the Statue of Liberty), and the ceremony itself in Las Vegas, the capital of American kitsch – it is the marriage of contrasting symbols: conquest and freedom.

Directors/Scenario	13 minutes
Catherine Addov	Color
Jean François d'Arrere	Age range 9–adult
Original Music	VHS $89
Christophe Heral	

Also available in French

637 If Brains Were Dynamite
The Sculpture of Mark Prent

Hanging like hindquarters in a meat freezer, bloody butchered human torsos and limbs simultaneously rivet and repel viewers of this film's opening footage. Mark Prent is a Canadian artist whose exhibitions always provoke outrage and have resulted in violent reactions and trials for obscenity. They also reveal the latent sadism of a certain section of the public – his *Man Strapped in an Electric Chair* could be 'executed' by pulling a handle to activate the chair, and Canadians were ready to queue for two hours to take a turn. The film illustrates this, but it allows us to enter into the artist's work and understand its personal implications: all these bodies are his own and have been cast in resin during a molding session which comes close to torture. They are then brought to life with frightening, painstaking care and accuracy, painted, given hair or a glass eye. Mark Prent has the support of his father and his wife, but in the absence of buyers he has gone into exile in Berlin. The film examines the relationship between aesthetic and ethical qualities, the Jewish memory, and individual complicity in power and in sadism.

'…provides an interesting look at the creative process, and it is also timely in its presentation of the question of government support for controversial, other-than-mainstream art. The technical quality is very good. Recommended for art library collections and for library media collections dealing with social issues.'
Video Rating Guide for Libraries, USA

For more information see page 297

Directors	28 minutes
Peter Bors	Color
Thom Burstyn	Age range 18–adult
	Film $693 Rental $199
	VHS $99

638 The Paradise of Cornelius Kolig

The uncategorizable artist Cornelius Kolig lives and works today in the same small community in which he was born and grew up, on the border of Italy, Austria and Slovenia. Preoccupied with the environment – both the natural, organic environment and the artificial, industrial (and often polluting) one – his works may take the form of a huge road-side hoarding of a heart, a strange machine for exploding shoes, or a gruesome collection of artificial body parts. He is obsessed with plastics, and the play between reality and artificiality, high art and shocking vulgarity. At times his work is close to that of the younger Canadian artist Mark Prent (see 637). Kolig has constructed for himself a bizarre studio-house. The lush garden which he tends lovingly is dominated by an ominous sheet-metal tower into which the artist can climb. In a large gallery-room, meanwhile, he holds a permanent display of his assemblages. Rituals fascinate him, especially the 'ordinary' rituals of everyday life. He is obsessed both with the human body and with human religion and spirituality. Amazingly, in a local Catholic church, he has mounted an outrageously iconoclastic installation, to the bewilderment of the visitors. In his work he seeks to realize an 'ironic paradise' of plastic beauty. Clearly something of social misfit, Kolig celebrates the 'uselessness' of art. Sensitive, lyrical, reflective, this film conveys the curious atmosphere surrounding this eccentric and solitary creator – and leaves intact the ultimate mysteriousness of his vocation.

Directors	43 minutes
Helga Ripper	Color
Fred Dickermann	Age range 17–adult
Participant	VHS $119
Cornelius Kolig	

Also available in German

► 638
Cornelius Kolig
Contemporary icon

►► 613
Antoni Miralda
Unfolding the bride's trousseau

635 Sculpture Australia

In sculpture as in the other arts, Australia has achieved a world reputation in recent years, though often at the cost of losing some of its most gifted artists to other countries. In this film Tim Burstall examines the Australian sculptors working in Australia and overseas, analyzes their attitudes and asks them to sum up their views about modern sculpture. Among the artists who appear is Ken Reinhart, juxtaposing plastic, sheet-metal and electric-light globes to create strange tributes to the technological world. Many other, less radical sculptors also talk and show their work, providing a unique insight into this often misunderstood art.

Director	30 minutes
Tim Burstall	Color
Original music	Age range 12–adult
Don Burrows	Film $623 Rental $189

636 Pleasures and Dangers
Six Women Artists at an Exciting Stage in their Careers

Six women gaining international success. This film is a portrait of their working lives in England, France and their home country, New Zealand. *Pleasures and Dangers* provides a lively introduction to new trends in the arts – from painting to animation, from feature films to giant photographs. The work of these artists is bold and colorful. They draw on the widest range of sources, from the images of television and advertising to ancient myths and symbols, and they explore issues of sex and gender in a way that is rich and unpredictable. They are Alexis Hunter, painter; Alison Maclean, film-maker; Julia Morison, painter; Lisa Reihana, animator; Merylyn Tweedie, mixed-media artist; and Christine Webster, photographer.

Director	52 minutes
Shirley Horrocks	Color
Writers	Age range 16–adult
Shirley Horrocks	Film $903 Rental $269
Roger Horrocks	VHS $129
Narrator	
Angela D'Audney	
Original music	
Johnathon Besser	
Award	
Bronze Apple,	
Oakland, California	

661 Image of Light
The Photography of Sir George Pollock

'For me, light is the most exciting thing there is … all life depends on it … it actually is the energy which maintains life on earth. As a maker of images, I feel privileged that photography allows me to use the life-giving energy directly in my work. I want to celebrate the joy of light … the objects that I put in front of my lenses are really only devices for controlling light. In one sequence I developed the idea of light and of the colors of light as creative forces. These forces grow, and they're soon strong enough to form an order…' George Pollock has given 'visual concerts' in Europe, Australia, South Africa and the United States, as well as all over Britain. The film has very little narration.

Director	16 minutes
Anthony Roland	Color
Original music	Age range 12–adult
Keith Winter	Film $553 Rental $169
	VHS $79
Participant	
George Pollock	

614 The Ritual Art of Siim-Tanel Annus

During his time as a student, Siim-Tanel Annus became a member of an influential circle of artists and theorists, grouped around Tonis Vint. Although he had already undergone a long artistic development, he was still thought of as a 'young artist.' He is thus a 'phenomenon,' without age, without period, and outside trends. From the beginning he has created drawings – sensitive, abstract images composed of tiny dots. Later he created geometric forms in black and white. He threw himself into performance art before it became common in Estonia in the 1980s; his 'garden parties' caused scandals. Birds, sun, moon, energy, earth, water, air – all these were personified in his performances, as his pictures had been intended to represent 'Light in Paradise.' His actions are ritualistic, rich in symbolism, but everything is subordinate to the creation of a visual image by the artist.

Director	10 minutes
Jaanus Nogisto	Color
Original music	Age range 10–adult
Peeter Vähl	VHS $69
Also available in Estonian	

618 Processing the Signal
Video Art, Technology, Artists and Audience

A documentary made in America in 1988 and 1989 that brings together some of the most innovatory artists of video art – Bill Viola, Nam June Paik, Kit Fitzgerald, Paul Garrin, John Sanborn, Marie Perillo and Zbigniew Rybczynski among others. Covering video installations, 'satellite art,' video performance and the penetration of video art into conventional television, *Processing the Signal* is a discussion about these artists' ideas and opinions.

Director/Scenario	Awards
Marcello Dantas	Cine Golden Eagle,
	Washington DC
Participants	Best Video on Art,
Peer Bode	New York
Paul Garrin	Best Video, Paris
Kit Fitzgerald	Best Production, Brazil
John Hanhardt	
Nam June Paik	38 minutes
Marie Perillo	Color
Zbigniew Rybczynski	Age range 11–adult
John Sanborn	
Ira Schneider	VHS $119
Bill Viola	
Reynold Weidenaar	
Dean Winkler	

773 Visions of Future Living

This film presents architecture of the future, on land, in the ocean and in space. It moves outside America to include France, Switzerland and the Caribbean. We visit a futuristic home entirely controlled by a 'house-brain' in Florida, meet avant-garde architects on the Côte d'Azure, witness underwater 'self-growing' construction experiments in the Virgin Islands. We watch a French ocean-architect working in a diving cell in his office on a boat in Paris, and then accompany him on his underwater sightseeing vessel in the Mediterranean. Finally we meet the architect of the Space Station in Houston, USA. Fascinating original shots of space evoke a future which our children may experience one day: living on a space station, in orbit or on a colony on the moon – or even the planet Mars.

Part of the series *Architectural Adventures*

Director/Scenario	44 minutes
Ray Müller	Color
Also available in German	Age range 15–adult
	VHS $119

619 Play it Again, Nam
Portrait of Nam June Paik,
the Inventor of Video Art

Musician, thinker, theorist, friend of John
Cage, Stockhausen and Georges Maciunas,
Nam June Paik has transformed the use of
electronics as an art medium, challenging
our notions about what can be expected
from works of art.

Director/Scenario Jean-Paul Fargier	**Not for sale in the USA**
Original music/ Narration Ulrich Lask	**26 minutes** **Color** **English narration with a few subtitles**
Participant Nam June Paik	**Age range 9–adult** **VHS $99**

666 Krzysztof Wodiczko: Projections
Transforming Façades of Buildings
into Political, Public Art

The image of a homeless person
materializes on a Boston war monument.
A swastika suddenly appears on the
South African Embassy in London. A city
watches skeletal hands play a tuneless dirge
on a war museum in Pittsburgh. These are
just some of the controversial 'projections'
created by Polish artist Krzysztof Wodiczko,
who transforms buildings and structures
into political, public art. This documentary
intercuts scenes of Wodiczko preparing a
public projection in Jerusalem in 1991
with other projections in Europe and
North America. Each reflects the artist's
involvement in a broad range of political
issues: a blistering attack in Edinburgh on
Margaret Thatcher's economic policies; a
reflection on American–Canadian free
trade at a Toronto water filtration plant;
a street-level protest against the problem
of homelessness in New York through a
controversial prototype mobile shelter.
Interestingly, the only site where Wodiczko
is denied permission for a projection is
Montreal, at the Promenades de la
Cathédrale, despite his participation in
the city's *Cent Jours d'Art Contemporain.*
This innovative film reflects the personal
and political aspects of Wodiczko's art.

Director/Scenario Derek May	**55 minutes** **Color**
National Film Board of Canada	**Age range 14–adult** **Film $973** Rental $289 **VHS $139**

▲ 666
Krzysztof Wodiczko
Projection onto
Hirshhorn Museum,
Washington DC

▲ 614
Siim-Tanel Annus
Light performance art

23 1880 to the present

Modern Architecture and Design

In the modern period, perhaps more than in any other, progressive ideas have cross-fertilized between the fine and applied arts. The roots of this tendency can be seen in Art Nouveau and in the Arts and Crafts tradition of nineteenth-century England, and it came to fruition in *De Stijl*, the Bauhaus and their influence.

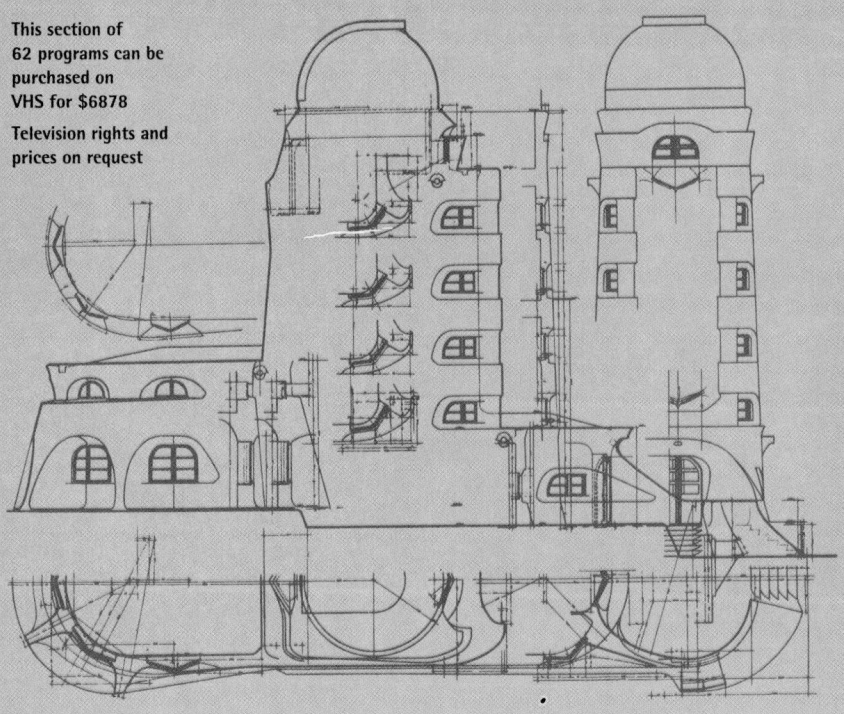

In the twentieth century, more than ever before, architects and designers have sought to make creations that stand as artistic statements, while, equally, fine artists have aspired to extend their practice to influence the whole environment, physical and conceptual, in which we live. Buildings and interiors have become artworks, while paintings and sculptures have tended to become 'environmental.' Thus artists such as Mondrian, Balla, Schwitters or Dubuffet have created total artistic habitats from their art. Others, such as Max Bill or van Doesburg, have practiced architecture and design alongside their painting. Such a state of affairs, however, has made for controversy. Art as 'total experience' has had its opponents, while architecture as 'artistic statement' has frequently been found an arrogant imposition on its users (see *Janus*, page 263, and *Beaubourg*, page 302). And there may yet be lessons to be learned from the traditional buildings of Africa or the spontaneous environmental art of graffiti.

History of Architecture and Design 1890–1939

This Open University/BBC series constitutes a thorough reinvestigation of the origins and theory of the modern movement in architecture and design. It combines a survey of the major developments during the period in Europe, Russia and America with several detailed case studies of themes or individual architects, and enables the viewer to understand the relationship between architecture and design in its historical context.

This series of 23 programs can be purchased on VHS for $2227 Reference S18

---

700   What is Architecture? An Architect at Work

Have you ever imagined designing your own home? Architect Geoffrey Baker describes how he planned his house in Ponteland, a village near Newcastle-upon-Tyne, listing the various features he wanted to incorporate and showing the preliminary sketches he made, together with buildings that influenced his choice. He admits a particular debt to Le Corbusier and his 1924 houses for workers, based on a cube. We explore a scale model of the house and see how the particular site chosen for it influenced the design; and finally we tour the finished house, paying special attention to the materials and colors Baker used. By seeing how the mind of one particular architect works, we are offered an insight into the thinking of architects in general.

Part of the series *History of Architecture and Design 1890–1939*

Director	25 minutes
Edward Hayward	**Black and white**
Presenter/Writer	**Age range 18–adult**
Dr Geoffrey Baker	**VHS $99**
Open University/BBC	

---

701   The Universal International Exhibition, Paris 1900

A mammoth – and some would say, chaotic – event, the Universal International Exhibition held in Paris in 1900 can be seen as a late celebration of nineteenth-century values, imperialism and eclecticism. It included displays of real live 'natives' from the colonies and real camels, a complete medieval French village and its inhabitants reconstructed on the Right Bank, and buildings ranging from Serbian Byzantine and English Jacobean to Austrian Gothic. But the exhibition was also intended to look forward to the new century: an elevated electric railway surrounded the site, and it held examples of what the general public considered to be the last word in modern architecture and design, epitomized by the Art Nouveau. Contemporary Pathe News film, still photographs and writings show us the tangle of artistic ideas from which the modern movements of the twentieth century were to emerge.

Part of the series *History of Architecture and Design 1890–1939*

Director	25 minutes
Nick Levinson	**Black and white**
Presenter/Writer	**Age range 18–adult**
Tim Benton	**VHS $99**
Open University/BBC	

---

702   Charles Rennie Mackintosh: Hill House

A detailed look at the inside and outside of Hill House, Helensburgh, near Glasgow, with its panoramic view of the Clyde, built by Mackintosh for the publisher Walter Blackie in 1903. In *Memories of Charles Rennie Mackintosh,* Blackie described how he came to commission the house after seeing Mackintosh's Glasgow School of Art. How did the relationship between client and architect and the client's individual needs affect the style of the house, and how are its interior and exterior design related to each other? Also how much, or how little, did traditional Scottish forms of architecture influence Mackintosh's work?

Part of the series *History of Architecture and Design 1890–1939*

Director	25 minutes
Nick Levinson	**Color**
Presenter/Writer	**Age range 18–adult**
Sandra Millikin	**VHS $99**
Open University/BBC	

703 Industrial Architecture: AEG and Fagus Factories

The problems of turning industrial buildings into architecture are illustrated in two German factories built by two different architects just before the First World War. At first the gigantic monumentalism of Behrens' AEG turbine factory seems very different from the delicate glass envelope of Gropius's Fagus shoe-last factory; but we find that Gropius was in fact indebted to Behrens in many ways, although his handling of glass in the façades was all his own, and revolutionary. Both men were interested in the ideas of K F Schinkel, an early nineteenth-century Neo-classical architect, and we can trace a continuity of classical architectural ideas through the still recognizable columns and pediments of Behrens to the less recognizable but still essentially classical forms of the Fagus factory.

Part of the series *History of Architecture and Design 1890–1939*

Director	**25 minutes**
Nick Levinson	**Color**
Presenter/Writer	**Age range 18–adult**
Tim Benton	**VHS $99**
Open University/BBC	

704 Frank Lloyd Wright: The Robie House

A guided tour of one of Wright's masterpieces, a splendid private house built for industrialist Frederick Robie in South Woodlawn, Chicago. The Robie house was the culmination of Wright's 'prairie house' style, so-called because its low horizontal lines were meant to blend with the flat landscape all around. Designed as a number of 'space blocks' grouped around a central core, the area that was architecturally shaped included the balconies, terrace, court and garden – Wright's aim was to create not merely a house, but a whole environment. He even took command of all the details of the interior, and designed stained glass, fabrics and furniture for it. He was convinced that buildings have a profound effect on the people who inhabit them, so that the architect, whether he realizes it or not, is really a molder of humankind.

Part of the series *History of Architecture and Design 1890–1939*

Director	**25 minutes**
Edward Hayward	**Color**
Presenter/Writer	**Age range 18–adult**
Sandra Millikin	**VHS $99**
Open University/BBC	

705 RM Schindler: The Lovell Beach House

In the mid- and late twenties two houses were built for the same patron, Dr Philip Lovell of Los Angeles, by two different Austrian architects who had each emigrated to America and spent time working as assistants to Frank Lloyd Wright. The Beach House at Newport Beach, south of Los Angeles, was designed by Rudolf Schindler, and incorporated several devices for healthy living specially requested by Dr Lovell. The other building is the Health House near Hollywood, designed by Richard Neutra; and the work of both men can be seen as closer to the emergent 'International Style' than to that of Wright, their ex-teacher.

Part of the series *History of Architecture and Design 1890–1939*

Director	**25 minutes**
Edward Hayward	**Color**
Presenter/Writer	**Age range 18–adult**
Sandra Millikin	**VHS $99**
Open University/BBC	

706 Erich Mendelsohn: The Einstein Tower

The Einstein Tower in Potsdam near Berlin is considered a key Expressionist building – its curved, organic forms depart from all traditional expectations of what a tower should look like. We trace the genesis of its design back to Erich Mendelsohn's letters and sketches sent from the front during the First World War. The rounded irregular forms of the tower were inspired by his passion for music and his interest in Einstein's revolutionary ideas; but the technical problems were daunting in the extreme. It is a tribute to the brilliance of Mendelsohn and the enthusiasm of his client, Dr Freundlich, that such a complex and beautiful concept ever actually materialized.

Part of the series *History of Architecture and Design 1890–1939*

Director	**25 minutes**
Nick Levinson	**Black and white**
Presenter/Writer	**Age range 16–adult**
Dennis Sharp	**VHS $99**
Open University/BBC	

704
Frank Lloyd Wright
The Robie House

703
Walter Gropius, Adolf Meyer,
Eduard Werner
Fagus Shoe-last Factory

The Bauhaus at Weimar, 1919–23

This was the most famous school of architecture, craftsmanship and design in modern times, and has had a huge influence on art-school education all over the world. In its early days it was in Weimar, Germany (it later moved twice and was closed down by the Nazis in 1933). George Adams was a student during the Weimar period. He discusses the attitude of the students toward their work, prevailing trends in art, and their famous tutors, who included Itten and van Doesburg. Some rare artefacts made at the Bauhaus during the early 1920s are also displayed and studied, including tea sets, textiles, silverware and furniture; part of the Bauhaus's importance was that it did not draw back from tackling the problems of mass-production.

Part of the series *History of Architecture and Design 1890–1939*

Director	25 minutes
Edward Hayward	Black and white
Presenter/Writer	Age range 18–adult
Tim Benton	VHS $99
Open University/BBC	

Berlin Siedlungen

Berlin is famous for its innovative pre-war housing estates, or *Siedlungen.* On location in Berlin, we trace their development from the picturesque garden-city style of Staaken, built in 1914, to the work of Taut at Britz and of several architects including Gropius, the director of the Bauhaus, at Siemensstadt just before the war. The later developments boldly proclaim the identity of the Marxist housing associations which built them, in contrast to the more traditional design of neighboring estates. Despite their large-scale composition, made up of blocks of flats, the garden-city ideal is never far away. Open balconies, trees and gardens help to make these some of the best housing estates ever built.

Part of the series *History of Architecture and Design 1890–1939*

Director	25 minutes
Nick Levinson	Color
Presenter/Writer	Age range 18–adult
Tim Benton	VHS $99
Open University/BBC	

The Weissenhof Siedlung, Stuttgart 1927

The Weissenhof *Siedlung,* or exhibition estate, was built near Stuttgart in Germany in 1927 as a solid manifesto of modern movement architects, a demonstration of their abilities in the field of housing. The white stuccoed, flat-roofed buildings were designed by men who would later become well-known: Peter Behrens, Gropius, Mies van der Rohe, Oud and Le Corbusier. Weissenhof soon achieved fame – some would say, notoriety – and was generally taken to be the first public exhibition of what was later called 'International Style.' Examining a number of houses at Weissenhof, we ask how far the architecture matches up to the architects' ideas of the logical use of modern materials, and how far it fulfils their uninhibited and uncompromising search through their building for 'new ways to live.'

Part of the series *History of Architecture and Design 1890–1939*

Director	25 minutes
Edward Hayward	Color
Presenter/Writer	Age range 18–adult
Tim Benton	VHS $99
Open University/BBC	

The International Exhibition of Arts, Paris 1925

The International Exhibition of Modern Decorative and Industrial Arts, to give it its full title, was a curious mixture. Many of the commercial and national pavilions displayed both avant-garde and more conventional design, often with an emphasis on craftsmanship and exotic materials. Two buildings were outstanding: Melnikov's Russian Pavilion, and Le Corbusier's Esprit Nouveau Pavilion. Hidden away in a less than prominent position, this 'cellular living unit' was made of simple industrial materials and was completely free of decoration. Infinitely extendable, it brought the latest technology to bear on the problem of mass housing.

Part of the series *History of Architecture and Design 1890–1939*

Director	25 minutes
Nick Levinson	Black and white
Presenter/Writer	Age range 18–adult
Tim Benton	VHS $99
Open University/BBC	

Adolf Loos

The Czech architect Adolf Loos was also a journalist and a theorist of art. Most of his work was done in Austria, France, Germany and Switzerland, but he was a great admirer of Britain's and America's social systems and in consequence an admirer of their architecture too. He was capable of adapting ideas from Charles Rennie Mackintosh, for example, to suburban Vienna. His elegant and individual designs were remarkable for their use of space, and sensitive and sophisticated use of materials. We tour some of his shops and houses in Vienna, including the Goldmann and Salatsch store, Knize's Gentleman's Outfitters, and the Scheu and Moller houses.

Part of the series *History of Architecture and Design 1890–1939*

Director	25 minutes
Edward Hayward	Color
Presenter/Writer	Age range 18–adult
Tim Benton	VHS $99
Open University/BBC	

712 Le Corbusier: Villa Savoye

Le Corbusier famously called his private
houses 'machines à habiter,' or machines
to be lived in. Perhaps he wanted to imply
that they were so different from other
houses that they constituted a new form
altogether. Certainly that is what we are
likely to feel when we approach his
Villa Savoye near Paris, finished in 1930.
The house is empty now, but stands as one
of the most impressive monuments to
Le Corbusier's ideas about architecture
and the modern movement in general.
A low square box resting on 'stilts' of
reinforced concrete, it reveals his interest
in ocean liners and his preoccupation
with abstract 'space blocks.' Photographs
of the house when occupied give some
idea of what it was like to live in – not
'mechanized living,' but a 'design for living.'

Part of the series *History of Architecture
and Design 1890–1939*

Director	**25 minutes**
Nick Levinson	**Color**
Presenter/Writer	**Age range 18–adult**
Tim Benton	**VHS $99**
Open University/BBC	

713 English Flats of the Thirties

A comparison of two examples of designs
of flats in 1930s England. One is Quarry Hill
Estate in Leeds, a huge council-housing
scheme scheduled for demolition. After
showing us the back-to-back streets from
which the tenants of Quarry Hill were likely
to have come, the narrator explains how
the new estate adopted the most advanced
contemporary ideas of both construction
and social engineering, and discusses
whether or not it was a success. In contrast,
we then examine Highpoint I, a luxury block
in London, designed in the grand manner
for much richer tenants. In spite of the gulf
between their tenants' incomes, we can see
great similarities between the two projects,
and also considerable differences between
those and tower blocks being built on the
Continent at the same time.

Part of the series *History of Architecture
and Design 1890–1939*

Director	**25 minutes**
Edward Hayward	**Black and white**
Presenter/Writer	**Age range 18–adult**
Tim Benton	**VHS $99**
Open University/BBC	

◀◀ 709
Le Corbusier, Pierre Jeanneret
Axonometric plan,
Weissenhof Siedlung

▲ 712
Le Corbusier
Villa Savoye

▲ 713
Berthold Lubetkin
Highpoint I

Connell, Ward and Lucas was one of the leading Modernist architectural partnerships in the 1930s. Amyas Connell himself is interviewed about his house 'High and Over' in Amersham, which has many features reminiscent of the International Style, but which also has design affinities with Italian villas – Connell reveals that he was influenced by Michelangelo as well as by the International movement. Then we move on to Moor Park in Rickmansworth, designed by Basil Ward, and discuss its design in detail, particularly the use of pilotis and other hallmarks of the modern movement. Finally we ask how far the British public of the time was prepared to accept such modern house designs.

Part of the series *History of Architecture and Design 1890–1939*

Director	**25 minutes**
Edward Hayward	**Color**
Presenter/Writer	**Age range 18–adult**
Dr Geoffrey Baker	**VHS $99**
Open University/BBC	

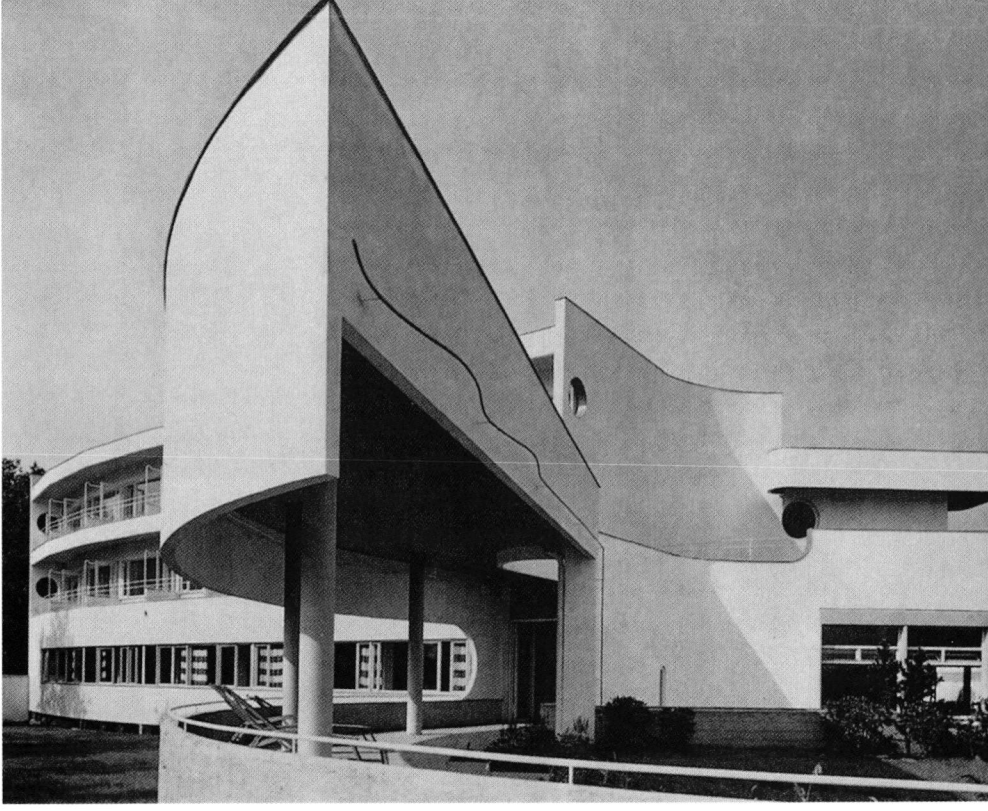

The least well-known period of German architect Hans Scharoun's career is his work in the 1930s. After the First World War he had emerged as an Expressionist; he soon moved on to the International Style, but unusually he did not abandon the sculptural and 'expressionistic' elements of his early work. Here we look at three houses he built during the thirties; unlike many of his contemporaries, Scharoun stayed in Germany and continued to practice under the Nazis, although in a restricted capacity. The Schminke house of 1933 must be one of the last great International Style buildings in Germany; however, the Scharf and Mohrmann houses, designed in 1939, show Scharoun reverting to vernacular forms and materials on the exteriors while creating some of the most exciting open-plan interiors of the modern movement.

Part of the series *History of Architecture and Design 1890–1939*

Director	**25 minutes**
Nick Levinson	**Color**
Presenter/Writer	**Age range 18–adult**
Tim Benton	**VHS $99**
Open University/BBC	

The Brighton Museum, England, houses a unique collection of 1920s French and English furniture. It is arranged in sets to show the marriage between furniture and interior design emphasized by some designers of the period. Examining individual pieces in detail, we pay particular attention to the way they were manufactured, and conclude that the new metal furniture needed just as high a degree of craftsmanship as more traditional wooden items. And we investigate the influence of French designers on English craftsmen after the 1925 Paris Exhibition of Modern Decorative and Industrial Arts.

Part of the series *History of Architecture and Design 1890–1939*

Directors	**25 minutes**
Patricia Hodgson	**Black and white**
Bennett Maxwell	**Age range 18–adult**
Presenter/Writer	**VHS $99**
Tim Benton	
Open University/BBC	

Deanery Gardens fits its environment, the red-brick Thames-side village of Sonning, to perfection. Its designer Edwin Lutyens, perhaps the greatest British architect of the last one hundred years, created buildings that are supremely English in character: a tour of Deanery Gardens emphasizes its traditional aspects and the influences such as the Art and Crafts movement that went into his work. And yet it is also possible to see Lutyens as a classical designer, for his buildings are as logically and consciously planned as they could possibly be – a fact which their appearance of mellowed red-brick, tiles and half-timbering is apt to conceal.

Part of the series *History of Architecture and Design 1890–1939*

Director	**25 minutes**
Edward Hayward	**Black and white**
Presenter/Writer	**Age range 18–adult**
Dr Geoffrey Baker	**VHS $99**
Open University/BBC	

718   The London Underground

In the 1930s the London Underground Railway, so often felt today to be dirty, inefficient and obsolescent, was seen as highly efficient and a symbol of the future, almost a form of fantasy. Here we visit the three stations at the northern end of the Piccadilly line, built in the 1930s by the architect Charles Holden. Cockfosters, a piece of concrete-and-glass functionalism which manages to adapt itself to a semi-rural environment, Oakwood, with its striking use of London Transport 'house style', and Southgate, with its integration of different kinds of transport, are structures perfectly fitted to their function; they also encapsulate the image of the underground in the 1930s.

Part of the series *History of Architecture and Design 1890–1939*

Director	**25 minutes**
Edward Hayward	**Black and white**
Presenter/Writer	**Age range 18–adult**
Dr Geoffrey Baker	**VHS $99**
Open University/BBC	

719   'Moderne' and 'Modernistic'

By the mid 1930s the International Style was in full swing, but it was too revolutionary and austere to attract most of the British public. They wanted something showier and more exotic, especially for commercial buildings like factories, cinemas, and holiday-spirited seaside architecture; and they found it in the 'moderne' and 'modernistic' styles with their mixture of ingredients, often part-Egyptian, part-classical and part-modern. Thomas Wallis's Hoover factory, a classical composition with exotic decoration, is compared with the Le Corbusier Modernist style, which entirely rejects ornamentation. Seaside architecture is illustrated in Blackpool and Frinton, from fairground moderne to buildings by Joseph Emberton and Oliver Hill, which merge into the International Style proper.

Part of the series *History of Architecture and Design 1890–1939*

Director	**25 minutes**
Nick Levinson	**Black and white**
Presenter/Writer	**Age range 18–adult**
Dr Geoffrey Baker	**VHS $99**
Open University/BBC	

720   The Other Tradition

Despite the achievements of the modern movement, the greater part of between-the-wars architecture in Britain remained traditional, exemplified by buildings such as Manchester City Library and Liverpool Cathedral. Country-house designs of the period also show how little the modern movement had gained ground. Some modern buildings were appearing, of course, and they are contrasted with the traditional styles and also those buildings influenced by Scandinavian and Dutch developments. In conclusion we focus on the simplified classicism of the winning design by Grey Wornum for the Royal Institute of British Architects building: conservative tradition modified by Modernist taste, a symbol of the restrained excellence appreciated by the profession.

Part of the series *History of Architecture and Design 1890–1939*

Director	**25 minutes**
Miriam Rapp	**Black and white**
Presenter/Writer	**Age range 18–adult**
Dr Geoffrey Baker	**VHS $99**
Open University/BBC	

▼ 715
Hans Scharoun
Workers Collective Hostel
for the single and
newly married

▲ 719
Thomas Wallis
Hoover Factory

721   The Suburban Style

The semi-detached house has largely been ignored as an architectural form, but that has never affected its popularity with house-buyers. Touring Ilford, near London, we examine the design of suburban houses and the factors that shaped the suburbs – for example, the growth of 'estates' and the availability of transport to take their inhabitants to work. In particular we examine and contrast an Edwardian terraced house and a 1928 'semi'; the Edwardian house was built to accommodate servants, and the decoration of the front contrasts with the rougher, cheaper aspect of the back, while the 1928 house is differently planned and relatively undecorated. Perhaps the 'semi' has been unfairly neglected by the world of architecture?

Part of the series *History of Architecture and Design 1890–1939*

Director	**25 minutes**
Patricia Hodgson	**Color**
Presenter/Writer	**Age range 18–adult**
Stephen Bayley	**VHS $99**
Open University/BBC	

722   The Housing Question

The social effects of architecture are examined through three post-war British housing estates. London County Council's Alton West estate at Roehampton, built in the fifties, was a testimony to the survival of interest in Le Corbusier's ideas, often blamed for the failure of modern architecture. Did the estate have a chance of becoming an attractive environment to live in? Trellick Tower in north Kensington, London, is a thirty-six-story building of impressive sculptural form, but how successful is it? The architect denies the theory that vandalism is linked to a lack of individuality in architectural design. Finally the Byker program in Newcastle appears to be something quite new for Britain.

Part of the series *History of Architecture and Design 1890–1939*

Director	**25 minutes**
Nick Levinson	**Black and white**
Presenter/Writer	**Age range 18–adult**
Stephen Bayley	**VHS $99**
Open University/BBC	

El Lissitzky
Constructivist of the Russian Avant-Garde

Leo Lorez portrays the work of the Soviet Constructivist El Lissitzky as an architect, photographer, painter, typographer and designer of exhibitions. Lissitzky's life was that of a pre-war cosmopolitan. Born in 1890 in Smolensk, he went to Germany to study architecture in Darmstadt. He returned to Russia when Marc Chagall invited him to teach at the Vibetsk Art School. Under the influence of the Russian revolution and its fantastic vision of a future to be designed afresh, he became one of the most important artists of the avant-garde led by Malevich. In the 1920s he came in contact with the German Dadaist circle around Kurt Schwitters and Hans Arp. He created his 'Prouns', a new kind of visual grammar or unit of visual phenomena, which he declared to be 'changing stations' from the two-dimensionality of the canvas to the three-dimensionality of architecture. His architectural projects which were never executed – the Lenin Tribune, a podium from which Lenin could address the masses, and the Wolkenbügel, a skyscraper in Moscow – are realized here by computer animation and shown as if at the sites they were originally planned for. The video draws on authentic picture and sound material, including sequences from Vertov's famous films and original quotes from Lissitzky himself, to portray him as a central figure in classical modern art.

'The cinematography is sharp, distinct, and well lit. Narration is kept to a minimum… Lissitzky's legacy has such a contemporary but classic feel and appearance. Adults, students, and the general public will enjoy this portrait of the artist. For many, Lissitzky will be a serendipitous discovery. Recommended for both public library and college collections.'
Video Rating Guide for Libraries, USA

Director/Scenario	**88 minutes**
Leo Lorez	**Color and**
Also available in German	**black and white**
	Age range 14–adult
	VHS $189

Movable Steel Bridges
Historical Survey: Draw, Bascule, Lift and Swing Bridges

Movable Steel Bridges starts with a historical survey of known and unknown, beautiful, rare and exceptional movable bridges all over the world, and then examines the four main types of movable bridge – the drawbridge, the bascule bridge, the lift bridge, including the roll-on roll-off bridge, and the swing bridge. The structural and mechanical aspects of bridge construction are extensively dealt with, as are subjects such as windloading and hydraulics.

'This is visually very well done. Bridges are seen from angles not available to casual viewers, through the eyes of those who see beauty in mechanism. There are several diagrams that help explain the overall principles of how these bridges work.'
Video Rating Guide for Libraries, USA

Director	**78 minutes**
Nico NG Muyen	**Color**
Delft University	**Age range 14–adult**
of Technology	**VHS $179**
Also available in Dutch and French	

The Man with Modern Nerves
Adolf Loos, Pioneer Architect

The model used in this animated rhythmic fantasy is based on sketches of terraced Mexican pyramids done by Adolf Loos in 1923 for a design for a city hall in Mexico. Known for the purity and simplicity of his style, Adolf Loos is one of the pioneers of modern architecture. This film was conceived without narration.

Directors/Scenario	**8 minutes**
Bady Minck	**Black and white**
Stefan Stratil	**Age range 14–adult**
Original music	**Film $483** Rental $149
Andre Wergenthaler	**VHS $69**

502B **The Rietveld Schröder House**
Restoration of a *De Stijl* Interior and Exterior

In 1924 Mrs Schröder-Schräder of Utrecht commissioned the architect Gerrit Rietveld to build a house for her. Today the result of their co-operation – for the design was truly a combined effort – is considered a monument to Modernism and the purest expression of the principles of *De Stijl*. Mrs Schröder lived in the house until her death in 1985; she was ninety-five years old. Toward the end of her life she decided that she wanted the house to be restored as far as possible to its original condition, and she asked Bertus Mulder, an architect who had worked for Rietveld in the past, to undertake this reconstruction process. The crucial elements of the 'new way of living' for which this house was a manifesto in 1925 – for example, the use of space and the system of sliding panels or walls especially created for Mrs Schröder – had disappeared during sixty years of use, repainting and redecoration; but twenty-four black and white photographs of the house taken shortly after it was built, together with the memories of Mrs Schröder and her three children, became Mulder's primary sources. There were others – for example, he found slivers of paint which revealed the original colors used. All the phases of his effort to reconstruct the house were filmed, and in the film he dwells particularly on the noteworthy aspects of Rietveld's architecture. In 1987 the house was opened to the public, and it is now a museum.

Director	**30 minutes**
Ike Bertels	**Color**
Restoration-architect	**Age range 16–adult**
Bertus Mulder	**VHS $99**
Also available in Dutch	

515 **The Bauhaus**
Its Impact on the World of Design

This film draws attention to the great social responsibility of town planners, architects and mass-production designers, whose job it is to design the cities, houses and goods that form humankind's everyday surroundings. It sets out to show that of all art institutions in the 1920s, the Bauhaus was the most intensive in its approach to the task of aestheticizing the modern technical world. At the same time it indicates the importance of design in general, for without it the human need for beauty would remain at least partly unsatisfied.

For more information see pages 132 and 133

Director	**19 minutes**
Detten Schliermacher	**Color**
Original music	**Age range 14–adult**
Hans Posegga	**Film $623** Rental $189
Also available in German	**VHS $89**

502 **Theo van Doesburg**
New Aesthetics for a New World

Theo van Doesburg is best known as a painter and as the founder and editor of the avant-garde magazine *De Stijl* (*The Style*, 1917–28). But van Doesburg was also active in other fields: literature, philosophy, architecture, typography. This film explores his life and work, with the emphasis on his architecture, through posthumous works and documentary evidence about the artist and his wife recently given to the Netherlands.

Director	**30 minutes**
Frank den Oudsten	**Color**
	Age range 14–adult
	Film $693 Rental $199
	VHS $99

503
El Lissitzky in his studio

502B
Gerrit Rietveld
The renovated Rietveld
Schröder House

972   Japonism, Part Two
Japanese Influences on Western Art:
Domestic Architecture and Ceramic Design

A brief examination of Japanese influence
on western architecture and applied arts.
David Leach, himself a ceramist and expert
on Japanese culture, talks about his father,
Bernard Leach, a pioneer in uniting oriental
and western traditions.

Director	**15 minutes**
Guido De Bruyn	**Color**
Also available in Dutch	**Age range 15–adult**
and French	**VHS $79**

The Roots of Modern Design in Finland

Celebrating the spirit of the 1930s, when
Scandinavian design first gained wide
acclaim, this film juxtaposes period movie
clips and documentary footage with images
of a wide range of Finnish architecture,
interior design and furnishings by Rivel
and many others. It explores the idealistic,
even naïve ideology of the day, with its
faith in the 'light, health and efficiency'
of Functionalism (or *funkkis,* as the Finns
call it), and in 'optimism with pragmatism.'
The film also charts the continued influence
of the epoch in the 'new functionalism'
of design today.

Director	**40 minutes**
Kaisa Blomstedt	**Color**
Writers	**Age range 16–adult**
Kaisa Blomstedt	**Film $693** Rental $199
Mikael Merenmies	**VHS $99**
Also available in Finnish	

742   Scandinavian Design:
The Lunning Prize 1951–70

When Frederik Lunning left his native
Denmark for the USA in the 1920s,
Scandinavian design was virtually unknown,
and few people believed that Lunning
could establish a market for Danish
porcelain and glass in New York – but by
1940 his business was flourishing. Then,
of course, the war cut off supplies from
Europe. After the war, in an effort to
replenish his depleted stock, Lunning sent
Kaj Dessau to find fresh merchandise in
Denmark, Sweden, Norway and Finland,
the only countries where industrial art still
flourished. Delighted with the quality of
what he found, Dessau felt that a showcase
for Scandinavian products should be set up
in the New York shop, and he also proposed
the establishment of an awards fund
for young artists who, despite the war and
its shortages, had persevered in the
creation of beauty and originality. The first
Lunning prize was awarded in 1951.

Director	**10 minutes**
Pekka Mandart	**Color and**
Original music	**black and white**
Pera Pirkola	**Age range 15–adult**
	VHS $69

822   Master of Glass

Master of Glass is a documentary about
an exceptional craftsman – Per Steen
Hebsgaard, the dynamic force behind an
amazing development in modern Danish
glass. For centuries glass pieces have been
joined together with lead alone, and this
could only be done in one dimension.
Medieval methods are still widely used in
works of art made from glass, but
Hebsgaard – who, incidentally, began his
working life installing double-glazing
before moving on to a firm that specialized
in stained glass – invented new techniques
that avoid the use of lead. Then he began
to invite the best Danish and foreign artists
to explore all the possibilities inherent in
glass, using new or old techniques to create
paintings, collages and even sculptures; one
of his aims, he says, was to liberate stained
glass from being used in churches alone.
Hebsgaard's success lies in his ability to
inspire and collaborate with other artists,
although he himself says 'at a very early
stage I realized that I could be number
thirty-five as an artist, and I wanted to be
number one as a craftsman.' The film
concentrates on two projects in particular.
One is a large sculpture in glass created
by Jan Sivertsen. Together Hebsgaard and
Sivertsen use silicone to assemble and
erect the fragile material at the FIAC art
exhibition in Paris. The second project,
with Bjørn Nørgaard, is a 23-foot-high
glass pavilion for a Danish brewery, made
of more than five thousand pieces of
colored and painted glass which are then
fired and leaded – a fitting challenge for
the 'master of glass.'

Director	**36 minutes**
Peter Christensen	**Color**
Participant	**Age range 14–adult**
Per Steen Hebsgaard	**VHS $109**
Writer	
Nanna Sten Jensen	
Original music	
Niels Hauge	
Also available in Danish	

Chichester Theological College

The building by Ahrends, Burton and Koralek in Chichester, England, is analyzed using live action, diagrams and animation, with particular reference to local and aesthetic, spatial and functional considerations. The second part of the video comprises a discussion between the presenter and the three architects.

'…a lot of good information about architecture…would be useful in teaching students about structure, design, and how buildings function within the environment they create…a good video to view or use as a teaching aid.'
Video Rating Guide for Libraries, USA

Director	**45 minutes**
Gavin Nettleton	**Color**
Consultant	**Age range 16–adult**
Dr Geoffrey Baker	**VHS $129**

761 **Public-sector Housing in Amsterdam 1900–91**

Every foreign visitor to Amsterdam notices its mixture of small-town cosiness and international character, but may not stop to consider the reason for it: unlike most city centers, which are full of offices and expensive privately owned houses, Amsterdam has kept and renewed public-sector housing in apparently unaffordable locations. Since early this century, Amsterdam's planners have aimed to sweep away the slums where the workers used to live. The painter J Sierhuis recalls his grandmother, who brought up eight or nine children in two rooms, several of them succumbing to TB before they reached adulthood. Different schools of architects had different ideas for public housing, some of them magnificently futuristic, but the devastation of the Second World War meant that quantity, not quality, was what the people demanded – sometimes with violence. Since the 1980s nineteenth-century neighborhoods have been restored or demolished and rebuilt while the inhabitants are temporarily rehoused. More than half the dwellings in the city are now in the public sector.

Director	**46 minutes**
Henk Raaf	**Color**
Also available in Dutch	**Age range 16–adult**
	VHS $129

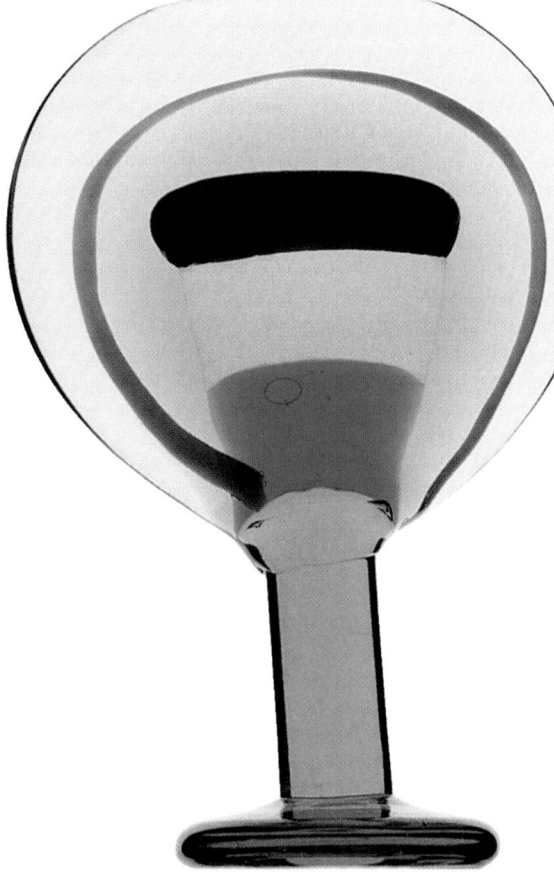

822
Bjørn Nørgaard
Fredericia Brewery
Pavilion

761
Michel de Klerk
Entrance detail, public housing, Amsterdam

742
Oiva Toikka
Lolipop

23 Modern Architecture and Design

197

735 Le Corbusier, Part One 1887–1929

Produced to celebrate the centenary of the birth of Swiss architect, town-planner, painter, sculptor and poet Charles-Edouard Jeanneret-Gris, known as Le Corbusier, this documentary is the first in the world to have been post-produced entirely in digital video. Moreover, the computer and 3-D techniques employed make it possible to visualize, in a realistic way, projects that the architect was unable to complete in his lifetime: his famous *City of Three Million Inhabitants* (1922) for instance, and the *Voisin* plan in Paris (1925). Twelve minutes of the work are devoted to the simulation of *in situ* scale models of the architect's most ambitious projects. This three-part documentary, based primarily on interviews granted to local radio stations by Le Corbusier in the 1950s, lets the artist speak for himself about his controversial 40-year career. Several previously unreleased archival documents, filmed architecture courses and 16mm pictures taken by the artist increase the viewer's understanding of the life and work of one of the greatest architects of our century. The first part focuses on the development of Le Corbusier's philosophy and work from the earliest days up to the *Villa Savoye*.

Director	**57 minutes**
Jacques Barsac	**Color**
	Age range 15-adult
Co-producers	
Antenne 2 La Sept	**VHS $139**
Mission Cable	
Gourmont	
INA	
RTSR	
Channel 4	
Thomson	
Foundation Le Corbusier	
Plan Construction	
Plan Recherche Image	
The Ministeries of Culture,	
Urbanism, Post and	
Telecommunications and	
Foreign Affairs	

Awards
Gold Medal, Academy
of Architecture, Paris
Grand Prix, International
Festival Films on Art, Paris
Grand Prix, Lausanne
Press Award, Lausanne

Also available in French

736 Le Corbusier, Part Two 1928–1936

The second part is devoted to urban planning and Le Corbusier's ambitious, unrealised projects.

54 minutes
Color
Age range 15-adult
VHS $139

737 Le Corbusier, Part Three 1945–1965

The third part features Le Corbusier's greatest accomplishments of the post-war years, from the *Unité d'Habitation* in Marseilles to the *Firminy Church*.

67 minutes
Color
Age range 15-adult
VHS $139

738 Le Corbusier 1887–1965

Short version combining 735, 736 and 737.

60 minutes
Color
Age range 15-adult
VHS $159

739 Le Corbusier: Villa La Roche

Tim Benton examines the history of Villa La Roche in Paris. Le Corbusier developed the site for the Swiss banker and art collector, Roal La Roche. Taking a detailed look at the finished house and comparing its present state with photographs taken in the 1920s, the program examines how the particular architectural forms came about.
The development of the plans and ideas for the house reflect the often divergent desires of the architect and clients, as well as Le Corbusier's involvement with the ideas and practice of purist art at the time, exemplified in the magazine *L'Esprit Nouveau*.

Part of the series
Modern Art, Practices and Debates

Director	**25 minutes**
Nick Levinson	**Color**
Presenter	**Age range 18-adult**
Tim Benton	**VHS $99**
Open University/BBC	

The Finnish architect Alvar Aalto (1898–1976) was one of this century's great reformers in architecture and interior design. Aalto's work demonstrates an intense individualism combined with clear-sighted understanding of the international architectural trends of his day. A striking characteristic of his work is a rationalism that is sensitive to both humankind and nature. So powerful was his personal style that there is no Aalto school of architecture, nor is it possible to identify any architects whose work had a particular influence on him, although from the realm of free-form architecture Frank Lloyd Wright stands out as a point of comparison, as does Le Corbusier. In his later years Alvar Aalto tried to avoid publicity and was rarely interviewed; he chose to speak through his work. This film includes his last interview for television. It shows major examples of his architecture – hospitals and industrial buildings as well as domestic projects – and also many of the furnishings and fittings on which his reputation largely rests. These were often created specifically for his interiors, but then would be adapted for general manufacture, frequently becoming acknowledged classics. Much of his furniture is still in production, and it is stylishly and imaginatively presented in this film.

For more information see page 264

Director	57 minutes
Piero Berengo Gardin	Color
	Age range 16–adult

Film $973 Rental $289
VHS $139

737
Le Corbusier
Unité d'Habitation, Marseilles

763
Alvar Aalto
Paimio Sanatorium
Sun deck

764 Homage to Humanity

The *Grande Arche* in Paris and its Architect

The *Grande Arche*, marking the bicentenary of the French revolution, was inaugurated at La Défense in the west of Paris on July 14, 1989. It is situated within the historic axis which includes the Louvre, the Tuileries, the Place de la Concorde, the Champs-Elysées, the Etoile and the Arc de Triomphe. The design, by Danish architect Johan Otto von Spreckelsen, was chosen in a competition initiated by President Mitterrand in 1982. Spreckelsen died in 1987 without seeing his work completed. In this portrait, made between 1983 and 1989, the architect describes his conception of the *Grande Arche*, and other buildings in Denmark. He also speaks of the joys and difficulties of working in Paris, and of his meeting with President Mitterrand, who followed the work's progress with great interest.

In Danish with English subtitles

Director/Scenario/ Narration	**45 minutes**
Dan Tschernia	**Color**
	Subtitles
Participant	**Age range 15–adult**
Johan Otto von Spreckelsen	**VHS $119**

◀◀ 764
Johan Otto von Spreckelsen
The Grande Arche, Paris

◥ 766
Jim Stirling
History Faculty, Cambridge

766   **Jim Stirling's Architecture**

James Stirling, born in 1926, was one of
the few British architects of this century to
receive undisputed recognition, even
though he was regarded as a rebel, and
worked outside the mainstream of modern
architecture. His completed projects in
Britain include the History Faculty at
Cambridge University; Leicester University
Engineering Department; Queen's Building,
Oxford, and mass construction housing at
Runcorn. In the film we see six of his major
schemes completed in the United Kingdom,
while Stirling explains his personal
philosophy, its democratic roots and his
respect for the individual.

Director	**50 minutes**
Ron Parks	**Color**
Participant	**Age range 15–adult**
Jim Stirling	**Film $903** Rental $269
Arts Council of	**VHS $129**
Great Britain	

767   **An Affirmation of Life**
       The Architecture of Moriyama

The Japanese-Canadian architect
Raymond Moriyama is the creator of
major, outstandingly individual buildings.
An Affirmation of Life takes us into
the serene, sweeping spaces of his
administrative center in Ontario, and,
most dramatically, into the Science North
Center at Sudbury – a building structured
like a snowflake spanning a huge cleft in
the bedrock. The cliff faces and natural
features are fully incorporated into the
modern construction, and local miners
were employed to create the underground
passages and chambers that are also a
part of the scheme. The program also looks
at the architect's design for a public
monument, the ceremonial bell presented
in gratitude to the people of Ontario by
its Japanese community. Moriyama himself
talks about his projects in a manner
deceptively, though engagingly, direct and
simple; in the past he has won a contract
in competition with other architects by
presenting no plans or specifications but
simply arriving in person to tell the clients
of his vision for their building. But clients
and colleagues of Moriyama speak in this
film of the depths hidden within this
seemingly very modern man, like the deep
cleft beneath his Sudbury building.
He has spent time in India, absorbing
Zen Buddhist principles, and is overridingly
concerned with our relationship with
nature, with ecology and the holistic
integration of human life with the greater
universe around us.

Director/Script	**27 minutes**
Alex Hamilton Brown	**Color**
	Age range 13–adult
	VHS $99

23 Modern Architecture and Design

201

765 Larsen – Light – Now
An Architect's Style and Approach

A profile of world-renowned Danish architect Henning Larsen. Among his works are the state secondary school of Haut-Taastrup, the municipal library at Gentofte, the Copenhagen School of Economics in Frederiksberg, the University of Trondheim, and the Foreign Affairs Ministry in Saudi Arabia. Our impressions of his architecture change with the changing of the light. Larsen did not always want to be an architect. He explains here what motivated his choice of vocation, and defines his style and approach.

In Danish with English subtitles

Director/Scenario | 45 minutes
Pi Michael | Color
 | Subtitles
Participant | Age range 15–adult
Henning Larsen |
 | VHS $119

769 Birth of a Hospital

An empty lot, bordered by a ring road and the Boulevard Sérurier at the Porte du Pré-Saint-Gervais in Paris: this is the site on which the government decided to construct a large hospital for children. Pierre Riboulet's project met with unanimous approval. For five months, from May to October 1980, the architect kept a daily journal. A new kind of hospital, a 'large curvilinear form,' a comforting space open to the city and to light, took shape on paper. Pierre Riboulet's tale is one of adventure, of a race against the clock, of obstacle courses – bureaucratic, economic, technical and aesthetic. This film adaptation of Riboulet's journal seeks to capture the architect's emotions as the project unfolds day by day.

Director | 67 minutes
Jean-Louis Comolli | Color
 | Age range 14–adult
Scenario/Participant |
Pierre Riboulet | Film $1113 Rental $299
 | VHS $159
Awards |
Scenario Grand Prix, |
Montreal |
Council of Europe Prize, |
Strasbourg |
Prize of the French Society |
of Architects, Bordeaux |
Prize of the European |
Documentary Biennale, Marseille |

768 The Seasons
Four Journeys into Raili and Reima Pietilä's Architecture

The Helsinki-based architect Raili Pietilä states that he does not want to deal with truth, in case the truth turns out to be 'a black hole where gravity is too great for anything to exist.' Rather, he seeks to steer around reality through metaphor, and to make buildings which are frameworks in which reality can exist. His highly individual approach to creating a building might involve exploring grammar, the structure of sentences, the narrative method of novels, or the identities of the seasons. He will listen to music in search of a formal 'theme.' He will study landscape, or the effect of wind and snow on water. All these will inform his design, so that the overall experience of a Pietilä environment will be rooted in a source which those who look at or live in it may never guess at. In this film he takes us around a range of his buildings. We see a residential complex set in a birch forest, in which the patterns of tree bark, trunks and foliage provide the motif for the façades. When building a modern city church, the architect's aim is to marry a sense of sanctuary and transcendence with a continued contact with the everyday world, seen through apertures and doorways, in contrast with the enclosed feeling of Gothic cathedrals. Finally, the architect revisits his Finnish Embassy building in India, built with traditional local labor methods, but designed to follow the patterns of Finland's snow-swept landscape. Here he speaks of the detachment any artist can feel for a long-finished work, enclosing a reality as mysterious to its creator as to anyone else who encounters it.

Director/Script | 35 minutes
Anssi Blomstedt | Color
 | Age range 14–adult
Original music |
Arvo Pärt | Film $763 Rental $199
 | VHS $109

765
Henning Larsen
Detail of interior,
Ministry of Foreign Affairs,
Riyadh

773
Roy Mason
Computer-controlled house
Xanadu, Florida

Architectural Adventures

Avant-garde House Designs in North America and Europe

These films are not about high-rise blocks or skyscrapers. Instead they show new possibilities of living for ordinary people. We all dream of ideal homes, but few venture to make these dreams come true.

This series of 3 programs can be purchased on VHS for $357 Reference S26

---

771 Dreams Come True

This film features people throughout America who have built their own homes from their own designs, without the help of an architect. We visit a special school in Maine which runs do-it-yourself courses covering all aspects of building one's own house. Then we meet people who have taken the course and tried to build their own house, seeing what they have achieved and what difficulties they encountered. Most important of all, the film shows many imaginative and extravagant examples of unusual homes in Maine, New York, California and New Mexico.

Part of the series *Architectural Adventures*

Director/Scenario
Ray Müller

Also available in German

44 minutes
Color
Age range 15–adult
VHS $119

---

772 New Horizons

This film is about architects and artists who have broken new ground, developing original ideas and using new building materials. We meet a sculptor in Texas who has spent his last ten years welding a poetic house of steel; we see underground homes in New Mexico whose designs were inspired by the cave dwellings of the Pueblo Indians; we visit a mysterious cluster of domes in southern California, and the 'habitable sculptures' of an architect in Texas which were designed to produce varied psychological feedback from those who live in them – for example, different lights or temperature can be activated automatically in response to prevailing or expected weather conditions.

Part of the series *Architectural Adventures*

Director/Scenario
Ray Müller

Also available in German

44 minutes
Color
Age range 15–adult
VHS $119

---

773 Visions of Future Living

This film presents architecture of the future, on land, in the ocean and in space. It moves outside America to include France, Switzerland and the Caribbean. We visit a futuristic home entirely controlled by a 'house-brain' in Florida, meet avant-garde architects on the Côte d'Azure, witness underwater 'self-growing' construction experiments in the Virgin Islands. We watch a French ocean-architect working in a diving cell in his office on a boat in Paris, and then accompany him on his underwater sightseeing vessel in the Mediterranean. Finally we meet the architect of the Space Station in Houston, USA. Fascinating original shots of space evoke a future which our children may experience one day: living on a space station, in orbit or on a colony on the moon – or even the planet Mars.

Part of the series *Architectural Adventures*

Director/Scenario
Ray Müller

Also available in German

44 minutes
Color
Age range 15–adult
VHS $119

'We are surrounded with things which we have not made and which have a life and structure different from our own: trees, flowers, grasses, rivers, hills, clouds. For centuries they have inspired us with curiosity and awe. They have been objects of delight. We have recreated them in our imaginations to reflect our moods. And we have come to think of them as contributing to an idea which we have called nature. Landscape painting marks the stages in our conception of nature. Its rise and development since the Middle Ages is part of a cycle in which the human spirit attempted once more to create a harmony with its environment.'
Kenneth Clark

24
Landscape into Art

This section of
20 programs can be
purchased on
VHS for $2120

Television rights and
prices on request

A huge proportion of the films in the Roland Collection deal to some extent with landscape. In titles concerning Renaissance artists the camera frequently penetrates to backgrounds of mountains and distant horizons, and several film-makers make a point of relating the works shown to the natural environment in which and upon which the artist dwelt (see for example Paula Modersohn-Becker, Van Eyck, Bruegel, Kandinsky). This section, however, selects a range of artists concerned with the depiction of landscape as a subject in its own right, in a tradition which began with the Northern Renaissance, reached its first heights with Dutch seventeenth-century painters, led to the sublime or picturesque scenery of Romanticism and the *plein-air* researches of Impressionism, and remains a potent theme for contemporary artists.

John Constable

The landscapes of John Constable are so familiar, so constantly on view, that it is difficult to believe that at the time he was painting landscape subjects were often considered inherently inferior to other genres – to portraits and, in particular, to grand historical, mythological or allegorical compositions. Since the Renaissance it had been assumed that, in depicting trees, fields, water and clouds, an artist could never achieve the heights of exaltation or the depths of seriousness that 'subject painting' was thought to guarantee. Constable, of course, benefited from and contributed to a rejection of narrative, anecdotal painting (witness the fall from fashion of Victorian 'conversation' painting). Notions of the sublime and the picturesque, the aesthetic or awe-inspiring emotions felt in viewing the 'raw' landscape, suggested ways in which pictures of such subjects could articulate profound human feelings. Indeed, with the erosion of the credibility of myth and religion for many, landscape often became the most viable medium for expressing spiritual realities.

355 Constable: The Changing Face of Nature

Leslie Parris, co-selector of the 1991 Tate Gallery Constable exhibition, introduces his hero with great knowledge lightly worn. 'We all know Constable,' he says. 'It is difficult to escape *The Haywain* as it trundles from one biscuit tin to another. But if we look instead at the real thing, we may find an artist more varied and more exciting than we imagined.' Largely filmed direct from the paintings themselves, this is a valuable introduction to Constable's art.

'Teachers, programmers, and independent students of art…will find this video useful.' *Video Rating Guide for Libraries,* USA

Writer/Presenter	**25 minutes**
Leslie Parris	**Color**
Audio Visual Unit	**Age range 14–adult**
The National Gallery	**VHS $99**

356 Constable: The Leaping Horse

John Constable was, with Turner, the foremost English landscape painter of the nineteenth century; *The Haywain* is his most famous picture. Of the green watermeadows and windswept skies of Suffolk he remarked, 'These scenes made me a painter.' Here we analyze his *Leaping Horse* in terms of landscape genre painting as a whole, and look at the skills and techniques available to the artist. We also consider the constraints and possibilities with which the landscape painter worked, including the current market in art and the ideas of Constable's contemporaries about how the countryside could be represented.

Part of the series
Culture and Society in Britain 1850–90

Director	**25 minutes**
Charles Cooper	**Color**
Presenter	**Age range 18–adult**
Briony Fer	**VHS $99**
Open University/BBC	

◀◀ 413, page 210
Claude-Oscar Monet
The Water-lily Pond

▲ 355
John Constable
Weymouth Bay

24 Landscape into Art

205

309A Claude

The Roman Landscape

'Calm beautiful and serene…' is how Turner, the great nineteenth-century landscape painter, described the landscapes of the seventeenth-century master, Claude Lorraine. This video examines the ways in which Claude drew his inspiration from classical and contemporary poetry, the remains of ancient, medieval and Renaissance Rome and the countryside around the city. Shot on location in Italy and from original paintings and drawings, it demonstrates not only the artist's powers of evocation but also the naturalism which dazzled his contemporaries, and caused Turner's rival Constable to claim that it was Claude who first taught him 'how to look at nature.'

Audio Visual Unit	**25 minutes**
The National Gallery	**Color**
	Age range 14–adult
	VHS $99

347 Caspar David Friedrich

In 1987 The National Gallery in London bought *Winter Landscape* by Caspar David Friedrich, a German landscape painter. Like so many of his paintings, it is full of a sense of mystery. Friedrich's paintings are not well known in Britain, and this was the first oil painting by him to enter a public collection in England. His life and the development of his extraordinary landscape imagery are the subjects of this production.

'…intelligent, informative, and tightly written…solid piece of artistic analysis… most useful to students of art'
Video Rating Guide for Libraries, USA

Writer/Presenter	**25 minutes**
William Vaughan	**Color**
Audio Visual Unit	**Age range 14–adult**
The National Gallery	**VHS $99**

348 Caspar David Friedrich: Landscape as Language

In Germany, as in England, landscape was the finest achievement of Romantic painting, and Friedrich is the outstanding German painter in this field. His landscapes symbolize and express subjective human experience; his approach to nature is naïve and his religious thought has a melancholy aspect. The pantheistic interpretation of landscape in Friedrich's art – that is to say, the sense of God informing the universe – made an important break with tradition.

For more information see page 232

Director	**18 minutes**
Dr Walter Koch	**Color**
Original music	**Age range 14–adult**
Pavel Blatny	**Film $623** Rental $189
Johannes G Fritsch	**VHS $89**

360 Turner

Credited with liberating color from its rôle of merely describing the subject of a painting, Turner evoked an intensity of feeling in his landscapes that future Impressionists and abstract artists were to try to capture years later. This internationally acclaimed film, which shows why Turner is regarded as the father of modern art, is a cinematographic essay on the most important period of Turner's work, the last twenty-five years. A selection made from ten thousand paintings illustrates Turner at the height of his creative powers. Most of the works filmed have never been photographed or exhibited before. The original music captures the ethereal quality of Turner's work. There is no narration.

'A first rate film. A very successful choice of the late Turner period at the time when, having become a master of color, his extraordinary qualities as a colorist are at their peak. Turner is depicted as a phenomenon…faithful color reproduction, richness of the music, and care and elegance of presentation.'
UNESCO

'Here is Turner exposed to public view in a way no exhibition, however ambitious, could match'
Art and Antiques Weekly, London

Director	**12 minutes**
Anthony Roland	**Color**
Original music	**Age range 12–adult**
Marius Constant	**Film $623** Rental $189
Awards	**VHS $89**
Silver Cup, Salerno	
Certificate of Merit, Vancouver	
Highly Commended, German Center for Film Classification	
Quality Award and Prize, French National Film Center	
Chriss Award, Columbus	
Koussivitzky Award, USA prize for the year's best piece of European contemporary music	

Corot

Like Constable, Corot was one of the first artists to take his easel out of doors. Like Constable again, he developed a new approach to landscape painting through his sensitive treatment of light, form and distance. This film is concerned with his visit to Rome in 1825 and his interest in Poussin. It shows his early historical compositions and his later landscapes; it also attempts to assess his place among other great landscape painters of the English, Dutch and Barbizon schools, such as Constable, Hobbema, Millet, and the impressionist Sisley.

Director/Writer
Roger Leenhardt

Original music
Guy Bernard

Awards
Quality Prize and
Quality Award,
French National Film Center

Also available in French

18 minutes
Color
Age range 12–adult

Film $623 Rental $189
VHS $89

24 Landscape into Art

207

400 Victor Hugo Drawings

Moody scenes of old castles in the mist, the moon on dark waters…Known as a great French writer, playwright and poet, Victor Hugo was also a remarkable draftsman. Unknown drawings, filmed from the only important collection of Hugo's work, reveal a world of mystery, poetry and dramatic power that is exceptionally cinematographic. More intimate and direct than Hugo's writings, these drawings have the power to take us into the gothic world of his imagination. There is no narration.

Director	**14 minutes**
Anthony Roland	**Black and white**
Original music	**Age range 12–adult**
Michel Phillipot	**Film $553** Rental $169
	VHS $79

386 Victorian Painting – Country Life and Landscapes

The most popular Victorian paintings were of the countryside – picturesque cottages, pretty milkmaids, perfect cattle. This unrealistic image of the English landscape is still with us, but as painters moved away from the towns which had been ravaged by the Industrial Revolution, they escaped as far as the Great Western Railway would take them, and found themselves in Cornwall. Here they contemplated the lessons learned from the French Impressionists, and Stanhope Forbes founded the Newlyn School. Victorian painting was moving into the twentieth century.

Part of the series *Painters to the People*

Director of photography	**26 minutes**
Edwin Mickleburgh	**Color**
Presenter/Writer	**Age range 15–adult**
Christopher Wood	**VHS $99**
Original music	
Ed Shearmur	

349 Arnold Böcklin
A Biography – His Vision of Nature

This is one of the most comprehensive films ever made about an artist. The fantastical work of the Swiss painter Arnold Böcklin, one of the great landscape painters of the nineteenth century, forms a keystone in the bridge from nineteenth-century Romantic and Neo-classical trends to the Modernism of the twentieth century. Yet, like many other influential artists of his era, Böcklin's reputation has not been high, his preoccupation with subject and symbol being incompatible with the prevailing picture of modern art as progressing away from 'content' toward the pure 'form' of abstraction. Böcklin's style, by contrast, was close to that of many Victorian artists in Britain, artists who were also derided for being narrative, fanciful, meticulous. Today, however, with the breakdown of such doctrinaire definitions of Modernism, the importance of Böcklin and his contemporaries is recognized anew.

For more information see page 80

Director/Writer	**96 minutes**
Bernhard Raith	**Color**
Narrator	**Age range 14–adult**
Peter Ustinov	**Film $1533** Rental $449
Award	**VHS $219**
Special Jury Prize, Montreal	

Also available in German

411 Renoir

Renoir's greatest fame came from his association with the French Impressionist painters of the later nineteenth century. The Impressionists captured their immediate surroundings in richly colored, fluently sketched canvases often executed out of doors rather than in the studio. But Renoir's long career encompassed a wide range of styles and there is a world of difference between the ambitious subject pictures he painted in the 1860s and the glowing nudes that he produced in the final years before his death in 1919. This video explores the full range of Renoir's extraordinary talent through detailed photography and an illuminating script by John House, one of the selectors of the Renoir exhibition seen in London, Paris and Boston.

Script	**28 minutes**
John House	**Color**
Narrator	**Age range 14–adult**
Sir Anthony Quayle	**VHS $99**

An awareness of the human need to identify with a specific place, an archetypal landscape to which one returns again and again, is fostered as an idea in the Alpine paintings of Giovanni Segantini. The myth of the mountains, releasing us from everyday life and confronting us with the eternal qualities of nature, transcends human existence so that we can see it as part of a cosmic wholeness. Such strong emotions are rendered in a non-sensationalist way in this film, which compares Segantini's vision with the actual landscape in a flow of quiet and rhythmical images. The paintings, the beauties of nature and the thoughts of the artist tell their own tale. Only a small amount of information is given in connection with place, time, motive and theme; art-historical, philosophical or theological interpretations are dispensed with. The medium of film, better than any other art form, links the immediate experience of nature, its translation into art, and its symbolic interpretation. Panoramic scenes are shot from the same positions in which Segantini installed his sometimes enormous canvases; the camera shows the real topography of a place, and then shifts easily into the world of the paintings.

For more information see pages 96 and 260

Director	**45 minutes**
Gaudenz Meili	**Color**
Writer	**Age range 14–adult**
Guido Magnaguagno	**Film $833** Rental $249
Also available in French,	**VHS $119**
Italian and Spanish	

▼ 400
Victor Hugo
Castles by the sea

▲ 418
Giovanni Segantini
Midday on the Alps

336A Poetry and Landscape

Professor John Barrell of Sussex University looks at eighteenth-century landscape paintings and poetry which describes landscapes, in the context of their social and political background. He argues that landscape was seen as a metaphor for society, providing either a justification for, or a critique of, the established order. The program falls into four parts:

1 The organization of eighteenth-century landscape painting to look like theatre sets and a comparison with equivalent techniques in poetry

2 The political significance of such a procedure, related to the different layers of society

3 The contrast in paintings between formalized landscape gardens and 'natural' landscape and its significance as a metaphor for degrees of freedom

4 The layering of society represented in rural poetry and in visual representations of rural life.

Part of the series *The Enlightenment*

Director	**25 minutes**
Robert Philip	**Color**
Presenter	**Age range 18–adult**
Professor John Barrell	**VHS $99**
Open University/BBC	

▼ 391
Claude-Oscar Monet
The Beach at Trouville,
detail

◥ 413
Claude-Oscar Monet
Bathers at La Grenouillère

▶▶ 397
Camille Pissarro
White Frost

391 Art in the Making: Impressionism

A group of pictures in The National Gallery, London, cleaned to restore the original brilliant colors and textures, exemplifies the aims and methods of the Impressionist painters. This video, filmed on location in France and England, looks at the Impressionists' color theories and their use of newly available pigments, and demonstrates the ways in which modern technology made possible the development of Impressionism.

'This high quality program provides a focused overview of a significant period in painting history...well scripted with high quality photography of the paintings. Lighting that shows the texture of the paint on the surface...recommended for audiences who are interested in learning more about how the impact of new materials and knowledge affect the way artists paint.'
Video Rating Guide for Libraries, USA

Part of the series *Art in the Making*

Presenter	**22 minutes**
James Heard	**Color**
Audio Visual Unit	**Age range 14–adult**
The National Gallery	**VHS $89**

413 Monet

Monet is often seen as the archetypal Impressionist painter, conveying unstructured, sensual impressions of 'real' scenes, but this view may be misleading. Paintings like *Bathers at La Grenouillère* and *Gare St Lazare* are not, perhaps, 'sliced from life', but are highly worked and tightly structured to produce an almost flat, decorative effect. In later years Monet worked more and more from inspiration provided by the famous water-garden he had made at Giverny, culminating in the great series of waterlily paintings; but even in these, it is possible to demonstrate that clear artistic principles of organization are at work. It seems that whatever his subject, Monet was well aware of the part that illusion and artifice must play in any work of art.

Part of the series *Modern Art and Modernism: Manet to Pollock*

Director	**25 minutes**
Tony Coe	**Color**
Presenter/Writer	**Age range 17–adult**
Dr Anthea Callen	**VHS $99**
Open University/BBC	

Impressionism and Post-Impressionism

What is an Impressionist? And how much
does one Impressionist have in common
with another? This is an attempt to explain
how categories like Impressionism and
Post-Impressionism come into being in
the minds of art historians, and to discover
whether the reputation of the artists to
whom they give these labels is distorted
when we assume that they share more
than a certain kind of technique.

Part of the series *Modern Art and
Modernism: Manet to Pollock*

Director	25 minutes
Charles Cooper	**Color**
Presenter/Writer	**Age range 17–adult**
Belinda Thomson	**VHS $99**
Open University/BBC	

397 **Pissarro**

During the 1880s, when he was already
more than fifty years old, Camille Pissarro
was forced to reassess and then change
the subject of his work. As this appraisal
shows, although he did not, or could not,
break away from the principles of
Impressionism to which he had hitherto
given his allegiance – he was the only
artist to show in all eight of the
Impressionist exhibitions – his increasing
commitment to left-wing political ideas
altered more than his outlook on life.
Now, as a painter of peasants and peasant
life, he faced new problems that were
both technical and ideological.

Part of the series *Modern Art and
Modernism: Manet to Pollock*

Director	25 minutes
Nick Levinson	**Color**
Presenter/Writer	**Age range 17–adult**
TJ Clarke	**VHS $99**
Open University/BBC	

426 Fauvism

By 1890 Matisse, who was to be the *chef d'école* of the Fauvist movement, had moved to Paris, where he shared a studio with Marquet (another of the future Fauves) right next to the River Seine. After a conventional beginning at the Ecole des Beaux Arts, Matisse studied at the studio of the painter Gustave Moreau, who preferred to develop imagination in his students rather than academic imitation. As early as 1896 Matisse was preoccupied with color, and trips to the Mediterranean, the 'land of light', encouraged him to persevere in this direction. Cézanne was another important influence, but other painters including Derain and Vlaminck were coming to share Matisse's attraction to light and color. In 1904, Matisse encountered Pointillist painters, including Paul Signac, at St Tropez, and he employed the technique for a few months. In 1905 he discovered the work of Gauguin; Fauvism was born during the Salon d'Automne exhibition where the works of Matisse, Marquet, Derain and Vlaminck were shown, and a wry critic named them *fauves,* or 'wild beasts.' The Fauvist artists did not form a homogeneous school, but they all tended to use the energetic power of light and color. If power and energy are indeed at the center of their works, then in some sense the Italian Futurists may be said to have taken over from them in expressing movement, power and exhilaration, as can be seen from the paintings of Carrà, Balla, Boccioni, Severini and Russolo, which are introduced toward the end of this film. It also features works by Moreau, Maillol, Dufy and others.

Part of the series
The Adventure of Modern Art

Director	**53 minutes**
Carlos Vilardebo	**Color**
Writers/Narration	**Age range 15–adult**
André Parinaud	**Film $1043** Rental $299
Carlos Vilardebo	**VHS $149**

Also available in French

◀◀ 660
Pamela Bone
Solitude, The Outer Hebrides

▼ 426
André Derain
Regent Street, London

660 Circle of Light
The Photography of Pamela Bone

This film without words is composed of Pamela Bone's unique photograhic transparencies. Her talent has been said to 'push photography beyond its own limits, liberating it to the status of an entirely creative art form.' Inspired by nature, and being more responsive to feeling than to thought, Miss Bone has sought to express the mystery and beauty of the inner vision through photographic means alone: landscape has the quality of a dream; children on the sea-shore have a sense of their own enchantment, trees are forboding and strange when night moves in their arms. It took Miss Bone twenty years to find the right technique and so overcome the limitations that photography would impose.

Director/Scenario	**32 minutes**
Anthony Roland	**Color**
Sound	**Age range 12–adult**
Elsa Stansfield	**Film $763** Rental $199
Delia Derbyshire	**VHS $109**
Award	
First Prize, Cork	

595 Bridget Riley

Though at first sight the dazzling paintings of the Op Artist Bridget Riley seem uncompromisingly abstract, this film brings out the clear relationship they have to landscape. The artist's early paintings are landscapes executed in a divisionist style relating to Seurat and Van Gogh. The perception of light in the landscape is her major preoccupation, and an early experience she describes of being engulfed in sunlight is important for her development. Throughout this film, sequences of hills, grasses and running water are alternated with those of the pictures, subtly bringing out the fact that the rhythms and resonances in her works are in tune with the natural environment.

For more information see page 129

Director/Writer	**28 minutes**
David Thompson	**Color**
Arts Council of	**Age range 12–adult**
Great Britain	**Film $693** Rental $199
	VHS $99

25
The Human Figure in Art

For centuries depictions of the human figure were prized more highly than those of still-life, animals or landscape, and from the Renaissance onward anatomy became a staple of the artist's training.

This section of 22 programs can be purchased on VHS for $2188
Television rights and prices on request

The human figure in art carries, in different ways and through different periods, a huge significance, being the most direct means by which art can address the human condition. In early societies its significance was supernatural, a rendering of gods or spirits in human form. Later, in the Renaissance, although Christianity provided the dominant social belief system, western art's obsession with the figure reflected an increasingly humanist outlook, with humankind at the center of the universe. The distortions of Modernist art, meanwhile, may be interpreted as reflecting human alienation, isolation and anguish (see for example the work of Francis Bacon).

Numerous films in the Roland Collection deal with figurative art; this section highlights some of those in which concern with representing the figure is most conspicuous.

Accorded divine status in the world of art, Michelangelo Buonarroti was a beginning and an end unto himself. Regardless of the media in which he worked – painting, sculpture or architecture – there is a breathtaking perfection to the finished product. This film marks the high point of the art film-making of Carlo Ragghianti. The most technically ambitious and innovative film on art in its period, *Michelangelo* is still unsurpassed as an exposition of an artist's vision in painting, architecture, drawing and sculpture. A camera was designed and built specifically for this film to achieve the sense of a completely free, fluid, infinitely varied viewpoint, weaving at will around the artist's forms. Our conception of the genius of Michelangelo is one of a master able to move between and within his various media, bending and twisting his forms freely into the dramatic contrapposto which marks the transition from late Renaissance to Mannerism. It is this soaring, spiralling fluency that Ragghianti's unique camera work, supported by music by Johann Sebastian Bach, conveys.

'Here we are confronted with the absolutely new and hitherto unexplored possibilities of the film camera in the analysis of artistic forms'
La Nazione, Florence

'Leaves an impression of weightlessness, even brevity, as well as force'
Corriere della Sera, Milan

'We can feel the thematic and stylistic unity in the art of Michelangelo'
La Stampa, Turin

Director/Narration	35 minutes each part
Carlo L Ragghianti	Age range 14–adult
Awards	Color
Exceptional Quality,	
Quality Prize,	**Each part**
Outstanding Merit,	Film $763 Rental $199
Italian Government	VHS $109

◀◀   410, page 218
      Edgar Degas
      Dancer practising

▶   230B
      Michelangelo
      Dawn

---

95   **Maya Terracotta Figurines**

The Mayas were founders of the most brilliant of the pre-Columbian civilizations. When their tombs on Jaina Island, off the north-west coast of Yucatán, were opened, they yielded many very fine, lively terracotta figurines, most of them in the forms of whistles and bells, representing nearly every strand of Mayan society – priests, chiefs on their thrones, warriors, ball-players, dancers, musicians, and craftsmen. Mostly produced in what is now Honduras, these figurines, with their dress, attitudes and expressions so carefully observed, are not only a record of Mayan society, but are invaluable for their artistic qualities too. This is a film without narration.

Directors	12 minutes
Carlos Saenz	Color
Slivia Garduno	Age range 8–adult
Original music	Film $553 Rental $169
Rocio Sanz	VHS $79

Michelangelo Buonarroti

Michelangelo's status for many as the greatest genius of western art rests on the long-standing conviction that the most important kind of painting, above still-life or landscape, is the rendering of the human form. While being an intensely religious period, the High Renaissance in Italy was also a period of burgeoning humanism, when human beings were gaining a new self-confidence and independence, and when even the divine and the spiritual were cast by artists in uncompromisingly corporeal form. The powerful anatomy and rippling musculature they painted typify this trend, which has in some ways continued up until today. The modern successors to Michelangelo's soaring, teeming heroes of the Sistine Chapel are the swooping and swirling Batman, Superman, and other superhuman giants of comic books.

273 Rubens, Part One

Classical Synthesis: Prophet of Modern Art

Starting from the wide-ranging and varied works of Peter Paul Rubens, this first part gives an overview of some of the most important periods and influences in the history of western painting. In Italy, where he stayed for eight years as a student, Rubens made antique and Renaissance culture his own. He was also aroused by the new Baroque style, which he brought back to Flanders and gave a typical Flemish character. Rubens is famous for his exuberant nudes. No one has rendered different types of nude better than he did: they are ecstatic, aesthetic and even ethereal. We see each type later in the work of other painters such as Watteau, Fragonard and Delacroix. We also see Rubens at work as a landscape painter, at which point it is easy to step from his work into the pre-Impressionist landscapes of Constable. At the end of the story, which also introduces us to Cubism, Futurism and even the beginnings of film, we recognize in Rubens a painter who brings life in all its variety to the canvas.

Part of the series
The Genius of Flemish Painting

Screenplay	**55 minutes**
Harold Van de Perre	**Color**
Director	**Age range 14–adult**
Anton Stevens	**VHS $139**

Also available in Dutch,
French and German

274 Rubens, Part Two

Celebrating the Art of Painting

The second part of this documentary deals mainly with Rubens's own *œuvre* and the evolution of his style. It is divided into three periods. The first concerns his early work: though still classical, it shows the influence of the Baroque. The paintings are clearly and easily interpreted and make full use of diagonal axes *(The Elevation of the Cross, The Descent from the Cross)*. Later he begins to give his own interpretation to the subjects he portrays. His composition becomes more complex, disturbing, and dynamic *(The Mystic Wedding of Saint Catharina, The Virgin Venerated by the Saints)*. In his third period Rubens breaks all bounds and dispenses with the rules of painting. We see an explosion of style in which composition becomes a whirlpool, the brush strokes swirl and dive, color vibrates in the light *(The Ascension of Mary)*. We also see Rubens at work in the studio among his pupils. How do we recognize the hand of the master? What techniques does he employ? How does he arrive at his lyrical style? Finally, Rubens's *Allegory of War* is compared with Picasso's *Guernica*.

Part of the series
The Genius of Flemish Painting

Screenplay	**55 minutes**
Harold Van de Perre	**Color**
Director	**Age range 14–adult**
Anton Stevens	**VHS $139**

Also available in Dutch,
French and German

365 Géricault: The Raft of the 'Medusa'

Painter and lithographer Théodore Géricault was the leader of the French Romantic movement; *The Raft of the 'Medusa'* was his most ambitious work. In this film we see how he consciously sought for 'headline' public events to provide a subject for a major work that would launch his career. The *Medusa*, a government vessel, had foundered off the West African coast, and 150 people tried to escape on a raft. After thirteen days, only fifteen were rescued alive. They had had nothing but a few drops of wine – and human meat – to sustain them. The tragedy was blamed on official negligence and created a political scandal. Géricault depicted the instant when the survivors first saw the rescue ship, and he went to extraordinary lengths to achieve authenticity: he interviewed survivors and drew their portraits, he had a model of the raft built, he even studied corpses in the morgue.

Director	**21 minutes**
Adrien Touboul	**Color**
Script	**Age range 12–adult**
Georges-Antoine Borias	**Film $623** Rental $189
Original music	**VHS $89**
Jacques Lasru	

◀ 273
Peter Paul Rubens
The Battle of the Amazons

▶▶ 370
Eugène Delacroix
Carrying an injured person

Delacroix
Human and Animal Movement Expressed
in Drawings

Born into an age marked by revolution and
extremes, Eugène Delacroix was an arch
romanticist; he was also one of the finest
French draftsmen, influencing not only
many of his contemporaries but also
modern masters such as Van Gogh,
Gauguin, Cézanne, Rodin and Matisse.
In this film, the theme of movement in
the human and animal form builds up
through tightly woven sequences to a
climax. Delacroix's drawings make us
understand the basic value of his art, his
intimate thoughts and his daring invention.
This is the only film of its kind made in
the famous Louvre Drawing Collection.
There is no narration.

'Delacroix is magic. We seem to be sharing
the artist's most intimate thoughts in a
strange land where the creativity of
Delacroix is perfectly matched with the
equally creative powers of the film-maker…
a very strong feeling for the artist's style,
ideas, and moods…notable for unity of
purpose and coherence, for synchronization
of visuals and music…shows real feeling
for the artist.'
Vancouver International Film Festival

'Startling musical score; excellent
photography; unusual treatment of subject;
artistically authentic…turned stills into a
moving scene showing the art and genius
of the artist…exciting…intimate; unity
like a poem.'
Canada's Documentary Film Festival

For more information see pages 225
and 237

Director
Anthony Roland

Original music
Marius Constant

Awards
Silver Cup, Salerno
Diplôme d'Honneur,
Cannes
First Prize, Canada's
International Film
Festival, Yorkton
Certificate of Merit,
Vancouver
Commended,
German Center for
Film Classification
Quality Award,
French National Film Center
Chriss Award, Columbus

13 minutes
Black and white
Age range 6–adult

Film $623 Rental $189
VHS $89

410 Degas' Dancers

In this film, as in other key titles in the Roland Collection, a meeting takes place between several media: the dance of Degas' subject matter, the dynamism of his draftsmanship, the drama of the score by Marius Constant, and the exploratory and expressive direction of the film-maker's camera work. The elements are mutually illuminating. Degas anticipates photographic and filmic qualities in his use of light and the 'verism' of his cropping and composition. The dancers 'draw' and compose in space, transposing music into visual form, which is in turn reinterpreted in the score, synchronized with Anthony Roland's moving, extemporizing camera work. This film, like others in the collection, collaborates with its subject in a way that complements and perhaps challenges more cerebral, analytical films in this and other sections. Where a more conventional narrator might hasten to make a didactic point about Degas – for example, about the frequent misery of girls forced into the 'marriage market' of ballet training – this film, with no narration, respects the silence and inscrutability of the artist's images. It permits us a slower, more meditative entry into the pictures, during which we may indeed come to sense tensions, ambivalences, even pain, existing simultaneously with delicacy and beauty.

Director
Anthony Roland
Documentation
Lilian Browse
Original music
Marius Constant
Awards
Silver Cup, Salerno
Chriss Award, Columbus

13 minutes
Black and white
Age range 10–adult
Film $623 Rental $189
VHS $89

420 Toulouse-Lautrec

Born the heir to a rich and aristocratic family, Henri de Toulouse-Lautrec seemed to have everything a young man could want – until an accident and bone disease left him with the head and torso of an old man and the legs of a dwarf. With true heroism he turned to drawing and painting the glittering life he could no longer share. He had been forced on to the sidelines, made to understand how society treats its outcasts; and this understanding can be seen in his portraits of the prostitutes he visited, the only women who were available to him. His life was a drama which he consciously lived to the full, dying at the age of thirty-seven from alcohol and venereal disease; but he rejected pity so rigorously that not even those who knew him best realized the weight of suffering he bore. This deeply moving film shows the artist as a man as well as a creative genius.

Director
Jacques Berthier
Narration
Henri Perruchot
Jacques Berthier
Original music
Pierre Spiers
Also available in French

14 minutes
Color
Age range 14–adult
Film $553 Rental $169
VHS $79

440 Paula Modersohn-Becker

Paula Modersohn-Becker was the most important woman artist of her day and one of the main forerunners of Expressionism. She lived in Worpswede, in the fens north-east of Bremen in Germany. Little water-courses often dividing, a sand-dune set on the flat marsh, brown moorland, black canals – the power of the landscape is central to her work; it roused in her the faculty to see things as simple, big and monumental. 'If one only could, one should write down the people and the landscape in a sign-language … the great simplicity of form, that is the wonder.' Her diary, which became famous for the way it documented her development, is used for this film's narration. 'I feel how my work startles people. Still … it is the vividness with which one grasps the object which makes beauty in art.' Despite the influence of the Worpswede landscape, figure painting and portraiture remained a staple of Modersohn-Becker's work. Her most famous painting is probably the reclining nude *Mother and Child*, and she has been lauded by feminist art critics for her warm and empathetic representations of the female form.

Director
Friedhelm Heyde
Awards
International Status,.
German Government
Highly Commended,
German Center
for Film Classification
Also available in German

12 minutes
Color
Age range 14–adult
Film $553 Rental $169
VHS $79

504B Re/Visions: Mexican Mural Painting

The Mexican Muralist movement is the artistic child of post-revolutionary Mexico. Octavio Paz clearly distinguishes the political and ideological elements of the paintings of Diego Rivera, David Alfaro Siqueiros and José Clemente Orozco from their strictly pictorial content. The poet also places the works of these Mexican artists in the wider context of modern world painting. The dynamism of their figures, the distortions and emphatic compositions and the explicit social content of the Muralists' work put them firmly in the Expressionist camp. Some of their works bear comparison with European artists such as Beckmann or Edvard Munch, and perhaps also influenced later artists such as Jackson Pollock. Paz explains how Mexican Muralism was closely linked with the Mexican revolution, which gave the nation a new sense of identity and an impulse to return to its origins; and we learn how José Vasconcelos, Minister for Education, involved creative artists from all the media in the reconstruction of Mexico's identity.

Part of the series
Mexico through the Eyes of Octavio Paz

Director	**56 minutes**
Hector Tajonar	**Color**
Presenter/Writer	**Age range 14–adult**
Octavio Paz	**VHS $139**

Special collaboration
Marie José Paz

Original music
Mario Lavista

Also available in Spanish

508 Käthe Kollwitz

Käthe Kollwitz was the most powerfully emotional German artist of this century; this film describes her life and work, and stresses the timelessness and humanity of her art. Its very personal narration is taken wholly from the artist's own diaries. The suffering of Berliners in the 1890s, the cruelty and senselessness of the First World War, in which Kollwitz lost a son, and the anguish of the Second World War are vividly portrayed. Most of her best works are tragic and many of them specifically pacifist. This was a pioneering art film, and the honesty of its approach is unsurpassable.

Director	**16 minutes**
Herbert Apelt	**Black and white**
Original music	**Age range 13–adult**
Oskar Sala	**Film $693** Rental $199
Also available in German	**VHS $99**

219

Pablo Picasso was born in Malaga, Spain, in 1881, and studied art in Barcelona and Madrid. He moved to Paris in 1904 and rapidly became known as an artist with outstanding innovative powers. Between 1908 and 1914 he developed Cubism in close collaboration with Georges Braque. The value of this film is that it records the comprehensive exhibition of Picasso's sculptures at the Tate Gallery, London, works rarely seen together. It includes works from all periods and in a variety of materials and styles: figurative heads and figures in bronze; sheet metal, wire and tube constructions made with the Spanish sculptor Julio González; a series of massive modelled heads with exaggerated features, dating from the 1930s; the witty assemblages of found materials (the *Bull's Head,* the *Baboon*); ceramic sculptures of the late 1940s and 1950s; and the 'folded' works of the 1960s, in which sheet metal is used as paper. The commentary, written by Sir Roland Penrose, and accompanied by photographs of Picasso at work, describes the various influences – African art, Cubism, Mediterranean fables – on the sculptor and offers some personal interpretations. The film, above all, is a celebration of Picasso's unique ability to transform ordinary materials, even household objects, into poetic statements.

Director/Writer	**27 minutes**
Roland Penrose	**Color**
Narration	**Age range 14–adult**
Jill Balcon	**Film $693** Rental $199
Arts Council of	**VHS $99**
Great Britain	

401　Rodin

At his death, Rodin was the most famous artist in the Western world but the critical reception of his works was far from positive. As a sculptor making public works, Rodin was exposed to public criticism. The modernity of his works was ridiculed by critics. Even his famous *Thinker* and his *Balzac* attracted scorn and, in the case of the *Thinker*, physical violence. The explicit sexuality of Rodin's sculpture was often seen as scandalous but contemporary taste was tolerant of the erotic as long as it represented the female form. Nude women were ubiquitous in nineteenth-century art. Rodin's *Balzac* sexualized the male form; critical anger did not focus directly on its phallic nature, but saw the sculpture as incomprehensible. Rodin's career marks the transition from the public role of the nineteenth-century sculptor to the more private consumption of modern art.

Part of the series
Modern Art, Practices and Displays

Director	**25 minutes**
Nick Levinson	**Color**
Presenter	**Age range 18–adult**
Annie Wagner	**VHS $99**
Open University/BBC	

519　Dina in the King's Garden
Maillol Sculpture

The sculptor Aristide Maillol was born in the South of France, a man of the Mediterranean, which is itself associated with classical and ancient civilization. He studiously turned his back on the turmoil of our times, reasoning that an attempt to reinterpret the old myths in a twentieth-century manner was perhaps the best way of coming to terms with his own times. As his theme he chose opulent earth goddesses, rich luxuriant mother figures, nubile country girls. He modeled these women in a lifelong variation on the theme of natural bounty. One of his most famous models was Dina, and now a great number of bronze statues of Dina are to be seen in the Tuileries gardens of the Louvre, the former royal palace in Paris. Nothing more romantic and poetic can be imagined than these great bronze women of the South, redolent with heat and lazy passion, in the snow-chilled gardens of the North. There is no narration.

Director	**10 minutes**
Dominique Delouche	**Color**
Music	**Age range 12–adult**
Richard Strauss	**Film $483** Rental $149
Award	**VHS $69**
Quality Award, French	
National Film Center	

Henry Moore

The organic forms of Henry Moore's art, despite their frequent relation to landscape, essentially refer to the human figure. Moore recalls the poignant childhood experience of having to rub his mother's back with medicinal oils, and he has elsewhere recollected walking to school, mesmerized by the rounded forms of the calves of the children walking ahead of him. These very personal memories indicate why the undulations of the human body remain his major inspiration.

580   **Henry Moore, London 1940–42**
The Series of Shelter Drawings

This film features the explicitly figurative imagery of Moore's famous wartime bomb-shelter drawings, depicting the heads, torsos and limbs of the people of London taking refuge from air-raids in the tunnels of the city's subway system. The figures are likened, through the artist's distortions, to the pebbles, hillsides and valleys of an idyllic, peaceful Britain, which seems so far from urban, war-devastated London, yet with which they have some strange communion through their burrowing into the bowels of the earth. In his benign and essentially rural humanism, in the face of modern wars and the modern world they heralded, Moore is close to others of his generation working in other media: the poets Auden or Betjeman, and the composer Britten. There is no narration.

'A revelation: a strength and force disclosed, a mastery made clear'
Sunday Times, London

'…pictures of exceptional quality. Silently the film demonstrates that great art can easily dispense with commentary, and the value of the drawings is thus enhanced.'
UNESCO

'…captures these drawings and their detail with great mastery…the editing is outstanding. With the aid of music which is very impressive…the film has succeeded in reproducing the essential feature of these drawings, which is not dependent on the representation of terror itself…but solely on the greatness and dignity of man…'
German Center for Film Classification

'It's uncanny, Anthony Roland, the master of the montage and dissolve…The film melts moment by moment into a living and breathing homage to the people of London.'
Michigan Education Journal

For more information see pages 160 and 290

Director
Anthony Roland

Original music
Marius Constant

Awards
Silver Cup, Salerno
Honor Award, Vancouver
Certificate of Honor, Leipzig
Special Excellence, Mannheim
Exceptional Merit, Yorkton
Quality Award and Quality Prize, French National Film Center
Highly Commended, German Center for Film Classification
Chriss Award, Columbus

12 minutes
Black and white
Age range 14–adult

Film $553 Rental $169
VHS $79

221

599A Francis Bacon: Paintings 1944–62

The film opens with images that recur in Francis Bacon's paintings – Muybridge photographs of animals in motion, stills from Eisenstein's *The Battleship Potemkin*, a Rembrandt self-portrait, and *Pope Innocent X* by Velázquez. The remainder of the film presents Bacon's interpretation of such images during the period 1944–62. There is no commentary, but through a combination of music, camera movement and editing, the film accentuates the violence and menace of the paintings, and gives an impression of their emotional power.

Director/Writer David Thompson	**11 minutes** **Color** **Age range 17–adult**
Music Elizabeth Lutyens	**Film $553** Rental $169 **VHS $79**
Arts Council of Great Britain	

599 Francis Bacon

Francis Bacon was one of the world's greatest post-war artists. After 1944, when he made his first triptych *Studies for Three Figures at the Base of a Crucifixion*, Bacon painted more than twenty triptychs. This video was shot at the Tate Gallery's exhibition of Bacon's work and focuses on the thirty-six panels that make up twelve of the major works. The images are illuminated by a sound track which is based on an interview given by Bacon himself. Artists often find it difficult to discuss their work, but here Bacon talks about his paintings with great clarity. He explores the themes of morality, realism and sexuality that always preoccupied him. The result gives an insight into the pictures, the way they are made and the way Bacon saw them.

'Invaluable…the expertly detailed visual analysis of the imagery leaves the viewer with the uncomfortable but exhilarating sense that Bacon's macabre *œuvre* has been left to percolate under one's own skin. The feeling is transcending…a must-see for serious art students and a compelling experience for the neophyte.'
Video Rating Guide for Libraries, USA

For more information see page 117

Director/Script Richard Francis	**28 minutes** **Color** **Age range 17–adult** **VHS $99**

600 Josef Herman Drawings

The great British realist painter Josef Herman portrays working men – coal-miners in Wales, grape-harvesters in Burgundy, Portuguese fishermen and farm laborers. He gives man's immemorial struggle for existence the quality of an epic. His form is simple and monumental, his drawing, as he says himself, 'true to experience rather than observation.' His subject, the immense dignity of the manual laborer in contact with the realities of nature, is a dying one in an age of automation; and the film mirrors the epic quality of his work. There is no narration. This is a film which proves that it is up to individuals to feel what is great in art rather than blandly to accept the opinions of others.

'With his violent pen and brush it is a visual triumph of labor. The director has deliberately chosen the rhythm of the laborer and the effect is monumental' UNESCO

For more information see page 244

Director Anthony Roland	**15 minutes** **Black and white** **Age range 12–adult**
Original music Louis Saguer	**Film $553** Rental $169 **VHS $79**
Awards Quality Award, French National Film Center Chriss Award, Columbus	

◀◀ 599
Francis Bacon
Pope II

◀ 600
Josef Herman
Two Peasants in the Field

621 Calder's Circus

Alexander Calder's fascination with the circus began in his mid-twenties, when he published illustrations in a New York journal of Barnum and Bailey's Circus, for which he held a year's pass. It was in Paris in 1927 that he created the miniature circus celebrated in this film – tiny wire performers, ingeniously articulated to walk tightropes, dance, lift weights, and engage in acrobatics in the ring. The Parisian avant-garde would gather in Calder's studio to see the circus in operation. It was, as critic James Johnson Sweeney noted, 'a laboratory in which some of the most original features of his later work were to be developed.' This film exudes the great personal charm of Calder himself, moving and working the tiny players like a ringmaster, while his wife winds up the gramophone in the background. *The Circus* is now housed at the Whitney Museum in New York.

For more information see page 158

Director	**19 minutes**
Carlos Vilardebo	**Color**
Presenter	**Age range 5–adult**
Alexander Calder	**Film $693** Rental $199
	VHS $99

626 Chadwick

British sculptor Lynn Chadwick flatly refuses to discuss the meanings, associations or possible interpretations of his distinctive metallic figures. Yet, clearly, adapting and distorting the human form is one of the most effective and provocative strategies an artist can adopt to win a response from the public. Unlike the rounded figures of certain sculptors from the generation preceding his own (with the possibly influential exception of Jacob Epstein's famous *Rock Drill*), Chadwick's characters are spiky, angular, abrasive and crystalline. Sometimes they recall crustaceans or insects, sometimes armored warriors or science-fiction aliens. Faces are blank facets, expressionless. Chadwick shares these qualities with other sculptors of his time, both in Britain (Armitage and Butler) and internationally (see for example *Sculpture Australia*, 635, *Spoleto*, 640). Protests at a dehumanized world? Expressions of alienation? The artist remains dourly inscrutable behind his own blank mask of a welder's visor.

For more information see page 162

Director/Writer	**51 minutes**
Barrie Gavin	**Color**
Original music	**Age range 14–adult**
Toru Takemitsu	**Film $903** Rental $269
	VHS $129

664 Bernard Faucon: Fables

A Photographer's Use of Eighty-three Window Mannequins

This film describes the world of Bernard Faucon and the story of the mannequins which appeared in his photographs from 1977 to 1981. In 1989, he assembled, restored, dressed and placed them in front of the camera for the last time. On March 22, 1990, the eighty-three mannequins left France for their final retreat, the Nanasai Museum in Kyoto, Japan. Faucon describes his beginnings and his 'encounters' with his mannequins. Over fifty unpublished photographs are presented.

Director/Scenario	**44 minutes**
Jean Real	**Color**
Participant	**Age range 12–adult**
Bernard Faucon	**Film $833** Rental $249
Original music	**VHS $119**
Pierre Boeswilwald	

Also available in French

26
Animals in Art

Along with the human form, animals were subjects of the earliest art ever created. For prehistoric artists, beasts represented food but were also sacred, spiritual beings. Animals remained a vital component of all art in all cultures. With the Renaissance, the depiction of animals themselves (important in much classical and medieval art) was neglected in favor of supposedly more elevated subjects, yet re-emerged in the eighteenth century with artists such as Stubbs, with his animal 'portraits', and became part of the Romantic vocabulary with artists such as Géricault and Delacroix. The representation of animals also played an important (and often overlooked) rôle in the development of Modernism, which often sought subjects far away from the anecdotal or heroic allegories of academicism.

This section of
5 programs can be
purchased on
VHS for $435
Television rights and
prices on request

10 **Tassili N'Ajjer**
Prehistoric Rock Paintings of the Sahara

Four thousand years ago the people who inhabited the Tassili N'Ajjer, a group of mountains in the eastern Sahara, painted the rocks with scenes of their daily life. There can be little doubt that the animal images they produced were part of a magic ritual to ensure a successful hunt – perhaps for men of that time there was no clear distinction between image and reality, so they believed that by making a picture of an animal they brought the animal itself within their grasp. From the thousands of pictures they left we learn that the desert then was no desert at all: it was a place of flourishing community life, of flowers and waterholes and herds of antelope. To our eyes these vivid and colorful scenes look astonishingly 'modern', preserved as they have been by the dry climate.

'Very beautiful, with a very fine subject'
UNESCO

Director	**16 minutes**
Jean-Dominique Lajoux	**Color**
Narration	**Age range 6–adult**
Max-Pol Fouchet	**Film $553** Rental $169
Original music	**VHS $79**
Maurice Le Roux	
Awards	
Gold Medal, Venice	
Bronze Medal, Bilbao	
Quality Award and Prize,	
French National Film Center	

338 **George Stubbs**
The Most Original and Searching of All Animal Painters

Stubbs, labeled 'Mr Stubbs the Horse Painter,' was undervalued for far too long. Now he is recognized as the equal of his contemporaries, Gainsborough and Reynolds. He is the most original and searching of all animal painters, whether his subject is a brood-mare and foal, a monkey or a poodle. He is also a portraitist, as much a master of the art of class-distinction in eighteenth-century England as he is of the anatomy of the horse. This is a unique record of the most important exhibition of Stubbs ever held, described by the *Times Educational Supplement* as 'wild, exotic and modern.'

Script	**26 minutes**
Simon Wilson	**Color**
Tate Gallery	**Age range 12–adult**
	VHS $99

370 **Delacroix**
Human and Animal Movement Expressed in Drawings

Delacroix, along with his colleagues Barye, the animal sculptor, and Géricault, the inveterate painter and rider of horses, was obsessed by animals. For these artists, as sometimes for Stubbs in England, animals were a key symbol of Romanticism, representing force and instinct as opposed to human civilization and rationality. Stunning sequences of animal drawings feature in this film. There is no narration.

'Delacroix is magic. We seem to be sharing the artist's most intimate thoughts in a strange land where the creativity of Delacroix is perfectly matched with the equally creative powers of the film-maker… a very strong feeling for the artist's style, ideas, and moods…notable for unity of purpose and coherence, for synchronization of visuals and music…shows real feeling for the artist.'
Vancouver International Film Festival

For more information see pages 77 and 237

Director	Awards
Anthony Roland	Silver Cup, Salerno
Original music	Diplôme d'Honneur, Cannes
Marius Constant	First Prize, Canada's International Film Festival, Yorkton
	Certificate of Merit, Vancouver
	Commended, German Center for Film Classification
	Quality Award, French National Film Center
	Chriss Award, Columbus
	13 minutes
	Black and white
	Age range 6–adult
	Film $623 Rental $189
	VHS $89

⚡ 370
Eugène Delacroix
Tiger attacking horse

◀◀ 338
George Stubbs
The Milbanke and Melbourne Families

▲ 498
Franz Marc
Blue Horse I

498 **Franz Marc**

The great German painter Franz Marc may be regarded as one of the originators of modern art. With his friend Kandinsky he founded the avant-garde 'Blue Rider' group. Marc wrote that 'the irreligious humanity which lived all around me did not excite my true feelings, whereas the virgin feeling for life of the animal world set alight everything good in me.' Animals, particularly horses, are central in his work; at first they are symbols of nature, but later they become the messengers of a higher spiritual world.

Director	**21 minutes**
Goltz van Helmholt	**Color**
Narration	**Age range 14–adult**
Dr K H Rothe	**Film $623** Rental $189
Original music	**VHS $89**
Karl von Feilitzsch	
Award	
Highly Commended,	
German Center for	
Film Classification	
Also available in German	

530 **Picasso: Romancero du Picador**
Pen and Wash Drawings of the Bullfight

For Picasso, animals were symbols of instinctual power and mythic representations of archetypal life forces, as they had been for Renaissance artists earlier still. In particular Picasso seems to have identified with the bull or Minotaur as embodying a heavy but also poignant power. There are traces of classicism, too – echoes of Greek vase painting, for example – in his brilliant depictions of the bull in his bullfight scenes. This film concentrates on a series of virtuoso pen drawings of bullfights, strung together into a narrative.

For more information see pages 152 and 241

Director	**13 minutes**
Jean Desvilles	**Black and white**
Narration	**Age range 12–adult**
Michel Leiris	**Film $553** Rental $169
Original music	**VHS $79**
Georges Delerue	
Awards	
Grand Prix, Vancouver	
Quality Award,	
French National Film Center	
Also available in French	

In every culture, in every age, art has gone hand in hand with religion, and image-making has had a spiritual significance. This has been true since the time of prehistoric cave paintings.

27
Religious Art

This section of
31 programs can be
purchased for $3573
as 30 titles on VHS
plus 1 title on film

Television rights and
prices on request

In our age, an age of growing secularism, art can be seen as charting the anguish of humanity's loss of faith, or even, perhaps, becoming itself a new religion (as the attitude of Lissitzky, Arp, Marc and others suggests). For other observers, the decline of a spiritual dimension in human life is simply echoed by a general decline in contemporary artistic expression.

The films in this section concentrate on the Middle Ages and the Renaissance, when Christianity and art were in total accord, and aesthetic brilliance and intense piety were thought to be synonymous.

111 Romanesque Architecture of Alsace
Men of Stone, Men of Faith
see page 32

112 Romanesque Architecture of Burgundy
Eve, Stone and the Serpent
see page 32

113 Romanesque Architecture of Languedoc
Aude: Crossroads of the Romanesque
see page 33

114 Romanesque Architecture of Normandy
Narrow Naves, Mighty Vessels
see page 33

115 Romanesque Architecture of Poitou-Charente
Stone, Mystery and Light
see page 33

116 Romanesque Architecture of Provence
The 'Three Sisters'
see page 33

117 Pierres d'Etoiles (Gems of Stone)
Romanesque Art in Medieval France and Spain

The *pierres d'étoiles* or 'gems of stone' were the stages of the pilgrim route from Aubrac to Santiago de Compostela. This film about sacred sites of Romanesque art in France and Spain is divided into four parts: *The Resurrection, The Paths of Eternity, The Sphere of the Stars,* and *The Courses of the Sea.* It analyzes the Visigothic, Carolingian and Mozarabic influences on Romanesque style in the context of this network of sacred sites – Sainte-Foy de Conques, Perse, Bessuéjouls, Sainte-Marie de Souillac, Saint-Pierre de Moissac, Eunate, San Millan de la Cogolla, San Miguel de la Escalada, Foncebadon, Leboreiro, Santiago de Compostela, and Castro de Barona. Finally, it examines the spiritual and material considerations that influenced the fertile imagination of Romanesque sculptors and architects.

Director	54 minutes
Gerard Raynal	Color
Original music	Age range 14–adult
David Hykes	Film $1043 Rental $299
Also available in French	VHS $149

98 Carved in Ivory

Between the seventh and twelfth centuries a highly sophisticated tradition of carving in ivory developed in Britain, beginning in the monasteries before their devastation by the Vikings and continuing until it was superseded by the French style in the twelfth century. In this film Lord Clark argues that, at its height, the English tradition was characterized by a sense of humanity lacking in its European counterparts. The earliest pieces shown, including the 'non-style' of the Frank's Casket and other examples in the Celtic or 'folk-wandering' cursive style, pre-date the classic period. Lord Clark illustrates this classic era, the hundred years around the Norman Conquest, with ivories from Winchester, a Giottesque nativity scene, small figures which show a 'complete disregard for conventional grace' and a small box which attains a 'classic grandeur worthy of a great Renaissance fresco.' The eleventh century saw the gradual revival of the cursive style, but while some pieces reveal a cold ornamental 'un-British' style, others continue the classic tradition, including in particular a 'Tau' cross from Winchester and a crozier made in Canterbury. Lord Clark sees the ensuing dominance of the French style as an end to a period in which the anonymous English sculptures were the best in the world. *Carved in Ivory* was filmed at the exhibition 'Ivory Carvings in Early Medieval England 700–1200' at the Victoria and Albert Museum, and Kilpeck Church, Herefordshire.

Director	30 minutes
Michael Gill	Color
Narration	Age range 14–adult
Lord Clark	Film $693 Rental $199
Arts Council of	VHS $99
Great Britain	

215, page 230
Guido Mazzoni
Mary, detail of statue
after restoration

150
Bourges Cathedral:
character from hell

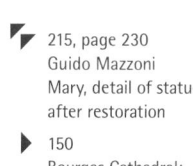

150 Visions of Light
Gothic Stained Glass

For medieval western society, Christianity was the overriding structural force. No area of life was untouched by it, and artists did not seek to be individual, original or subversive, or to give expression to private vision; they were the servants of religious authority, employed to convey the Christian message and thus reinforce society's coherence and stability. The stained-glass windows in the cathedral at Bourges in France are superb examples of how this art form was used to illustrate the Bible for people who could not read, as well as to light up formerly dim interiors: a stained-glass cinema of the Middle Ages. They tell, in the simplest of human terms, the Gospel stories, beginning with the birth of the world, when God ordered the sun to warm the earth and brilliantly colored birds and strange animals burst out upon scenes of fantastic vegetation. And together with the creations of God, they show the works of man – cities and buildings, and houses, and tables, chairs and cups – everyday things, all recreated by the unknown window painters, so that what they intended for the instruction of the people of their own time serves to tell us, now, how they lived.

Directors/Narration	15 minutes
Louis Cuny	Color
M Malvaux	Age range 9–adult
Original music	Film $553 Rental $169
Marcel Dellanoy	VHS $79

173 Van Eyck, Part One
Beauty in All Its Mystery

Part One deals exclusively with *The Adoration of the Lamb* polyptych (a picture or relief made up of two or more panels) in St Baaf's Cathedral, Ghent, believed to be the work of both Van Eyck brothers. This masterpiece is often described as an all-encompassing painted inventory of man and his world-view. But the film-makers go beyond iconography: entranced by the glowing vitality of the work, they try to explore the mystery of beauty itself. At the International Monte Carlo Television Festival in February 1990, Part One was honored with the URTI prize. URTI (International Radio and Television University) groups together around fifty official radio and television broadcasters whose objective is to promote the increase of cultural programing on the small screen. The jury praised the quality of direction, the rhythm and the contemplative approach to the work, referring to it as a breakthrough in television viewing.

Part of the series
The Genius of Flemish Painting

Screenplay	**55 minutes**
Harold Van de Perre	**Color**
Director	**Age range 14–adult**
Anton Stevens	**VHS $139**
Award	
URTI Prize, Monte Carlo	

Also available in Dutch, French and German

174 Van Eyck, Part Two
The Mystery of Painting

In the second part, three masterpieces by the younger of the two brothers, Jan Van Eyck, are studied: *The Madonna with Chancellor Rolin, The Madonna with Canon Van der Paele* and *The Marriage of Arnolfini*. By comparing these paintings with the Italian School of the same period, with contemporary Flemish and even with ancient Egyptian works, the film-makers try to clarify the abstract idea of 'style.'

Part of the series
The Genius of Flemish Painting

Screenplay	**55 minutes**
Harold Van de Perre	**Color**
Director	**Age range 14–adult**
Anton Stevens	**VHS $139**
Award	
Best Educational	
Documentary,	
International Festival	
of Art Films	
UNESCO, Paris	

Also available in Dutch, French and German

175 Beaune: Rogier van der Weyden

Considering its size, nowhere in the whole of western Europe was richer in the later Middle Ages than Burgundy; but the ostentation and extravagance of the wealthy only served to highlight the misery of the poor, who were dependent on their charity. Nicholas Rolin, Chancellor to Philip the Good, built the Hôtel de Dieu at Beaune in the fifteenth century, as a combined hospital and chapel for the sick, the aged and the poor. For the chapel, Rolin commissioned Rogier van der Weyden to create a many-paneled painting of the Last Judgment, which was unshuttered only on holy days. This powerful work of art – the good flying heavenwards to eternal bliss, the wicked pulled down to the fiery depths of hell – was a stark reminder to the invalids that they must always be prepared to meet their God...

Director/Narration	**15 minutes**
Jacques Berthier	**Color**
Original music	**Age range 14–adult**
Pierre Spiers	**Film $553** Rental $169
Also available in French	**VHS $79**

178 Ecce Homo
Richly Painted and Gilded Wood Sculptures

Already two centuries old in France and Italy, Gothic art reached eastern Europe much later. The most beautiful examples are to be found in Czechoslovakia; the richly painted and gilded wood sculptures of the birth, life, death and resurrection of Christ were made (as the Romanesque sculptures had been several hundred years before) by anonymous craftsmen, telling the simple people who could neither read nor write the basic stories of the New Testament. The most humble peasants could relate what they saw – birth, suffering, death – to their own life in their village, while the color and richness of the robes and diadems, more splendid than anything they were used to, served to impress the Gospel story on their mind. Too often today our notion of Gothic art and architecture is one of static forms and pale, neutral colors. Such restrained qualities, however, are due to the bleaching of age and the deliberate Puritan 'toning down' of original colors to suit post-Reformation tastes. In their day Romanesque and Gothic churches and cathedrals were ablaze with color, closer to the scintillation of Byzantine churches and Moslem temples than to the piously whitewashed northern church interiors we know today. The statuary was painted in gaudy and life-like color, and was carried in processions down aisles and out into the streets, draped in finery and flickering in the light of candles. Church ritual and pageantry had the immediacy and drama then that films have for modern audiences. This film shows rare statues which have retained their original colors, and restores to them something of their processional drama and mystery through the control of camera-angle and cinematic technique. Anthony Roland considers it to be one of the jewels of his collection. There is no narration.

Director	**9 minutes**
Bruno Sefranka	**Color**
Award	**Age range 12–adult**
Merit of Honor,	**Film $483** Rental $149
Bergamo	**VHS $69**

◀ 173
Van Eyck
The Knights of Christ
detail of the left wing of
The Adoration of the Lamb
polyptych

▼ 180
Fra Angelico
*The Entombment of
Christ*

180 **Fra Angelico**

The work of this Florentine painter is one
of the glories of the early Renaissance.
His spacious, richly colored compositions
are at once human and profound in their
religious feeling. An early example of
experiments in films on art, the film
presents a critical analysis of Fra Angelico's
style, which blended traditional Gothic
forms with the revolutionary ideas of his
contemporaries, Masaccio and Brunelleschi.

Director/Narration Carlo L Ragghianti	**10 minutes** **Color**
Original music Giorgio Fabor	**Age range 14–adult**
Award Exceptional Quality, Italian Government	**Film $483** Rental $149 **VHS $69**

Jean Fouquet

Jean Fouquet is probably the best known of all fifteenth-century illuminators, mingling as he does, like later artists such as Rembrandt or Friedrich, detailed attention to the observed world and the society surrounding him with intense religious content. Rembrandt and Friedrich, however, in seventeenth-century Holland and nineteenth-century Germany respectively, were seeking to keep religious sentiment alive within increasingly secular artistic developments. Fouquet, by contrast, was seeking to inject the actuality of his observation into a living, all-embracing religious tradition. It is from such artists, who clothed the characters of the Gospels in the fashions of their own times, and set them against contemporary backgrounds, that we acquire our automatic mental picture of Christian events acted out in medieval costume – a tradition strengthened by the Pre-Raphaelites, who themselves looked back to artists like Fouquet.

---

210 **Jean Fouquet**

Jean Fouquet was one of the greatest artists of the fifteenth century. Among his patrons was Etienne de Chevalier, Grand Treasurer of France, who commissioned from him a *Book of Hours*: a strange mixture of amusing picture book and devotional manual, linking the chronicles of Christianity to the hours of the day. Fouquet conceived this *Book of Hours* long before he began to work at it. Round each central picture, illustrating some incident from the life of Christ or the Virgin or some other important story from the Bible, he painted scenes of the places he and his patron had known in the king's service – Touraine and Italy, the castle of Vincennes, the streets of Paris. And, where it was appropriate, he portrayed people of his time, anticipating the liberties later Renaissance painters were to take with religious subject matter.

Director/Narration	**15 minutes**
Jacques Berthier	**Color**
Original music	**Age range 14–adult**
Pierre Spiers	**Film $553** Rental $169
Also available in French	**VHS $79**

---

215 **Guido Mazzoni**
The Master of Ecclesiastical Lifesize Statuary Groups

While following the restoration of the monumental *Porrini* group by Guido Mazzoni, this documentary also presents an overview of the sculptures of this marvellous but little-known Renaissance artist.

Director	**30 minutes**
Marco Speroni	**Color**
	Age range 14–adult
Original music	
Angelo Bergamini	**VHS $99**
Also available in Italian	

237
View of Santa Maria delle
Grazie, Venice

300
Rembrandt Harmensz van Rijn
The Young Christ with
the Elders in the Temple, detail

---

237 **Venice and Antwerp,**
Part Two: Forms of Religion

In the sixteenth century religion had a far greater impact on society in general; it dominated many aspects of life now presided over by government and social services. On location in Venice and Antwerp, we see that the two great cities were no exception to this rule; and yet, despite the supremacy of the Catholic Church, vital minorities such as Jews, Greeks and Germans were allowed relative freedom to practice their own religions.

Part of the series
Culture and Belief in Europe 1450–1600

Director	**25 minutes**
Nick Levinson	**Color**
Presenter	**Age range 18–adult**
David Englander	**VHS $99**
Open University/BBC	
Also available in Spanish	

300 **Rembrandt's Christ**
Drawings of the Life of Christ

Anthony Roland's *Rembrandt's Christ* is a difficult film to define. More penetrating and demanding than a simple celebration of Rembrandt's drawings (though it is certainly that too), yet more imaginative and poetic than any formal study of the artist's graphic work, the film takes the form of a seamless sequence of images choreographed to the specially composed music of Henry Barraud. The central theme is provided by Rembrandt's depictions of Christ, which have never before been gathered together in this way; 160 drawings from sixty-two collections in twelve countries were drawn upon for the film. Rembrandt is shown to be one of the great geniuses of graphic art, and at a time when the authenticity of many of his canvases is being questioned, it is perhaps appropriate to look again to the more intimate medium of his drawings for an insight into the artist's real character. The film reveals the huge breadth of his techniques, from subtly modeled tone to almost violent pen strokes, sensitive fine line, or the almost oriental virtuosity of brush and ink (picked up in Barraud's occasionally somewhat oriental, staccato score). The film intersperses the images of Christ with other biblical motifs, and, significantly, with scenes of landscape and street life of Rembrandt's Holland: children at play, crowds gathering, men and women going about their business. The artist's models are his friends, neighbors and family. The multi-layered nature of the film reflects the interconnections between Old and New Testaments, between past and present, and above all between sacred and secular life, which were universally felt in Rembrandt's day, particularly in Protestant Holland, where religion was being brought from the confines of church ceremony into the wider world of daily life. Thus in the film we see, for example, a parent and child such as those observed countless times by the artist in a domestic setting. Yet Rembrandt's addition of an angel to the scene immediately gives a biblical dimension, and in the same spirit the film director juxtaposes images from other drawings with it – images of violence that might anticipate the Massacre of the Innocents or Abraham's sacrifice of Isaac.

Henry Barraud's score, meanwhile, gives musical expression to the concept of Christ as at once human and divine. There is no narration.

'Of universal interest … penetrates very deeply … the mystery of creative activity in an artist of genius. And the result is a masterly film, which can, like a poem by Andrew Marvell or a sonata by Scarlatti, bear endless repetition, each time yielding something fresh and valuable to the spirit.'
Arts Review, London

'An extremely important work in the history of film … an aesthetic work as an end in itself … the spectator will feel extraordinarily enriched by deep thought and new ideas'
From the book *Christo nel Mondo,* Assisi

Director	**40 minutes**
Anthony Roland	**Black and white**
Original music	**Age range 14–adult**
Henry Barraud	**Film $763** Rental $199
Awards	**VHS $109**
Art Documentary of	
the Year, Assisi	
Chriss Award, Columbus	

305 **Rembrandt – The Bible**

Rembrandt's last years were spent entirely alone, but his love of art and of his fellow man made him unconquerable. As an illustrator of the Bible he is unsurpassed; he brooded over every episode of it in the light of his own experience, and gave to it a vivid and dramatic form. In consequence he is really the only great Protestant artist.

'Lord Clark achieves the impossible. He cuts away the cant from culture and makes it understandable to millions.'
Daily Express, London

Part of the *Kenneth Clark Rembrandt* series

Writer/Narrator	**30 minutes**
Kenneth Clark	**Color**
Director	**Age range 14–adult**
Colin Clark	**Film $693**

310   **Via Dolorosa (Stations of the Cross)**
Early Baroque Lifesize Sculpture in Slovakia

We normally associate the Baroque style with high art by sophisticated sculptors and painters, although it was often intended to impress a religious message on the common people as well as the intelligentsia. This film, however, focuses on what could be called 'folk baroque', created by artisans – lifelike carvings making up an extraordinary Stations of the Cross series at Rimov, a remote mid-seventeenth-century shrine in southern Bohemia. Here, a series of twenty-five white chapels, ranged over a five-mile route, contain lifesized figures enacting the fourteen traditional scenes from the last hours along the 'way of sorrows' leading up to Christ's crucifixion. The creation of the series was conceived and organized by a Jesuit, Jan Gurre, and throughout the Baroque period the Jesuit influence almost succeeded in turning art into a propaganda tool for the Counter-Reformation. Overwhelming church environments were created with all-encircling images and staggeringly illusionistic painted ceilings, which, combined with impassioned pulpit performances, were designed to sweep the congregation into unquestioning religious fervor. There was a general urge toward a 'total art' that involved the audience completely (opera was developing at the same time). This is powerfully demonstrated by the work shown in this film, which is a kind of forerunner of modern 'environment' and 'installation' art. Tellingly, as we pass the figures in the film, experiencing them as did the pilgrims to the shrine, the total work is described in terms of its 'actors', its 'sets' and its 'director', emphasizing its dramatic, even cinematic force.

Director	11 minutes
Hugo Huska	**Black and white**
Original music	**Age range 14–adult**
Vladimír Brabec	**Film $483** Rental $149
	VHS $69

483B   **The Moscow Kremlin, Part One**
The Walls, Towers and Cathedrals

Christianity in Russia under the Tsars created art and architecture as spectacular as that produced anywhere else in Europe – icons, church regalia, cathedrals, ornamented gospels and holy books, murals and ceiling paintings on biblical themes…All are celebrated in this film, which was made in pre-Glasnost Russia but manages to illuminate the historical importance of the religious art of the church fathers of the old regime. The film provides rare images of works and buildings still little known in the West.

Part of the series *The Moscow Kremlin*

Director/Script	**30 minutes**
Vladimir Benidiktov	**Color**
Art Video International	**Age range 14–adult**
Also available in Russian	**VHS $99**

330   **Star of Bethlehem**
Baroque Woodcarvings – Neapolitan Crib Figures

Although the Church in the eighteenth century was losing its hold over the minds of scientists and philosophers, it was able to keep a grip on the imagination of simpler people by telling them the stories of their faith in a way which was easy for them to understand. The most important story, of course, was that of the birth of Christ; but to the peasants of southern Italy who knew nowhere but their own villages, it was useless to talk of inns in Bethlehem or the Roman governor of Judea. The Church therefore had local woodcarvers make figures, none more than a handspan high, of the Holy Family, dressed in the familiar clothes of the peasants' own time and place. The three shepherds who come to worship the newborn baby are obviously based on three local shepherds; the innkeeper who has 'no room' is a grasping Neapolitan; and Herod and his soldiers massacring the innocents are dressed as Turks, the cruellest enemy of whom the peasants would have heard, or as Moslems, the arch-enemies of Christianity. There is no narration.

Director	**12 minutes**
Dr Doederlein	**Color**
Original music	**Age range 6–adult**
Mark Lothan	**Film $483** Rental $149
	VHS $69

348   **Caspar David Friedrich:**
Landscape as Language

In Germany, as in England, landscape was the finest achievement of Romantic painting, and Friedrich is the outstanding German painter in this field. His landscapes symbolize and express subjective human experience; his approach to nature is naïve and his religious thought has a melancholy aspect. The pantheistic interpretation of landscape in Friedrich's art – that is to say, the sense of God informing the universe – made an important break with tradition. At first glance, many of the landscapes of Caspar David Friedrich may not strike us as religious in theme. They depict empty moorlands, becalmed ships, lone trees on the horizon, perhaps a ruined church or churchyard gate. His technique is often stunningly illusionistic, recreating the visual world in a way which we might think earthly rather than spiritual. Yet, as Walter Koch is at pains to reveal here, all the artist's works carry an intense contemplative atmosphere, in the light of which we come to perceive a symbolism also at work – each lone tree, spire or mast is a recollection of Calvary, and each threshold, gateway or vista stretching before us speaks of entry into an eternal, spiritual world. As in another film in this section, *Rembrandt's Christ,* in which seemingly 'secular' landscapes are juxtaposed with biblical events to reveal the religious intensity which the artist sensed was manifest in the 'neutral', natural world, so here we are shown Friedrich's pantheistic notion of nature embodying the divine.

Director	**18 minutes**
Dr Walter Koch	**Color**
Original music	**Age range 14–adult**
Pavel Blatny	**Film $623** Rental $189
Johannes G Fritsch	**VHS $89**

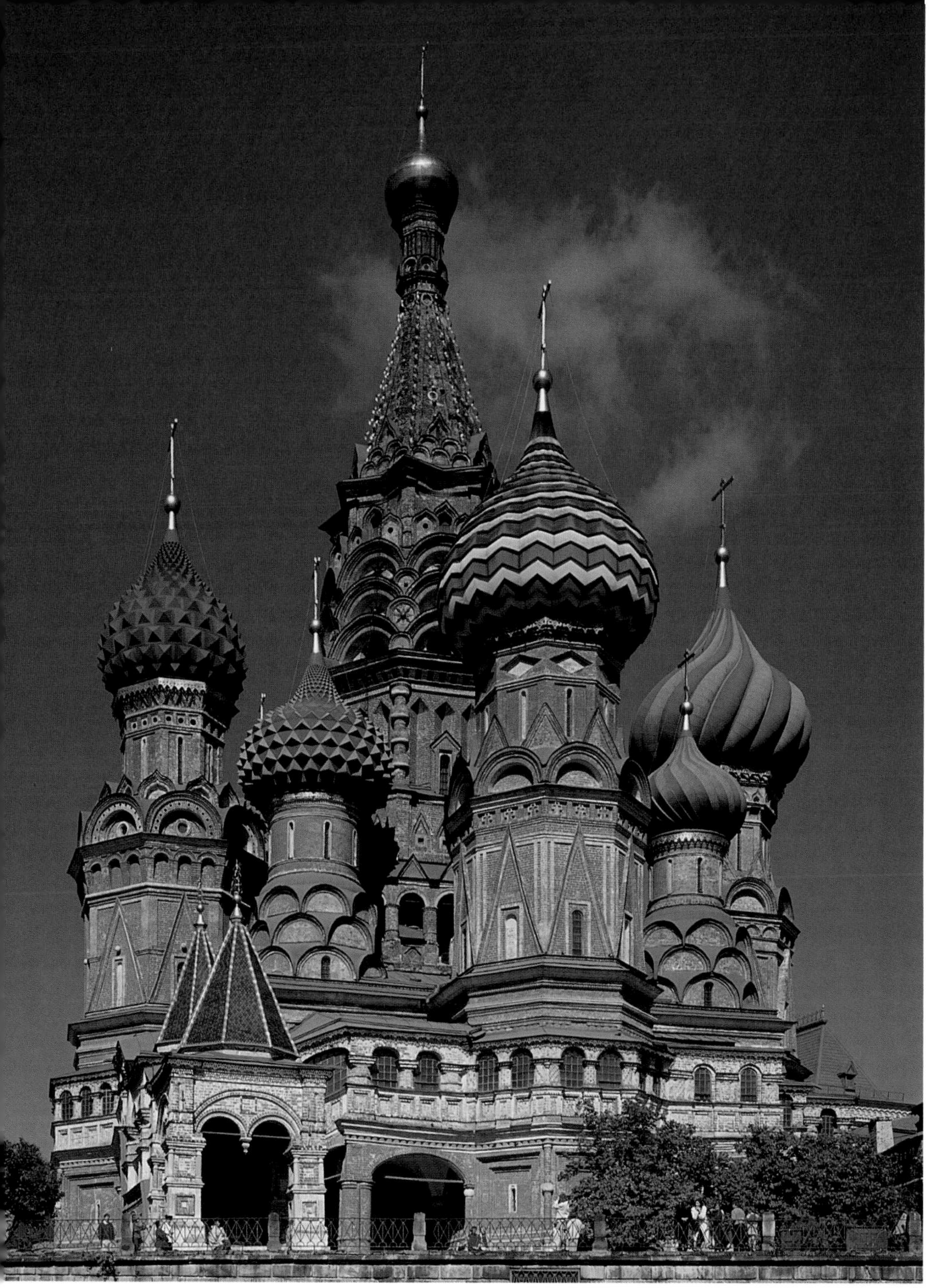

373 **The Victorian High Church**
see page 87

374 **Victorian Dissenting Chapels**
see page 87

375 **Religion and Society in Victorian Bristol**
see page 87

902 **In Memoriam**
The Archaeology of Graveyards
see page 278

136 **The Master Builders:**
The Construction of a Great Church
see page 278

176 **Buildings and Beliefs**
Medieval Social Structure and Spirituality
see page 279

313 **Chapels: The Buildings of Nonconformity**
Baptist, Unitarian, Quaker, Methodist
and Others
see page 279

490C **Your Church: A Threshold to History**
see page 279

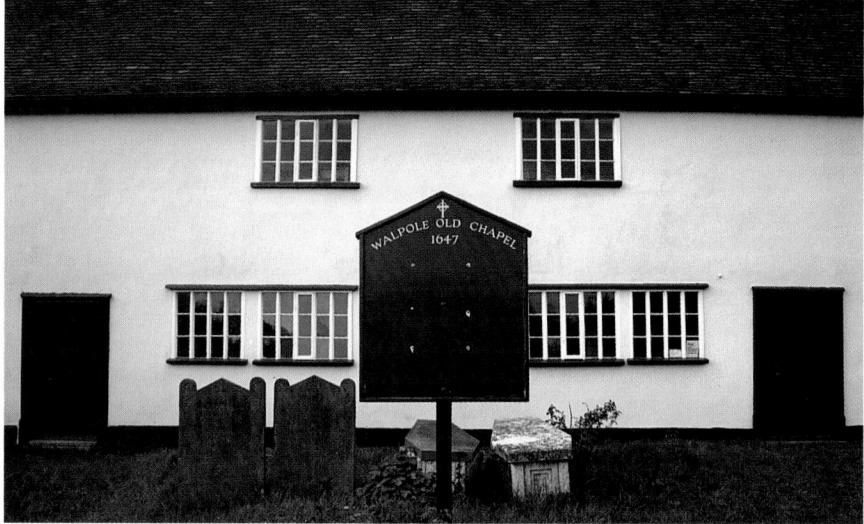

▲ 483B
St Basil's Cathedral, Moscow

▶ 313, page 279
Methodist Chapel, Walpole

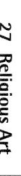

28
Drawing and the Graphic Arts

Films about drawing and the graphic arts make up a major part of the Roland Collection. For many painters and sculptors, drawing is the fundamental discipline behind their art. For other artists, drawing or print-making may be their major or even their only activity.

This section of 48 programs, excluding the series 'Draw with Don', page 274, can be purchased on VHS for $4592

Television rights and prices on request

While drawing frequently allows the viewer greater access to the artist's thinking and working processes than a highly finished painting or sculpture, film is an equally searching, analytical medium in which to follow those creative processes. In several of the films in this section (for example, those on Degas, Delacroix and Herman) we see a drawing 'assembled' in a way analogous to that in which the artist constructed it. Elsewhere the camera travels across the surface, or penetrates into the drawing's illusionistic depth, to reveal the means by which the illusion is effected. The 'story-board' of Rembrandt's biblical drawings comes alive on the screen. Steinlen's or Daumier's brilliant 'reportage' of social life becomes moving footage. Again and again, the strengths of the artists in this section are brought out by the force and coherence their drawings retain, even when projected on to the big screen or relayed through the television screen on which the modern audience is used to seeing the latest and most sophisticated visual excitements.

The force of graphic art, we are reminded, often lies in its economy of means, its monochromatic tonality, its honesty, its mystery.

485 What is a Good Drawing?

This educational film, with its clear
visuals and highly informative narration,
encourages an understanding and
appreciation of the art of drawing. The
great draftsman of every period will find
his own theme, his own symbols – and
his drawings express what he has to say
in a medium that everyone with eyes can
understand. In a really good drawing, it
is obvious that the artist does not follow
a formula, but invents an ever-varying
repertoire of graphic signs. And every
great draftsman can be recognized by his
handwriting, by the degree of flow and
rhythm, of sharpness and crispness he
imparts to his line. If he can impress his
own personal style of drawing on every
subject, he has forced the world around
him to see his own vision. Included in
the film are drawings by Neolithic man,
Pisanello, Botticelli, Raphael, Tintoretto,
Michelangelo, Holbein, Dürer, Rembrandt,
Tiepolo, Watteau, Fragonard, Goya, Ingres,
Delacroix, Victor Hugo, Millet, Degas,
Toulouse-Lautrec, Cézanne, Barlach, Picasso,
Henry Moore and Josef Herman.

Director	18 minutes
Anthony Roland	Black and white
Selection/Narration	Age range 12–adult
Dr Henry Roland	Film $623 Rental $189
	VHS $89

140 Villard de Honnecourt, Builder of Cathedrals

The thirty-three pages of this parchment
'album', covered with notes and drawings,
speak directly to us of a world about which
we know very little. Villard de Honnecourt,
thirteenth-century architect, engineer and
journalist, 'greets you and bids all of those
laboring at the tasks described in this book
to pray for his soul and remember him
kindly, for herein-contained is information
of great value' – not only about the
practical problems of stone and timberwork,
but also what he saw on his travels around
France and to Hungary, his working
sketches for the cathedrals he built or
planned along the way, and the principles
of the Gothic architecture which expressed
so magnificently the spirit of his times.

Directors/Narration	15 minutes
Georges Rebillard	Black and white
Yves Thaler	Age range 14–adult
Award	Film $553 Rental $169
Quality Prize,	VHS $79
French National Film Center	

290 Matthew Merian
European Engraver and Historian

In the work of the Basle-born engraver
Matthew Merian, we have an example of
graphic art at its most documentary. Merian,
part cartographer, part topographer, part
social scientist, used his art as a kind of
visual journalism, to record for posterity the
spread of city and country life, the political
traumas and the daily round in the first
half of the seventeenth century in Europe.
He worked in Paris, Frankfurt and a host of
other towns, particularly in Germany and
the Low Countries. His panoramas teem
with incidents like modern-day comic
strips. We get a glimpse of an engraver's
tools and copper plates in use – when this
film was made in the late 1950s, the
narrator described the 'burins, scrapers,
crayons, the tools of the copperplate
engraver' as those of an art 'nowadays
almost forgotten.' Today, after a resurgence
of interest in print-making, the tools of
the intaglio printer are once more widely in
use among artists (see *Etching*, page 245).

For more information see page 60

Director	15 minutes
Th N Blomberg	Black and white
Original music	Age range 12–adult
Horst Dempwolff	Film $553 Rental $169
Awards	VHS $79
International Status,	
German Government	
Highly Commended,	
German Center for	
Film Classification	

◀◀ 780, page 245
Hattori Kumiko
Fish Plant

▶ 485
Ernst Barlach
Russian Courtship

Rembrandt

'The judgment of [Rembrandt's] contemporaries, divided and inconsistent as it was in regard to his paintings, was unanimous and unrestrained in praise of his art of drawing...Rembrandt's idea of drawing as an instantaneous reaction to visual stimulation or impulsive expression of inner vision seemed something new and stupendous to his contemporaries [such as] fellow countryman Arnold Houbraken: "With regard to art, he was prolific in ideas, hence quite frequently there can be seen a large number of different studies of one and the same subject, full of variations with regard to character, attitudes and arrangements of garments...pen sketches on paper in which the emotions of the soul caused by different events are shown so artistically and clearly in their essential features that it is a marvel to look at. Anger, hatred, grief, joy, and so on, everything is delineated so naturally that one can read in the penstrokes what each one wants to say."...Drawings vibrate in the trembling life of radiant lines, which lend them not only the fluorescence of colour, but also a diaphanous quality as if the life of the soul would sublimate the body. Awe and majesty, love and faithful devotion are expressed.'
Otto Benesch

More penetrating and demanding than a simple celebration of Rembrandt's drawings (though it is certainly that too), yet more imaginative and poetic than any formal study of the artist's graphic work, this film takes the form of a seamless sequence of images choreographed to the specially composed music of Henry Barraud. The central theme is provided by Rembrandt's depictions of Christ, which have never before been gathered together in this way; 160 drawings from sixty-two collections in twelve countries were drawn upon for the film. Rembrandt is shown to be one of the great geniuses of graphic art.

'Of universal interest...penetrates very deeply...the mystery of creative activity in an artist of genius. And the result is a masterly film, which can, like a poem by Andrew Marvell or a sonata by Scarlatti, bear endless repetition, each time yielding something fresh and valuable to the spirit.'
Arts Review, London

'An extremely important work in the history of film...an aesthetic work as an end in itself...the spectator will feel extraordinarily enriched by deep thought and new ideas'.
From the book *Christo nel Mondo,* Assisi

For more information see page 56

Director	**40 minutes**
Anthony Roland	**Black and white**
Original music	**Age range 14–adult**
Henry Barraud	**Film $763** Rental $199
Awards	**VHS $109**
Art Documentary of	
the Year, Assisi	
Chriss Award, Columbus	

▲ 300
Rembrandt Harmensz van Rijn
Christ Crucified between the Two Thieves

▶▶ 370
Eugène Delacroix
Sketch from the Louvre collection

Human and Animal Movement
Expressed in Drawings

'The great French painter, whose work marks the beginning of modern art, and whom – to name only a few – Cézanne, Manet, Renoir, Van Gogh, considered as their master, has left a vast number of drawings, which remained unknown to the public until after his death. Less finished and complete than his pictures, they show in a striking way the genius of Delacroix, the boldness of his imagination, the complete independence from convention and school tradition. Every time he drew is proof of the revolution he started. He opened the eyes of his generation, his influence reaching far beyond his own time and country.' In these words the scholar Kurt Badt, one of this century's first 'discoverers' of Delacroix's drawings, introduced them to the public in the 1940s. This film, however, makes use of techniques not available to the authors of the few books on Delacroix as a draftsman. As Edouard Roditi first acclaimed it in the New York journal *Art Voices,* 'Anthony Roland has tried, in his film on Delacroix, to suggest to us the workings of the artist's mind by revealing the world of his drawings as if it were the real or imagined world that Delacroix depicts. Out of the four thousand Delacroix drawings in the collection of the Paris Louvre, Roland photographed four hundred, then used eighty-three of these in the film as it is now shown. Within a wash-drawing landscape, [the] camera slowly retreats from a close-up of details in the background to the foreground, when at last we see the whole drawing as if we were looking back on the way that we ourselves have just traveled. In a quick-cut sequence of stills of various sketches of animals in action, we gain the impression of watching real animals at play, as the artist saw them when he sketched them. The continuity of such an art movie is poetic, in terms of the aesthetics of the motion-picture…As a work of art in itself, such a film helps one to understand and appreciate an artist's work far more subtly and dramatically than any more traditional art-documentary.' There is no narration.

'Delacroix is magic. We seem to be sharing the artist's most intimate thoughts in a strange land where the creativity of Delacroix is perfectly matched with the equally creative powers of the film-maker… a very strong feeling for the artist's style, ideas, and moods…notable for unity of purpose and coherence, for synchronization of visuals and music…shows real feeling for the artist.'
Vancouver International Film Festival

'Startling musical score; excellent photography; unusual treatment of subject; artistically authentic…turned stills into a moving scene showing the art and genius of the artist… exciting…intimate; unity like a poem.'
Canada's Documentary Film Festival

For more information see pages 77 and 225

Director
Anthony Roland

Original music
Marius Constant

Awards
Silver Cup, Salerno
Diplôme d'Honneur, Cannes
First Prize, Canada's International Film Festival, Yorkton
Certificate of Merit, Vancouver
Commended, German Center for Film Classification
Quality Award, French National Film Center
Chriss Award, Columbus

13 minutes
Black and white
Age range 6–adult

Film $623 Rental $189
VHS $89

390 Daumier

Of all the visual wits of the nineteenth century, none was more sharp or observant than the painter, sculptor and engraver Honoré Daumier. He was jailed early in his career for caricaturing King Louis-Philippe as Gargantua, wolfing the taxes paid by the little people, but his time in the dank cells of St Pélagie prison seems only to have fueled his left-wing beliefs. He took the part of the common man against kings and princes, of the poor against the rich, of social justice against inequality. He mocked those whom he considered to be on the wrong side, and in doing so he gave enormous pleasure to their opponents. But his canvases, which today are worth millions, were ignored by the art-lovers of his time, and he was often faced with the direst poverty himself.

Directors/Writers
Roger Leenhardt
Henry Sarrade

Original music
Guy Bernard

Award
Special Mention, Locarno

Also available in French

15 minutes
Black and white
Age range 12–adult

Film $553 Rental $169
VHS $79

400 Victor Hugo Drawings

Moody scenes of old castles in the mist, the moon on dark waters… Known as a great French writer, playwright and poet, Victor Hugo was also a remarkable draftsman. Unknown drawings, filmed from the only important collection of Hugo's work, reveal a world of mystery, poetry and dramatic power that is exceptionally cinematographic. More intimate and direct than Hugo's writings, these drawings have the power to take us into the Gothic world of his imagination. There is no narration.

Director
Anthony Roland

Original music
Michel Phillipot

14 minutes
Black and white
Age range 12–adult

Film $553 Rental $169
VHS $79

405 Modern Mexican Art

Words and painting meet on the television screen to deliver an enriching vision of the painter José Maria Velasco, a great but little known portraitist, Hermenegildo Bustos, and José Guadalupe Posada, the engraver. Octavio Paz illuminates the creations of these masters of the nineteenth century. Posada's engravings, executed for the press, captured and caricatured the personalities and political and social events of his day in a style somewhere between eighteenth-century political cartoons and Germanic Expressionism of the twentieth century.

Part of the series
Mexico through the Eyes of Octavio Paz

Director
Hector Tajonar

Presenter/Writer
Octavio Paz

Special collaboration
Marie José Paz

Original music
Mario Lavista

Also available in Spanish

56 minutes
Color
Age range 14–adult

VHS $139

Edgar Degas

Though also a great painter and sculptor, Degas once remarked that he was 'born to draw.' Influenced at first by the refined draftsmanship of Holbein and Ingres, Degas' mature drawings, shown in this film, are closer to the style of Lautrec, but in the end unique to the artist himself.

The English draftsman, Randolph Schwab, who promulgated Degas' work to generations of artists from his influential position at the Slade School, London, has observed of the master's late drawings, 'design and movement, light and color, have become more important to him than the rigorous rendering of solid form. Characteristic are the strong diagonals in the composition, the "cutting" of figures by the margin, and the sense of character in the face...'

▼ 400
Victor Hugo
Castle ruins

▲ 410
Edgar Degas
Front View of Dancer

410 Degas' Dancers

In this film, as in other key titles in the Roland Collection, a meeting takes place between several media: the dance of Degas' subject matter, the dynamism of his draftsmanship, the drama of the score by Marius Constant, and the exploratory and expressive direction of the film-maker's camera work. The elements are mutually illuminating. Degas anticipates photographic and filmic qualities in his use of light and the 'verism' of his cropping and composition. The dancers 'draw' and compose in space, transposing music into visual form, which is in turn reinterpreted in the score, synchronized with Anthony Roland's moving, extemporizing camera work. This film, like others in the collection, collaborates with its subject in a way that complements and perhaps challenges more cerebral, analytical films in this and other sections. Where a more conventional narrator might hasten to make a didactic point about Degas – for example, about the frequent misery of girls forced into the 'marriage market' of ballet training – this film, with no narration, respects the silence and inscrutability of the artist's images. It permits us a slower, more meditative entry into the pictures, during which we may indeed come to sense tensions, ambivalences, even pain, existing simultaneously with delicacy and beauty. There is no narration.

Director
Anthony Roland

Documentation
Lilian Browse

Original music
Marius Constant

Awards
Silver Cup, Salerno
Chriss Award, Columbus

13 minutes
Black and white
Age range 10–adult

Film $623 Rental $189
VHS $89

239

415 Seurat Drawings

Seurat's drawings, like those of other great artists – Rembrandt and Daumier, for example – contain his talent in its entirety. This film brings together nearly all of Seurat's drawings and demonstrates how Pointillism can work in monochrome; looking at them, the pleasures of color seem to lose their importance. Nothing is more interesting than to see great artists reveal themselves in their drawings. Something seems to be created out of nothing in this naked confrontation between the artist and his medium. Seurat advances with infinite caution; yet however methodical his approach, the passion and the vigor are never lost, the reserve and the ardor reinforce one another. This deliberate, sophisticated, almost monumental art is frequently inspired by the most ephemeral, banal reality – by figures of anonymous passers-by in the street. These drawings have surprising dramatic force: the strange, precise silhouettes, moving in a kind of tragic silence, make one think of ghosts, soon to melt back into the darkness from which they have briefly emerged. There is very little narration.

Director	**17 minutes**
Anthony Roland	**Black and white**
Music	**Age range 12–adult**
Claude Debussy	**Film $623** Rental $189
	VHS $89

430 At the Foot of the Tree
A Homage to Steinlen

The Swiss-born painter, lithographer and draftsman Alexander Steinlen devoted his life to furthering the cause of justice and liberty. His mission was to express the opinions and reveal the suffering of those who could not speak for themselves, the inarticulate people and the cabhorses and carthorses of Paris. His work comments on the evils of his time – the imprisonment of children, the poverty of the workers, the horrors of war. He drew for magazines such as the anarchist *La Feuille*, considered dangerously revolutionary, and in consequence he often had to escape incognito from the authorities in Paris. However, the more lyrical and pleasing aspects of the simple working life, in the countryside where he hid himself and also in the city, are also celebrated in his work. The bold historical and political approach of this film to its subject ensures the viewer's complete involvement.

Director/Narration	**24 minutes**
Alain Saury	**Black and white**
Poem	**Age range 14–adult**
Jean Rictus	**Film $623** Rental $189
Original music	**VHS $89**
Henri Sauget	
Awards	
Special Diploma, Bergamo	
Quality Award,	
French National Film Center	

Also available in French

508 Käthe Kollwitz

Käthe Kollwitz was the most powerfully emotional German artist of this century; this film describes her life and work, and stresses the timelessness and humanity of her art. Its very personal narration is taken wholly from the artist's own diaries, and the suffering of Berliners in the 1890s, the cruelty and senselessness of the First World War, in which Kollwitz lost a son, and the anguish of the Second World War are vividly portrayed. Most of her best works are tragic and many of them specifically pacifist. This was a pioneering art film, and the honesty of its approach is unsurpassable.

Director
Herbert Apelt

Original music
Oskar Sala

Also available in German

16 minutes
Black and white
Age range 13–adult

Film $693 Rental $199
VHS $99

530 Picasso: Romancero du Picador
Pen and Wash Drawings of the Bullfight

From another related film in the Roland Collection, *The Forceful Gaze* (531), we learn how the artist, after days of curious lethargy following a visit to a bullfight, suddenly rose from his bed and executed – in two furious hours of creativity – the whole of his famous Toromaquia series of matador scenes. The theme of the bullring was indeed a favorite one with him, explored especially through etchings, drawings, engravings and lino-cuts. With the sharp tools of the engraver – brush, etching needle and pen – Picasso executed his strokes with the graceful precision, panache and flamboyance of a matador wielding spear, sword and cloak. Based on Picasso's most Spanish series of drawings, this short film is a fusion of art and music. The drawings depict the bullfight, that tragic confrontation between life and death, between man and beast. They reveal the mounted picador whose *picas* test the bull's bravery, the graceful and heroic matador, the public hooting and applauding in turn. Picasso, Spanish-born, depicts his types with the sardonic eye of a Goya, such as the chaste *señorita* in her mantilla, guarded by a shawled and crone-like duenna. Dissolves and camera movement trace the vigorous drawings, blending with the clamor of the arena, rousing bullfight marches, piercing flamenco coplas and dances accompanied by guitar and castanets. This creates a sense of action in a film which requires minimal narrative. The brilliance of Picasso, the Spanish spirit, and the drama of the bullfight merge.

For more information see pages 152 and 225

Director
Jean Desvilles

Narration
Michel Leiris

Original music
Georges Delerue

Awards
Grand Prix, Vancouver
Quality Award,
French National Film Center

Also available in French

13 minutes
Black and white
Age range 12–adult

Film $553 Rental $169
VHS $79

28 Drawing and the Graphic Arts

241

Max Ernst

Among Surrealist artists, the German Max Ernst was one of those most concerned with graphic techniques – developing, for example, his 'frottage' method by making rubbings of textured surfaces (see film 560). In *Kindness Week,* we see him delighting in the networks of hatched lines employed in Victorian engraved illustrations – a lattice-work of contours intended to be an 'invisible' method of creating depth and volume, but which Ernst subtly transforms into a conspicuously formal quality as he animates the curiously stilted figures from the illustrations.

For more information see page 140

570 Kindness Week (Max Ernst)

Max Ernst was one of the young men who returned from the 1914–18 war ready to reject all the standards and customs which society had hitherto taken for granted. If culture and religion had led to nothing better than the past four years of misery and horror, they argued, then it was time to give anarchy and unreason a chance. This film is about the series of 182 collage engravings which illustrate Ernst's irrational novel *Kindness Week,* divided into seven sequences which each represent a day of the week. By animating these fantasy engravings on film, the artist was able to bring yet another absurd element to his protest against reason. The quality of the animation is superb, and the entire film was personally approved by Max Ernst.

'Here the surrealist climate is recreated. High spirits and non-conformism are taken to the limits of the fantastic and of plastic inventiveness.'
UNESCO

Director	**19 minutes**
Jean Desvilles	**Black and white**
Narration	**Age range 12–adult**
Max Ernst	**Film $623** Rental $189
Original music	**VHS $89**
Georges Delerue	
Award	
Quality Award,	
French National Film Center	
Also available in French	

575 Steinberg

Without narrative, this film takes us on an enchanting path through the American artist Saul Steinberg's witty world of characters, animals and everyday objects, teaching us along the way the delights of drawing with line. Quite close to the doodling most of us indulge in, Steinberg's technique is friendly and unforbidding, yet the artist is clever, thought-provoking and disciplined. In placing himself at the service of the graphic work, the film-maker has created a system of analogies in which lines become movement on the screen. The composer, for his part, has adapted to a similar discipline which is just as strict. From the point of view of production, the film has been conceived as a long journey through the drawings, which are juxtaposed as if in an immense fresco.

'The director has made use of all the resources at the disposal of the cinema to communicate a form of dynamic humor'
UNESCO

Director	**14 minutes**
Peter Kassowitz	**Black and white**
Original music	**Age range 9–adult**
Bernard Parmegiani	**Film $553** Rental $169
	VHS $79

594 Adventures in Perception
The Work of the Graphic Artist
Maurits Escher

The work of the graphic artist Maurits Escher is a play on perspectives: it creates an illusion of the impossible. Boundaries expand to infinity, floors become ceilings and vice versa. He repeats forms in an ever-changing perspective, and creates a circle of metamorphosis. Escher's world derives its structure from a lucid intelligence, from a tremendous imagination and from prodigious craftsmanship. It is a revelation, of vital importance to the study of graphic design.

Director	**21 minutes**
Han van Gelder	**Color**
Award	**Age range 14–adult**
First Prize, Cork	**Film $693** Rental $199
Also available in	**VHS $99**
Dutch, French, German	
and Spanish	

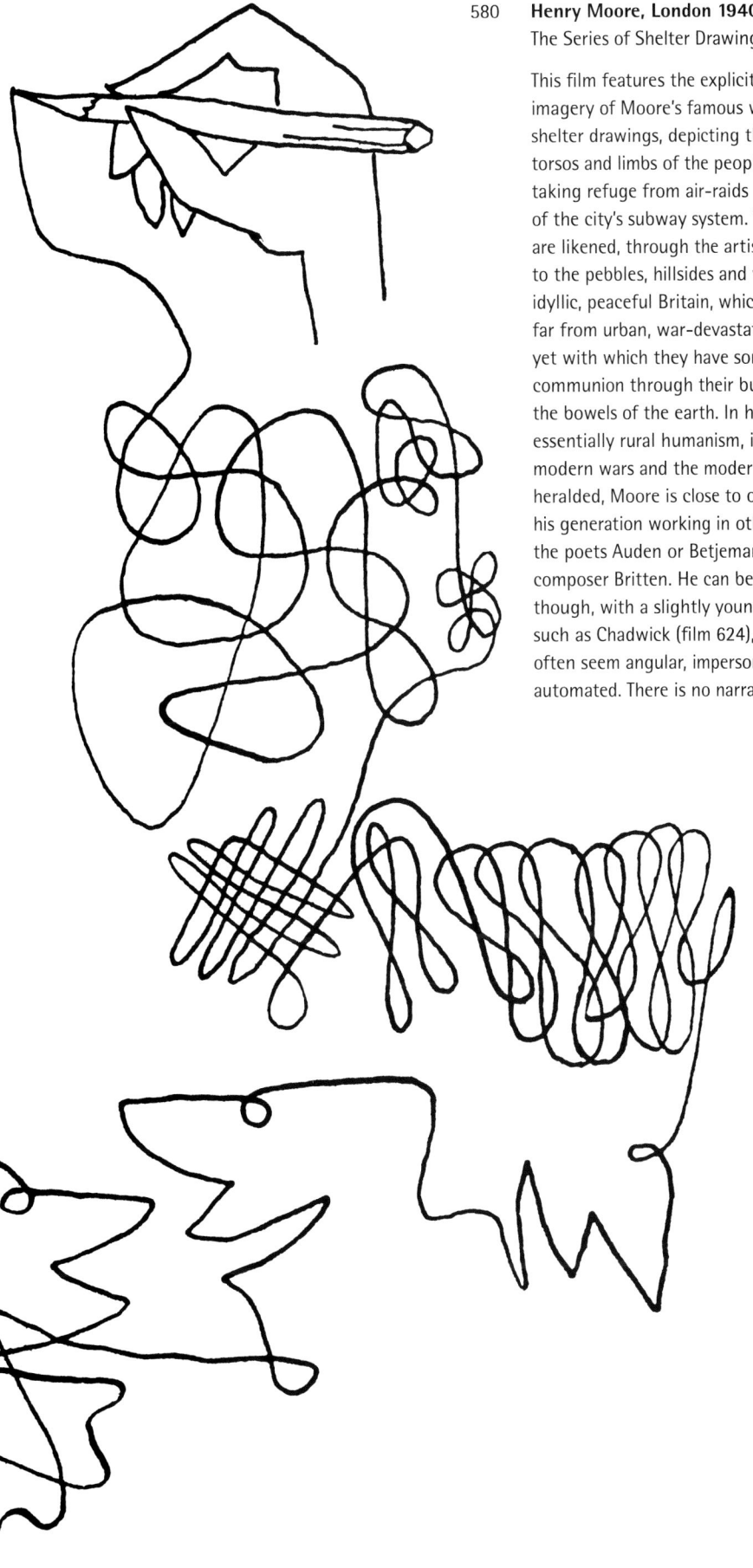

580 Henry Moore, London 1940–42

The Series of Shelter Drawings

This film features the explicitly figurative imagery of Moore's famous wartime bomb-shelter drawings, depicting the heads, torsos and limbs of the people of London taking refuge from air-raids in the tunnels of the city's subway system. The figures are likened, through the artist's distortions, to the pebbles, hillsides and valleys of an idyllic, peaceful Britain, which seems so far from urban, war-devastated London, yet with which they have some strange communion through their burrowing into the bowels of the earth. In his benign and essentially rural humanism, in the face of modern wars and the modern world they heralded, Moore is close to others of his generation working in other media: the poets Auden or Betjeman, and the composer Britten. He can be contrasted, though, with a slightly younger sculptor such as Chadwick (film 624), whose figures often seem angular, impersonal, and automated. There is no narration.

'…pictures of exceptional quality. Silently the film demonstrates that great art can easily dispense with commentary, and the value of the drawings is thus enhanced. The newsreel sequences at the beginning and the end contribute in producing an impressive atmosphere.'
UNESCO

'…captures these drawings and their detail with great mastery…the editing is outstanding. With the aid of music which is very impressive and, at the same time, discreet, the film has succeeded in reproducing the essential feature of these drawings, which is not dependent on the representation of terror itself, nor on any particular milieu or the like, but solely on the greatness and dignity of man, as preserved in these catacombs of terror.'
German Center for Film Classification

'A revelation: a strength and force disclosed, a mastery made clear'
Sunday Times, London

'It's uncanny, Anthony Roland, the master of the montage and dissolve…The film melts moment by moment into a living and breathing homage to the people of London.'
Michigan Education Journal

For more information see pages 160 and 290

Director
Anthony Roland

Original music
Marius Constant

Awards
Silver Cup, Salerno
Honor Award, Vancouver
Certificate of Honor,
Leipzig
Special Excellence,
Mannheim
Exceptional Merit,
Yorkton
Quality Award and
Quality Prize,
French National Film Center
Highly Commended,
German Center for
Film Classification
Chriss Award, Columbus

12 minutes
Black and white
Age range 14–adult

Film $553 Rental $169
VHS $79

580
Henry Moore
Four Grey Sleepers

575
Saul Steinberg
Endless drawing

Josef Herman

Born in Poland in 1911, Josef Herman has
spent most of his creative life in Britain.
Graduating from Warsaw's school of art in
1932, he traveled first to Brussels, then to
Glasgow, London and the Welsh mining
valleys, finally settling in London. There,
while never courting notoriety, he has
nevertheless been one of the major
presences in the art community. His work
is Expressionist in flavor, and he has strong
affinities with Belgian Expressionists such
as Permeke and De Smet. His subjects tend
to be taken from the lives of workers –
miners or laborers in the fields. He is thus
the heir to artists such as Millet or Daumier.
Herman has continued to travel widely,
depicting labor throughout the world.
In very recent years his paintings have
documented the feminist anti-nuclear
protests at Greenham Common, indicating
that Herman perceives the feminist and
ecological 'revolutions' to be extensions of
the socialist vision of his earlier work.

600 **Josef Herman Drawings**

The great British realist painter
Josef Herman portrays working men –
coal-miners in Wales, grape-harvesters
in Burgundy, Portuguese fisher-folk and
farm laborers. He gives man's immemorial
struggle for existence the quality of an
epic. His form is simple and monumental,
his drawing, as he says himself, 'true to
experience rather than observation.'
His subject, the immense dignity of the
manual laborer in contact with the
realities of nature, is a dying one in an age
of automation; and the film mirrors the epic
quality of his work. This is a film which
proves that it is up to individuals to feel
what is great in art rather than blandly
to accept the opinions of others.
There is no narration.

'With his violent pen and brush it is a
visual triumph of labor. The director has
deliberately chosen the rhythm of the
laborer and the effect is monumental'
UNESCO

Director
Anthony Roland

Original music
Louis Saguer

Awards
Quality Award, French
National Film Center
Chriss Award, Columbus

15 minutes
Black and white
Age range 12–adult

Film $553 Rental $169
VHS $79

973   Japonism, Part Three

Japanese Influences on Western Art:
Gesture of the Brush

In recent years, the exchanges between
Japanese and western art have been
bi-directional. Pierre Alechinsky explains,
for example, how the post-war art of the
West has been influenced by Japanese
calligraphy, and Japanese artist Chinjo Saito
reveals his debt to Europe's CoBrA group.

Director	**15 minutes**
Guido De Bruyn	**Color**
Also available in Dutch	**Age range 15–adult**
and French	**VHS $79**

**780   The Urban Bonsai:
Contemporary Japanese Prints**

Unlike traditional Japanese art,
contemporary Japanese prints still find
little recognition worldwide. They are a
profoundly modern as well as beautiful
medium. By means of interviews with
the artists about their background and
techniques, this film reflects on the
seventy-five works featured in the College
Women's Association of Japan Traveling
Print Show, and shows how much insight
they give into modern Japanese society.

Director/Writer	**42 minutes**
Takashi Usui	**Color**
College Women's	**Age range 14–adult**
Association of Japan	**VHS $119**
Also available in Japanese	

825   Screenprinting

The video concentrates on how screenprints
are made but, like others directed by Gavin
Nettleton, it also follows the creation of a
work by the artist Jane Sampson. She talks
during the introduction about the medium
and explains why she chooses to work with
screenprints. The practical topics covered
include the basic equipment, stencils, direct
photo emulsion, washing and preparing the
mesh, applying the emulsion, exposing it in
the print down frame with UV light and
then washing out the unexposed areas,
retouching and printing the next color, inks
and bases for printing, racking and removal
of the stencil and cleaning the screen. The
booklet expands on the video. At the end
the artists Brendan Neiland, Harvey Daniels,
Sue Gollifer and Terry Gravett discuss why
they enjoy making screenprints.

Director	**33 minutes**
Gavin Nettleton	**Color**
Writer/Consultant	**Age range 12–adult**
Harvey Daniels	**VHS and booklet $99**

830   Etching

This video introduces us to the artist
Sandy Sykes, who works from her studio
in Essex, England. She also spends some
time at the University of Brighton with
Terry Gravett developing an etching in a
series about dragons. The creation of this
work demonstrates a number of techniques,
including basic etching, engraving,
drypoint, aquatint and some of Sandy's own
processes. We follow these from the initial
drawing, through the degreasing, coating of
the plate, smoking, tracing, etching and
cleaning-off the ground, to the inking and
printing of all three plates involved in the
production of the final work. The booklet
expands on the video.

'…a very good illustration of how an
etching develops through its various stages.
The individual artist will also find this a very
helpful introduction to the craft of etching.
At each step we are shown the materials
and tools needed, reminded of safety
factors, and guided step by step through
each phase of the project. This video is a
class act. Sykes is knowledgeable and
personable. Excellent photography makes it
easy to follow the informative and logically
structured demonstrations. Liberal use of
close-ups further clarify the methods
presented…recommended for school,
college, and public libraries. As well as
providing valuable information for the
artist, it will also be of interest as
background information on the process of
etching to the non-artist.'
Video Rating Guide for Libraries, USA

Director	**40 minutes**
Gavin Nettleton	**Color**
Writers/Consultants	**Age range 12–adult**
Gavin Nettleton	**VHS and booklet $109**
Terry Gravett	

600
Josef Herman
Miners' Brass Band

973
Georges Mathieu
Sketch for jewelry design

Comics, the Ninth Art

A panorama of comics worldwide, from the turn of the century to the present day.

The world of comic-strip illustrations, while in many ways consciously the reverse of 'high culture', exhibits enormous richness and invention in terms of imagery, technique and iconography; and it draws, directly or indirectly, on sources throughout the history of art. Its earliest manifestations in the 1920s are closely related to the Art Nouveau and Belle Epoque styles of artists like Alphonse Mucha or Toulouse-Lautrec, who were themselves poster designers and graphic illustrators. Numerous other artists of the period supplied the fast-growing press with incisive, 'story-telling' cartoons. Comic-strips proper – from *Dick Tracy* and *Buck Rogers* to *Batman* and *Superman* employ graphic tricks and tropes familiar from Goya, Piranesi, Gustave Doré, Daumier and Félician Rops. Chinese narrative scrolls and Japanese prints by Utamaro, Hokusai and others continue to be re-echoed in comics, as do the styles of Nabis and Post-Impressionist artists, who were, in turn, influenced by oriental art. Expressionism and Surrealism give much to the comic artist. Likewise one can spot borrowings from the Mexican woodcuts of Posada. Comics also provide some of the most telling social documents of the modern age, reflecting the fantasies and archetypes of the passing decades, and providing either an escape from, or a commentary upon, the social and political situations of their readers. Familiar to us all from earliest childhood, comics, the classic 'enemies of schoolwork', nevertheless have a huge amount to tell us about art and life.

This series of 13 programs can be purchased on VHS for $1287 Reference S20

Series consultants
Antonio Altawiba
Lorenzo Diaz
Dennis Gifford
Maurice Horn
Kosei Ono
Richard Marshall

'The scope is international and extensive… Emphasis is on how the events of these decades shaped the comics of the time… it provides an interesting approach to the times it covers. Recommended for art libraries.'
Video Rating Guide for Libraries, USA

781 **Comics, the Ninth Art**

Telling stories and making up exciting tales
is probably an activity as old as humankind,
and representing them pictorially certainly
pre-dates civilization (and may even be
one of its causes). Inventing characters
and giving them form; causing them to
experience incredible adventures in
fantastic worlds; creating entire universes
in careful detail; mixing painting with
writing, the past with the present and
future; combining reality with fiction and
dreams with desires – and capturing it all
on a square of paper – is the world of the
comic artist. This film explores the relatively
short history of the form, which, despite
the criticism routinely leveled against it,
has become one of the pillars of twentieth-
century mass culture. Famous comic-strip
creators discuss their even more illustrious
progeny. And even those who think
they know all about the vignette may
be surprised to discover extraordinary
originality from unlikely sources.

Part of the series *Comics, the Ninth Art*

Director
Alejandro Vallejo

Script
Carmen Dominquez
Alejandro Vallejo
Maite Ruiz de Austri

Also available in French
and Spanish

28 minutes
Color
Age range 9–adult

VHS $99

782 **1900**
1900–1920

The year 1900 marks the meridian between
the Victorian era and our own, modern
world. In the two decades that followed –
which included both the Great War and
the October Revolution – the old ways
were lost for ever. A new, Modernist style
furnished concrete evidence that the
twentieth century was to be a new,
forward-looking era. The apotheosis of
the popular press as a mass medium
provided a secure framework within
which the graphic artist, the cartoonist,
the caricaturist and the illustrator joined
together to develop comics – the ninth art-
form. Maurice Horn is interviewed and
the film features Yellow Kid, Little Nemo,
Krazy Kat and the Katzenjammer Kids.

Part of the series *Comics, the Ninth Art*

Director
Alejandro Vallejo

Script
Carmen Dominquez
Alejandro Vallejo
Maite Ruiz de Austri

Also available in
French and Spanish

28 minutes
Color
Age range 9–adult

VHS $99

783 **To Be Continued...**
1920–1930

This period saw the appearance of the serial
comic. Founded by the *Chicago Tribune* and
the *New York Daily News*, the King Features
Syndicate sponsored and distributed, on a
nationwide basis, satirical, humorous, family
and situational strips, each (frequently
nail-biting) episode of which ended with
the immortal words 'To be continued…'
The film includes interviews with Dennis
Gifford and Maurice Horn and features
Little Orphan Annie, Betty Boop, Gasoline
Alley, Felix the Cat and Popeye.

Part of the series *Comics, the Ninth Art*

Director
Alejandro Vallejo

Script
Carmen Dominquez
Alejandro Vallejo
Maite Ruiz de Austri

Also available in French
and Spanish

28 minutes
Color
Age range 9–adult

VHS $99

With the ending of the Second World War and the coming of the new, suspicious atomic age, many comic strips, which had been a valuable propaganda tool during the preceding conflict, began to display an ever more ideological and political bias. The onset of the Cold War proper ushered in the bitter era of McCarthyism and the witch-hunts – the 'reds under the bed' syndrome – and neither comic strips nor their authors were to prove altogether immune to this pervasive influence. The film includes interviews with Charles Schulz, Harvey Kurtzman and Mort Walker, and features Peanuts, Beetle Bailey, Dan Dare, Jeff Hawke and Andy Capp.

Part of the series *Comics, the Ninth Art*

Director	**28 minutes**
Alejandro Vallejo	**Color**
Script	**Age range 9–adult**
Carmen Dominquez	**VHS $99**
Alejandro Vallejo	
Maite Ruiz de Austri	

Also available in French and Spanish

---

784 **The Adventure Begins**
1930–40

The bright, hedonistic strains of the Charleston – the signature tune of the early twenties – were already fading into the background as this boisterous and oddly neurotic decade approached its close. In 1927 Charles Lindbergh achieved the first solo non-stop crossing of the Atlantic east-bound, from New York to Paris. The entire world began to experience a growing passion for travel and its necessary concomitant, high adventure. Comics of the period faithfully mirrored this fantasy, with the first appearances of the hard-bitten detective strip, and exotic escapades in a variety of far-away colonial settings. Nor was fantasy adventure limited to planet Earth: comic-strip heroes and heroines experienced danger, terror and delight in outer space – as, vicariously, did their millions of eager readers. The film includes interviews with Burne Hogarth, Lee Falk and Hergé, and features Tarzan, Dick Tracy, Flash Gordon, Terry and the Pirates and Tintin.

Part of the series *Comics, the Ninth Art*

Director	**28 minutes**
Alejandro Vallejo	**Color**
Script	**Age range 9–adult**
Carmen Dominquez	**VHS $99**
Alejandro Vallejo	
Maite Ruiz de Austri	

Also available in French and Spanish

---

785 **Double Identity**
1940–50

Probably the most famous and enduring creation from the comic-strip artist's brush is the super-hero, who came into being in the years leading up to the Second World War. Two conditions of a true super-hero (or heroine) were the possession of special, superhuman powers, and a double identity, usually as an apparently normal, even meek, individual. The (often difficult) maintenance of this vital secret is one of the best-loved pillars of all super-hero plotlines – doing good by stealth in its ultimate form. During the global conflict which followed, the super-heroes joined up on the Allied side and saw much exotic 'action', which, while doing little for the real Allied war effort, contributed solidly to morale by providing favorite reading for many combat soldiers. The film includes interviews with Jack Kirby and Will Eisner, and features Superman, Batman, Spirit, Spirou and Lucky Luke.

Part of the series *Comics, the Ninth Art*

Director	**28 minutes**
Alejandro Vallejo	**Color**
Script	**Age range 9–adult**
Carmen Dominquez	**VHS $99**
Alejandro Vallejo	
Maite Ruiz de Austri	

Also available in French and Spanish

---

787 **Love is All You Need**
1960–68

The sixties saw the epicenter of pop culture moving away from the United States. European comic artists adopted the brash sixties style, heralding a grand revival of the form. Lushly produced albums, seductive yet assertive heroines, and a new determination to experiment, all led to a notable improvement in the quality of European comics and the creation of a faithful mass of adult followers. The film includes interviews with Jean Claude Forest, Jean Michel Charlier and Ibañez, and features James Bond, Modesty Blaise, Barbarella, Asterix, Blueberry and Mort Cinder.

Part of the series *Comics, the Ninth Art*

Director	**28 minutes**
Alejandro Vallejo	**Color**
Script	**Age range 9–adult**
Carmen Dominquez	**VHS $99**
Alejandro Vallejo	
Maite Ruiz de Austri	

Also available in French and Spanish

| 788 | **Comix** | 789 | **L'Imagination au Pouvoir** | 790 | **No Future?** |

788 **Comix**
1960–75

The US 'underground' of the late sixties and early seventies provided a wry alternative to the super-hero tradition, using a deliberately sleazy black-and-white style as a vehicle for a series of ferocious attacks on a society with whose forms of conduct, manners and values the authors were totally at odds. In common with many other pop forms of the time, the underground 'comix' tradition was disseminated through channels other than the established publishing houses, often in conjunction with the hippy movement, in the form of fanzines. The film includes interviews with Jack Kirby, Harvey Kurtzman, Gilbert Shelton and Richard Corben, and features Spiderman, Little Annie Fanny, Vampirella, Conan, Fabolous, Furry Freak Brothers and Den.

Part of the series *Comics, the Ninth Art*

Director
Alejandro Vallejo

Script
Carmen Dominquez
Alejandro Vallejo
Maite Ruiz de Austri

Also available in
French and Spanish

28 minutes
Color
Age range 9–adult

VHS $99

789 **L'Imagination au Pouvoir**
1968–75

In May 1968 the students of Paris began to rip up cobblestones to throw at the authorities; this, with other disturbances elsewhere in Europe, made it seem for a while as if a new, youth-led, Europe-wide revolution was in the offing. The movement found its most effective modes of expression in music and comic-books. Imagination became the watchword, and provided fertile soil for a mature style of comic authorship and production, wholly adult in tone. The Euro-comic at last broke through the barricades of intellectual opinion – which had hitherto regarded it as a mere consumer product – and so came, at last, to be viewed as a cultural phenomenon in its own right, thanks in part to the increasing importance and authority of the scriptwriters. The film includes interviews with Quino, Uderzo, Gotlib, Mœbius and Druillet, and features Valentina, Corto Maltese, Mafalda, Sturmtruppen and Hom.

Part of the series *Comics, the Ninth Art*

Director
Alejandro Vallejo

Script
Carmen Dominquez
Alejandro Vallejo
Maite Ruiz de Austri

Also available in French
and Spanish

28 minutes
Color
Age range 9–adult

VHS $99

790 **No Future?**
1975–85

As George Orwell's fateful 1984 drew closer, the arms race gathered momentum and the horizons of the future grew ominously dark. Cruise missiles, SS20s, nuclear power, ecological worries, rising unemployment and ever-shoddier goods at ever-increasing prices all contributed to the sombre *Zeitgeist* of the times. To the crash of badly tuned guitars, the punk (anti-)movement spread throughout the western world. Meanwhile the old dream of a united Europe took a few hesitant steps forward. European comics of the time naturally reflected these preoccupations. Meanwhile, along with the new recognition of their cultural status, came the eclipse of the importance of the characters in favor of their creators. The film includes interviews with Tanino Liberatore, Horacio Altuna, Enki Bilal and Milo Manara, and features Ran Xerox, Giusseppe Bergman, La Femme Piège, Judge Dredd and Los Pasajeros del Tiempo.

Part of the series *Comics, the Ninth Art*

Director
Alejandro Vallejo

Script
Carmen Dominquez
Alejandro Vallejo
Maite Ruiz de Austri

Also available in French
and Spanish

28 minutes
Color
Age range 9–adult

VHS $99

漫画、漫画

791 Born in the States
1975–85

For the USA, the early seventies represented one of the unhappiest periods in the country's history – it was being painfully and belatedly appreciated that not all wars are winnable. Yet for a young country in the process of celebrating its two hundredth birthday, disillusionment could not last long – there was still life in the American Dream. The worst of the oil crisis seemed to be passing, and once again the dollar took its place as the world's strongest currency. The super-heroes were still around, but in regenerated form, more human and fallible, asking questions, tackling social issues like drugs and ecological disasters, and powered by the big specialist publishers like DC and Marvel. Meanwhile, the independent comics carried on, faithful to the spirit of the underground tradition. The film includes interviews with July Simons, Howard Chaykin, Alan Moore and Beto Hernandez, and features X-men, Ronin, Watchmen, Love and Rockets and Elf Quest.

Part of the series *Comics, the Ninth Art*

Director
Alejandro Vallejo

Script
Carmen Dominquez
Alejandro Vallejo
Maite Ruiz de Austri

Also available in French
and Spanish

28 minutes
Color
Age range 9–adult

VHS $99

792 Manga, Manga
1985–90

Mangas are a new Japanese cultural manifestation – enormous (300 pages plus) adults-only comic books produced to high qualitative levels and, even more astoundingly, on a weekly basis. This is a publishing phenomenon unique in the world, and reveals yet another fascinating side of the Japanese national character. The film includes interviews with Osamu Tezuka, Kosei Ono, Go Nagai, Hiroshi Hirata and Goseki Kojima, and features Atom (Astro Boy), Mazinger Z, Lone Wolf and Cub, Akira and Devilman.

Part of the series *Comics, the Ninth Art*

Director
Alejandro Vallejo

Script
Carmen Dominquez
Alejandro Vallejo
Maite Ruiz de Austri

Also available in French
and Spanish

28 minutes
Color
Age range 18–adult

VHS $99

793 What's Next?
1985–2000

The comic as we know it today is a child of the early twentieth century, but that century is now passing. What may (or may not) lie ahead is the subject of this film: young, often highly experimental authors, now at last coming into their own? The application of semiconductor-based publishing technology to the production of images and comic books? Ever more avant-garde design? The film discusses the work of Paolo Baciliero, Mathias Schulteiss, Kissler, Loustal, Beb Deum and Götting.

Part of the series *Comics, the Ninth Art*

Director
Alejandro Vallejo

Script
Carmen Dominquez
Alejandro Vallejo
Maite Ruiz de Austri

Also available in French
and Spanish

28 minutes
Color
Age range 9–adult

VHS $99

Great Artists in the World of Comics

Why each author created his work; his development and the graphic techniques he uses.

The history and development of the comic book as an artistic entity in its own right is thoroughly covered in the series *Comics, the Ninth Art.* But although this form is often created by a collaborative team – artist and scriptwriter, often with a specialist 'inker' as well – it is the work of the former which gives the comic its 'look'; and by common consent the artistry, imagination and technical skills of the person who draws the pictures and executes the author/scriptwriter's plotline are the most compelling factors in the success or otherwise of any particular title. In many cases, indeed, no collaboration has taken place: the finished comic represents the work of a single person. In some cases their work has been venerated by several generations of aficionados. In each of the thirteen twenty-eight minute episodes of this series – analytical rather than documentary – one of these 'greats' is interviewed in depth about his life, work and development of style.

801   Eisner

Born in the USA, of Austro-Jewish ancestry, Will Eisner is one of the great thirties' pioneers of the comics movement – an independent-minded perfectionist with great insight into human passions. Throughout his wide range of subjects and plots – from thrillers to everyday dramas – he demonstrates intelligence, humor, sensitivity and brilliance.

Part of the series
Great Artists in the World of Comics

Director	28 minutes
Gustavo Mtz Smith	Color
Original music	Age range 12–adult
Caelo del Rio	VHS $99
Also available in French and Spanish	

802   Breccia

One of the most unsettling of comics artists, Argentina's Alberto Breccia is also one of the genuine veterans, with fifty years' experience of challenging the conventions in favor of his own demanding artistic path.

Part of the series
Great Artists in the World of Comics

Director	28 minutes
Gustavo Mtz Smith	Color
Original music	Age range 12–adult
Caelo del Rio	VHS $99
Also available in French and Spanish	

792
Manga, Manga
Title graphics

793
Character from
What's Next?

801
Will Eisner

251

803 Schulz

Forty years ago American Charles Schulz created one of the most famous and enduring comic strips of all time – *Peanuts*, aka Charlie Brown, starring the even more renowned dog Snoopy (of Red Baron fame).

Part of the series
Great Artists in the World of Comics

Director	**28 minutes**
Alejandro Vallejo	**Color**
Original music	**Age range 12–adult**
Caelo del Rio	**VHS $99**

Also available in French
and Spanish

804 Altuna

An extraordinary creator of atmospheres, Horacio Altuna of Argentina specializes in the depiction of the immediate future – science fiction for the day after tomorrow. He is also a fierce champion of social causes and a vehement critic of society.

Part of the series
Great Artists in the World of Comics

Director	**28 minutes**
Gustavo Mtz Smith	**Color**
Original music	**Age range 12–adult**
Caelo del Rio	**VHS $99**

Also available in French
and Spanish

805 Mœbius

An heroic voyager into inner space, France's Mœbius journeys through his own mind in search of a quiet and tranquil place to stop, take out his pencil, and begin work; the drawings are his testament that other, parallel worlds do exist.

Part of the series
Great Artists in the World of Comics

Director	**28 minutes**
Alejandro Vallejo	**Color**
Original music	**Age range 12–adult**
Caelo del Rio	**VHS $99**

Also available in French
and Spanish

806 Schulteiss

Perhaps the bitterest – at any rate, least sentimental – of all comics creators, Germany's Mathias Schulteiss invents characters who aim, not for heroics, but for survival in a cruel world where morality has become hopelessly confused with hypocrisy and treachery, where desperation rather than any desire for justice rules.

Part of the series
Great Artists in the World of Comics

Director	**28 minutes**
Iñigo Rotaetxe	**Color**
Original music	**Age range 12–adult**
Caelo del Rio	**VHS $99**

Also available in French
and Spanish

807 Manara

The disciple of Pratt, Mœbius and Federico Fellini, Italy's Milo Manara is an intensely critical artist, using eroticism and adventure in his work to denounce hypocrisy, oppression and alienation of the individual.

Part of the series
Great Artists in the World of Comics

Director	**28 minutes**
Gustavo Mtz Smith	**Color**
Original music	**Age range 16–adult**
Caelo del Rio	**VHS $99**

Also available in French
and Spanish

◄◄ 812
Alan Moore

◣◥ 803
Charles Schulz

▶ 809
Enki Bilal

СПАСИБО
РОДНОМУ СТАЛИНУ

808 Chaykin

One of the main pillars of the revival of comics in the USA, Howard Chaykin uses unashamed violence and cynicism, presented by means of versatile and dynamic graphics.

Part of the series
Great Artists in the World of Comics

Director	28 minutes
Iñigo Rotaetxe	Color
Original music	Age range 12–adult
Caelo del Rio	VHS $99

Also available in French and Spanish

809 Bilal

Creating a world where reality and fantasy exist side-by-side – even intermingled – the Frenchman Enki Bilal's unique style is a series of drawn chronicles of astounding precision – an unforgettably 'alive' effect which remains on the retina of the mind.

Part of the series
Great Artists in the World of Comics

Director	28 minutes
Alejandro Vallejo	Color
Original music	Age range 12–adult
Caelo del Rio	VHS $99

Also available in French and Spanish

810 Schuiten

An unsettling, innovative Belgian artist who creates imaginary worlds full of historical and aesthetic references from the recent past. Schuiten's interest in architecture and other physical settings is always present in his work.

Part of the series
Great Artists in the World of Comics

Director	28 minutes
Gustavo Mtz Smith	Color
Original music	Age range 12–adult
Caelo del Rio	VHS $99

Also available in French and Spanish

811 Liberatore

A radical with a hard-hitting style, Italy's Liberatore produces illustrations that reveal an everyday and disquieting search for Beauty and the Beast. Internationally recognized for 'Ran Xerox', he is said by some to be the Michelangelo of the medium.

Part of the series
Great Artists in the World of Comics

Director	28 minutes
Gustavo Mtz Smith	Color
Original music	Age range 12–adult
Caelo del Rio	VHS $99

Also available in French and Spanish

812 Moore

British scriptwriter Alan Moore has served to revolutionize the world of comics from a literary point of view. His work on traditional characters and new series has raised the level of comics, taking them to new groups of cultured and more demanding readers.

Part of the series
Great Artists in the World of Comics

Director	28 minutes
Alejandro Vallejo	Color
Original music	Age range 12–adult
Caelo del Rio	VHS $99

Also available in French and Spanish

813 Prado

Miguel Angel Prado represents a new era in the Spanish comic strip, reflecting a vision, both ironic and cruel, of Spanish society. He combines tenderness with common violence, using a graphical style that is both original and highly mobile.

Part of the series
Great Artists in the World of Comics

Director	28 minutes
Gustavo Mtz Smith	Color
Original music	Age range 12–adult
Caelo del Rio	VHS $99

Also available in French and Spanish

28 Drawing and the Graphic Arts

253

'From today painting is dead!' These words, which greeted the discovery of photography, proved far from true.

29
The Photographic Image

This section of
9 programs can be
purchased on
VHS for $1011

Television rights and
prices on request

The emergence of the medium of photography hastened the development of Modernist art, by clarifying the fact that the aim of art was never mere verisimilitude, and by beginning a fruitful interaction between photography and other arts. The radically cropped compositions of an artist like Degas paralleled effects occurring in photographs, while painters such as Bonnard and Vuillard employed photography in creating their paintings. Much later, photorealist artists (for example, Brendan Neiland) self-consciously emulated photographic effects, and photomontage artists created what were often politically loaded images from photographs. Photography itself, meanwhile, quickly came to be thought of as an art form in its own right, photographers often manipulating their imagery far beyond the bounds of the traditional representational image (see films 660 and 661, pages 213 and 256). Recent decades, too, have seen the emergence of the video camera as an artistic tool, creating worlds of curious, often caustic moving images (see films 618 and 619, pages 184–5).

Man Ray

2b Rue Ferou, Paris

This film was made in order to preserve the Parisian studio of the Surrealist artist Man Ray. For twenty-six minutes we are invited to discover what lives on in the silence, under the dust of a place out of time. Since the death of the artist in 1976, everything has remained in place: paintbrushes, canvases, cameras, the darkroom, sculptures, mail, an array of unusual objects, the bedroom. Juliet, Man Ray's muse and companion for over twenty years, remembers. She alone is able to talk about what lives on in the studio. She takes us back to share in his ideas and his friendships – with Duchamp, Giacometti, Breton, Eluard, Paulhan, Dali, and Buñuel. The film is a testimony to a life lived and an art very much alive. It visits, post-mortem, an extraordinary world. The studio was destroyed in December 1989.

Director	**26 minutes**
François Levy-Kuentz	**Color**
Scenario	**Age range 14–adult**
Stephan Levy-Kuentz	
François Levy-Kuentz	**VHS $99**
Participant	
Juliet Man Ray	

---

532 **Picasso: A Portrait**

The Man behind the Legend

The whole world knows Picasso the genius, but has never been able to agree about Picasso the man. Was he monster or oracle, malevolent or full of wisdom? In 1951 the director Edward Quinn, working as a photographer in the south of France, met Picasso at a ceramics exhibition and was allowed to take his picture. Picasso liked the results and gave Quinn permission to visit and photograph him regularly at home and at work, while he continued painting, drawing, sculpting or relaxing with his family and friends. None of the numerous sessions was set up – Picasso simply carried on with his own life and Quinn observed without interfering. The result is this diary of images, revealing as nothing else could Picasso's fascinatingly vital personality and the way he drew on his everyday experience for artistic inspiration.

Director/Writer	**60 minutes**
Edward Quinn	**Black and white**
Narrator	**Age range 14–adult**
Roland Penrose	**Film $903** Rental $269
Also available in French	**VHS $129**

660
Pamela Bone
Begonia and Butterfly

568
Man Ray
Head, after an 'Autochrome'

---

636 **Pleasures and Dangers**

Six Women Artists at an Exciting Stage in their Careers

Six women gaining international success. This film is a portrait of their working lives in England, France and their home country, New Zealand. *Pleasures and Dangers* provides a lively introduction to new trends in the arts – from painting to animation, from feature films to giant photographs. The work of these artists is bold and colorful. They draw on the widest range of sources, from the images of television and advertising to ancient myths and symbols, and they explore issues of sex and gender in a way that is rich and unpredictable. They are Alexis Hunter, painter; Alison Maclean, film-maker; Julia Morison, painter; Lisa Reihana, animator; Merylyn Tweedie, mixed-media artist; and Christine Webster, photographer.

Director	**52 minutes**
Shirley Horrocks	**Color**
Writers	**Age range 16–adult**
Shirley Horrocks	**Film $903** Rental $269
Roger Horrocks	**VHS $129**
Narrator	
Angela D'Audney	
Original music	
Johnathon Besser	
Award	
Bronze Apple,	
Oakland, California	

---

660 **Circle of Light**

The Photography of Pamela Bone

This film without words is composed of Pamela Bone's unique photographic transparencies. Her talent has been said to 'push photography beyond its own limits, liberating it to the status of an entirely creative art form.' Inspired by nature, and being more responsive to feeling than to thought, Miss Bone has sought to express the mystery and beauty of the inner vision through photographic means alone: landscape has the quality of a dream; children on the sea-shore have a sense of their own enchantment, trees are forboding and strange when night moves in their arms. It took Miss Bone twenty years to find the right technique and so overcome the limitations that photography would impose.

Director/Scenario	**32 minutes**
Anthony Roland	**Color**
Sound	**Age range 12–adult**
Elsa Stansfield	**Film $763** Rental $199
Delia Derbyshire	**VHS $109**
Award	
First Prize, Cork	

661 Image of Light
The Photography of Sir George Pollock

'For me, light is the most exciting thing
there is...all life depends on it...it actually
is the energy which maintains life on earth.
As a maker of images, I feel privileged
that photography allows me to use the
life-giving energy directly in my work.
I want to celebrate the joy of light...the
objects that I put in front of my lenses are
really only devices for controlling light.
In one sequence I developed the idea of
light and of the colors of light as creative
forces. These forces grow, and they're
soon strong enough to form an order...'
George Pollock has given 'visual concerts'
in Europe, Australia, South Africa and the
United States, as well as all over Britain.
The film has very little narration.

Director
Anthony Roland

Original music
Keith Winter

Participant
George Pollock

16 minutes
Color
Age range 12–adult

Film $553 Rental $169
VHS $79

664 Bernard Faucon: Fables
A Photographer's Use of Eighty-three
Window Mannequins

This film describes the world of Bernard
Faucon and the story of the mannequins
which appeared in his photographs from
1977 to 1981. In 1989, he assembled,
restored, dressed and placed them
in front of the camera for the last time.
On March 22, 1990, the eighty-three
mannequins left France for their final
retreat, the Nanasai Museum in Kyoto,
Japan. Faucon describes his beginnings
and his 'encounters' with his mannequins.
Over fifty unpublished photographs
are presented.

Director/Scenario
Jean Real

Participant
Bernard Faucon

Original music
Pierre Boeswilwald

Also available in French

44 minutes
Color
Age range 12–adult

Film $833 Rental $249
VHS $119

665 The Fresson Process
Photo Prints Using Carbon, a Unique
Technique Offers Artistic Possibilities

This photographic printing process using
coal makes it possible to obtain paper
prints that do not deteriorate in light and
which have a very special luminosity and
grain. The well-known photographers
Batho, Horvat, Tourdjman and Faucon
discuss this printing process. Bernard
Faucon takes a photograph of one of the
Lubéron hills, which then reappears in the
Fresson studio. Michel Fresson uses this
photograph and the subsequent laboratory
work on it to comment on and explain the
originality and history of the process which
was developed by his grandfather and
adapted by his father for color printing.
Bernard Plossu, again using the Fresson
method, traces a black and white print back
in time to the moment that the photograph
was taken. The key factors that induce
many artists to associate their work with
the renown and quality of the Fresson
tradition are the technical and artistic
possibilities which this process offers.

Director/Scenario
Jean Real

Also available in French

30 minutes
Color
Age range 12–adult

Film $693 Rental $199
VHS $99

29 The Photographic Image

666 Krzysztof Wodiczko: Projections

Transforming Façades of Buildings into
Political, Public Art

The image of a homeless person
materializes on a Boston war monument.
A swastika suddenly appears on the South
African Embassy in London. A city watches
skeletal hands play a tuneless dirge on a
war museum in Pittsburgh. These are just
some of the controversial 'projections'
created by Polish artist Krzysztof Wodiczko,
who transforms buildings and structures
into political, public art. This documentary
intercuts scenes of Wodiczko preparing
a public projection in Jerusalem in 1991
with other projections in Europe and
North America. Each reflects the artist's
involvement in a broad range of political
issues: a blistering attack in Edinburgh on
Margaret Thatcher's economic policies; a
reflection on American–Canadian free
trade at a Toronto water filtration plant;
a street-level protest against the problem
of homelessness in New York through
a controversial prototype mobile shelter.
Interestingly, the only site where Wodiczko
is denied permission for a projection
is Montreal, at the Promenades de la
Cathédrale, despite his participation in
the city's *Cent Jours d'Art Contemporain.*
This innovative film reflects the personal
and political aspects of Wodiczko's art.

Director/Scenario	**55 minutes**
Derek May	**Color**
National Film Board	**Age range 14–adult**
of Canada	**Film $973** Rental $289
	VHS $139

666
Krzysztof Wodiczko
The Border Projection,
Part Two,
at Centro Cultural Tijuana

667
Peter Kennard
Falklands Medal
Photomontage

667 Photomontage Today: Peter Kennard

This video examines one particular tendency
in the history of photomontage, the analysis
of the world in political terms. The film is
divided into three sections. The first looks
at the effect of layout and juxtaposition
on the meaning of images. It highlights the
difference between the 'variety show' of
a color magazine, and the impact of a John
Heartfield montage, or the slaughterhouse
scene in *The Hour of the Furnaces,* in which
individual images are made to interact to
produce new meanings. The second section
examines the mechanics of photomontage
construction, and its ability to say more
about reality than a simple photograph.
The third section considers possible uses
for political photomontage, in campaigns,
on posters, in books, newspapers and
magazines. The video focuses on the work
of British photomontagist Peter Kennard,
probably best known for his anti-nuclear
stance. In each section Kennard talks about
his own practice, and shows how some of
his photomontages were conceived,
constructed and distributed. The film
reveals how photomontage can provide
a critique of the reality represented in
conventional advertising and the media:
by unmasking this mediated view of the
world it becomes a political act. Kennard's

work is discussed in relation to other
photomontagists, such as John Heartfield
and Hans Staek who have, in their own
ways, used the juxtaposition of images to
make political statements. Underlying these
practices is the conviction that, in order to
use images to change lives, you first have
to change the images themselves.

'...best used to stimulate discussion
about the difference between propaganda
and political art, or as an introduction for
high school and college students creating
their own photomontages using either
cameras or images from magazines.
For adults wishing to create montages,
this is a needed purchase. There will always
be a need for political photomontages.
This videotape can be used in art, English,
contemporary issues, and photography
classes. And for any school wishing
to teach thinking skills, this is a needed
addition to the collection.'
Video Rating Guide for Libraries, USA

Directors	**35 minutes**
Chris Rodrigues	**Color**
Ron Stoneman	**Age range 14–adult**
Advisors	**VHS $109**
Mike Coker	
John Underwood	
Arts Council of	
Great Britain	

Increasingly, nowadays, we are made aware of the importance of our relationship with the environment that we inhabit – the whole planet – and we hear that modern civilization is causing drastic damage to the ozone layer, the rainforests, the oceans, in fact the whole eco-system. Late in the day, and all too reluctantly, we are beginning to face our ecological responsibilities, and to look to cultures and to periods in the past when nature and humankind seemed to exist in harmony.

30
Art, Architecture and the Environment

This section of
26 programs can be
purchased on
VHS for $2954

Television rights and
prices on request

The films in this section look at architecture that damages the environment and continues the industrial aggression of the twentieth century; at a 'new age' of architecture that by contrast is caring in its use of the earth's resources, and that seeks wholeness in its philosophy; at traditional African building in which such principles have never been abandoned; and at artists who have taken their works out of commercial galleries and into the landscape, to make statements of 'eco-consciousness' and solidarity with more ancient world-wisdom.

13 Prehistoric Sites
From Stonehenge to the Moorlands of
Western Britain

Prehistoric sites are often difficult to
understand; this video looks at a wide
variety – from Stonehenge, in Wiltshire,
England, to less well-known monuments
high on the moorlands of western Britain –
and helps to explain them. It also sets
out to tell part of the story of the ancient
peoples who built them. We can see
the evidence – tools, stone buildings,
earthworks, burial chambers, stone circles
and long lines of upright stones – but
how are we to interpret it? Many clues
are pointed out to help work out what
the monuments might have been used
for. Reconstruction paintings of prehistoric
times bring to life the remains of ancient
communities: the makers of these
structures were farmers, and we assume
that the henges had ritual and religious
significance in their lives. The construction
of the later hillforts of the Iron Age,
including Maiden Castle, is also looked at.
An excavation of a long barrow is used to
show how much of the evidence that we do
have has been recovered by archaeological
investigation. We also see a school party
using a detailed map as they set out to
explore a monument. The video ends by
making clear just how many such ancient
remains there are. It is a useful general
guide to any study of prehistory.

Part of the series *Looking at…*

English Heritage	**20 minutes**
	Color
	Age range 11–14
	VHS $89

88 Of Leaves and of Earth
Traditional Tribal Architecture
of the Cameroon

Cameroon is a country where men
and women continue to construct their
own habitats according to ancestral
methods and in perfect harmony with
the environment in which they live.
From the shores of Lake Chad to the great
equatorial forest, our guides are the writer
André Gide, a pygmy school-teacher, the
chief of a mountain tribe, and the sultan
of the Kotokos. In addition to architecture,
social customs and dance are examined. As
well as being an informative documentary,
this film is an extraordinary creation of
atmosphere. Retracing a route followed by
Gide in 1926, with excerpts from a journal
and clips of film made on the trip, we gain
a unique insight into the fascination and
peculiar tristesse that exotic cultures have
held for many modern European artists
and writers.

Director	**45 minutes**
Dominique Theron	**Color**
Awards	**Age range 6–adult**
Canton Prize, Lausanne	**Film $833** Rental $249
City of Bordeaux Prize,	**VHS $119**
FIFARC and FIDEM Awards	

Also available in French

▼ 88
Tribal village, Cameroon

▲ 92
Palenque, Chapas, Mexico

91 Pre-Columbian Art in Mexico

Octavio Paz speaks of his childhood in
Mixoac, now a suburb of Mexico City.
An Aztec shrine nearby was 'a kind of
doorway that led to another part of
Mexican tradition that I didn't know and
could only guess at… mine, yet also distant
from me.' Paz introduces us to the complex
cosmology of the Aztecs, their notions of
time and space, and their symbols, such
as the zigzag serpent motif, representing
the duality of the life force – rise and
fall, growth and death. Also featuring
prominently in this film are the great
pyramids of Tenayuca, Chichén-Itzá,
Teotihuacán and Tajín. We learn that the
Mesoamerican religions all share the notion
that the gods have sacrificed themselves
to create the world, and that human beings
must worship so as to keep the gods alive.
For these peoples there was no art for
art's sake. All the forms in their art and
architecture have symbolic meaning.

Part of the series
Mexico through the Eyes of Octavio Paz

Director	**56 minutes**
Hector Tajonar	**Color**
Presenter/Writer	**Age range 14–adult**
Octavio Paz	**VHS $139**
Special collaboration	
Marie José Paz	
Original music	
Mario Lavista	

Also available in Spanish

92 In Search of the Mayas

An introduction to the geographical area
of Mesoamerican culture which gave birth
to the pre-Hispanic civilizations of Mexico.
Origins and characteristics are discussed:
the idea of nature, communication with the
gods, the complex theocratic organization
and the symbolic nature of their artistic
expressions. The cultures of the Olmecs,
Mayas, Mixtecs and Zapotecs are examined
through a reconstruction of their
architecture, sculpture, painting, ceramics
and craftsmanship in precious metals.

Part of the series *The Art of Mexico*

Director	**56 minutes**
Hector Tajonar	**Color**
Narrator	**Age range 14–adult**
Ricardo Montalban	**VHS $139**
Original music	
Mario Lavista	

Also available in Spanish

605
Andy Goldsworthy
Poppies
Collected from a roadside verge
Each petal licked and pressed onto another
To make a line
Calm
Became windy
Line broken
Shrivelling in the sun

609
Richard Ray Whitman
in a scene from the film

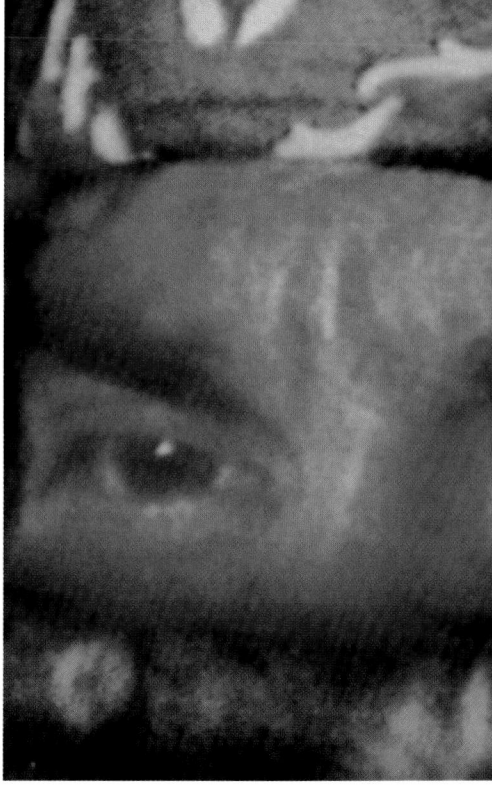

93   The Aztec Sun

The film deals with the pre-Columbian art of the groups of people from Mexico's high central plateau and the Gulf of Mexico. The plastic arts of the Totonac, Toltec and Mexican cultures reveal the continuity of a deeply religious and warlike view of the universe. The violence and beauty of these creations express a dramatic encounter with a mythical reality. The identity of Mesoamerica was preserved for centuries through this extraordinary view of the cosmos.

Part of the series *The Art of Mexico*

Director	**56 minutes**
Hector Tajonar	**Color**
Narrator	**Age range 14–adult**
Ricardo Montalban	**VHS $139**
Original music	
Mario Lavista	

Also available in Spanish

418   Giovanni Segantini: Life and Work

Today Giovanni Segantini (1858–99) is known, as 'the painter of idyllic life.' The frequent reproduction of his paintings in the form of popular prints has contributed to this rather superficial judgment. Yet the appeal of Segantini's work reflects not only a longing for an idyllic world but also a need for harmony and security, for transcendence. This film points up the tension between social reality and an idealized, perfectly balanced, paradisial world. Its starting point is Segantini's last work, *Growing – Being – Dying* (or birth, life, death). Besides taking the course of life as their subject, these three paintings also follow the course of the seasons and correspond with three places that were crucial for Segantini – Soglio, Scharberg and Maloja. Each still holds memories of Segantini's life, which the film evokes. Segantini was a myth-seeker, and he gave his longings artistic form, one that still fascinates and satisfies a large public.

For more information see pages 96 and 209

Director	**45 minutes**
Gaudenz Meili	**Color**
Writer	**Age range 14–adult**
Guido Magnaguagno	**Film $833** Rental $249
Also available in French,	**VHS $119**
Italian and Spanish	

605   Nature and Nature: Andy Goldsworthy

Andy Goldsworthy, a contemporary sculptor now living in Scotland, has for years been exploring various sites of the world, leaving behind sculptures that are in harmony with the environment. His materials are drawn from nature itself and his works, like many natural things, are essentially ephemeral. For Goldsworthy, seeing and understanding nature is a way of renewing our links with the earth. Here we meet him in the Scottish countryside with Colin Renfrew, head of Cambridge University's Department of Archaeology. The two men discover surprising similarities between their interest in and approach to nature.

Director/Scenario	**17 minutes**
Camille Guichard	**Color**
Narrators/Participants	**Age range 7–adult**
Andy Goldsworthy	**Film $623** Rental $189
Colin Renfrew	**VHS $89**

30 Art, Architecture and the Environment

Snow Dream
Gigantic Snow Sculpture

Silence, darkness, cold. Three men working wordlessly in the isolation of a snow-covered, mountainous landscape, sawing, cutting and shaping a huge cube of frozen snow. One of the men is French-Canadian sculptor Réal Bérard, the others his assistants. This film allows us to be spectators at the creation of a work of art far from any art gallery or civic square, a work seemingly made for the satisfaction of its creators alone. Extremes of heat and cold, fire and ice, are contrasted in this film: the men warm themselves all through the night at the campfire, even with the cigarettes they light. The monument they sculpt seems to be a synthesis of Eskimo and Aztec styles and imagery – broad faces, schematic birds, zigzag patterns, blocky forms. The film gives us a brief sequence of the finished work existing mysteriously in the world as the musical score picks up the plaintive theme one of the trio has been playing on a mouth organ by the fire. We see the sculpture survive a dramatic electric storm and torrential rain. Then its makers, still wordless, engulf it in a blazing conflagration. Impermanence would seem to be a major theme of this film, impermanence and the elemental forces at work in life and art.

Director/Writer Claude Grenier	**22 minutes** **Color**
Sculptor Réal Bérard assisted by Nick Burns Jim Tallosi	**Age range 8–adult** **Film $623** Rental $189 **VHS $89**
Original music Normand Roger	
National Film Board of Canada	

606 **Jean Verame:**
The New Adventurers

The film is about the unique adventure of a man creating a work of art in the Moroccan desert near Tafraout. During a period of three months, Jean Verame utilized eighteen tons of blue, violet, red and white paint to cover part of the Anti-Atlas mountains. His project, fully supported by King Hassan II, is a striking piece of art. His work and his presence are not without effects on the local ethnic group, the Berbers, whose women still go veiled in front of every man, though they are the working force of the region. Often compared to Christo, Jean Verame offers a different approach to contemporary painting: his mountains will last for at least 100 years.

Director Andrzej Kostenko	**52 minutes** **Color**
Participants Jean Verame The population of Tafraout (Morocco)	**Age range 12–adult** **Film $1043** Rental $299 **VHS $149**
Also available in French	

609 **A Day So Red**
Homage to the American Indians

All the artists portayed in this video work in different media. Richard Ray Whitman, a photographer, comes from the Yuchi tribe; painter Dan Daminga belongs to the Hopi people; Emmi Whitehorse is a Navajo painter; the Apache Bob Haozous makes constructed, sometimes fetish-like sculptures, while Edgar Heap of Birds, of the Ponca tribe, is a mixed-media artist. As will be evident, these artists are not practicing the traditional arts of their peoples, but using the language of contemporary art to articulate the relationship between their cultural past and present, to testify to their identity, and perhaps to heal the wounds of cultural displacement and discontinuity. Each short video segment takes a raw, matter-of-fact, unrhetorical look at an artist against the traditional music of his or her tribe. This footage does not offer a polished tribute to celebrities of the art world, but gives glimpses of personalities 'living' their art.

Director Pierre Lobstein	**42 minutes** **Color**
Award Leonardo de Vinci Prize, French Ministry of Foreign Affairs	**Age range 13–adult** **VHS $99**

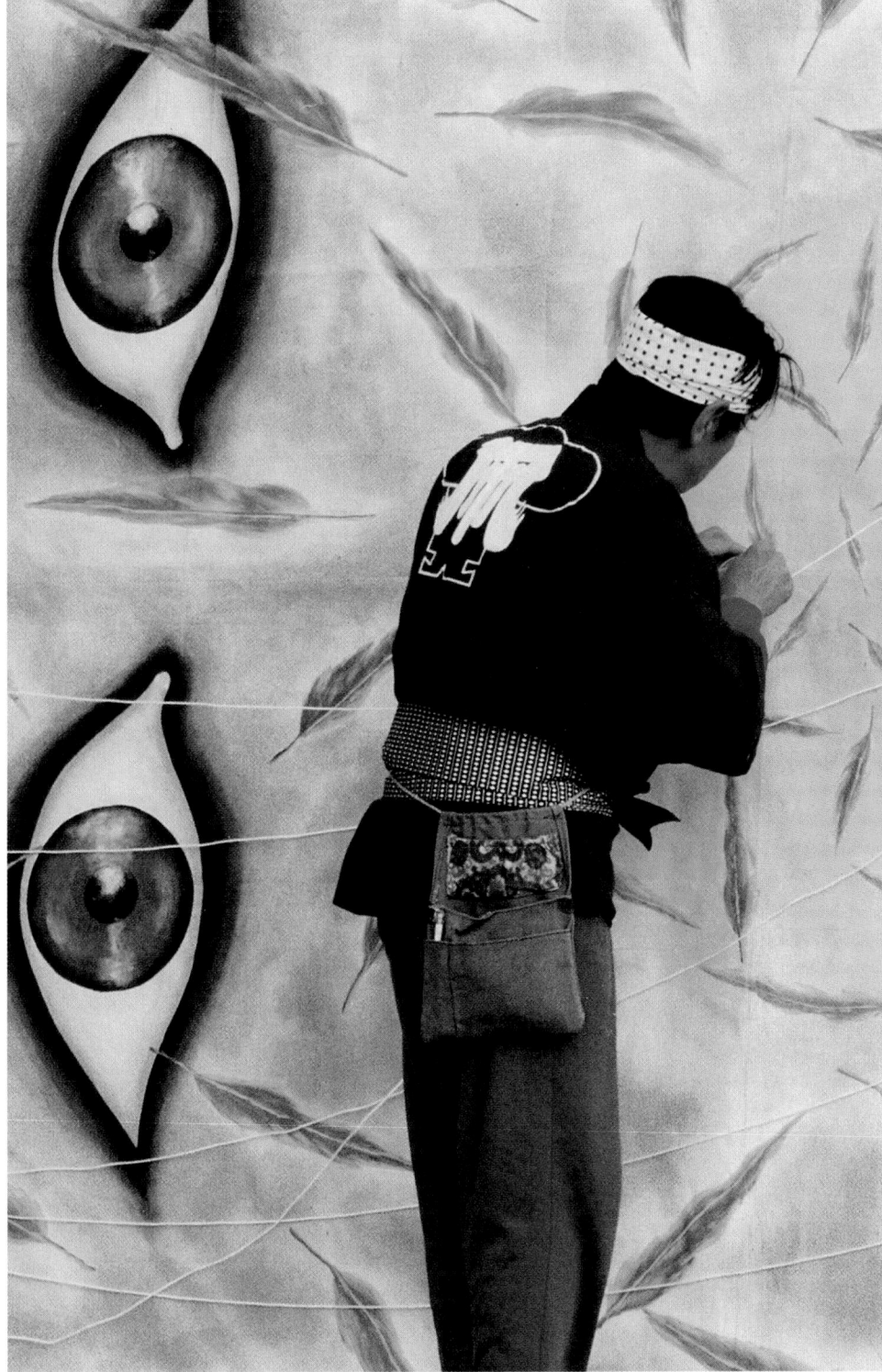

Pictures for the Sky
Famous Artists Design Kites

Working in conjunction with Japanese master kite-makers, a hundred famous artists from twenty countries all over the world created 'art kites' to turn the sky above Himeji, Japan, into a playground for their world of paintings. *Pictures for the Sky* documents one of the most fascinating international art spectacles of recent years, and is unique in its attractive presentation of a wide range of new works by important representatives of contemporary art. Artists featured include Robert Rauschenberg, Emilio Vedova, Niki de Saint Phalle, Panamarenko, Horst Antes, Frank Stella, Daniel Buren, Kumi Sugai, José de Guimarães, Otto Herbert Hajek, Salome, Tom Wesselmann, Antoni Tàpies, Per Kirkeby, Bukichi Inoue, Chema Cobo, Graham Dean, Griska Bruskin, Rupprecht Geiger, Paul Wunderlich, Mimmo Paladino, Karel Appel, General Idea, Olle Kaks, Zvi Goldberg, Imre Bak, Karl Otto Götz, Ulrike Rosenbach, Kenny Scharf, Gregorij Litischevskij, Sadamasa Motonaga, Tadanori Yokoo, Klaus Staeck, Franz Erhard Walther, and Ivan Rabuzin.

Director/Script	**30 minutes**
Markus Zollner	**Color**
Original sound	**Age range 8–adult**
Jan Kollwitz	**Film $693** Rental $199
Also available in	**VHS $99**
Dutch, French, German,	
Italian, Japanese,	
Portuguese and Russian	

◀ 612
Chema Cobo
*The Power of
No-Disappointment*

614 The Ritual Art of Siim-Tanel Annus

During his time as a student, Siim-Tanel Annus became a member of an influential circle of artists and theorists, grouped around Tonis Vint. Although he had already undergone a long artistic development, he was still thought of as a 'young artist.' He is thus a 'phenomenon', without age, without period, and outside trends. From the beginning he has created drawings – sensitive, abstract images composed of tiny dots. Later he created geometric forms in black and white. He threw himself into performance art before it became common in Estonia in the 1980s; his 'garden parties' caused scandals. Birds, sun, moon, energy, earth, water, air – all these were personified in his performances, as his pictures had been intended to represent 'Light in Paradise.' His actions are ritualistic, rich in symbolism, but everything is subordinate to the creation of a visual image which the artist conceives of just as he does most of his graphic works.

Director	10 minutes
Jaanus Nogisto	Color
Original music	Age range 10–adult
Peeter Vähl	VHS $69

Also available in Estonian

627 The Spinney by Jean Dubuffet

Without narration, we follow all the different stages leading up to the unveiling of *The Spinney,* a monumental sculptural work by Jean Dubuffet, on June 18, 1988 in Flaine, Haute Savoie, France – the location chosen by Dubuffet himself.

'…an inspiration for artists…can at times be mesmerizing…highly artistic…fits together in unexpected ways. This is a video that art discussion groups or those into surrealism may enjoy.'
Video Rating Guide for Libraries, USA

For more information see page 163. Films 503D and 582 also feature Dubuffet's work.

Director	16 minutes
Nedjima Scialom	Color
	Age range 12–adult
	VHS $79

491 Europa Nostra
The Threat to and Protection of the European Heritage

This multi-award-winning film has been financed by contributions from a number of European governments and the European Economic Community. Shot in fifteen countries in western and eastern Europe, it touches upon all aspects of conservation, including lost treasures, restoration, new uses for old buildings and new construction, both harmonious and incongruous, traffic (congestion, parking and pedestrian areas), the pressures of tourism, unsightly advertising and other 'eyesores', technical and financial problems, and the activities of local authorities and conservation societies.

'…a beautiful film, directed and edited with great flair and skill. From its opening montage of glories that have survived the assaults of war, decades of neglect and the depredations of developers, to its end above the water of threatened Venice, the changes of pace and the violence of contrasts keep your eyes very wide open. Teachers of history, social studies, liberal studies and current affairs will find obvious uses for the film. *Europa Nostra* is a powerful indictment of those whose judgment of our architectural inheritance is determined by whether they will make money faster by knocking it down rather than allowing it to stand for our pleasure. The quality of our lives is our responsibility – and that is a political and moral lesson every school should teach. *Europa Nostra* is as good an aid as you will get for putting it across.'
Times Educational Supplement, London

Director	24 minutes
Charles Mapleston	concise version
Narration	Color
Michael Middleton	Age range 12–adult
Awards	Film $693 Rental $199
Gold Award,	VHS $99
Special Award,	
British Architectural	
Heritage Year	
Silver Plaque, Chicago	
Grand Prize, Silver Trophy,	
South Africa	
First Award BISFA, London	
First Prize, Ouistreham	
Bronze Award,	
Interfilm Award, Berlin	

493 Janus
Europe's Architectural Heritage: A Call to Action

Janus highlights the dangers threatening the magnificent buildings, civic architecture and urban environment, both ancient and modern, which belong to all Europeans. Its objective is to demonstrate forcefully the fact that our architectural heritage is as much at the mercy of ourselves as of architects, planners and government departments; and it asserts that at different times each one of us may display indifference or concern, admiration or neglect. *Janus* is strong medicine. It is meant to make you think – and it does! There is no narration.

Director	36 minutes
Anthony Wilkinson	Color
Original music	Age range 8–adult
John Scott	Film $833 Rental $249
	VHS $119

610A Walls, Walls
The Murals of Los Angeles

A documentary about the murals of Los Angeles: who paints them, who looks at them, who pays for them? The capital of talking pictures has talking walls, through which the people of Los Angeles speak. Naïve, violent, poetic frescos, full of color and humor, reveal the adventure of the city and its inhabitants – black, Mexican, Puerto Rican – images of America caught in the melting-pot at one specific moment in history. Most of these murals will already have been destroyed; only in this film do they still live on.

Director/Writer/Narrator	81 minutes
AGNES VARDA	Color
Awards	Age range 12–adult
Grand Prix, Florence	Film $1323 Rental $399
Prix Joseph von Sternberg,	VHS $189
Mannheim	

Also available with French subtitles

Paris: Story of a City
Medieval to Modern within a Century

In 1853 Napoleon III appointed
Baron Georges-Eugène Haussmann, a
lawyer and civil servant, to the post of
prefect of the Seine *département* of France.
His brief was to improve Paris's planning,
and for the following two decades he swept
away acres of rambling medieval streets
and substituted his own concept of a
modern city – wide, straight boulevards
with imposing façades, converging at major
junctions marked by monuments, public
buildings and points of importance such as
city gates or railway stations. Paris became
the yardstick by which all European cities
were judged. This film was made to mark
the centenary of the death of Baron
Haussmann in 1891. Historian Francis Loyer
combs the city, scrutinizing objects that
are so familiar we no longer see them:
a wooden shutter, the angle of a street,
a carving on a façade. 'Haussmannism' is
often seen as a kind of urban vandalism
presaging the great modern devastations
in the name of progress; it can also look
like totalitarian imposition by an authority
eager to control and police its populace and
to suppress revolution. In this film, however,
Haussmann's scheme is considered as a
rigorous and coherent means of controlling
the growth of a city.

Director
Stan Neumann

Scenario
Stan Neumann
Francis Loyer

Art historian
Francis Loyer

Awards
Grand Prix, Bordeaux
Environmental Film
of the Year,
National Geographic,
Washington DC

Also available in French

52 minutes
Black and white
Age range 14–adult

Film $903 Rental $299
VHS $129

263A

The Roland Collection

◀◀ 623
Richard Serra
Fulcrum

623 Smithson and Serra: Beyond Modernism?

Robert Smithson and Richard Serra both
believed that sculpture should have a dialog
with its environment. Two sculptures of
Richard Serra are shown in an urban
environment – *Fulcrum* in the Broadgate
development at Liverpool Street in London
and *Tilted Arc* in New York – the latter has
since been destroyed. *Spin Out*, a tribute
to Robert Smithson, is in a rural site at
the Kroller-Muller Museum in Holland.
Robert Smithson's work is represented
by *Broken Circle, Spiral Hill*, which is
in a disused quarry in Northern Holland.
Smithson, who died in 1973, greatly
influenced Serra's work.

Part of the series
Modern Art, Practices and Debates

Director	**25 minutes**
GD Jayalakshmi	**Color**
Presenter	**Age range 18–adult**
Paul Wood	**VHS $99**
Participant	
Richard Serra	

Open University/BBC

403 Paris, Spectacle of Modernity

The program is presented by three art
historians, all experts on different aspects
of nineteenth-century French art and
urbanism, who display their own particular
methodology. Francis Frascina's approach
is informed by a Marxist view of history
in which the reconstruction of Paris under
its prefect Baron Haussmann is seen as
determined by the political and economic
forces of capitalism. Tim Benton explores
the history of urban development and
outlines the positive improvements against
the social cost of such rapid change.
Hollis Clayson's argument centers on the
huge public concern over the growth of
prostitution in the city. The program
suggests ways in which these historical
interpretations can inform our reading of
Impressionist art in the 1870s.

Part of the series
Modern Art, Practices and Debates

Director	**25 minutes**
Nick Levinson	**Color**
Presenters	**Age range 18–adult**
Francis Frascina	**VHS $99**
Tim Benton	
Hollis Clayson	

Open University/BBC

547 Public Murals in New York

At the height of the Depression in the USA,
Franklin D Roosevelt was elected president.
As part of the New Deal program, the
Federal Art Project employed artists to
paint public murals. There were over 200
in New York alone. The program visits the
sites of some of the murals: *The Pursuit
of Happiness* by Vertis Hayes in Harlem
Hospital, showing phases of life among
Negro people in Africa and America;
The Development of Medicine by William
Palmer (two parts remain) in Queens
General Hospital, New York; the only
abstract work, done for the Williamsburgh
Housing Project but now removed to the
Brooklyn Museum; James Brooks' *Flight* at
La Guardia Airport; and James Michael
Newell's *The History of Western Civilization*
at Evander Childs High School.

Part of the series
Modern Art, Practices and Debates

Director	**25 minutes**
GD Jayalakshmi	**Color**
Presenter	**Age range 18–adult**
Dr Jonathan Harris	**VHS $99**

Open University/BBC

263B

763 Alvar Aalto

The Finnish architect Alvar Aalto
(1898–1976) was one of this century's
great reformers in architecture and interior
design. Aalto's work demonstrates an
intense individualism combined with clear-
sighted comprehension of the international
architectural trends of his day. A striking
characteristic of his work is rationalism,
but a rationalism that is sensitive to nature
and the place of humanity within it.
He considered that architecture must serve
people, not theories, and that it is a
discipline involving 'all fields of human
endeavour.' Working often in his native
Finland, or with materials originating there,
he was adamant that the structures made
by and for human beings must be in
harmony with the environment, and he
was always at pains to use natural
substances, such as the wood that is
so plentiful in Scandinavia.

For more information see page 199

Director	**57 minutes**
Piero Berengo Gardin	**Color**
	Age range 16–adult
	Film $973 Rental $289
	VHS $139

767 An Affirmation of Life
The Architecture of Moriyama

The Japanese-Canadian architect
Raymond Moriyama is the creator of major,
outstandingly individual buildings.
An Affirmation of Life takes us into the
serene, sweeping spaces of his
administrative center in Ontario, and, most
dramatically, into the Science North Center
at Sudbury – a building structured like a
snowflake spanning a huge cleft in the
bedrock. The cliff faces and natural features
are fully incorporated into the modern
construction, and local miners were
employed to create the underground
passages and chambers that are a part of
the scheme. The program also looks at the
architect's design for a public monument,
the ceremonial bell presented in gratitude
to the people of Ontario by its Japanese
community. Moriyama himself talks about
his projects in a manner deceptively,
though engagingly, direct and simple; in the
past he has won a contract in competition
with other architects by presenting no
plans or specifications but simply arriving
in person to tell the clients of his vision for
their building. But clients and colleagues
of Moriyama speak in this film of the
depths hidden within this seemingly very
modern man, like the deep cleft beneath
his Sudbury building. He has spent time in
India, absorbing Zen Buddhist principles,
and is overridingly concerned with our
relationship with nature, with ecology
and the holistic integration of human life
with the greater universe around us.

Director/Script	**27 minutes**
Alex Hamilton Brown	**Color**
	Age range 13–adult
	VHS $99

768 The Seasons
Four Journeys into Raili and
Reima Pietilä's Architecture

The Helsinki-based architect Raili Pietilä
states that he does not want to deal with
truth, in case the truth turns out to be
'a black hole where gravity is too great for
anything to exist.' Rather, he seeks to
steer around reality through metaphor, and
to make buildings which are frameworks
in which reality can exist. His highly
individual approach to creating a building
might involve exploring grammar, the
structure of sentences, the narrative
method of novels, or the identities of the
seasons. He will listen to music in search
of a formal 'theme.' He will study landscape,
or the effect of wind and snow on water.
All these will inform his design, so that the
overall experience of a Pietilä environment
will be rooted in a source which those who
look at or live in it may never guess at.
In this film he takes us around a range of
his buildings. We see a residential complex
set in a birch forest, in which the patterns
of tree bark, trunks and foliage provide
the motif for the façades. When building
a modern city church, the architect's aim
is to marry a sense of sanctuary and
transcendence with a continued contact
with the everyday world, seen through
apertures and doorways, in contrast to
the enclosed feeling of Gothic cathedrals.
Finally, the architect revisits his Finnish
Embassy building in India, built with
traditional local labor methods, but
designed to follow the patterns of Finland's
snow-swept landscape. Here he speaks of
the detachment any artist can feel for
a long-finished work, enclosing a reality
as mysterious to its creator as to anyone
else who encounters it.

Director/Script	**35 minutes**
Anssi Blomstedt	**Color**
	Age range 14–adult
Original music	**Film $763** Rental $199
Arvo Pärt	**VHS $109**

763
Alvar Aalto
Paimio Sanatorium,
Finland, corner detail

772
Robert Bruno
Steel House in construction
Lubbock, Texas

Architectural Adventures
Avant-Garde House Designs in North America and Europe

These films are not about high-rise blocks or skyscrapers. Instead they show new possibilities of living for ordinary people. We all dream of ideal homes, but few venture to make these dreams come true.

This series of 3 programs can be purchased on VHS for $357 Reference S26

---

771 Dreams Come True

This film features people throughout America who have built their own homes from their own designs, without the help of an architect. We visit a special school in Maine which runs do-it-yourself courses covering all aspects of building one's own house. Then we meet people who have taken the course and tried to build their own house, seeing what they have achieved and what difficulties they encountered. Most important of all, the film shows many imaginative and extravagant examples of unusual homes located in Maine, New York, California and New Mexico.

Part of the series *Architectural Adventures*

Director/Scenario
Ray Müller
Also available in German
**44 minutes
Color
Age range 15–adult
VHS $119**

---

772 New Horizons

This film is about architects and artists who have broken new ground, developing original ideas and using new building materials. We meet a sculptor in Texas who has spent his last ten years welding a poetic house of steel; we see underground homes in New Mexico whose designs were inspired by the cave dwellings of the Pueblo Indians; we visit a mysterious cluster of domes in southern California, and the 'habitable sculptures' of an architect in Texas which were designed to produce varied psychological feedback from those who live in them – for example, different lights or temperature can be activated automatically in response to prevailing or even to expected weather conditions.

Part of the series *Architectural Adventures*

Director/Scenario
Ray Müller
Also available in German
**44 minutes
Color
Age range 15–adult
VHS $119**

---

773 Visions of Future Living

This film presents architecture of the future, on land, in the ocean and in space. It moves outside America to include France, Switzerland and the Caribbean. We visit a futuristic home entirely controlled by a 'house-brain' in Florida, meet avant-garde architects on the Côte d'Azure, witness underwater 'self-growing' construction experiments in the Virgin Islands. We watch a French ocean-architect working in a diving cell in his office on a boat in Paris, and then accompany him on his underwater sightseeing vessel in the Mediterranean. Finally we meet the architect of the Space Station in Houston, USA. Fascinating original shots of space evoke a future which our children may experience one day: living on a space station, in orbit or on a colony on the moon – or even the planet Mars.

Part of the series *Architectural Adventures*

Director/Scenario
Ray Müller
Also available in German
**44 minutes
Color
Age range 15–adult
VHS $119**

30 Art, Architecture and the Environment

31
Films for Younger Audiences

All films in the Roland Collection are given audience age-guides and many, even when not made specifically for younger audiences, will be found eminently suitable for children, whose approach to the unfamiliar and challenging in art is often more receptive and unprejudiced than that of adults.

This section of
63 programs,
excluding the series
'Comics, the Ninth Art',
pages 246–50, can be
purchased on
VHS for $5087

Television rights and
prices on request

Many films in this section have little or no narration, offering broad, unintimidating access to their subjects, which parents and teachers can use with children at many levels. Some titles offer irresistible stimulus to practical play and creativity. *Calder's Circus*, for example, shows how simple media such as wire, cork and tin can be used to create figures and animals, while *Pictures in the Sky* provides the perfect prelude to kite-making and kite-flying. Other films encourage collage, drawing, modeling and exploration of the environment.

10 Tassili N'Ajjer
Prehistoric Rock Paintings of the Sahara

Four thousand years ago the people who inhabited the Tassili N'Ajjer, a group of mountains in the eastern Sahara, painted the rocks with scenes of their daily life. Why? Probably they were making magic; we can only guess. But from the hundreds of thousands of pictures they left (nowhere else is prehistoric art to be found in such abundance) we learn that the desert then was no desert at all: it was a place of flourishing community life, of flowers and waterholes and herds of antelope. To our eyes these vivid and colorful humans and animals in motion, farming and hunting and making war, look astonishingly 'modern', preserved as they have been by the dry climate. Today, however, they are in danger, since many have been defaced by tourists and some have already entirely disappeared. To film this invaluable record of the paintings, some of the most recent technical developments in the art of film have been used to capture some of the most ancient images we still have. At the very dawning of artistic activity, the images human beings create are bound up with the politics and economics of their existence – the animals they hunt, the forces, natural and supernatural, that sustain their lives, the battles they fight. Their pictures are inscribed on the very fabric of the environment they inhabit – the rocks and cave walls – prefiguring the graffiti or public murals of today, giving expression to social concerns and passions.

'Very beautiful, with a very fine subject' UNESCO

Director	16 minutes
Jean-Dominique Lajoux	**Color**
Narration	**Age range 6–adult**
Max-Pol Fouchet	**Film $553** Rental $169
Original music	**VHS $79**
Maurice Le Roux	
Awards	
Gold Medal, Venice	
Bronze Medal, Bilbao	
Quality Award and Prize,	
French National Film Center	

267, page 282
Educational event
at Kirby Hall

95
Mayan chieftan

88 Of Leaves and of Earth
Traditional Tribal Architecture of the Cameroon

Cameroon is a country where men and women continue to construct their own habitats according to ancestral methods and in perfect harmony with the environment in which they live. From the banks of Lake Chad to the great equatorial forest, our guides are French writer André Gide, a pygmy school-teacher, the chief of a mountain tribe, and the sultan of the Kotokos. In addition to architecture, social customs and dance are examined. As well as being an informative documentary, this film is an extraordinary creation of atmosphere. Retracing a route followed by Gide in 1926, with excerpts from a journal and clips of film made on the trip, we gain a unique insight into the fascination and peculiar tristesse that exotic cultures have held for many modern European artists and writers.

Director	45 minutes
Dominique Theron	**Color**
Awards	**Age range 6–adult**
Canton Prize, Lausanne	**Film $833** Rental $249
City of Bordeaux Prize,	**VHS $119**
FIFARC and FIDEM Awards	

Also available in French

95 Maya Terracotta Figurines

Making images of figures – of people – is one of our most basic instincts. Faces and bodies are the first things the child draws. The objects shown in this film are whistles, bells, ornaments – all shaped into human figures, originating from around what is present-day Honduras. The Mayan peoples who occupied this area around AD 500 depicted in their pottery priests, nobles, dancers, soldiers, musicians, craftsmen – every member of their society. This, like many in the Roland Collection, is an excellent film for the young to make drawings from – recalling as many 'types' as they can from what they have seen, or 'freezing frame' to copy a certain figure. Young students in any pottery class will also be inspired by the notion of useful everyday objects made in the forms of contemporary characters. There is no narration.

Directors	12 minutes
Carlos Saenz	**Color**
Slivia Garduno	**Age range 8–adult**
Original music	**Film $553** Rental $169
Rocio Sanz	**VHS $79**

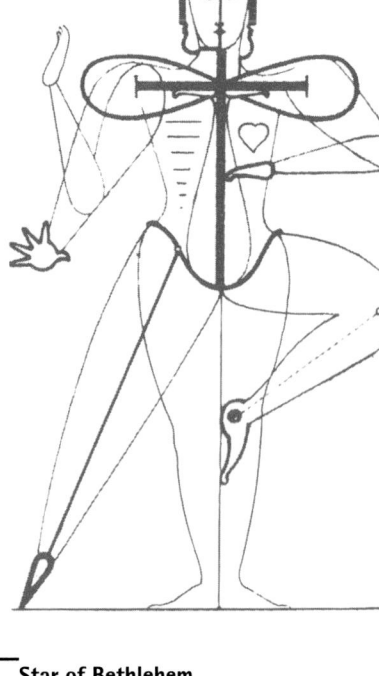

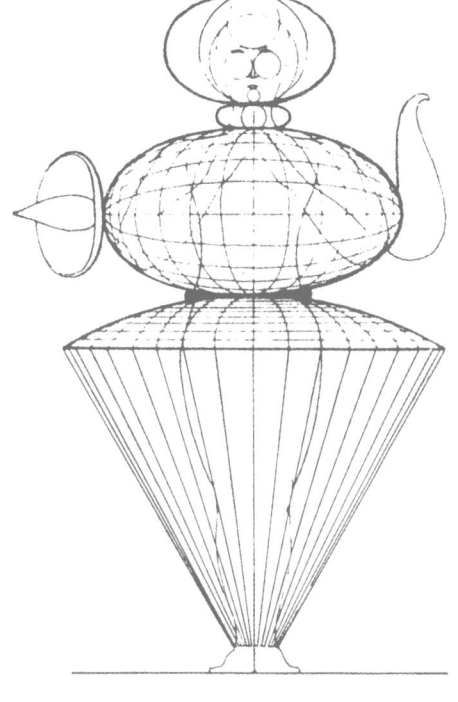

150   **Visions of Light**
Gothic Stained Glass

For medieval western society, Christianity was the overriding structural force. No area of life was untouched by it, and artists did not seek to be individual, original or subversive, or to give expression to private vision; they were the servants of religious authority, employed to convey the Christian message and thus reinforce society's coherence and stability. The stained-glass windows in the cathedral at Bourges in France are superb examples of how this art form was used to illustrate the Bible for people who could not read, as well as to light up formerly dim interiors: a stained-glass cinema of the Middle Ages. They tell, in the simplest of human terms, the Gospel stories, beginning with the birth of the world, when God ordered the sun to warm the earth and brilliantly colored birds and strange animals burst out upon scenes of fantastic vegetation. And together with the creations of God, they show the works of humankind – cities and buildings, and houses, and tables and chairs and cups – everyday things, all recreated by the unknown window painters, so that what they intended for the instruction of the people of their own time serves to tell us, now, how they lived.

Directors/Narration	**15 minutes**
Louis Cuny	**Color**
M Malvaux	**Age range 9–adult**
Original music	**Film $553** Rental $169
Marcel Dellanoy	**VHS $79**

330   **Star of Bethlehem**
Baroque Woodcarvings – Neapolitan Crib Figures

Although the Church in the eighteenth century was losing its hold over the minds of scientists and philosophers, it was able to keep a grip on the imagination of simpler people by telling them the stories of their faith in a way which was easy for them to understand. The most important story, of course, was that of the birth of Christ; but to the peasants of southern Italy who knew nowhere but their own villages, it was useless to talk of inns in Bethlehem or the Roman governor of Judea. The Church therefore had local woodcarvers make figures, none more than a handspan high, of the Holy Family, dressed in the familiar clothes of the peasants' own time and place. The three shepherds who come to worship the newborn baby are obviously based on three local shepherds; the innkeeper who has no room is a grasping Neapolitan; and Herod and his soldiers massacring the innocents are dressed as Turks, the cruellest enemy of whom the peasants would have heard, or as Moslems, the arch-enemies of Christianity. There is no narration.

Director	**12 minutes**
Dr Doederlein	**Color**
Original music	**Age range 6–adult**
Mark Lothan	**Film $483** Rental $149
	VHS $69

389   **Parliamentarians: Daumier Sculpture**

Honoré Daumier is better known to most people as a graphic artist, and perhaps as a painter, than as a sculptor, yet he created many sculptures, which often preceded the lithographs and drawings that relate to them. His modeled heads of politicians, originally painted in polychrome (though also cast in bronze) are part caricatures of notables of the time and part physiological human 'types.' Using creative lighting, sound and camera work, the film brings alive the *Parliamentarians* and other works by Daumier, setting them in dramatic context and deploying the figures almost as if they are in a puppet theater. This is one of the many rare film discoveries which the Roland Collection has brought out of undeserved obscurity.

Director	**18 minutes**
Jiri Jahn	**Black and white**
Scenario	**Age range 9–adult**
Eric Legler	**Film $623** Rental $189
Original music	**VHS $89**
Rolf Kuhl	

Also available in German

517 **Man and Mask**
Oskar Schlemmer and the Bauhaus Stage

Oskar Schlemmer did not confine his activities at the Bauhaus to painting and teaching sculpture. He also wanted to put his ideas about ballet into practice, and in 1922 he did so in public for the first time. He planned to free the stage from the trappings of tradition in order to give expression to the 'pure idea.' The central theme of his work was the relation between humankind and space, and the mediator between these two was to be the dancer, stripped of his individual identity by the use of costumes and masks. This documentary film, made with the artistic advice of Oskar Schlemmer's widow, presents an historically faithful, precise reconstruction of some of his dances. More than any other film, it gives a sense of what Bauhaus teaching was really like, and is truly important to an understanding of the origins of contemporary dance.

For more information see page 135

Director	27 minutes
Margarete Hasting	Color
	Age range 10–adult
Original music	
Eric Fersti	Film $693 Rental $199
	VHS $99

570 **Kindness Week (Max Ernst)**

Max Ernst's humorous and illogical collages of figures and objects from Victorian engravings are perhaps less bewildering to audiences today than when they were made between the wars. The 'zany' qualities of Surrealism (see section 18), of which Ernst was a leading practitioner, have become familiar through advertising and television humor. Nevertheless there is great mystery in Ernst's work, which may disorientate children less than adults, who are more attached to the convention and logic that Surrealism seeks to subvert.

'High spirits and non-conformism are taken to the limits of the fantastic.'
UNESCO

Director	19 minutes
Jean Desvilles	Black and white
	Age range 12–adult
Narration	
Max Ernst	Film $623 Rental $189
	VHS $89
Original music	
Georges Delerue	
Quality Award,	
French National Film Center	
Also available in French	

269

621
Alexander Calder
Lion and lion-tamer from
Calder's Circus, 1926–31

575
Saul Steinberg
Sketches

594   **Adventures in Perception**

The Work of the Graphic Artist
Maurits Escher

The visual puzzles and games of Maurits
Escher have a permanent fascination for
viewers of all ages. He explores graphic
puns and optical illusions, and creates
'impossible' illusions which contradict logic
and expectation. He plays with all kinds
of artistic conventions. In Escher there
are elements of Surrealism (see section 18),
of the Op Art of Vasarely (page 129), and of
the self-conscious visual conjuring of
Steinberg (opposite), though unlike the
latter, Escher's sensibility is precise and
intricate, rather than relaxed and whimsical.

Director	21 minutes
Han van Gelder	**Color**
Award	**Age range 14–adult**
First Prize, Cork	**Film $693** Rental $199
Also available in Dutch,	**VHS $99**
French, German and Spanish	

600   **Josef Herman Drawings**

Leading British artist Josef Herman draws
workers, fishermen, peasants in fields and
miners, with boldness, simplicity, force,
but also subtlety and feeling. His figures
are often built from the most basic
elements of light and shade, line and tone,
almost as if he is shuffling and adding
elements in a collage – an exercise which
young viewers of this film may be inspired
to try. Without any narration, the film takes
us into his rich, silent world of laborers
which is becoming all but lost to us, in our
'post-industrial' cities.

'With his violent pen and brush it is a
visual triumph of labor. The director
has deliberately chosen the rhythm of the
laborer and the effect is monumental.'
UNESCO

For more information see page 244

Director	15 minutes
Anthony Roland	**Black and white**
Original music	**Age range 12–adult**
Louis Saguer	**Film $553** Rental $169
Awards	**VHS $79**
Quality Award,	
French National Film Center	
Chriss Award, Columbus	

621   **Calder's Circus**

Alexander Calder's fascination with the
circus began in his mid-twenties, when he
published illustrations in a New York
journal of Barnum and Bailey's Circus, for
which he held a year's pass. It was in Paris
in 1927 that he created the miniature
circus celebrated in this film – tiny wire
performers, ingeniously articulated to walk
tightropes, dance, lift weights, and engage
in acrobatics in the ring. The Parisian
avant-garde would gather in Calder's studio
to see the circus in operation. It was, as
critic James Johnson Sweeney noted,
'a laboratory in which some of the most
original features of his later work were to
be developed.' This film exudes the great
personal charm of Calder himself, moving
and working the tiny players like a
ringmaster, while his wife winds up the
gramophone in the background. *The Circus*
is now housed at the Whitney Museum
in New York.

Director	19 minutes
Carlos Vilardebo	**Color**
Presenter	**Age range 5–adult**
Alexander Calder	**Film $693** Rental $199
	VHS $99

630 **The Genesis of a Sculpture**
Adam-Tessier

In this animated film, without ever seeing the sculptor or his hands at work with the chisel, we follow the magical transformation of the stone's contours, as layers are chipped away to reveal a face – and then, mysteriously, partly to eradicate it again. Many young viewers will learn an important lesson about art when they ask why, after nearly having the sculpture realistically 'finished', the artist seems to take it back to a less defined form.

'The technique of this research film of great integrity is remarkable. The care taken to be truthful extends almost to complete frankness. This is a courageous film.'
UNESCO

Directors	**13 minutes**
Olivier Clouzot	**Black and white**
Julien Pappe	**Age range 10–adult**
Music	**Film $483** Rental $149
Anton Webern	**VHS $69**
Awards	
Mention d'Excellence,	
Cannes	
Biennale Prize, Paris	

605 **Nature and Nature: Andy Goldsworthy**

Andy Goldsworthy, a contemporary sculptor now living in Scotland, has for years been exploring various sites of the world, leaving behind sculptures that are in harmony with the environment. His materials are drawn from nature itself and his works, like many natural things, are essentially ephemeral. For Goldsworthy, seeing and understanding nature is a way of renewing our links with the earth. Here we meet him in the Scottish countryside with Colin Renfrew, head of Cambridge University's Department of Archaeology. The two men discover surprising similarities between their interests in and approaches to nature.

Director/Scenario	**17 minutes**
Camille Guichard	**Color**
Narrators/Participants	**Age range 7–adult**
Andy Goldsworthy	**Film $623** Rental $189
Colin Renfrew	**VHS $89**

575 **Steinberg**

Without narrative, this film takes us on an enchanting path through the American artist Saul Steinberg's witty world of characters, animals and everyday objects, teaching us along the way the delights of drawing with line. Quite close to the doodling we all indulge in, Steinberg's technique is friendly and unforbidding, with no attempt at the 'realistic' effects we too often think of as 'proper' draftsmanship. Yet the artist is clever, thought-provoking and disciplined. Few, after seeing this film, will be able to resist picking up a pencil.

'The director has made use of all the resources at the disposal of the cinema to communicate a form of dynamic humor'
UNESCO

For more information see page 171

Director	**14 minutes**
Peter Kassowitz	**Black and white**
Original music	**Age range 9–adult**
Bernard Parmegiani	**Film $553** Rental $169
	VHS $79

607 **Snow Dream**
Gigantic Snow Sculpture

Silence, darkness, cold. Three men working wordlessly in the isolation of a snow-covered, mountainous landscape, sawing, cutting and shaping a huge cube of frozen snow. One of the men is French-Canadian sculptor Réal Bérard, the others his assistants. This film allows us to be spectators at the creation of a work of art far from any art gallery or civic square, a work seemingly made for the satisfaction of its creators alone. Extremes of heat and cold, fire and ice, are contrasted in this film: the men warm themselves all through the night at the campfire, even with the cigarettes they light. The monument they sculpt seems to be a synthesis of Eskimo and Aztec styles and imagery – broad faces, schematic birds, zigzag patterns, blocky forms. The film gives us a brief sequence of the finished work existing mysteriously in the world as the musical score picks up the plaintive theme one of the trio has been playing on a mouth organ by the fire. We see the sculpture survive a dramatic electric storm and torrential rain. Then its makers, still wordless, engulf it in a blazing conflagration. Impermanence would seem to be a major theme of this film, impermanence and the elemental forces at work in life and art.

Director/Writer	**22 minutes**
Claude Grenier	**Color**
Sculptor	**Age range 8–adult**
Réal Bérard	**Film $623** Rental $189
assisted by	**VHS $89**
Nick Burns	
Jim Tallosi	
Original music	
Normand Roger	
National Film Board	
of Canada	

612 Pictures for the Sky
Famous Artists Design Kites

Working in conjunction with Japanese master kite-makers, a hundred famous artists from twenty countries all over the world created 'art kites' to turn the sky above Himeji, Japan, into a playground for their world of paintings. *Pictures for the Sky* documents one of the most fascinating international art spectacles of recent years, and is unique in its attractive presentation of a wide range of new works by important representatives of contemporary art. Artists featured include Robert Rauschenberg, Emilio Vedova, Niki de Saint Phalle, Panamarenko, Horst Antes, Frank Stella, Daniel Buren, Kumi Sugai, José de Guimarães, Otto Herbert Hajek, Salome, Tom Wesselmann, Antoni Tàpies, Per Kirkeby, Bukichi Inoue, Chema Cobo, Graham Dean, Griska Bruskin, Rupprecht Geiger, Paul Wunderlich, Mimmo Paladino, Karel Appel, General Idea, Olle Kaks, Zvi Goldberg, Imre Bak, Karl Otto Götz, Ulrike Rosenbach, Kenny Scharf, Gregorij Litischevskij, Sadamasa Motonaga, Tadanori Yokoo, Klaus Staeck, Franz Erhard Walther and Ivan Rabuzin.

Director/Script Markus Zollner	30 minutes Color
Original sound Jan Kollwitz	Age range 8–adult Film $693 Rental $199 VHS $99
Also available in Dutch, French, German, Italian, Japanese, Portuguese and Russian	

488 'I Know I'm Wrong, Ask My Friends, They Say the Same Thing'
Children Portray Picasso

An art teacher in Paris asks his students, aged ten to fifteen, to paint a portrait of Picasso. The results, and their comments, are astonishing. The spontaneity and humorous lack of respect they display contrast strongly with any traditional approach to culture.

This film is in French with English subtitles.

Director Pierre Levy	10 minutes Color
Also available in Dutch, German, Italian, Japanese, Portuguese and Russian	Age range 5–adult Film $483 Rental $149 VHS $69

803 Schulz
The Creator of the Cartoon Character 'Peanuts'

Forty years ago American Charles Schulz created one of the most famous and enduring comic strips of all time – *Peanuts*, aka Charlie Brown, starring the even more renowned dog Snoopy (of Red Baron fame).

From the series
Great Artists in the World of Comics

Director Alejandro Vallejo	28 minutes Color
Original music Caelo del Rio	Age range 12–adult VHS $99
Also available in French and Spanish	

Comics, the Ninth Art

A panorama of comics worldwide, from the turn of the century to the present day.

This series of 13 programs can be purchased on VHS for $1287 Reference S20

See pages 246–50

612
Niki de Saint Phalle
Art kite
The Bird in Love

612
José Guimarães
Art kite
Figure of Don Sebastião
carrying large blue snake

788
Comix
Title graphics

793
What's Next?

31 Films for Younger Audiences

273

Draw with Don

Don Conroy is an Irish author, children's TV presenter and leading wildlife artist, and he has written several children's books. This series focuses on techniques of drawing and painting. Encouraging creativity above all, Don skillfully balances instruction with fun.

This series of
22 programs
can be purchased
on VHS for $1518
Reference S22

Each part

12 minutes
Color
Age range 5–12

VHS $69

Director
Bob Corkey

Presenter/Writer
Don Conroy

Original music
Rowan Johnson

841 **Making Shapes**

How to build up a picture using simple shapes.

842 **Cartoon Forms**

The art of drawing cartoons using simple shapes. Don shows us how to draw a cartoon witch and an owl.

843 **Coloring Cartoons**

Don adds more life to his cartoons using watercolors and colored crayons.

844 **Caricatures**

What they are and how to draw them.

845 **Pen and Ink Techniques**

Don shows us the way to construct drawings of birds and people using pen and ink.

846 **Pen and Brush Techniques**

Don creates mystical landscapes and shows us the skills involved in using pen and brush.

847 **Nature Drawings**

Capturing a natural scene on paper.

848 **Drawing Animals**

Capturing a subject close to Don's heart, nature and the beauty of animals such as the badger.

849 **Drawing Birds**

Using simple shapes again, Don takes us through the stages of drawing birds successfully.

850 **Painting Birds**

Painting without drawing first.

851 **Landscape Painting**

Sketching in and painting a landscape.

852 **Creative Painting**

Some tricks of the trade demonstrated by Don with the aid of some salt and a candle.

853 **Creative Drawing**

Dramatic illustration – with the aid of some more tricks of the trade.

854 **Poster Lettering**

All you need to know about poster lettering – and more.

855 **Poster Drawing**

Making the most of the paper to create an eyecatching poster.

856 **Making a Collage**

Abstract pictures using simple shapes.

857 **Fun Techniques**

Forget about paintbrushes, pens and even pencils for this painting.

858 **Painting on Stones**

How to have fun and be imaginative while painting stones.

859 **Theme Painting**

Don shows us how to paint a story.

860 **Sketching People**

Different sketches using different techniques.

861 **Painting 1**

Don creates two very simple mood paintings using different types of artboard.

862 **Painting 2**

The beauty of a wildlife landscape and hints on how to create one.

▶ 900
Castle Acre Priory,
Norfolk, England

Archaeological Detectives

A series that shows how enjoyable investigating evidence can be, for children to watch on their own or in class groups.

This series of 3 programs can be purchased on VHS for $257
Reference S29

---

900   **The Mystery**

The Mystery is about investigating ruined buildings, asking questions, making a detailed record of the evidence and attempting to reach conclusions. Looking for the evidence from the past can be carried out in much the same way as the police work, collecting evidence for a crime. Here Sally and Gavin, young archaeological detectives, tackle the mystery of Castle Acre Priory, Norfolk, England, aided by a team of local police. Their first task is to get an idea of the site's size and complexity. Where is the entrance? They have to discover by observation and questioning whether the buildings they are examining were ever lived in. What are the clues – fireplaces, stairs, upper floors? What sort of people lived there? The police detectives help Sally and Gavin take an accurate record of the 'scene.' At police headquarters they continue their investigations. Armed with photographs, notes and a plan of the site, they continue to question the evidence and compare it with what they find in reference books and other records. An exciting and fast-moving documentary which will help children develop skills of observation and encourage questioning before they visit an ancient site or building – the ideas presented here can be applied to any site or group of buildings from any period in the past.

Part of the series *Archaeological Detectives*

Director/Writer	12 minutes
Patrick Redsell	Color
Presenter/Narrator	Age range 8–14
Mike Corbishley	VHS $69
English Heritage	

---

901   **Bits and Bodies**

Archaeologists have to piece together fragments of evidence from the past and use detective skills to reach accurate conclusions. In this exciting documentary, three teams of children develop similar skills in an entertaining way, investigating objects and sifting the evidence before them while competing for the title of 'Champion Detectives.' All the games can easily be set up as classroom exercises. Handling and analyzing everyday objects is a way of active learning which develops a wide range of skills like recognizing and classifying, recording and examining, explaining and forming conclusions. The teams begin by sorting objects accurately into categories, such as stone, clay and bone, like finds on an archaeological site. This involves handling, comparing and questioning – for example, is the object made of one material or several? The Lost Luggage Game and the Feely Bag Game call for teamwork to solve a problem with a variety of mystery objects. Others investigate portraits, looking at facial expressions, clothes and background detail, or unfamiliar artefacts, deciding for example whether they are hand- or machine-made. In the Skeleton Game, surviving clues build up a picture of the person when they were living – what can a ring or a coin tell us? For the Brushes Game, the team must choose and label items for a museum display. After playing three different games each, a final question round decides the championship.

Part of the series *Archaeological Detectives*

Director/Writer	33 minutes
Patrick Redsell	Color
Presenter/Narrator	Age range 9–14
Mike Corbishley	VHS $109
English Heritage	

490D   **Clues Challenge**

One of the biggest problems for visitors to the ruins of our past is making sense of what is left. *Clues Challenge* is an entertaining introduction to archaeological detective work. In this fast-moving documentary Alice and Daniel face the challenge of becoming archaeological detectives. They have to investigate three different modern houses, answer set questions, carry out an investigation and collect clues. The first house is fully furnished but empty of people. They are asked to work out who lives there. They search the house for clues, take photographs and make notes. (Question: do the toys indicate a boy or a girl?) The second house is a bungalow with no furniture in it. Here it is less obvious which are the bedrooms. They have to search harder for clues and be more observant. Again they have to work out what the rooms might have been used for. (Question: what do the marks on the flooring show?) Finally they are taken to a new building site, where the site foreman shows them round. Their challenge is to work out what the building is going to be from seeing the foundations alone. By asking children to look for 'evidence' in surroundings which are familiar to them, *Clues Challenge* helps to prepare them for recording and reaching conclusions about the buildings and objects of the past.

Part of the series *Archaeological Detectives*

Director/Writer	14 minutes
Patrick Redsell	Color
Presenter/Narrator	Age range 9–14
Mike Corbishley	VHS $79
English Heritage	

Evidence on Site

Investigative learning by looking at the evidence of the past, for classroom viewing either before or after a site visit.

This series of 6 programs can be purchased on VHS for $484 Reference S30

---

14 Grimes Graves
Neolithic Flint Mines and the Techniques of Flint Knapping

The strange landscape of pits and mounds known as Grimes Graves near Thetford in Norfolk, England, is the site of one of Britain's earliest industries, flint mining, and its associated craft of flint knapping. This industry was carried on in the area within living memory – the craft survived long enough to be filmed in the 1940s and historic footage of this is included. Next, the mines are investigated and examined for evidence of how neolithic miners extracted the flint – the pits are the filled-in entrances to mine shafts. A school party is shown beginning their investigation of the mines. A professional flint knapper, John Lord, takes the viewer on a tour of the mines, including one of the deepest that is not open to the public. The flint is found underground embedded in the chalk, and the best is at the bottom of the pit, 60 feet down. Here tunnels lead off the central chamber into a maze of galleries beyond. John Lord demonstrates how the neolithic miners must have worked, using antler picks, by scraping away the chalk to loosen the large flint boulders. In the last part of the video he demonstrates the skills needed to make an axe head by using a pebble to split the flintstone and shape it. Finally the cutting edge of the axe head is put on, using an antler to flake off smaller pieces.

Part of the series *Evidence on Site*

Director/Writer	**12 minutes**
Philip Sugg	**Color**
English Heritage	**Age range 6–14**
Also available in French	**VHS $79**

---

16 Working on the Evidence: Maiden Castle
Modern Archaeology at the Iron Age Hillfort

A group of young people visit the hillfort of Maiden Castle in Dorset, England, and think themselves back in time. They realize that archaeology is all about building up a picture of what life was like in the past. The archaeologist at work explains the techniques of modern archaeology and what his team is actually doing at Maiden Castle. Reconstruction paintings based on real evidence help to show life in the Iron Age, and so does a visit to an experimental farm which uses the farming 'technology' employed by people over two thousand years ago. The children work on the evidence on site and in the local museum in Dorchester. Through a series of 'dissolves' they are transformed into the Iron Age people who defended the fort and the Roman soldiers who stormed it, while archive film shows Sir Mortimer Wheeler giving a vivid analysis of the battle of AD 43, based on what he learned from his excavations.

Part of the series *Evidence on Site*

Director/Writer	**20 minutes**
David Collison	**Color**
English Heritage	**Age range 9–14**
Also available in French	**VHS $89**

◀ 14
Demonstration of flint knapping

◀ 490B
Dover Castle
View from the north

◀ 16
Protectors of Maiden Castle reconstruction drawing

99B Castles of Northumberland

This video has been designed for use in five sections. The first part, *Siting a Castle*, opens by setting the context for castle building. Children are shown how to relate the building to the landscape and to understand that castles were built both to control the land and to give security. Siting was crucial, especially if the castle's rôle was largely defensive. In the second section, *Elements of a Castle*, we are introduced to the two basic earthworks common to most castles of the period, the motte and bailey. To these are added buildings such as the keep, curtain wall, towers, stables and outhouses. *Defending a Castle* forms the third section. All castles had various lines of defence: defended entrances such as barbicans and gateways with drawbridge and portcullis were combined with strong walls and towers. We also learn the best way of attacking castles. The fourth section introduces the skills of observation and deduction involved in *Looking at a Wall*. We are shown how to look for clues to alterations and how stone was used. Lines of old roofs, doorways, fireplaces, slots for timber floor supports and other construction clues can be seen. The final section, *A Place to Live In*, looks at a fortified manor house before moving on to larger castles. We see where families lived in a castle and how it could be both a home and a refuge in times of attack.

Part of the series *Evidence on Site*

Director	**24 minutes**
Frank Harris	**Color**
Writer	**Age range 9–15**
Michael Scarborough	**VHS $99**
Narrator	
Judi Dench	
English Heritage	

138 Building an Abbey: Rievaulx
Approaching Technology through an
Historic Building

Rievaulx is a twelfth-century Cistercian
abbey set in a beautiful and secluded valley
in North Yorkshire, England. Children from
a local primary school are shown looking
for clues to the design and engineering
problems faced by the monks who built this
large group of buildings. A great deal can
be learned from looking carefully at both
the buildings and the remains of fallen
masonry. For example, it is possible to work
out how the monks built such tall columns
and high walls. We see how the buttresses
and pinnacles, beautiful as they are, have
more than a mere decorative function,
being an integral part of the engineering.
Weight, stresses and load-bearing in a
vaulted stone roof are introduced through
the medium of an instructive children's
game. While the magnificent nave and choir
are the central core of Rievaulx, the remains
of the extensive monastic buildings are also
examined for clues to the way of life of the
monks who lived, worked and worshiped
here. Evidence of the hearths, the kitchens
and refectory all add to our understanding
of how they lived. The film is a stepping-off
point for a multi-disciplinary study of the
history of any abbey or cathedral.

Part of the series *Evidence on Site*

Director	14 minutes
Frank Harris	Color
Writer	Age range 8–15
Michael Scarborough	VHS $79
English Heritage	

312 Evidence on Site: Boscobel House
Where Charles II Hid from Parliament

An introduction to a house where Charles II
hid from the Roundheads. Boscobel, near
Wolverhampton, England, was an isolated
hunting lodge in a forest when the future
king fled there after his defeat at Worcester
in 1651. While Parliament's forces searched
the area, Charles, dressed in servant's
clothes, hid in an oak tree and later in a
priest's hole within the house. This single
dramatic event acted like a time-bomb on
Boscobel. When the story became public
after Charles's coronation, seventeenth-
century tourists flocked to see the oak tree,
tearing off branches as souvenirs and
eventually killing it – but the house was
unaffected. Not until it was sold in the early
nineteenth century did the time-bomb
explode. The new owners celebrated
Boscobel's past by remodeling the house
as they thought it might have been in
Charles's time. Their view of history was
an entertaining mixture of fact and fiction,
so many features of the house are not what
they seem to be, and need close inspection
before one can assess their origins. This
documentary explains the complicated
history of the house, and the effects of an
historic event on a quiet country dwelling.
It also raises questions about how we look
at the past which are applicable to any site.

Part of the series *Evidence on Site*

Director/Writer	10 minutes
Philip Sugg	Color
English Heritage	Age range 9–14
	VHS $69

490B Dover Castle: The Key to England

Dover Castle in Kent is one of the largest
and strongest castles in Britain, dominating
the shortest passage from the continent of
Europe to England. The clifftop site has
been fortified for two thousand years:
the medieval castle follows the outline of
an Iron Age hill fort. The keep is the
strongest of its time. It was built both as a
residence for the king and as a stronghold.
This was the first castle to make great use
of wall towers, projecting in front of and
above the walls. A large range of residential
buildings which included a great chamber
and hall for the king were built within inner
walls around the keep. After the French laid
siege to the castle in 1216 and undermined
one of the towers, further changes were
made to strengthen the defences. Major
alterations were made later when the castle
was adapted to the needs of heavy guns
during the Napoleonic wars. The look of the
castle was changed by cutting down the
towers to make gun platforms and to clear
the line of fire from the keep. Later changes
came when the castle became part of the
wider artillery fortifications of Dover
harbor. It continued to be modernized
through the two world wars, and was in
the front line of the Dunkirk evacuation.

Part of the series *Evidence on Site*

Central Office	12 minutes
of Information	Color
English Heritage	Age range 11–17
	VHS $69

Frameworks of Worship

A series looking at ways in which archaeologists gather and use information.

This series of 5 programs can be purchased on VHS for $455 Reference S31

902 **In Memoriam**
The Archaeology of Graveyards

Graveyards and cemeteries provide an educational source of unparalleled richness: ecology, archaeology, demography, art and social history can all be approached through the evidence they yield. Monuments and burial customs have developed over the last thousand years, and attitudes to death have changed as well. Memorials reflect a community but do so in different ways at different times. In the Middle Ages, overnight vigils with the deceased were common, as were funeral feasts and celebrations. The growth of towns in the eighteenth century led to the establishment of large cemeteries. York public cemetery is divided between Anglican believers, nonconformists and unbelievers. In the nineteenth century death became an industry, with commercially run cemeteries, undertakers and monument makers. There is a wealth of information in graveyards, giving insights into fashions in Christian names, tombstone design, the size of families, child mortality, paupers' graves – all human life, and death, is here. Churchyards are also valuable reserves for wildlife. A carefully managed churchyard can provide habitats for many different insects, butterflies, birds, wild flowers and plants.

This program is particularly suitable for teacher training.

Part of the series *Frameworks of Worship*

Director	**21 minutes**
John Murray	**Color**
Writer	**Age range 16–adult**
Richard Morris	**VHS $89**
Presenter	
Roberta Gilchrist	
English Heritage	

136 **The Master Builders:**
The Construction of a Great Church

Medieval builders produced some of the finest structures that the world has seen in terms of technical sophistication, engineering skill, grace in design, and sheer size. This video follows the building of a cathedral from the earliest stages of fundraising and planning to its construction from the foundations to the roof. By looking at the existing fabric of Beverley Minster, England, in an archaeological light, we can reconstruct some of the methods used to design and build it. Firstly a present-day architect shows how the master builders used the principle of proportional geometry to develop the complicated design with a minimum of equipment. Excavations show evidence of how the foundations support the colossal weight of the building and overcome the problems of the ground beneath. A draftsman uses modern techniques to create a template for cutting the stone, basing it on surviving working drawings. Construction methods are shown, including the use of scaffolding and cranes, and the building of curved arches to form an interior framework, and flying buttresses to stop the walls from bulging. Many of the individual tool marks left by the masons, plumbers and joiners survive today and help to date the various stages in the building project. Finally, the cracks in the central tower serve as a reminder that not even the master builders were infallible.

Part of the series *Frameworks of Worship*

Director	**21 minutes**
John Murray	**Color**
Writer	**Age range 8–15**
Richard Morris	**VHS $89**
Presenter/Narrator	
Roberta Gilchrist	
English Heritage	

176 Buildings and Beliefs
Medieval Social Structure and Spirituality

This exploration of a typical parish church –
All Saints, York, England – shows how much
can be learned about the social and
religious beliefs of those who built it and
extended it over the centuries. The starting
point is the structure itself. The surviving
fabric can tell us a great deal about the
sequence of construction; a model is used
to show the development and enlargement
of the building and its division into
different parts. All Saints was situated in
the industrial part of the city – evidence
of various trades and industries can be
seen in the symbols on coffin lids. Further
evidence comes from written records such
as fourteenth-century wills, which contain
a wealth of information about funeral
arrangements and bequests for
improvements to the church – these
indicate the increasing prosperity of the
local merchants and tradesmen. New glass
windows were inserted, and the aisles were
divided and widened to put in more side
chapels so that masses could be said for
the departed who had left money for the
purpose. At one time there were five
separate altars. Merchants also gave money
for the establishment of a hospice for
the poor and sick. Altogether the fabric
of the building, together with its records,
is a rich source of historical information.

This program is particularly suitable for
teacher training.

Part of the series *Frameworks of Worship*

Director	**20 minutes**
John Murray	**Color**
Writer	**Age range 16–adult**
Richard Morris	**VHS $89**
Narrator	
Roberta Gilchrist	
English Heritage	

313 Chapels: The Buildings of Nonconformity
Baptist, Unitarian, Quaker, Methodist
and Others

Chapels commemorates the three-
hundredth anniversary of the passing of
the Act of Toleration in England in 1689
by celebrating varied local buildings which
often receive little attention. The Act
stimulated the building of chapels for all
types of Nonconformist worship; *Chapels*
compares the archaeology of remaining
buildings of different denominations and
asks what these reveal about the kinds of
religious practices they sheltered and about
how the chapels are related to the human
and industrial landscape of villages and
towns. Baptist and Unitarian chapels, for
example, are compared with contemporary
Church of England chapels of ease (built for
the convenience of remote parishioners)
and Quaker meeting houses. Early primitive
Methodist houses in which the 'Ranters'
preached are contrasted with the cavernous
grandeur of Victorian Methodist churches
built in major industrial towns like York.
Chapels relates to a wide range of studies:
history, geography, religion, conservation
and social development. It is also of
importance to planners and architects, and
to chapel-goers, in an age when many
Nonconformist buildings face redundancy,
and thousands have already disappeared.

This program is particularly suitable for
teacher training.

Part of the series *Frameworks of Worship*

Director/Writer	**18 minutes**
John Murray	**Color**
Writer	**Age range 16–adult**
Richard Morris	**VHS $89**
Narrator	
Roberta Gilchrist	
English Heritage	

490C Your Church: A Threshold to History

What can looking at an ordinary parish
church – this example is in rural North
Yorkshire, England – tell us about its
history? Four specialists talk about their
approach to the evidence; the video is
designed to be viewed in sections. Firstly,
the churchyard: the tombstones are vital
evidence. Their inscriptions must be
recorded now, before weathering destroys
them. Then the fabric of the church: much
can be learned from careful observation,
making measurements and drawings
and taking photographs. The viewer is
introduced to ground-based remote sensing
techniques, which involve electronic
scanning and computer enhancement of
images; and tree-ring dating techniques
are employed to help date a sequence of
bell frames in the tower. The third section
explores the archaeological evidence
of another church that was demolished
to make way for a supermarket. The
development of the building is traced from
the earliest wooden structure through to
the greatly enlarged Victorian church.
The last section shows the church as part
of the wider landscape in which it was built.
Traces of earlier agricultural communities
who worshiped there can still be seen in
the form of roads, tracks, boundary
banks, medieval field cultivation strips,
and later park land.

This program is particularly suitable for
teacher training.

Part of the series *Frameworks of Worship*

Director	**23 minutes**
John Murray	**Color**
Writer/Narration	**Age range 16–adult**
Richard Morris	**VHS $99**
English Heritage	
Award	
Winner Channel 4,	
British Archaeological	
Awards	

Looking at...

A series looking at real sites and investigating the clues left behind.

This series of 3 programs can be purchased on VHS for $257 Reference S32

<table>
<tr><td>13</td><td>

Prehistoric Sites
From Stonehenge to the Moorlands of Western Britain

Prehistoric sites are often difficult to understand; this video looks at a wide variety, from Stonehenge, in Wiltshire, England, to less well-known monuments high on the moorlands of western Britain, and helps to explain them. It also sets out to tell part of the story of the ancient peoples who built them. We can see the evidence – tools, stone buildings, earthworks, burial chambers, stone circles and long lines of upright stones – but how are we to interpret it? Many clues are pointed out to help work out what the monuments might have been used for. Reconstruction paintings of prehistoric times bring to life the remains of ancient communities: the makers of these structures were farmers, and we assume that the henges had ritual and religious significance in their lives. The construction of the later hillforts of the Iron Age, including Maiden Castle, is also looked at. An excavation of a long barrow is used to show how much of the evidence that we do have has been recovered by archaeological investigation. We also see a school party using a detailed map as they set out to explore a monument. The video ends by making clear just how many such ancient remains there are. It is a useful general guide to any study of prehistory.

Part of the series *Looking at...*

English Heritage

20 minutes
Color
Age range 11–14
VHS $89

</td><td>99A</td><td>

Looking at a Castle
The Complex Arrangements of Medieval Life

The remains of the fortifications and domestic quarters of Goodrich Castle, near Ross-on-Wye, Hereford and Worcester, England, show the complex arrangements of life in a medieval castle. The presenter acts as a detective, identifying and reading the clues which the building contains. For example, how was the castle defended against attack? There is a pit for a drawbridge; sockets and grooves in the gatehouse point to doors and a portcullis; and there are 'murder holes' and arrow slits. A castle is essentially a collection of houses with a strong outer wall. But where are the houses? Looking carefully, it is possible to see angles where roofs, long since gone, were once sealed and joined to the main structure. Fireplaces and the remains of the ovens reveal where the kitchen was, and there is evidence for a covered way that provided a service passage between houses and kitchen. Looking up at the different floor levels in the towers and large buildings enables the presenter to show that there was space here for five separate households. A useful introduction to castles in general, since most medieval castles have layouts similar to Goodrich's.

Part of the series *Looking at...*

English Heritage

14 minutes
Color
Age range 9–13
VHS $79

</td><td></td></tr>
</table>

▨◣ 13
Castlerigg stone circle,
England

◀ 99A
Artist's impression of
an Anglo-Saxon
lady of the manor

137 **Looking at an Abbey**
How Cistercian Monks Organized their Lives

The partly ruined Rievaulx Abbey in North
Yorkshire, England, has a lot to tell the
visitor about monastic life. There were many
different orders of Cistercian monks, but
they all followed the same rule laid down
by St Benedict. Moreover, the layout of
monasteries followed a common plan.
The communities lived round a central
cloister, a kind of village green, with a
covered way all round. The spiritual center
of their lives was worship, and so the most
important building was the cross-shaped
church to the north of the cloister. The
Cistercians were a self-sufficient order:
at Rievaulx they had up to five hundred lay
brethren, who farmed the lands but were
not permitted to worship with the monks –
they had to stay behind a screen which
divided the church in two. It is possible
to see where the dormitories, kitchens,
refectory and infirmary were, and also
how the Chapter House was reduced in
size and rebuilt as the numbers of monks
at Rievaulx dwindled over the centuries.
The community was advanced for its time:
in particular, it made provision for an
unusually effective sewerage system.

Part of the series *Looking at...*

Narration	**17 minutes**
Howard Williams	**Color**
	Age range 8–15
English Heritage	**VHS $89**

31 Films for Younger Audiences

281

◄◄ 267
Educational event
at Kirby Hall

◄ 634
Stirling Clark
Sculptor in residence
at Dover Castle

118   The Norman Conquest of England

The Norman Conquest was not just a political or military achievement: it altered the language, the landscape and the building styles of England. Who were the Normans? They were really French-speaking Vikings, who controlled large parts of Italy, Sicily and Antioch in Syria as well as conquering England and parts of Scotland and Ireland. To protect and control their conquest they built a vast number of motte and bailey castles. At first these were wooden structures, but many were later developed further in stone. The most impressive of all is the Tower of London, begun in 1068 as a simple earth fort and developed to display the importance of the king. The Normans also erected a great many ecclesiastical buildings, such as Rochester Cathedral. Norman features are pointed out – many churches were later altered, so their Norman features are no longer obvious. Examples shown include Durham Cathedral, the tiny church of Kilpeck in Hereford and Worcester, and a Norman house in Lincoln that has the same shaped windows and doors as the churches. The landscape also holds many clues to the Norman Conquest. Besides the ditches, mottes and earth banks of the early castles, there are the remains of the great open fields preserved as ridge and furrow strips. Then there are the royal forests the Normans created, such as the New Forest. The *Domesday Book* is a great property survey of the kingdom; and a glance at the dictionary shows many words still in everyday use that were originally Norman French. The clues to the conquest are still all around us.

English Heritage

15 minutes
Color
Age range 8–15
VHS $79

267   The Past Replayed: Kirby Hall
A Living History Project for Special-needs Schoolchildren

Special-needs schoolchildren experience a day out in the sixteenth-century at Kirby Hall, Northamptonshire, England. The first part of this video is an account of the planning and organization that preceded the event: the teachers attended courses to study music, dancing, costume-making, cooking and the history of Kirby Hall. Next, the children were given careful preparation for the day in the classroom. This part of the video also includes a brief resumé of the day's events and a look at the follow-up work carried out by the schools. The second part of the video is intended for classroom use; it is a detailed record of the day itself. Each child was dressed in authentic costume, and took part in two work groups in order to experience different aspects of life in a grand country house in 1590. Lunch was authentic too – the pea soup was not popular! In the afternoon each school presented some aspect of their work as the last event of the day.

This program is particularly suitable for teacher training.

Director
Alan McPherson

English Heritage

38 minutes
Color
Age range 9–13
VHS $99

311   Teaching on Site:
Seventeenth-century Merchants' Houses

The visit of a group of six-year-old children to two seventeenth-century merchants' houses in Great Yarmouth, Norfolk, England. Their teacher had already visited the site and planned how the children should prepare in school for their outing, what they should do during the visit, and the follow-up work they could do afterwards. Beforehand, they were encouraged to compare houses from past centuries with those they were used to themselves, and to develop skills of observation which would be useful on the day. A local museum education service provided relevant objects which they could handle and familiarize themselves with in the classroom. Their work in the medieval houses built on the comparisons the children had been making between old and new, but the historic buildings and the variety of objects displayed in them also helped them to imagine what life might have been like in the past. The class worked in three small groups on observation, artwork and creating stories – work which was shared in the whole class back at school, in discussion, writing, art and technology lessons, the class teacher showing how this was a useful progression from the visit itself. This video will be useful for teachers wishing to investigate the possibility of using the historic environment for their teaching.

This program is particularly suitable for teacher training.

Director
Patrick Redsell

English Heritage

19 minutes
Color
Age range 6–9
VHS $89

Evidence of Our Lives shows how children can develop skills by recording, researching and interpreting their local environment. The preparations for the building of a new reservoir in the Roadford Valley in Devon, England, provide an ideal opportunity for children to work alongside archaeologists in their study of the history of a valley. Firstly a modern, furnished house is explored for the evidence it offers of the way of life of its present-day inhabitants, contrasting this from an archaeologist's viewpoint with earlier dwellings. Then we see the children working in the valley to gather what evidence they can find there. We discover that interpreting evidence is a skill that requires constant revision as further evidence comes to light, but that with careful work we can begin to draw a realistic picture of the past.

Director	27 minutes
Timothy Taylor	Color
English Heritage	Age range 9–15
	VHS $99

634   Historic Site: A Sculptor's View

What is a 'candlepoise'? The Normans' version of a table lamp, of course – according to Stirling Clark, sculptor-in-residence during 1991 at Dover Castle, Kent, England. Clark's brief was to base his own two- and three-dimensional work on aspects of the castle, and to develop and teach programs of art, design and technology for visiting schools and colleges which would help them use Dover Castle as a source of pattern, texture and form for their work. The video records his own sculptures which include a *Siege Chair*, a daunting wheeled seat of oak beams and rusting iron, the *King Eggcup*, a unique example of Norman breakfastware displaying impregnable stonework, strategically placed arrowslits and a lightly boiled egg, and the *Candlepoise* itself. It shows him working with visiting groups of adult-education students and children of different ages; their productions include a curious selection of neckties decorated with patterns drawn from close observation of stonework around the castle. School groups go on to produce their own design-based classroom work. Although the work of the sculptor and his visitors is based on Dover Castle, the ideas expressed during his residency and recorded here could be applied to any historic building or site.

This program is particularly suitable for teacher training.

Director	23 minutes
Alan McPherson	Color
Writer	Age range 5–16
Jonathan Barnes	VHS $99
Original music	
Neil Ardley	
English Heritage	

904   Rescuing Our Past

Buried evidence from the past can easily be destroyed and lost for ever; and not only town or city sites of archaeological importance come under threat. Country sites are in danger too, and from more than just motorway construction or mineral extraction. Modern farming uses deep plowing that can be very destructive, especially as most archaeological evidence in the countryside lies only inches below the surface of the ground. This video centers around 'rescue archaeology' at an Anglo-Saxon site in North Yorkshire which is about to be plowed up. After an introductory section it divides into three parts. The first, *Discovery*, shows the main methods archaeologists employ in deciding where to dig. The second, *Recovery*, explores the main techniques of excavation, showing the different ways of recovering information about buildings, the remains of people, their clothes and personal belongings, and environmental evidence. Computers are used more and more in the field, in conjunction with electronic surveying techniques. In the third section, *Reconstruction*, all the information gathered during the excavation is put together to give a picture of the past, showing us what kind of houses these Anglo-Saxons lived in. A reconstruction illustration shows an Anglo-Saxon woman wearing clothes and with other possessions including brooches and her handbag, and accompanied by a dog, all of which were discovered in the dig.

Director/Writer	12 minutes
Alan McPherson	Color
Original music	Age range 9–15
Neil Ardley	VHS $79
English Heritage	

Since the dawning of the age of psychoanalysis we have known that art provides a window on to the subconscious life of its creators. The passionate Romantics with their preoccupation with erotic power and with death, the anguished Expressionists, the Surrealists with their use of 'automatic writing' and dream imagery, the Abstract Expressionists who recorded their emotive outpourings on canvases splattered like the ink-blots of the psychiatrist Rorschach – all these invite us to read in them the patterns of the human psyche.

32
Art and the Subconscious

This section of 17 programs can be purchased on VHS for $1903

Television rights and prices on request

◀◀ 503C
Jackson Pollock
Autumn Rhythm

▲ 506
Edvard Munch
Anxiety

503C American Abstraction

When the United States became isolated by the Second World War, American art started to find its own way. Influenced by the possibilities represented in the psychic automatism of the Surrealists, a new 'frenetic' art was created, based on the 'gesture', on a direct communication between the artist and his canvas. Painting was now 'physical', the best example being Jackson Pollock's action painting. Other painters started action painting as well, and Willem De Kooning added a sensuality to his works that the puritanical society he lived in had previously forbidden, but which he could get away with through Abstraction.

For more information see page 114

Part of the series
The Adventure of Modern Art

Director	53 minutes
Carlos Vilardebo	Color
Writers/Narration	Age range 15–adult
André Parinaud	**Film $1043** Rental $299
Carlos Vilardebo	**VHS $149**

Also available in French

506 Edvard Munch: The Restless Years

The Restless Years deals with the life and work of Edvard Munch from his birth in 1863 to the mental and physical breakdown he suffered in 1908. It covers the years when Munch was an eager student of art, a frequenter of intellectual circles, a visitor to the artistic capitals of Europe and, above all, a prolific painter. The narrative sets Munch's development as a painter in the context, first of his early life and dramatic emotional experience, and later against the background of changes in the artistic and intellectual life of Europe. Many of Munch's paintings are examined in detail, and the commentary is interspersed with readings from Munch's own writing about his work. Particular attention is paid to the works that make up *The Frieze of Life*, Munch's most important project, on which he worked for almost thirty years.

'Both the artistic and technical quality of the video are high. The colors are subtle and the close-ups emphasize both the bold and the intentionally blurry features. Edvard Munch's words contrast clearly with the well modulated voice of the narrator.'
Video Rating Guide for Libraries, USA

Director	21 minutes
Brian Taylor	Color
Narration	Age range 14–adult
Christine Newton	**VHS $89**

507 Edvard Munch: The Frieze of Life

'We should no longer paint interiors with men reading and women knitting. We should paint living people who breathe, feel, suffer and love.' This manifesto, written in 1889 by the twenty-six-year-old Norwegian artist Edvard Munch, was implemented by him throughout the 1890s in major works on the universal themes of love, anxiety and death, linked in a 'symphonic arrangement' he titled *The Frieze of Life*. Shot on location in Norway and from original paintings and graphic works, the commentary is mainly drawn from Munch's own writings.

Director	24 minutes
Jonathan Wright Miller	Color
Original music	Age range 14–adult
Peter Kiely	**VHS $99**
Audio Visual Unit	
The National Gallery	

285

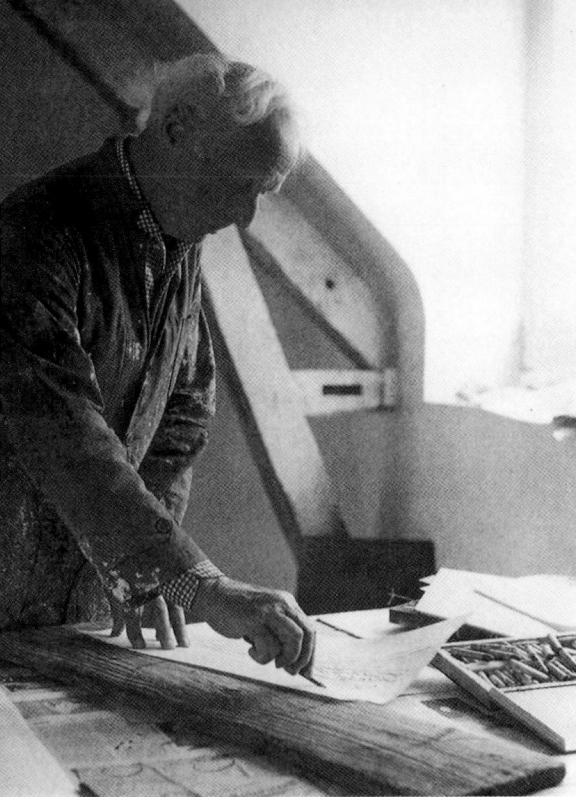

◀ 560
Max Ernst working on
a frottage (rubbing) in
his studio

▶▶ 509
James Ensor
The Unusual Masks

560 Max Ernst: Journey into the Subconscious

The inner world of the great painter Max Ernst is the subject of this film. One of the principal founders of Surrealism, Max Ernst explores the nature of materials and the emotional significance of shapes to combine with his collages and netherworld canvases. The director and Ernst together use the film creatively as a medium to explain the artist's own development.

'A very beautiful film...the great enchanter...casts a spell over his public... a poetry of high quality, fairy-like without being imprecise, leads one ultimately into surrealism.'
UNESCO

Directors	**12 minutes**
Peter Schamoni	**Color**
Dr C Lamb	**Age range 12–adult**
Narration/Voice	**Film $553** Rental $169
Max Ernst	**VHS $79**
Original music	
Hans Posegga	

Awards
Grand Prix, Oberhausen
Highly Commended,
German Center for
Film Classification

562 Max Ernst and the Surrealist Revolution

The program examines the relationship between the revolutionary rhetoric of Surrealist literature and the works of Max Ernst, which are not evidently about revolutionary subjects. The link is the process whereby Ernst and other Surrealists arrived at their imagery. Ernst developed the techniques of collage, grattage and frottage, which relied on 'random' events suggesting or establishing images. The Surrealist revolution lies in this organized artistic expression of the subconscious – to use Ernst's own words, in 'the synthesis of objective and subjective life'.

Part of the series
Modern Art, Practices and Debates

Director	**25 minutes**
Jeremy Cooper	**Color**
Presenter	**Age range 18–adult**
David Batchelor	**VHS $99**
Contributors	
Professor Dawn Ades	
Dr Sarah Wilson	
Open University/BBC	

509 'I'm Mad, I'm Foolish, I'm Nasty'
A Self-portrait of James Ensor

In this film we see how James Ensor, an acknowledged initiator of Expressionism, begins with an essentially Impressionist style, but gradually introduces more fantastical, scatological subject matter, a 'caricature' drawing style and physical paint-handling and more artificial color. The influence on his imagery and color of the spectacular shells, the exotic masks and grotesques sold in his parents' and uncle's souvenir shops in his native Ostend is suggested in the film, as is the atmospheric protean presence of the sea. Subtly suggested are the anxieties and melancholia at work under the surface of Ensor's life. We are left to speculate on the rôle of his dominating mother, and of his dissolute father who died when the artist was a young man. Death, and a strangely whimsical eroticism are his recurrent preoccupations. He never married, and he stayed with his mother until the age of fifty-five: she gave him money for paint, but she never appreciated what he did with it. The demon-ridden, grotesque world of his paintings is peopled with carnival figures, skeletons and masked men – but the masks are true faces, showing the depravity which is normally hidden in everyday life. Critics labeled him 'mad, foolish and nasty.'

'...impressive video...approaches Ensor's work as he might have approached the subject himself...leads us directly into the personality of the artist, discovering the imagery...intercutting a feast of rich details from paintings and sketches with photos of the artist at the same locations occupied by his subjects...a remarkable and poetic portrait of the artist who prefigured Expressionism. The producer's vision and Ensor's vision blend into one unified whole. Its lean, economical editing lets every shot add meaning to the next. This is one of the finest videos on an artist you're likely to see. It is highly recommended.'
Video Rating Guide for Libraries, USA

For more information see page 148

Director/Script	**55 minutes**
Luc de Heush	**Color**
Texts	**Age range 14–adult**
James Ensor,	**Film $1043** Rental $299
extracts from letters,	**VHS $149**
speeches and orations	
Ensor's voice	
John Boyle	
Narrator	
Richard Wells	
Original music	
Denis Pousseur	

Awards
Best Documentary,
Belgium
Selected European Cinema,
Berlin
Directors' Grand Prix,
UNESCO Paris

Also available in Dutch
and French

561 Surrealism

Dada, the nihilistic precursor of Surrealism, was deliberately anti-art and anti-sense, intended to outrage and scandalize. Characteristic of it were Marcel Duchamp's 'readymades' – everyday objects elevated to the status of art by the mere decision of the artist to call them such – or his reproduction of the *Mona Lisa* decorated with a moustache and an obscene caption. As Dada burnt itself out, Surrealism was born, chiefly through the efforts of the writer André Breton. In both literature and painting Surrealism explores the same themes: the exaltation of dreams, the love of madness and revolt. De Chirico painted landscapes which provoke disorientation in the viewer. New materials were called into service to aid the discovery of the unusual: collages of photos and illustrations, or the rubbing of textures, by Max Ernst; splashes of ink and automatic drawing by André Masson. Miró revealed the mysteries and qualities of the void by placing just a few traces or ideograms on a canvas. Meanwhile Magritte and Tanguy painted in a much more traditional, meticulously illusionistic manner, but created images that are fantastical, alogical. Dali's techniques were similar, yet his intentions were more extreme and outrageous; and following the Surrealist dictum, 'art is an attitude of mind', he was as provocative in his lifestyle as in his paintings. As the Second World War approached, many of the movement's artists fled to America. The Surrealist spirit was never so intense again.

Also featured are Balla, Arp, Schwitters, Picabia and many others.

Part of the series
The Adventure of Modern Art

Director	**53 minutes**
Carlos Vilardebo	**Color**
Writers/Narration	**Age range 15–adult**
André Parinaud	**Film $1043** Rental $299
Carlos Vilardebo	**VHS $149**

Also available in French

567B Dali and Surrealism

'As beautiful as the chance encounter of a sewing machine and an umbrella on an operating table', Surrealism aimed to free the artist from the dictates of moral, aesthetic or intellectual concerns, to create from the unhampered subconscious. During the late 1920s and early 1930s, Salvador Dali became one of the leading Surrealists, producing memorable Surrealist images such as the famous 'soft watches'. But although Dali and the Surrealists shared an interest in the functioning of the subconscious, and in subverting traditional realism, in other ways they diverged widely: some at least of the Surrealists were aiming at an art which could be practiced by anyone, without training, and this was part of their attempt to link the movement with Marxism, whereas Dali continued to base his work on fine technique – and eventually returned to the Catholic Church.

Part of the series *Modern Art and Modernism: Manet to Pollock*

Director	**24 minutes**
Robert Philip	**Color**
Presenter/Writer	**Age range 18–adult**
David Batchelor	**VHS $99**
Open University/BBC	

▲ 561
Giorgio de Chirico
The Uncertainty of the Poet

511 Part of the Struggle

Art and Politics in the Weimar Republic

Rarely in modern times has art been more intimately involved with the social and political world than during the years of the Weimar Republic in Germany. Expressionism, the vanguard movement before the First World War, created works of spiritual vitality with a strong emotional content. The Expressionists believed that an artistic revolution could help bring about social and political change by transforming the individual. Realism was rejected in favor of a subjective search for an inner reality. But the horror of the First World War and the subsequent political turmoil in Germany thrust many artists into a new relationship with society. The Weimar Republic was formed in 1919 and collapsed in 1933 with Hitler's accession to power. *Part of the Struggle* focuses on the relationship between avant-garde art and left-wing politics during a period of unprecedented social and economic upheaval. It looks in detail at artists based in Dresden and the formation of such political art movements as the Red Group in 1923 and the Association of Revolutionary Artists in 1928. The film uses a minimum of commentary and the artists' own words are heard in dramatized 'interviews' in which actors portray Georg Grosz, Otto Dix, Hans and Lea Grundig and Otto Nagel. It covers the Dada explosion, the abortive German revolution, when Dix, Grosz and Heartfield joined the Spartacists, the move away from Dada towards Verism and the *Neue Sachlichkeit* (the 'New Objectivity'), and finally the Nazis' infamous exhibition of these artists' work as 'degenerate art.'

'For one seeking information about the Weimar era in art and politics, this is one of those titles that belongs in both public and educational libraries. *Part of the Struggle* will probably find a grateful audience in high school students through adults seeking to understand conditions following the First World War. Recommended.'
Video Rating Guide for Libraries, USA

Directors	36 minutes
Norbert Bunge	Color
Ron Orders	Age range 14–adult
Arts Council of Great Britain	Film $763 Rental $199
	VHS $109

569 IMAGO Meret Oppenheim

For many younger women artists Meret Oppenheim is a rôle-model, because of the way she lived her life and realized her creative freedom. She won early fame in the thirties with her *Fur-lined Teacup*, but then experienced a long creative crisis. In the middle of the 1950s she regained her self-confidence and quietly began a new phase of productivity. At the end of the sixties her work was rediscovered, and she gained new recognition. Meret Oppenheim considered herself a seismograph of the spiritual landscape – one who, being rooted in the past and future, kept the passage to the unconscious open. She had a deep trust in the unconscious and throughout her life she recorded her dreams, which she used as a source of guidance and self-knowledge. She also strongly believed that art has no gender, and strove to balance and unite the opposite sides of her psyche, the spiritual-female and spiritual-male, an effort that was reflected in her appearance and in the dreams of her last years. She felt that, ever since the establishment of patriarchy, the female principle had been devalued and projected on to women. Because of this disturbed balance, she felt that a new direction in the evolution of mankind is needed, where the female principle is not devalued and humanity arrives at wholeness. The makers of this film were friends of Meret Oppenheim and had planned to make the film with her. After her death in 1985 they went ahead on their own, basing the narration, spoken by Glenda Jackson, on the artist's own words, taken from her letters, writings and poems, and on conversations with her family and friends. It tells the story of her life, but it is also a supremely poetic presentation of the themes that dominated her art.

Directors/Writers	Awards
Pamela Robertson-Pearce	Outstanding Quality Prize,
Anselm Spoerri	The Swiss Film Board
	Gold Apple Award,
Narration	Oakland
based on texts, letters,	Grand Prix, Mulhouse
dreams and poems by	Honorary Mention, Paris
Meret Oppenheim	
	Also available in French
Narrator	German, and Spanish
Glenda Jackson	

90 minutes
Color and
black and white
Age range 16–adult

Film $1393 Rental $399
VHS $199

570 Kindness Week (Max Ernst)

Max Ernst was one of the young men who returned from the 1914-18 war ready to reject all the standards and customs which society had hitherto taken for granted. If culture and religion had led to nothing better than the past four years of misery and horror, they argued, then it was time to give anarchy and unreason a chance. This film is about the series of 182 collage engravings which illustrate Ernst's irrational novel *Kindness Week*, divided into seven sequences which each represent a day of the week. By animating these fantasy engravings on film, the artist was able to bring yet another absurd element to his protest against reason. The quality of the animation is superb, and the entire film was personally approved by Max Ernst.

'Here the surrealist climate is recreated. High spirits and non-conformism are taken to the limits of the fantastic and of plastic inventiveness.'
UNESCO

Director	19 minutes
Jean Desvilles	Black and white
	Age range 12–adult
Narration/Voice	
Max Ernst	Film $623 Rental $189
	VHS $89
Original music	
Georges Delerue	
Award	
Quality Award, French National Film Center	
Also available in French	

580   Henry Moore: London 1940–42

The Series of Shelter Drawings

Eliminating all narration, this film explores, on several metaphoric levels, the very nature of human consciousness and creativity. With the image of people descending, before a blitz, to spend a night in the subterranean, artery-like tubes of the subway system, the film draws us into the artist's inner mind, where the creative process occurs, and also into subconscious levels of experience – a dream world where fears and anxieties coexist with a curious stillness. We gain an insight here into how Moore's interests related for a while to those of the Surrealists. The film is calm, yet charged, an atmosphere complemented by the delicate yet tense music of Marius Constant.

'…pictures of exceptional quality. Silently the film demonstrates that great art can easily dispense with commentary, and the value of the drawings is thus enhanced. The newsreel sequences at the beginning and the end contribute in producing an impressive atmosphere.'
UNESCO

'A revelation: a strength and force disclosed, a mastery made clear'
Sunday Times, London

'It's uncanny, Anthony Roland, the master of the montage and dissolve…The film melts moment by moment into a living and breathing homage to the people of London.'
Michigan Education Journal

For more information see pages 160 and 221

Director	12 minutes
Anthony Roland	**Black and white**
Original music	**Age range 14–adult**
Marius Constant	**Film $553** Rental $169
Awards	**VHS $79**
Silver Cup, Salerno	
Honor Award, Vancouver	
Certificate of Honor, Leipzig	
Special Excellence, Mannheim	
Exceptional Merit, Yorkton	
Quality Award and Quality Prize, French National Film Center	
Highly Commended, German Center for Film Classification	
Chriss Award, Columbus	

596   The Reality of Karel Appel

The reality of the painter Karel Appel is an overcrowded, possessed and frantic world, a barbaric age in which he can only paint as a barbarian – as he says in this film. His paintings are gaudy, his colors vivid, and he slaps them on the canvas as if in a duel, using his brushes, paints, putty-knife and his hands as weapons. Appel was preoccupied and influenced throughout his career by the art of psychotics, naïves and 'outsiders'.

For more information see page 116

Director	15 minutes
Jan Vrijman	**Color**
Awards	**Age range 13–adult**
Golden Bear, Berlin	**Film $623** Rental $189
Gran Premio, Bergamo	**VHS $89**
Silver Medal, Barcelona	
Silver Medal, La Felguera	

805   Mœbius

An heroic voyager into inner space, France's great comics artist Mœbius journeys through his own mind in search of a quiet and tranquil place to stop, take out his pencil, and begin work; the drawings are his testament that other, parallel worlds do exist.

From the series
Great Artists in the World of Comics

Director	28 minutes
Alejandro Vallejo	**Color**
Original music	**Age range 12–adult**
Caelo del Rio	**VHS $99**
Also available in French and Spanish	

615 Eugène Ionesco: Voices, Silences

As a man of letters, Ionesco is best known for his contributions to the theater, notably *La Cantatrice Chauve* (*The Bald Prima Donna*), *Les Chaises* (*The Chairs*) and *Le Roi Se Meurt* (*Exit the King*). When he tires of the clamor of words, Eugène Ionesco starts painting. In a studio in St Gall, Switzerland, he exudes colors and forms as he would words, and he never stops talking, confronting us, laughing at us or himself, expressing the same anxieties and dreams, and interpreting excerpts from his plays. Tragicomic beings appear on the paper: there are false masks and real faces, knights clad in black or sheathed in a multicolored armor; there are the branches of unknown trees, and bursts of grim laughter, and hieroglyphics. Sometimes he accepts a question, shares a confidence, a wink, a smile, then he takes up his brush, leaves time in suspension and traces a line.

'A film of rare quality…The director succeeds in playing down his own rôle, the better to bring out the connections between painting and speech, the image and the voice, abstract thought and the irrepressible burgeoning forth of forms.'
La Libre Belgique, Brussels

'An extraordinarily vivid portrait…'
Le Soir, Brussels

'A very fine film…'
Pourquoi pas?, Brussels

'…creativity and old age…a new creative language aptly documented in this video… the artist's own statements and his reading from plays, essays, and fiction on the nature of art, creativity, and aging are worth listening to. Skillful camera weaving of paintings, the artist at work, and the artist musing on creativity in dramatic settings… imbued with intelligence, wit, and wisdom.'
Video Rating Guide for Libraries, USA

Director	**61 minutes**
Thierry Zeno	**Color**
Scenario	**Age range 18–adult**
Thierry Zeno with	**Film $1043** Rental $299
the collaboration	**VHS $149**
of Eugène Ionesco	
Narrator/Participant	
Eugène Ionesco	
Also available in French	

965 Drawn by Experience
Art Therapy with Victims of War

'When you start drawing, you are going to lose control. Someone said to me, my drawings don't lie.' An art therapist explains how her job is to help people to search for the past, to lay down their burden of hidden memories and feelings by expressing them visually. Her clients are people who have lived through wars, often as children, and they may have spent many years unconsciously repressing recollections of the terror and pain they suffered. Drawing and modeling can lead them gradually to unbury and release these feelings; and even when the subject matter is painful, the process itself, which may take months or even years, can still be enjoyable. However, as the therapist points out, 'art therapy has got nothing to do with artistic achievement. It is the authenticity that counts.'

This program is particularly suitable for teacher training.

Director	**21 minutes**
Joke Stephan	**Color**
Script/Research	**Age range 17–adult**
Truus Wertheimer-Cahen	**VHS $99**
Advisor	
FA Begeman	
ICODO Foundation	
Also available in Dutch	

◀◀ 580
Henry Moore
Tube Shelter Perspective

▼ 973
Julius Bissier

973 Japonism, Part Three
Japanese Influences on Western Art:
Gesture of the Brush

In recent years, the exchanges between Japanese and western art have been bi-directional. Pierre Alechinsky explains, for example, how the post-war art of the West has been influenced by Japanese calligraphy, and Japanese artist Chinjo Saito reveals his debt to Europe's CoBrA group.

Director	**15 minutes**
Guido De Bruyn	**Color**
Also available in Dutch	**Age range 15–adult**
and French	**VHS $79**

33
Art Appreciation

Most of the films on art in the Roland Collection are, fundamentally, exercises in appreciation. The collection as a whole was conceived of as an aid to enriching aesthetic experience. The films in this section, however, are some that deal consciously with our understanding of, enjoyment of and benefit from works of art.

This section of 10 programs can be purchased on VHS for $1010

Television rights and prices on request

487 **The Artist's Eye: Bridget Riley's Selection from The National Gallery**

Bridget Riley demonstrates the power of color as a structural element in picture-making. She discusses questions central to her own work, while at the same time illuminating the art of the past. Paintings by Titian, Veronese, El Greco, Rubens, Poussin and Cézanne are used as examples.

Audio Visual Unit	**26 minutes**
The National Gallery	**Color**
	Age range 14–adult
	VHS $99

489 **Art for Whose Sake?**

Original artists of any time and place first shock the eye, then convert it to a fresh way of seeing the familiar. The shock is not always pleasant; but when it passes, the artist can say, 'Now, look!' and the world around us appears different. It may take us time to see the world as the artist saw it.

Director	**14 minutes**
Sam Napier-Bell	**Color**
Art advisor	**Age range 12–adult**
Laurence Bradbury	**Film $553** Rental $169
	VHS $79

485 **What is a Good Drawing?**

This educational film, with its clear visuals and highly informative narration, encourages an understanding and appreciation of the art of drawing. The great draftsman of every period will find his own theme, his own symbols – and his drawings express what he has to say in a medium that everyone with eyes can understand. In a really good drawing, it is obvious that the artist does not follow a formula, but invents an ever-varying repertoire of graphic signs. He can be recognized by his handwriting, by the degree of flow and rhythm, of sharpness and crispness he imparts to his line. Included in the film are drawings by Neolithic man, Pisanello, Botticelli, Raphael, Tintoretto, Michelangelo, Holbein, Dürer, Rembrandt, Tiepolo, Watteau, Fragonard, Goya, Ingres, Delacroix, Victor Hugo, Millet, Degas, Toulouse-Lautrec, Cézanne, Barlach, Picasso, Henry Moore and Josef Herman.

Director	**18 minutes**
Anthony Roland	**Black and white**
Selection/Narration	**Age range 12–adult**
Dr Henry Roland	**Film $623** Rental $189
	VHS $89

393 **The Impressionist Surface**

Dr Paul Smith reviews influential theories of Impressionism. Clement Greenberg's Modernist criticism argued that Impressionism was a critical stage in the movement toward flatness and abstraction. In contrast TJ Clark saw flatness in Impressionism as carrying meaning about the nature of modern life and as signifying modernity itself. Paul Smith rejects both explanations as over-simplified. Flatness, the use of individual brush strokes, was a way of rendering 'sensations.' Pissarro and Monet used scientific color theories to achieve greater impact and immediacy in their work. Cézanne's work also showed that the world depicted depended on the surface depicting it. His work testifies to a struggle to hold colors and surface in balance. Degas' depiction of realistic social and sexual life depends on the artifical or factitious technique of representing it. These artists wanted to convey the sensations provoked by nature, not just a notion of 'flatness.'

Part of the series
Modern Art, Practices and Debates

Director	**25 minutes**
Nick Levinson	**Color**
Presenter	**Age range 18–adult**
Dr Paul Smith	**VHS $99**
Open University/BBC	

381 **The Pre-Raphaelites**

Christopher Wood presents a very personal view of paintings from the reign of Queen Victoria. In this program, he tells how he discovered Pre-Raphaelite paintings for himself. At the time they were unfashionable and hidden away in the basements of galleries. The magic names of Rossetti, Millais and Holman Hunt revealed their secrets, and he learned of the tragedy behind one particular painting.

Part of the series *Painters to the People*

Director of photography	**26 minutes**
Edwin Mickleburgh	**Color**
Presenter/Writer	**Age range 15–adult**
Christopher Wood	**VHS $99**
Original music	
Ed Shearmur	

618 **Processing the Signal**
Video Art, Technology, Artists and Audience

A documentary made in America that brings together some of the most innovatory artists of video art – Bill Viola, Nam June Paik, Kit Fitzgerald, Paul Garrin, John Sanborn, Marie Perillo and Zbigniew Rybczynski among others. Covering video installations, 'satellite art,' video performance and the penetration of video art into conventional television, *Processing the Signal* is a discussion about these artists' ideas and opinions.

Director/Scenario	Awards
Marcello Dantas	Cine Golden Eagle,
Participants	Washington DC
Peer Bode	Best Video on Art,
Paul Garrin	New York
Kit Fitzgerald	Best Video, Paris
John Hanhardt	Best Production, Brazil
Nam June Paik	**38 minutes**
Marie Perillo	**Color**
Zbigniew Rybczynski	**Age range 11–adult**
John Sanborn	**VHS $119**
Ira Schneider	
Bill Viola	
Reynold Weidenaar	
Dean Winkler	

551 **On Pictures and Paintings**

Charles Harrison conducts us on a tour of selected works in the Tate Gallery, London, exploring different ways of thinking about how works of art represent and, in that sense, have meaning. We tend to expect paintings to be pictures, even though this expectation is not always justified (Kandinsky). Some works represent without being pictures at all (abstracts – Poliakoff). Harrison considers what makes a painting 'modern,' starting with Cézanne and moving through Braque, Grosz, Dali, Miró, Jack Smith and Leger, to show how the illusionistic devices of painting become decoupled from the rational compositional themes within which they had previously been controlled.

Part of the series
Modern Art, Practices and Debates

Director	**25 minutes**
Jeremy Cooper	**Color**
Presenter	**Age range 18–adult**
Charles Harrison	**VHS $99**
Open University/BBC	

◀◀ 485
Antoine Watteau
Man Bending Forward

293

486 Genesis

Observations on the Creation of
Five Works of Art

Dealing with the parallels and inter-
relationships between all the arts,
Genesis can be seen as a 'keynote' film
in the Roland Collection. The film examines
the making of works of art by the poet
Ida Gerhardt, the painter Armando,
the choreographer Hans Van Manen, the
composer Reinbert de Leeuw and the
sculptor Carel Visser. With enormous
subtlety and dignity, the director intertwines
the thematic threads that make up the
fabric of her film. The poet's opening works
speak of stones being taught to dance –
and we see the choreographer guiding
dancers through an extemporization as he
evolves a new work. We see too the feet
of the painter enacting an unconscious
shuffle across the studio floor as his canvas
progresses. On his tape recorder the
painter plays jazz improvisations, while
elsewhere a sculptor, improvising a piece
from found objects and car parts,
is whistling meditatively to himself.
Meanwhile, a composer mulls over problems
of tempo and melody, working toward a
choral composition. Cutting between the
parallel activities of its five creative
protagonists, all of whom share in a kind of
fellowship, though they never meet, the
film gradually lingers longer on each artist,
thus increasing the effect of surprise and
revelation as each time we suddenly switch
again to 'catch up' with the choral work,
the painting, or the poem in progress, and
are left in suspense over the delicate
balancing act of the sculpture, or the tense
development of the dance. Very discreetly
the director allows the sound track from
each sequence to carry over into the next,
in which another artist is being shown, thus
enhancing the sense of creative parallelism.
The film is full of suggestive details.
The creators' hands are a point of focus –
the poet's with its pen, the painter's with
brush or spatula, the composer's, directing
with a conductor's baton, the sculptor's
with a welding rod, the choreographer's
with its perpetual cigarette.

Metaphorical images relating to the
creative process recur subtly through the
film. The road – along which the poet walks
and the sculptor cycles (and it is *car* parts
he uses in his work) – suggests the *journey*
of artistic creation. 'How can I get him
over there?' agonizes the choreographer,
considering the passage of a dancer across
the stage. It is perhaps too literal to suggest
that when we see the poet's road blocked
with flooding water, a 'creative block' is
being alluded to. But another recurrent
image is certainly that of the bridge –
the poet is seen standing on bridges; one
dancer's body creates a bridge supporting
another's; the sculptor's work itself is a kind
of bridge; and when the painter (supported
on the arches of his clogs) squeezes paint
out on newspaper, it is on to a picture of
a bridge or aqueduct. The symbolism of the
film is not literal or heavy, but within the
reflective silence of artistic activity which
is conveyed so well, the potential creative
charge of every aspect of the artists'
environments is brought home to the
viewer. Another issue which emerges is
that of collaboration in the creative process.
The choreographer and composer work
respectively with dancers and vocalists,
who are in some way the 'raw material' that
they manipulate. The sculptor visits scrap
merchants and blacksmiths, even abattoirs
(and consults his faithful 'assistant', Moses,
a bull terrier), yet he appears quite solitary.
The poet and painter work in isolation.
All these artists, however, are involved with
interaction, at first with their chosen media,
then with the wider world when their works
are performed, published or exhibited.

'This quality video could be used in art
classes or in community art programs as
well as being enjoyed by individuals'
Video Rating Guide for Libraries, USA

Director/Scenario
Cherry Duyns

Awards
Golden Calf,
Dutch Filmdays
Best Documentary,
Uppsala
Gold Plaque, Chicago

Also available in Dutch,
French and Spanish

57 minutes
Color
Age range 14–adult
Film $1043 Rental $299
VHS $149

**424 Dreams of Beautiful Japan –
Van Gogh and Ukiyo-e**

Le Père Tanguy, one of Vincent Van Gogh's
best-known works, is a portrait of the
proprietor of an art supply shop in France.
In the background of this nineteenth-
century portrait we are surprised to see
six different Japanese prints, or ukiyo-e,
unmistakably featuring Japanese scenes
and objects, including cherry blossom,
a Japanese courtesan, Mount Fuji, and
a cluster of morning-glory. What inspired
Van Gogh to include these ukiyo-e in the
background of the portrait? This program
explores the fascinating relationship
between Vincent Van Gogh and the Japan
of his dreams, as each of the six ukiyo-e in
the background of *Le Père Tanguy* is traced
back through the 'Japonism' movement of
Van Gogh's Paris to its Japanese origin.

NHK Broadcasting Center
Also available
in Japanese

45 minutes
Color
Age range 14–adult
VHS $129

971   Japonism, Part One

Japanese Influences on Western Art:
Ukiyo-e/Japonitis/Mood of Light/
Return to the Linear

The western world's fascination with Japan
since 1854 (when her ports were forcibly
opened to the rest of the world by the
US Navy) has caused almost every major
artist up to the end of the last century to
adopt the styles, techniques and ideas of
the Japanese model. This film examines
Japanese influences in the works of the first
and second generations of Impressionists,
including Van Gogh, Gauguin, the Nabis
and Toulouse-Lautrec, and provides a
starting-point for analyzing the influence
of Japanese art on Art Nouveau.

Director
Guido De Bruyn

Also available in Dutch
and French

30 minutes
Color
Age range 15–adult
VHS $99

972   Japonism, Part Two

Japanese Influences on Western Art:
Domestic Architecture and Ceramic Design

A brief examination of Japanese influence
on western architecture and applied arts.
David Leach, himself a ceramist and expert
on Japanese culture, talks about his father,
Bernard Leach, a pioneer in uniting oriental
and western traditions.

Director
Guido De Bruyn

Also available in Dutch
and French

15 minutes
Color
Age range 15–adult
VHS $79

973   Japonism, Part Three

Japanese Influences on Western Art:
Gesture of the Brush

In recent years, the exchanges between
Japanese and western art have been
bi-directional. Pierre Alechinsky explains,
for example, how the post-war art of the
West has been influenced by Japanese
calligraphy, and Japanese artist Chinjo Saito
reveals his debt to Europe's CoBrA group.

Director
Guido De Bruyn

Also available in Dutch
and French

15 minutes
Color
Age range 15–adult
VHS $79

424
Vincent Van Gogh
Le Père Tanguy

971
The Wave
French, circa 1900

For a full understanding of art it is imperative to know something of how it is 'used' by society – how, and why, and by whom it is bought and sold, treasured in museums, presented in exhibitions. Certain films in this section profile major museums and public collections, looking at their historical, political and sociological rôles. Others center on the issues raised in art dealing, and on the presentation of different kinds of exhibition to the public.

34
Dealers, Exhibitions, Museums and Critics

This section of
32 programs can be
purchased on
VHS for $3068

Television rights and
prices on request

482 **London, Center of the World's Art Trade**

Produced with the enthusiastic co-operation
of selected London art dealers, this film
was directed by a dealer turned film-maker.
Not surprisingly, therefore, it offers a
privileged view of the art trade not usually
accessible to the public. This fascinating
subject is treated in an intimate manner,
conveying the mounting excitement at
an auction as well as behind-the-scenes
discussions among dealers. Rare works of
art are seen in some of the better-known
galleries, in contrast with less expensive
items in the street markets. Included in
the film are works of art by Veronese,
Rembrandt, Van Dyck, Largillière, Boucher,
Fragonard, Turner, Sisley, Pissarro, Degas,
Monet, Bonnard, Kokoschka, Sutherland,
and Henry Moore. Also featured are
Greek and Persian pottery and French and
English eighteenth-century furniture.

Director   **25 minutes**
Anthony Roland   **Color**
                           Age range 12–adult
                           Film $693 Rental $199
                           VHS $99

◀◀ 481A, page 305
Robert Venturi and
Denise Scott-Brown
Sainsbury Wing
The National Gallery, London

▼ 482
Oskar Kokoschka
*View of London from
Shell Centre*

637 **If Brains Were Dynamite**
The Sculpture of Mark Prent

Central to this film which investigates the
work of controversial young Canadian artist
Mark Prent are the legal and moral issues
that arise when a gallery attempts to
exhibit work that certain sectors of the
public find offensive, or in bad taste. Prent's
deliberately 'shock-horror' installations
feature realistic life-casts of lashed,
lacerated bodies and severed limbs. We hear
the artist, his dealer and the scholarly
supporters of his work speaking out in his
defence, and describing the hostility which
eventually led Prent to seek artistic asylum
in Germany's less censorious art world.

'...provides an interesting look at the
creative process, and it is also timely in
its presentation of the question of
government support for controversial,
other-than-mainstream art. The technical
quality is very good. Recommended for
art library collections and for library media
collections dealing with social issues.'
Video Rating Guide for Libraries, USA

For more information see page 164

Directors   **28 minutes**
Peter Bors   **Color**
Thom Burstyn   **Age range 18–adult**
                           Film $693 Rental $199
                           VHS $99

34. Dealers, Exhibitions, Museums and Critics

612 Pictures for the Sky
Famous Artists Design Kites

Working in conjunction with Japanese master kite-makers, a hundred famous artists from twenty countries all over the world created 'art kites' to turn the sky above Himeji, Japan, into a playground for their world of paintings. *Pictures for the Sky* documents one of the most fascinating international art spectacles of recent years, and is unique in its attractive presentation of a wide range of new works by important representatives of contemporary art. Artists featured include Robert Rauschenberg, Emilio Vedova, Niki de Saint Phalle, Panamarenko, Horst Antes, Frank Stella, Daniel Buren, Kumi Sugai, José de Guimarães, Otto Herbert Hajek, Salome, Tom Wesselmann, Antoni Tàpies, Per Kirkeby, Bukichi Inoue, Chema Cobo, Graham Dean, Griska Bruskin, Rupprecht Geiger, Paul Wunderlich, Mimmo Paladino, Karel Appel, General Idea, Olle Kaks, Zvi Goldberg, Imre Bak, Karl Otto Götz, Ulrike Rosenbach, Kenny Scharf, Gregorij Litischevskij, Sadamasa Motonaga, Tadanori Yokoo, Klaus Staeck, Franz Erhard Walther and Ivan Rabuzin.

Director/Script Markus Zollner	**30 minutes** **Color**
Original sound Jan Kollwitz	**Age range 8–adult** **Film $693** Rental $199
Also available in Dutch, French, German, Italian, Japanese, Portuguese and Russian	**VHS $99**

587 Kinetics
The Record of an Exhibition

The film is based on an exhibition of kinetic artists of many nationalities – Takis, Jesús Raphael Soto, Jean Tinguely, Kenneth Martin, Philip Vaughan *et al* – at the Hayward Gallery, London, in 1970. Kinetic art takes many forms and can be traced to an age-old interest in automata, epitomized by the search for perpetual motion. The film sees this art as a celebration of man-made and natural dynamics, questioning our modes of perception and rejecting the distinction between illusion and reality. Much of the film is given to an exploration of dazzling play of light and movement in the exhibition: pieces that move automatically, some of which require spectator participation, structures of metal and plastic, electronic equipment using neon, ultra-violet and stroboscopic lights.

Director Lutz Becker	**14 minutes** **Black and white**
Narration John Adar	**Age range 12–adult**
Arts Council of Great Britain	**Film $553** Rental $169 **VHS $79**

742 Scandinavian Design:
The Lunning Prize 1951–70

When Frederik Lunning left his native Denmark for the USA in the 1920s, Scandinavian design was virtually unknown, and few people believed that Lunning could establish a market for Danish porcelain and glass in New York – but by 1940 his business was flourishing. Then, of course, the war cut off supplies from Europe. After the war, in an effort to replenish his depleted stock, Lunning sent Kaj Dessau to find fresh merchandise in Denmark, Sweden, Norway and Finland, the only countries where industrial art still flourished. Delighted with the quality of what he found, Dessau felt that a showcase for Scandinavian products should be set up in the New York shop, and he also proposed the establishment of an awards fund for young artists who, despite the war and its shortages, had persevered in the creation of beauty and originality. The first Lunning prize was awarded in 1951.

Director Pekka Mandart	**10 minutes** **Color and**
Original music Pera Pirkola	**black and white** **Age range 15–adult** **VHS $69**

590 Vasarely

This film is a rare document from the period when, in both Europe and America, Abstraction in various forms was becoming dominant, and Victor Vasarely was pioneering 'Op Art.' The film was made at the time of one of the artist's early exhibitions at the progressive Denise René Gallery in Paris – René herself makes a fleeting appearance in Op Art couture. With a soundtrack of contemporary music, and without narration, the film-maker has sought to create a vibrant composition of rhythms and contrasts in the spirit of Vasarely.

Director Peter Kassovitz	**9 minutes** **Black and white**
Original music Ianis Xenakis	**Age range 12–adult** **Film $483** Rental $149 **VHS $69**

▲ 742
Tapio Wirkkala
Laminated Birch Leaf

▶▶ 587

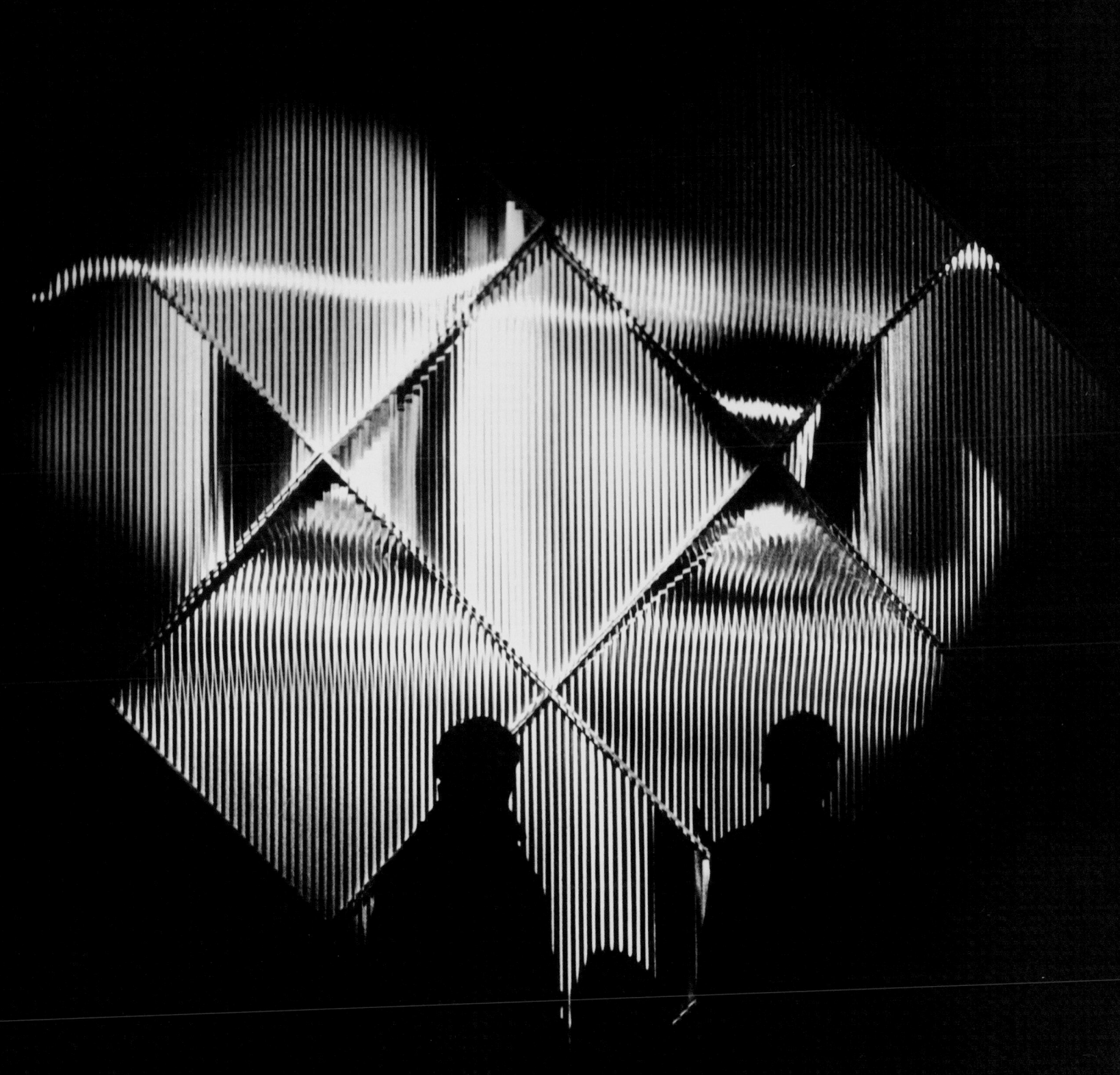

639 Submarine
Dreams and Passions of Tom McKendrick

Artist and sculptor Tom McKendrick grew up in the shipbuilding town of Clydebank near Glasgow, Scotland. *Submarine* was the name of his multi-media exhibition in Glasgow, and in this documentary he explains his childhood obsession with a device that could 'goe under water unto the bottome and come up again at your plaisure' (as it was described in 1578) and with its development into the deadly weapon of today. The submarine relies on invisibility; it operates by stealth. 'These things are really ugly but that's part of their attraction for me. They're powerful and they're brutal and they're vulnerable at the same time.' Clydebank was almost completely destroyed by bombing in 1941, and McKendrick's artistic vision was shaped by a community scarred physically and emotionally. He left school at fifteen to start work in the world-famous John Brown's shipyard, becoming a 'loftsman,' a trade now obsolete, but as the yard experienced its final death-throes, in common with Clydebank shipbuilding as a whole, McKendrick moved on to the Glasgow School of Art. He is now an artist of international importance, with paintings on display all over the world.

'Bring together an artist as articulate as Tom McKendrick and a film-maker as visually eloquent as Mark Littlewood, and you get an art film of exceptional quality – one which conveys the ideas and the imagery of the artist, and even the texture of his work. *Submarine* is an extraordinarily vivid exploration of McKendrick's obsession with one of the deadliest and darkest of man's inventions. While he claims that the submarine has no aesthetic qualities, he is clearly committed to demonstrating that is has. The whole subject is steeped in paradox. As he says, the submarine's method of stealthily stalking its prey may seem to be the epitome of cowardice and yet immense courage is required to endure the claustrophobic conditions inside a submarine being bombarded by depth charges. By the same token, the ugly carcases of the thousands of submarines which lie in the depths around these islands are the tombs of heroes. One of the most impressive sequences in the film begins with McKendrick in his native Clydebank, standing on the derelict stocks on which some of the greatest ships in the world were built. He recalls that on that seemingly insignificant row of planks, the *Lusitania* took shape. She was to be the first major victim of the submarine, going down with 1,000 passengers, and this film shows the U-boat commander's entry in his log book, recording how he could not fire another torpedo into the struggling throng of people in the water. What has this to do with art? McKendrick brings out the way that man's resourcefulness and creativity are matched by his infinite capacity for destruction, and the final image in the film is chilling in the extreme. The film draws its inspiration and much of its imagery from Tom McKendrick's *Submarine* exhibition which is touring Scotland, but the cross-cutting with actuality film is very effectively done – for example, the sequences in McKendrick's studio have a marvelously physical quality. Music and sound are used very imaginatively and the photography is of a quality that one has come to expect of Mark Littlewood. He has good reason to be proud of this film.'
Scotsman, Edinburgh, 1990

'An artistic triumph…gives the fleeting impression of other people's lives passing before your eyes…full of atmosphere from the hidden depths'
Glasgow Herald

Director
Mark Littlewood

Narrator/Participant
Tom McKendrick

Original music
John Russell
Tom McKendrick

Awards
Best Film,
Nova Scotia
Best Portrait,
Montreal

52 minutes
Color
Age range 12–adult
Film $903 Rental $269
VHS $129

▲ 639
Tom McKendrick
Part of *Submarine*
multi-media exhibition

533 Picasso the Sculptor

This film records the comprehensive exhibition of Picasso's sculptures at the Tate Gallery, London, works rarely seen together, from all periods and in a variety of materials and styles: figurative heads and figures in bronze; sheet metal, wire and tube constructions; a series of massive modeled heads from the 1930s; the witty assemblages of found materials (the *Bull's Head*, the *Baboon*); ceramic sculptures of the late 1940s and 1950s; and the 'folded' works of the 1960s, in which sheet metal is used as paper. The commentary, accompanied by photographs of Picasso at work, describes the various influences – African art, Cubism and Mediterranean fables. The film, above all, is a celebration of Picasso's unique ability to transform ordinary materials, even household objects, into poetic statements.

Director/Writer	27 minutes
Roland Penrose	Color
Narrator	Age range 14–adult
Jill Balcon	Film $693 Rental $199
Arts Council of	VHS $99
Great Britain	

592 Lichtenstein in London

This film is a record of Roy Lichtenstein's retrospective show 'The American Dream' at the Tate Gallery, London, and includes a wide range of his comic-strip paintings, some of his caricatures of modern styles, notably those of Picasso and Mondrian, and a few sculptures. The diverse opinions of members of the public interviewed at the exhibition reveal the controversy surrounding Lichtenstein's work at that time. Lichtenstein talks about the rôle of the cliché in his art, and his attempt to counteract the lack of sensitivity in commercial art while deliberately using the same restricted imagery, materials and conventions. He describes his wish to develop a similar clichéd style for his 'copies' of other artists' work, creating something which is both a caricature and also a genuine statement in its own right.

Director	20 minutes
Bruce Beresford	Color
Scenario	Age range 12–adult
David Sylvester	Film $623 Rental $189
Narration	VHS $89
Roy Lichtenstein	
Arts Council of	
Great Britain	

640 Sculpture in the City – Spoleto

Spoleto is a medieval Italian city, the ancient capital of Lombardy. Each year it has a festival of the arts, and its streets, squares, steps and old buildings are filled with new sculpture; on entering the city the visitor passes under a giant triumphal arch by the American Alexander Calder. This unusual film shows how the modern sculpture achieves new meaning and proportion when placed in outdoor settings within a city which already contains every style of architecture and design from Roman relic to Baroque. Included in the film are sculptures by Marino Marini, Laurens, Perez, Germaine Richier, Giacomo Manzu, Lynn Chadwick, Alexander Calder, Pietro Consagra, Ettore Colla, Nino Franchina, Alberto Viani, Leonardo Leoncillo, Hans Arp, Henry Moore.

Director	11 minutes
P Schivazap	Color
Award	Age range 12–adult
Exceptional Quality,	Film $483 Rental $149
Italian Government	VHS $69

483 The Queen's Pictures
Royal Collectors through the Centuries

Over the centuries kings and queens of Great Britain have created the greatest private collection of works of art in the world. Today it includes some seven thousand paintings, among them works by Bruegel, Holbein, Van Dyck, Rembrandt, Vermeer, Claude, Canaletto, Gainsborough and Reynolds. The foundations of the royal collection were laid in the sixteenth century by Henry VIII and his daughter Elizabeth I, while the enthusiasm and discernment of collectors such as Charles I and the Prince Regent (later George IV) helped to create the artistic climate of their day, in Britain and beyond. *The Queen's Pictures* traces the growth of the collection and includes location shots at Hampton Court, Windsor, Osborne House, Kensington Palace and the Banqueting House, Whitehall, London.

Author	24 minutes
Caroline Crichton-Stuart	Color
Audio Visual Unit	Age range 12–adult
The National Gallery	VHS $99

353 **A View from the Mountains:**
The Oscar Reinhart Foundation

Set in the heart of Europe, Switzerland shares much of the culture of its neighbors, yet retains its distinct individuality, shaped by the mountains to which it owes its existence. The Oscar Reinhart Foundation in Winterhur, while containing magnificent paintings from other countries, also houses a local collection celebrating that special 'view from the Alps.' This video, filmed on location in Switzerland and from original paintings, illustrates work by many of the major and unfamiliar artists exhibited there – Swiss painters such as Wolf, Böcklin and Hodler, the great Romantic artists Runge and Friedrich, the Austrian Waldmüller and others – and records the landscape which inspired some of their greatest works.

Audio Visual Unit
The National Gallery

20 minutes
Color
Age range 14–adult
VHS $89

484 **Beaubourg: The Pompidou Center, Paris**

Can one control art which criticizes 'the system' by absorbing it into the system, and elevating it to the status of the official avant-garde? And is that what the authorities were trying to do in Paris when they built the Centre Georges Pompidou after the upheavals of 1968? The students on the streets of Paris were demanding a social and cultural revolution; their ideas were apparently expressed in the founding of 'Beaubourg,' but at the same time its collections and exhibitions showcase French culture and France's importance as the perennial home of modern, and post-modern, art. So is Beaubourg an expression of cultural and political freedom, or is it really a symbol of central control?

Part of the series *Modern Art and Modernism: Manet to Pollock*

Director
Nick Levinson
Presenter/Writer
Michael Baldwin
Open University/BBC

25 minutes
Color
Age range 18–adult
VHS $99

502B **The Rietveld Schröder House**
Restoration of a *De Stijl* Interior
and Exterior

In 1924 Mrs Schröder-Schräder of Utrecht commissioned the architect Gerrit Rietveld to build a house for her. Today the result of their co-operation – for the design was truly a combined effort – is considered a monument to Modernism and the purest expression of the principles of *De Stijl*. Mrs Schröder lived in the house until her death in 1985; she was ninety-five years old. Toward the end of her life she decided that she wanted the house to be restored as far as possible to its original condition, and she asked Bertus Mulder, an architect who had worked for Rietveld in the past, to undertake this reconstruction process. The crucial elements of the 'new way of living' for which this house was a manifesto in 1925 – for example, the use of space and the system of sliding panels or walls especially created for Mrs Schröder – had disappeared during sixty years of use, repainting and redecoration; but twenty-four black and white photographs of the house taken shortly after it was built, together with the memories of Mrs Schröder and her three children, became Mulder's primary sources. There were others – for example, he found slivers of paint which revealed the original colors used. All the phases of his effort to reconstruct the house were filmed, and in the film he dwells particularly on the noteworthy aspects of Rietveld's architecture. In 1987 the house was opened to the public, and it is now a museum.

Director
Ike Bertels
Restoration-architect
Bertus Mulder
Also available in Dutch

30 minutes
Color
Age range 16–adult
VHS $99

◀ 502B
Gerrit Rietveld
Interior of
Rietveld Schröder House

▶▶ 484
Renzo Piano and
Richard Rogers
The Pompidou Center,
Paris

540 Picasso: Joie de Vivre

Picasso's joy in living is revealed in the Picasso Museum at Antibes. In the summer of 1946, the whole of Europe was recovering from the strain of the war years. Picasso was staying in the south of France where the medieval and long-empty castle at Antibes was offered to him with the idea of making it a permanent Picasso museum. For four months the master worked at sculpture, painting, pottery and covering the walls of the castle with vast murals, each a paean of praise to the new life coming to fruition about him.

Director
Jacques Berthier

Narration
Henri Perruchot
Jacques Berthier

Original music
Pierre Spiers

Also available in French

12 minutes
Color
Age range 12–adult

Film $483 Rental $149
VHS $69

567 Theater of Memory: The Dali Museum

Theater of Memory shows the unique theater museum in Catalonia that brings together the works of the self-styled Surrealist genius Salvador Dali. It does not present a conventional survey of the artist's career, but aims to show the museum itself as a work of art. Everything in it is important and significant; nothing is incidental. The voice-over is by Dali himself. He speaks of his pride at being Catalan, of his love for his 'muse' Gala, and of his collaborations with the artist Antoni Pitxot, for whom rock and granite are an obsession. Dali guides us (and a mysterious little girl in a sailor-suit who 'shadows' us throughout) past gilded statues and manikins, past curious columns of tyres, and up and down staircases guarded by bizarre automatons. We see the Mae West Room in which the furnishings create the illusion of huge lips, and we see Dali's Cadillac, which, he boasts, is one of only six of its kind, others being owned by Roosevelt, Clark Gable and Al Capone. Dali tells us of the alchemist's fascination with creating gold, and of his own parallel obsession with creating the perfect illusion through his immaculate painting technique, by which he claims (presumably in opposition to Expressionism) to have 'saved modern painting from slackness and chaos.'

Director
Joan Mallarach

Script
Jesus Garay
Joan Mallarach

Original music
Javier Navarrete

Also available in Spanish

32 minutes
Color
English narration
Some subtitles
Age range 10–adult

VHS $109

376 A New Museum in South Kensington

The story of the development of the new museum buildings which eventually, in the early years of the twentieth century, became the Victoria and Albert Museum. The idea for the museum grew out of Prince Albert's Great Exhibition of 1851, which had attracted over six million visitors, and out of the government's wish to improve the education of British designers. The fascinating if fractured growth of the buildings reflects the parallel growth of the museum's status from its beginnings as a rather suspect pioneering venture, and also the development of taste between 1850 and 1890. It also illustrates conflicting contemporary attitudes toward the economics of education and manufacture, craftsmanship and collecting, and bringing art to the people – or at least to those who had the leisure to visit museums.

Part of the series
Culture and Society in Britain 1850–90

Director
Tony Coe

Presenter/Writer
Colin Cunningham

Open University/BBC

25 minutes
Color
Age range 17–adult

VHS $99

◀ 376
Aston Webb
Victoria and Albert Museum,
London

◥ 481
Edward Middleton Barry
The dome of the Barry Rooms
The National Gallery, London

481   **Art for Pleasure's Sake**

This introductory film about The National Gallery in London, which houses one of the world's finest collections of pictures, gives some details of the history of the gallery and how some of its pictures were acquired. The film also includes an interview with the director at the time the film was made, Michael Levey.

From the series
The National Gallery – A Private View

Director
Henry Lewes

Writer/Narration
Edwin Mullins

28 minutes
Color
Age range 12–adult

Film $693 Rental $199
VHS $99

481A   **The Much-Loved Friend?**
A Portrait of The National Gallery

This film looks at the history and rôle of The National Gallery, London, through the eyes of those who work in it and visit it: trustees such as the Prince of Wales, the director Neil MacGregor, the artist Howard Hodgkin, architects Robert Venturi and Denise Scott-Brown, and members of the public. Archive footage is combined with a behind-the-scenes look at the gallery's work, especially the scientific and conservation departments.

Director
Nicholas Rossiter

Research
Randall Wright

Consultant
Christoper Cook

Original music
Carol Canning

47 minutes
Color
Age range 13–adult

VHS $119

481B   **Pictures in Pictures**
Themes and Variations at The National Gallery

The paintings featured in this video, all on display in The National Gallery, do not share a theme or subject, they were not painted in a particular period, nor do they come from the same country or region. They do however have one thing in common: the picture within a picture. Pictures in pictures can give an artist the opportunity to imitate other artists' styles, they can provide us with information on the way paintings were once displayed or, like plays, they can pass comment on the main action or subject. They can also allude seriously or playfully to notions of reality and resemblances. Pictures in pictures show artists turning their attention to the very art that they practice.

Audio Visual Unit
The National Gallery

25 minutes
Color
Age range 13–adult

VHS $99

The Moscow Kremlin
A Monument to Russian Culture and Architecture

This series of 3 programs can be purchased on VHS for $297 Reference S27

483B The Moscow Kremlin, Part One
The Walls, Towers and Cathedrals

Begun eight and a half centuries ago, the development of the Kremlin, ancient seat of the Russian Tsars, is traced in this film from oak-wood fort to the red-brick fifteenth-century eminence seen today. Also explored is the Kremlin's huge Cathedral of the Assumption, begun in 1497 by the Grand Duke Ivan III using an Italian architect to bring the latest building styles from western Europe. It was here that generations of Russian patriarchs and Tsars were crowned, and in their turn buried beneath opulent tombs. The film features icon and mural paintings by, among others, Andrei Rubilov and his pupils, by Dionysus, and by his son Theodysius. Within walls of just over a mile in circumference, the Kremlin consists of a multitude of buildings and chambers: the Bell Tower that announced momentous decrees of state, or warned of uprisings or invasion; the seventeenth-century canopied turret from which Tsars surveyed their subjects in Red Square; the Armoury, holding mementoes and cannon from the famous 1812 victory over Napoleon; the seventeenth-century Archangel Cathedral, dedicated to the Archangel Mikhail, protector of Russia. The diversity of architectural style in the Kremlin is explained in this film in terms of the cosmopolitan range of builders called upon to add to the edifice over the centuries. Many of them were Italian, and at least one – Christopher Galloway in the seventeenth-century – was British.

Part of the series *The Moscow Kremlin*

Director/Script	**30 minutes**
Vladimir Benidiktov	**Color**
Art Video International	**Age range 14–adult**
Also available in Russian	**VHS $99**

483C The Moscow Kremlin, Part Two
The Tower-chambers and Palaces

This film highlights a few of the especially notable features of the Kremlin's dense cluster of buildings. We begin with the fifteenth-century gold-domed Grand Ducal Palace, with its white-faced stone walls which reflect the Italian origins of its architect. (The cosmopolitan nature of European culture from the Middle Ages right up to the late Renaissance is repeatedly seen in the films on Moscow in this section.) This building, we learn, witnessed many momentous decisions in Russian political history, including the unification of Russia and the Ukraine. We are taken through the 'Golden Grille,' with its magnificent metalwork, which guards the seventeenth-century Tirimar Chamber. We enter the nineteenth-century Kremlin Hall, 145 feet high (and only two stories), which contains an incomparable collection of furniture, and decoration bewildering in its eclectic style, from classical and baroque to imitations of the French châteaux of Louis XIV. The film sketches the historical events to which such buildings provided the backdrop – right up to the Victory Parade of 1945.

Part of the series *The Moscow Kremlin*

Director/Script	**30 minutes**
Vladimir Benidiktov	**Color**
Art Video International	**Age range 14–adult**
Also available in Russian	**VHS $99**

483D The Moscow Kremlin, Part Three
The Armoury: Countless Treasures of the Russian Tsars

This film focuses on the Russian State Armoury in the Kremlin, and its staggering collection of metalwork, jewelery, arms and armor. Though there are many medieval pieces, the collection is especially strong in sixteenth- and seventeenth-century western work, and in European metalwork and silverware up to the mid-nineteenth century. Ceremonial crowns are a special feature, such as the celebrated 'Jericho Cap' helmet, or the crown of Ivan the Terrible. There are also many snuff-boxes, a collection of enameled miniature portraits (one of Peter the Great), silver chalices, censers, a twelfth-century Byzantine cross, and a jewel-encrusted gospel, again made for Ivan the Terrible and housed in the Cathedral of the Annunciation. The collection of English silverware is better than any in England itself, due to the ironic fact that Cromwell melted down so much silver during a republican revolution of a kind that would not come to Russia until the twentieth century.

Part of the series *The Moscow Kremlin*

Director/Script	**30 minutes**
Vladimir Benidiktov	**Color**
Art Video International	**Age range 14–adult**
Also available in Russian	**VHS $99**

483B
The Kremlin, Moscow

483C
The Kremlin, Moscow

327 **Classical Sculpture and the Enlightenment**

The Grand Tour took many people of taste and wealth to Italy in the eighteenth century and encouraged the collecting of antique works of art. This program concentrates on one important British collector, Charles Townley, whose collection of marbles is in the British Museum. Gerard Vaughan of Oxford University talks to Colin Cunningham of the Open University about a number of Townley's most important marbles. They discuss the problems of interpreting the subject of sculptures and the question of restoration. Publications illustrating Greek and Roman works of art influenced British taste, as did the displays of the works themselves. Among the volumes shown are the works from Pompeii and Herculaneum published by the King of Naples.

Part of the series *The Enlightenment*

Director	25 minutes
Robert Philip	Color
Presenters	Age range 18–adult
Colin Cunningham	VHS $99
Gerard Vaughan	
Open University/BBC	

484A **Musée d'Orsay**

This program looks at how an old disused railway station in Paris, the Gare d'Orsay, was converted into an important museum housing art from Daumier and Millet to the Impressionists and Post-Impressionists. It also tries to understand the relationship between avant-garde art and kitsch and the reasons for the museum's hanging policy. It enables the student to discover that a museum space is not neutral – there are specific historical and art historical reasons behind the way pictures are hung.

Part of the series
Modern Art, Practices and Debates

Director	25 minutes
GD Jayalakshmi	Color
Presenter	Age range 18–adult
Tim Benton	VHS $99
Contributors	
Michel Laclotte	
Roland Schaer	
Madeleine Reberious	
Open University/BBC	

87 **The Colonial Encounter**

Past and Present Ways of Representing and Categorizing the Culture of Ex-French Colonies in Africa

In the first part of the program Annie Coombes looks at the ways in which the culture and history of the French colonies have been represented to a western European audience since the turn of the nineteenth century. These issues are introduced through an interview with Joseph Adando, conducted at the Musée de l'Homme, Paris. Annie Coombes considers the organization and content of exhibitions, and the images of colonial culture disseminated by the popular press and a growing tourist industry. The program focuses on the representations of two African colonies, Dahomey (now the state of Benin) and Algeria. Dahomey was made a French colony in 1893, while Algeria was occupied in 1830. The representation of these two cultures is considered in the context of the colonial displays in the Trocadero Museum, Paris, and the displays and exhibits in the Paris World Fair of 1900. Annie Coombes goes on to consider how forms of ethnographical display and categorization have been developed in the organization of two modern collections: the Rockefeller Collection in the Metropolitan Museum in New York, and the Museum of Mankind in London. She argues that the former tends to emphasize the formal qualities of these colonial objects, encouraging us to evaluate them in terms of western artistic criteria, whereas some of the displays in the Museum of Mankind may encourage us to engage with the contradiction inherent in western consumption of the artefacts and history of non-western colonial cultures.

Part of the series
Modern Art, Practices and Displays

Director	25 minutes
Nick Levinson	Color
Presenter	Age range 18–adult
Annie Coombes	VHS $99
Open University/BBC	

551 **On Pictures and Paintings**

Charles Harrison conducts us on a tour of selected works in the Tate Gallery, London, exploring different ways of thinking about how works of art represent and, in that sense, have meaning. Some works represent without being pictures at all (abstracts – Poliakoff). Harrison considers what makes a painting 'modern,' starting with Cézanne and moving through Braque, Grosz, Dali, Miró, Jack Smith and Leger, to show how the illusionistic devices of painting become decoupled from the rational compositional themes within which they had previously been controlled.

Part of the series
Modern Art, Practices and Debates

Director	25 minutes
Jeremy Cooper	Color
Open University/BBC	Age range 18–adult
	VHS $99

484B **The Museum of Modern Art**

This program on the Museum of Modern Art has several contributors – a founding member of the museum, the architect Philip Johnson; the present Director of Paintings, Kirk Varnedoe; an art critic who protested against the museum's policy during the Vietnam era, Lucy Lippard; an art historian, Linda Nochlin, and an artist refused by the museum, Leon Golub. They are interviewed about how and why MOMA became one of the most important art institutions of the twentieth century. And behind the glamor, what sort of place is it? Do art institutions like MOMA harbor an élite culture or do they make 'high art' democratically available to everyone? Does MOMA promote specifically American values, thereby becoming a vehicle of American imperialism? Is Modernism as a movement over and, if so, has MOMA become a fossilized museum? Is there a different rôle that MOMA could perform in today's Post-modernist world?

Part of the series
Modern Art, Practices and Debates

Director	25 minutes
GD Jayalakshmi	Color
Presenter	Age range 18–adult
Francis Frascina	VHS $99
Open University/BBC	

583 Art and the Left

US Artists Politicized by the Impact of Vietnam, Civil Rights and Feminism

Francis Frascina interviews artists, critics and museum curators active in the resistance to the Vietnam War and racism in the USA. It begins with the vivid testimony of Nancy Spero and Martha Rosler, who changed their art practices in response to their opposition to US involvement in Vietnam. Other artists and critics recall the legacy of 1968.

Part of the series
Modern Art, Practices and Debates

Director	**25 minutes**
NL and GD Jayalakshmi	**Color**
Participants	**Age range 18–adult**
Nancy Spero	**VHS $99**
Martha Rosler	
Lucy Lippard	
Rudolf Baranik	
Leon Golub	
Mary Kelly	
May Stevens	
Marcia Tucker	
Kinshasha Conwill	

Open University/BBC

503E Jackson Pollock: Tim Clark and Michael Fried in Conversation

Art historian TJ Clark and art critic Michael Fried in the past occupied opposing positions. Clark was the eminent advocate of the social history of art, based on a Marxist approach which saw art as produced in a socio-economic context. Fried, on the other hand, was an arch-Modernist, believing art to be about itself alone, separate from social meaning. Now, however, the two have moved closer. Clark accepts the canonical greatness of Pollock's work and Fried no longer claims that art functions only in an 'optical' way.

Part of the series
Modern Art, Practices and Debates

Directors	**25 minutes**
GD Jayalakshmi	**Color**
Nick Levinson	**Age range 18–adult**
Presenter	**VHS $99**
Paul Wood	

Open University/BBC

482A Greenberg on Art Criticism

Art historian TJ Clark interviews Clement Greenberg, well-known art critic, about writing art criticism and asks what are the essential qualities that make for great art in the modern period.

Part of the series
Modern Art, Practices and Debates

Director	**25 minutes**
Nick Levinson	**Color**
GD Jayalakshmi	**Age range 18–adult**
Open University/BBC	**VHS $99**

482B Greenberg on Jackson Pollock

In conversation with art historian TJ Clark, Clement Greenberg, art critic, speaks of his first meeting with the painter Jackson Pollock. He discusses Pollock's early work – successes and failures – his methods as a painter and his last years.

Part of the series
Modern Art, Practices and Debates

Directors	**25 minutes**
Nick Levinson	**Color**
GD Jayalakshmi	**Age range 18–adult**
Open University/BBC	**VHS $99**

▲ 482B
Jackson Pollock
Blue Poles: Number 11,
detail

34 Dealers, Exhibitions, Museums and Critics

35
Conservation and Preservation

The preservation and conservation of works of art and architecture is a major and a proper concern of the guardians of cultural heritage worldwide. The films in this section range from impassioned calls for conservational vigilance to informative studies of archaeological and fine-art restoration processes.

This section of
13 programs can be
purchased on
VHS for $1357

Television rights and
prices on request

27   Borobudur: Beyond the Reach of Time
Final Stages of Restoring Indonesia's
Great Shrine

Dating from a thousand years ago, the
temple of Borobudur stands in Java, a 400-
feet-square terraced pyramid festooned
with stone carvings and reliefs featuring
five hundred figures of Buddha. The carvings
tell stories of his life, and the film retells
the myths of Buddhism. It also charts the
enormous reconstruction and restoration
project to which Borobudur has been
subjected in recent years, having suffered
erosion by the elements and subsidence.

Director	**32 minutes**
Francine Vande Wiele	**Color**
Narration	**Age range 14–adult**
Brian Fetherstone	**Film $763** Rental $199
Principal adviser	**VHS $109**
Professor Dr Haryati	
Soebadio	
UNESCO	
Also available in	
French, Portuguese,	
Russian and Spanish	

30   Nubia '64
Saving the Temples of Ancient Egypt

The ancient Egyptians built colossal temples
and shrines along the banks of the River
Nile. When the modern rulers of Egypt
decided to dam the Nile in Nubia, to ensure
regular irrigation along 600 miles of its
course, they knew that the river's level was
bound to rise and rise until some of these
monuments were completely submerged.
Only a huge exercise in conservation, in
which the experts of many nations had to
co-operate, could save these priceless
treasures from death by water. What had
taken hundreds of years and thousands of
slaves to build had to be moved and
reassembled in months on the new banks of
the Nile. Presented as a human document
rather than as art history, this film will
fascinate old and young viewers alike.
Locations featured include the Aswan Dam,
the Tomb of Pennenout, the Temple of Deer,
the Shrine of Gaarf Hussein, the Temple of
Dakka, the Temple of Ramses, the Temple of
Philae, the Temple of Abu Simbel, the Temple
of Amada and the Temple of Kalaboha.

Director	**42 minutes**
Robert Genot	**Color**
Narration	**Age range 12–adult**
Desroches-Noblecourt	**Film $833** Rental $249
Award	**VHS $119**
Grand Prix, Cannes	

◀◀ 226, page 310
Leonardo da Vinci
*Virgin and Child
with St Anne and
the Infant St John*, detail

▲ 30
Abu Simbel, Egypt
Dismantling one of the
Osiriao pillars, entrance hall
of the Great Temple

309

111 Romanesque Architecture of Alsace
Men of Stone, Men of Faith

'Architecture is the only art where I can enter into the interior. All the other arts keep me on the outside. A master builder, whether he be a monk or a layman…when he builds a temple, he knows that a kind of hymn will emanate from the internal spaces. I can pray in any temple as long as the architects and builders gave it that rhythm which brings me silence, meditation and peace…I believe that Romanesque architecture is the most authentic manifestation of the mentality and soul of the people who lived in the eleventh and twelfth centuries. Life wasn't funny; when a little bit of happiness was found somewhere it was taken advantage of to the detriment of civil and religious laws. The important thing was not to get caught…but that was a period when people were straightforward, they sinned heavily, and they repented a great deal! One didn't cheat. What was white was white, what was black was black …one didn't attempt to justify oneself!' In such terms the monk Brother Pascal takes us engagingly into the world of Romanesque Alsace, and provides the philosophical and social background for what develops into a discussion of the conservation of medieval buildings. Churches looked at include those of Ottmarsheim, Murbach, Epfig, Rosheim, and Neuwiller-les-Saverne.

Part of the series *French Romanesque*

Director	**26 minutes**
Alain Schwarzstein	**Color**
Historian	**Age range 14–adult**
Roland Oberle	**Film $693** Rental $199
Participant	**VHS $99**
Brother Pascal	
Series concept/Producer	
Clara Ford	
Also available in French	

114 Romanesque Architecture of Normandy
Narrow Naves, Mighty Vessels

Abbot Le Legard, ecclesiastic and builder at the Abbey of La Lucerne, brings back to life the great figures of Romanesque creation in Normandy. The legend and reality in the story of William the Conqueror are blended in the course of this evocation of the period. Cerisy, Jumièges, St Etienne and the Trinité of Caen, Essay, St Martin de Boscherville – these are the great medieval buildings the film examines. Abbot Le Legard deals with the technical issues of restoration and reconstruction, as well as those of aesthetic appreciation. He conveys his respect for and responsiveness to all that the Romanesque has left us.

Part of the series *French Romanesque*

Director	**26 minutes**
Bernaud Saint-Pierre	**Color**
Historian	**Age range 14–adult**
Maylise Bayle	**Film $693** Rental $199
Participant	**VHS $99**
Abbot Le Gard	
Series concept/Producer	
Clara Ford	
Also available in French	

215 Guido Mazzoni
The Master of Ecclesiatical Lifesize Statuary Groups

While following the restoration of the monumental *Porrini* group by Guido Mazzoni, this documentary also presents an overview of the sculptures of this marvellous but little-known Renaissance artist.

Director	**30 minutes**
Marco Speroni	**Color**
Original music	**Age range 14–adult**
Angelo Bergamini	**VHS $99**
Also available in Italian	

226 The Restoration of a Leonardo da Vinci

The *Virgin and Child with St Anne and the Infant St John,* Leonardo da Vinci's famous cartoon of 1506/8 which had been at The National Gallery in London since 1962, was attacked with a shotgun on July 17, 1987. This video, compiled from footage exclusive to The National Gallery, offers a unique and fascinating insight into the methods of a modern conservator and those of past centuries, and into the working practices of Leonardo himself.

Audio Visual Unit	**20 minutes**
The National Gallery	**Color**
	Age range 12–adult
	VHS $89

▶ 215
Guido Mazzoni
Statue during restoration

493 Janus

Europe's Architectural Heritage:
A Call to Action

Janus highlights the dangers threatening
the magnificent buildings, civic architecture
and urban environment, both ancient and
modern, which belong to all Europeans.
Its objective is to demonstrate forcefully
the fact that our architectural heritage is
as much at the mercy of ourselves as of
architects, planners and government
departments; and it asserts that at
different times each one of us may display
indifference or concern, admiration
or neglect. *Janus* is strong medicine.
It is meant to make you think – and it does!
There is no narration.

Director	**36 minutes**
Anthony Wilkinson	**Color**
Original music	**Age range 8–adult**
John Scott	**Film $833** Rental $249
	VHS $119

491 Europa Nostra

The Threat to and Protection of the
European Heritage

This multi-award-winning film has been
financed by contributions from a number
of European governments and the European
Economic Community. Shot in fifteen
countries in western and eastern Europe,
it touches upon all aspects of conservation,
including lost treasures, restoration, new
uses for old buildings and new construction,
both harmonious and incongruous, traffic
(congestion, parking and pedestrian areas),
the pressures of tourism, unsightly
advertising and other 'eyesores,' technical
and financial problems, and the activities of
local authorities and conservation societies.

'...a beautiful film, directed and edited with
great flair and skill. From its opening
montage of glories that have survived the
assaults of war, decades of neglect and the
depredations of developers, to its end above
the water of threatened Venice, the changes
of pace and the violence of contrasts keep
your eyes very wide open. Teachers of
history, social studies, liberal studies and
current affairs will find obvious uses for
the film. *Europa Nostra* is a powerful
indictment of those whose judgment of our
architectural inheritance is determined by
whether they will make money faster by
knocking it down rather than allowing it
to stand for our pleasure. The quality of our
lives is our responsibility – and that is a
political and moral lesson every school
should teach. *Europa Nostra* is as good an
aid as you will get for putting it across.'
Times Educational Supplement, London

Director	**24 minutes**
Charles Mapleston	**concise version**
Narration	**Color**
Michael Middleton	**Age range 12–adult**
Awards	**Film $693** Rental $199
Gold Award,	**VHS $99**
Special Award,	
British Architectural	
Heritage Year	
Silver Plaque, Chicago	
Grand Prize, Silver Trophy,	
South Africa	
First Award BISFA, London	
First Prize, Ouistreham	
Bronze Award,	
Interfilm Award, Berlin	

311

The Fall and Rise of Mackintosh

The reputation of the great Glasgow builder Charles Rennie Mackintosh, designer of the Glasgow School of Art, the so-called 'first building of the modern movement,' had fallen so low twenty-five years ago, when film-maker Murray Grigor helped to found the 'Friends of Toshie' society, that few of the city's inhabitants even knew his name – as Grigor established when he conducted a vox pop in George Square. But today, sixty years after his death, Mackintosh is a real force in world architecture and design. How has this revolution come about? And is there a danger that the real genius of Mackintosh's style will be crushed beneath a modern avalanche of pastiche and parody? This film highlights the restoration of Mackintosh's work (as well as his reputation), including the painstaking recreation of Glasgow's Miss Cranston's Tea Rooms.

For more infromation see page 105

Director/Writer Murray Grigor	**52 minutes**
	Color
Original music David McNiven	**Age range 14–adult**
	VHS $129

Interviews/Discussions
Filippo Alison, Italy
Edward Cullinan, UK
Hans Hollein, Austria
Stanley Tigerman, USA
Aldo Van Eyck, Netherlands
Professor Andrew Macmillan, UK
Professor Isi Metzstein, UK
Bruno del Priori, Italy

Special work
Arata Isosaki, Japan

The Rietveld Schröder House

502B

Restoration of a *De Stijl* Interior
and Exterior

In 1924 Mrs Schröder-Schräder of Utrecht commissioned the architect Gerrit Rietveld to build a house for her. Today the result of their co-operation – for the design was truly a combined effort – is considered a monument to Modernism and the purest expression of the principles of *De Stijl*. Mrs Schröder lived in the house until her death in 1985; she was ninety-five years old. Toward the end of her life she decided that she wanted the house to be restored as far as possible to its original condition, and she asked Bertus Mulder, an architect who had worked for Rietveld in the past, to undertake this reconstruction process. The crucial elements of the 'new way of living' for which this house was a manifesto in 1925 – for example, the use of space and the system of sliding panels or walls especially created for Mrs Schröder – had disappeared during sixty years of use, repainting and redecoration; but twenty-four black and white photographs of the house taken shortly after it was built, together with the memories of Mrs Schröder and her three children, became Mulder's primary sources. There were others – for example, he found slivers of paint which revealed the original colors used. All the phases of his effort to reconstruct the house were filmed, and in the film he dwells particularly on the noteworthy aspects of Rietveld's architecture. In 1987 the house was opened to the public, and it is now a museum.

Director	30 minutes
Ike Bertels	Color
Restoration-architect	Age range 16–adult
Bertus Mulder	VHS $99

Also available in Dutch

494
Hampton Court Palace,
England
Devastation after the fire

After the Fire: The Restoration of Hampton Court Palace

494

One disastrous night in March 1986 fire gutted an entire wing of Hampton Court Palace, Henry VIII's beautiful riverside retreat near London which was later modernized by Christopher Wren. The problem of replacing the irreplaceable – not only the building itself, but Grinling Gibbons carvings, painted ceilings and the canopy of William III's throne – was solved by a working party of architects, historians and other experts, who turned to the technology of the future to recreate the work of past masters. Through a delicate balance of science and age-old craft, builders and carvers, blacksmiths and stonemasons, painting and textile conservators are skillfully restoring the damaged fabric of this most popular of royal palaces.

Director	30 minutes
Judy Davidson	Color
Writer	Age range 12–adult
Claire Peterken	Film $693 Rental $199
Narrator	VHS $99
John Hedges	

Also available in
Arabic, French and
Latin American Spanish

Art Restoration

495

Layers of dirt are lifted from a small picture largely ignored for centuries – and a masterpiece by Raphael is revealed. X-radiography discovers a second figure behind the first in a sixteenth-century royal portrait. High technology establishes for police or auction rooms whether priceless pottery is real or fake. Science can analyze works of art and restore them to their original perfection – or so it seems. But in restoration, something of the past is always lost. Will the judgments that restorers make today stand up to the scrutiny of future generations?

Directors	30 minutes
Iain Softley	Color
Phil Jones	Age range 13–adult
Writer	VHS $99
Christine Leeson	
Narrator	
Cheryl Campbell	

Also available in
Arabic, French and
Latin American Spanish

Physics and Fine Art

496A

The Scientific Examination of Paintings

This video takes us behind the scenes of The National Gallery in London to show how science is used in the investigation and conservation of works of art. New techniques are being developed all the time. For example, infra-red reflectography can penetrate to the lowest levels of a painting to show the 'underdrawing' with which the artist began his work – and the style of the underdrawing can be a very valuable guide to the authenticity of a picture. X-rays can be used to examine the whole picture; and the video reveals how a portrait by Goya was painted over another on the same canvas. It is also possible to discover and analyze the actual materials the artist used; then if restoration is necessary, the restorers know exactly what to use. In a portrait by Rembrandt of his mistress, was the red he used a cheaper mixture of two pigments rather than the more expensive pure vermilion? Paintings are fragile things; they may start to deteriorate as soon as they leave the studio. A subject of Sir Joshua Reynolds, watching the color drain out of his painted face during his own lifetime, claimed that Reynolds had 'made his paintings die before the man.' But scientific control of the gallery environment can slow down this deterioration. Without science, knowledge of how artists of the past worked, what paints they used, and how we should best preserve their paintings would be meager indeed.

Audio Visual Unit	30 minutes
The National Gallery	Color
Institute of Physics	Age range 14–adult
	VHS $99

The playwright Tom Stoppard has observed that 'technique without ideas gives us wicker baskets; ideas without technique gives us modern art.' In fact, while the distinction between arts and crafts and the rôle of technique within them is an area of controversy among contemporary craftspeople and artists, most fine art involves technical skills, and most crafts can be carried to the level of an art. Certainly the training of a traditional African carver or a sculptor working on a Romanesque church would have been almost entirely a training in practical techniques, yet the inspiration and expression in their works is undeniable.

36
Techniques of the Artist

Artists at Work
Art and Craft Techniques

This section of 30 programs, excluding the series 'Draw with Don', page 274, can be purchased on VHS for $3160

Television rights and prices on request

In the nineteenth century the Arts and Crafts movement sought to reintroduce handicraft techniques into manufacturing to raise design products to the level of art. Clearly, as long as artists and designers continue to produce physical objects of any kind, issues of technique will remain important.

This section features films which look at technique, whether giving insights into the procedures of artists and craft workers of the past and present, or giving in-depth introductions to specific art and craft techniques.

486 Genesis

Observations on the Creation of
Five Works of Art

Genesis shows how a work of art which
begins its life in the imagination of an
artist takes shape on paper or on canvas,
in voices or car parts or on stage in the
form of a ballet. The artists whose works
of art were observed from the initial stages
to completion are the poet Ida Gerhardt,
the painter Armando, the choreographer
Hans Van Manen, the composer Reinbert de
Leeuw, with a piece for sixteen voices by
György Ligeti, and the sculptor Carel Visser.
The audience sees and hears nothing
but the process of creation – the genesis
of works of art.

'This quality video could be used in art
classes or in community art programs as
well as being enjoyed by individuals.'
Video Rating Guide for Libraries, USA

For more information see page 294

Director/Scenario Cherry Duyns	57 minutes Color
Awards	Age range 14–adult
Golden Calf, Dutch Filmdays	Film $1043 Rental $299 VHS $149
Best Documentary, Uppsala	
Gold Plaque, Chicago	
Also available in Dutch, French and Spanish	

602 Brendan Neiland: Evolution of a Commission

This program explores two important
aspects of the life of an artist, the
commissioning of a work by a major
institution and the artist's professional
practice. It features Brendan Neiland,
a well-established British artist whose
work is in collections throughout the world.
We follow the progress of one of Neiland's
paintings commissioned by British Rail,
from the start of the commissioning
process through the many stages of
creation to the reproduction and display
of the work as a poster on King's Cross
Station, London. We also see how Neiland
practices as a professional artist and we
investigate his relations with his gallery and
private clients. Art critics from the *Sunday
Times* and the *Financial Times* talk about
Neiland's work, the commercial aspects of
art and how the artist has to compromise in
fulfilling the needs of a commission, and
Neiland's family, who talk about his success
and how it has impinged on their lives.

Director Gavin Nettleton	37 minutes Color Age range 12–adult VHS $119

973 Japonism, Part Three

Japanese Influences on Western Art:
Gesture of the Brush

In recent years, the exchanges between
Japanese and western art have been
bi-directional. Pierre Alechinsky explains,
for example, how the post-war art of the
West has been influenced by Japanese
calligraphy, and Japanese artist Chinjo Saito
reveals his debt to Europe's CoBrA group.

Director Guido De Bruyn	15 minutes Color Age range 15–adult
Also available in Dutch and French	VHS $79

639, page 318
Tom McKendrick at work

973
Christian Dotremont
Automated writing
A Lapp Winter's Day…

595 Bridget Riley

Perceptual art is concerned with the effects
and processes of what, in this film, Bridget
Riley calls 'the great privilege of sight'.
'Looking,' as she puts it, 'is a pleasure –
a continual pleasure.' From the black and
white paintings of the early 1960s
which first established her international
reputation, to her increasing concern with
the self-generating luminosity of pure
color, the film traces her 'exploration of the
truth of what one can see.' In the studio,
we see her working on a painting – finding
that visual structure which from basic and
simple elements will release complex effects
of energy, movement, space, light and
'induced' color through the physical act of
looking. Certain artists – Van Gogh, Seurat,
Monet and the Futurists – are particularly
important to her. But the film also shows
the inspiration she has always drawn
from certain types of visual experiences
in nature. 'Painting,' as Bridget Riley says,
'has to obey the laws of painting.' But
for her that is a process parallel to nature,
dependent on our day-to-day experience
of the joy of using our eyes.

Director/Writer David Thompson	28 minutes Color
Arts Council of Great Britain	Age range 12–adult Film $693 Rental $199 VHS $99

627 The Spinney by Jean Dubuffet

Without narration, we follow all the
different stages leading up to the unveiling
of *The Spinney*, a monumental sculptural
work by Jean Dubuffet, on June 18, 1988,
in Flaine, Haute Savoie, France – the
location chosen by Dubuffet himself.

'…an inspiration for artists…can at
times be mesmerizing…highly artistic…
fits together in unexpected ways.
This is a video that art discussion groups
or those into surrealism may enjoy.'
Video Rating Guide for Libraries, USA

For more information see page 163

Director Nedjima Scialom	16 minutes Color Age range 12–adult VHS $79

36 Techniques of the Artist

626   **Chadwick**

Lynn Chadwick achieved international recognition in 1956 when he won the First Prize for Sculpture at the Venice Biennale. At that time, Chadwick was simply one of the new generation of talented English sculptors; now he is widely acknowledged as the successor to Henry Moore. Chadwick was born in 1914 and began his working life as an architectural draftsman. His later work as a furniture and textile designer led him to sculpture, and he developed an original sculptural technique and a personal vocabulary of fabulous beasts, totemic forms and majestic double figures. For the last thirty years, Chadwick has lived at Lypiatt Manor, deep in the heart of Gloucestershire, keeping his distance from the art world. Despite his use of the human figure, he describes his work as abstract; beyond this he is reluctant to analyze its deeper meaning. Director Barrie Gavin spent some days watching Chadwick at work on a new project, two figures ascending and descending a staircase. By following the process of drawing, the construction of the armature (the metal skeleton used to support the clay or wax during the making of a sculpture), to the foundry and finished piece, this film gives an insight into the artist's physical and mental approach to his work.

For more information see page 162

Director/Writer Barrie Gavin	**51 minutes**
Original music Toru Takemitsu	**Color**
	Age range 14–adult
	Film $903 Rental $269
	VHS $129

620   **Sculpture 58, the Story of a Creation**
Bernhard Heiliger

In his Berlin studio, Bernhard Heiliger traces the designs for the large sculpture group to be positioned outside the German Pavilion at the Brussels World Fair. We follow the development from the clay maquette (small model) to the original plaster model. Apart from the physical handicraft involved, we also become aware of the artist's struggle for expression. This is a film without narration, an unsurpassable example of the type of film which shows the artist in the process of creation, ideal for helping the viewer to understand the structure of a sculpture.

Director Herbert Seggelke	**12 minutes**
	Color
Original music Boris Blacher	**Age range 12–adult**
	Film $553 Rental $169
Awards Honor Award, Bergamo Honor Award, Cork Culture Award, German Government Highly Commended, German Center for Film Classification	**VHS $79**

▼ 620
Bernard Heiliger
Maquettes in the
corner of his studio

◀ 620
Bernard Heiliger
Standing figures

630   **The Genesis of a Sculpture**

Adam-Tessier

This film employs a fascinating technique to show the various stages of a sculpture produced by Maxim Adam-Tessier. There is no narration, but the viewer is able to see the sculptor's hesitations, his choices – and his regrets.

'The technique of this research film of great integrity is remarkable. The care taken to be truthful extends almost to complete frankness. This is a courageous film.'
UNESCO

For more information see page 271

Directors	13 minutes
Olivier Clouzot	Black and white
Julien Pappe	Age range 10–adult
Music	Film $483 Rental $149
Anton Webern	VHS $69
Awards	
Mention d'Excellence,	
Cannes	
Biennale Prize, Paris	

---

605   **Nature and Nature: Andy Goldsworthy**

Andy Goldsworthy, a contemporary sculptor now living in Scotland, has for years been exploring various sites of the world, leaving behind sculptures that are in harmony with the environment. His materials are drawn from nature itself and his works, like many natural things, are essentially ephemeral. For Goldsworthy, seeing and understanding nature is a way of renewing our links with the earth. Here we meet him in the Scottish countryside with Colin Renfrew, head of Cambridge University's Department of Archaeology. The two men discover surprising similarities between their interests in and approaches to nature.

Director/Scenario	17 minutes
Camille Guichard	Color
Narrators/Participants	Age range 7–adult
Andy Goldsworthy	Film $623 Rental $189
Colin Renfrew	VHS $89

---

607   **Snow Dream**

Gigantic Snow Sculpture

Silence, darkness, cold. Three men working wordlessly in the isolation of a snow-covered, mountainous landscape, sawing, cutting and shaping a huge cube of frozen snow. One of the men is French-Canadian sculptor Réal Bérard, the others his assistants. This film allows us to be spectators at the creation of a work of art far from any art gallery or civic square, a work seemingly made for the satisfaction of its creators alone. Extremes of heat and cold, fire and ice, are contrasted in this film: the men warm themselves all through the night at the campfire, even with the cigarettes they light. The monument they sculpt seems to be a synthesis of Eskimo and Aztec styles and imagery – broad faces, schematic birds, zigzag patterns, blocky forms. The film gives us a brief sequence of the finished work existing mysteriously in the world as the musical score picks up the plaintive theme one of the trio has been playing on a mouth organ by the fire. We see the sculpture survive a dramatic electric storm and torrential rain. Then its makers, still wordless, engulf it in a blazing conflagration. Impermanence would seem to be a major theme of this film, impermanence and the elemental forces at work in life and art.

Director/Writer	22 minutes
Claude Grenier	Color
Sculptor	Age range 8–adult
Réal Bérard	Film $623 Rental $189
assisted by	VHS $89
Nick Burns	
Jim Tallosi	
Original music	
Normand Roger	
National Film Board	
of Canada	

---

637   **If Brains Were Dynamite**

The Sculpture of Mark Prent

Hanging like hindquarters in a meat freezer, bloody butchered human torsos and limbs simultaneously rivet and repel viewers of this film's opening footage. Mark Prent is a Canadian artist whose exhibitions always provoke outrage and have resulted in violent reactions and trials for obscenity. They also reveal the latent sadism of a certain section of the public – his *Man Strapped in an Electric Chair* could be 'executed' by pulling a handle to activate the chair, and Canadians were ready to queue for two hours to take a turn. The film illustrates this, but it allows us to enter into the artist's work and understand its personal implications: all these bodies are his own and have been cast in resin during a molding session which comes close to torture. They are then brought to life with frightening, painstaking care and accuracy, painted, given hair or a glass eye. Mark Prent has the support of his father and his wife, but in the absence of buyers he has gone into exile in Berlin. The film examines the relationship between aesthetic and ethical qualities, the Jewish memory, and individual complicity in power and in sadism.

For more information see page 297

Directors	28 minutes
Peter Bors	Color
Thom Burstyn	Age range 18–adult
	Film $693 Rental $199
	VHS $99

---

638   **The Paradise of Cornelius Kolig**

In the Gail Valley, Carinthia, in Austria, Cornelius Kolig has for years been creating his 'paradise', a place where architecture, flowers, pictures and sounds unite to form a synthesis of the arts – a creative 'free space' where artistic activity becomes a sacramental act.

For more information see page 182

Directors	43 minutes
Helga Ripper	Color
Fred Dickermann	Age range 17–adult
Participant	VHS $119
Cornelius Kolig	

Also available in German

639 Submarine

Dreams and Passions of Tom McKendrick

Artist and sculptor Tom McKendrick, whom we watch at work throughout this film, grew up in the shipbuilding town of Clydebank near Glasgow, Scotland. *Submarine* was the name of his multi-media exhibition in Glasgow, and in this documentary he explains his childhood obsession with a device that could 'goe under water unto the bottome and come up again at your plaisure' (as it was described in 1578) and with its development into the deadly weapon of today. The submarine relies on invisibility; it operates by stealth. 'These things are really ugly but that's part of their attraction for me. They're powerful and they're brutal and they're vulnerable at the same time.' Clydebank was almost completely destroyed by bombing in 1941, and McKendrick's artistic vision was shaped by a community scarred physically and emotionally. He left school at fifteen to start work in the world-famous John Brown's shipyard, becoming a 'loftsman', a trade now obsolete, but as the yard experienced its final death-throes, in common with Clydebank shipbuilding as a whole, McKendrick moved on to the Glasgow School of Art. He is now an artist of international importance, with paintings on display all over the world.

'…exceptional quality'
Scotsman, Edinburgh

'An artistic triumph…gives the fleeting impression of other people's lives passing before your eyes'
Glasgow Herald

For more information see page 300

Director	52 minutes
Mark Littlewood	Color
Narrator/Participant	Age range 12–adult
Tom McKendrick	Film $903 Rental $269
Original music	VHS $129
John Russell	
Tom McKendrick	
Awards	
Best Film, Nova Scotia	
Best Portrait, Montreal	

661 Image of Light

The Photography of Sir George Pollock

This film has very little narration, but shows us, close-up, a creative photo-artist at work. 'For me, light is the most exciting thing there is…all life depends on it… it actually is the energy which maintains life on earth. As a maker of images, I feel privileged that photography allows me to use the life-giving energy directly in my work. I want to celebrate the joy of light… the objects that I put in front of my lenses are really only devices for controlling light. In one sequence I developed the idea of light and of the colors of light as creative forces. These forces grow, and they're soon strong enough to form an order…' George Pollock has given 'visual concerts' in Europe, Australia, South Africa and the United States, as well as all over Britain.

Director	16 minutes
Anthony Roland	Color
Original music	Age range 12–adult
Keith Winter	Film $553 Rental $169
Participant	VHS $79
George Pollock	

664 Bernard Faucon: Fables

A Photographer's Use of Eighty-three Window Mannequins

This film describes the world of Bernard Faucon and the story of the mannequins which appeared in his photographs from 1977 to 1981. In 1989, he assembled, restored, dressed and placed them in front of the camera for the last time. On March 22, 1990, the eighty-three mannequins left France for their final retreat, the Nanasai Museum in Kyoto, Japan. Faucon describes his beginnings and his 'encounters' with his mannequins. Over fifty unpublished photographs are presented.

Director/Scenario	44 minutes
Jean Real	Color
Participant	Age range 12–adult
Bernard Faucon	Film $833 Rental $249
Original music	VHS $119
Pierre Boeswilwald	

Also available in French

666 Krzysztof Wodiczko: Projections

Transforming Façades of Buildings into Political, Public Art

The image of a homeless person materializes on a Boston war monument. A swastika suddenly appears on the South African Embassy in London. A city watches skeletal hands play a tuneless dirge on a war museum in Pittsburgh. These are just some of the controversial 'projections' created by Polish artist Krzysztof Wodiczko, who transforms buildings and structures into political, public art. This documentary intercuts scenes of Wodiczko preparing a public projection in Jerusalem in 1991 with other projections in Europe and North America. Each reflects the artist's involvement in a broad range of political issues: a blistering attack in Edinburgh on Margaret Thatcher's economic policies; a reflection on American–Canadian free trade at a Toronto water filtration plant; a street level protest against the problem of homelessness in New York through a controversial prototype mobile shelter. Interestingly, the only site where Wodiczko is denied permission for a projection is Montreal, at the Promenades de la Cathédrale, despite his participation in the city's *Cent Jours d'Art Contemporain*. This innovative film reflects the personal and political aspects of Wodiczko's art.

Director/Scenario	55 minutes
Derek May	Color
National Film Board	Age range 14–adult
of Canada	Film $973 Rental $289
	VHS $139

768 The Seasons

Four Journeys into Raili and Reima Pietilä's Architecture

The Helsinki-based architect Raili Pietilä states that he does not want to deal with truth, in case the truth turns out to be 'a black hole where gravity is too great for anything to exist.' Rather, he seeks to steer around reality through metaphor, and to make buildings which are frameworks in which reality can exist. His highly individual approach to creating a building might involve exploring grammar, the structure of sentences, the narrative method of novels, or the identities of the seasons. He will listen to music in search of a formal 'theme.' He will study landscape, or the effect of wind and snow on water. All these will inform his design, so that the overall experience of a Pietilä environment will be rooted in a source which those who look at or live in it may never guess at. In this film he takes us around a range of his buildings. We see a residential complex set in a birch forest, in which the patterns of tree bark, trunks and foliage provide the motif for the façades. When building a modern city church, the architect's aim is to marry a sense of sanctuary and transcendence with a continued contact with the everyday world, seen through apertures and doorways, in contrast with the enclosed feeling of Gothic cathedrals. Finally, the architect revisits his Finnish Embassy building in India, built with traditional local labor methods, but designed to follow the patterns of Finland's snow-swept landscape. Here he speaks of the detachment any artist can feel for a long-finished work, enclosing a reality as mysterious to its creator as to anyone else who encounters it.

Director/Script Anssi Blomstedt	**35 minutes**
	Color
Original music Arvo Pärt	**Age range 14–adult**
	Film $763 Rental $199
	VHS $109

764 Homage to Humanity

The *Grande Arche* in Paris and its Architect

The *Grande Arche* marking the bicentenary of the French revolution was inaugurated at La Défense in the west of Paris on July 14, 1989. It is situated within the historic axis which includes the Louvre, the Tuileries, the Place de la Concorde, the Champs-Elysées, the Etoile and the Arc de Triomphe. The design, by Danish architect Johan Otto von Spreckelsen, was chosen in a competition initiated by President Mitterrand in 1982. Spreckelsen died in 1987 without seeing his work completed. In this portrait, made between 1983 and 1989, the architect describes his conception of the *Grande Arche,* and other buildings in Denmark. He also speaks of the joys and difficulties of working in Paris, and of his meeting with President Mitterrand, who followed the work's progress with great interest.

In Danish with English subtitles

Director/Scenario/ Narration Dan Tschernia	**45 minutes**
	Color
	Subtitles
Participant	**Age range 15–adult**
Johan Otto von Spreckelsen	**VHS $119**

765 Larsen – Light – Now

An Architect's Style and Approach

A profile of world-renowned Danish architect Henning Larsen. Among his works are the state secondary school of Haut-Taastrup, the municipal library at Gentofte, the Copenhagen School of Economics in Frederiksberg, the University of Trondheim and the Foreign Affairs Ministry in Saudi Arabia. Our impressions of his architecture change with the changing of the light. Larsen did not always want to be an architect. He explains here what motivated his choice of vocation, and defines his style and approach.

In Danish with English subtitles

Director/Scenario Pi Michael	**45 minutes**
	Color
	Subtitles
Participant Henning Larsen	**Age range 15–adult**
	VHS $119

▼ 765
Henning Larsen
Ministry of Foreign Affairs,
Riyadh, Saudi Arabia

Art in the Making

Over the last fifty years the techniques of X-ray and infra-red photography have led to rapid advances in the investigation of paintings, and so have new methods of distinguishing paint layers and analyzing pigments. It is now possible to find out an exhilarating, indeed at times disconcerting, amount about how 'Old Masters' painted. Many of these developments were pioneered in The National Gallery's scientific and conservation departments. The aim of this series is to bring these findings before a wider public and to present the information alongside the paintings themselves.

This series of
3 programs
can be purchased
on VHS for $267
Reference S6

163   **Art in the Making:**
        Italian Painting before 1400

Filmed in Siena and at The National Gallery, London, this video examines the methods and techniques of Tuscan panel paintings of the fourteenth century. Using the detailed instruction in Cennino Cennini's *Libro dell'Arte* (c1397), experts from The National Gallery conservation and framing departments demonstrate the many stages of creating an altarpiece, including making gesso, water gilding, burnishing, pigment grinding, and painting with egg tempera. The demonstrations are linked with paintings by Duccio, Nardo and Jacopo di Cione.

Part of the series *Art in the Making*

Presenter   **20 minutes**
James Heard   **Color**
Audio Visual Unit   **Age range 14–adult**
The National Gallery   **VHS $89**

The following book of the same title gives an extensive overview of the subject – an ideal companion to the video.

164   **Art in the Making:**
Book   **Italian Painting before 1400**

In Italy between 1270 and 1370 the whole tradition of European painting underwent a radical and enduring change of direction. Through their study of The National Gallery's rich holdings of works from the early Renaissance, the authors examine the materials and techniques of painting which effected this transformation. They survey the primarily religious function of the works commissioned, the system of patronage, the operation of painters' guilds and contracts of employment and the organization of workshops. This is followed by a comprehensive and very readable account of panel-painting techniques. The substantial sections on pigments and color represent original research done at the gallery. The book discusses great masterpieces of this period, with full-page color reproductions, cross-sections showing layers of paint and gilding and their composition, X-rays, infra-red photographs and reflectograms.

Authors from   **10.75 x 8.75 inches**
The National Gallery   **273 x 224 mm**
                       236 pages
                       303 illustrations
                       174 in color

                       Book $33

▼ 163
Method of Tuscan panel
painting of the
fourteenth century

◤ 391
Pierre-Auguste Renoir
The Seine at Asnières

296   Art in the Making: Rembrandt

Rembrandt is universally recognized as
an artist of intense feeling, but here less
well-known aspects of the seventeenth-
century Dutch master are revealed.
He was a brilliant craftsman and his
calculated painting methods, studio
organization and ingenious use of certain
pigments, as well as his dramatic use
of thick, impasted color, are all explored
through The National Gallery's own
unrivalled collection.

Part of the series *Art in the Making*

Presenter	**20 minutes**
James Heard	**Color**
	Age range 12–adult
Audio Visual Unit	
The National Gallery	**VHS $89**

The following book of the same title gives
an extensive overview of the subject –
an ideal companion to the video.

297   **Art in the Making: Rembrandt**
Book

The National Gallery's Rembrandts have
a remarkable chronological spread,
representing most of his major concerns
and preoccupations as a mature painter.
This book describes Rembrandt's technical
procedures – how he prepared his canvases
and panels, first laid in the composition,
made alterations on the canvas, and so on –
which enables the authors to make a major
contribution to the controversial issue of
establishing an authentic Rembrandt œuvre.
The book presents an account of the
subject matter of each painting and fully
illustrated technical analyses. There is also
a chronology of Rembrandt's life and
important works; essays on training and
studio practice in the Netherlands, and on
Rembrandt's painting materials and
techniques; a survey of his paint medium;
a glossary and an extensive bibliography.

Authors from	**10.75 x 8.75 inches**
The National Gallery	**273 x 224 mm**
	160 pages
	189 illustrations
	88 in color
	Book $33

391   Art in the Making: Impressionism

A group of pictures in The National Gallery,
London, cleaned to restore the original
brilliant colors and textures, exemplifies
the aims and methods of the Impressionist
painters. This video, filmed on location
in France and England, looks at the
Impressionists' color theories and their
use of newly available pigments, and
demonstrates the ways in which modern
technology made possible the development
of Impressionism.

'This high quality program provides a
focused overview of a significant period
in painting history…well scripted with
high quality photography of the paintings,
lighting that shows the texture of the
paint on the surface, both important
characteristics of this style…recommended
for audiences who are interested in learning
more about how the impact of new
materials and knowledge effect the way
artists paint.'
Video Rating Guide for Libraries, USA

Part of the series *Art in the Making*

Presenter	**22 minutes**
James Heard	**Color**
	Age range 14–adult
Audio Visual Unit	
The National Gallery	**VHS $89** Rental $39

The following book of the same title gives
an extensive overview of the subject –
an ideal companion to the video.

392   **Art in the Making: Impressionism**
Book

While Impressionist art appears to be
effortless and spontaneous, it actually
involves an intricate and varied approach
to painting. This book investigates how
Impressionist paintings were made and
what materials were used. Impressionist
artists came to the fore during a period of
dramatic change in patterns of artistic
training and patronage. The book begins
with an essay that sets their techniques
within the wider context of French
nineteenth-century painting. The authors
discuss such subjects as open-air painting,
the Impressionist use of color, and the
paint layers and surfaces of Impressionist
paintings. Focusing in particular on the
new synthetic pigments that became
available in tubes, the authors show how
this development allowed artists to free
themselves from traditional studio
practice and to render their subject matter
more vividly. Fifteen paintings from
The National Gallery are examined, using
X-rays, infra-red photography, and the
analysis of pigments and paint media.
An analysis of the artists' palette,
a chronology, biographies of the artists
discussed, a glossary and an extensive
bibliography complete this interesting
and valuable work.

Authors from	**10.75 x 8.75 inches**
The National Gallery	**273 x 224 mm**
	228 pages
	316 illustrations
	218 in color
	Book $33

667 Photomontage Today: Peter Kennard

This video examines one particular tendency in the history of photomontage, the analysis of the world in political terms. The film is divided into three sections. The first looks at the effect of layout and juxtaposition on the meaning of images. It highlights the difference between the 'variety show' of a color magazine and the impact of a John Heartfield montage, or the slaughterhouse scene in *The Hour of the Furnaces,* in which individual images are made to interact to produce new meanings. The second section examines the mechanics of photomontage construction, and its ability to say more about reality than a simple photograph. The third section considers possible uses for political photomontage, in campaigns, on posters, in books, newspapers and magazines. The video focuses on the work of British photomontagist Peter Kennard, probably best known for his anti-nuclear stance. In each section Kennard talks about his own practice, and shows how some of his photomontages were conceived, constructed and distributed. The film reveals how photomontage can provide a critique of the reality represented in conventional advertising and the media: by unmasking this mediated view of the world it becomes a political act. Kennard's work is discussed in relation to other photomontagists, such as John Heartfield and Hans Staek who have, in their own ways, used the juxtaposition of images to make political statements. Underlying these practices is the conviction that, in order to use images to change lives, you first have to change the images themselves.

Directors	**35 minutes**
Chris Rodrigues	**Color**
Ron Stoneman	**Age range 14–adult**
Advisors	**VHS $109**
Mike Coker	
John Underwood	
Arts Council of	
Great Britain	

822 Master of Glass

Master of Glass is a documentary about an exceptional craftsman – Per Steen Hebsgaard, the dynamic force behind an amazing development in modern Danish glass. For centuries glass pieces have been joined together with lead alone, and this could only be done in one dimension. Medieval methods are still widely used in works of art made from glass, but Hebsgaard – who, incidentally, began his working life installing double-glazing before moving on to a firm that specialized in stained glass – invented new techniques that avoid the use of lead. Then he began to invite the best Danish and foreign artists to explore all the possibilities inherent in glass, using new or old techniques to create paintings, collages and even sculptures; one of his aims, he says, was to liberate stained glass from being used in churches alone. Hebsgaard's success lies in his ability to inspire and collaborate with other artists, although he himself says 'at a very early stage I realized that I could be number thirty-five as an artist, and I wanted to be number one as a craftsman.' The film concentrates on two projects in particular. One is a large sculpture in glass created by Jan Sivertsen. Together Hebsgaard and Sivertsen use silicone to assemble and erect the fragile material at the FIAC art exhibition in Paris. The second project, with Bjørn Nørgaard, is a 23-foot-high glass pavilion for a Danish brewery, made of more than five thousand pieces of colored and painted glass which are then fired and leaded – a fitting challenge for the 'master of glass.'

Director	**36 minutes**
Peter Christensen	**Color**
Participant	**Age range 14–adult**
Per Steen Hebsgaard	**VHS $109**
Writer	
Nanna Sten Jensen	
Original music	
Niels Hauge	
Also available in Danish	

815 Artists' Techniques

Any work of art is determined first and foremost by the materials available to the artist and his ability to manipulate them. Here we examine five paintings, Gleyre's *Lost Illusions,* Renoir's *La Parisienne,* Manet's *Déjeuner sur l'Herbe,* Monet's *Autumn at Argenteuil,* and Cézanne's *Mountains Seen from L'Estaque,* for the techniques which each artist employed: the application of paint, the use of color, the brushwork and the type of lighting. Only when these technical limitations are taken into account can one begin to understand what the artist's vision really was.

Part of the series *Modern Art and Modernism: Manet to Pollock*

Director	**23 minutes**
Tony Coe	**Color**
Presenter/Writer	**Age range 17–adult**
Dr Anthea Callen	**VHS $89**
Open University/BBC	

▶▶ 667
Peter Kennard
Defended to Death
Photomontage

Draw with Don series

Don Conroy is an Irish author, children's TV presenter and leading wildlife artist, and he has written several children's books. This series focuses on techniques of drawing and painting. Encouraging creativity above all, Don skillfully balances instruction with fun.

See page 274

841	**Making Shapes**
842	**Cartoon Forms**
843	**Coloring Cartoons**
844	**Caricatures**
845	**Pen and Ink Techniques**
846	**Pen and Brush Techniques**
847	**Nature Drawings**
848	**Drawing Animals**
849	**Drawing Birds**
850	**Painting Birds**
851	**Landscape Painting**
852	**Creative Painting**
853	**Creative Drawing**
854	**Poster Lettering**
855	**Poster Drawing**
856	**Making a Collage**
857	**Fun Techniques**
858	**Painting on Stones**
859	**Theme Painting**
860	**Sketching People**
861	**Painting 1**
862	**Painting 2**

This series of 22 programs can be purchased on VHS for $1518
Reference S22

Each part
12 minutes
Color
Age range 5–12
VHS $69

---

820 Enameling

The video starts with a short history of enameling and introduces the subject as a whole. Major techniques are explained such as basse taille, cloisonné, champlevé, plique-à-jour and painted enamel.
The program was shot in the studio of Jane Short, a young English enameler and jeweler who talks us through the design, making and coloring of a piece using a number of techniques. The second part takes the principal stages in greater detail, many of the demonstrations being given by Ros Conway, another English enameler, whose collaboration with Hugh O'Donnell has produced some of the finest work in enamel in the 1980s. The making of a piece is again shown from the preparation of the metal, through the packing to the firings and the final grinding and polishing. The booklet expands on the videos and gives additional information on techniques, the workshop, tools and equipment, materials, water, grinding, acidulation, keeping enamels, color samples, kiln temperatures, packing, laying, keeping a notebook, metals, design, problems and hazards.

'This is a serious, non-slick, instructional production…an excellent teaching tool for an instructor who guides a class through the details. The technical aspects of the program are very good; close-up details of the artist at work are plentiful. There is no information lacking in this thoughtfully produced work. Recommended for public libraries with craft collections.'
Video Rating Guide for Libraries, USA

'The tightness of the text and the filming, the extraordinary deftness of Jane Short, and the dedication of both enamelers to their craft make compulsive viewing. The success of the videos inspires the hope that documentary-makers will take up the challenge. They will find it difficult to better the filming of these techniques.'
Crafts Magazine, London

Director	**Part 1 29 minutes**
Gavin Nettleton	**Part 2 28 minutes**
Writers/Consultants	**Color**
Ros Conway	**Age range 12–adult**
Jane Short	**VHS and booklet $139**

---

830 Etching

This video introduces us to the artist Sandy Sykes, who works from her studio in Essex, England. She also spends some time in Brighton with Terry Gravett developing an etching in a series about dragons. The creation of this work demonstrates a number of techniques, including basic etching, engraving, drypoint, aquatint, and some of Sandy's own processes. We follow these from the initial drawing, through the degreasing, coating of the plate, smoking, tracing, etching and cleaning-off the ground, to the inking and printing of all three plates involved in the production of the final work. The booklet expands on the video.

'…a very good illustration of how an etching develops through its various stages. The individual artist will also find this a very helpful introduction to the craft of etching. At each step we are shown the materials and tools needed, reminded of safety factors, and guided step by step through each phase of the project. This video is a class act. Sykes is knowledgeable and personable. Excellent photography makes it easy to follow the informative and logically structured demonstrations. Liberal use of close-ups further clarify the methods presented…recommended for school, college, and public libraries. As well as providing valuable information for the artist, it will also be of interest as background information on the process of etching to the non-artist.'
Video Rating Guide for Libraries, USA

Director	**40 minutes**
Gavin Nettleton	**Color**
Writers/Consultants	**Age range 12–adult**
Gavin Nettleton	**VHS and booklet $109**
Terry Gravett	

825 Screenprinting

The video concentrates on how screenprints are made, but, like others directed by Gavin Nettleton, it also follows the creation of a work. The artist Jane Sampson talks during the introduction about the medium and explains why she chooses to work with screenprints. The practical topics covered include the basic equipment, stencils, direct photo emulsion, washing and preparing the mesh, applying the emulsion, exposing it in the print down frame with UV light and then washing out the unexposed areas, retouching and printing the next color, inks and bases for printing, racking and removal of the stencil and cleaning the screen. The booklet expands on the video. At the end the artists Brendan Neiland, Harvey Daniels, Sue Gollifer and Terry Gravett discuss why they enjoy making screenprints.

Director	33 minutes
Gavin Nettleton	Color
Writer/Consultant	Age range 12–adult
Harvey Daniels	VHS and booklet $99

827 Lithography

This video-based learning package is a practical guide to the creation of lithographic prints. It is intended for artists wishing to become involved in printmaking and who need to understand the basic principles of lithography. The programme covers both stone and zinc plates and features Harvey Daniels, who was head of the printmaking course at the University of Brighton for many years. He prints simple images off both stone and metal plates. Aspects of lithography covered include the preparation of the stone and plates, graining and 'prepping,' making marks on the surface, etching, gumming, and printing off direct and offset presses. Multicolored printing and the collaboration with a commercial printer are also shown. The accompanying booklet, written by Ann d'Arcy Hughes, expands on the processes shown in the video and offers a useful comparison between those used on plates and on stones.

Director	39 minutes
Gavin Nettleton	Color
	Age range 12–adult
	VHS and booklet $109

835 Stonecarving

This video-based teaching package is intended for those embarking on a sculpture course. It gives an insight into the practicalities of carving stone and the creation of a piece of sculpture, and will also be of interest to anyone studying art. The video follows the creation of a work by Peter Randall-Page commissioned for a major shopping center in Britain. The work commemorates the European Year of the Environment. Peter describes how the stone is quarried, transported and delivered to his studio. We watch the moving and positioning of the stone and how it is roughed out with a variety of hand and power tools. Peter explains how he finds the form within the stone and scales up from the maquette, or model, and how he develops the work using the angle grinder, punches and points, hammers, claw-tools and pneumatic tools. Finally he refines the form and polishes the surface. The video ends with his thoughts on stone and reviews some of his work in this most enduring material. The booklet expands on the video.

'…has strong educational value. Explanations of carving terminology and demonstrations of tool use and safety gear add to the value of this learning experience…suited for college and adult education classes.'
Video Rating Guide for Libraries, USA

Director	43 minutes
Gavin Nettleton	Color
Writer/Consultant	Age range 12–adult
Peter Randall-Page	VHS and booklet $119

▲ 835
Peter Randall-Page
Where the Bee Sucks

37
Archaeology

Archaeology only developed as a true science in the nineteenth century. Prior to that, its roots are in the plunder of wars and conquests, in the exotica amassed by western explorers and, in the eighteenth century, by well-to-do cultural 'tourists' traveling to the Orient or to the Mediterranean in pursuit of an idea of classicism.

This section of 29 programs can be purchased on VHS for $2591

Television rights and prices on request

Archaeology proper developed out of the realization that it was more informative to study objects in their contexts, rather than in isolation, and that, in the earth beneath us, the remains of generations are preserved in successive levels, which can be identified and analyzed through the technique of stratigraphy. What had been an amassing of booty, or an egocentric accumulation of private collections, became the self-effacing vocation of the archaeologist; the names of even the most eminent, such as Sir Leonard Wooley, the great archaeologist of the kingdom of Ur in Sumeria are rarely mentioned.

Many titles in this section deal with the great areas of archaeological discovery: the temples and cities of Egypt, Mesopotamia, the Mediterranean, or the cathedrals, castles, churches and houses of medieval Europe. Others, particularly in the *English Heritage* series (made for young learners, but very worthwhile for their parents and teachers too), open up the principles of archaeology into a broadly creative, fact-gathering attitude to the world all around us. Even our own homes can be studied as 'historic' sites...

◀◀ 40B
Persepolis, Iran
Northern staircase of the
Central Palace, detail

▲ 40B
*The Archers of
Darius the Great*, detail
Enamelled bricks

Film and Video Series

This section gives summary information about the series offered by the Roland Collection: twenty-nine series on art and architecture, and four on modern literature and philosophy. A thumb-nail sketch of each series is followed by page references to the full catalog entries for individual programs.

It also includes profiles of three key producers, which give fascinating insights into how their films are made and the thinking behind their work.

S1 Ancient Cultures of Mesopotamia

The earliest beginnings of western civilization, five thousand years ago in Mesopotamia, are explored in these films shot on location in present-day Iraq. Spectacular images of ancient sites and museum treasures reveal the Sumerian kingdom of Ur, the fortress-temple town of Hatra and the legendary city of Babylon; one film focuses on the Assyrian era through the life of King Assurnasirpal, and another follows the story of Islamic architecture.

See pages 20–1
5 programs
25 minutes each
Film $4950*
VHS $495

S2 The Art of Mexico

Mexican art from its dawning to the twentieth century. The first two programs look at several pre-Columbian cultures in different areas of Mesoamerica, showing how views of the universe were expressed in the art and architecture. The third describes events after the Spanish conquest and the evangelization, asking how far the indigenous and western traditions became integrated. The last shows how the country reacted to the artistic movements of the nineteenth and twentieth centuries, and how the War of Independence and the revolution infused so much of Mexican art with an enduring nationalism.

See pages 27, 60, 83
4 programs
56 minutes each
VHS $556

S3 Mexico through the Eyes of Octavio Paz

Visiting an Aztec shrine near his childhood home came as a revelation to Octavio Paz, the writer and presenter of this series on Mexican art. In the earliest program he guides us around sights such as the great pyramids of Tenayuca, Chichén-Itzá and the Coatlicue colossal figure in Mexico City, explaining the complex cosmology of the Aztecs. In later programs he introduces us to the little-known masters of nineteenth-century Mexican painting, and the more widely appreciated post-revolutionary Muralist movement. The final program focuses on contemporary Mexican painters, showing them at work in their studios and discussing what they owe to their Central American heritage.

See pages 27, 83, 107, 167
4 programs
56 minutes each
VHS $556

S4 French Romanesque

Each of these six films visits a different area of France and looks at the variety of architecture to be found there around a thousand years ago, exploring not only the buildings themselves but also the religious beliefs that gave rise to the creations of this fascinating epoch.

See pages 32–3
6 programs
26 minutes each
Film $5940*
VHS $594

S5 The National Gallery – A Private View

Using the virtually unrivaled holdings of western painting in The National Gallery, London, the story of European art is presented from its beginnings until the rise of Modernism. With films such as *Baroque Painting in France and Italy*, *The Age of Rembrandt* and *The Northern Renaissance*, all the major threads in this immense tapestry are presented in their true colors.

See pages
37, 41–3, 49, 55,
59–61, 75, 78, 305
12 programs
28 minutes each
Film $11880*
VHS $1188

S6 Art in the Making

How exactly were 'Old Masters' produced? This series from The National Gallery, London, examines methods used in Italy before 1400 and by Rembrandt and the Impressionists, concentrating on the actual techniques of the artists. X-ray and infra-red photography have made it possible to distinguish paint layers and analyze pigments as never before; these videos not only demonstrate the techniques of painting but relate them to the kind of expressive purpose required in each case.

See pages 320–1
3 programs
20 to 22 minutes
VHS $267

S7 The Genius of Flemish Painting

Focusing on the major figures – the Van Eycks, Bruegel and Rubens – this series examines the achievements of Flemish painting across two centuries, from the staggering perfection of the Van Eycks' *Adoration of the Lamb* to the Baroque style of Rubens.

See pages 38, 51, 59
6 programs
50 to 55 minutes
VHS $834

S8 Culture and Belief in Europe 1450–1600

This comprehensive series examines the relationship between religion, art and society: how did these elements affect each other in different parts of the continent and how were they related to the political and economic issues of the day? The viewer is swept from the Suleimaniye in Istanbul to the Escorial outside Madrid, from Strasbourg to Shropshire, from Venice and Antwerp to Fontainebleau and Rome.

See pages
45–7, 49, 50–2
13 programs
24 to 25 minutes
VHS $1287

* Revised price

S9   Kenneth Clark Rembrandt series

Five highly acclaimed films which reveal the character of Rembrandt, often called the greatest artist who ever lived. They follow the course of his genius from his early, rebellious period through his successful middle age to the isolation of his late maturity. Kenneth Clark, the illustrious writer and narrator of this series, devotes the whole of the last film to Rembrandt's work as an illustrator of the Bible, which made him, some say, 'the only great Protestant artist.'

See page 57   5 programs
                            30 minutes each
                            Film $4950*

S10   The Age of Baroque

This series investigates the varied manifestations of the Baroque ideal, from intense theatricality and concern with the grotesque to a more reflective style. The diversity of these ideas is reflected in their geographical range, with the more flamboyant examples occurring predominantly in the south. The series traces the spread of the Baroque across western Europe, and to Latin America, Russia and colonial India.

See pages 63–5   6 programs
                            60 minutes each
                            Film $9540*
                            VHS $954

S11   The Enlightenment

This absorbing subject is explored through studies of painters such as Chardin and Hogarth and architect-designers like Robert Adam, as well as on a more general level, considering attitudes to nature, the relationship between poetry and landscape painting, or what family life was like in a French château during the Age of Reason.

See pages 68–71B   16 programs
                            23 to 25 minutes
                            VHS $1584

S12   Culture and Society in Britain 1850–90

Ten fascinating studies of Victorian art and architecture, seen in the context of the society from which it sprang. Public, private and religious buildings, such as Manchester Town Hall, the artists' houses in London's Melbury Road, Anglo-Catholic churches and Dissenting chapels, are scrutinized for the light they shed on the lives of those who owned and used them.

See pages 85–9   10 programs
                            25 minutes each
                            VHS $990

S13   Painters to the People

Rediscovered and fashionable once more, like other things Victorian, the painting of that era has always intrigued the writer and art historian Christopher Wood. His first, secret love was for the magic of the Pre-Raphaelites, but other films in the series concentrate on the realist visions of men like Fildes, Holl and Herkomer, on artists like Alma-Tadema who dreamed of ancient Greece and Rome, and others who took up the challenge of the French Impressionists. This is a comprehensive survey of a huge subject, filled with little-known delights.

See pages 90–1   6 programs
                            26 minutes each
                            VHS $594

S14   La Grande Epoque

Before it was dramatically curtailed by the blow that fell on Europe in 1914, Art Nouveau spread across the continent and beyond. These films explore the aesthetic and social factors that caused the restless 'new style' to be adopted with such vigor from Vienna to Mexico City, from Paris to Cape Town. A rich and varied survey of a rich and varied movement and its leading personalities, including composers like Mahler and Debussy, as well as architects, designers and painters.

See pages 102–3   4 programs
                            60 minutes each
                            Film $6360*
                            VHS $636

S15   Western Art 1700–1970

Taking the year 1700 as the point at which western art truly began to diversify, the series provides a broad outline of this complex subject, making it an excellent general introduction for younger audiences.

See pages   4 programs
75, 99, 145, 154   19 to 26 minutes
                            Film $3860*
                            VHS $386

S16   Modern Art and Modernism:
           Manet to Pollock

This series charts the amazing course of Modernism, beginning with Manet and the other Impressionists. Some films are devoted to individual masters such as Monet, Beckmann and Duchamp, while others deal with movements like Surrealism and Cubism which forcibly broke the mold of tradition. The texture of the series is enriched with studies of the artists' techniques and the social and critical milieu against which their often heroic advances were achieved.

See pages   16 programs
94–6, 98–9, 112, 114,   24 to 25 minutes
119, 121, 126, 131,   VHS $1584
142–3, 150, 302

S17   The Adventure of Modern Art

Starting with the explosion of Fauvism, this series takes us through many of the more challenging manifestations of the modern movement. It traces the progress of Abstraction and the innovations of the Cubists and Surrealists, and also covers more recent developments such as Pop and the diverse ways in which many contemporary artists have sought to define reality.

See pages   13 programs
98, 107, 113–5,   53 minutes each
119, 123, 130–1, 139,   Film $19370*
151, 167, 177–8   VHS $1937

History of Architecture and Design 1890–1939

The first video attempts to define the rôle of the architect by portraying the thoughts of Geoffrey Baker as he designs and builds his own house. Thereafter, the series surveys the progress of Modernism, incorporating studies of such key figures as Le Corbusier, Lloyd Wright and Mackintosh, looking at individual buildings to highlight their achievements. Other videos are more general in scope, covering topics such as suburban style, English furniture, and the problems of building contemporary mass housing.

See pages 188–93   23 programs
25 minutes each

VHS $2227

S19   **Modern Art, Practices and Debates**

The many controversies to which the modern movement has given birth are reflected in this long and varied series. Aesthetic subjects such as the theories and techniques of Impressionism or the expressive nature of Matisse's work stand alongside more polemical inquiries into feminism in art, the meaning of art criticism (in an interview with Clement Greenberg) or the effect of left-wing politics on the art of 1960s America.

See pages   21 programs
80, 83A, 95, 97–8,   25 minutes each
114, 119, 124, 130,   VHS $2079
141, 151A–B, 198,
263B, 307A–B

S20   **Comics – The Ninth Art**

These programs trace the astonishing rise of the comic from 1900 to the present day, investigating the ways in which comics can mirror the times around them as well as fulfilling their rôle as vehicles of fantasy. The final program, entitled *What's Next?*, looks at how new publishing technology will develop this fascinating medium in the future.

See pages 246–50   13 programs
28 minutes each

VHS $1287

S21   **Great Artists in the World of Comics**

A wide-ranging exploration of the work of some of the top creators of comic design past and present, chosen from all over the world, which demonstrates the high level of expression attainable in this form. From the political to the erotic to the purely aesthetic, the series leaves the viewer in no doubt about the amazing talents of these artists, each of whom is profiled in a separate program.

See pages 251–3   13 programs
28 minutes each

VHS $1287

S22   **Draw with Don**

A wonderful series for children. Irish wildlife artist Don Conroy demonstrates different techniques for painting and drawing subjects from landscapes and animals to cartoons and posters. Every program seeks to extend the young artist's creativity, balancing the required discipline with a keen sense of fun.

See page 274   22 programs
12 minutes each

VHS $1518

S26   **Architectural Adventures**

This series studies the ways in which people outside the mainstream have tried to broaden the possibilities of architecture. One program profiles a school which teaches do-it-yourself house building. Another describes people who have broken new ground in building – for example, a Texan sculptor who spent ten years welding a 'house of steel' – and the third ponders the creative alternatives that will be available to architects in the future, such as a home entirely controlled by a 'house-brain,' or a colony on the moon.

See page 203   3 programs
44 minutes each

VHS $357

S27   **The Moscow Kremlin**

This series takes an in-depth look at the ancient seat of the Tsars, following the progress of its buildings from wooden fort to the red-brick structure that we know today. And the viewer is also guided around the fabulous treasures the Kremlin contains, such as staggering collections of jewelry, metalwork, arms and armor, enameled miniatures and ceremonial crowns.

See page 306   3 programs
30 minutes each

VHS $297

S28   **The Beautiful City of Moscow**

The amazing architectural and cultural history of Moscow, from the construction of major churches and palaces in the time of Ivan the Terrible, through the development in the eighteenth and nineteenth centuries of country estates, which are now islands of quiet surrounded by the city, to the early twentieth century, a period of great architectural transition and complexity.

See pages   4 programs
53, 72, 75, 104   30 minutes each

VHS $396

S29   **Archaeological Detectives**

Intended for children, these three programs are filled with ingenious ways to stimulate their interest in archaeology. Rôle-playing 'detective' games, examining mystery objects and visiting different kinds of modern houses to guess what sort of people live there are only some of the methods used in preparing young people for field trips to ancient sites to observe and record evidence of the past. For class and individual viewing.

See page 275   3 programs
12, 14 and 33 minutes

VHS $257

S30 Evidence on Site

An educational series which gives an all-round introduction to the study of the past through the investigation of historic sites. Subjects include a group of young people visiting archaeologists at Maiden Castle, Dorset, England, who suddenly find themselves transported back into a 're-created' past; a discussion of the best place to build a medieval castle; and methods of discovering what the day-to-day life of monks in Rievaulx Abbey, North Yorkshire, would have been like.

See pages 276–7   6 programs
                        10 to 24 minutes
                        VHS $484

S31 Frameworks of Worship

What can be learned from the physical evidence that remains today about what religious life was like in the past? In this series all kinds of church buildings, from cathedrals to graveyards, are examined, clearly demonstrating the fascinating ways in which the archaeologist can piece together historical information about any kind of site.

See pages 278–9   5 programs
                        18 to 23 minutes
                        VHS $455

S32 Looking at...

Stonehenge and less well-known prehistoric sites, a medieval castle and a Cistercian abbey are investigated in these three programs. The series forms a useful guide to employing the 'detective' techniques of archaeology on any ancient site, to find out what social structures may have given it that form and no other.

See pages 280–1   3 programs
                        14, 17 and 20 minutes
                        VHS $257

S40 Literature in the Modern World

Focusing on a wide range of challenging literary texts, this series examines the forces that have shaped twentieth-century English literature: modernism, post-colonialism and cultural images of gender are discussed in relation to novels, poetry and plays.

See pages 388–9   14 programs
                        24 to 90 minutes
                        VHS $1386

S41 Writers Talk: Ideas of Our Time

Produced by the Institute of Contemporary Arts, London, this series constitutes a unique literary resource, which reflects the diversity of English-language writing today. Each program features a well-known writer talking with another writer or critic – Isabel Allende in conversation with Marina Warner, Edward Said with Salman Rushdie, Toni Morrison with AS Byatt... Friends and professionals, writing in many different genres, get to the heart of their lives and work.

See pages 376–85   106 programs
                        25 to 61 minutes
                        VHS $8374

S42 Writers on Writing: Creative Writing Course

A six-part course in video and print for teachers of English and students aged fifteen and over, based on edited conversations between writers at the Institute of Contemporary Arts, London. The videos and study guide with forty-eight task sheets provide source material on the writing process, including methods, themes, language, genre and form; supporting material for course work or independent study; and insight into the work of contemporary writers ranging from Maya Angelou to Harold Pinter and Maurice Sendak.

See pages 386   6 programs and
                        104-page booklet
                        20 to 28 minutes
                        VHS $594

S43 Spirit of Freedom

A spectacular four-part documentary by the eminent writer and thinker Bernard-Henri Levy, exploring twentieth-century history and the part played by intellectuals – writers, poets, artists and scientists who have espoused the causes of freedom and revolution, from Emile Zola to Jean-Paul Sartre and Fidel Castro. The Dreyfuss Affair, the Bolshevik Revolution, the rise of Fascism, Stalinism and Nazism, the turbulent 1960s, the Cultural Revolution in China, the Vietnam War and Third-World rebellions – all are brought vibrantly to life.

See page 387   4 programs
                        52 minutes each
                        VHS $596

English Heritage

English Heritage is a national public body, appointed by the government, responsible for the conservation of England's architectural and archaeological heritage. It is actively concerned with the preservation of the monuments, sites and landscapes of the 'historic environment.' In addition to looking after such places itself, it makes grants to individual property owners, and also makes grants for the excavation of sites under threat, like the Roman town of Heybridge in Essex, recently facing 'redevelopment.' In the production of films and other educational materials on the historic environment English Heritage is foremost in Britain, and probably in Europe, seeing this as part of the service it was set up to provide.

Most of its films are made for five- to sixteen-year-olds or their teachers. Some films, such as the *Archaeological Detectives* series, are aimed directly at children, although teachers should watch them too. Films which look at individual sites, like *Grimes Graves* or *Dover Castle: The Key to England*, are meant to be viewed by children either as an introduction to the site or during follow-up work. Lately, however, English Heritage has concentrated mainly on teacher-training films, to be used either in training colleges or during in-service training, showing how the historic environment can be used as a resource for all main school subjects, not just history.

Mike Corbishley is executive producer of many of English Heritage's films, and presenter of several. He was an archaeologist and a teacher for twenty years himself, and has strong views on what can go wrong when an expert in any field tries to collaborate with a film-maker. Either the expert has script control, he says, in which case the script is likely to be too dense and the film too tightly packed with images, or the film-maker takes over and makes what he considers a good film ('that's a lovely shot') at the expense of its aim or subject. Although Mike believes it is important not to interfere with the creative process flowing between director, crew and participants in a film, he is always present during the filming, much of the editing and the final edit of the film, to guard against both these pitfalls.

His favorite of all the films he's made, and it's included in the Roland Collection, is *Clues Challenge*. 'It takes a simple idea,' he says, 'that archaeologists have to work like detectives: when they're looking at ancient structures, they have to use their own experience and their common sense to make deductions from what they see. As a teacher, I used to invent activities for pupils that would show them what that meant, using their own everyday environment. So, the kids in the film are taken first to a modern house, left as if the family who lives there has just gone out shopping, and asked what it tells them. Do children live here, how old are they, have they got animals? OK, we say, that was easy. Now, here's an empty house – a bit harder. What was this room used for? The lino here is a different color, they must have had furniture standing over it. There was a television in this room, there's the socket. Finally, we take them to a building site, and show them just the foundations of a house. How many rooms is it going to have, where will the stairs be, is there a garage? And then they and the children watching realize that this is what archaeologists *do*. They start at this end – with the foundations.

'I especially like this film because it puts a simple idea across so clearly. It's even been used in universities, by professors with undergraduate archaeology students.'

The children in English Heritage films are not actors, and it's easy for child viewers to identify with them. They are chosen from screen tests held at ordinary schools, or a whole group of real pupils are featured, doing a real project. 'We say to the teacher, we want to make a film about, say, maths, or technology, and the historic environment. So, *you* devise a strategy using a castle, for example, and we'll film you, and at the end you'll have a proper project and we'll have a film. It's one of our principles – we show real work, not just bits of action staged for the camera.'

The National Gallery

Staff at the Audio Visual Unit:
Jacquie Footer
Joan Lane
Marcus Latham
Carol McFadyen

Video, an increasingly important educational medium both in the home and in the classroom, is particularly useful in the study of paintings. The National Gallery is unique among British national museums and galleries in having its own video production unit, which, with its unlimited access to original paintings from every period, is able to film details unnoticed even to gallery visitors. The unit draws on the art-historical and technical expertise of National Gallery staff, and thus can present the latest results of scholarship or the scientific examination of important pictures, and illustrate a variety of Old Master techniques.

Since the late 1980s, the Audio Visual Unit has been making videos related to the permanent collection or to temporary exhibitions. However, all the National Gallery videos stand alone as introductions to their subjects. The unit does not wait until an exhibition is in place before beginning to film: they begin work months or even years ahead of its arrival. First a script is commissioned, perhaps from the National Gallery's curator of the exhibition or from the outside consultant who is selecting works for the exhibition and preparing its catalog. The unit and author work on this draft script before setting off on location. With *Manet: The Heroism of Modern Life*, for example, the footage shot on location documents Manet's visit to Spain, complementing the exhibition by giving a new angle on its theme and resulting in a film which can be shown alongside it and have an independent life after the exhibition ends. In *An Eye for Detail*, buildings that are still standing today are compared with their portrayal in Early Netherlandish paintings. *The Queen's Pictures* includes location shots at Hampton Court Palace, Windsor Castle, Osborne House, Kensington Palace and the Banqueting House, Whitehall, London.

When examining a painting in detail, as Joan Lane, head of the unit, explains, it is necessary to film the painting itself, not a transparency. Texture, depth and surface cannot be examined properly at one remove, and to make a precise art-historical point, a study of a tiny detail like the hands or nose in a portrait might be

vital. So if the painting is not in the gallery, the unit visits it 'at home.' On discovering that the technical and creative processes of painting were not a subject much explored by other film-makers, the Unit went ahead with the *Art in the Making* series, which investigates pre-1400 paintings, Old Masters and Impressionist works using X-rays, infra-red photography and other techniques pioneered in the gallery's scientific and conservation departments.

The question of who should present films like these is a thorny one. Joan Lane believes that curators or other experts on the subject of the film usually do the job best, even though they are not front-of-camera professionals. 'Actors can't always get the right inflection or convey real authority,' she says. 'A lot of glossy productions are based round celebrity presenters. Ours are based round the works of art. We find voice-overs are less distracting.'

The production staff of the unit, at present four people, are able to work with enormous flexibility and unique experience of art gallery requirements to cover a range of projects from unstructured filming for archival purposes to full broadcast-quality programs.

One of the National Gallery videos, *Art in the Making: Italian Painting before 1400*, received the Small Unit Award from the British Educational Television Association in 1991. Two others, *Constable: The Changing Face of Nature* (in collaboration with the Tate Gallery) and *The Queen's Pictures*, were selected for showing at the Montreal Film Festival in 1992 and 1993 respectively. Through the Roland Collection, the videos are seen frequently at international exhibitions, for instance in Munich in July 1993. And they are highly praised by critics – the *Video Rating Guide for Libraries* described *The Queen's Pictures*, to take one example, as 'glorious and authoritative.'

Three series producers The National Gallery

335

Open University

The Open University was set up in Britain twenty-five years ago, in partnership with the British Broadcasting Corporation, to pioneer the system of open and distance learning for adults that is so well known today. Since then open universities round the world have modelled themselves on it, with the help of British OU advisers. Television programs are an integral part of the sophisticated learning system by which students study at home. These are made by the BBC, which provides production, operational, engineering and support facilities at the OU's Production Centre, in cooperation with the university's academic staff.

About 200,000 students are registered at any one time for undergraduate, postgraduate and continuing education courses. But in addition to the OU's 'official' students, the BBC estimates that six to eight million people watch the OU's broadcasts every week. The university is required by its charter to promote the educational well-being of the wider community, and research shows that a large percentage of students who enrol were originally members of this 'drop-in' audience, attracted by the popular appeal of so many of the programs.

'Of course we want the programs we make to be accessible to the general public,' says Charles Cooper, producer of several OU series, such as *Culture and Belief in Europe 1450–1600*. 'It's part of our brief – otherwise, we wouldn't be an *open* university. And I get a lot of letters from the public about my programs as feedback!'

All the producers of OU programs are academically well qualified, many being subject specialists in their own right, and are full members of university faculties. Charles Cooper trained first as an art historian, but even as an undergraduate he had a great love for film. 'Painting and film, they're both image-making,' he says.

The production of an Open University course can take two or three years to complete. OU producers play a vital rôle in advising the course team on the best way to convey the educational concepts through the medium of television.

'Our programs bring together disciplines which aren't normally associated, like literature, history of art, music,' says Charles Cooper. 'That's rare in higher education, and we may have as many as forty-five experts pooling their expertise on a series.' Among the production staff at the OU Production Centre is a wide spread of scientists, mathematicians, technologists, social scientists, educationalists and specialists in the humanities, trained to work to BBC standards on all programs.

Back in the 1970s, everyone's image of an OU program was of a bearded man in a dreadful shirt standing in front of a blackboard: an attempt to transfer the lecture room to the student's home. But nowadays that's entirely out of date – the film *Educating Rita* did a lot to show the OU in a different light! Program production techniques have long since moved away from studio-based material towards location work. 'We like to go on location, especially to places our students are unlikely to be able to visit,' says Charles Cooper. 'To go somewhere like Seville or Toulouse, so that they can see for themselves what they look like – three minutes of location footage can tell a hundred times more about the atmosphere or sense of scale than ten or twelve flat photographs. It's surrogate experience.'

When it comes to presenters, he believes (in common with Joan Lane of The National Gallery, London) that 'real people' – enthusiastic experts who are amateurs in front of the camera – convey love and knowledge of a subject better than professional presenters. They're not all OU academics, though. 'When we went to Istanbul (for *Ottoman Supremacy: The Suleimaniye*) we were very lucky to get Godfrey Goodwin, the author and art historian who is a world authority on Ottoman architecture. He almost single-handedly began the active research into it, and he was working at the university in Istanbul at the time. If we haven't got a homegrown expert on any subject, we go out and find the very best person for the job.'

Indexes

The catalog entries for the films and videos on art and architecture have been comprehensively indexed to help you find the programs you need as quickly and easily as possible.

The General Index lists every production under its title. It also has entries for people featured in the programs, including artists, architects and many historical figures; for countries and place names; and for foreign language versions. Other entries group together productions that deal with a particular art form, such as painting, photography or ceramics, or with art movements and styles, such as Art Nouveau or Biedermier. Subject entries cater for all interests, from 'animals in art,' 'archaeology' and 'art therapy' to 'urban studies,' 'war' and 'women in art.'

This section also lists country of origin and production dates for all Roland Collection titles.

The Key to the Collection gives a chronological listing of films and videos on art and architecture (see pages 412–29); it also lists Roland Collection videos on modern literature by author (pages 430–32) and by title (page 433).

General index

- Film and video titles are in bold type
- Catalog numbers are in large type
- Page numbers are in small type
- Where titles appear more than once in the catalog, the text of the catalog entry is fully indexed on the first appearance only

1900 782 104 247

A

Aalto, Alvar
    Alvar Aalto 763 199 264
    also featured in 553 154
abbeys see monasteries
Abstract Expressionism 554 114 131
Abstraction
    Abstract Expressionism 554 114 131
    Abstraction 497 123 137
    Abstraction: The Experience 503D 115 131
    American Abstraction 503C 114 130 285
    also featured in 498 124, 500 125, 501–2 124,
        503 128, 516 128, 518 126, 527 150,
        528 126, 553 154, 581 177, 590 129,
        595 129, 598 130
Action Painting 503C 285, 553 154
Adam, Robert
    The Hand of Adam 339 72
    Kedleston Hall (Robert Adam) 328 71B
Adam-Tessier, Maxim, **The Genesis of a Sculpture**
    630 164 271 317
Adami, Valerio 601 167
Adams, George 707 134
Adler, Kathleen, **Berthe Morisot: An Interview
    with Kathleen Adler** 417 98
Adolf Loos 711 190
The Adventure: Artists on Art 584 178
The Adventure Begins 784 248
The Adventure of Modern Art series
    Abstraction 497 123 137
    Abstraction: The Experience 503D 115 131
    The Adventure: Artists on Art 584 178
    American Abstraction 503C 114 130 285
    Contemporaries – The Quest for Reality
        601 167
    Contemporary Expression 512B 113
    Cubism 521 119
    Expressionism 504 107
    Fauvism 426 98 213
    New Realities 541 151
    Pop Art: The Test of the Object 581 177
    The Sixties: The Art in Question 582 177
    Surrealism 561 139 288
Adventures in Perception 594 170 242 270
AEG turbine factory 703 189
An Affirmation of Life 767 201 264
African art and architecture
    The Colonial Encounter 87 25
    Of Leaves and of Earth 88 25
    The Shape of Darkness 85A/B 25
    Tassili N'Ajjer 10 15
**After the Fire: The Restoration of Hampton
    Court Palace** 494 313

The Age of Baroque series 314–19 63–5
The Age of Leonardo and Raphael 225 43
The Age of Rembrandt 295 55
The Age of Rubens 275 59
The Age of Titian 223 42
Ahrends, Burton and Koralek 760 197
Aillaud, Gilles 601 167
Albers, Joseph 503D 115
Albert, Prince Consort of England 372 86, 376 89
The Albert Memorial 372 86
Alechinsky, Pierre 512B 113, 973 170
Alehjadino 317 65
Alembert, Jean d' 322 71A
Alexander the Great 40A/B 19
Algeria 87 25
All the World on Stage 314 63
Alma-Tadema, Sir Lawrence 385 91
Alsace, **Romanesque Architecture of Alsace**
    111 32 310
Altuna, Horacio, **Altuna** 804 252
Alvar Aalto 763 199 264
Ambleside, Merz-bau 563–563A 141
America
    pre-Columbian 90–3 27, 95 27
    see also Canada, Latin America, United States
American Abstraction 503C 114 130 285
American Indians 609 180 261
Amersham, 'High and Over' 714 192
Amsterdam, public-sector housing 761 197
ancient civilizations see Egypt, Etruscan tombs,
    Greek art and architecture, Hittites, Indonesia,
    Mesopotamia, Roman art and architecture,
    Sassanian art and architecture
Ancient Cultures of Mesopotamia series
    21–5 20–1
And They Sang a New Song 125 34
**Angelica Kauffmann, RA, and the Choice of
    Painting** 333A 71B
Angelico, Fra
    Fra Angelico 180 41 229
    also featured in 179 41
Anglican church, Anglo-Catholicism
    see Church of England
animals in art
    Constable: The Leaping Horse 356 76
    Delacroix 370 225
    Drawing Animals 848 274
    Franz Marc 498 124
    George Stubbs 338 225
    Innocents: Images in Hogarth's Painting
        335 71
    Picasso: Romancero du Picador 530 225
    Tassili N'Ajjer 10 225
animated films
    The Genesis of a Sculpture 630 271
    Kindness Week (Max Ernst) 570 140
    The Man with Modern Nerves 730 194

The Roland Collection　　　■ Film and video titles are in bold type　　■ Catalog numbers are in large type　　■ Page numbers are in small type

The Roland Collection

353

Index of film and video titles

- Film and video catalog numbers are in large type
- Page numbers are in small type

For chronological listing of titles by catalog number see pages 412–29

■ Film and video catalog numbers are in large type   ■ Page numbers are in small type

■ Film and video catalog numbers are in large type   ■ Page numbers are in small type

Index of directors

Index of Scriptwriters

- Film and video catalog numbers are in large type

- Page numbers are in small type

Index of narrators and presenters

- Film and video catalog numbers are in large type
- Page numbers are in small type

Index of composers of commissioned music

- Film and video catalog numbers are in large type
- Page numbers are in small type

Index of awards

- Film and video catalog numbers are in large type

- Page numbers are in small type

Catalog number	Page number	Country of origin	Year of production	Roland film release	Roland video release / Rerelease (r)
10	15	France	1962	1968	1986
13	15	Britain	1982		1993
14	15	Britain	1988		1993
16	17	Britain	1987		1993
20	17	France	1963	1968	1986
21	20	Finland	1988	1995	1993
22	20	Finland	1988	1995	1993
23	21	Finland	1988	1995	1993
24	21	Finland	1988	1995	1993
25	21	Finland	1988	1995	1993
27	22	Indonesia/Netherlands	1983	1994	1993
30	30	France	1965	1968	1986
40A	19	Germany	1963	1968	1986
40B	19	Germany	1963	1968	1986
50	22	France	1957	1968	1986
70	23	Italy	1957	1968	1986
80	23	Italy	1958	1968	1986
85A	25	France	1966	1968	1986
85B	25	France	1966	1968	1986
87	25	Britain	1993		1995
88	25	France	1989	1994	1993
90	27	Germany	1959	1968	1986
91	27	Mexico	1989		1996
92	27	Mexico	1990		1993
93	27	Mexico	1990		1993
95	27	Mexico	1962	1968	1986
98	29	Britain	1975	1994 r	1994 r
99A	29	Britain	1980		1993
99B	30	Britain	1989		1993
100	30	France	1956	1968	1986
110	30	France	1958	1968	1986
111	32	France	1989	1995	1994
112	32	France	1989	1995	1994
113	33	France	1989	1995	1994
114	33	France	1989	1995	1994
115	33	France	1989	1995	1994
116	33	France	1989	1995	1994
117	31	France	1990	1995	1995
118	31	Britain	1982		1993
119	31	Britain	1984		1993
120	34	Italy	1955	1968	1986
123	34	Austria	1988		1995
125	34	USA	1987		1993
130	34	France	1961	1968	1986
136	35	Britain	1991		1993
137	35	Britain	1980		1993
138	35	Britain	1988		1993
140	36	France	1964	1968	1986
150	36	France	1955	1968	1986
160	36	Italy	1963	1968	1986
163	37	Britain	1989		1992
165	37	Britain	1975	1977	1986
170	38	France	1963	1968	1986
171	38	Britain	1992		1994
173	38	Belgium	1990		1992
174	38	Belgium	1990		1992
175	39	France	1963	1968	1986
176	39	Britain	1990		1993
178	39	Czech Republic	1966	1968	1986
179	41	Britain	1975	1977	1986
180	41	Italy	1955	1968	1986
200	41	Italy	1954	1968	1986
205	49	Britain	1975	1977	1986
210	41	France	1963	1968	1986
215	42	Italy	1991		1995
220	42	Italy	1961	1968	1986
223	42	Britain	1975	1977	1986
225	43	Britain	1975	1977	1986
226	43	Britain	1990		1992
230A	44	Italy	1964	1968	1986
230B	44	Italy	1964	1968	1986
232	45	Austria	1987		1995
233	45	Britain	1991		1993
236	49	Britain	1991		1993
237	49	Britain	1991		1993
238	50	Britain	1991		1993
240	50	Germany	1964	1968	1986
242	50	Britain	1991		1993
244	51	Belgium	1991		1992
245	51	Belgium	1991		1992
246	51	Britain	1991		1993
252	46	Britain	1991		1993
254	46	Britain	1991		1993
256	46	Britain	1991		1993
259	47	France	1991	1996	1996
260	47	Britain	1991		1993
261	47	Britain	1991		1993
265	52	Britain	1991		1993
266	52	Britain	1991		1993
267	52	Britain	1991		1993
269	53	Russia	1991		1996
270	53	Slovakia	1963	1968	1986
271	53	Germany	1982		1996
273	59	Belgium	1991		1992
274	59	Belgium	1991		1992
275	59	Britain	1975	1977	1986
289	60	Netherlands	1963	1992 r	1992 r
290	60	Germany	1956	1968	1986
295	55	Britain	1975	1977	1986
296	55	Britain	1990		1992
298	56	Britain	1992		1993
300	56	France	1964	1964	1986
301	57	Britain	1974	1977	
302	57	Britain	1974	1977	
303	57	Britain	1974	1977	
304	57	Britain	1974	1977	
305	57	Britain	1974	1977	
306	60	Mexico	1990		1996
307	60	Britain	1975	1977	1986
309	61	Britain	1975	1977	1986
309A	61	Britain	1994		1994
310	61	Czech Republic	1965	1968	1986
311	66	Britain	1991		1993
312	276	Britain	1990		1993
313	279	Britain	1989		1993
314	63	France/Germany/Italy	1982	1996	1993
315	63	France/Germany/Italy	1982	1996	1993
316	64	France/Germany/Italy	1982	1996	1993
317	65	France/Italy/Germany	1982	1996	1993
318	65	France/Italy/Germany	1982	1996	1993
319	65	France/Italy/Germany	1982	1996	1993
320	67	France	1966	1968	1986
322	71A	Britain	1993		1995
323	68	Britain	1980		1993
324	71A	Britain	1991		1995
325	68	Britain	1980		1993
326	71A	Britain	1993		1995
327	71A	Britain	1993		1995
328	71B	Britain	1993		1995
329	71B	Britain	1993		1995
330	67	Germany	1953	1968	1986
333	68	Britain	1980		1995
333A	71B	Britain	1993		1995
334	69	Britain	1980		1993
335	71	Britain	1980		1993
336	71	Britain	1980		1993
336A	71B	Britain	1993		1995
337	71B	Britain	1980		1993
337A	71B	Britain	1993		1995
338	72	Britain	1984		1992
339	72	Britain	1975	1995	1993
340	72	Germany	1960	1968	1986
341	72	Russia	1991		1996
342	75	Britain	1974	1974	1986
343	75	Russia	1991		1996
345	75	Britain	1975	1977	1986
346	93	Britain	1975	1977	1986
347	82	Britain	1990		1992
348	82	Germany	1973	1977	1986
349	80	Switzerland	1987	1995	1995
350	81	USA	1989	1995	1992
351	81	Austria	1990		1994
353	82	Britain	1993		1994
355	76	Britain	1991		1992
356	76	Britain	1987		1993
360	76	France	1964	1964	1986
365	77	France	1963	1968	1986
370	77	France	1962	1962	1986
371	85	Britain	1988		1993
372	86	Britain	1987		1993
373	87	Britain	1987		1993
374	87	Britain	1987		1993
375	87	Britain	1987		1993
376	89	Britain	1987		1993
377	89	Britain	1987		1993
378	89	Britain	1988		1993
379	89	Britain	1988		1993
380	78	France	1965	1968	1986
381	90	Britain	1990		1993
382	90	Britain	1990		1993
383	91	Britain	1990		1993
384	91	Britain	1990		1993
385	91	Britain	1990		1993
386	91	Britain	1990		1993
389	79	Germany	1958	1996	1996
390	79	France	1958	1968	1986
391	93	Britain	1990		1992
393	293	Britain	1992		1995
394	94	Britain	1992		1993
395	94	Britain	1985		1993
397	94	Britain	1985		1993
400	79	France	1964	1964	1986
401	80	Britain	1991		1995
402	83A	France	1991	1993	1993
403	83A	Britain	1992		1995
405	83	Mexico	1989		1996
406	83	Mexico	1990		1995
410	95	France	1964	1964	1986
411	95	Britain	1989		1994
412	95	Britain	1992		1995
413	95	Britain	1983		1993
414	147	Britain	1993		1994
415	96	Britain	1977	1977	1986
416	96	Britain	1985		1993
417	98	Britain	1992		1995
418	96	Switzerland	1990	1995	1994
420	97	France	1963	1968	1986
424	97	Japan	1992		1995
425	98	Britain	1985		1993
426	98	France	1980	1994	1994

Catalog number	Page number	Country of origin	Year of production	Roland film release	Roland video release / Rerelease (r)
430	99	France	1963	1968	1986
440	147	Germany	1963	1968	1986
445	99	Britain	1974	1974	1986
456	102	Belgium/France/Germany/Spain	1985	1996	1995
457	103	Belgium/France/Germany/Spain	1985	1996	1995
458	103	Belgium/France/Germany/Spain	1985	1996	1995
459	103	Belgium/France/Germany/Spain	1985	1996	1995
460	103	France	1965	1968	1986
463	101	Spain	1991		1993
464	101	Spain	1991		1993
465	104	Austria	1990		1993
468	104	Russia	1991		1996
470	105	Britain	1965	1968	1986
471	105	Britain	1991		1993
480	104	France	1965	1968	1986
481	305	Britain	1975	1977	1986
481A	305	Britain	1991		1993
481B	305	Britain	1993		1994
482	297	Britain	1969	1969	1986
482A	307B	Britain	1981/92		1995
482B	307B	Britain	1981/92		1995
483	301	Britain	1991		1992
483B	306	Russia	1991		1996
483C	306	Russia	1991		1996
483D	306	Russia	1991		1996
484	302	Britain	1985		1993
484A	307A	Britain	1991		1995
484B	307B	Britain	1992		1995
485	235	Britain	1973	1973	1986
486	294	Netherlands	1988	1993	1993
487	293	Britain	1989		1992
488	272	France	1983	1995	1995
489	293	Britain	1967	1977	1986
490	194	Netherlands	1990		1992
490B	277	Britain	1981		1993
490C	279	Britain	1987		1993
490D	275	Britain	1990		1993
491	263	Britain	1976	1977	1986
493	263	Britain	1974	1977	1986
494	313	Britain	1990		1994
495	313	Britain	1992		1994
496A	313	Britain	1992		1994
497	123	France	1980	1994	1994
498	124	Germany	1964	1968	1986
500	125	Germany	1961	1968	1986
501	124	Netherlands	1973	1994r	1992r
501A	136	Britain	1992		1995
502	124	Netherlands	1985	1994r	1992r
502B	136	Netherlands	1988		1993
502D	127	Netherlands	1972	1996r	1995r
503	128	Germany	1987		1992
503C	114	France	1980	1994	1994
503D	115	France	1980	1994	1994
503E	114	Britain	1993		1995
504	107	France	1980	1994	1994
504B	107	Mexico	1989		1996
505	109	Germany	1973	1973	1986
506	109	Britain	1983		1992
507	109	Britain	1993		1993
508	109	Germany	1961	1968	1986
509	110	Belgium	1990	1995	1993
510	111	Germany	1965	1968	1986
511	112	Britain	1985	1993r	1993r
512	112	Britain	1985		1993
512B	113	France	1980	1994	1994
513	114	Italy	1965	1968	1986
515	133	Germany	1967	1973	1986
516	128	Britain	1987		1992
517	135	Germany	1967	1973	1986
518	126	Germany	1967	1968	1986
519	157	France	1966	1968	1986
520	149	France	1963	1968	1986
521	119	France	1980	1994	1994
524	150	Britain	1985		1993
525	151A	Britain	1993		1995
527	150	Britain	1985		1993
528	126	Britain	1985		1993
529	119	Britain	1985		1993
530	152	France	1961	1968	1986
531	152	France	1991		1995
532	152	France	1969	1994	1994
533	153	Britain	1968	1994r	1994r
534	151B	Britain	1993		1995
535	151B	Britain	1992		1995
540	153	France	1965	1968	1986
541	151	France	1980	1994	1994
543	154	Britain	1989		1994
546	154	Britain	1981	1994r	1994r
547	151A	Britain	1992		1995
551	151A	Britain	1993		1995
552	145	Britain	1974	1974	1986
553	154	Britain	1974	1974	1986
554	114	Britain	1985		1993
555	120	Britain	1987	1994r	1992r
557	121	Britain	1985		1993
558	139	Britain	1978	1993r	1993r
559	139	Britain	1978	1993r	1993r
560	140	Germany	1964	1968	1986
561	139	France	1980	1994	1994
562	286	Britain	1992		1995
563	141	Norway	1991		1993
563A	141	Norway	1976	1994	1994
564	142	USA	1982	1993r	1993r
565	142	Britain	1985		1993
567	143	Spain	1991		1992
567B	143	Britain	1985		1993
567C	143	Mexico	1993		1994
568	144	France	1989		1992
569	289	Switzerland	1989	1995	1994
570	140	France	1961	1968	1986
570A	289	Switzerland	1989		1995
571	289	Switzerland	1989		1995
572	145	Germany	1968	1968	1986
574	145	Denmark	1990		1992
575	171	France	1965	1968	1986
580	160	France	1963	1963	1986
581	177	France	1980	1994	1994
582	177	France	1980	1994	1994
583	307B	Britain	1992		1995
584	178	France	1980	1995	1995
587	178	Britain	1970	1995r	1995r
590	129	France	1960	1968	1986
592	168	Britain	1981	1995r	1995r
593	169	Britain	1977	1995r	1995r
594	170	Netherlands	1970	1992r	1992r
595	129	Britain	1979	1992r	1992r
596	116	Netherlands	1962	1992r	1992r
597	117	France	1990		1994
598	130	Britain	1986		1993
599	117	Britain	1989		1994r
599A	117	Britain	1963	1995r	1995r
600	173	France	1964	1964	1986
601	167	France	1980	1994	1994
602	174	Britain	1991		1993
603	174	New Zealand	1988	1994	1993
605	164	France	1991	1993	1993
606	179	France	1985	1996	1996
607	180	Canada	1983	1993	1993
608	180	France	1988	1995	1995
609	180	France	1988		1993
610A	180	France	1980	1994r	1993r
610B	181	Germany	1990		1993
611	167	Mexico	1989		1996
612	181	Germany	1989	1996	1993
613	182	France	1992		1996
614	184	Estonia	1991		1994
615	172	Belgium	1987	1992	1992
618	184	Brazil	1989		1993
619	185	France	1990		1995
620	158	Germany	1958	1968	1986
621	158	France	1961	1994r	1993r
623	263B	Britain	1992		1995
625	162	Britain	1985		1992
626	162	Britain	1990	1992	1992
627	163	France	1988		1992
630	164	France	1963	1968	1986
634	283	Britain	1991		1993
635	164	Australia	1969	1969	1986
636	184	New Zealand	1991	1994	1994
637	164	Canada	1976	1993	1993
638	182	Austria	1992		1995
639	165	Britain	1990	1993	1993
640	164	Italy	1968	1968	1986
660	213	Britain	1972	1972	1986
661	184	Britain	1974	1974	1986
664	223	France	1990	1996	1996
665	256	France	1987	1993	1993
666	185	Canada	1991	1993	1993
667	257	Britain	1982	1994r	1994r
700	188	Britain	1975		1993
701	188	Britain	1975		1993
702	188	Britain	1975		1993
703	189	Britain	1975		1993
704	189	Britain	1975		1993
705	189	Britain	1975		1993
706	189	Britain	1975		1993
707	190	Britain	1975		1993
708	190	Britain	1975		1993
709	190	Britain	1975		1993
710	190	Britain	1975		1993
711	190	Britain	1975		1993
712	191	Britain	1975		1993
713	191	Britain	1975		1993
714	192	Britain	1975		1993
715	192	Britain	1975		1993
716	192	Britain	1975		1993
717	192	Britain	1975		1993
718	193	Britain	1975		1993
719	193	Britain	1975		1993
720	193	Britain	1975		1993
721	193	Britain	1975		1993
722	193	Britain	1975		1993
730	194	Austria	1988	1993	1993
735	198	France	1987		1996
736	198	France	1987		1996
737	198	France	1987		1996
738	198	France	1989		1996
739	198	Britain	1992		1995
741	137	Finland	1989	1993	1993
742	196	Finland	1992		1993
760	197	Britain	1980		1992
761	197	Netherlands	1991		1992
763	199	Finland	1972	1994	1993

Country of origin, production and release dates

Catalog number	Page number	Country of origin	Year of production	Roland film release	Roland video release	Rerelease (r)
764	200	Denmark	1989		1993	
765	202	Denmark	1990		1993	
766	201	Britain	1973	1996	1995	
767	201	Canada	1985		1993	
768	202	Finland	1987	1994	1993	
769	202	France	1991	1996	1996	
771	203	Germany	1984		1996	
772	203	Germany	1984		1996	
773	203	Germany	1984		1996	
780	245	Japan	1991		1995	
781	247	Spain	1990		1993	
782	247	Spain	1990		1993	
783	247	Spain	1990		1993	
784	248	Spain	1990		1993	
785	248	Spain	1990		1993	
786	248	Spain	1990		1993	
787	248	Spain	1990		1993	
788	249	Spain	1990		1993	
789	249	Spain	1990		1993	
790	249	Spain	1990		1993	
791	250	Spain	1990		1993	
792	250	Spain	1990		1993	
793	250	Spain	1990		1993	
801	251	Spain	1991		1996	
802	251	Spain	1991		1996	
803	252	Spain	1991		1996	
804	252	Spain	1991		1996	
805	252	Spain	1991		1996	
806	252	Spain	1991		1996	
807	252	Spain	1991		1996	
808	253	Spain	1991		1996	
809	253	Spain	1991		1996	
810	253	Spain	1991		1996	
811	253	Spain	1991		1996	
812	253	Spain	1991		1996	
813	253	Spain	1991		1996	
815	322	Britain	1985		1993	
820	324	Britain	1987		1992	
822	322	Denmark	1990		1993	
825	325	Britain	1987		1993	
827	325	Britain	1993		1994	
830	324	Britain	1990		1992	
835	325	Britain	1988		1992	
841	274	Ireland	1990		1993	
842	274	Ireland	1990		1993	
843	274	Ireland	1990		1993	
844	274	Ireland	1990		1993	
845	274	Ireland	1990		1993	
846	274	Ireland	1990		1993	
847	274	Ireland	1990		1993	
848	274	Ireland	1990		1993	
849	274	Ireland	1990		1993	
850	274	Ireland	1990		1993	
851	274	Ireland	1990		1993	
852	274	Ireland	1990		1993	
853	274	Ireland	1990		1993	
854	274	Ireland	1990		1993	
855	274	Ireland	1990		1993	
856	274	Ireland	1990		1993	
857	274	Ireland	1990		1993	
858	274	Ireland	1990		1993	
859	274	Ireland	1990		1993	
860	274	Ireland	1990		1993	
861	274	Ireland	1990		1993	
862	274	Ireland	1990		1993	
900	275	Britain	1991		1993	
901	275	Britain	1990		1993	
902	278	Britain	1990		1993	
903	283	Britain	1991		1993	
904	283	Britain	1988		1993	
965	291	Netherlands	1990		1993	
971	295	Belgium	1990		1996	
972	295	Belgium	1990		1996	
973	295	Belgium	1990		1996	
1004	390	Britain	1987		1995	
1005	390	Britain	1986		1995	
1006	390	Britain	1987		1995	
1010	390	Britain	1987		1995	
1041	387	France	1990		1994	
1042	387	France	1990		1994	
1043	387	France	1990		1994	
1044	387	France	1990		1994	
1051	388	Britain	1990		1995	
1052	388	Britain	1990		1995	
1053	388	Britain	1990		1995	
1054	388	Britain	1989		1995	
1055	388	Britain	1989		1995	
1057	388	Britain	1990		1995	
1058	389	Britain	1990		1995	
1059	389	Britain	1990		1995	
1060	389	Britain	1990		1995	
1061	389	Britain	1990		1995	
1062	389	Britain	1991		1995	
1063	389	Britain	1990		1995	
1064	389	Britain	1991		1995	
1065	389	Britain	1990		1995	
W01	377	Britain	1986		1986	
W016	384	Britain	1986		1986	
W021	381	Britain	1986		1986	
W028	384	Britain	1986		1986	
W029	384	Britain	1986		1986	
W1	377	Britain	1984		1986	
W2	377	Britain	1984		1986	
W3	377	Britain	1984		1986	
W4	377	Britain	1986		1986	
W5	377	Britain	1984		1986	
W6	378	Britain	1985		1986	
W7	378	Britain	1984		1986	
W8	378	Britain	1986		1986	
W9	378	Britain	1986		1986	
W10	379	Britain	1985		1986	
W11	379	Britain	1985		1986	
W12	380	Britain	1985		1986	
W13	380	Britain	1986		1986	
W14	380	Britain	1985		1986	
W15	380	Britain	1985		1986	
W16	380	Britain	1986		1986	
W17	380	Britain	1986		1986	
W18	381	Britain	1986		1986	
W19	381	Britain	1984		1986	
W20	381	Britain	1986		1986	
W21	381	Britain	1986		1986	
W22	381	Britain	1985		1986	
W23	382	Britain	1985		1986	
W24	382	Britain	1985		1986	
W25	382	Britain	1985		1986	
W26	382	Britain	1986		1986	
W27	383	Britain	1985		1986	
W28	384	Britain	1985		1986	
W29	384	Britain	1985		1986	
W30	384	Britain	1985		1986	
W31	384	Britain	1984		1986	
W32	384	Britain	1985		1986	
W33	385	Britain	1986		1986	
W34	385	Britain	1984		1986	
W35	385	Britain	1984		1986	
W36	385	Britain	1985		1986	
W37	385	Britain	1985		1986	
W38	385	Britain	1985		1986	
W39	385	Britain	1985		1986	
W40	377	Britain	1986		1989	
W41	377	Britain	1987		1989	
W42	377	Britain	1987		1989	
W43	377	Britain	1987		1989	
W44	377	Britain	1987		1989	
W45	378	Britain	1987		1989	
W46	378	Britain	1988		1989	
W47	378	Britain	1987		1989	
W48	378	Britain	1987		1989	
W49	378	Britain	1987		1989	
W50	378	Britain	1987		1989	
W51	378	Britain	1988		1989	
W52	378	Britain	1988		1989	
W53	379	Britain	1988		1989	
W54	385	Britain	1989		1989	
W55	379	Britain	1987		1989	
W56	379	Britain	1988		1989	
W57	379	Britain	1987		1989	
W58	379	Britain	1988		1989	
W59	380	Britain	1988		1989	
W60	380	Britain	1987		1989	
W61	380	Britain	1987		1989	
W62	380	Britain	1987		1989	
W63	380	Britain	1987		1989	
W64	381	Britain	1987		1989	
W65	381	Britain	1987		1989	
W66	382	Britain	1988		1989	
W67	382	Britain	1987		1989	
W68	382	Britain	1988		1989	
W69	382	Britain	1987		1989	
W70	382	Britain	1988		1989	
W71	382	Britain	1988		1989	
W72	382	Britain	1988		1989	
W73	383	Britain	1988		1989	
W74	383	Britain	1988		1989	
W75	383	Britain	1987		1989	
W76	383	Britain	1986		1989	
W77	383	Britain	1987		1989	
W78	383	Britain	1987		1989	
W79	383	Britain	1987		1989	
W80	383	Britain	1986		1989	
W81	383	Britain	1987		1989	
W82	384	Britain	1988		1989	
W83	384	Britain	1987		1989	
W84	384	Britain	1987		1989	
W85	385	Britain	1988		1989	
W86	385	Britain	1988		1989	
W87	385	Britain	1988		1989	
W88	379	Britain	1988		1989	
W89	383	Britain	1988		1989	
W90	383	Britain	1989		1995	
W91	377	Britain	1989		1995	
W92	381	Britain	1989		1995	
W93	378	Britain	1989		1995	
W94	385	Britain	1989		1995	
W95	380	Britain	1989		1995	
W96	381	Britain	1989		1995	
W97	379	Britain	1989		1995	
W98	384	Britain	1989		1995	
W99	379	Britain	1989		1995	
W100	379	Britain	1989		1995	
W101	379	Britain	1989		1995	
WOW1	386	Britain	1988		1989	
WOW2	386	Britain	1988		1989	
WOW3	386	Britain	1988		1989	
WOW4	386	Britain	1988		1989	
WOW5	386	Britain	1988		1989	
WOW6	386	Britain	1988		1989	

Videos on Modern Literature

The Roland Collection includes some of the
best series on contemporary literature and
philosophy available on video.

A separate catalog for **Writers Talk:
Ideas of Our Time**, giving biographical details of
each writer, is available on request.

All prices include non-theatrical institutional
public performance use with lending rights.

Writers Talk
Ideas of Our Time

One of the most important literary resources currently available on video.

Each video in the series features a writer talking with another writer or critic. In these conversations friends and professionals, who have one thing in common – a love of writing and literature – get to the very heart of their lives and their work. Many of the videos contain questions from a live audience. The writers speak in their own time, with little editing and no censorship.

The videos may be used in a variety of ways. As part of an educational program they will inspire and bring students closer to an international body of writers. They may be used as the basis for creative writing courses. As part of a public library resource they will lead new readers to established and new writers.

The videos are produced by ICA Video at the Institute of Contemporary Arts (ICA), London. Recent titles have received generous sponsorship by 'The Guardian' newspaper.

This series of
106 programs
can be purchased
on VHS for $8374
Reference S41

Television rights and
prices on request

Available on request: an illustrated catalog with biographical details and cross referencing index for the following subject categories:

African writing
American Indian writing
Australian writing
Black women's writing
Canadian writing
Caribbean writing
Cartoons
Children's books
The cut-up method
The detective story
Drama
Emigration and displacement
Fairy tales and myths
Film-making
Hebrew writing
History
The historical novel
Humor
Illustration
Irony and satire
Japanese writing
Landscape
Latin American writing
Magical realism
The modern tradition
Mothers and children in literature
The oral tradition
Palestinian writing
Poetry
Poetry for children
Polish writing
Political responsibilities of the writer
Post-modernism
Psychiatry
Realism
Religion and belief
The role of the writer
Science-fiction
Structuralist and deconstructionist criticism
The short story
Televisual culture
Travel writing
The war and the anti-war novel
Writing for television
Writing about sex
Women's writing

All videos are in color VHS $79 each

◀ Chinua Achebe
Kathy Acker

▼ Maya Angelou

W42 Aharon Appelfeld

with Clive Sinclair

Writing in Hebrew
Writing to expunge memory
Finding a language to express tragedy
28 minutes   The Jews and assimilation

W43 Margaret Atwood

with Hermione Lee

Themes of women 'breaking out'
Visual imagery as inspiration
Literature informed by fairy tales
Writing as a woman from
the male point of view
Mythology in contemporary literature
53 minutes   Using humor

W3 Gillian Avery
Penelope Farmer
Jill Paton Walsh

with Heather Neill

'Literary' writing for children
Death, grief, torment in children's books
Fantasy and magic
45 minutes   The child as reader

W40 Dannie Abse

with Elaine Feinstein

Influence of Dylan Thomas
Fifties' English poetry
Sixties' American poetry
Development of metaphor
Political responsibility
47 minutes   Welsh and Jewish heritage

W01 Chinua Achebe

with Nuruddin Farah

Translation
African and Nigerian identity
Choosing a language in which to write
39 minutes   Nigerian oral tradition

W41 Kathy Acker

with Angela McRobbie

Post-structuralist and post-modern writing
Influence of William Burroughs
Seventies' American punk culture
40 minutes   The cut-up method

W1 Brian Aldiss
Christopher Priest

with Lisa Appignanesi

The science-fiction genre
Sources of stories
The writer/reader relationship
41 minutes   Movements in magical realism

W91 Isabel Allende

with Marina Warner

Women as storytellers
Soap operas
Goodness outweighing evil in Chile
40 minutes   Magical realism

W2 Martin Amis

with Ian McEwan

Money in literature, folklore and history
Threat of annihilation
Changing characteristics
36 minutes   of the hero in literature

W4 Maya Angelou

Writing through the black experience
The human spirit in adversity
31 minutes   Prose and poetry readings

W44 Paul Bailey

with Margaret Walters

Writing about old people
Using humor to write about tragedy
Charles Dickens as inspiration
Homosexuality in twentieth-century literature
Impact of First World War
30 minutes   on contemporary culture

W5 JG Ballard

with Matthew Hoffman

Using childhood memories in fiction
Landscapes in science fiction
Inspiration of surrealist painters
'Empire of the Sun' as
45 minutes   thinly veiled autobiography

▲
AS Byatt

◀
Melvyn Bragg
William Burroughs

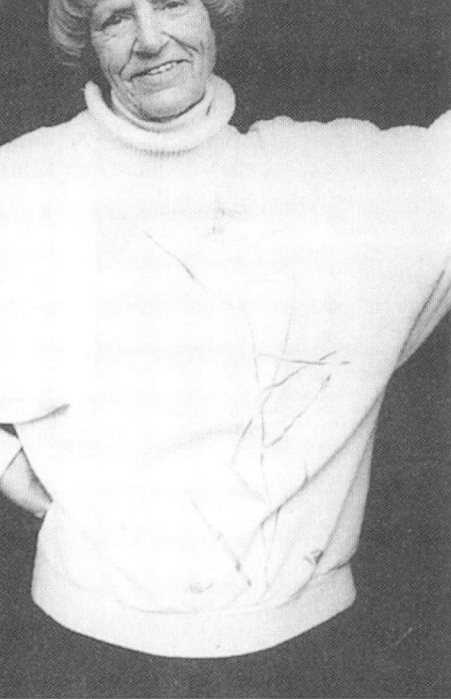

Monica Dickens

▶

G Cabrera Infante
JP Donleavy

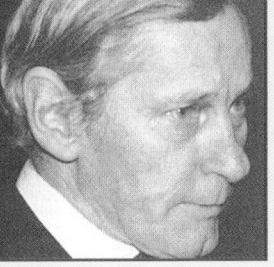

Nadine Gordimer
Allen Ginsberg

William Gaddis

W59 **Louise Erdrich**
Michael Dorris
with Paul Bailey

Being an American Indian in the United States
Oral and tribal traditions
Writing as a method of self-discovery
27 minutes   Collaborative writing

W60 **Elaine Feinstein**
with AS Byatt

Female sexuality and dependence
Cultism in the twentieth century
Poetry, the novel, short stories and plays
36 minutes   Border as metaphor

W95 **First novels**
Deborah Levy
Geoff Dyer

Publishing a first novel
The city and the dispossessed
From non-fiction to fiction
40 minutes   Exile from South Africa

W61 **Marilyn French**
with Sarah Dunant

Power structures and patriarchy
Male/female relationships
Mother/daughter relationships
Childraising
49 minutes   Sexuality and pregnancy

W13 **William Gaddis**
with Malcolm Bradbury

Time and place in the novel
Political and cultural climate
of contemporary America
The novel as entertainment and moral text
32 minutes   Religion

W14 **Maggie Gee**
with Sheila McCleod

Pollution
Role of reviewers
Experimenting with style
Difficulties of writing about happiness
46 minutes   Nuclear war

W15 **Penelope Gilliatt**
with Penelope Lively

Structure and language across the forms
The short story
Childhood experiences and memories
38 minutes   Writing about places

W16 **Allen Ginsberg**
with RD Laing

The intimacy of poetry
Relationship between poems and dreams
61 minutes   Role of meditation

W62 **Nadine Gordimer**
with Margaret Walters

Motives for writing a political novel
Africa's landscapes
Writing in exile
South African black consciousness movement
45 minutes   How to end a book

W12 **Mary Gordon**
Margaret Drabble

Writing about mothers and children
First descriptions of breastfeeding
in English literature
Writing from a child's point of view
41 minutes   Books as child substitutes

W63 **Prabhu Guptara**
with Naseem Khan

The control and use of
channels of communication
Historical function of black writing
39 minutes   Language and text

W17 **Elizabeth Hardwick**
with Malcolm Bradbury

The modern movement
Post-war American aestheticism
What makes a good writer?
America as custodian of European culture
33 minutes   Writing styles

▲
George V Higgins

▶
Kazuo Ishiguro

◀
Joseph Heller

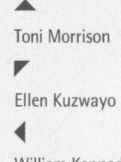

Toni Morrison

Ellen Kuzwayo

William Kennedy

All videos are in color VHS $79 each

▶
Marge Piercy

▼
Ben Okri

◀
Michèle Roberts

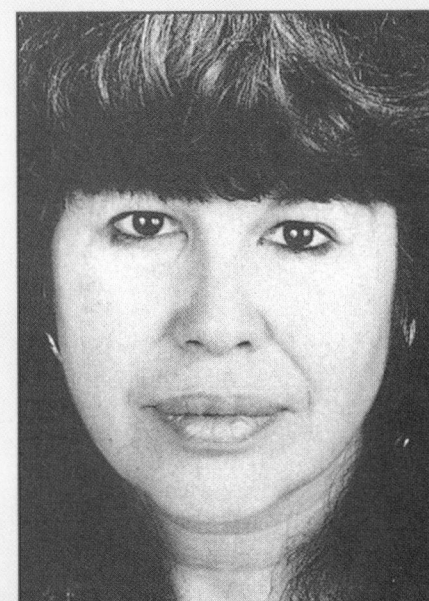

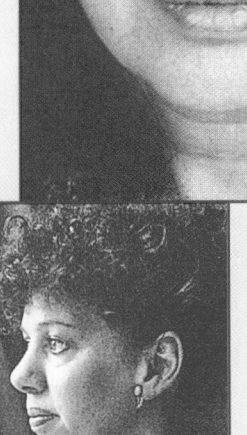

383

W82 Graham Swift

with David Profumo

Storytelling
Drawing upon emotion and intellect
Writing as therapy
41 minutes   Exploring the unknown

W028 Edward Said

with Salman Rushdie

Displacement, landlessness and exile
Palestinian women
Zionism and Palestine
79 minutes   Western attitudes

W83 Emma Tennant

with James Buxton

The English view of the imagination
Women writers
Characteristics of European writers
Writing as storytelling
Pluralism in contemporary culture
35 minutes   Voices and styles

W28 Maurice Sendak

with Paul Vaughan

Ingredients of successful children's stories
The role of monsters
Writing and illustrating for children
Drawing upon family as inspiration
46 minutes   Adapting books for opera

W29 Wole Soyinka

The erosion of moral rights in climates of fear
Artists working within societies
in which they are banned
Impact of African sculpture on Western art
Socio-political injustices in Africa
Impact of African culture on America
Creative responses to oppression in America
61 minutes   The nuclear bomb

**W32 D M Thomas
Wendy Perriam
Clare Boylan**

Sex in literature
The issue of pornography
55 minutes   Style and vocabulary

W029 Mongane Serote

with Edward Blishen

Black South African writing
Poetry versus fiction
Childhood reading
The English language in African literature
38 minutes   South Africa and the short story

W30 Stephen Spender

with Al Alvarez

The role of creative-writing courses
Twentieth-century English poetry
The poet with a sacred mission
Characteristics of the American poet
53 minutes   Friendship with WH Auden

W98 Three Cuban poets

Eliseo Diego
César Lopez
Pedro Pérez Sarduy

Contemporary Cuban poetry
Three different voices
40 minutes   Writing and cultural traditions

**W016 Janice Shinebourne
Beryl Gilroy**

with Susheila Nasta

Landscapes in Caribbean literature
Writing with no literary precedent
Women in Caribbean literature
The English language in Caribbean writing
53 minutes   Color and race

W31 Ralph Steadman

with Peter Fuller

Motives for writing 'Sigmund Freud'
Extending the parameters of cartooning
Drawing caricatures
52 minutes   Using satire in pictures

W84 Colin Thubron

with Malise Ruthven

The impossibility of writing
about one's own society
The 'grand' tradition of English travel writing
Motives for being a travel writer
35 minutes   Use of notebooks and journals

W33 John Updike
with Claire Tomalin

Personal and domestic themes
Updike as chronicler of the New World
Writing about sex
Small-town life as the site of drama
50 minutes   God

W34 Mario Vargas Llosa
with John King

Mass culture and modernism
Satire and farce
The Latin American novelist's role in politics
Latin American romanticism
50 minutes   Role of intellectuals

W85 Nirmal Verma
with Gita Sahgal

Writing from a child's perspective
Themes of human deprivation
Impact of history on the individual
35 minutes   Using soliloquy

W35 Gore Vidal
with Lorna Sage

Americans and their history
Impact of the televisual culture
Ambition and power in the United States
42 minutes   'Lincoln'

W54 Marina Warner
with Lisa Appignanesi

The history contained in ephemera
Women and virginity
Influences of Catholicism
Women's history within fairy tales
40 minutes   Gender and separation

W36 Fay Weldon
Deborah Moggach

How to write for television
Creating tension and drama
Essential ingredients for successful screenplays
41 minutes   The role of actors and directors

W86 Fay Weldon
with Valerie Grove

Writing about motherhood
Writing which challenges the status quo
Writing as a woman about men
The male/female relationship
Fiction's inability to contain reality
50 minutes   The sacred and the profane

W37 Arnold Wesker
with David Edgar

Writing from a working-class perspective
Changing role of drama
English playwrights of the fifties
55 minutes   Political drama

W38 Raymond Williams
with Michael Ignatieff

Being a socialist novelist
Using a historical canvas
Cultural influence on consciousness
History's entanglement with the psyche
51 minutes   Themes of betrayal

W87 Tom Wolfe
with Peter York

Post-modernism in American culture
The effect of the metropolis
on contemporary culture
Experimental literature in the United States
The birth of 'New Journalism'
Using journalistic techniques in the novel
55 minutes   Art, architecture and the critic

W94 Writing Biography
Carol Easton
Victoria Glendinning

Biographies of friends
Biographies of writers
40 minutes   Research

W39 Writing for Children
Robert Leeson
Maurice Sendak
Gillian Avery
Penelope Farmer
Jill Paton Walsh

Experimental children's writing
Writing within a moral context
The relationship between fantasy and realism
48 minutes   Functions of children's books

▶ Gore Vidal

▼ Mario Vargas Llosa
John Updike

◣ Tom Wolfe

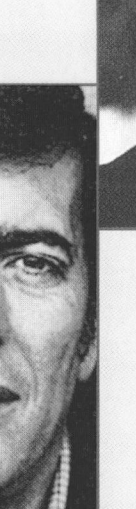

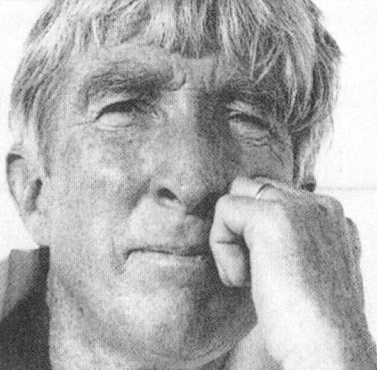

Writers on Writing
Creative Writing Course

Six videos with 104-page booklet with 48 tasksheets

The writers in the series include

Dannie Abse
Chinua Achebe
Brian Aldiss
Martin Amis
Maya Angelou
Margaret Atwood
JG Ballard
John Berger
Raymond Briggs
Margaret Drabble
Elaine Feinstein
Maggie Gee
Nadine Gordimer
Mary Gordon
George Higgins
Kazuo Ishiguro
PD James
Lena Kennedy
Robert Leeson
Deborah Moggach
Wendy Perriam
Marge Piercy
Harold Pinter
Christopher Priest
Ruth Rendell
Michèle Roberts
Salman Rushdie
Maurice Sendak
Mongane Serote
Janice Shinebourne
John Updike
Mario Vargas Llosa
Gore Vidal
Fay Weldon
Arnold Wesker

This series of
6 VHS videos and
104–page booklet
can be purchased
for $594
Reference S42

Each part

Color
Age range 15–adult

VHS $99
includes 104–page
booklet

'Writers on Writing' is a major resource in video and print designed to stimulate creative writing and literary appreciation. It is based on edited conversations between writers discussing their work at the Institute of Contemporary Arts in London. This creative writing course is designed for teachers of English and students aged fifteen and over. It consists of six twenty to twenty-eight minute videos and a study guide with forty-eight tasksheets.

The course aims to bridge the gap between the professional author and the student writer by raising shared issues such as methods, themes, language, genre and form. It provides:

■ source material on the writing process to encourage reflection and discussion about how to write

■ supporting materials for course work or for the independent student to develop the craft of writing

■ insight into the work of contemporary writers; their discussion of their own writing will encourage students to read with greater understanding

A teacher could build a year's course around the videos and tasksheets, or they can be used individually. This flexibility also makes the course ideal for adult evening classes and self-study. The study guide covering the whole course is supplied with each video. Additional copies can be obtained from the Roland Collection.

WOW1 — Beginnings – Inspiration – The role of the writer

■ The ingredients of writing
■ Keeping a writing record
■ Beginnings
■ What is inspiration?
■ Looking at other writers' work
24 minutes ■ The role of the writer

WOW2 — Writing from personal experience – Subjects

■ Finding subjects to write about
■ Subjects and themes
■ Discovering what you have to say
■ Looking at other writers' work
■ Autobiographical writing
■ Writing to persuade
■ Writing fantasy
28 minutes ■ Personal writing

WOW3 — Methods – Drafting – Research

■ Planning a piece of writing
■ Methods and research
■ How you write
■ Using research
■ Looking at other writers' work
20 minutes ■ Follow-up work

WOW4 — Character – Setting – Plot

■ Defining the terms
■ Using character, setting and plot
■ Looking at other writers' work
■ Characters and settings
■ Place and atmosphere
■ Building a character
23 minutes ■ Plot structure

WOW5 — Form – Genre

■ Choice of form and genre
■ Thinking about form
■ Thinking about genre
■ Looking at other writers' work
■ Experimenting with form
25 minutes ■ Experimenting with genre

WOW6 — Language – Audience

■ Style and audience
■ Language
■ Audience and readership
■ Looking at translation
■ Looking at other writers' work
■ Experimenting with language
23 minutes ■ Writing for different audiences

Spirit of Freedom

A four-part documentary by Bernard-Henri Lévy

Bernard-Henri Lévy, eminent writer, essayist and thinker, and well-known personality, wrote and presents this account of this century's most influential intellectuals, their attempts to foster their visions of freedom, and the confrontation of their ideals with historical and political reality. Their story is intricately intertwined with the evolution of the twentieth century.

The term 'intellectual' covers writers, poets, artists and scientists, who through their work, writings and public stances have committed themselves to their ideals, and in so doing have substantially shaped the history of our age. They have travelled the world in search of the absolute, espousing revolutionary causes, navigating between truth and lies, often triumphing, often stumbling.

Spirit of Freedom retraces their steps, from the Dreyfus Affair, which captured public opinion at the turn of the century, the Bolshevik Revolution, the rise of Fascism, Stalinism and Nazism, through the turbulent 1960s, the Cultural Revolution in China, the Vietnam War, and Third-World rebellions. Emile Zola, André Gide, André Malraux, Jean-Paul Sartre, Albert Camus, Lenin, Stalin, Castro are among the protagonists of the series; Claude Lévi-Strauss, Claude Lanzman (director of the film 'Shoah'), Regis Debray, who was Che Guevara's comrade-in-arms, Klaus Croissant (lawyer of the infamous Baader-Meinhoff Group) are among those interviewed.

Rich archival footage, interviews, voice-over narration and on-location filming vibrantly bring these events, and the people who made them happen, to life. BHL accompanies viewers on an odyssey from Paris to the USSR, Berlin, Algeria, Beijing … Each episode focuses on one specific wave of thought in its historical and chronological context.

Not available
in the USA

This series of
4 programs
can be purchased
on VHS for $596
Reference S43

Writer/Presenter
Bernard-Henri Lévy

Director
Alain Ferrari

Also available in French

Each part

52 minutes
Color
Age range 17–adult

VHS $149

1041 **Part One: Great Expectations**
Dawn from the East:
The Communist Temptation

The poets, artists, philosophers and scientists who, galvanised by the Alfred Dreyfus affair, were the first to be termed 'intellectuals.' The First World War and the Bolshevik Revolution further impelled them to find the answer to a better world, leading many of them, such as the Surrealists, in 1927, to harken to the tempting call of Communism.

1042 **Part Two: Days of Contempt**
Fascism and the Nazis

The story of Fascism and resistance to it. At the heart of this episode are writers whose names are linked with liberty – André Malraux, Ernest Hemingway, André Gide – as well as others who belong to the darker side of history.

1043 **Part Three: Lost Illusions**
Breaking from Stalin

In the aftermath of the Second World War, through post-colonialism and Third World revolution to Vietnam, Communist socialism has fought to free itself from the Stalinist yoke. In a time of violent upheaval, Jean-Paul Sartre, Albert Camus and Regis Debray were among those engaged in a bitter struggle with history.

1044 **Part Four: The Demise of the Prophets**
Re-inventing the Model

The program begins with May 1968; the Left is at the height of its triumph. Maoism, Baader-Meinhoff terrorism, Cambodia … Although the hushed crowd at Jean-Paul Sartre's funeral procession in 1980 is large and reverent, this event marks a turning point. Today's intelligentsia has become isolated, introverted; human rights has become its sole cause. Could it be that the intellectual is a dying breed?

Literature in the Modern World

The relevance of literary study in the modern world is highlighted in this stimulating series, which focuses on a wide range of challenging literary texts.

This series of 14 programs can be purchased on VHS for $1386 Reference S40

1051 'Endgame' by Samuel Beckett

Samuel Beckett's second drama, *Endgame*, is a play in which nothing happens once – unlike his first play, *Waiting for Godot*, in which nothing happens twice. It is not a play about chess in any explicit sense, but it does feature a lovable, if curmudgeonly, old man in a dustbin. It *is* funny, and it is a classic of modern literature.

Director
Tony Coe

Open University/BBC

90 minutes
Color
Age range 18–adult
VHS $99

1052 English, Whose English?

Professor Graham Martin, Open University, investigates some ways in which images of England were developed in the late nineteenth and early twentieth centuries as a means of justifying and maintaining imperialism, against increasing doubt and conflict about Britain's imperial ambitions. He examines the roles played by archive footage, newsreels, feature films and travelogues, by English literature – Virginia Woolf, Rupert Brooke, Kipling and *The Wind in the Willows* – by the monarchy, the countryside and that most English of sports, cricket. He ends by looking at the apparent break in the continuity of English literature provoked by Modernism and by reactions to the Great War, exemplified by Virginia Woolf's *Mrs Dalloway* and TS Eliot's *The Waste Land* – both works were later absorbed into a redefined concept of English literature.

Director
Tony Coe

Presenter
Professor Graham Martin

Actors
Hilary Cromie
Stephen Earle

Open University/BBC

24 minutes
Color
Age range 18–adult
VHS $99

1053 What was Modernism?

Professor Frank Kermode and Barbara Everett consider the question 'what was modernism?' in relation to TS Eliot's *The Waste Land* and Virginia Woolf's *Mrs Dalloway*. The language of Modernist poetry and novels, the use of allusions and structure in Modernist literature, and the implications for the reader are all subjects of discussion, as is the idea that Modernism arose out of a specific historical context – the First World War.

Director
G D Jayalakshmi

Participants
Professor Frank Kermode
Barbara Everett

Open University/BBC

24 minutes
Color
Age range 18–adult
VHS $99

1054 Crossing the Border: Images of England in the 1930s

This program examines how England and Englishness were portrayed in the 1930s in poetry, advertisements, photographs and film. The 1930s, whilst a time of doom, gloom and unemployment, brought new opportunities, including the use of the countryside for relaxation and pleasure, rather than work. Auden, rejecting the nostalgic view of the better days of Georgian poetry, was interested in recent human industrial activity and relationships. The program's final eight minutes comprise extracts from the film *Nightmail*, showing the attempt to unite rural south with industrial north, incorporating working and middle classes.

Director
Betty Talks

Presenter
Angus Calder

Open University/BBC

24 minutes
Color
Age range 18–adult
VHS $99

1055 Left and Write: Recalling the 1930s

Linked with film 1054, *Crossing the Border*, which shows how writers, poets and film-makers viewed England and Englishness, this video looks outwards from England to a wider European perspective. Three writers – Julian Symons, Sir Stephen Spender and Naomi Mitchison – recall how it felt to be a writer on the left and the issues that mattered to them. Four topics are discussed: sex, including homosexuality and censorship; politics – the 1930s were a time of intense political commitment; Spain – the Spanish Civil War was a focal point for many 1930s writers; and writing, an assessment of the political commitment of themselves and their contemporaries from the viewpoint of the late 1980s.

Director
Betty Talks

Narrator
Benjamin Whitrow

Participants
Julian Symons
Sir Stephen Spender
Naomi Mitchison

Open University/BBC

24 minutes
Color
Age range 18–adult
VHS $99

1057 In the Market Place

This program analyzes the market pressures that determine the production of literature. It focuses on Jeanette Winterson, who adapted her first novel, *Oranges are Not the Only Fruit*, for serialization on television, to general critical acclaim. Through interviews with Jeanette Winterson, literary agent Pat Kavanagh, editor Liz Calder and bookseller Jane Cholmeley, the publishing business is explained.

Director
Charles Cooper

Participants
Jeanette Winterson
Pat Kavanagh
Liz Calder
Jane Cholmeley

Open University/BBC

24 minutes
Color
Age range 18–adult
VHS $99

1058 Empire and Nation: The Re-fashioning of Literature

The program looks at the relationship between Britain and India from an Indian perspective. Presented by Susie Tharu, an Indian academic who teaches English literature in Hyderabad, it traces the history of one Indian poem, *Radhika Santwanam*, from the eighteenth century to Independence. The complex relationship between Britain and India is explored, showing how modern India is a product of British colonialism. Shot in New Delhi, Madras, Hyderabad and Thanjavur, the program analyzes the rise of a new middle class in India, which dresses more 'modestly', studies English literature and appreciates Western values, as embodied in British architecture in India.

Director	24 minutes
G D Jayalakshmi	Color
Presenter	Age range 18–adult
Susie Tharu	VHS $99

Open University/BBC

1059 Serjeant Musgrave at the Court

In 1959 John Arden's *Serjeant Musgrave's Dance* was put on at the Royal Court theatre, London. The program explores the theatrical and political background of the late 1950s by interviewing people concerned with this production and the Royal Court, intercut with archive material. John Arden explains why he wrote the play; Lindsay Anderson discusses the problems and challenges of directing it; Ian Bannen talks about how he approached the character of Serjeant Musgrave; Jocelyn Herbert describes Brecht's influence on her set designs; and Bill Gaskill explores the political and artistic ideas of the 'new' writers of the 1950s who were involved with the Royal Court.

Director	24 minutes
Betty Talks	Color
Participants	Age range 18–adult
John Arden	VHS $99
Lindsay Anderson	
Ian Bannen	
Jocelyn Herbert	
Bill Gaskill	

Open University/BBC

1060 Born into Two Cultures?

Chinua Achebe and R K Narayan discuss their experiences as writers – what it means to be born into one culture and language, yet to write in the English language, giving us special insights into the problem of operating in two distinct cultures.

Director	24 minutes
G D Jayalakshmi	Color
Presenters	Age range 18–adult
Chinua Achebe	VHS $99
R K Narayan	

Open University/BBC

1061 Caribbean Poetry: The Literary and Oral Traditions

Three poets, James Berry, David Dabydeen and Jackie Kay, discuss the varied traditions of poetry in the Caribbean and look at two distinct strands of poetry, the oral and the literary, and how they have affected poets writing in Britain.

Director	24 minutes
Amanda Willett	Color
Narrator	Age range 18–adult
Anne-Marie Grey	VHS $99
Participants	
James Berry	
David Dabydeen	
Jackie Kay	

Open University/BBC

1062 The Gentle Sex?

A televisual essay examining some of the ways in which cultural images of gender in the twentieth century have arisen. Material from many sources offers a historical justification for Simone de Beauvoir's view of woman as 'other.' Other interrelated pressures, such as class and race, are also considered. Extracts from Toni Morrison's *Song of Solomon* and Grace Nichols's *Spell Against Too Much Male White Power* are used to explore the literary implications of representations of gender in the modern world.

Director	24 minutes
Mags Noble	Color
Presenter	Age range 18–adult
Dinah Birch	VHS $99

Open University/BBC

1063 Changing Voices

Building on the theoretical overview in film 1062, *The Gentle Sex?*, four women poets, Elizabeth Jennings, Fleur Adcock, Carol Rumens and Grace Nichols, debate the issues of feminist literary theory in their own terms. They discuss feminism, being a poet, being a mother, language, politics and readers, and each poet reads one of her poems.

Director	25 minutes
Betty Talks	Color
Participants	Age range 18–adult
Fleur Adcock	VHS $99
Elisabeth Jennings	
Grace Nicols	
Carol Rumens	

Open University/BBC

1064 The Next Five Minutes: Literature and History

Interviews with Martin Amis, Angela Carter and J G Ballard explore how these writers have dealt with the history of the world since 1945. How can writers present the reality of potential apocalypse? And should they try? The program concludes with an extract from Martin Amis's novel *London Fields*.

Director	24 minutes
Beth Martin	Color
Participants	Age range 18–adult
Martin Amis	VHS $99
Angela Carter	
J G Ballard (archive)	

Open University/BBC

1065 Brecht on Stage

Professor Hans Mayer worked closely with Brecht on the original production of *Mother Courage and Her Children*. Here he discusses how it was staged and the work of Brecht at the Berliner Ensemble.

Director	24 minutes
Amanda Willett	Color
Presenter	Age range 18–adult
Professor Hans Mayer	VHS $99
Helene Weigel	
Carl Weber	

Open University/BBC

Introduction to Literature

Four programs which investigate how language works – in everyday life, in literature and in particular literary forms, such as poetry and the detective novel.

1004 Language and Literature

With the help of Professor Umberto Eco, best-selling author, we investigate the difference between everyday language and the language of literature. Does everyday language tend to do our thinking for us, because we use linguistic stereotypes and fail to notice the inherited historical meanings of words? And is that the difference between it and literary language, which, as Eco argues, is 'language which draws attention to itself'? This idea is tested on William Blake's poem *The Sick Rose*, and we discover that while no 'correct' interpretation of the meaning of a poem can ever be established, it will still have a basic area of meaning which must be observed. We conclude that writers use literary language to question received ideas in the world of everyday language, and perhaps to change that world.

Presenter	24 minutes
Graham Martin	Color
with Umberto Eco	Age range 18–adult
Director	VHS $99
Tony Coe	

Open University/BBC

1005 Poetry: Language and History

An inquiry into the relationship between language and its historical context. We discover why Seamus Heaney's *Broagh* and Yeats's *Easter 1916* are political as well as landscape poems; we also consider the relative importance of the sound of a poem and its meaning. Can one admire the technical ability of a poet like Dryden whilst disagreeing with what he says? And are we in fact really incapable of grasping what he says, since we can't rid ourselves as readers of our own historical context? Do we always reinterpret works written in the past in the light of our own time, instead of learning more about the times they came out of?

Presenter	24 minutes
Graham Martin	Color
Director	Age range 18–adult
Tony Coe	VHS $99

Open University/BBC

1006 Narrative

Umberto Eco, author of the medieval murder mystery *The Name of The Rose*, suggests that all novels are a sort of detective story. We are invited to test that theory by examining a dramatized scene from Chapter Three of Dickens's *Hard Times*, to see the ways in which the author builds up our expectations of and predictions about the way in which the story will end. We see how the scene reminds us of the very opening of the book, and also points forward to several later scenes. We are also reminded of the context in which many of Dickens's books were produced: they were published as magazine serials, and he also read them aloud to audiences. Umberto Eco concludes by affirming the importance of the detective novel.

Presenter	24 minutes
Graham Martin	Color
with Umberto Eco	Age range 18–adult
Director	VHS $99
Tony Coe	

Open University/BBC

1010 Signs of the Times – Umberto Eco

In this program Umberto Eco is shown in his country house, in an art gallery and in various locations around the ancient town of Urbino, discussing *The Name of the Rose* and the ideas behind it. These include the history of semiotics – the branch of linguistics which deals with signs and symbols – and the way in which we understand the world around us by reading the 'signs' it gives us, much as Eco's sleuth, the English monk William of Baskerville, reads the clues which help him to solve the series of murders in *The Name of the Rose*.

Presenter	24 minutes
Umberto Eco	Color
Director	Age range 18–adult
Anne Diack	VHS $99

Open University/BBC

The Making of the Roland Collection

From producer to distributor to end-user:
this section pays tribute to the role of the
production companies that make the films and
videos distributed by the Roland Collection, and
to some of the educational institutions that
benefit from them – clients may be fascinated
to see the extent of grass-roots support the
collection has generated in the United States.
The 'Highlights' take a brief look at the
background to the collection – its creation and
the innovative ways in which it has expanded
the audience for films on art – and at exciting
future developments.

Australia

Film Australia
Malcolm Otton

Austria

Minck/Stratil
ORF

Belgium

BRT
RTBF
Simple Productions
VAR
Vision on Art
Zeno Film

Brazil

Magneto

Anthony Roland gratefully acknowledges the enthusiastic co-operation of the production companies whose films are included in the Roland Collection. Their representatives have helped in many ways – for example with exhaustive screenings of productions, finalizing contracts for the titles selected by Anthony Roland, clearing rights where applicable, obtaining negatives and video masters, making available foreign-language versions, and assisting with the making of English-language versions.

Almost all of the productions are distributed on an exclusive basis.

Canada

Briston Productions
International Tele-Film
National Film Board of Canada

Czech Republic

Ceskoslovenska Televize
Kratky Film Praha Barrandov

Denmark

Danmarks Radio
Sorensen Film

Estonia

Estonian Television

Finland

Filkas
Finn Image

France

Antenne 2
Anthony Roland Films
Atelier du Film
Canal Plus
Célia Film
Centre Georges Pompidou
Ciné Tamaris
5 Continents
Cité des Sciences
Delegations au Développement et
        aux Formations
Editions Cinégraphiques
Equipage and Final Touch
Films ABC
Films du Cyprès
Films du Jeudi
Films du Prieure
Films du Saturne
Films du Touraine
Films Michel François
Films Roger Leenhardt
Gaumont
Institut du Monde Arabe
Institut Géographique National
Institut National de l'Audiovisuel
Institut Pédagogique National
ITUD, Paris
Jean-Claude Lubtchansky
KAFE
La Sept
Les Films d'Ici
Les Films de l'Iris
Made in Europe Productions
Maison de la Culture du Havre
Magic Films
Maria la Hardouin
Ministry of Culture
Ministry of Foreign Affairs
Ministry of Post and Telecommunications
Ministry of Urbanism
Mission Cable
ORSTOM
ORTF
Pas Sage Image
Pathé Télévision
Pierre Lobstein

Plan Construction
Plan Recherche Image
Productions Tanit
Regards Productions
Salto Productions
Service de la Recherche ORTF
SIPRO
Soleluna Films
Terra Luna Films
Thomson
TIP TV
Tracol Film
3 Plus Productions
UNESCO

Germany

Arts Media
Bayerischer Rundfunk
Blomberg
Brussels Avenue
Cine-International
Deutsche Condor Film
DOC Reporters
Euphono Film
Film Studio W Leckebusch
Gareis Film
Herbert Apelt
Hossfeld
Igel Film
Justin Goltfried
Karl F de Vogt
Klanz Ertz
Marcus Zollner
M2T
Polytel International
Peter Schamoni
Ray Muller
Rota Film
Telepool
Tri Star
Unda Film
Utopia Film
ZDF
Zeiss Film

Great Britain

Anthony Roland Films
Arts Council of Great Britain
Ashwood Educational Productions
Barony Film and Television
Basic Films
Brighton Polytechnic
Channel Four Television
Cinecontact
Educational Films of Scotland
Educational Media International
English Heritage
Europa Nostra
Fellowbetter
Inner London Education Authority
Institute of Contemporary Arts
James Garrett
Jane Balfour Films
John Halas
Louis R Annaud
National Gallery
Open University/BBC
Pacesetter Films
Tate Gallery
Television Entertainment
Visual Heritage
Visual Publications
World Wide Pictures

Ireland

Videoactive

Italy

Giorgio Patara
MOANA, Rome
Officinema
RAI
Romor Film

Japan

College Women's Association of Japan
Media International Corporation
NHK

Mexico

Museo Nacional de Antroplogía
Protele

Morocco

Radiotélévision Marocaine

Netherlands

Delft University of Technology
Horizon Film Productions
Jan Vrijman
Multifilm Nico Crama
Netherlands Information Service
NV Han van Gelder
Raaf Film
Wonten Snip

New Zealand

Meridan Film
New Zealand Film Commission
TVNZ

Norway

Statens Filmsentral

Russia

Art Video International

Slovakia

Bratislavia Film Studios
Studio Kratkych Filmov

Spain

Episa
Provideo
TVE

Switzerland

Gaudenz Meili
RTSI
RTSR
T & C Edition AG

USA

Arcadia Pictures
Caldwell/Enrico
Lewis Jacobs
Wayne Schowalter

The impetus for the collection was generated by Anthony Roland's nationwide lecture tour of the United States, where he presented five films that he had directed to museums and universities in twenty-eight cities. The response from art educators was an overwhelming demand for readily accessible films on art. Anthony Roland took up the challenge to search out and select the finest films available and to distribute them worldwide. This involved extensive work at film laboratories around the world, making negatives compatible with US standards.

The Roland Collection was launched as an official cultural event of the Olympics in Mexico City. Since then the collection has supplied programs to over four thousand clients in eighty-two countries, and to two hundred film festivals, as well as creating unique festivals of films on art in their own right.

The Art Film Centre was set up in central London: for two years two cinemas were dedicated to showing films on art, bringing together members of most of the capital's art associations, and art-lovers from across Europe, who came to spend whole weekends at the centre.

The Guardian paid tribute to 'the magnitude of Anthony Roland's fait

A mobile art museum, named Artscope, was created, consisting of sixteen open-air cinemas, with a 6,400 seating capacity. Its month-long world premiere at the Edinburgh Festival was a huge success.

The Scotsman called Artscope 'the most extraordinary spectacle to be seen anywhere in the festival'.

This was followed by a five-week US premiere on the National Mall in Washington DC, and a New York City summer season.

'Artscope is a three-dimensional catalo

'Artscope … a unique amalgam of international talent.'
The Smithsonian Associate

'Anthony Roland believes commercial distributors don't screen the world's best films. So he's come up with a way to take great films directly to the people. His solution transforms any large park or city square into an open-air arena containing sixteen separate film screens. The result is a festival of art, film, music and bacchanal all rolled into one'
Special Events Report, Chicago

Other festivals organized by the Roland Collection include a three-day festival at the National Gallery Art Book Fair in London; a five-day festival of rare films on art for the International Council of Museums in Quebec City; 106 screenings over four days using twenty screening rooms at the Munich Medianet (an international market of audiovisual and interactive programs for culture and education).

Using forty large video monitors, 500 programs on art have been presented over a number of days at numerous shows:
- Museums and Heritage show, London
- MILIA (International Publishing and New Media Market), Cannes
- Salon International des Techniques Museographiques, Lille
- Audiovisual Creative Fair, Brussels
- European Council of International Schools, Montreux

nd to his choice of films that combine

'intrinsic filmic quality with worthy subject-matter,' and in the *Times* the sculptor Henry Moore wrote: 'that it required the enterprise and courage of one individual to bring such a concept into being is a matter for amazement;' the *Sunday Times* acclaimed Anthony Roland as a 'one-man UNESCO.'

The Roland Collection also exhibits intermittently at numerous annual conventions:
- American Library Association (ALA)
- College Art Association (CAS), USA
- International Council of Museums (ICOM)
- International Federation of Library Associations and Institutions (IFLA)
- International Film and Programme Market for TV, Video, Cable and Satellite (MIPCOM), France
- International Television Programme Market (MIPTV), France
- National Art Education Association (NAEA), USA
- National Association of Television Programming Executives (NATPE), USA
- National Society for Education in Art and Design (NSEAD), UK

f Roland's film collection. Looking like a campfire-circle for culture vultures… the atmosphere is glorious'
Washington Post

'Artscope… the best of all possible things to see.'
New York Magazine

Further exciting developments of the collection are in preparation: an interactive resource catalog on the World Wide Web (Internet) offering new film and video productions each week and giving access to the very heart of the Roland Collection. A CD-ROM version of the catalog is also being planned.

Alabama

Lurleen Wallace State Junior
College
State College
University
James Faulkner State Junior
College
Art Association
City Schools
Independent Presbyterian
Church
Museum of Art
Southern College
University of Alabama
Shelby County Board of
Education
University of North Alabama
Marshall County Materials
Center
Museum of Art
Oakwood College
University
Bishop State Community
College
University of South Alabama
University
Auburn University at
Montgomery
Museum of Fine Arts
High School
High School
Montgomery High School
College
State University
The University of Alabama
Tuskegee Institute
University of Alabama

Alaska

Alaska Pacific University
School District
University of Alaska
University of Alaska
University of Alaska
University of Alaska
Chukchi College
Matanuska Susitna
Community College
Prince William Sound
Community College

Arizona

Unified School
Cochise College
University of Arizona
School District 1
Northern Arizona University
Window Rock School District 8
Community College
Elementary Schools
Mohave Community College
Arizona Lutheran Academy
Arizona State University
Maricopa Community College
Phoenix College
Public Library
Rio Salado Community College
Scottsdale Schools
Thunderbird High School
Union High School District 210
Embry-Riddle Aeronautical
University
Prescott College
Center of the Arts
Horizon High School
Public Schools
Arizona State University
Marcos de Niza High School
Union High School District
Amphitheater Public Schools
Fine Arts
Pima Community College
University of Arizona
Arizona Western College

Arkansas

Henderson State College
Northwest Arkansas
Community College
Hendrix College
City Schools
High School
University of Arkansas
East Arkansas Community
College
Westark Community College
Arkansas Art Center
Humanities Resource Center
University of Little Rock
High School
Northeast High School
Public Schools
University of Arkansas
John Brown University
Arkansas State University

California

College of Alameda
Pacific Union College
Unified School District
Ferman Chambers
Cabrille College
High School District
Humbolt State University
Robert Woodruff Arts
Center Incorporated
Pacific College
Pacific University
California State College Library
High School
College of Notre Dame
Moffitt Library
Pacific Film Archive
University Art Museum
Woodbury University
San Diego State University
High School
California State University
High School

High School
California State University
Hilltop High School
Southwestern College
Sweetwater Community
College
Harvey Mudd College
Huntley Bookstore
Pitzer College
Scripps College
Unified School District
San Bernardino Valley College
Mount Diable Unified School
District
Orange County College
West Valley High School
Library
High School
Cypress College
University of California
Los Angeles County Public
Library
Cuyamaca College
Grossmont College
College of the Redwoods
Solano City Community
College District
Unified School District
College of the Redwoods
Fort Bradd High School
Fremont Ohlone College
California State University
City College
Pacific College
State College
Unified School District
California State University
Fullerton College
Unified School District
Professional Media Service
Corporation
Community College
Citrus College
Stanford University
Joint Union High School
Centinela Valley High School
District

Chabot College
Moreau High School
South County Community
College
College
University of California
Unified School District
Flintridge Prep School
Museum of Art
Community College District
Grossmount Union High
School District
Biola University
Antelope Valley Community
College District
Unified School District
California State University
City College
County Museum of Art
Gipson Hoffman and Pancione
Jack Healy Productions
Mount St Mary's College
Preferred Equities Corporation
Public Library
Public Schools
Sigma International
Corporation
Unified School District
University High School
University of Southern
California
East Union High School
Yuba Community College
District
Archdiocese of San Francisco
College
Highlands School
Saddleback College Library
Saddleback Valley Unified
School District
Yosemite Community College
District
Schools
Moorpark College
Peninsular College
Seaside High School
Isaac Newton Graham School
St Frances High School
Union High School
Thousand Oaks Library

California State University
Holmes Junior High School
California College of Arts and
Crafts
College Prep School
Lamy College
Public Library
Mira Costa College
Unified School District
Unified School District
Warehouse
County Public Library
Unified School District
House Fellowship of Friends
Butte College
Union High School District
College of the Desert
Main Library
PVLD
Area Community College
District
Norton Simon Museum of Art
Westridge School
Unified School District
El Dorado County Office of
Education
El Dorado Schools
Diablo Valley College
Pleasanton School
Unified School District
High School
Shasta Tehama Trinity Joint
Community College
San Mateo City Schools
Sequoia High School
California Baptist College
Community College
University of California
Sierra College
California State College –
Sopoma
American River College
California State University
City College
Consumnes River College
Croker Art Gallery
State College
Hartnell College
Notre Dame High School
Moorpark College

Colorado

Connecticut

Delaware

District of Columbia

Florida

Northfield
Sunset Ridge School
Oak Park and River Forest
High School
Oglesby
Illinois Valley Community
College
Palatine
Harper College
Palos Hills
Amos Alonze Stagg School
District
Moraine Valley Community
College
Park Ridge
Main Township High School
Peoria
Lakeview Museum of Arts and
Sciences
Pekin
Community High School
River Grove
Triton College
Riverside
Broadfield High School
Rockford
Art Museum
Rockford College
Rock Island
Augustana College Library
Roscoe
Illinois State Museum
J Iguchi and Company
Lincoln Land Community
College
Sangamon State University
Springfield Art Association
South Holland
South Suburban College
Springfield
Lincoln Land Community
College
Sugar Grove
Wavbonsee Community
College
Tinley Park
Victor J Andrew High School
Tomms
School District 5
University Park
Governors State University
Urbana
Champaigne County Schools
University of Illinois at Urbana
Wadsworth
The Pyramid
Waterloo
Community Unit School
District 5
Wauconda
Community School District
Waukegan
Holy Child High School
Wheaton
High School
Wheaton College
Wilmette
Harper School
Loloya Academy
Regina High School
Winetka
New Trier High School East
Winnebago
Art Guild of Rockford

Indiana

Bedford
College Center
Bloomington
Indiana University
Cambridge
City Western Wayne Schools
Chesterton
Duneland School Corp
Columbus
North High School
Crawfordsville
Wabash College
Crown Point
High School
Decatur
Bellmont High School
Elkhart
Community School
Evansville
College of Evansville
Indiana Vocational Technical
College
Fort Wayne
Museum of Art – Purdue
University
Franklin
Franklin College
Gary
Public Library
Goshen
College
High School
Greencastle
De Pauw University
Hanover
Duggan Library
Indianapolis
Adams Elementary School
Allen County Public Library
Avon High School
Ben Davis Junior High School
Herron Museum of Art
Public Library
University of Indianapolis
Muncie Ball
State University
Notre Dame
St Mary's College
University of Notre Dame
Oakland
City College
Rensellar
St Joseph's College
Richmond
Earlham College
Terre Haute
Indiana State University
Upland
Taylor University
Valparaiso
High School
Lutheran University
Association Incorporated
University Association
Vincennes
University
West Lafayette
Purdue University
Wabash Valley Education
Center

Iowa

Ames
Community School District
Iowa State University
Beitendorf
Mississippi Bend Area
Education Agency
Scott Community College
Boone
DMACC
Burlington
Great River Area Education
Agency
Ceder Falls
Area 7 Media Services
State College of Iowa
University of Northern Iowa
Ceder Rapids
Coe College
First Lutheran Church
First Presbyterian Church
Kenwood Park Presbyterian
Church
Kirkwood Community College
Mount Mercy College
Clarinda
Iowa Western Community
College
Clinton
Mt St Clare College
Creston
Southwestern Community
College
Davenport
Art Gallery
Community School District
St Ambrose College
Decorah
Luther College
Des Moines
Art Center
Iowa State University
Drake
Grand View College
University
Varsity Theatre
Dubuque
Clarke College
Elkader
Keystone AEA Media Center
Emmetsburg
Iowa Lakes Community
College
Forest City
Waldorf College
Fort Dodge
Iowa Central Community
College
Grinell
Grinell College
Iowa City
University of Iowa
Marshalltown
Community College
Community Schools
Mason City Board of
Education
Senior High School
Muscatine
Schools
Ottumwa
Educational Media Center
Pella
Central College

Sioux City
Briar Cliff College
Dordt College
Morningside College
Storm Lake
Buena Vista College
Truro
Community School District
Waverly
Wartburg College

Kansas

Abilene
Schools
Baldwin City
Community Arts Council
Coffeyville
Community College
Colby
Community College
Dodge City
St Mary of the Plains College
El Dorado
Butler County Community
College
Circle Gallery and Frame Shop
Heston
Heston College
Highland
Community College
Hutchinson
Community Junior College
Kansas City
Community College
Lawrence University of Kansas
Public Library
Lindsborg
Bethany College
Manhattan
Kansas State University
Marysville
Unified School District
North Newton
Bethel College
Overland
Blue Valley Service Center
Johnson County Community
College
Otis-Bison High School
Pittsburg
Kansas State College
State University
Salina
Public Schools Mission
Unified School District 305
Shawnee
Art Museum
Mission Public Schools
State University
Sterling
Sterling College
Topeka
High School
Topeka and Shawnee County
Public Library
Washburn University
Wichita
College Continuing Education
State University
Public Library

Kentucky

Berea
College
Bowling Green
Western Kentucky University
Corington
Board of Education
Elizabethtown
High School
Frankfort
Bondurant Middle School
Department of Libraries
Hodgenville
La Rue County Junior High
School
Hopkinsville
Community College Library
Lexington
University of Kentucky
Louisville
Bellarmine College
Downtown Library
JB Speed Art Museum
Jefferson County Board of
Education
Southern High School
Translyvania University
Trinity High School
University of Louisville
Morehead
State University
Mount Vernon
Family Life Center School
Murray
State University
Paducah
Community College
Richmond
Eastern Kentucky University
Williamsburg
Cumberland College
Wilmore
Asbury College

Louisiana

Alexandria
Central Louisiana Art
Association Incorporated
Baton Rouge
Southern University
Covington
Christ Episcopal School
Metairie Park
Country Day School
New Orleans
Delgado Community College
Isidore Newman School
Louisiana State University
Museum of Art
Tulane University School of
Architecture
University of New Orleans
Shreveport
Barnwell Garden and Art
Center
Meadows Museum of Art
Southern University
Slidell
Pope John Paul II High School

Maine

Augusta
Cony High School
Bangor
Husson College
Bethel
Gould Academy
Brewer
High School
Brunswick
Bowdoin College
Falmouth
High School
Farmington
University of Maine
Gorham
University of Maine at
Portland
University of Southern Maine
Lewiston
Bates College
Machias
University of Maine
Madawaska
High School
Madison
High School
Oqunquit
Barn Gallery Association
Orono
University of Maine
Portland
School of Art
University of South Maine
Westbrook College Library
Sabattus
Oak Hill High School
Sanford
High School
South Portland
South Portland School
University Heights
University of Maine at
Augusta
Waterville
Colby College

Maryland

Annapolis
Anne Arundel Public School
US Naval Academy
Baltimore
Dundalle Community College
Essex Community College
Goucha College
John Hopkins University
Loyola Notre Dame Library
McDonogh School
Morgan State University
Museum of Art
New Community College of
Baltimore
University of Maryland
Walters Art Gallery
Bel Air
John Carroll School
Brooklandsville
St Paul's School
Catonsville
Catonsville Community College
Chesterton
Washington College
Clarksville
Board of Education of Howard
County

Owosso
Emery Pratt Company
Petoskey
Public Schools
Pinconning
Area Schools
Plymouth
High School
Pontiac
School District
Portage
Central High School
Port Huron
St Clair County Community
College
Rochester
Oakland University
Roscommon
Kirtland Community College
Sault Ste Marie
Lake Superior State College
Public Schools
Spring Arbor
College of Spring Arbor
Traverse City
Northwest Michigan College
Trenton
High School
Union Lake
Oakland Community College
University Center
Saginaw Valley College
Warren
Macomb Community College
Ypsilanti
Eastern Michigan University

Minnesota

Aitkin
High School
Bloomington
Abraham Lincoln High School
Normandale Community
College
Normandale State Junior
College
Brooklyn Center
Brooklyn Park
High School
North Hennepin Community
College
Burnsville
High School
Chaska
High School
Collegeville
St John's University
Diamond Path
Independent School District
Duluth
College of St Scholastica
East High School
University of Minnesota
Eagan
Cedar Elementary School
Eden Prairie
High School
Edina
East Senior High School
Furgus Falls
Community College
Grand Rapids
Hasca Community College
Itasca Community College
Hibbing
Community College
Lester Prairie
Public School
Little Canada
Roseville Area Middle School
Long Lake
Orono High School
Minneapolis
Breck School
College of Art and Design
Community College
Institute of Arts
Media Resource Center
Museum of Art
North Hennepin State Junior
College
Seven Arts
Society of Fine Arts
Technical Institute
University of Minnesota
Walker Art Center
Minnetonka
High School
Moorhead
Concordia College
State University
New Hope
Independent School
New Ulm
Dr Martin Luther College

Northfield
Carleton College
St Olaf College
Red Wing
Central High School
Richfield
Public Schools
Rochester
Community College
Public Library
Roseville
Northwestern College Library
St Cloud
State University
St Joseph
College of St Benedict
St Louis Park
Public Schools
St Paul
College of Associated Art
College of St Catherine
College of St Thomas
Concordia College
Edgewood Junior High School
Gustavas Adolphus College
Hamline University
MacAlester College
Public Schools
University of Minnesota
St Peter
Gustavus Adolphus College
Stewartville
High School
Two Harbors
Lake Superior School
Virginia
Independent School District
Watertown
Mayer High School
West St Paul
Henry Sibley High School
White Bear Lake
Lakewood Community College
White Bear High School
Willmar
Junior High School
Winona
St Mary's College
State College
Worthington
Community College State
Junior College

Mississippi

Cleveland
Delta State College
Fulton
Itawamba Community College
Greenville
Media Center
Gulfport
Gulf Coast Junior College
Hattieburg
University of Southern
Mississippi
Jackson
Millsaps College
Public School District
State University
Larrel
Roger Library and Museum of
Art
Lorman
Alcorn A and M College
Meridian
Junior College
Mississippi
Mississippi University
Mississippi State
Mitchell Memorial Library
Raymond
Community College District
Hinds Junior College
Senatobia
Northwest Mississippi
Community College
Northwest Mississippi Junior
College

Missouri

Boonville
R-I High School
Canton
Culver-Stockton College
Cape Girardeau
Southeast Missouri State
University
Chesterfield
Parkway School District
Clayton
School District of Clayton
Columbia
Columbia College
David Hickman High School
University of Missouri
Columbus
Rock Bridge High School
State College for Women
Stevens College
Hillsboro
Jefferson College
Jefferson City
Lincoln University
Kahoka
Clark County R-I Schools
Kansas City
Barston School
Christian Education
Committee
Exhibits USA
Hallmark Cards
Lincoln College Prep
Lion Creek Archaeological
Museum
Nelson-Atkins Art Museum
Nelson Gallery of Art
Pembroke Hill School

Kirksville
Northeast Missouri State
University
Kirkwood
High School
Lexington
High School
Liberty
William Jewell College
Maryville
Northwest Missouri State
University
Monet
Board of Education
North Kansas City
High School
Raymond
Hinds Community College
District
Richmond Heights
Christian Brothers College
High School
Rolla
University of Missouri-Rolla
St Charles
Francis Howell School
St Louis
City Art Museum
Community College
Country Day School
Harris-Stowe State College
Incarnate Word Academy
Library
Instructional Resources
Junior College District
Mary Institute
National Art Education
Association
St Louis College of Pharmacy
Thomas Jefferson Library
University of Missouri
Washington University
Webster College
Webster University
Whitfield School
Sedalia
State Fair Community College
Springfield
Baptist Bible College
Drury College
Southwest Missouri State
University
Warren
Macomb City Community
College
Warrenburg
Central Missouri State College

Montana

Billings
Eastern Montana College
Senior High School
Bozeman
Montana State University
Great Falls
College of Great Falls
Helena
Helena School District 1
Kalispell
Flathead Valley Community
College
School District 5
Miles City
Community College
Missoula
University of Montana

Nebraska

Alliance
Senior High School
Beatrice
Southeast Community College
Bellevue
Mission Junior High
Columbus
Central Community College
Fremont
Junior High
Midland Lutheran College
Grand Island
Bennett Martin Public Library
Lincoln Art Museum
Public Schools
University of Nebraska
Lincoln
University of Nebraska
Norfolk
Northeast Community College
Omaha
College of St Mary
Josslyn Art Museum
Metropolitan Technical
Community College
Public Schools
University of Nebraska at
Omaha
West Side School
Seward
Concordia Teachers College
Wayne
State College

Nevada

Carson City
School District
Las Vegas
Clark County School District
Minotaur Fine Art
University of Nevada Las
Vegas
Reno
High School
Robert McQueen High School
Library
University of Nevada
Washoe County School District

New Hampshire

Concord
High School
Durham
University of New Hampshire
Exeter
Phillips Academy
Gilford
Middle-High School
Hampton
Winnacunnet High School
Hanover
Dartmouth College
Henniker
New England College
Hollis
Elementary School
Keene
Public Library
Manchester
Currier Gallery of Art
University of New Hampshire
Newport
High School
Plymouth
State College
Tamworth
Arts Council

New Jersey

Aberdeen
Matawan-Aberdeen Regional
School District
Annandale
North Hunterdon Regional
High School
Bedminster
Clarence Dillon Library
Bergenfield
Free Public Library
Bernardsville
Public Library
Blackwood
Camden County College
Blairstown
North Warren Regional High
School Library
Bloomfield
Bloomfield College
Bogota
High School
Boonton
High School
Cherry Hill
Public Schools
Convent Station
College of St Elizabeth
Cranford
Public Schools
Union County College
Delran
High School
Deptford Township
Gloucester County College
Dover
County College of Morris
East Orange
Upsala College
Edison
Middlesex County College
Elizabeth
Pingry School
Englishtown
Freehold Regional High School
District

Farmingdale
Schools
Flanders
Mount Olive High School
Glassboro
State College
Glen Ridge
High School
Hamburg
Wallkill Valley Region High
School District
High Bridge
Hunterdon County Audio
Holmdel
High School
St John Vianney Region High
School
Irvingston
High School
Jackettstown
Centenary College
Jersey City
Academic High School
St Peter's College
State College
Kearny
High School
Lakehurst
Manchester Township High
School
Lawrenceville
Rider College Schools
Lincroft
Brookdale Community College
Livingston
Newark Academy
Madison
Drew University
Mahwah
Ramapo College
Maplewood
School District of South
Orange
Mays Landing
Atlantic Community College
Mendham
Free Public Library
W Morris Mendham High
School
Millburn
Education Center
Monmouth Junction
South Brunswick High School
Montclair
Art Museum
Kimberley Academy
Montvale
Passack Hills High School
Morristown
High School
Newark
Essex County College
New Brunswick
Rutgers University
New Providence
High School
Newton
High School
North Bergen
High School
High School North
North Branch
Raritan Valley Community
College

Norwood
American Overseas Book
Company Incorporated
Oakland
Indian Hills High School
Paramus
Bergen Community College
Board of Education
Paramus High School
Paterson
Passaic County Community
College
Pemberton
Burlington County College
Perth Amboy
High School
Piscataway
Rutgers University
Pomona
Stockton State College
Princeton
Day School
International Schools Services
Stuart Country Day School of
the Sacred Heart
University Art Museum
Randolf Township
County College of Morris
Red Bank
High School
Ridgewood
High School
Somerset
Franklin Township Board of
Education
Sparta
High School
Summit
Oak Knoll School
Teaneck
High School
Toms River
Ocean County College
Trenton
Department of Education
State of New Jersey
Fisher Junior High School
Ryder College
State College
Union
Kean College of New Jersey
Upper Montclair
State College
Upper Saddle River
Cavallini Middle School
Vernon
Township High School
Wayne Valley
High School
William Paterson College
Westfield
Board of Education
West Long Branch
Shore Regional High School
West Orange
Mountain High School
Wildwood
High School

New Mexico

Albuquerque
Albuquerque Academy
University of New Mexico
Farmington
Northwest New Mexico Media
Consortium
Gallup
University of New Mexico
Hobbs
New Mexico Junior College
Las Cruces
New Mexico State University
School District 2
Las Vegas
New Mexico Highlands
University
Montezuma
Armand Hammer United
World College of the
American West
Portales
Enmu Library
Santa Fe
Institute of American Indian
Arts
St John's College
Shiprock
Navajo Community College

New York

Albany
College of St Rose
Colonic Central High School
Institute of History of Art
New York State Education
Department
Plaza Manager's Office ESP
University of the State of New
York
Alfred
State University College of
Ceramics
Amherst
Daemen College
Sweet Home High School
Auburn
Cayuga Community College
Aurora
Wells College Library
Ballston Spa
High School
Batavia
Genesee Community College
Bedford
Fox Lane High School
Belmore
Mepham High School
Binghamton
Broome Community College
Roberson Memorial Center
State University of New York
Brentwood
Academy of St Joseph
Briarcliff Manor
King's College
Pace University
Brockport
Albright-Knox Art Gallery
Daemen College
State University College
Bronxville
Sarah Lawrence College

Buffalo
D'Youville College
State University
Villa Maria College
Canandaigra
Community College of the
Finger Lakes
Canton
HC Williams High School
St Lawrence University
Cazenovia
Cazenovia College
Central Valley
Monroe-Woodbury High
School
Chappaqua
Horace Greeley High School
Cheektowaga
Cleveland Hill UFSD
John F Kennedy High School
Clinton
Hamilton College Library
Cobleskill
State University of New York
College of Agriculture and
Technology
Corning
Corning Community College
Museum of Glass
Corona
New York Hall of Science
Cortland
State University College
Delhi
State University of New York
College of Agriculture and
Technology
Delmar
Dromitory Authority State of
New York
Dixhills
Ambassador Book Service
Dobbs Ferry
High School
Eastchester
Tuckahoe Union Free School
District
East Hampton
Guild Hall Museum
East Meadow
Schools
East Syracuse
Minoa
Elmira
Elmira College
Steele Memorial Library
Endicott
Union-Endicott High School
Endwell
Maine Endwell Senior High
School
Fallsway
Sullivan Correctional Facilities
Floral Park
Sewanhaka High School
Forest Hills
FDS Art World
Fredonia
State University College
Fulton
G Ray Bodley High School
Junior High
Garden City
Mineola Senior High School
Nassau Community College
Genesco
State University College

Geneva
Hobart and Smith Colleges
Hobart and William Colleges
Glens Falls
Adirondack Community
College
Hyde Collection
Granville
Junior/Senior High School
Greenville
Long Island University
Hannibal
High School
Hauppauge
Ballen Booksellers
International Incorporated
Hawthorne
Union Free School District
Hempstead
Hofstra University
Hillburn
Suffern High School
Hilton
High School
Hyde Park
FD Roosevelt High School
Irvington
High School
Islip
Public Library
Terrace Junior High School
Ithaca
Cornell University
Ithaca College
Jamaica
St John's University
York College
Jamestown
Chautauqua Cattaraugus
Library System
Katonah
John Jay High School
The Katonah Gallery
Kenmore
Town of Tonawands Public
School
Kingston
Lock Stock and Barrel
Myron J Michael Junior High
School
Lafargeville
Central School
Lawrence
High School
Lawrence Middle School
Lebanon Springs
New Lebanon Central School
Lewiston
Coutts Library Services
Incorporated
Liberty
Central School District
Locust Valley
Friends Academy
Long Beach
City Schools
Long Island
Dowling College
Garden City High School
The Bridgehampton High
School
Loudonville
Siena College
Lowville
Central School District

Malone
North Country Community
College
Manhasset
High School
Marion
Central School
Medford
Patchogue-Medford Schools
Middleton
Orange County Community
College
Millbrook
Bennett College
Mineola
Arts Project Junior High
School
Monroe
Area Medical Assoc
Montauk
Public School
Moravia
High School
Newburgh
Mt St Mary College
New City
Central School District
New Hyde Park
Herricks Senior High School
New Paltz
State University College
Ulster BOCES
New Rochelle
Blessed Sacrament - St Gabriel
High School
College of New Rochelle
Iona College
New York City
Art and Antiques
Artists Rights Society
Art of the Western World
Art Student League
Bronx Community College
Library
Brooklyn College
Brooklyn Eastern District High
School
Brooklyn Museum
Brooklyn Public Library
Chemiakine Metaphysical Arts
Incorporated
City College
City of New York Department
of Parks and Recreation
Columbia University
Cooper Union
Dalton School
Doubleday
Fashion Institute of
Technology
First NY International Festival
of Arts
Fordham University
Gould Paper Corporation
Gramavision Incorporated
Greenwich House Pottery
Guggenheim Museum
Harper and Row Publishers
Herbert Lehman College
High School of Music and Art
Hunter College
Insight Media Incorporated
Institute of International
Education
John Jay College

Laboratory Institute of
Merchandising
Manhattan College
Medgar Evers College
Metropolitan Museum of Art
Museum of Modern Art
Museum of the American
Indian
New York University
Orion and Gloval Chartering
Company Incorporated
Phillip Morris Incorporated
Polytechnic Prep County Day
School
Program for Art on Film
Prospect Park Brooklyn
Public Library
Queens Borough Public Library
Queens College of the City of
New York
Riverside Schools
Roy Emmons Associates
Sarah Lawrence College
School of Visual Arts
Seven Arts Association
Spence School
State University of New York
Maritime College
Teachers College
Teachers and Writers
Collaborative
Typony Marketing Company
Visual Resources Incorporated
Whitney Museum of American
Art
Northport
High School
Norwich
City Schools
Oakdale
Dowling College
Oneonta
State University College
Orchard Park
Educational Services
Erie Community College
Oswego
State University College
State University of New York
College at Oswego
Oyster Bay
High School
Painted Post
Corning Painted Post Area
School
West High School
Philadelphia
Indian River Central School
Pittsburgh
State University College
Pleasantville
High School
Poplar Ridge
Southern Cayuga Central
School
Port Washington
Paul D Schriber High School
Potsdam
Central School District
Clarkson University
State University College at
Potsdam
Purchase
State University of New York
Rensselser
East Greenbush Community
Library

Rhinebeck
Thinebeck Central School
Rochester
Arcadia High School
College of Liberal Arts
Concetta Glass Studio
Greece Central School District
Institute of Technology
Monroe Community College
Museum and Science Center
Nazareth College of Rochester
Rochester Regional Library
Council
St Joseph Fisher College
University of Rochester
Rockville Centre
South Side High School
Roslyn
Bryant Library
Rye
County Day School
Rye High School
St Bonaventure
University – Library
Sanborn
Niagara County Community
College
Saratoga Springs
Skidmore College
Schenectady
Linton High School
Niskayuna Central Schools
Union College
Seaford
High School
Union Free School District
Selden
Suffolk County Community
College
Sodus
High School Central School
Southampton
Long Island University
Sparkhill
St Thomas Aquineas College
Staten
Wagner College
Stony Brook
State University of New York
Stone Ridge
Ulster County Community
College
Suffern
Rockland Community College
Syosset
High School
Syracuse
Henninger Media Center
Le Moyne College Library
Onondaga County Public
Library
Syracuse University
Westhill High School
Thornwood
Westlake High School
Troy
Emma Willard School
Hudson Valley Community
College
Rensselaer Polytechnic
Institute
Russel Sage College
Uniondale
St Pius X Prep Seminar

Utica
Mohawk Valley Community
College
Munson-Williams Peoctor
Institute
Valhalla
Westchester Community
College
Wantagh
High School
Wappingers Falls
Central Schools
Wayland
Central School
West Babylon
Senior High
Westbury
Wheatley Schools
West Sayville
High School
West Seneca
Central School
White Plains
Westchester Art Workshop
Wilson
Central School

North Carolina

Asheville
University of North Carolina
Boone
Appalachian State University
State Teachers College
Watauga High School
Brevard
College Corporation
Carthage
Sandhills Community College
Chapel Hill
University of North Carolina
Charlotte
Central Piedmont
Charlotte Community College
Charlotte-Mecklenburg School
James Turner
Mint Museum of Art
University of North Carolina
China Grove
Junior High
Cullowhee
Western Carolina University
Davidson
Davidson College
Durham
County Schools
Duke University
North Carolina Central
University
Technical Institute
Elon College
Library
Fayetteville
Fayetteville State University
Methodist College
Technical Community College
Gastonia
Arts Center/TRC
Goldsboro
Wayne Community College
Greensboro
DC Heath and Company
Greensboro College
Guildford County Schools
University of North Carolina

Greenville
East Carolina University
Pitt Community College
High Point
College
Jamestown
Guilford Technical Community
College
Laurinburg
St Andrews Presbyterian
College
Lexington
Davidson County Community
College
Louisberg
Louisberg College
Madison
Western Rockingham City
Schools
Misenheimer
Pfeiffer College Incorporated
Montreat
Anderson College
Morehead City
Carteret Community College
Murphy
Tri County Community College
New Bern
Tryon Palace Restoration
Raleigh
Carlyle Campbell Library
Haywood Community College
St Mary's College
State Library of North Carolina
Wake County Board of
Education
Salisbury
Rowan Cabarrus Community
College
Spartanburg
Converse College
Spindle
Isothermal Community College
Statesville
Mitchell Community College
Wake Forest
Southeast Baptist Theological
Seminary
Waynesville
Haywood County Public
Library
Whiteville
Southeastern Community
College
Williamston
Martin Community College
Wilson
Atlantic Christian College
Barton College
City Technical College
Wingate
Wingate College
Winston-Salem
Forsyth Technical Institute
Mount Tabor High School
Wake Forest University
Yanceyville
Bartlett Yances High School

North Dakota

Bismarck
Century High School
University of Mary
Bottineau
North Dakota State University
School District 1
Devils Lake
School District 1
Fargo
NDSU Art Gallery
NDSU Department of Design
Grand Forks
University of North Dakota
Jamestown
Jamestown College
Minot
State University
Valley City
State University
Williston
University of North Dakota

Ohio

Ada
Ohio Northern University
Akron
Art Institute
Art Museum
Board of Education
Summit County Public Library
University of Akron
Ashland
Ashland College
Ashtabula
Campus Library
Athens
Ohio University
Bay Village
High School
Bellbrook
Stephen Bell Elementary
School
Berea
Baldwin-Wallace College
Boardman
High School
Bowling Green
State University
Brunswick
High School
Canton
Art Institute
Central Catholic High School
Walsh College Library
Cedarville
College Library
Celina
Wright State University
Chardon
Notre Dame Academy
Chillicothe
Ohio University
Union-Scioto Local Schools
Cincinnati
Archbishop Moeller High
School
Art Academy of Cincinnati
Bible College and Seminary
Claude Courter Education
Center
Deer Park City School District
McAuley High School
Moeller High School
Museum Association

403

Williamsport
Pennsylvania College of
Technology
Williamsport Area School
District
York
William Penn Senior High
School
York College of Pennsylvania
York College Library
Youngwood
Westmoreland Community

Puerto Rico

Bayamon
Universidad de Puerto Rico
Cayey
Colegio Universitario de Cayey
Mayaguez
Upper Mayaguez Campus
Old San Juan
University of the Sacred Heart
Ponce
University of Puerto Rico
Rio Piedras
Colegio San Ignacio de Loyola
University of Puerto Rico
San German
International American
University of Puerto Rico
San Juan
Institut de Cultura
Puertorriquera
Liga Estudiantes de Arte de
San Juan
Santurce
St John's School
Universidad del Sagrado
Corazon

Rhode Island

Barrington
High School
Bristol
Roger Williams College
Cranston
High School East
Johnston
Atwood Pediatrics
Kingston
University of Rhode Island
Lincoln
Council of the Arts
Newport
Art Association
Salve Regina College
Providence
Brown University
Lasalle Academy
Providence College
Rhode Island School of Design
Rhode Island
College of Rhode Island
Rhode Island School of Design
State of Rhode Island and
Providence
Smithfield
Community College of Rhode
Island
New England Institute of
Technology
Warwick
Bryant College
Woonsocket
Education Department

South Carolina

Allendale
University of South Carolina
Camden
Kershaw County School
District
Charleston
College
Cheraw
High School
Clemson
Emery A Cunnin Architecture
Library
University
Columbia
College of Columbia
Museum of Art and Science
South Carolina State Library
University of South Carolina
Conway
Horry County School District
Due West
Erskine College
Florence
Florence School
Francis Marion College
Greenville
School District of Greenville
County
Technical College
Greenwood
Lander College
Lancaster
University of South Carolina
Spartanburg
City Schools
Converse College
University of South Carolina
Wofford College
Wake Forest
Southeast Baptist Theological
Seminals

South Dakota

Aberdeen
Northern State College
Brookings
South Dakota State University
Rosebud
Sinte Gleska College
Sioux Falls
Augustana College
Spearfish
Black Hills State College
Vermillion
University of South Dakota

Tennessee

Chattanooga
Hunter Museum of Art
State Technological
Community College
Tennessee Temple University
University of Tennessee at
Chattanooga
Clarksville
Felix G Woodward Library
Cookeville
Putnam County Board of
Education
Tennessee Technological
University
Dyer
Gibson County High School
Gallatin
Volunteer State Community
College
Greeneville
Tusculum College
Harriman
Roane State Community
College
Jackson
State Community College
Union University
Johnson City
East Tennessee State
University Library
Knoxville
Johnson Bible College
Knox County School
Museum of Art
University of Tennessee
Webb School of Knoxville
Martin
University of Tennessee
Memphis
Academy of Arts
Dixon Gallery and Gardens
Harding Academy of Memphis
Memphis City Schools
Memphis State University
Rhodes College
St Mary's Episcopal School
Murfreesboro
Middle Tennessee State
University
Nashville
Belmont College
David Lipscomb University
George Peabody College of
Teachers
Metropolitan Board of
Education
Sarratt Art Center
Vanderbilt University
Wharton Middle School

Texas

Abilene
Christian College
Hardin-Simmons University
Addison
Trinity Christian Academy
Alpine
Sul Ross State University
Alvin
Junior College
Amarillo
College Bookstore
Public Schools
Arlington
University of Texas
Austin
Community College
Media Center
St Edward's University
St Stephen's Episcopal School
The University of Texas at
Austin
University Interscholastic
League
University of Texas Press
Baytown
Lee College
Beaumont
Art Museum
Beaumont Independent School
District
Lamar University
Big Spring
Howard County Junior College
District
Brownsville
Independent School District
Texas Southmost College
Burleson
High School
Canyon
West Texas State University
Carthage
Panola College
College Station
College of Architecture and
Design
Texas A and M University
Commerce
East Texas State University
Copperas Cove
Copperas Cove Independent
School District
Junior High School
Corpus Christi
Art Foundation Incorporated
Del Mar College
Corsicana
Navarro College
Dallas
Mountain View College
Museum of Fine Arts
Public Library
Richland College
St Mark's School
Southern Methodist University
Denton
North Texas University
South Texas Woman's
University
Edinburg
Pan American University

El Paso
Community College
El Paso Independent School
District
Museum of Art
Public Schools
University of Texas at El Paso
Yselta Independent School
Farmers Branch
Brookhaven College
Fort Worth
Ammon Carter Museum
Kimbell Art Museum
Tarrant County Junior College
Texas Christian University
Texas Wesleyan College
Western Hills High School
Freeport
Brazosport Independent
School District
Gary
Public Schools
Georgetown
Southwestern University
Grapevine
High School Library
Haskell
Independent School District
Houston
Baptist University
Houston Community College
System
Houston Education Service
Center
Jane Long Middle School
Library
Museum of Fine Arts
Rice University
Texas Southern University
University of Houston at Clear
Lake
University of Houston –
Downtown
Hurst
Tarrant City Junior College
Irving
Independent School District
Jacksonville
Lon Morris College
Katy
Independent School District
Killeen
Independent School District
Kingwood
North Harris County College
Klein
Independent School District
Lancaster
Cedar Valley College
Laredo
American School Foundation
Guadalajara AC
Longview
Pine Tree Independent School
District
The Trinity School of Texas
Lubbock
Texas Technical University
Lufkin
Angelina College
Lufkin High School
Macogdochen
State University
Manchester
University of New Hampshire
Marshall
East Texas Baptist University

Mesquite
Eastfield College
Midland
College
Museum of the Southwest
Mount Pleasant
Independent School District
Northeast Texas Community
College
Nacogduches
Stephen Austin State
University
Odessa
College of Odessa
Paris
Junior College
Pasadena
Independent School District
San Jacinto College
Plano
Collin County Community
College
Independent School District
Port Arthur
Independent School District
Richardson
University of Texas at Dallas
Rosenberg
Lamar Junior High School
San Angelo
Angelo State University
Education Service Center
Region XV
San Antonio
Academic Enrichment
Alamo Heights High School
Incarnate Word College
Pudder Middle School
St Mary's University Academic
Library
St Philip's College
San Antonio College
Trinity University
University of Texas
Ursuline Academy
San Marcos
Southwest Texas State
University
Seguin
Texas Lutheran College Library
Sherman
Austin College
Public Schools
Stephenville
Tarleton State University
Temple
Junior College
Texaskana
East Texas State University
Tyler
Junior College
Victoria
University of Houston –
Victoria
Waco
Baylor University
McLennan Community College
Waco High School
Waxahachie
School District
Weatherford
College of Weatherford
Wichita Falls
Midwestern State University
Wichita Falls Museum and Art
Center

Utah

Alpine Instructional Media
  Center
Utah State University
Weber State University
Public Library
Utah Valley Community
  College
Brigham Young University
Salt Lake Community College
School District
University of Utah
Nebo School District

Vermont

Bennington College
Mount Anthony Union High
  School
Community College of
  Vermont
Mount Abraham V High
  School
Champlain College
Trinity College of Vermont
University of Vermont
St Michael's College
Mount Mansfield Union High
  School
RFD
Southern Vermont Art Center
Southern Vermont Artists
  Incorporated
Marlboro College
College of Middlebury
Mill River High School
Green Mountain College
Windham College
Academy

Virginia

City Public Schools
Northern Virginia Community
  College
North Virginia Community
  College
Marymount University
Randolph Macon College
Virginia Polytechnic Institute
  and State University
Virginia Technical College
Sullins College
Adult Education Center
Albemarle County Schools
University of Virginia
Public Schools
Public Schools
Longwood College
George Mason Junior Senior
  High School
Emory and Henry College
College of Hampden–Sydney
University
Eastern Memonite College
James Madison University
Instructional Materials Center
St Paul's College
Lylburn Downing Middle
  School
Washington and Lee University
Central Virginia Community
  College
Liberty University
Lynchburg City Schools
Randolph Macon Woman's
  College
Foxcroft School
Christopher Newport
  University
Old Dominion University
Virginia Wesleyan College
Virginia State University
University
Southwest Virginia
  Community College

J Sargeant Reynolds
  Community College
Presbyterian School of
  Christian Education
Shape High School
Virginia Commonwealth
  University
Virginia Museum of Fine Arts
Virginia State Library
City School Board
Virginia Western Community
  College
Roanoke College
Mary Baldwin College
College of Sweet Briar
City Schools
First Colonial High School
College of William and Mary
Colonial Williamsburg
  Foundation
Williamsburg Regional Library

Virgin Islands

University of the Virgin Islands

Washington

Grays Harbor College
Green River Community
  College
Northwest Indian College
Public Library
Western Washington
  University
West Washington State
  College
Whatcom Community College
Whatcom Museum of History
  of Art
Trinity Western University
Olympic College
Centralia College
Eastern Washington State
  College
Eastern Washington University
  Library
Central Washington University
Community College
Kentridge Senior High School
Lake Washington Vocational-
  Technological
South Whidbey High School
Edmonds Community College

School District 400
Senior High School
Skagit Valley College
Evergreen State College
South Puget Sound
  Community College
Wenatchee Valley College
  North
Washington State University
Renton School District
Art Museum
Central Community College
Seattle Pacific University
Shoreline Community College
South Seattle Community
  College
University of Washington
Gonzaga University
School District 81
Spokane Falls Community
  College
Bellarmine Prep School
Fort Steilacoom Community
  College
Pacific Lutheran University
Pierce College at Fort
  Steilacoom
Tacoma Community College
University of Puget Sound
Public School
Whitman College
Valley College
Valley Community College

West Virginia

Concord College
College of Bethany
State College
Art Gallery
Davis and Elkins College
State College
Cabell County Board of
  Education
Huntington Galleries
Marshall University
West Virginia University
State College

Wisconsin

Lawrence University
Board of Education Joint
  District 1
School
St Norbert College
  Incorporated
University of Wisconsin
McKenna Middle School
Prep University Wisconsin
Southwest Wisconsin
  Technical College
Ashwaubenon Public Schools
Preble High School
University of Wisconsin
High School
College Community Library
Kenosha Gateway Technical
  Institute
Lac Courte Oreilles Ojibwa
University of Wisconsin
Mount Senario College
Logan Middle School
University of Wis-La Crosse
Area Board of Education
  District 4
Area Technical College
Dept of Public Instruction
Metropolitan School District
University of Wisconsin
District Schools
University of Wisconsin State
Senior High School
Art Center
Area Technical College
Bay View High School
Cardinal Stritch College
Institute of Art and Design
Marquette University
Mount Mary College
Pius XI High School
Public Library
St Gall Adult Learning Center
University of Wisconsin
Wisconsin Lutheran College
Lakeland Union High School
Paine Art Center
Parkview School

University of Wisconsin
Racine Unified School
William Horlick High School
University of Wisconsin
School District
Senior High School
University of Wisconsin
University of Wisconsin
Senior High School
Middle School
Carroll College
Senior High School
Leigh Yawkey Woodson Art
  Museum
Wausau West High School
High School
University of Wisconsin
Wisconsin State University
Union High School
Lincoln High School
Rapids Board of Education

Wyoming

College of Casper
Laramie County Community
  College
University of Wyoming
Central Wyoming College
College
Freemont County School
  District 24
Crook County School District

Ordering Made Easy

The Key to the Collection provides a summary of technical details and all the information necessary to place an order; it also makes it easy to select films on the basis of art discipline, period and age range. Programs on art and architecture and film and video series are listed chronologically by catalog number, while videos on modern literature are listed alphabetically by author. At a glance you will find:

- art disciplines by color code
- description page numbers
- series cross references
- recommended audience age range
- price list

Further details of prices, availability and services offered by the Roland Collection are given on pages 434–5, including:

- rental prices
- television use
- stock footage
- preview service

This section also includes a guide for teachers in the USA on how video acquisition can be funded through the United States National Visual Arts Standards scheme.

In a pioneering initiative to improve art education in America, National Visual Arts Standards (NVAS) have been drawn up, setting out what every schoolchild should know and be able to do in visual arts, dance, theater and music. The standards are part of the *Goals 2000: Educate America Act*, which provides over 10 billion dollars for state and local education reform programs. Individual teachers and school districts can apply for funds if they can show their courses fulfil the standards.

The Roland Collection of Films and Videos on Art represents a major resource that can help art educators implement the scheme, which is outlined opposite. The Key to the Collection (pages 412–29) shows which content standard areas and age ranges are covered by individual programs.

In a message to members, the president of the US National Art Education Association stressed the importance of the scheme:

'National standards in visual art, music, dance and theater are now firmly placed among the goals to be met by the year 2000 for all children K-12 in the United States. Art is accepted as one of the "basics" – a goal for which art educators have worked, pleaded, written and spoken for decades… We've never had this status before… We've never had this kind of money before… We've never had these resources before.

'The first point I want to make is that the goals are options for districts and states; the moneys from the legislation will flow to the states and to districts; the standards… are voluntary, not mandatory. What this means to you is that the emphasis… will shift from the federal and national level to the state and local level. The leadership needed to employ the national goals, to capture the funds, to utilize the standards, is going to be… your responsibility.

'You need to seek ways in which the goals can be replicated in your state and schools; find out the procedures for using the funds in your state and individual schools; and use the standards and other resources… I hope you take this very important challenge.'

Excerpts of president's message from NAEA News, *June 1994, courtesy NAEA*

Grades Kindergarten–4

To meet the standards, students must learn vocabularies and concepts associated with various types of work in the visual arts and must exhibit their competence at various levels in visual, oral, and written form.

In grades Kindergarten–4, young children experiment enthusiastically with art materials and investigate the ideas presented to them through visual arts instruction. They exhibit a sense of joy and excitement as they make and share their artwork with others. Creation is at the heart of this instruction. Students learn to work with various tools, processes and media. They learn to co-ordinate their hands and minds in explorations of the visual world. They learn to make choices that enhance communication of their ideas. Their natural inquisitiveness is promoted, and they learn the value of perseverance.

As they move from kindergarten through the early grades, students develop skills of observation, and they learn to examine the objects and events of their lives. At the same time, they grow in their ability to describe, interpret, evaluate and respond to work in the visual arts. Through examination of their own work and that of other people, times and places, students learn to unravel the essence of artwork and to appraise its purpose and value. Through these efforts, students begin to understand the meaning and impact of the visual world in which they live.

Grades 5–8

In grades 5–8, students' visual expressions become more individualistic and imaginative. The problem-solving activities inherent in art making help them develop cognitive, affective and pyschomotor skills. They select and transform ideas, discriminate, synthesize and appraise, and they apply these skills to their expanding knowledge of the visual arts and to their own creative work. Students understand that making and responding to works of visual art are inextricably interwoven and that perception, analysis and critical judgement are inherent to both.

Their own art making becomes infused with a variety of images and approaches. They learn that preferences of others may differ from their own. Students refine the questions that they ask in response to artworks. This leads them to an appreciation of multiple artistic solutions and interpretations. Study of historical and cultural contexts gives students insights into the rôle played by the visual arts in human achievement. As they consider examples of visual artworks within historical contexts, students gain a deeper appreciation of their own values, the values of other people, and the connection of the visual arts to universal human needs, values and beliefs. They understand that the art of a culture is influenced by aesthetic ideas as well as by social, political, economic and other factors. Through these efforts, students develop an understanding of the meaning and import of the visual world in which they live.

Grades 9–12

In grades 9–12, students develop deeper and more profound works of visual art that reflect the maturation of their creative and problem-solving skills. Students understand the multifaceted interplay of different media, styles, forms, techniques and processes in the creation of their work.

Students develop increasing abilities to pose insightful questions about contexts, processes and criteria for evaluation. They use these questions to examine works in the light of various analytical methods and to express sophisticated ideas about visual relationships using precise terminology. They can evaluate artistic character and aesthetic qualities in works of art, nature and human-made environments. They can reflect on the nature of human involvement in art as a viewer, creator and participant.

Students understand the relationships among art forms and between their own work and that of others. They are able to relate understandings about the historical and cultural contexts of art to situations in contemporary life. They have a broad and in-depth understanding of the meaning and import of the visual world in which they live.

409

Content standards	1 Understand and apply media, techniques and processes	2 Use knowledge of structures and functions	3 Choose and evaluate a range of subject matter, symbols and ideas
Grades Kindergarten–4 **Student achievement standards**	**a** know the differences between materials, techniques and processes **b** describe how different materials, techniques and processes cause different responses **c** use different media, techniques and processes to communicate ideas, experiences and stories **d** use art materials and tools in a safe and responsible manner	**a** know the differences among visual characteristics and purposes of art in order to convey ideas **b** describe how different expressive features and organizational principles cause different responses **c** use visual structures and functions of art to communicate ideas	**a** explore and understand prospective content for works of art **b** select and use subject matter, symbols and ideas to communicate meaning
Grades 5–8 **Student achievement standards**	**a** select media, techniques and processes; analyze what makes them effective or not effective in communicating ideas; and reflect upon the effectiveness of their choices **b** intentionally take advantage of the qualities and characteristics of art media, techniques and processes to enhance communication of their experiences and ideas	**a** generalize about the effects of visual structures and functions and reflect upon these effects in their own work **b** employ organizational structures and analyze what makes them effective or not effective in the communication of ideas **c** select and use the qualities of structures and functions of art to improve communication of their ideas	**a** integrate visual, spatial and temporal concepts with content to communicate intended meaning in their artworks **b** use subjects, themes and symbols that demonstrate knowledge of contexts, values and aesthetics that communicate intended meaning in artworks
Grades 9–12 **Student achievement standards**	**Proficient** **a** apply media, techniques and processes with sufficient skill, confidence and sensitivity that their intentions are carried out in their artworks **b** conceive and create works of visual art that demonstrate an understanding of how the communication of their ideas relates to the media, techniques and processes they use **Advanced** **c** communicate ideas regularly at a high level of effectiveness in at least one visual arts medium **d** initiate, define and solve challenging visual arts problems independently using intellectual skills such as analysis, synthesis and evaluation	**Proficient** **a** demonstrate the ability to form and defend judgements about the characteristics and structures to accomplish commercial, personal, communal, or other purposes of art **b** evaluate the effectiveness of artworks in terms of organizational structures and functions **c** create artworks that use organizational principles and functions to solve specific visual arts problems **Advanced** **d** demonstrate the ability to compare two or more perspectives about the use of organizational principles and functions in artwork and to defend personal evaluations of these perspectives **e** create multiple solutions to specific visual arts problems that demonstrate competence in producing effective relationships between structural choices and artistic functions	**Proficient** **a** reflect on how artworks differ visually, spatially, temporally and functionally, and describe how these are related to history and culture **b** apply subjects, symbols and ideas in their artworks, and use the skills gained to solve problems in daily life **Advanced** **c** describe the origins of specific images and ideas and explain why they are of value in their artwork and in the work of others **d** evaluate and defend the validity of sources for content and the manner in which subject matter, symbols and images are used in the students' works and in significant works by others

4 Understand the visual arts in relation to history and cultures	5 Reflect upon and assess the characteristics and merits of their work and the work of others	6 Make connections between visual arts and other disciplines

a know that the visual arts have both a history and specific relationships to various cultures

b identify specific works of art as belonging to particular cultures, times and places

c demonstrate how history, culture and the visual arts can influence each other in making and studying works of art

a understand there are various purposes for creating works of visual art

b describe how people's experiences influence the development of specific artworks

c understand there are different responses to specific artworks

a understand and use similarities and differences between characteristics of the visual arts and other arts disciplines

b identify connections between the visual arts and other disciplines in the curriculum

---

a know and compare the characteristics of artworks in various eras and cultures

b describe and place a variety of art objects in historical and cultural contexts

c analyze, describe and demonstrate how factors of time and place (such as climate, resources, ideas and technology) influence visual characteristics that give meaning and value to a work of art

a compare multiple purposes for creating works of art

b analyze contemporary and historic meanings in specific artworks through cultural and aesthetic inquiry

c describe and compare a variety of individual responses to their own artworks and to artworks from various eras and cultures

a compare the characteristics of works in two or more art forms that share similar subject matter, historical periods, or cultural context

b describe ways in which the principles and subject matter of other disciplines taught in the school are interrelated with the visual arts

---

Proficient

a differentiate among a variety of historical and cultural contexts in terms of characteristics and purposes of works of art

b describe the function and explore the meaning of specific art objects within varied cultures, times and places.

c analyze relationships of works of art to one another in terms of history, aesthetics and culture, justifying conclusions made in the analysis and using such conclusions to inform their own art making

Advanced

d analyze and interpret artworks for relationships among form, context, purposes and critical models, showing understanding of the work of critics, historians, aestheticians and artists

e analyze common characteristics of visual arts evident across time and among cultural/ethnic groups to formulate analyses, evaluations and interpretations of meaning

Proficient

a identify intentions of those creating artworks, explore the implications of various purposes, and justify their analyses of purposes in particular works

b describe meanings of artworks by analyzing how specific works are created and how they relate to historical and cultural contexts

c reflect analytically on various interpretations as a means for understanding and evaluating works of visual art

Advanced

d correlate responses to works of visual art with various techniques for communicating meanings, ideas, attitudes, views and intentions

Proficient

a compare the materials, technologies, media and processes of the visual arts with those of other arts disciplines as they are used in creation and types of analysis

b compare characteristics of visual arts within a particular historical period or style with ideas, issues, or themes in the humanities or sciences

Advanced

c synthesize the creative and analytical principles and techniques of the visual arts and selected other arts disciplines, the humanities, or the sciences

USA National Visual Art Standards

Recommendations for implementation of standards

Grades K-4 (Ages 5-10)	Grades 5-8 (Ages 10-14)	Grades 9-12 (Ages 14-18)	1	2	3	4	5	6	Painting	Drawing and graphics	Sculpture	Architecture and design	Photography and video art	Period covered / Artists' dates	Catalog number	Title	Preview video (see page 435)	Series reference (see pages 428-9)	Availability codes (outside USA see page 434)	Audience / Recommended age range	Running time in minutes Color (c) / Black and white (b/w)	Revised prices 16mm film sale	16mm film rental USA and Canada only	VHS video sale
■	■	■		2		4			■					Prehistoric	10	Tassili N'Ajjer pages 15, 25, 225, 267	P1			6–adult	16 c	$790	$169	$79
	■	■				4							■	Prehistoric	13	Prehistoric Sites pages 15, 259, 280	P1A	S32		11–14	20 c			$89
■	■	■				4						■		Neolithic	14	Grimes Graves pages 15, 276	P1B	S30		6–14	12 c			$79
■	■	■				4							■	Iron Age–AD 43	16	Working on the Evidence pages 17, 276	P1B	S30		9–14	20 c			$89
	■	■			3	4					■			Neolithic–AD 400	20	The Origins of Art in France page 17	P1			12–adult	38 b/w	$990	$199	$99
	■	■				4					■	■		3000–2000 BC	21	The Sumerian Kingdom of Ur page 20	P2A	S1		14–adult	25 c	$990	$199	$99
	■	■				4					■	■		2000–500 BC	22	Babylon – The Gate of the Gods page 20	P2A	S1		14–adult	25 c	$990	$199	$99
	■	■				4					■	■		883–859 BC	23	Assurnasirpal – The Assyrian King page 21	P2A	S1		14–adult	25 c	$990	$199	$99
	■	■				4					■	■		400 BC–AD 300	24	Hatra page 21	P2A	S1		14–adult	25 c	$990	$199	$99
	■	■				4						■		3000 BC–AD 1985	25	The Mesopotamian Heritage of Islamic Architecture page 21	P2A	S1		14–adult	29 c	$990	$199	$99
	■	■				4					■	■		AD 900–1000	27	Borobudur: Beyond the Reach of Time pages 22, 309	P10C			14–adult	32 c	$1090	$199	$109
	■	■				4					■	■		3500 BC–AD 1000	30	Nubia '64 pages 19, 309	P2		A15	12–adult	42 c	$1190	$249	$119
	■	■				4					■	■		3000 BC–AD 600	40A	Digging for the History of Man, Part One page 19	P1			12–adult	30 c	$990	$199	$99
	■	■				4					■	■		3000 BC–AD 600	40B	Digging for the History of Man, Part Two page 19	P1			12–adult	25 c	$990	$199	$99
	■	■		2					■			■		1500–400 BC	50	Greek Pottery page 22	P2			12–adult	19 c	$890	$189	$89
	■	■									■			300–100 BC	70	Etruscan Tombs of Volterra page 23	P2			14–adult	11 c	$690	$149	$69
	■	■				4			■					200 BC–AD 79	80	Pompeii, City of Painting page 23	P2			12–adult	12 c	$790	$169	$79
	■	■			3	4		6			■			1000–1900	85A	The Shape of Darkness, Part One page 25	P3			12–adult	26 b/w	$890	$189	$89
	■	■			3	4		6			■			1000–1900	85B	The Shape of Darkness, Part Two page 25	P3			12–adult	26 b/w	$890	$189	$89
		■				4					■			1000–1993	87	The Colonial Encounter pages 25, 307A	P32A	S19	A8	18–adult	25 c			$99
■	■	■	1			4							■	Traditional	88	Of Leaves and of Earth pages 25, 259, 267	P3A			6–adult	45 c	$1190	$249	$119
	■	■			3	4					■			400–1000	90	A Thousand and One Years Ago page 27	P3			12–adult	13 c	$790	$169	$79
	■	■			3	4						■	■	1200 BC–AD 1521	91	Pre-Columbian Art in Mexico pages 27, 259	P3G	S3		14–adult	56 c			$139
	■	■			3	4						■	■	1200 BC–AD 1521	92	In Search of the Mayas pages 27, 259	P3E	S2		14–adult	56 c			$139
	■	■			3	4						■	■	600 BC–AD 1521	93	The Aztec Sun pages 27, 260	P3E	S2		14–adult	56 c			$139
	■	■				4					■			500–700	95	Maya Terracotta Figurines pages 27, 215, 267	P3			14–adult	12 c	$790	$169	$79
	■	■				4					■			700–1200	98	Carved in Ivory pages 29, 227	P4A		A2	14–adult	30 c	$990	$199	$99
■	■			2		4							■	1100–1400	99A	Looking at a Castle pages 29, 280	P1A	S32		9–13	14 c			$79
■	■	■				4							■	1250–1500	99B	Castles of Northumberland pages 30, 276	P1B	S30		9–15	24 c			$99
	■	■			3	4					■	■		1000–1200	100	French Romanesque Art page 30	P3			12–adult	21 b/w	$890	$189	$89
	■	■			3	4			■			■		1000–1200	110	Romanesque Painters page 30	P3			12–adult	12 c	$690	$149	$69

USA National Visual Art Standards

K–4 (5–10)	5–8 (10–14)	9–12 (14–18)	1	2	3	4	5	6	Painting	Drawing and graphics	Sculpture	Architecture and design	Photography and video art	Period covered / Artists' dates	Catalog number	Title	Preview video	Series reference	Availability codes	Audience / Recommended age range	Running time (c/b/w)	Revised prices 16mm film sale	16mm film rental USA and Canada only	VHS video sale
	■	■		2	3	4					■	■		1000–1200	111	Romanesque Architecture of Alsace pages 32, 310	P3D	S4		14–adult	26 c	$990	$199	$99
	■	■		2	3	4					■	■		1000–1200	112	Romanesque Architecture of Burgundy page 32	P3D	S4		14–adult	26 c	$990	$199	$99
	■	■		2	3	4					■	■		1000–1200	113	Romanesque Architecture of Languedoc page 33	P3D	S4		14–adult	26 c	$990	$199	$99
	■	■		2	3	4					■	■		1000–1200	114	Romanesque Architecture of Normandy pages 33, 310	P3D	S4		14–adult	26 c	$990	$199	$99
	■	■		2	3	4					■	■		1000–1200	115	Romanesque Architecture of Poitou-Charente page 33	P3D	S4		14–adult	26 c	$990	$199	$99
	■	■		2	3	4					■	■		1000–1200	116	Romanesque Architecture of Provence page 33	P3D	S4		14–adult	26 c	$990	$199	$99
	■	■		2	3	4					■	■		950–1250	117	Pierres d'Etoiles pages 31, 227	P3B			14–adult	54 c	$1490	$299	$149
■	■	■				4						■		1066	118	The Norman Conquest of England pages 31, 282	P3C			8–15	15 c			$79
	■	■			3	4					■	■		1066–1200	119	English Romanesque Art page 31	P3A			12–18	56 c			$129
	■	■		2								■		1000–1300	120	Pisa, Story of a Cathedral Square page 34	P4			14–adult	11 c	$690	$149	$69
	■					4					■	■		1000–1250	123	The Romanesque in Austria page 34	P4A			15–adult	44 c			$119
	■	■			3	4		6			■	■		1188	125	And They Sang a New Song page 34	P3A			14–adult	28 c			$99
	■	■				4					■			1100–1800	130	Popular Art in Brittany page 34	P4			14–adult	19 b/w	$790	$169	$79
■	■	■	1										■	1200–1300	136	The Master Builders: The Construction of a Great Church pages 35, 278	P1B	S31		8–15	21 c			$89
■	■	■				4							■	1100–1200	137	Looking at an Abbey pages 35, 281	P1A	S32		8–15	17 c			$89
■	■	■	1										■	1100–1200	138	Building an Abbey: Rievaulx pages 35, 277	P1B	S30		8–15	14 c			$79
	■	■	1							■			■	1230–5	140	Villard de Honnecourt: Builder of Cathedrals pages 36, 235	P4			14–adult	15 b/w		$169	$79
■	■	■				4			■					1200–1300	150	Visions of Light pages 36, 227, 268	P4			9–adult	15 c	$790	$169	$79
	■	■		2									■	1196–1250	160	Antelami: The Baptistery of Parma page 36	P4			14–adult	16 c	$790	$169	$79
	■	■	1				5		■					1270–1400	163	Art in the Making: Italian Painting before 1400 pages 37, 320	P18A	S6		14–adult	20 c			$89
	■	■				4			■					1250–1450	165	The Birth of European Painting page 37	P16	S5		12–adult	28 c	$990	$199	$99
	■	■				4			■		■			1300–1500	170	Dijon: The Four Grand Dukes of Burgundy page 38	P4			14–adult	14 c	$790	$169	$79
	■	■		2	3		5		■					1422–64	171	An Eye for Detail page 38	P4A			14–adult	21 c			$89
	■	■		2		4	5		■					c1389–1441	173	Van Eyck, Part One pages 38, 228	P5C			14–adult	55 c			$139
	■	■		2		4	5		■					c1389–1441	174	Van Eyck, Part Two pages 38, 228	P5C			14–adult	55 c			$139
	■	■							■					1400–64	175	Beaune: Rogier van der Weyden pages 39, 228	P4			12–adult	15 c	$790	$169	$79
	■	■				4							■	1000–1500	176	Buildings and Beliefs pages 39, 279	P3C	S31		16–adult tt	20 c			$89
	■	■									■			1500–1600	178	Ecce Homo pages 39, 228	P4			12–adult	9 c	$690	$149	$69

USA National Visual Art Standards

Recommendations for implementation of standards — Content standards

Grades K–4 (Ages 5–10)	Grades 5–8 (Ages 10–14)	Grades 9–12 (Ages 14–18)	1	2	3	4	5	6	Painting	Drawing and graphics	Sculpture	Architecture and design	Photography and video art	Period covered / Artists' dates	Catalog number	Title	Preview video see page 435	Series reference see pages 428–9	Availability codes for use outside USA see page 434	Audience / Recommended age range / Teacher training (tt)	Running time in minutes / Color (c) / Black and white (b/w)	Revised prices 16mm film sale	16mm film rental USA and Canada only	VHS video sale
▫	■					4			■					1450–1500	179	Early Renaissance in Italy page 41	P16	S5		12–adult	28 c	$990	$199	$99
▫	■								■					1387–1455	180	Fra Angelico pages 41, 229	P5			14–adult	10 c	$690	$149	$69
▫	■								■					1416–98	200	Piero della Francesca page 41	P5			14–adult	10 c	$690	$149	$69
▫	■					4			■					1400–1550	205	The Northern Renaissance page 49	P16	S5		12–adult	28 c	$990	$199	$99
▫	■				3	4			■					1420–c80	210	Jean Fouquet pages 41, 230	P5			14–adult	15 c	$790	$169	$79
▫	■										■			1450–1518	215	Guido Mazzoni pages 42, 230, 310	P4A			14–adult	30 c			$99
▫	■				3		5		■					1444–1510	220	Botticelli's Calumny of Apelles page 42	P5			14–adult	12 c	$690	$149	$69
▫	■					4			■					1500–1600	223	The Age of Titian page 42	P17	S5		12–adult	28 c	$990	$199	$99
▫	■					4			■					1480–1530	225	The Age of Leonardo and Raphael page 43	P17	S5		12–adult	28 c	$990	$199	$99
▫	■											■		1506–8	226	The Restoration of a Leonardo da Vinci pages 43, 310	P18A			12–adult	20 c			$89
▫	■			2					■	■	■	■		1475–1564	230A	Michelangelo, Part One pages 44, 215	P6			14–adult	35 c	$1090	$199	$109
▫	■			2					■	■	■	■		1475–1564	230B	Michelangelo, Part Two pages 44, 215	P6			14–adult	35 c	$1090	$199	$109
	■			2									■	1508–80	232	The Miracle of Palladio page 45	P4A			15–adult	43 c			$119
	■					4						■	■	1450–1600	233	Rome under the Popes: Church and Empire page 45	P5A	S8	A8	18–adult	25 c			$99
	■					4							■	1450–1600	236	Venice and Antwerp, Part One: The Cities Compared page 49	P5A	S8	A8	18–adult	25 c			$99
	■					4							■	1450–1600	237	Venice and Antwerp, Part Two: Forms of Religion pages 49, 230	P5A	S8	A8	18–adult	25 c			$99
	■					4						■		1520–89	238	Christopher Plantin, Polyglot Printer of Antwerp page 50	P5A	S8	A8	18–adult	25 c			$99
▫	■				3	4			■	■				1497–1543	240	At the Turn of the Age: Hans Holbein page 50	P5			12–adult	13 c	$790	$169	$79
	■					4			■					1498–1574	242	Maarten van Heemskerck: Humanism and Painting in Northern Europe page 50	P5A	S8	A8	18–adult	24 c			$99
▫	■			2		4	5		■					c1525–69	244	Bruegel, Part One page 51	P5C	S7		14–adult	50 c			$139
▫	■			2		4	5		■					c1525–69	245	Bruegel, Part Two page 51	P5D	S7		14–adult	50 c			$139
	■					4			■					c1525–69	246	Pieter Bruegel and Popular Culture page 51	P5B	S8	A8	18–adult	24 c			$99
	■					4							■	1450–1600	252	Seville: The Edge of Empire page 46	P5B	S8	A8	18–adult	24 c			$99
	■					4							■	1450–1600	254	El Escorial: Palace, Monastery and Mausoleum page 46	P5B	S8	A8	18–adult	24 c			$99
	■					4							■	1450–1600	256	Ottoman Supremacy: The Suleimaniye, Istanbul page 46	P6A	S8	A8	18–adult	24 c			$99
▫	■					4					■			1536–90	259	Germain Pilon page 47	P6A			14–adult	15 c	$890	$189	$89
	■					4			■				■	1450–1600	260	Fontainebleau: The Changing Image of Kingship page 47	P5B	S8	A8	18–adult	24 c			$99
	■					4							■	1500–1600	261	Discovering Sixteenth-century Strasbourg page 47	P5A	S8	A8	18–adult	24 c			$99
	■					4							■	1500–1600	265	Shropshire in the Sixteenth Century page 52	P5B	S8	A8	18–adult	24 c			$99

USA National Visual Art Standards

K-4	5-8	9-12	CS1	CS2	CS3	CS4	CS5	CS6	Painting	Drawing and graphics	Sculpture	Architecture and design	Photography and video art	Period covered / Artists' dates	Catalog number	Title	Preview video	Series reference	Availability codes	Audience / Recommended age range / Teacher training	Running time / Color (c) / Black and white (b/w)	Revised prices 16mm film sale	16mm film rental USA and Canada only	VHS video sale
		■				4						■		1450–1600	266	Hardwick Hall: Power and Architecture page 52	P5B	S8	A8	18–adult	24 c			$99
■	■					4						■		1500–1600	267	The Past Replayed: Kirby Hall pages 52, 282	P1B			9–13 tt	38 c			$99
	■	■				4						■		1500–1700	269	Moscow: The Gold-domed Capital page 53	P6A	S28		14–adult	30 c			$99
	■	■				4						■		1500–1600	270	Renaissance Architecture in Slovakia page 53	P5			14–adult	12 c	$690	$149	$69
	■	■				4			■					1568–1625	271	Jan Bruegel the Elder page 53	P7A			12–adult	45 c			$119
	■	■		2	3	4	5		■					1577–1640	273	Rubens, Part One pages 59, 216	P5D	S7		14–adult	55 c			$139
	■	■		2	3	4	5		■					1577–1640	274	Rubens, Part Two pages 59, 216	P5D	S7		14–adult	55 c			$139
	■	■				4			■					1600–1650	275	The Age of Rubens page 59	P17	S5		12–adult	28 c	$990	$199	$99
	■	■				4			■					c1582–1666	289	Portrait of Frans Hals page 60	P7A			14–adult	17 c	$890	$189	$89
	■	■			3	4					■			1593–1650	290	Matthew Merian pages 60, 235	P7			12–adult	15 b/w	$790	$169	$79
	■	■				4			■					1600–90	295	The Age of Rembrandt page 55	P17	S5		12–adult	28 c	$990	$199	$99
	■	■	1				5		■					1606–69	296	Art in the Making: Rembrandt pages 55, 321	P18A	S6		12–adult	20 c			$89
	■	■			3				■					1606–69	298	Rembrandt: Painter of Stories page 56	P18A			12–adult	24 c			$99
■	■	■					5	6		■				1606–69	300	Rembrandt's Christ pages 56, 231, 236	P7			10–A	49 b/w	$1090	$199	$109
	■	■							■	■				1606–69	301	Rembrandt – The Self-Portraits page 57	P7G	S9		14–adult	30 c	$990	$199	
	■	■							■	■				1606–69	302	Rembrandt – The Rebel page 57	P7G	S9		14–adult	30 c	$990	$199	
	■	■							■	■				1606–69	303	Rembrandt – The Success page 57	P7G	S9		14–adult	30 c	$990	$199	
	■	■							■	■				1606–69	304	Rembrandt – The Withdrawal page 57	P7G	S9		14–adult	30 c	$990	$199	
	■	■			3				■	■				1606–69	305	Rembrandt – The Bible pages 57, 231	P7G	S9		14–adult	30 c	$990	$199	
	■	■				4			■			■		1521–1821	306	Mexico: The Grandeur of New Spain page 60	P3F	S2		14–adult	56 c			$139
	■	■				4			■					1560–1830	307	Spanish Art: El Greco to Goya page 60	P18	S5		12–adult	28 c	$990	$199	$99
	■	■				4			■					1600–1800	309	Baroque Painting in France and Italy page 61	P18	S5		12–adult	28 c	$990	$199	$99
	■	■			3				■					1600–82	309A	Claude: The Roman Landscape pages 61, 206	P9C			14–adult	25 c			$99
	■	■									■			1648–1705	310	Via Dolorosa (Stations of the Cross) pages 61, 232	P7			14–adult	11 b/w	$690	$149	$69
■						4						■		1600–1700	311	Teaching on Site pages 66, 282	P3C			6–9 tt	19 c			$89
■	■					4						■		1600–1820	312	Evidence on Site: Boscobel House pages 66, 277	P1B	S30		9–10	10 c			$69
		■				4						■		1689–1900	313	Chapels: The Buildings of Nonconformity pages 66, 279	P3C	S31		16–adult tt	18 c			$89
		■				4		6	■		■	■		1600–1800	314	All the World on Stage page 63	P7C	S10	A6	15–adult	60 c	$1590	$299	$159
		■				4		6	■		■	■		1600–1800	315	The Wizards of the Marvellous page 63	P7C	S10	A6	15–adult	60 c	$1590	$299	$159
		■				4		6	■		■	■		1600–1800	316	The Long Frontiers to the North page 64	P7D	S10	A6	15–adult	60 c	$1590	$299	$159

Recommendations for implementation of standards — Content standards 1 2 3 4 5 6

USA National Visual Art Standards

Recommendations for implementation of standards

Grades K–4 (Ages 5–10)	Grades 5–8 (Ages 10–14)	Grades 9–12 (Ages 14–18)	1	2	3	4	5	6	Painting	Drawing and graphics	Sculpture	Architecture and design	Photography and video art	Period covered / Artists' dates	Catalog number	Title	Preview video see page 435	Series reference see pages 428–9	Availability codes for use outside USA see page 434	Audience Recommended age range / Teacher training (tt)	Running time in minutes Color (c) / Black and white (b/w)	Revised prices 16mm film sale	16mm film rental USA and Canada only	VHS video sale
		■				4		6	■		■	■	■	1600–1800	317	The Southern Empire of Baroque page 65	P7D	S10	A6	15–adult	60 c	$1590	$299	$159
		■				4		6	■		■	■	■	1600–1800	318	From Rubens to Gainsborough page 65	P7E	S10	A6	15–adult	60 c	$1590	$299	$159
		■				4		6	■		■	■	■	1600–1800	319	The Baroque of Extremes page 65	P7E	S10	A6	15–adult	60 c	$1590	$299	$159
	▣	■			3			6	■					1687–1721	320	Antoine Watteau: The Melancholia of Pleasure page 67	P7			14–adult	18 c	$890	$189	$89
		■			3	4		6		■		■		1751–72	322	The Encyclopédie page 71A	P7I	S11	A8	18–adult	25 c			$99
		■			3	4	5		■					1700–1800	323	Chardin and the Female Image page 68	P7B	S11	A8	18–adult	24 c			$99
		■			3		5		■					1700–1800	324	Chardin and the Still Life page 71A	P7I	S11	A8	18–adult	25 c			$99
		■				4						■		1789	325	Montgeoffroy: Life in a Château page 68	P7B	S11	A8	18–adult	23 c			$99
		■				4						■		1700–1800	326	Frederick the Great and Sans Souci page 71A	P7I	S11	A8	18–adult	25 c			$99
		■				4					■			1500 BC–AD 1800	327	Classical Sculpture and the Enlightenment pages 23, 71A	P7I	S11	A8	18–adult	25 c			$99
		■										■		1759	328	Kedleston Hall (Robert Adam) page 71B	P7I	S11	A8	18–adult	25 c			$99
		■				4						■		1700–1800	329	Scotland and the Enlightenment page 71B	P7J	S11	A8	18–adult	25 c			$99
■	▣	■						6			■			1700–50	330	Star of Bethlehem pages 67, 232, 268	P7			6–adult	12 c	$690	$149	$69
		■				4			■	■		■		1726–1800	333	Freedom and Plenty: England through Foreign Eyes page 68	P7B	S11	A8	18–adult	25 c			$99
		■				4			■					1741–1807	333A	Angelica Kauffman, RA, and the Choice of Painting page 71B	P7J	S11	A8	18–adult	25 c			$99
		■				4						■		1747	334	A Little Gothick Castle page 69	P7B	S11	A8	18–adult	22 c			$99
		■			3	4			■					1697–1764	335	Innocents: Images in Hogarth's Painting page 71	P7B	S11	A8	18–adult	23 c			$99
		■		2								■		1735	336	English Landscape Gardens page 71	P7B	S11	A8	18–adult	24 c			$99
		■				4		6				■		1700–1800	336A	Poetry and Landscape pages 71B, 210	P7J	S11	A8	18–adult	25 c			$99
		■			3	4		6	■					1734–97	337	Joseph Wright of Derby: Images of Science page 71	P7B	S11	A8	18–adult	25 c			$99
		■				4		6			■			1700–1800	337A	Nature Displayed page 71B	P7J	S11	A8	18–adult	25 c			$99
	▣	■					5		■					1724–1806	338	George Stubbs pages 72, 225	P8A			12–adult	26 c			$99
	▣	■		2		4	5					■		1728–92	339	The Hand of Adam page 72	P9A			14–adult	33 c	$1090	$199	$109
	▣	■				4		6				■		1725–50	340	Royal Rococo page 72	P7			12–adult	13 c	$790	$169	$79
	▣	■				4						■		1650–1750	341	Moscow: Showing a Youthful Look to the World page 72	P6A	S28		14–adult	30 c			$99
	▣	■				4		6	■		■	■		1700–1900	342	The Multiplication of Styles 1700–1900 page 75	P19	S15		12–adult	26 c	$990	$196	$99
	▣	■				4						■		1700–1900	343	Moscow: In the Quiet of Its Country Estates page 75	P6A	S28		14–adult	30 c			$99
	▣	■				4			■					1720–1850	345	The British Achievement page 75	P18	S5		12–adult	28 c	$990	$196	$99
	▣	■				4			■					1800–1900	346	The Road to Modern Art pages 78, 93	P18	S5		12–adult	28 c	$990	$196	$99
	▣	■			3				■					1774–1840	347	Caspar David Friedrich pages 82, 206	P8A			14–adult	25 c			$99

USA National Visual Art Standards

K–4	5–8	9–12	1	2	3	4	5	6	Painting	Drawing and graphics	Sculpture	Architecture and design	Photography and video art	Period covered / Artists' dates	Catalog number	Title	Preview video see page 435	Series reference see pages 428–9	Availability codes for use outside USA see page 434	Audience / Recommended age range / Teacher training (tt)	Running time in minutes / Color (c) / Black and white (b/w)	Revised prices 16mm film sale	16mm film rental USA and Canada only	VHS video sale
	▪	■			3		5		■					1774–1840	348	Caspar David Friedrich: Landscape as Language pages 82, 206, 232	P8			14–adult	18 c	$890	$189	$89
		■			3		5		■					1827–1901	349	Arnold Böcklin 80, 208	P8E			14–adult	96 c	$2190	$449	$219
		■				4			■	■	■	■		1815–48	350	The Happiness of Still Life page 81	P8A			15–adult	27 c	$990	$199	$99
		■				4			■	■		■		1815–48	351	Biedermeier and Vormärz page 81	P8E			15–adult	25 c			$99
	▪	■			3				■					1800–1920	353	A View from the Mountains page 82	P9C			14–adult	20 c			$89
	▪	■							■					1776–1837	355	Constable: The Changing Face of Nature pages 76, 205	P8A			14–adult	25 c			$99
		■		2			5		■	■				1820s	356	Constable: The Leaping Horse pages 76, 85, 205	P8B	S12	A8	17–adult	25 c			$99
	▪	■		2			5	6	■					1775–1851	360	Turner pages 76, 206	P8			12–adult	12 c	$890	$189	$89
	▪	■				4	5		■	■				1791–1824	365	Géricault: The Raft of the 'Medusa' pages 77, 216	P8			12–adult	21 c	$890	$189	$89
■	▪	■	1				5	6	■					1798–1863	370	Delacroix pages 77, 217, 225, 237	P8			6–adult	13 b/w	$890	$189	$89
		■				4			■			■		1863–93	371	Cragside page 85	P8B	S12	A8	17–adult	25 c			$99
		■		2		4					■	■		1860s	372	The Albert Memorial page 86	P8B	S12	A8	17–adult	25 c			$99
		■				4						■		1823–90	373	The Victorian High Church page 87	P8B	S12	A8	17–adult	25 c			$99
		■				4						■		1780–1880	374	Victorian Dissenting Chapels page 87	P8B	S12	A8	17–adult	25 c			$99
		■				4						■		1840–1910	375	Religion and Society in Victorian Bristol page 87	P8C	S12	A8	17–adult	25 c			$99
		■				4						■		1857–99	376	A New Museum in South Kensington pages 89, 304	P8C	S12	A8	17–adult	25 c			$99
		■				4						■		1867–75	377	King Cotton's Palace: Manchester Town Hall page 89	P8C	S12	A8	17–adult	25 c			$99
		■				4						■		1780–1880	378	Rural Life: Image and Reality page 89	P8C	S12	A8	17–adult	25 c			$99
		■				4						■		1845–80	379	The Melbury Road Set page 89	P8C	S12	A8	17–adult	25 c			$99
	▪	■					5		■					1796–1875	380	Corot pages 78, 207	P8			12–adult	18 c	$890	$189	$89
		■			3		5		■					1848–80	381	The Pre-Raphaelites pages 90, 293	P8D	S13	A9	15–adult	26 c			$99
		■			3		5		■					1855–96	382	The Followers of the Pre-Raphaelites page 90	P8D	S13	A9	15–adult	26 c			$99
		■			3	4	5		■					1840–1910	383	Victorian Painting – Modern Life page 91	P8D	S13	A9	15–adult	26 c			$99
		■			3	4	5		■					1840–1900	384	Victorian Painting – High Life and Low Life page 91	P8D	S13	A9	15–adult	26 c			$99
		■			3	4	5		■					1840–1900	385	Victorian Painting – Aesthetes and Dreamers page 91	P8D	S13	A9	15–adult	26 c			$99
		■			3	4	5		■					1840–1917	386	Victorian Painting – Country Life and Landscapes pages 91, 208	P8D	S13	A9	15–adult	26 c			$99
	▪	■				4		6			■			1808–79	389	Parliamentarians: Daumier Sculpture pages 79, 268				14–adult	18 b/w	$890	$189	$89
	▪	■			3	4					■			1808–79	390	Daumier pages 79, 238	P8			12–adult	15 b/w	$790	$169	$79
	▪	■	1				5		■					1860s–1886	391	Art in the Making: Impressionism pages 93, 210, 321	P18A	S6		14–adult	22 c			$89

USA National Visual Art Standards

Grades K-4 Ages 5-10	Grades 5-8 Ages 10-14	Grades 9-12 Ages 14-18	1	2	3	4	5	6	Painting	Drawing and graphics	Sculpture	Architecture and design	Photography and video art	Period covered / Artists' dates	Catalog number	Title	Preview video see page 435	Series reference see pages 428-9	Availability codes for use outside USA see page 434	Audience Recommended age range / Teacher training (tt)	Running time in minutes Color (c) / Black and white (b/w)	Revised prices 16mm film sale	16mm film rental USA and Canada only	VHS video sale
	■			2			5		■					1860s–1886	393	The Impressionist Surface pages 97, 293	P32A	S19	A8	18–adult	25 c			$99
■	■				3	4			■					1860s	394	Manet: The Heroism of Modern Life page 94	P9A			14–adult	25 c			$89
	■						5		■					1865–81	395	Manet page 94	P20	S16	A8	17–adult	25 c			$99
	■					4			■					1880s	397	Pissarro pages 94, 211	P20	S16	A8	17–adult	25 c			$99
■	■						5	6		■				1802–85	400	Victor Hugo Drawings pages 79, 208, 238	P8			12–adult	14 b/w	$790	$169	$79
	■					4	5			■	■			1840–1917	401	Rodin pages 80, 220	P32A	S19	A8	18–adult	25 c			$99
■	■					4							■	1853–80	402	Paris: Story of a City page 83A	P9A			14–adult	52 b/w	$1290	$269	$129
	■					4			■				■	1853–80	403	Paris, Spectacle of Modernity pages 83A, 263B	P32A	S19	A8	18–adult	25 c			$99
■	■				3	4			■		■			1800–1990	405	Modern Mexican Art pages 83, 238	P3G	S3		14–adult	56 c			$139
■	■				3	4			■		■			1800–1990	406	Modern Mexico: The Artistic Identity page 83	P3F	S2		14–adult	56 c			$139
■	■	■		2			5	6	■	■				1834–1917	410	Degas' Dancers pages 95, 218, 239	P9			10–adult	13 b/w	$890	$189	$89
■	■								■					1841–1919	411	Renoir page 95				14–adult	28 c			$99
	■				3		5		■					1870s	412	The Bathers by Cézanne and Renoir: Modernism and the Nude page 95	P32A	S19	A8	18–adult	25 c			$99
	■						5		■					1840–1926	413	Monet pages 95, 210	P20	S16	A8	17–adult	25 c			$99
■	■						5		■					1844–1910	414	Surprised! The Paintings of Henri Rousseau pages 208, 268	P9C			13–adult	20 c			$89
■	■		1				5	6		■				1859–91	415	Seurat Drawings pages 96, 240	P9			12–adult	17 b/w	$890	$189	$89
	■			2		4			■					1859–91	416	Seurat page 96	P20	S16	A8	17–adult	24 c			$99
	■					4			■					1841–95	417	Berthe Morisot – An Interview with Kathleen Adler page 98	P32A	S19	A8	18–adult	25 c			$99
■	■				3		5		■	■				1859–99	418	Giovanni Segantini: Life and Work pages 96, 209, 260	P9A			14–adult	45 c	$1190	$249	$119
	■								■	■				1864–1901	420	Toulouse-Lautrec pages 97, 218	P9			14–adult	14 c	$790	$169	$79
■	■					4			■	■				1853–90	424	Dreams of Beautiful Japan – Van Gogh and Ukiyo-e pages 97, 294	P9B			14–adult	45 c			$119
	■								■					1860–1905	425	Impressionism and Post-Impressionism pages 98, 211	P20	S16	A8	17–adult	25 c			$99
	■								■					1903–8	426	Fauvism pages 98, 213	P15A	S17	A10	15–adult	53 c	$1490	$299	$149
■	■				3						■			1859–1923	430	At the Foot of the Tree pages 99, 240	P9			14–adult	24 b/w	$890	$189	$89
■	■				3		5		■					1876–1907	440	Paula Modersohn-Becker pages 147, 218	P9			14–adult	12 c	$790	$169	$79
■	■							6	■			■	■	1870–1907	445	One Hundred Years of Modern Art, Part One page 99	P19	S15		12–adult	19 c	$890	$189	$89
	■					4			■		■	■	■	c1890–1914	456	Burning with Life page 102	P10D	S14	A7	15–adult	60 c	$1590	$299	$159
	■					4			■		■	■	■	c1890–1914	457	The Enlightened Bourgeois page 103	P10D	S14	A7	15–adult	60 c	$1590	$299	$159
	■					4			■		■	■	■	c1890–1914	458	Art Nouveau page 103	P10E	S14	A7	15–adult	60 c	$1590	$299	$159
	■					4			■		■	■	■	c1890–1914	459	Final Vortex page 103	P10E	S14	A7	15–adult	60 c	$1590	$299	$159
■	■			2		4			■	■	■	■	■	1893–1925	460	Art Nouveau: Equivoque 1900 page 101	P10		A15	12–adult	14 c	$890	$189	$89

USA National Visual Art Standards

Column groups: USA National Visual Art Standards — Grades K–4 (Ages 5–10), Grades 5–8 (Ages 10–14), Grades 9–12 (Ages 14–18). Recommendations for implementation of standards — Content standards 1–6. Category columns: Painting, Drawing and graphics, Sculpture, Architecture and design, Photography and video art. (■ = solid mark, ▫ = light mark)

K–4	5–8	9–12	1	2	3	4	5	6	Painting	Drawing & graphics	Sculpture	Architecture & design	Photography & video art	Period covered / Artists' dates	Catalog number	Title	Preview video (p.435)	Series reference (pp.428–9)	Availability codes (p.434)	Audience / age range	Running time (c/b·w)	Revised prices 16mm film sale	16mm film rental USA & Canada	VHS video sale
	▫	■				4			■	■	■	■		1881–1914	463	Modernism in Barcelona page 101	P10B			12–adult	25 c			$99
	▫	■				4						■		1881–1914	464	Modernist Architecture in Barcelona page 101	P10B			14–adult	25 c			$99
	▫	■				4			■			■		1890–1914	465	Vienna 1900 page 104	P8E			14–adult	18 c			$89
	▫	■				4						■		1900–1914	468	Moscow 1910: Search for Truth page 104	P6A	S28		14–adult	30 c			$99
	▫	■				4			■			■		1868–1928	470	Charles Rennie Mackintosh page 105	P10			14–adult	22 c	$890	$189	$89
	▫	■					5					■		1868–1928	471	The Fall and Rise of Mackintosh pages 105, 312	P13B			14–adult	52 c			$129
	▫	■							■			■		1861–1942	480	Hectorologie page 104	P10			13–adult	12 c	$790	$169	$79
	▫	■							■			■			481	Art for Pleasure's Sake page 305	P16	S5		12–adult	28 c	$990	$199	$99
	▫	■							■			■			481A	The Much Loved Friend? A Portrait of The National Gallery page 305	P9C			13–adult	47 c			$119
	▫	■							■						481B	Pictures in Pictures page 305	P9C			13–adult	25 c			$99
	▫	■							■						482	London, Center of the World's Art Trade page 297	P15			12–adult	25 c	$990	$199	$99
		■		2			5		■						482A	Greenberg on Art Criticism page 307B	P32B	S19	A8	18–adult	25 c			$99
		■		2			5		■					1912–56	482B	Greenberg on Jackson Pollock page 307B	P32B	S19	A8	18–adult	25 c			$99
	▫	■							■					c1550–1980	483	The Queen's Pictures page 301	P18A			12–adult	24 c			$99
	▫	■				4						■		1300–1900	483B	The Moscow Kremlin, Part One: The Walls, Towers and Cathedrals pages 232, 306	P4B	S27		14–adult	30 c			$99
	▫	■				4						■		1300–1900	483C	The Moscow Kremlin, Part Two: The Tower-chambers and Palaces page 306	P4B	S27		14–adult	30 c			$99
	▫	■				4						■		1300–1900	483D	The Moscow Kremlin, Part Three: The Armoury: Countless Treasures of the Russian Tsars page 306	P4B	S27		14–adult	30 c			$99
		■				4			■			■			484	Beaubourg: The Pompidou Center, Paris page 302	P22	S16	A8	17–adult	25 c			$99
		■							■		■	■			484A	Musée d'Orsay page 307A	P32B	S19	A8	18–adult	25 c			$99
		■							■						484B	The Museum of Modern Art page 307A	P32B	S19	A8	18–adult	25 c			$99
	▫	■	1		3		5			■				Neolithic–AD 1970	485	What is a Good Drawing? pages 235, 293	P14			12–adult	18 b/w	$890	$189	$89
	▫	■	1				5	6	■		■			1988	486	Genesis pages 294, 315	P13C			14–adult	57 c	$1490	$299	$149
	▫	■		2			5		■					1520–1907	487	The Artist's Eye: Bridget Riley's Selections from The National Gallery page 293	P14A			14–adult	25 c			$99
■	▫	■					5		■	■				c1989	488	'I Know I'm Wrong, Ask My Friends, They Say the Same Thing' page 272				6–adult	10 c	$690	$149	$69
	▫	■					5		■					1870–1970	489	Art for Whose Sake? page 293	P13			12–adult	14 c	$790	$169	$79
	▫	■	1	2									■	1600–1985	490	Movable Steel Bridges page 194	P27B			14–adult	78 c			$179
	▫	■				4			■			■		Iron Age–AD 1945	490B	Dover Castle: The Key to England page 277	P3C	S30		11–17	12 c			$69

USA National Visual Art Standards

K-4	5-8	9-12	1	2	3	4	5	6	Painting	Drawing and graphics	Sculpture	Architecture and design	Photography and video art	Period covered / Artists' dates	Catalog number	Title	Preview video	Series reference	Availability codes	Audience / Teacher training (tt)	Running time / Color (c) Black and white (b/w)	16mm film sale	16mm film rental USA and Canada only	VHS video sale
		■				4							■	1100–1900	490C	Your Church: A Threshold to History page 279	P3C	S31		16–adult tt	23 c			$99
■	■	■				4							■	present	490D	Clues Challenge page 275	P1A	S29		9–14	14 c			$79
	■	■											■	1200–present	491	Europa Nostra pages 263, 311	P15			12–adult	24 c	$990	$199	$99
■	■	■											■	1200–present	493	Janus pages 263, 311	P15			8–adult	36 c	$1190	$249	$119
	■	■											■	1689/1986	494	After the Fire: The Restoration of Hampton Court Palace page 313	P10C			12–adult	30 c	$990	$199	$99
	■	■							■						495	Art Restoration page 313	P10C			13–adult	30 c			$99
	■	■						6	■						496A	Physics and Fine Art page 313	P10C			14–adult	30 c			$99
		■		2			5		■					1910–50	497	Abstraction pages 123, 137	P15B	S17	A10	15–adult	53 c	$1490	$299	$149
	■	■			3				■					1880–1916	498	Franz Marc pages 124, 225	P10			14–adult	21 c	$890	$189	$89
	■	■		2	3			6	■					1866–1944	500	Kandinsky pages 125, 147	P10			12–adult	15 c	$790	$169	$79
	■	■		2					■					1872–1944	501	Piet Mondrian pages 124, 136	P10A			14–adult	18 c	$890	$189	$89
		■		2			5		■					1872–1944	501A	Mondrian pages 124, 136	P32C	S19	A8	18–adult	25 c			$99
	■	■		2			5		■				■	1883–1931	502	Theo van Doesburg pages 124, 136, 195	P10A			14–adult	30 c	$990	$199	$99
		■		2									■	1924	502B	The Rietveld Schröder House pages 136, 195, 302, 313	P10C			16–adult	30 c			$99
	■	■				4			■	■	■		■	1917–25	502D	Art in Revolution page 127	P12B		A2	14–adult	50 c	$1390	$289	$139
	■	■		2		4		6	■	■	■	■	■	1890–1941	503	El Lissitzky pages 128, 194	P10A			14–adult	88 c			$189
		■		2			5		■					1930–50	503C	American Abstraction pages 114, 130, 285	P15C	S17	A10	15–adult	53 c	$1490	$299	$149
		■		2			5		■					1945–68	503D	Abstraction: The Experience pages 115, 131	P15C	S17	A10	15–adult	53 c	$1490	$299	$149
		■	1		3		5		■					1912–56	503E	Jackson Pollock: Tim Clark and Michael Fried in Conversation pages 114, 130, 307B	P32B	S19	A8	18–adult	25 c			$99
		■			3	4			■					1906–45	504	Expressionism page 107	P15B	S17	A10	15–adult	53 c	$1490	$299	$149
		■			3	4			■					1900–30	504B	Re/Visions: Mexican Mural Painting pages 107, 219	P3H	S3		15–adult	56 c			$139
	■	■			3	4			■					1905–11	505	Die Brücke page 109	P11			14–adult	24 c	$990	$199	$99
	■	■			3				■	■				1863–1944	506	Edvard Munch: The Restless Years pages 109, 285	P11A			14–adult	21 c			$89
	■	■			3		5		■	■				1863–1944	507	Edvard Munch: The Frieze of Life pages 109, 285	P9C			14–adult	24 c			$99
	■	■			3	4					■			1867–1945	508	Käthe Kollwitz pages 109, 219, 241	P11			14–adult	16 b/w	$990	$199	$99
	■	■			3	4	5		■				■	1860–1949	509	'I'm Mad, I'm Foolish, I'm Nasty' pages 110, 148, 286	P11A		A1	14–adult	55 c	$1490	$299	$149
	■	■			3	4			■					1867–1956	510	Emil Nolde page 111	P11			14–adult	12 c	$790	$169	$79
	■	■				4			■	■				1919–33	511	Part of the Struggle page 112	P11A		A2	14–adult	36 c	$1090	$199	$109
		■			3	4	5		■					1932–37	512	Beckmann page 112	P21	S16	A8	17–adult	25 c			$99
		■			3	4			■					1918–75	512B	Contemporary Expression page 113	P15B	S17		15–adult	53 c	$1490	$299	$149
	■	■			3	4			■					1886–1977	513	Kokoschka page 114	P11			14–adult	10 c	$690	$149	$69

USA National Visual Art Standards

Ages 5-10 (K-4)	Ages 10-14 (5-8)	Ages 14-18 (9-12)	Content standards (1-6)	Painting	Drawing & graphics	Sculpture	Architecture & design	Photography & video art	Period covered / Artists' dates	Catalog number	Title	Preview video (p.435)	Series ref (p.428-9)	Availability codes (p.434)	Audience age range	Running time (min)	16mm film sale	16mm film rental (USA/Canada)	VHS video sale
	■	■	2	■	■	■	■		1919–25	515	The Bauhaus pages 133, 195	P11			14–adult	19 c	$890	$189	$89
	■		2	■	■				*1895–1946*	516	A Memory of Moholy-Nagy pages 128, 134 Not available in the USA	P10A			14–adult	15 c			$89
■		■	2, 6					■	1922	517	Man and Mask: Oskar Schlemmer and the Bauhaus Stage pages 135, 269	P11			10–adult	27 c	$990	$199	$99
	■		3, 5, 6	■					*1878–1940*	518	Paul Klee pages 126, 135, 150	P12			14–adult	30 c	$990	$199	$99
	■					■			*1861–1944*	519	Dina in the King's Garden pages 157, 220	P12			12–adult	10 c	$690	$149	$69
	■		3, 5	■					*1881–1955*	520	Fernard Léger page 149	P12			12–adult	14 c	$790	$169	$79
	■		2, 5	■					1907–14	521	Cubism page 119	P15A	S17	A10	15–adult	53 c	$1490	$299	$149
	■		5	■					1907–27	524	Matisse page 150	P21	S16	A8	17–adult	24 c			$99
	■		2, 5	■					*1869–1954*	525	Matisse and the Problem of Expression page 151A	P32C	S19	A8	18–adult	25 c			$99
	■		3, 5	■					1940–60	527	Nicholson, Wallis and St Ives page 150	P22	S16	A8	17–adult	24 c			$99
	■		4	■					1918–19	528	Klee and the Munich Revolution pages 126, 150	P21	S16	A8	17–adult	25 c			$99
	■		5	■					1907–25	529	Cubism and Modernism page 119	P21	S16	A8	17–adult	25 c			$99
	■		6		■				1960	530	Picasso: Romancero du Picador pages 152, 225, 241	P12			12–adult	13 b/w	$790	$169	$79
	■			■					1967–73	531	Picasso: The Forceful Gaze page 152	P12A		A3	14–adult	26 c			$99
	■							■	1951–67	532	Picasso: A Portrait pages 152, 255	P12A			14–adult	60 b/w	$1290	$269	$129
	■					■			1925–70	533	Picasso, the Sculptor pages 153, 157, 220, 301	P12B		A2	14–adult	27 c	$990	$199	$99
	■		1, 2, 5	■	■				1912–13	534	Picasso's Collages 1912–13: The Problem of Interpretation pages 119, 151B	P32C	S19	A8	18–adult	25 c			$99
	■		3, 4, 5	■	■				1936–7	535	Picasso's Guernica page 151B	P32C	S19	A8	18–adult	25 c			$99
	■			■	■				1946	540	Picasso: Joie de Vivre pages 153, 304	P12			12–adult	12 c	$690	$149	$69
	■			■		■			1916–40	541	New Realities page 151	P15C	S17	A10	15–adult	53 c	$1490	$299	$149
	■		3	■					*1887–1985*	543	Chagall page 154	P12A			14–adult	28 c			$99
	■		3, 5	■					*1882–1967*	546	Edward Hopper page 154	P13E		A2	15–adult	49 c	$1290	$269	$129
	■		2, 4, 5	■				■	1930s	547	Public Murals in New York pages 151A, 263B	P32C	S19	A8	18–adult	25 c			$99
	■		2, 5	■					1890–1950	551	On Pictures and Paintings pages 151A, 293, 307A	P32D	S19	A8	18–adult	25 c			$99
	■		6	■		■	■		1907–30	552	One Hundred Years of Modern Art, Part Two page 145	P19	S15		12–adult	26 c	$990	$199	$99
	■		6	■		■	■		1930–70	553	One Hundred Years of Modern Art, Part Three page 154	P19	S15		12–adult	26 c	$990	$199	$99
	■		2, 5	■					1940–60	554	Abstract Expressionism pages 114, 131	P22	S16	A8	17–adult	24 c			$99
	■		4, 6	■	■	■	■	■	1909–44	555	Vita Futurista page 120	P11A		A2	16–adult	42 c	$1390	$289	$139
	■		2, 4	■					1909–30	557	Futurism, Modernity and Style page 121	P21	S16	A8	17–adult	24 c			$99

USA National Visual Art Standards

Grades K-4 (Ages 5-10)	Grades 5-8 (Ages 10-14)	Grades 9-12 (Ages 14-18)	CS1	CS2	CS3	CS4	CS5	CS6	Painting	Drawing and graphics	Sculpture	Architecture and design	Photography and video art	Period covered / Artists' dates	Catalog number	Title	Preview video (p.435)	Series ref (p.428-9)	Availability codes (p.434)	Audience / Teacher training	Running time Color(c)/b&w	16mm film sale	16mm film rental USA & Canada	VHS video sale
		■			3	4			■	■			■	1913–36	558	Europe after the Rain, Part One page 139	P13A		A2	17–adult	47 c	$1190	$249	$119
		■			3	4			■	■			■	1913–60s	559	Europe After the Rain, Part Two page 139	P13A		A2	17–adult	42 c	$1190	$249	$119
	■	■			3				■	■				1891–1976	560	Max Ernst: Journey into the Subconscious pages 140, 286	P13		A15	12–adult	12 c	$790	$169	$79
		■			3				■					1915–45	561	Surrealism pages 139, 288	P15A	S17	A10	15–adult	53 c	$1490	$299	$149
		■			3		5		■					1913–36	562	Max Ernst and the Surrealist Revolution pages 141, 286	P32C	S19	A8	18–adult	25 c			$99
	■	■	1				5	6	■		■			1887–1948	563	Merz: Kurt Schwitters page 141	P10B			14–adult	28 c			$99
	■	■	1				5		■	■	■			1940–48	563A	I Build My Time page 141	P13E		A2	14–adult	33 c	$1090	$199	$109
	■	■					5		■	■	■			1886–1968	564	Marcel Duchamp in His Own Words page 142	P13A			14–adult	34 c	$1090	$199	$109
		■					5		■	■	■			1886–1968	565	Duchamp page 142	P22	S16	A8	17–adult	21 c			$99
■	■	■			3				■	■	■		■	1904–89	567	Theater of Memory: The Dali Museum pages 143, 304	P10B			10–adult	32 c			$109
		■			3		5		■	■	■			1925–35	567B	Dali and Surrealism pages 143, 288	P21	S16	A8	17–adult	24 c			$99
		■			3				■	■	■		■	1904–89	567C	Salvador Dali: His Life through His Paintings page 143	P10B			16–adult	45 c			$129
	■	■			3				■	■	■		■	1890–1977	568	Man Ray pages 144, 255	P13A			14–adult	26 c			$99
		■			3				■	■	■			1913–85	569	IMAGO Meret Oppenheim pages 144, 175, 289	P13B			16–adult	90 c	$1990	$399	$199
	■	■	1		3			6		■				1934	570	Kindness Week (Max Ernst) pages 140, 242, 269, 289	P13			12–adult	19 b/w	$890	$189	$89
		■			3				■	■	■		■	1932–54	570A	IMAGO Meret Oppenheim, Part One: 1932–54 pages 144, 175, 289	N/A			16–adult	35 c			$109
		■			3				■	■	■		■	1959–85	571	IMAGO Meret Oppenheim Part Two: 1959–85 pages 175, 289	N/A			16–adult	35 c			$109
	■	■			3				■					1920–70	572	Realms of the Fantastic page 145	P13			14–adult	11 c	$690	$149	$69
		■			3	4			■					1908–	574	A Mental State pages 145, 171	P14A			18–adult	29 c			$129
■	■	■	1				5	6		■				1914–	575	Steinberg pages 171, 242, 271	P13			9–adult	14 b/w	$790	$169	$79
	■	■				4		6		■				1940–42	580	Henry Moore: London 1940–42 pages 160, 221, 243, 290	P13			14–adult	12 b/w	$790	$169	$79
		■			3	4	5		■		■			1954–74	581	Pop Art: The Test of the Object page 177	P15D	S17	A10	15–adult	53 c	$1490	$299	$149
		■			3	4	5		■		■			1960s	582	The Sixties: The Art in Question page 177	P15D	S17	A10	15–adult	53 c	$1490	$299	$149
		■			3	4			■	■				1960s	583	Art and the Left page 307B	P32B	S19	A8	18–adult	25 c			$99
		■			3		5		■		■			1965–75	584	The Adventure: Artists on Art page 178	P15E	S17	A10	15–adult	53 c	$1490	$299	$149
	■	■	1						■		■			1967–70	587	Kinetics pages 178, 298	P12B		A2	12–adult	23 b/w	$790	$169	$79
	■	■		2				6	■	■				1908–	590	Vasarely pages 129, 168, 298	P13			12–adult	9 b/w	$690	$149	$69
	■	■			3		5		■					1923–	592	Lichtenstein in London pages 168, 301	P13E		A2	12–adult	21 c	$890	$189	$89
	■	■			3		5		■					1937–	593	Tom Phillips page 169	P13E		A2	14–adult	50 c	$1390	$289	$139

USA National Visual Art Standards

Recommendations for implementation of standards — Content standards 1 2 3 4 5 6

K-4	5-8	9-12	CS1	CS2	CS3	CS4	CS5	CS6	Painting	Drawing & graphics	Sculpture	Architecture & design	Photography & video art	Period covered / Artists' dates	Catalog number	Title	Preview video	Series ref	Availability codes	Audience / age range	Running time	16mm film sale	16mm film rental (USA & Canada)	VHS video sale
	■	■		2			5		■	■				1898–1972	594	Adventures in Perception — pages 170, 242, 270	P13C			14–adult	21 c	$990	$199	$99
	■	■		2			5		■					1931–	595	Bridget Riley — pages 129, 170, 213, 315	P14B		A2	12–adult	28 c	$990	$199	$99
	■	■					5		■					1921–	596	The Reality of Karel Appel — pages 116, 170, 290	P13C			13–adult	15 c	$890	$189	$89
	■	■					5		■					1930–	597	Antonio Saura: Confessions — pages 117, 171	P14F		A11	14–adult	26 c			$99
	■	■					5		■					1932–	598	Howard Hodgkin: A Study — pages 130, 172	P13C			12–adult	16 c			$89
	■				3				■					1909–92	599	Francis Bacon — pages 117, 172, 222	P13C			17–adult	28 c			$99
	■				3		5		■					1944–62	599A	Francis Bacon: Paintings 1944–62 — pages 117, 172, 222	P13E		A2	17–adult	11 c	$790	$169	$79
■	■	■	1				5	6		■				1911–	600	Josef Herman Drawings — pages 173, 222, 244, 270	P13			10–adult	15 b/w	$790	$169	$79
	■				3		5		■	■	■			1970–85	601	Contemporaries – The Quest for Reality — page 167	P15E	S17	A10	15–adult	53 c	$1490	$299	$149
	■	■	1						■	■			■	1941–	602	Brendan Neiland: Evolution of a Commission — pages 174, 315	P14B			12–adult	37 c			$119
	■	■			3	4			■					1919–87	603	Victory over Death: The Paintings of Colin McCahon — page 174	P13D		A4	14–adult	52 c	$1290	$269	$129
■	■	■	1								■			1991	605	Nature and Nature: Andy Goldsworthy — pages 164, 178, 260, 271, 317	P14D			5–adult	16 c	$890	$189	$89
	■	■							■	■				1939–	606	Jean Verame: The New Adventurers — pages 179, 261	P13F			12–adult	52 c	$1490	$299	$149
■	■	■									■			c1989	607	Snow Dream — pages 180, 261, 271, 317	P14D		A17	8–adult	22 c	$890	$189	$89
	■	■			3				■					1934–	608	Paya et Talla — page 180	P14F			14–adult	30 c	$1090	$199	$109
	■	■			3	4			■		■		■	1989	609	A Day So Red — pages 180, 261	P14D			13–adult	42 c			$99
	■	■		2	3	4			■	■		■		1982	610A	Walls, Walls — pages 180, 263	P14E		A12	12–adult	81 c	$1890	$399	$189
	■	■				4			■					1989	610B	The Paintings Came Tumbling Down — page 181	P14E			12–adult	15 c			$79
	■	■			3				■		■			1930–90	611	Contemporary Mexican Art — page 167	P3H	S3		14–adult	56 c			$139
■	■	■							■				■	1989–90	612	Pictures for the Sky — pages 181, 262, 272, 298	P14D			8–adult	30 c	$990	$199	$99
■	■	■		2	3						■	■		1986–92	613	Un Mariage d'Amour — page 182	P13F			9–adult	13 c			$89
■	■	■			3			6	■		■			c1990	614	The Ritual Art of Siim-Tanel Annus — pages 184, 263	P14D			10–adult	10 c			$69
	■				3			6	■	■				1987	615	Eugène Ionesco: Voices, Silences — pages 172, 291	P13D		A1	18–adult	61 c	$1490	$299	$149
	■	■	1		3								■	1989	618	Processing the Signal — pages 184, 293	P14C		A19	11–adult	38 c			$119
■	■	■											■	1990	619	Play It Again, Nam — page 185 — Not available in the USA	P14E		A18	9–adult	26 c			$99
	■	■	1					6			■	■		1915–	620	Sculpture 58, the Story of a Creation — pages 158, 316	P14			12–adult	12 c	$790	$169	$79
■	■	■	1								■			1926–31	621	Calder's Circus — pages 158, 223, 270	P12A		A10	5–adult	19 c	$990	$199	$99

USA National Visual Art Standards

Grades K-4 Ages 5-10	Grades 5-8 Ages 10-14	Grades 9-12 Ages 14-18	\<th colspan>						Painting	Drawing and graphics	Sculpture	Architecture and design	Photography and video art	Period covered / Artists' dates	Catalog number	Title	Preview video see page 435	Series reference see pages 428-9	Availability codes for use outside USA see page 434	Audience Recommended age range / Teacher training (tt)	Running time in minutes Color (c) Black and white (b/w)	Revised prices 16mm film sale	16mm film rental USA and Canada only	VHS video sale
			1	2	3	4	5	6																
		■		2			5				■			c1990	623	**Smithson and Serra: Beyond Modernism?** pages 158, 263B	P32D	S19	A8	18–adult	25 c			$99
	■	■		2							■			1924–	625	**Anthony Caro** page 162	P13D			12–adult	26 c			$99
	■	■	1								■			1914–	626	**Chadwick** pages 162, 223, 316	P14B			14–adult	51 c	$1290	$269	$129
	■	■	1								■			1901–85	627	**The Spinney by Jean Dubuffet** pages 163, 263, 315	P13D			12–adult	16 c			$79
■	■	■	1					6			■			1920–	630	**The Genesis of a Sculpture** pages 164, 271, 317	P14			10–adult	13 b/w	$690	$149	$69
■	■	■				4					■				634	**Historic Site: A Sculptor's View** page 283	P3C			5–16 tt	23 c			$99
		■	1								■			1960–70	635	**Sculpture Australia** pages 164, 184	P14			12–adult	30 c	$890	$189	$89
	■		1		3				■		■		■	c1990	636	**Pleasures and Dangers** pages 184, 255	P14C		A4	16–adult	52 c	$1290	$269	$129
	■		1		3		5				■			1947–	637	**If Brains Were Dynamite** pages 164, 182, 297, 317	P14A			18–adult	28 c	$990	$199	$99
	■				3		5				■			1942–	638	**The Paradise of Cornelius Kolig** pages 182, 317	P14F			17–adult	43 c			$119
	■	■			3	4			■		■			1990	639	**Submarine** pages 165, 300, 318	P14B			12–adult	52 c	$1290	$269	$129
	■	■									■			c1966–70	640	**Sculpture in the City – Spoleto** pages 164, 301	P13			12–adult	11 c	$690	$149	$69
	■	■			3			6					■	1972	660	**Circle of Light** pages 213, 255	P14			12–adult	32 c	$1090	$199	$109
	■	■	1					6					■	1928–	661	**Image of Light** pages 184, 256, 318	P14			12–adult	16 c	$790	$169	$79
	■	■		2	3								■	1977–90	664	**Bernard Faucon: Fables** pages 223, 256, 318	P14F			12–adult	44 c	$1190	$249	$119
	■	■	1										■	c1987	665	**The Fresson Process** page 256	P14A			14–adult	30 c	$990	$199	$99
	■	■			3	4							■	1943–	666	**Krzysztof Wodiczko: Projections** pages 185, 257, 318	P14C		A17	14–adult	55 c	$1390	$289	$139
	■	■	1		3	4							■	1949–	667	**Photomontage Today: Peter Kennard** pages 257, 322	P14A		A2	14–adult	35 c			$109
		■		2						■		■		1970s inspired by 1920s–30s	700	**What is Architecture? An Architect at Work** page 188	P23	S18	A8	18–adult	25 b/w			$99
		■			3	4						■		1900	701	**The Universal International Exhibition, Paris 1900** pages 101, 188	P23	S18	A8	18–adult	25 b/w			$99
		■		2			5					■		1903	702	**Charles Rennie Mackintosh: Hill House** pages 105, 188	P23	S18	A8	18–adult	25 c			$99
		■					5					■		c1913	703	**Industrial Architecture: AEG and Fagus Factories** page 189	P23	S18	A8	18–adult	25 c			$99
		■		2			5					■		1908	704	**Frank Lloyd Wright: The Robie House** page 189	P23	S18	A8	18–adult	25 c			$99
		■		2			5					■		1923–7	705	**RM Schindler: The Lovell Beach House** page 189	P23	S18	A8	18–adult	25 c			$99
		■		2			5					■		1914–18	706	**Erich Mendelsohn: The Einstein Tower** pages 113, 189	P24	S18	A8	18–adult	25 b/w			$99
		■		2		4						■		1919–23	707	**The Bauhaus at Weimar, 1919–23** pages 134, 190	P24	S18	A8	18–adult	25 b/w			$99
		■		2								■		1914–27	708	**Berlin Siedlungen** page 190	P24	S18	A8	18–adult	25 c			$99

USA National Visual Art Standards

For prices in United Kingdom and Australia see page 434

Grades K–4 Ages 5–10	Grades 5–8 Ages 10–14	Grades 9–12 Ages 14–18	CS 1	CS 2	CS 3	CS 4	CS 5	CS 6	Painting	Drawing and graphics	Sculpture	Architecture and design	Photography and video art	Period covered / Artists' dates	Catalog number	Title	Preview video see page 435	Series reference see pages 428–9	Availability codes for use outside USA see page 434	Audience Recommended age range / Teacher training (tt)	Running time in minutes Color (c) / Black and white (b/w)	Revised prices 16mm film sale	16mm film rental USA and Canada only	VHS video sale
	■			2								■		1927	709	The Weissenhof Siedlung Stuttgart 1927 page 190	P24	S18	A8	18–adult	25 c			$99
	■											■		1925	710	The International Exhibition of Arts, Paris 1925 page 190	P24	S18	A8	18–adult	25 b/w			$99
	■			2			5					■		*1873–1933*	711	Adolf Loos page 190	P24	S18	A8	18–adult	25 c			$99
	■			2			5					■		1929–31	712	Le Corbusier: Villa Savoye page 191	P25	S18	A8	18–adult	25 c			$99
	■											■		1930s	713	English Flats of the Thirties page 191	P25	S18	A8	18–adult	25 b/w			$99
	■											■		1930s	714	English Houses of the Thirties page 192	P25	S18	A8	18–adult	25 c			$99
	■			2			5					■		1933–39	715	Hans Scharoun page 192	P25	S18	A8	18–adult	25 c			$99
	■											■		1920s	716	English Furniture page 192	P25	S18	A8	18–adult	25 b/w			$99
	■						5					■		1899	717	Edwin Lutyens: Deanery Gardens page 192	P25	S18	A8	18–adult	25 b/w			$99
	■											■		1930s	718	The London Underground page 193	P26	S18	A8	18–adult	25 b/w			$99
	■											■		1930s	719	'Moderne' and 'Modernistic' page 193	P26	S18	A8	18–adult	25 b/w			$99
	■											■		1918–39	720	The Other Tradition page 193	P26	S18	A8	18–adult	25 c			$99
	■											■		1920s	721	The Suburban Style page 193	P26	S18	A8	18–adult	25 c			$99
	■											■		1950s	722	The Housing Question page 193	P26	S18	A8	18–adult	25 b/w			$99
▫	■											■	■	1923	730	The Man with Modern Nerves page 194	P27A			14–adult	8 b/w	$690	$149	$69
	■			2			5		■	■		■	■	1887–1929	735	Le Corbusier, Part One 1887–1929 page 198	P26A			15–adult	57 c			$139
	■			2			5		■	■		■	■	1928–37	736	Le Corbusier, Part Two 1928–1936 page 198	P26A			15–adult	54 c			$139
	■			2			5		■	■		■	■	1945–65	737	Le Corbusier, Part Three 1945–1965 page 198	P26B			15–adult	67 c			$139
	■			2			5		■	■		■	■	*1887–1965*	738	Le Corbusier 1887–1965 (short version combining 735, 736, 737) page 198	P26B			15–adult	60 c			$159
	■			2			5		■			■		1920s	739	Le Corbusier: Villa La Roche page 198	P32D	S19	A8	18–adult	25 c			$99
	■			2								■		1930s	741	The Flame of Functionalism pages 137, 196	P27			16–adult	40 c	$990	$199	$99
	■											■		1951–70	742	Scandinavian Design: The Lunning Prize 1951–70 pages 196, 298	P27			15–adult	9 c			$69
	■						5					■		1980s	760	Chichester Theological College page 197	P27A			16–adult	45 c			$129
	■					4						■		1900–91	761	Public Sector Housing in Amsterdam 1900–91 page 197	P27B			16–adult	46 c			$129
	■			2			5					■		*1898–1976*	763	Alvar Aalto pages 199, 264	P27			16–adult	57 c	$1390	$289	$139
	■			2	3						■	■		1983–9	764	Homage to Humanity pages 200, 319	P27D			15–adult	45 c			$119
	■			2							■	■		*1925–*	765	Larsen – Light – Now pages 202, 319	P27A			15–adult	45 c			$119
	■			2								■		*1926–92*	766	Jim Stirling's Architecture page 201	P27B		A2	15–adult	50 c	$1290	$269	$129
▫	■			2	3		5					■		*1929–*	767	An Affirmation of Life pages 201, 264	P27A			13–adult	27 c			$99
▫	■			2				6				■		*1923–93*	768	The Seasons pages 202, 264, 319	P27A			14–adult	35 c	$1090	$199	$109
▫	■			2			5				■	■		1980	769	Birth of a Hospital page 202				14–adult	67 c	$1590	$299	$159

USA National Visual Art Standards

Grades K-4 (Ages 5-10)	Grades 5-8 (Ages 10-14)	Grades 9-12 (Ages 14-18)	CS1	CS2	CS3	CS4	CS5	CS6	Painting	Drawing and graphics	Sculpture	Architecture and design	Photography and video art	Period covered / Artists' dates	Catalog number	Title	Preview video see page 435	Series reference see pages 428-9	Availability codes for use outside USA see page 434	Audience Recommended age range / Teacher training (tt)	Running time in minutes Color (c) / Black and white (b/w)	Revised prices 16mm film sale	16mm film rental USA and Canada only	VHS video sale
		■			3								■	1977–81	771	Dreams Come True pages 203, 265	P27C	S26		15–adult	44 c			$119
		■			3								■	1979–83	772	New Horizons pages 203, 265	P27C	S26		15–adult	44 c			$119
		■			3								■	1982–6	773	Visions of Future Living pages 184, 203, 265	P27C	S26		15–adult	44 c			$119
	■	■	1							■				c1990	780	The Urban Bonsai: Contemporary Japanese Prints page 245	P9B			14–adult	42 c			$119
■	■	■			3	4				■				1900–2000	781	Comics, the Ninth Art page 247	P29	S20		9–adult	28 c			$99
■	■	■			3	4				■				1900	782	1900 pages 104, 247	P29	S20		9–adult	28 c			$99
■	■	■			3	4				■				1900–20	783	To Be Continued... page 247	P29	S20		9–adult	28 c			$99
■	■	■			3	4				■				1930–40	784	The Adventure Begins page 248	P29	S20		9–adult	28 c			$99
■	■	■			3	4				■				1940–50	785	Double Identity page 248	P29A	S20		9–adult	28 c			$99
■	■	■			3	4				■				1950–60	786	Fifty, Fifty page 248	P29A	S20		9–adult	28 c			$99
■	■	■			3	4				■				1960–8	787	Love is All You Need page 248	P29A	S20		9–adult	28 c			$99
■	■	■			3	4				■				1960–75	788	Comix page 249	P29A	S20		9–adult	28 c			$99
■	■	■			3	4				■				1968–75	789	L'Imagination au Pouvoir page 249	P29B	S20		9–adult	28 c			$99
■	■	■			3	4				■				1975–85	790	No Future? page 249	P29B	S20		9–adult	28 c			$99
■	■	■			3	4				■				1975–85	791	Born in the States page 250	P29B	S20		9–adult	28 c			$99
		■			3	4				■				1985–90	792	Manga, Manga page 250	P29B	S20		18–adult	28 c			$99
■	■	■			3	4				■				1985–2000	793	What's Next? page 250	P29B	S20		9–adult	28 c			$99
	■	■	1		3		5			■				present	801	Eisner page 251	P30	S21		12–adult	28 c			$99
	■	■	1		3		5			■				present	802	Breccia page 251	P30	S21		12–adult	28 c			$99
	■	■	1		3		5			■				present	803	Schultz pages 252, 272	P30	S21		12–adult	28 c			$99
	■	■	1		3		5			■				present	804	Altuna page 252	P30	S21		18–adult	28 c			$99
	■	■	1		3		5			■				present	805	Moebius pages 252, 290	P30A	S21		12–adult	28 c			$99
	■	■	1		3		5			■				present	806	Schulteiss page 252	P30A	S21		18–adult	28 c			$99
		■	1		3		5			■				present	807	Manara page 252	P30A	S21		18–adult	28 c			$99
	■	■	1		3		5			■				present	808	Chaykin page 253	P30A	S21		12–adult	28 c			$99
	■	■	1		3		5			■				present	809	Bilal page 253	P30B	S21		16–adult	28 c			$99
	■	■	1		3		5			■				present	810	Schuiten page 253	P30B	S21		12–adult	28 c			$99
	■	■	1		3		5			■				present	811	Liberatore page 253	P30B	S21		16–adult	28 c			$99
	■	■	1		3		5			■				present	812	Moore page 253	P30B	S21		12–adult	28 c			$99
	■	■	1		3		5			■				present	813	Prado page 253	P30B	S21		12–adult	28 c			$99
		■	1						■					1843–80	815	Artists' Techniques pages 99, 322	P20	S16	A8	17–adult	23 c			$89
	■	■	1											present	820	Enameling page 324	P28			12–adult	57 c			$139
	■	■	1											c1990	822	Master of Glass pages 196, 322	P14E			12–adult	36 c			$109
	■	■	1							■				present	825	Screenprinting pages 245, 325	P28			12–adult	33 c			$99
	■	■	1							■				present	827	Lithography page 325	P28B			12–adult	39 c			$109
	■	■	1							■				present	830	Etching pages 245, 324	P28A			12–adult	40 c			$109
	■	■	1									■		present	835	Stonecarving page 325	P28A			12–adult	43 c			$119

USA National Visual Art Standards

Grades K–4 (Ages 5–10)	Grades 5–8 (Ages 10–14)	Grades 9–12 (Ages 14–18)	Content standards 1	2	3	4	5	6	Painting	Drawing and graphics	Sculpture	Architecture and design	Photography and video art	Period covered / Artists' dates	Catalog number	Title	Preview video see page 435	Series reference see pages 428–9	Availability codes for use outside USA see page 434	Audience Recommended age range / Teacher training (tt)	Running time in minutes Color (c) Black and white (b/w)	Revised prices 16mm film sale	16mm film rental USA and Canada only	VHS video sale
■	■		1							■				present	841	Making Shapes page 274	P31	S22	A13	5–12	12 c			$69
■	■		1							■				present	842	Cartoon Forms page 274	P31	S22	A13	5–12	12 c			$69
■	■		1							■				present	843	Coloring Cartoons page 274	P31	S22	A13	5–12	12 c			$69
■	■		1							■				present	844	Caricatures page 274	P31	S22	A13	5–12	12 c			$69
■	■		1							■				present	845	Pen and Ink Techniques page 274	P31	S22	A13	5–12	12 c			$69
■	■		1							■				present	846	Pen and Brush Techniques page 274	P31	S22	A13	5–12	12 c			$69
■	■		1							■				present	847	Nature Drawings page 274	P31	S22	A13	5–12	12 c			$69
■	■		1							■				present	848	Drawing Animals page 274	P31	S22	A13	5–12	12 c			$69
■	■		1							■				present	849	Drawing Birds page 274	P31	S22	A13	5–12	12 c			$69
■	■		1						■					present	850	Painting Birds page 274	P31	S22	A13	5–12	12 c			$69
■	■		1						■					present	851	Landscape Painting page 274	P31	S22	A13	5–12	12 c			$69
■	■		1						■					present	852	Creative Painting page 274	P31A	S22	A13	5–12	12 c			$69
■	■		1							■				present	853	Creative Drawing page 274	P31A	S22	A13	5–12	12 c			$69
■	■		1							■				present	854	Poster Lettering page 274	P31A	S22	A13	5–12	12 c			$69
■	■		1							■				present	855	Poster Drawing page 274	P31A	S22	A13	5–12	12 c			$69
■	■		1						■	■				present	856	Making a Collage page 274	P31A	S22	A13	5–12	12 c			$69
■	■		1						■	■				present	857	Fun Techniques page 274	P31A	S22	A13	5–12	12 c			$69
■	■		1						■					present	858	Painting on Stones page 274	P31A	S22	A13	5–12	12 c			$69
■	■		1						■					present	859	Theme Painting page 274	P31A	S22	A13	5–12	12 c			$69
■	■		1							■				present	860	Sketching People page 274	P31A	S22	A13	5–12	12 c			$69
■	■		1						■					present	861	Painting 1 page 274	P31A	S22	A13	5–12	12 c			$69
■	■		1						■					present	862	Painting 2 page 274	P31A	S22	A13	5–12	12 c			$69
■	■	■											■	1000–1200	900	The Mystery page 275	P1A	S29		8–14	12 c			$69
■	■	■												present	901	Bits and Bodies page 275	P1A	S29		9–14	33 c			$109
		■												900–1900	902	In Memoriam page 278	P3C	S31		16–adult tt	21 c			$89
■	■	■												present	903	Evidence of Our Lives page 283	P!A			9–15	27 c			$99
■	■	■												Anglo–Saxon	904	Rescuing Our Past page 283	P1A			8–15	12 c			$79
		■			3			6	■					1990	965	Drawn by Experience page 291	P14F			17–adult	21 c			$99
		■		2					■	■			■	1854–1920	971	Japonism, Part One pages 97, 104, 295	P9B			15–adult	30 c			$99
		■		2									■	1970–80	972	Japonism, Part Two pages 196, 295	P9B			15–adult	15 c			$79
		■		2					■	■				1870–80	973	Japonism, Part Three pages 170, 245, 291, 295, 315	P9B			15–adult	15 c			$79

USA National Visual Art Standards

Recommendations for implementation of standards

Ages 5–10	Ages 10–14	Ages 14–18	Content standards	Painting	Drawing and graphics	Sculpture	Architecture and design	Photography and video art	Period covered / Artists' dates	Series number	Title	Preview video	Series reference	Availability codes	Audience	Running time	16mm film sale	16mm film rental	VHS video sale
▫	■		4			■	■		3000 BC–AD 1985	S1	**Ancient Cultures of Mesopotamia** pages 20–1 / 5 programs, numbers 21–5	P2A	S1		14–adult	129 c	$4950	$995	$495
▫	■		3 4	■		■	■		1200 BC–AD1990	S2	**The Art of Mexico** pages 27, 60, 83 / 4 programs, numbers 92, 93, 306, 406	P3E P3F	S2		14–adult	224 c			$556
▫	■		3 4	■		■	■		1200 BC–AD1990	S3	**Mexico through the Eyes of Octavio Paz** pages 27, 83, 107, 167 / 4 programs, numbers 91, 405, 504B, 611	P3G P3H	S3		14–adult	224 c			$556
▫	■		2 3 4			■	■		1000–1200	S4	**French Romanesque** pages 32–3 / 6 programs, numbers 111–16	P3D	S4		14–adult	156 c	$5940	$1194	$594
▫	■		4	■					1250–1975	S5	**The National Gallery – A Private View** pages 37, 41–3, 49, 55, 59–61, 75, 78, 305 / 12 programs, numbers 165, 179, 205, 223, 225, 275, 295, 307, 309, 345, 346, 481	P16 P17 P18	S5		12–adult	336 c	$11880	$2388	$1188
▫	■	1	5	■					1270–1886	S6	**Art in the Making** pages 320–1 / 3 programs, numbers 163, 296, 391	P18A	S6		14–adult	62 c			$267
▫	■		2 4 5	■					1422–1640	S7	**The Genius of Flemish Painting** pages 38, 51, 59 / 6 programs, numbers 173, 174, 244, 245, 273–4	P5C P5D	S7		14–adult	320 c			$834
	■		4	■	■	■	■		1450–1600	S8	**Culture and Belief in Europe 1450–1600** pages 45–7, 49, 50–2 / 13 programs, numbers 233, 236–8, 242 246, 252, 254, 256, 260–1, 265–6	P5A P5B P6A	S8	A8	18–adult	325 c			$1287
▫	■		3	■	■				*1606–69*	S9	**Kenneth Clark Rembrandt Series** page 57 / 5 programs, numbers 301–5	P7G	S9		14–adult	150 c	$4950	$995	
	■		4 6	■		■	■		1600–1800	S10	**The Age of Baroque** pages 63–5 / 6 programs, numbers 314–19	P7C P7D/E	S10	A6	15–adult	360 c	$9540	$1794	$954
	■		4	■	■	■	■		1700–1800	S11	**The Enlightenment** pages 68–71B / 16 programs, numbers 322–9, 333–7A	P7B P7I/J	S11	A8	18–adult	350 c			$1584
	■		4	■		■	■		1850–90	S12	**Culture and Society in Britain 1850–90** pages 85–9 / 10 programs, numbers 356, 371–9	P8B P8C	S12	A8	17–adult	250 c			$990
	■		3 4 5	■					1848–1910	S13	**Painters to the People** pages 90–1 / 6 programs, numbers 381–6	P8D	S13	A9	15–adult	156 c			$594
	■		4	■	■	■	■		c1890–1914	S14	**La Grande Epoque** pages 102–3 / 4 programs, numbers 456–9	P10D P10E	S14	A7	15–adult	240 c	$6360	$1196	$636
▫	■		6	■		■	■		1700–1970	S15	**Western Art 1700–1970** pages 75, 99, 145, 154 / 4 programs, numbers 342, 445, 552–3	P19	S15		12–adult	97 c	$3860	$783	$386
	■		3 4 5	■					1860–1956	S16	**Modern Art and Modernism: Manet to Pollock** pages 94–6, 98–9, 112, 114, 119, 121, 126, 131, 142–3, 150, 302 / 16 programs, numbers 395, 397, 413, 416, 425, 484, 512, 524, 527–9, 529, 554, 557, 565, 567B, 815	P20 P21 P22	S16	A8	17–adult	400 c			$1584

Prices worldwide in US $

For institutional non–theatrical public performance use with lending rights

USA National Visual Art Standards

Grades K–4 Ages 5–10	Grades 5–8 Ages 10–14	Grades 9–12 Ages 14–18	CS 1	CS 2	CS 3	CS 4	CS 5	CS 6	Painting	Drawing and graphics	Sculpture	Architecture and design	Photography and video art	Period covered / Artists' dates	Series number	Title	Preview video see page 435	Series reference	Availability codes for use outside USA see page 434	Audience Recommended age range / Teacher training (tt)	Running time in minutes Color (c) / Black and white (b/w)	Revised prices 16mm film sale	16mm film rental USA and Canada only	VHS video sale
		■		2	3	4	5		■		■			1903–85	S17	**The Adventure of Modern Art** pages 98, 107, 113–5, 119, 123, 130–1, 139, 151, 167, 177–8 / 13 programs, numbers 426, 497, 503C–D, 504, 512B, 521, 541, 561, 581, 582, 584, 601	P15A P15B P15C P15D P15E	S17	A10	15–adult	689 c	$19370	$3887	$1937
	■			2			5						■	1890–1939	S18	**History of Architecture and Design 1890–1939** pages 188–93 / 23 programs, numbers 700–22	P23/4 P25/6	S18	A8	18–adult	575 c +b/w			$2277
	■			2	3	4	5		■				■	1860–1993	S19	**Modern Art, Practices and Debates** pages 80, 83A, 95, 97–8, 114, 119, 124, 130, 141, 151A–B, 198, 263B, 307A–B / 21 programs, numbers 87, 393, 401, 403, 412, 417, 482A–B, 484A–B, 501A, 503E, 525, 534–5, 547, 551, 562, 583, 623, 739	P32A P32B P32C P32D	S19	A8	18–adult	525 c			$2079
■	□	■			3	4					■			1900–2000	S20	**Comics, the Ninth Art** pages 246–50 / 13 programs, numbers 781–93	P29 P29A/B	S20		9–adult	364 c			$1287
	□	■	1		3		5				■			1990	S21	**Great Artists in the World of Comics** pages 251–3 / 13 programs, numbers 801–13	P30 P30A P30B	S21		12–adult	364 c			$1287
■	□		1						■	■					S22	**Draw with Don** page 274 / 22 programs, numbers 841–62	P31 P31A	S22	A13	5–12	264 c			$1518
	■				3								■	1977–86	S26	**Architectural Adventures** page 203 / 3 programs, numbers 771–3	P27C	S26		15–adult	132 c			$357
	□	■				4							■	1300–1900	S27	**The Moscow Kremlin** page 306 / 3 programs, numbers 483B–D	P4B	S27		14–adult	90 c			$297
	□	■				4							■	1300–1925	S28	**The Beautiful City of Moscow** pages 53, 72, 75, 104 / 4 programs, numbers 269, 341, 343, 468	P6A	S28		14–adult	120 c			$396
■	□	■												1000–1990	S29	**Archaeological Detectives** page 275 / 3 programs, numbers 490D, 900–1	P1A	S29		8–14	59 c			$257
■	□	■				4							■		S30	**Evidence on Site** pages 276–7 / 6 programs, numbers 14, 16, 99B, 138, 312, 490B	P1B P3C	S30		6–17	92 c			$484
	■					4							■	900–1900	S31	**Frameworks of Worship** pages 278–9 / 5 programs, numbers 136, 176, 313, 490C, 902 (useful for teacher training)	P1B P3C	S31		16–adult tt	103 c			$455
■	□	■				4							■	Prehistoric– AD 1400	S32	**Looking at...** pages 280–1 / 3 programs, numbers 13, 99A, 137	P1A	S32		9–15	51 c			$257
	■													1800–1990	S40	**Literature in the Modern World** pages 388–9 / 14 programs, numbers 1051–65	P34A P34B/C	S40	A8	18–adult	403 c			$1386
	■													present	S41	**Writers Talk: Ideas of Our Time** pages 376–85 / 106 programs, numbers W01–W101	WPC	S41	A14	15–adult	4481 c			$8374
	■													present	S42	**Writers on Writing: Creative Writing Course** page 386 With 104 page booklet containing 48 task sheets / 6 programs, numbers WOW1–WOW6	PWOW	S42	A14	15–adult tt	143 c			$594
	■													1894–1989	S43	**Spirit of Freedom** page 387 / 4 programs, numbers 1041–44 / Not available in North America	P37A P37B	S43		17–adult	208 c			$596

	Period covered	Catalog number	Title	Compilation video of excerpts	Series reference see pages 428–9	Availability codes for use outside USA see page 434	Audience Recommended age range / Teacher training (tt)	Running time in minutes / Color (c) / Black and white (b/w)	VHS video sale For UK and Australia see page 434
A	present	W40	**Dannie Abse** with Elaine Feinstein, page 377		S41		15–adult	47 c	$79
	present	W01	**Chinua Achebe**, page 377	WPC	S41		15–adult	39 c	$79
	present	W41	**Kathy Acker** with Angela McRobbie, page 377		S41		15–adult	40 c	$79
	present	W1	**Brian Aldiss** and Christopher Priest, page 377		S41		15–adult	41 c	$79
	present	W91	**Isabel Allende** with Marina Warner, page 377	WPC	S41		15–adult	40 c	$79
	present	W2	**Martin Amis** with Ian McEwan, page 377		S41		15–adult	36 c	$79
	present	W4	**Maya Angelou**, page 377	WPC	S41		15–adult	31 c	$79
	present	W42	**Aharon Appelfeld** with Clive Sinclair, page 377	WPC	S41		15–adult	28 c	$79
	present	W43	**Margaret Atwood** with Hermione Lee, page 377	WPC	S41		15–adult	53 c	$79
	present	W3	**Gillian Avery, Penelope Farmer, Jill P Walsh**, page 377		S41		15–adult	45 c	$79
B	present	W44	**Paul Bailey** with Margaret Walters, page 377	WPC	S41		15–adult	30 c	$79
	present	W5	**JG Ballard** with Matthew Hoffman, page 377		S41		15–adult	45 c	$79
	present	W45	**Nina Bawden** with Edward Blishen, page 378	WPC	S41		15–adult	36 c	$79
	present	W6	**Quentin Bell** with Edward Blishen, page 378		S41		15–adult	43 c	$79
	present	W7	**John Berger** with Lisa Appignanesi, page 378		S41		15–adult	43 c	$79
	present	W46	**Quentin Blake** with Heather Neill, page 378		S41		15–adult	24 c	$79
	present	W47	**William Boyd** with Susan Richards, page 378		S41		15–adult	35 c	$79
	present	W48	**Malcolm Bradbury** with AS Byatt, page 378		S41		15–adult	39 c	$79
	present	W49	**Melvyn Bragg** with Frank Delaney, page 378		S41		15–adult	43 c	$79
	present	W93	**Howard Brenton** with Donna Soto-Morettini, page 378		S41		15–adult	40 c	$79
	present	W50	**Raymond Briggs** with Barry Took, page 378		S41		15–adult	47 c	$79
	present	W51	**Anthony Burgess** with AS Byatt, page 378		S14		15–adult	53 c	$79
	present	W52	**William Burroughs** with Kathy Acker, page 378		S41		15–adult	36 c	$79
	present	W8	**André Brink** with Christopher Hope, page 378		S41		15–adult	37 c	$79
	present	W9	**AS Byatt** with Iris Murdoch, page 378		S41		15–adult	47 c	$79
C	present	W10	**G Cabrera Infante** with Mario Vargas Llosa, page 379		S41		15–adult	45 c	$79
	present	W53	**Peter Carey** with Margaret Walters, page 379	WPC	S41		15–adult	45 c	$79
	present	W11	**Angela Carter** with Lisa Appignanesi, page 379		S41		15–adult	49 c	$79
D	present	W101	**Fred D'Aguiar** with Carol Phillips, page 379		S41		15–adult	30 c	$79
	present	W88	**Robertson Davies** with Edward Blishen, page 379		S41		15–adult	40 c	$79
	present	W55	**Farrukh Dhondy** with HO Nazareth, page 379		S41		15–adult	37 c	$79
	present	W56	**Monica Dickens** with David Cook, page 379	WPC	S41		15–adult	40 c	$79
	present	W99	**Elisio Diego** with Ana de Skalon, page 379		S41		15–adult	40 c	$79
	present	W97	**E L Doctorow** with Margaret Walters, page 379		S41		15–adult	40 c	$79
	present	W57	**JP Donleavy** with Frank Delaney, page 379		S41		15–adult	45 c	$79
	present	W58	**Maureen Duffy** with Elaine Feinstein, page 379	WPC	S41		15–adult	45 c	$79

Writers Talk
Ideas of Our Time

	Period covered	Catalog number	Title	Compilation video of excerpts	Series reference see pages 428–9	Availability codes for use outside USA see page 434	Audience Recommended age range Teacher training (tt)	Running time in minutes Color (c) Black and white (b/w)	VHS video sale For UK and Australia see page 434
E	present	W100	Buchi Emecheta with Susheila Nasta, page 379	WPC	S41		15–adult	40 c	$79
	present	W59	Louise Erdrich and Michael Dorris with Paul Bailey, page 380		S41		15–adult	27 c	$79
F	present	W60	Elaine Feinstein with AS Byatt, page 380		S41		15–adult	36 c	$79
	present	W95	First Novels: Deborah Levy and Geoff Dyer with Chris Mitchell, page 380		S41		15–adult	40 c	$79
	present	W61	Marilyn French with Sarah Dunant, page 380	WPC	S41		15–adult	49 c	$79
G	present	W13	William Gaddis with Malcolm Bradbury, page 380		S41		15–adult	32 c	$79
	present	W14	Maggie Gee with Sheila McCleod, page 380	WPC	S41		15–adult	46 c	$79
	present	W15	Penelope Gilliat with Penelope Lively, page 380		S41		15–adult	38 c	$79
	present	W16	Allen Ginsberg with RD Laing, page 380	WPC	S41		15–adult	61 c	$79
	present	W62	Nadine Gordimer with Margaret Walters, page 380	WPC	S41		15–adult	45 c	$79
	present	W12	Mary Gordon and Margaret Drabble, page 380		S41		15–adult	41 c	$79
	present	W63	Prabhu Guptara with Naseem Khan, page 380		S41		15–adult	39 c	$79
H	present	W17	Elizabeth Hardwick with Malcolm Bradbury, page 380		S41		15–adult	33 c	$79
	present	W19	Joseph Heller with Michael Kustow, page 381		S41		15–adult	39 c	$79
	present	W18	George V Higgins with Malcolm Bradbury, page 381		S41		15–adult	32 c	$79
	present	W64	Russell Hoban with Dee Palmer, page 381		S41		15–adult	36 c	$79
	present	W96	Christopher Hope with Penelope Fitzgerald, page 381		S41		15–adult	40 c	$79
I	present	W92	John Irving with Liz Calder, page 381		S41		15–adult	40 c	$79
	present	W20	Kazuo Ishiguro with Clive Sinclair, page 381	WPC	S41		15–adult	35 c	$79
J	present	W021	Howard Jacobson with John Walsh, page 381		S41		15–adult	50 c	$79
	present	W65	PD James with AS Byatt, page 381	WPC	S41		15–adult	33 c	$79
K	present	W21	Ryszard Kapuscinski with Fred Bailey, page 381		S41		15–adult	39 c	$79
	present	W22	Lena Kennedy, page 381	WPC	S41		15–adult	25 c	$79
	present	W66	William Kennedy with Noah Richler, page 382		S41		15–adult	50 c	$79
	present	W23	Ellen Kuzwayo with Hilda Bernstein, page 382	WPC	S41		15–adult	48 c	$79
L	present	W24	RD Laing with Anthony Clare, page 382	WPC	S41		15–adult	51 c	$79
	present	W25	Robert Leeson with Mary Cadogan, page 382		S41		15–adult	45 c	$79
	present	W67	Penelope Lively with Nicholas Bagnall, page 382	WPC	S41		15–adult	43 c	$79
	present	W26	Alison Lurie with Malcolm Bradbury, page 382		S41		15–adult	22 c	$79
M	present	W68	Making Children's Picture Books, page 382		S41		13–adult	44 c	$79
	present	W69	Ian McEwan with Martin Amis, page 382		S41		15–adult	52 c	$79
	present	W70	Michael Moorcock with Colin Greenland, page 382		S41		15–adult	40 c	$79
	present	W71	Toni Morrison with AS Byatt, page 382	WPC	S41		15–adult	42 c	$79
	present	W72	John Mortimer with Michael Billington, page 382		S41		15–adult	41 c	$79
N	present	W73	Gloria Naylor with Nicholas Shakespeare, page 383	WPC	S41		15–adult	36 c	$79

Writers Talk Ideas of Our Time	Period covered	Catalog number	Title	Compilation video of excerpts	Series reference see pages 428–9	Availability codes for use outside USA see page 434	Audience Recommended age range Teacher training (tt)	Running time in minutes Color (c) Black and white (b/w)	VHS video sale For UK and Australia see page 434
O	present	W90	**Joyce Carol Oates** with Hermione Lee, page 383	WPC	S41		15–adult	40 c	$79
	present	W74	**Ben Okri** with Edward Blishen, page 383		S41		15–adult	36 c	$79
P	present	W75	**Marge Piercy** with Nikki Gerrard, page 383	WPC	S41		15–adult	46 c	$79
	present	W27	**Harold Pinter** with Benedict Nightingale, page 383		S41		15–adult	48 c	$79
	present	W76	**Michael Powell** with Chris Peachment, page 383		S41		15–adult	45 c	$79
R	present	W77	**Jeremy Reed** with Nicky Singer, page 383		S41		15–adult	44 c	$79
	present	W78	**Ruth Rendell** with PD James, page 383	WPC	S41		15–adult	40 c	$79
	present	W79	**Michèle Roberts** with Giuliana Schiavi, page 383	WPC	S41		15–adult	39 c	$79
	present	W80	**Mike Rosen**, page 383		S41		13–adult	41 c	$79
	present	W81	**Salman Rushdie** with Charlotte Cornwall, page 383	WPC	S41		15–adult	46 c	$79
	present	W89	**Salman Rushdie** with WL Webb, page 383		S41		15–adult	47 c	$79
S	present	W028	**Edward Saïd** with Salman Rushdie, page 384		S41		15–adult	79 c	$79
	present	W28	**Maurice Sendak** with Paul Vaughan, page 384	WPC	S41		15–adult	46 c	$79
	present	W029	**Mongane Serote** with Edward Blishen, page 384		S41		15–adult	38 c	$79
	present	W016	**Janice Shinebourne** and Beryl Gilroy, page 384		S41		15–adult	53 c	$79
	present	W29	**Wole Soyinka**, page 384		S41		15–adult	61 c	$79
	present	W30	**Stephen Spender** with Al Alvarez, page 384		S41		15–adult	53 c	$79
	present	W31	**Ralph Steadman** with Peter Fuller, page 384		S41		15–adult	52 c	$79
	present	W82	**Graham Swift** with David Profumo, page 384		S41		15–adult	41 c	$79
T	present	W83	**Emma Tennant** with James Buxton, page 384	WPC	S41		15–adult	35 c	$79
	present	W32	**DM Thomas, Wendy Perriam, Clare Boylan**, page 384		S41		15–adult	55 c	$79
	present	W98	**Three Cuban Poets: Elosio Diego, Cesar Lopez and Pedro Perez Sarduy** with Ana de Skalon, page 384		S41		15–adult	40 c	$79
	present	W84	**Colin Thubron** with Malise Ruthven, page 384	WPC	S41		15–adult	35 c	$79
U	present	W33	**John Updike** with Claire Tomalin, page 385		S41		15–adult	50 c	$79
V	present	W34	**Mario Vargas Llosa** with John King, page 385		S41		15–adult	50 c	$79
	present	W85	**Nirmal Verma** with Gita Sahgal, page 385		S41		15–adult	35 c	$79
	present	W35	**Gore Vidal** with Lorna Sage, page 385		S41		15–adult	42 c	$79
W	present	W54	**Marina Warner** with Lisa Appignanesi, page 385	WPC	S41		15–adult	40 c	$79
	present	W36	**Fay Weldon** and Deborah Moggach, page 385		S41		15–adult	41 c	$79
	present	W86	**Fay Weldon** with Valerie Grove, page 385		S41		15–adult	50 c	$79
	present	W37	**Arnold Wesker** with David Edgar, page 385		S41		15–adult	55 c	$79
	present	W38	**Raymond Williams** with Michael Ignatieff, page 385		S41		15–adult	51 c	$79
	present	W87	**Tom Wolfe** with Peter Yorke, page 385	WPC	S41		15–adult	55 c	$79
	present	W94	**Writing Biography: Carol Easton and Victoria Glendinning** with Lisa Appignanesi, page 385		S41		15–adult	40 c	$79
	present	W39	**Writing for Children**, page 385		S41		13–adult	48 c	$79

	Period covered	Catalog number	Title	Compilation video of excerpts	Series reference see pages 428–9	Availability codes for use outside USA see page 434	Audience Recommended age range Teacher training (tt)	Running time in minutes	Color (c) Black and white (b/w)	VHS video sale For UK and Australia see page 434
Writers on Writing Creative Writing Course	present	WOW1	Beginnings – Inspiration – Role of the Writer, page 386	PWOW	S42		15–adult	24 c		$99
	present	WOW2	Writing from Personal Experience – Subjects, page 386	PWOW	S42		15–adult	28 c		$99
	present	WOW3	Methods – Drafting – Research, page 386	PWOW	S42		15–adult	20 c		$99
	present	WOW4	Characters – Setting – Plot, page 386	PWOW	S42		15–adult	23 c		$99
	present	WOW5	Form – Genre, page 386	PWOW	S42		15–adult	25 c		$99
	present	WOW6	Language – Audience, page 386	PWOW	S42		15–adult	23 c		$99
Introduction to Modern Literature	present	1004	Language and Literature, page 390	P33		A8	18–adult	24 c		$99
	present	1005	Poetry: Language and History, page 390	P33		A8	18–adult	24 c		$99
	present	1006	Narrative, page 390	P33		A8	18–adult	24 c		$99
	present	1010	Signs of the Times: Umberto Eco, page 390	P33		A8	18–adult	25 c		$99
Spirit of Freedom	1894–1930	1041	Great Expectations: Dawn from the East, page 387 Not available in North America	P37A	S43		17–adult	52 c		$149
	1922–45	1042	Days of Contempt: Fascism and the Nazis, page 387 Not available in North America	P37A	S43		17–adult	52 c		$149
	1925–54	1043	Lost Illusions: Breaking from Stalin, page 387 Not available in North America	P37B	S43		17–adult	52 c		$149
	1955–89	1044	The Demise of the Prophets: Re-inventing the Model, page 387 Not available in North America	P37B	S43		17–adult	52 c		$149
Literature in the Modern World	1957	1051	End Game by Samuel Beckett, page 388	P34A	S40	A8	18–adult	90 c		$99
	1880–1930	1052	English Whose English?, page 388	P34A	S40	A8	18–adult	25 c		$99
	1925–40	1053	What was Modernism?, page 388	P34A	S40	A8	18–adult	24 c		$99
	1930s	1054	Crossing the Border: Images of England in the Thirties, page 388	P34B	S40	A8	18–adult	24 c		$99
	1930s	1055	Left and Write: Recalling the Thirties, page 388	P34B	S40	A8	18–adult	24 c		$99
	1990	1057	In the Market Place, page 388	P34B	S40	A8	18–adult	24 c		$99
	1750–1945	1058	Empire and Nation: The Re-fashioning of Literature, page 389	P34B	S40	A8	18–adult	24 c		$99
	1950s	1059	Serjeant Musgrave at the Court, page 389	P34B	S40	A8	18–adult	24 c		$99
	present	1060	Born into Two Cultures?, page 389	P34C	S40	A8	18–adult	24 c		$99
	present	1061	Caribbean Poetry: Literary and Oral Traditions, page 389	P34C	S40	A8	18–adult	24 c		$99
	present	1062	The Gentle Sex?, page 389	P34C	S40	A8	18–adult	24 c		$99
	present	1063	Changing Voices, page 389	P34C	S40	A8	18–adult	24 c		$99
	present	1064	The Next Five Minutes: Literature and History, page 389	P34C	S40	A8	18–adult	24 c		$99
	1941	1065	Brecht on Stage, page 389	P34C	S40	A8	18–adult	24 c		$99

Supplementary price information

For a complete price list, see the Key to the Collection, pages 412–33.

Prices are subject to change without prior notice.

Rights information

Prices are for institutional use and include non-commercial, non-theatrical, public performance and lending rights. Television use is not included, but see page 435. Prices for individual home use are available upon request.

Worldwide prices

The price list gives prices for use worldwide in US dollars. If ordering from the UK or Australia, please use the conversion table opposite.

Rental prices

Film and video rental is available in the USA and Canada only. Film rental prices are given in the price list. For video rental prices, please use the conversion table opposite.

Terms of payment

■ United States, United Kingdom and Australia: thirty days net for institutions; for individuals, cash with order, as below.

■ rest of world: cash with order; cheques in US dollars payable on a US or UK bank; most credit cards accepted. Proforma invoices sent on request.

VHS video sale / VHS video rental

Worldwide	United Kingdom only ex VAT	Australia only	USA and Canada only
$69	£39	Aus $53	$39
$79	£45	Aus $60	$39
$89	£49	Aus $69	$39
$99	£56	Aus $76	$49
$109	£59	Aus $84	$49
$119	£67	Aus $92	$59
$129	£73	Aus $99	$59
$139	£79	Aus $107	$69
$149	£85	Aus $115	$69
$159	£89	Aus $123	$79
$169	£95	Aus $130	$79
$179	£99	Aus $138	$89
$189	£105	Aus $146	$89
$199	£110	Aus $154	$99
$219	£122	Aus $169	$99

Shipping and handling

	Worldwide	United Kingdom	Australia
16mm film sale	courier charge	courier charge	courier charge
16mm film rental	USA and Canada only: US $16	not available	not available
VHS video sale	US $7	£4	Aus $6
8 or more (each)	US $3.50	£2	Aus $3
VHS video rental	USA and Canada only: US $11	not available	not available
VHS video preview	US $7	£4	Aus $6
Books (each)	US $7	£4	Aus $6
Resource guide (each)	US $8	£5	Aus $8

Availability

USA and Canada

All Roland Collection films and videos are available for sale or rent in North America, with six exceptions:

■ titles 516, 619 are not for sale in the USA

■ titles 1041, 1042, 1043, 1044 are not for sale in the USA and Canada

Outside the USA

Please check the availability code against some titles in the Key to the Collection, pages 412–33, before ordering. The availability code is given in the third column after the program title.

A1 **Outside** North America, UK and Eire by special request

A2 Not for sale in the EC

A3 Not for sale in French-speaking countries or Japan

A4 Not for sale in New Zealand or South Africa

A5 Not for sale **outside** English-speaking countries

A6 Not for sale in German- or French-speaking countries, Italy, Africa or ex-French colonies or French-speaking Canada

A7 Not for sale as **A6** but also Spain and Latin America

A8 For sale in the UK for individual home study use. Not for sale to institutions in the UK. Not for sale in Spain, South America (except Chile), Australia, New Zealand, Japan, Pakistan, Hong Kong, Macau, China, Malaysia, Singapore, Brunei, Indonesia, Thailand and Taiwan. For any countries of the African Continent please enquire.

A9 Not for sale in South Africa

A10 Not for sale in Italy, Israel, French-speaking countries or French-speaking Canada

A11 Not for sale in France or Spain

A12 Not for sale in French-speaking countries

A13 Not for sale in Northern Ireland and Eire

A15 Not for sale **outside** the USA

A16 Not for sale **outside** the USA and Canada

A17 Not for sale in Canada, Germany or Italy

A18 Not for sale **outside** Japan, Far East, Europe and English-speaking countries

A19 Not for sale **outside** English-speaking countries and the African Continent

Options and services

Unconditional guarantee

The Roland Collection has used its best endeavors to make its own excellent film negatives and video 1-inch masters as well as to be accurate in the description of each program. Should customers for any reason feel that their purchase does not satisfy their needs, we will credit them, replace the title or make a refund, as requested.

Conditions of use

Roland Collection films and videos are copyright. The making of an archive copy or duplicating in whole or part is not permitted.

Exhibition use

If the Roland Collection videos are used continuously as part of an exhibition, a weekly royalty equivalent to the VHS purchase price is payable. If there are only two showings a day, no royalty fee is payable. In some cases permission may be granted for production of a 'one-off' laser disc to simplify continuous automated exhibition use.

Television use

Most of the programs are available for educational television use and some for commercial television use, but all require prior clearance. Clearance and permission fees depend upon the intended use.

Film and video formats

On request, U-matic and Beta SP videos are also available. Laser disc, CD-ROM and other electronic formats are being considered for a number of titles. 35mm film (normal and widescreen) may be specially ordered for some films.

International TV systems

When ordering a video, please specify where a tape will be used so that we can ensure that it is compatible with your TV system. In addition to VHS, U-matic and Beta SP cassette formats, there are different types of television signal in operation throughout the world. The two most common systems are NTSC, used in North America, most of South America, Japan and part of the Middle East, and PAL, used in the UK, Australia, South Africa, parts of South America, Malaysia and most of Western Europe.

There is a 20 per cent price supplement on all videos for systems other than standard NTSC and standard PAL.

Commerical and educational services

Foreign language versions

Many titles are available in different languages: see the language of your choice in the General Index. There is a 20 per cent surcharge for language versions other than English.

Stock footage

Stock footage may be purchased for educational and commercial use. Please indicate your interest and we will advise which productions are available for footage sale. Our entire collection of thirty-five million images is available with a visual time code, facilitating location of appropriate footage.

Transcripts of narrations

Transcripts are available for many titles (some also in foreign language versions). These have proved an invaluable support to educators preparing class activities as well as to television program directors looking for stock footage. Prices vary from US $7 to $30 each, including shipping and handling.

Program notes

Cultural background program notes are available for forty-two titles, price US $12 including shipping and handling.

Preview service

We offer a unique service to qualified institutional buyers: several complete titles are available on the same VHS preview tape. The titles on each preview cassette relate in period or thematically, or are the work of a single producer. Visual time codes give instant title access.

To locate the preview tape you need, look up the catalog number of your chosen program in the Key to the Collection, pages 412–33; the number of the preview video is given in the first column after the program title.

Preview tapes must be returned within ten days of receipt, with payment of return postage and insurance at US $200 per tape. Previews not returned will be considered as purchased and invoiced at the retail cost per title. Shipping and handling charge $7 per tape.

Artspectrum

A two-hour-long opportunity to experience the sights and sounds of the Roland Collection. Complete sequences of $1^1/_2$–3 minutes from fifty-six programs on art and architecture demonstrate the vast range of teaching materials available. A visual time code offers a fast way to locate each title. Available as VHS preview or for sale at US $69 to institutional and private buyers.

WPC
Writers Talk: Ideas of Our Time

Preview compilation of 82 minutes with sequences of 1–$3^1/_2$ minutes from thirty-three programs on individual writers. A visual time code makes it easy to locate each writer. Available as VHS preview or for sale at US $69 to institutional and private buyers.

Bill to

Ship to

	Bill to		Ship to
organization		organization	
department		department	
address		address	
city		city	
state/zip		state/zip	
country		country	
telephone		telephone	
fax		fax	
date		date	
purchase order number		for the attention of	
for the attention of			

The Roland Collection

USA

22-D Hollywood Avenue
Ho-Ho-Kus
New Jersey 07423

Freephone
1 800 597 6526
1 800 59 ROLAND

Telephone
201 251 8200

Fax
201 251 8788

England

Peasmarsh
East Sussex
TN31 6XJ

Telephone
01797 230 421
Intl +44 1797 230 421
From the USA
011 44 1797 230 421

Fax
01797 230 677
Intl +44 1797 230 677
From the USA
011 44 1797 230 677

catalog number	title	rental dates required	Quantity required 16mm film	VHS video	price per title	total

USA

Shipping and handling

		subtotal	
Film sale @ $11	Video rental @ $11	shipping and handling	
Film rental @ $16	Video preview @ $7		
Video sale @ $7	Books @ $7		
8 or more @ $3.50	Resource guide @ $8	**grand total**	

Access □   Visa □   Mastercard □   American Express □

payment by

credit card number ⊔⊔⊔⊔ ⊔⊔⊔⊔ ⊔⊔⊔⊔ ⊔⊔⊔⊔   expiry date _____

cardholder's name _____   cardholder's signature _____